DUMBARTON OAKS
MEDIEVAL LIBRARY

Daniel Donoghue, General Editor

LIFE OF THE VIRGIN MARY

JOHN GEOMETRES

DOML 77

Life of the Virgin Mary

JOHN GEOMETRES

Edited and Translated by

MAXIMOS CONSTAS
and
CHRISTOS SIMELIDIS

DUMBARTON OAKS
MEDIEVAL LIBRARY

HARVARD UNIVERSITY PRESS
CAMBRIDGE, MASSACHUSETTS
LONDON, ENGLAND
2023

Printed in the United States of America

First Printing

Library of Congress Cataloging-in-Publication Data available from the Library of Congress at https://lccn.loc.gov/2022038055

ISBN 978-0-674-29080-8 (cloth : alk. paper)

Contents

Introduction

John Geometres: Life and Works

John Geometres (ca. 935–ca. 1000) was one of the most highly accomplished writers of the Byzantine period. He flourished in Constantinople during the second half of the tenth century, where he was an imperial military officer, the poet laureate of his day, and a precursor of the eleventh-century Byzantine literary renaissance.[1] His brilliant career at the court came to an end when he fell out of favor under Basil II (in or around 985), but he continued his literary work as a leading member of an elite religious confraternity associated with the church of the Mother of God in the Kyros district of the capital.[2] It was in this church that the Mother of God appeared to the late-antique liturgical poet Romanos the Melodist, and where he was later buried. The confraternity was likely founded in memory of Romanos and continued his devotion to the Virgin through the production of poems, hymns, and homilies in her honor.

Though Geometres wrote on a variety of themes and subjects, the majority of his writings are religious in nature.[3] These include a poetic rendering *(metaphrasis)* of the biblical odes; epigrams on icons and frescoes; scholia on the ora-

tions of Gregory of Nazianzus; a compendium of the ascetic life in classicizing tetrastichs; five prosodic hymns to the Virgin; a lengthy oration on the Annunciation; and a homiletic treatise written for the feast of the Dormition, conventionally known as the *Life of the Virgin,*[4] which is edited and translated in this present volume. A series of elaborate meditations on the events of Mary's life, the *Life of the Virgin* is arguably the single most important witness to Marian doctrine and devotion ever produced in the Byzantine world.[5]

The *Life of the Virgin Mary*

Geometres's *Life of the Virgin* is the most outstanding example of several biographies and literary treatments of the Mother of God written in the middle Byzantine period.[6] These biographies include the late eighth- or early ninth-century *Life of the Theotokos* by Epiphanios the Monk;[7] the ninth-century Marian homilies of George of Nikomedia;[8] the tenth-century *Life of the Virgin* by Symeon Metaphrastes;[9] and a late tenth-century Georgian redaction of Geometres's *Life of the Virgin* produced by Euthymios the Athonite.[10] In this rare example of a Byzantine scholar reworking a contemporary and complex rhetorical text, Euthymios's aim was to simplify Geometres's *Life* in order to make it accessible to a wide Georgian readership.[11]

Biographies of the Virgin were without precedent in the early Byzantine tradition, and Epiphanios is often considered the creator of the genre.[12] Geometres gave the new genre its fully realized form, combining biblical texts, apocryphal literature, and material from patristic homilies in a monumental synthesis of two vast literary and liturgical cy-

cles, namely, the cycle of Mary's birth and childhood, and the cycle of her death, burial, and translation in divine glory to heaven.[13]

The *Life of the Virgin* is an elaborate farewell discourse delivered on the annual commemoration of the Virgin's death (or "Dormition") celebrated on August 15, an occasion which provided Geometres with the opportunity to recount in detail his subject's entire life. The material is presented in chronological order and organized largely around the Marian feasts of the Byzantine ecclesiastical year (as well as the feasts of Christ at which the Virgin was historically present, for example, the Nativity and the Crucifixion). Geometres begins his discourse with the history and genealogy of Mary's parents, after which he describes her upbringing in the temple, followed by the events recorded in the Gospels (her betrothal to Joseph, the Annunciation, Visitation, Nativity, the Meeting with Simeon, the Wedding at Cana, and so on), bringing the main narrative to a close with an extended treatment of the Dormition. After this, he briefly recounts the transfer of the Virgin's garments to Constantinople during the reign of Leo I (ruled 457–474) and then concludes with elaborate praises and prayers of thanksgiving to the Mother of God and her son.

Throughout the *Life,* Geometres makes frequent references to "today's feast" and the "feast we are now celebrating." However, the sheer length of the work, which runs to nearly forty-five thousand words, makes it unlikely that it was read in its present form at a feast or vigil of the Dormition. Instead, it may have been originally delivered in a shorter form (possibly in separate sections over the course of an all-night vigil) and subsequently revised and expanded,

which may perhaps account for the author's references to his "study" of earlier Marian literature and to his oration as a "written" work (*Life* 2).[14]

In his attempt to date the *Life,* Antoine Wenger noticed that in the course of the closing prayer to the Virgin (*Life* 129), Geometres asks for deliverance from "acts of fratricide," and he concluded that the *Life* was written during the tumultuous period between 976 (the death of John Tzimiskes) and 989 (the defeat of Bardas Skleros). Wenger also thought that Geometres was alluding to a particularly acute phase of civil war and internecine conflict, perhaps the rebellion of Bardas Phokas (987–989).[15] Marc Lauxtermann argued further that this closing prayer in the *Life* bears comparison with Geometres's poem "On the Rebellion" (εἰς τὴν ἀποστασίαν), which apparently also refers to Halley's Comet and is thus dated to 989.[16]

We believe, however, that Dmitry Korobeynikov is correct in finding an earlier dating more probable, namely, the aftermath of the murder of Nikephoros II Phokas (December 10–11, 969) by his nephew and comrade John I Tzimiskes, whose coconspirators might be "the sheep" that "have turned into beasts" mentioned by Geometres (*Life* 129). The murder was followed by the Rus' advance on Constantinople and the first rebellion of Nikephoros II's nephew Bardas Phokas (supported by his father, Leo Phokas) in the spring of 970.[17] Moreover, the acts of "impiety" (ταῖς ἀσεβείαις) mentioned here by Geometres likely refer to the *epitimion,* a prohibition from entering church grounds—and, *ipso facto,* from coronation—imposed by Patriarch Polyeuktos on Tzimiskes, who accepted it. In what is unlikely to be a coincidence, Geometres's words echo the speech Polyeuk-

tos addressed to Tzimiskes after the murder, and correspond exactly to Leo the Deacon's description of the murder of Nikephoros II as "an unholy and abominable deed, loathsome to God" (θεοστυγὲς καὶ ἀνόσιον μῦσος).[18] Further, and again according to Korobeynikov, Geometres's reference to "savage beasts from without" (these are not the same as the "sheep" that "have turned into beasts" mentioned above) very likely refers to pagan invaders who can be identified with the Rus' warriors under Svyatoslav, who advanced rapidly on Constantinople soon after the murder of Nikephoros. The period from the assassination of Nikephoros through the end of the ensuing civil war, lasting from December 11, 969 to the autumn of 970, was the only opportunity in the tenth century when pagan invaders could have threatened Constantinople itself. No such pagan threat was posed to the capital in the period from 976 to 989 (though in 988/9 Vladimir of Rus' invaded the Crimea and took Cherson).[19]

The historical context outlined above serves to identify the event that Geometres describes in the *Life's* closing paragraph. However, the dating proposed for this event (969–970) does not secure the actual date of the *Life*'s composition, since there is no way of knowing if it was more or less already complete at the time of the events it alludes to in its final prayers, or whether Geometres had previously delivered sections of it as independent homilies.

Though the *Life* survives in only a small number of manuscripts, this does not reflect the full history of the text and its influence. The transmission of the *Life* involved several manuscripts that are no longer extant, and it is evident that the Byzantine editors of the work had already collated vari-

ous copies of it by the time of the earliest surviving witnesses (see the Note on the Text). About eighty years after Geometres's death, excerpts from the *Life* were included in Niketas of Heraclea's *Catena on Luke,* which is the largest and richest of Niketas's compilations and arguably his greatest work.[20] Geometres is cited alongside leading patristic writers, indicating that, not long after his death, he was considered a theological authority. Thomas Aquinas produced a Latin translation of Niketas's *Catena,* which was influential on his own commentary on the Gospel of Luke. The eleventh-century literary critic Michael Psellos was familiar with Geometres's work and acknowledges his insight and intelligence.[21] The inclusion of the *Life of the Virgin* in Vaticanus graecus 504 is yet another testimony to the work's importance. This twelfth-century codex is a massive theological compendium containing the works of the most prominent patristic and Byzantine theological writers: Basil of Caesarea, Gregory of Nazianzus, Gregory of Nyssa, John Chrysostom, Dionysios the Areopagite, Maximos the Confessor, and John of Damascus, culminating with the *Life of the Virgin* by Geometres.[22]

Language and Style

John Geometres has been rightly praised for his verbal artistry in both verse and prose.[23] His virtuosic *Life of the Virgin* surely captured the attention of its audience through its inventive and mellifluous wordplay, profusion of rich and vivid imagery, and compelling exegetical and theological arguments. These features are well illustrated in a passage from the end of chapter 65 ("Thus he both purifies us . . . adopted

sons together with himself"), which contains parallelisms in the structure of cola (ἡμᾶς καθαίρει—ἡμῖν καθαίρεται, "purified us—is purified by us"; εὐθέως . . . ἐκ τοῦ ὕδατος—μετ' ὀλίγον τοῦ μνήματος, "immediately . . . from the water—soon . . . from the tomb"), and *polyptoton,* that is, repetitions of the same words both in different cases (φθορᾶς . . . φθορᾷ φθορὰ . . . φθορᾶς) and in compounds (διαφθορᾶς), or of repeated prepositions in compounds (συναναφέρων . . . συναφθαρτίζων . . . συνυιοθετούμενος).

As these densely placed figures—playing out over the course of only a few lines—illustrate, the *Life* is replete with impressive rhetorical devices.[24] Geometres enjoys the effect of words with similar sounds (for example, μαινομένην καὶ λυμαινομένην in 129) and the use of the same verb with different prepositions (for instance, παραβάλλειν . . . παραβάλλειν . . . ὑπερβάλλειν in 69, or σύστειλον . . . περίστειλον in 121). Very rare words (περιθυρέω, "to be about the entrance," in 90; προσκιάζω, "foreshadow," at 23), hapax legomena (φιλοπαρθενία, "love of virginity," in 10, 23, and 125; ἀνάκραμα, "a blending," in 9), or unique forms of known verbs (such as συνιστέον in 6, from σύνοιδα, "to know well," which confused scribes) are also used and further elevate the high register of the text's vocabulary.

Geometres's Greek is elaborate, refined, and often dense and obscure; his rhetorical style tends toward the labyrinthine, through the use of lengthy and complex sentences. Some of his linguistic and stylistic habits are likely to have been representative of the trends of his time, which have not yet been fully established by modern scholarship, and thus a comprehensive study of these trends in light of larger developments in written Medieval Greek remains a schol-

arly desideratum. It should also be noted that the *Life* was not intended to be read and studied in the way we treat it today, but rather to be read aloud, with pauses and (likely) vocal modulations suggested by the numerous punctuation signs found in the manuscripts. In its original context, the text of the *Life* would have been delivered in short phrasal units, and with a different "rhetorical logic" that would have been readily recognized and followed by a cultivated Byzantine audience.[25] It follows, then, that Geometres's language and style were not determined solely by his own education, talents, and training, but by the expectations of his audience, which is likely to have included erudite members of the lay confraternity attached to the church of the Mother of God in the Kyros district.[26]

Scholars have long recognized that the *Life* is not a conventional work of hagiography but is shaped in the form of something like a sequence of homilies. However, this does not break the strong biographical and narrative threads that unite these sections into a single work, which can also be read as a treatise. This is especially the case when Geometres presents historical arguments (in one instance based on his reading of the first-century Jewish historian Josephus) or engages in extended theological debates and wants to forward his own confidently held views.[27] At the same time, the text in many places also reads like a panegyric in praise of the Virgin's heroic contests and her array of unsurpassable qualities and virtues.[28]

Geometres's highly rhetorical and poetic language, often driven by personal religious devotion and emotional intensity, at times lends itself to extravagant and exaggerated expression. Examples include his alignment of Mary with God

the Father, both of whom "gave" their son "over to death" (124); or calling the Virgin "another intercessor" (παράκλητος, 126), a term used by Christ as a designation of the Holy Spirit (John 14:16).[29] As noted below, Geometres is careful to qualify such statements that cannot always be taken *prima facie* as fixed points of doctrine.

Theological Themes

If the *Life of the Virgin* is a literary and rhetorical masterpiece designed to captivate, delight, and impress its audience, it is also a work of exceptional theological sophistication animated by deeply felt devotion to the Mother of God. Throughout the work, Geometres maintains that the events of Mary's life are "mysteries" that can be grasped only through an act of "contemplation" (θεωρία), which he achieves through an elaborate theological expansion of the New Testament, drawing out the implications of the incarnation for Mary's life, which is uniquely bound to the life of her son.

In the Byzantine theological tradition, confession of faith in Jesus Christ as the incarnate son of God the Father does not in any way exclude his mother according to the flesh, making Mariology an integral aspect of Christology. From this point of view, Mary's title of "Theotokos" (God-bearer) is simply the other side of the biblical teaching that "the Word became flesh" (John 1:14). The Council of Ephesus (431 CE), which bestowed this title on Mary, did so precisely because her human nature guaranteed the truth of the incarnation. The theology of the Council of Chalcedon (451 CE) led to further developments in Marian doctrine and de-

votion, since its "communication of properties" between human and divine nature gave her a full share in the transformative power of her son's divine life and work.

In the eighth and ninth centuries, these theological principles figured prominently in the Orthodox response to Iconoclasm, when the doctrine of the incarnation required heightened attention to the physical and spiritual unity of the incarnate Word with his human mother.[30] To demonstrate the reality of Christ's humanity, iconophile theologians emphasized the reality of his sufferings, which led to a corresponding emphasis on the sufferings of his mother, who was the source of that humanity.[31] When these "affective" features became part of the theological understanding of Mary, they were fully informed by established Christological doctrine.[32] Mary's maternal compassion, her suffering, and other ostensibly emotional responses were not highlighted for their own sake but were understood in light of the transformation of her human nature in and through the incarnation. The result was that "affective" Marian piety was inwardly structured by the doctrine of the incarnation, while the doctrine of the incarnation became infused with the spirit of piety and devotion.

This is the theological tradition that Geometres inherited, and which he made the principal theme of his *Life of the Virgin,* namely, the ontological solidarity uniting the human mother with her divine-human son. In chapter 72, Geometres compares this union not only to the inseparability of a body from its shadow but also, and rather strikingly, to the hypostatic union, that is, to the inseparable unity of divinity and humanity within Christ himself. He is, however, careful to qualify this bold analogy with the adverb "virtually"

(σχεδόν), and the acknowledgment that the consubstantiality of mother and son in terms of their shared human nature does not lead to a confusion of their personal identities (since "they were separate according to hypostasis"). However, this does not prevent the unity of the mother's "every deed, relationship, and disposition" with those of her son. By virtue of her divine maternity, Mary mirrors the activities of her son throughout all the stages of his earthly life and especially at the time of his passion. Because Christ suffered for human beings, this must also be reflected in the experience of his mother, though their suffering is not symmetrical: "she also suffered together (συνέπασχε) with him, and indeed, if it is not too daring a thing to say, she suffered more than he did." Once again, Geometres ventures a bold formulation but not without qualification, indicating that he knows the parameters of orthodox Christological doctrine and the extent to which he can speculatively overstep its boundaries.

His account of Mary's suffering at the crucifixion, death, and burial of her son is surely one of the more remarkable narrative sequences in the entire *Life* and, in chapter 124, unsurprisingly calls forth some of his most daring claims. For Geometres, Mary is not simply the mother of the redeemer but contributes personally to the work of redemption. Like God the Father, she too gives her son over to death. Her suffering adds something to the sufferings of Christ or at the very least extends them. That Mary "co-suffers" with Christ has led some Roman Catholic theologians to argue that Geometres "forcefully affirms" the notion that Mary is a "co-redeemer" with Christ.[33] However, such a reading ignores the fact that Geometres disassociates

(through an associative wordplay) Christ from the Virgin (λύτρον, "ransom," vs. λυτήριον, "deliverance") and that the assistance offered by her is wholly dependent on salvation in Christ, while the latter in no way depends on the suffering of his mother.[34]

Though space does not allow for a full treatment of this question, Geometres is perhaps building on the logic of participation in the sufferings of Christ adumbrated by Paul in the New Testament: "I rejoice in my sufferings for your sake, and complete in my flesh what is lacking in Christ's afflictions" (Colossians 1:24; compare 2 Corinthians 4:10, 1 Peter 4:13). Not unlike Geometres, John Chrysostom understood this passage to mean that the apostles suffered more than Christ, who promised them that they "will also do the works that I am doing, and even greater things than these" (John 14:12).[35] The participation of the saints in the sufferings of Christ constitutes the form and measure of their assimilation to God, and thus the Mother of God's imitation of Christ may simply be a difference of degree and not of kind.[36] However, that Geometres felt obliged to carefully qualify these claims indicates that they were potentially controversial or at the very least without established precedent, but here we must let the matter rest.

After the resurrection and ascension, Mary, who had previously served as the leader of Christ's female disciples, now takes on a new role. While maintaining her connection to Christ, she assumes leadership of the early Church, becoming the "protector, teacher, and sovereign of all, of his friends and disciples, and of both men and women," taking "upon herself the cares of all" (96). With Christ's departure from this world, Mary's ontological solidarity with her son as-

sumes even greater importance, since she takes the place of Christ who is physically absent: all the disciples had "in place of the Lord's bodily presence the one who gave birth to his body" (96). As the leader of the new community, Mary organizes all apostolic activity, and "just as she had once suffered with her son, so too she suffered again with his heralds and disciples," for "she was already their common mother," so that when "they were bound in chains, she was bound together with them," in spirit being imprisoned with Peter and struck by the stones thrown at Stephen (97). The crowning "mystery" of her life is her death and translation to heaven, when she is exalted beyond every creature, becoming the "common mother of all" and "something even greater than a mother, for just as her nature is above nature, so too is her relationship and goodwill toward human beings" (105). It is now that she becomes fully a mediator to Christ and an intercessor for the world, "a second mediator between us and the first mediator, a God-bearing human being between us and the man-bearing God" (123), "lavishly bestowing munificence on all" (126).

The Dormition

The *Life of the Virgin* was composed for delivery on the annual commemoration of the Virgin's repose celebrated on August 15 and known as the Dormition. The recounting of this event is at once the high point of the *Life,* the lengthiest section of the entire work, and exceptionally rich in theological ideas and concepts. The section as a whole may be divided into three parts of unequal length. The first part (103–19) is a detailed narration of the Dormition, from the

initial appearance of the angel to Mary, through her death, burial, translation, and empty tomb, interspersed with numerous and often lengthy digressions (on the presence of Dionysios the Areopagite at her funeral, on various theories regarding Paul's ascent to the third heaven, the location of paradise, the transfer of the Virgin's vestments to Constantinople, and so on). The second part (119–21) offers a balanced theological consideration of Mary's death. Geometres frames his remarks by affirming that all things pertaining to the Virgin "unfolded in a manner beyond and even contrary to nature" (120), including her death. When she died, her spirit departed from her body, which latter was solemnly placed in a tomb, where it remained incorrupt. Three days later, her body was translated from the grave to heaven in a manner befitting the mother of God, for she was "raised up to the heavens . . . before the resurrection, just as we will be raised after the resurrection. And she was raised in her entirety, just as her son was" (120), though unlike him, her soul and body were separated and translated to heaven at different times where they were finally reunited. Geometres explicitly rejects the notion that Mary was immortal and affirms that her death, like her maternity, guarantees the reality of the human nature of her son. He further argues that the Virgin's translation to heaven is a figure of human nature's final, eschatological encounter with Christ, so that "this present ascension" is "proof of the future resurrection" (121). At the same time, the events surrounding Mary's Dormition serve as a model for the spiritual life through the symbolic death and resurrection of the soul enacted through asceticism. Geometres draws his discourse to a conclusion in the third part (122–28). He sings the praises

of summer and in particular of the day (122–23), which he intriguingly compares to astronomical events in the constellation Virgo. This is followed by the concluding section, which contains a series of prayers to Christ and the Virgin (124–25), an exuberant celebration of her miracles and intercessory powers (126–28), and a prayer for protection and deliverance from civic unrest that concludes the entire work, which Geometres offers to the Mother of God in gratitude for the many gifts she has given him.

This volume is the collaborative work of the coauthors, Maximos Constas and Christos Simelidis. The critical edition of the Greek text, the English translation, the Introduction, the Note on the Text, the Notes to the Translation, and the Notes to the Text were jointly planned, drafted, and brought to completion by the two authors.

We are foremost indebted to our editors, Alexander Alexakis and Richard Greenfield, as well as to Nicole Eddy, for numerous helpful suggestions for improvement. Andrew Faulkner graciously read the entire text and offered insightful remarks on the translation. We are thankful to Mary B. Cunningham, who kindly gave us her forthcoming translation of Epiphanios's *Life of the Theotokos,* and a copy of her new book prior to publication. Throughout our work on this volume, we received valuable help from Dimitrios A. Christidis, Dmitry Korobeynikov, Thamar Otkhmezuri, Georgi Parpulov, Dimitrios Skrekas, and Nigel G. Wilson. Annaclara Cataldi Palau kindly lent us her microfilm of MS Genoa, Biblioteca Franzoniana, Urbanus 32. At an early stage in the project, Vassa Countouma generously provided us

with documents from the Antoine Wenger archive in Paris. Special assistance on a number of points was offered by Tikhon Alexander Pino, Fr. Panayiotis Hasiakos, Vasiliki Limberis, and Chance Bonar, who assisted in the compilation of the index. We are grateful to Bishop Joachim Cotsonis and Hilary Rogler of the Holy Cross library for their assistance and support, as well as to Fr Maximos's research assistants, Lukas Buhler and Anthony Ladas. Opportunities to present and discuss different aspects of this project took place at Saint Vladimir's Orthodox Theological Seminary, Dumbarton Oaks, Oxford University, the Aarhus Institute of Advanced Studies, and the International Conference, "The Virgin Beyond Borders."

Notes

1 For a biographical study, see Marc D. Lauxtermann, "John Geometres: Poet and Soldier," *Byzantion* 68 (1998): 356–80.

2 On which, see Paul Magdalino, "The Liturgical Poetics of an Elite Religious Confraternity," in *Reading in the Byzantine Empire and Beyond,* ed. Teresa Shawcross (Cambridge, 2018), 116–32.

3 For Geometres's works, see Emilie Marlène van Opstall, *Jean Géomètre: Poèmes en hexamètres et en distiques élégiaques* (Leiden, 2008), 15–17; Emilie Marlène van Opstall and Maria Tomadaki, "John Geometres: A Poet around the Year 1000," in *A Companion to Byzantine Poetry,* ed. Wolfram Hörandner, Andreas Rhoby, and Nikos Zagklas (Leiden, 2019), 191–211; and Christos Simelidis, "Two *Lives of the Virgin:* John Geometres, Euthymios the Athonite, and Maximos the Confessor," *Dumbarton Oaks Papers* 74 (2020): 129–34.

4 See Martin Jugie, *La mort et l'assomption de la Sainte Vierge* (Rome, 1944), 317n1: "Ce discours de Jean est très long et constitue une veritable *Vie* de la Vierge."

5 See the assessments of Antoine Wenger, "L'intercession de Marie en orient du VIe au Xe siècle," *Études mariales* 23 (1966): 51–75, at 66: "Jean le

Géomètre . . . est l'auteur d'une *Vie de la Vierge* qui est à notre sens la somme mariale de la théologie mariale byzantine"; and Jane Baun, "Why Should We Read Middle Byzantine Fathers?," in *A Celebration of Living Theology: A Festschrift in Honour of Andrew Louth,* ed. Justin A. Mihoc and Leonard Aldea (London and New York, 2014), 59–74, at 66–67: "John Geometres' *Life of the Virgin* . . . constitutes a veritable doctrinal essay on the mission of the Virgin, and the history of Marian doctrine and devotion is incomplete without it."

6 "Biography" here is used as a term of convenience; see Simon Claude Mimouni, *Les traditions anciennes sur la Dormition et l'Assomption de Marie* (Leiden and Boston, 2011), 75, who correctly notes that the Middle Byzantine *Lives* of the Virgin are a literary genre "somewhere between hagiography and homiletics."

7 The text is extant in two versions: Albert Dressel, *Epiphanii monachi et presbyteri edita et inedita* (Paris and Leipzig, 1843), 13–44; and PG 120:186–216, which reprints the 1774 edition by Giovanni Mingarelli.

8 Available in PG 100:1336–504.

9 Vasilii Vasil'evich Latyshev, *Menologii anonymi Byzantini saeculi X quae supersunt,* vol. 2, *Menses Iunium, Iulium, Augustum continens* (Saint Petersburg, 1912; repr., Leipzig, 1970), 345–83. It is not clear if Symeon's *Life* was a source for, or to the contrary was based on, the *Life* by Geometres; for a summary of this question, see Mary B. Cunningham, *The Virgin Mary in Byzantium, c.400–1000: Hymns, Homilies and Hagiography* (Cambridge, 2021), 197n101.

10 For an English translation, see *The Life of the Virgin: Maximos the Confessor,* trans. Stephen Shoemaker (New Haven, 2012). It had long been mistakenly thought that Euthymios's Georgian translation was made from a lost work by Maximos the Confessor; for a thorough study of this question, see Christos Simelidis, "Two *Lives of the Virgin.*"

11 The Notes to the Translation of this volume are not the place for detailed comments on Euthymios's reworking of the *Life.* However, for ease of reference and study we have aligned the chapter divisions of the original Greek text with those of the Georgian version; for more about this, see the Note on the Text.

12 See Epiphanios, *Life of the Theotokos:* "There have been many panegyrists of the Theotokos among the Holy Fathers, but not one among them

elaborated her life and times truly and accurately, from her upbringing to her death. . . . Thus, we will provide something in simple language for those who long for the facts about her" (ed. Dressel, *Epiphanii monachi,* 13–14). We are thankful to Mary Cunningham for providing us with a copy of her forthcoming translation of the *Life* by Epiphanios.

13 As indicated in the Notes to the Translation, Geometres's sources include Gregory of Nyssa, Amphilochios of Iconium, Ps.-Basil of Caesarea, John Chrysostom, Dionysius the Areopagite, Epiphanios the Monk, George of Nikomedia, John of Damascus, Josephus, as well as significant literary borrowings from other patristic writers, especially Gregory of Nazianzus.

14 Marian homilies delivered in sections or serially over the course of an all-night vigil are attested through the ninth century, but it is not clear if this practice continued into the tenth; see Célestin Marie Bernard Chevalier, "Les trilogies homilétiques dans l'elaboration des fêtes Mariales. 650–850," *Gregorianum* 18 (1937): 361–78.

15 Antoine Wenger, *L'Assomption de la T. S. Vierge dans la tradition byzantine du VIe au Xe siècle* (Paris, 1955), 193.

16 See Lauxtermann, "John Geometres," 364; for the poem, see Maria Tomadaki, "Ιωάννης Γεωμέτρης, Ιαμβικά Ποιήματα: Κριτική έκδοση, μετάφραση και σχόλια" (PhD diss., University of Thessaloniki, 2014), 56–59 (text and translation), 266–70 (commentary).

17 Karl Benedikt Hase, *Leonis diaconi Caloënsis historiae libri decem,* Corpus scriptorum historiae Byzantinae (Bonn, 1828), 84–126; Hans Thurn, *Ioannis Scylitzae Synopsis historiarum,* Corpus fontium historiae Byzantinae, Series Berolinensis 5 (Berlin, 1973), 279–94; Jean-Claude Cheynet, *Pouvoir et contestations à Byzance (963–1210)* (Paris, 1990; online, 1996), no. 6, pp. 24–25, http://books.openedition.org/psorbonne/3844. Although the rebellion of the two Bardases (Phokas and Skleros) in 987–989 is traditionally portrayed as a civil war, it is doubtful that the Byzantines would have viewed it as a fratricide (ἀδελφοκτονία), so strongly associated with Cain and Abel; see, for example, Epiphanios, *Ancoratus,* ed. Karl Holl, *Epiphanius (Ancoratus und Panarion),* Die griechischen christlichen Schriftsteller der ersten drei Jahrhunderte 25 (Leipzig, 1915), p. 172, line 20; and Theodor Büttner-Wobst and Anton Gerard Roos, eds., *Excerpta historica iussu imp. Constantini Porphyrogeniti confecta,* vol. 2, part 1, *Excerpta de virtutibus et vitiis* (Berlin, 1906), p. 5, line 21. No rebellion in the tenth century is described in this

kind of language in any of the histories and chronicles; and Basil II and Bardas Skleros (or Bardas Phokas) were neither related to each other nor on equal footing in the eyes of the government.

18 Leo the Deacon, *History* 5.9, ed. Hase, *Leonis diaconi Caloënsis,* p. 90, lines 12–13, trans. Alice-Mary Talbot and Dennis F. Sullivan, *The History of Leo the Deacon: Byzantine Military Expansion in the Tenth Century* (Washington, DC, 2005), 140. See also Skylitzes, *History* 2, ed. Thurn, *Ioannis Scylitzae Synopsis,* p. 285, lines 25–26, trans. John Wortley, *John Skylitzes: A Synopsis of Byzantine History, 811–1057* (Cambridge, 2010), 272: "the hands [of John I] were dripping with the steaming blood of a newly slain kinsman" (ἀτμίζοντι ἔτι τῷ συγγενικῷ αἵματι σταζομένας τὰς χεῖρας ἔχοντα). Skylitzes ascribes these words to Polyeuktos's speech to John I after the murder of Nikephoros. Like fratricide (ἀδελφοκτονία), the expression "blood of a kinsman" (τῷ συγγενικῷ αἵματι) clearly alludes to Genesis 4:10.

19 Dmitry Korobeynikov, personal correspondence with the authors, October 10, 2021.

20 Niketas incorporated nearly fifty excerpts from Geometres's *Life of the Virgin* and oration on the Annunciation, as well as excerpts from Symeon Metaphrastes, the only other tenth-century writer included in the collection; for references, see the Note on the Text.

21 Paul Gautier, ed., *Michaelis Pselli, Theologica* (Leipzig, 1989), vol. 1, p. 181, lines 101–4; see Simelidis, "Two *Lives of the Virgin,*" 135; and Stratis Papaioannou, "Ioannes Sikeliotes (and Ioannes Geometres) Revisited," *Travaux et Memoires* 23 (2019): 659–92, at 678–79.

22 On this manuscript, see the Note on the Text. It is noteworthy that the *Life*'s account of the Passion was excerpted in the thirteenth-century codex Ambrosianus gr. E 100 supp. Other sections may have also circulated independently as sermons or readings for feast days of the Theotokos and Christ; see Shoemaker, *The Life of the Virgin,* 161–64, which indicates that the Georgian version of the *Life* was broken up into separate sections and read throughout the liturgical year.

23 See, for example, Charles Barber, "Reading the Garden in Byzantium: Nature and Sexuality," *Byzantine and Modern Greek Studies* 16 (1992): 1–20, at 9–10.

24 It is worth citing a few more characteristic examples: καὶ νῦν ἐν τῷ πάθει τὴν αὐτὴν ἀπαθεστάτην τὲ ὁμοῦ καὶ συμπαθεστάτην ἀπέδειξε (*antithesis,* 73); τὸ ἀνδρωδέστατον αὐτὸ τῆς ἀνανδροτάτης (*antithesis,* 74);

κεκαμωμένων ταῖς μάστιξι . . . νενεκρωμένων τοῖς πάθεσι (*isocolon,* 85); τὸ κοινὸν ἱλαστήριον, τὸ φρικτὸν μυστήριον, τὸ καινὸν τῆς θείας ἑνώσεως καὶ τῆς ἀνθρωπίνης ἀναπλάσεως ἐργαστήριον (*homoioteleuton,* 111); ἅρπασον καὶ τὴν διὰ νεφελῶν τῶν μαθητῶν ἁρπαγὴν εἰς ἀπόδειξιν τῆς τελευταίας καὶ βεβαίας καὶ τῶν ἐσχάτων Χριστοῦ μαθητῶν ἐπὶ νεφελῶν ἁρπαγῆς (*figura etymologica and polyptoton,* 121).

25 The phrase "rhetorical logic" is from Roderich Reinsch, "What Should an Editor Do with a Text Like the 'Chronographia' of Michael Psellos?," in *Ars Edendi,* ed. Alessandra Bucossi and Erika Kihlman, vol. 2 (Stockholm, 2012), 131–54, at 145.

26 See Magdalino, "Liturgical Poetics"; and Simelidis, "Two *Lives of the Virgin,*" 133 and 137–38.

27 On Geometres's self-confidence and the authoritative manner in which he expresses some of his views, see Simelidis, "Two *Lives of the Virgin,*" 130 and 152–53.

28 See the remarks of Wenger, *L'Assomption,* 186; Jane Baun, *Tales from Another Byzantium: Celestial Journey and Local Community in the Medieval Greek Apocrypha* (Cambridge, 2007), 283; and Cunningham, *The Virgin Mary in Byzantium,* 23.

29 Geometres was capable of making unusual and unexpected remarks: in his encomium of the apple, he juxtaposed the healing qualities of a rotten apple with Christ; see Simelidis, "Two *Lives of the Virgin,*" 132, 147–48, 150–51.

30 For discussion, see Ioli Kalavrezou, "Images of the Mother: When the Virgin Mary Became *Meter Theou,*" *Dumbarton Oaks Papers* 44 (1990): 165–72; Niki Tsironis, "The Mother of God in the Iconoclastic Controversy," in *Mother of God: Representations of the Virgin in Byzantine Art,* ed. Maria Vassilaki (Athens, 1999), 27–39; and Kathleen Corrigan, "Text and Image on an Icon of the Crucifixion at Mount Sinai," in *The Sacred Image East and West,* ed. Robert Ousterhout and Leslie Brubaker (Urbana and Chicago, 1995), 45–62.

31 This was a theological strategy first used against the anti-Chalcedonians; see, for example, Anastasios of Sinai, *Hodegos* 12.1, ed. Karl-Heinz Uthemann, *Anastasii Sinaitae Viae dux,* Corpus Christianorum Series Graeca 8 (Turnhout, 1981), 201–2.

32 So-called "affective" Marian piety is a feature of medieval Marian devotion not entirely applicable to Byzantine Marian piety; see Sarah McNamer, *Affective Meditation and the Invention of Medieval Compassion* (Philadelphia, 2010); and Maximos Constas, "Abba Poemen and Mary at the Cross: On the Origins of Byzantine Devotion to the Mother of God," in *Lament as Performance in Byzantium,* ed. Niki Tsironis and Theofili Kampianaki (London, forthcoming).

33 See, for example, Wenger, *L'Assomption,* 406n1; and Jean Galot, "La plus ancienne affirmation de la corédemption mariale: Le témoignage de Jean le Géomètre," *Recherches des science religieuse* 45 (1957): 187–208. While some Roman Catholic theologians carefully qualify Mary's *participation* in the divine economy of salvation, the notion that "Mary's intense sufferings were amassed in such an interconnected way that was not only a proof of her unshakable faith, but also a contribution to the redemption of all, and were mysteriously and supernaturally fruitful for the redemption of the world" (John Paul II, *Salvifici Doloris* 25, apostolic letter, February 11, 1984) would seem to make the redemptive work of Christ contingent on the emotional response of a human being, and as such has no parallel in Byzantine theological thought.

34 See Simelidis, "Two *Lives of the Virgin,*" 148.

35 John Chrysostom, *Homily* 4, on Colossians (PG 62:326), and *Homily* 1, on 2 Corinthians (PG 61:387). See also the interpretation of Colossians 1:24 by Photios of Constantinople, *Epistle* 253, ed. B. Laourdas and L. G. Westerink, *Photii patriarchae Constantinopolitani Epistulae et Amphilochia* (Leipzig, 1983–1988), vol. 2, pp. 190–93; and the Photian fragment on the same verse preserved in the *catena,* ed. Karl Staab, *Pauluskommentare aus der griechischen Kirche* (Münster, 1933), 631–32.

36 See Maximos the Confessor, *Ambigua* 21.14–15, ed. Nicholas [Maximos] Constas, *On Difficulties in the Church Fathers: The Ambigua,* Dumbarton Oaks Medieval Library 28 and 29 (Cambridge, MA, 2014), vol. 1, pp. 441–45. See also the discussions in Lars Thunberg, *Microcosm and Mediator: The Theological Anthropology of Maximus the Confessor* (Chicago, 1995), 22–36; and Adam G. Cooper, *The Body in St Maximus the Confessor: Holy Flesh, Wholly Deified* (Oxford, 2005), 241–50.

LIFE OF THE VIRGIN MARY

Ἐξόδιος ἢ προπεμπτήριος εἰς τὴν Κοίμησιν τῆς ὑπερενδόξου Δεσποίνης ἡμῶν Θεοτόκου, τοῦ μακαρίου Ἰωάννου τοῦ Γεωμέτρου

Θαρρεῖν μὲν τὸν λόγον ἐπ' ὀλίγον κἂν ἦν, εἰ, ὥσπερ ἡ προκειμένη πρὸς εὐφημίαν παντὸς ἦν ὑπερηρμένη καὶ τρόπου καὶ φύσεως, οὕτω δὴ καὶ γλῶττα παρῆν παντὸς ὑπερκειμένη λόγου καὶ πάσης τέχνης τὲ καὶ δυνάμεως· ἢ τό γε δεύτερον, εἰ κἄν, ὥσπερ προπεμπομένης ὑλική τε γλῶσσα καὶ ἄϋλος ἀγγέλων ἅμα καὶ ἀποστόλων ἀνεκίρνα τὰ προπεμπτήρια, οὕτω καὶ νῦν ἑορταζομένης *πᾶν ὅσον ἐγκόσμιόν τε καὶ ὑπερκόσμιον* εἰς ἓν συνελθὸν καὶ συνεισενεγκὸν ὁμοῦ τὴν τέχνην καὶ τὴν φωνήν, μίαν συνετέλουν καὶ τὴν ᾠδήν. Ἦν γὰρ ἀξία μὲν οὐδὲ οὕτω. Πῶς γὰρ τῇ γε ὡς ἀληθῶς ἀξίᾳ καὶ μόνῃ καὶ θυγατρὶ καὶ μητρὶ καὶ νύμφῃ τοῦ ὄντος καὶ Δεσποίνῃ τῶν ὄντων, καὶ μηδὲ τοῖς χερουβὶμ τρανῶς θεατῇ μηδὲ τοῖς σεραφὶμ ἀρκετῶς ὑμνητῇ, μηδὲ καταληπτῇ ταῖς ἄλλαις ὅλαις ὑψηλοτέραις ἢ ταπεινοτέραις τάξεσιν, ἐγγυτέρα δ' ἂν ἴσως ἦν τῆς ἀξίας καὶ οὐ τοσούτῳ τῶν πραγμάτων ἀπελιμπάνετο; Ἐπεὶ δὲ καὶ ἄμφω

Funeral oration or farewell discourse for the Dormition of our most glorious Lady the Theotokos, by the blessed John Geometres

Prologue

It would have been possible, if only for a little while, for me to speak with confidence, if, that is, I possessed a tongue that transcended all speech and every human skill and power, just as the one who is set before us as the subject of our praise is exalted above every form of life and nature. Or if, in the second place, it happened that, just as when she was being carried in procession to her tomb, the material voices of the apostles blended with the immaterial voices of the angels in the singing of her funeral songs, so too now, when she is being honored by us at this feast, *all the powers on earth and those above the earth* came together in unison and combined their musical skill and voices in the singing of a single song. But even that would not be worthy of her. For how could it be possible for such a song to praise her worthily and not fall vastly short of its subject, seeing that it is addressed to one who is truly worthy, one who alone is the daughter, mother, and bride of the One who exists, and who herself is the Queen of all that exists, and who cannot be gazed upon directly even by the cherubim, nor praised sufficiently by the seraphim, nor comprehended by all the other ranks of angels, whether they be of higher or lower station?

ταῦτα, τὸ μὲν διὰ τὸ ὑπὲρ φύσιν, τὸ δὲ διὰ τὸ ὑπὲρ τὴν τάξιν ἢ τὸν καιρόν, ἀδύνατα—πείθομαι γάρ ποτε καὶ ἄμφω συνελθεῖν ταῦτα καὶ καθάπερ τῷ ταύτης υἱῷ οὕτω δὴ καὶ ταύτῃ *πᾶν γόνυ κάμψειν καὶ πᾶσαν γλῶσσαν καὶ ἐπιγείων καὶ οὐρανίων ἀνυμνῆσαι καὶ ἐξομολογήσασθαι*—πόσον τι χρὴ καὶ τῆς ἀξίας ἀποπεσεῖν οἴεσθαι νῦν τὸν μόνον ἐγχειροῦντα καὶ ὑλικὸν καὶ μηδὲ περὶ ταῦτα λαμπρὸν μηδὲ τῶν πολλῶν ἴσως πολὺ διαφέροντα;

Οὐ μὴν ἀλλ' οὐχὶ κἂν πάντῃ τῆς ἀξίας ἀπολειπώμεθα, ἤδη καὶ τῆς προθυμίας ὁμοῦ συναπολειψόμεθα. Τὸ μὲν γὰρ τῆς δυνάμεως καὶ ἀνεύθυνον, τὸ δὲ τῆς βουλήσεως καὶ ὑπεύθυνον· ἐπεὶ καὶ τῷ ταύτης υἱῷ, τὸ μὲν κατὰ δύναμιν πᾶν εὐπρόσδεκτον, τὸ δὲ ἀπροαίρετον καὶ ὑπόδικον, μᾶλλον δὲ καὶ ἀδύνατον, ὥσπερ τὸ κατ' ἀξίαν, οὕτω καὶ τὸ μὴ κατὰ δύναμιν αὐτὴν μακαρίζειν. Ὅπερ αὐτὴ πᾶσι καὶ κατὰ πᾶσαν γενεὰν προεθέσπισεν, ἄλλως θ' ὅτε καὶ μὴ μακαρίσαι μᾶλλον ἐκείνην ἐστίν, ἣν προλαβὼν οὕτως ὁ υἱὸς καὶ Θεὸς ἐμακάρισεν, ἢ μακαρίους μὲν ἀποδεῖξαι τοὺς λόγους οἳ μακαρίσαι τὴν μακαριωτάτην ἐκείνην προείλοντο, μακαρίους δὲ τούς τι τῶν ἐκείνης ἀκούοντας καὶ πιστεύοντας, μακάριον δὲ καὶ ἑαυτὸν τὸν ἐκείνῃ τι τῶν ἐκείνης αὐτῆς προσάγοντα κατὰ δύναμιν. Ἐπεὶ οὖν τοσαύτη μὲν πάντοθεν ἡ ἀνάγκη, τοσαῦτα δὲ καὶ τὰ κέρδη τῷ λόγῳ,

But since neither of these conditions is possible, the former because she transcends nature, and the latter because she transcends the ranks of angels, just as she transcends the occasion of our feast—though I am nevertheless convinced that at some point the earthly and the heavenly will indeed gather together, and then, just as in the case of her son, *every knee will bend and every earthly and heavenly tongue will praise and confess* her too—how much more must the present speaker now reckon that his own attempt to praise her will also fall short of its mark with respect to her worthiness, since it is merely earthly, devoid of any brilliance, and is not much different from the praise offered by ordinary speakers?

But even if I am entirely lacking in worthiness, I am not lacking in eagerness. The former depends on natural ability and thus is irreproachable, but the latter depends on desire and thus is subject to reproach for, to her son, whatever is within natural ability is acceptable, but choosing *not* to praise her would be censurable; indeed, it would be impossible, for just as we cannot praise and bless her according to her worthiness, neither can we also *not* praise and bless her according to our natural ability. This is what she had foretold regarding all people and every generation, especially when it is not possible to bless her more than her son and God blessed her by choosing her, but simply to demonstrate that the words chosen to bless the most blessed Theotokos are themselves blessed, just as they who hear and believe something from her life are blessed; and blessed too is he who offers to her, to the best of his ability, something from her life. Since, then, on all sides the need is so great, it follows that the benefits to be gained from the discourse are

αὐτὴν ἂν εἴη χρεών, τοῦ Λόγου τὴν Μητέρα τοῦ λόγου προστησαμένους, θαρρούντως ἐπαφεῖναι τῷ μεγάλῳ πελάγει τούτῳ τῆς εὐφημίας οὐχ᾽ ὁρίζοντι μὲν λογισμοῖς, οὔτε ἀνθρωπίνοις οὔτε δὲ οὐρανίοις, οὐκ ἀφορίζοντι δὲ ὅμως τοὺς μὴ τὸ πᾶν τέμνοντας οὐδὲ ἀχρειοῦντι τῷ λειπομένῳ τὸ ἀνυόμενον.

2 Ἔστι μὲν οὖν καὶ τοῦτο τῆς πάντα ταύτης ὑπερφυοῦς ὑπὲρ φύσιν· οὔτε γὰρ ἱστορίας οὔτε δὲ εὐφημίας ἔργον ἐκπληρῶσαι τοῖς ταύτην ἐνισταμένοις τὴν ὑπόθεσιν δυνατόν· οὔτε γὰρ πάντα ἢ γοῦν τὰ πλεῖστα περιλαβεῖν, ὅπερ ἱστορίας, οὔτε δὲ τοῖς περιλειφθεῖσι περιθεῖναί τι μέγεθος, ὅπερ εὐφημίας· πολλοῦ γε καὶ δεῖ, ὅπου γε μηδὲ κατ᾽ ἴσον ἐλθεῖν ἀλλὰ καὶ ἀμφοτέρων ἐκπεσεῖν ἀναγκαῖον, εἰ καὶ παραδόξως αὖθις ὁ λόγος ἀντιστρέφειν δύναται. Ὅ τε γὰρ ἱστορῶν εὐφημεῖ τὰ παντὸς ἐγκωμίου λέγων ἐπέκεινα, καὶ ὁ εὐφημῶν ἱστορεῖ μὴ ψιλῶς μόνον ἀλλὰ καὶ ἐνδεῶς, ὡς πολὺ τῶν πραγμάτων ἀπολειπόμενος· ὥσπερ δὴ καὶ ἡμῖν οὔτε πάντα περιληπτέον οὔθ᾽ ὧν περιλάβωμεν ἀπαιτητέον τὸ μέγεθος, ἀλλὰ τῶν ἀναγκαιοτέρων τὲ καὶ γνωριμωτέρων, εἰ δὲ καὶ ἄλλως εἰς ἔτι καὶ νῦν τοῖς πολλοῖς ἀγνοουμένων, ἀλλ᾽ ὧν οὐκ ὀλίγοι τῶν παλαιῶν οὐδὲ μικροί τινες μάρτυρες.

Τούτων οὖν κατ᾽ ἐπιδρομὴν καὶ δι᾽ ὅσων ἐξὸν ἐφαψαμένοις, οὕτω τῇ τε πανηγύρει τὰ πρόσφορα, καὶ τοῖς ποθοῦσι τῆς ἱστορίας τὰ καίρια, καὶ τῇ Παρθένῳ δὲ καὶ Θεοῦ

equally great, and those who champion in words the Mother of the Word, are obliged to set themselves loose upon this great sea of praise, which is not bounded by the power of reason, either human or heavenly; neither does it exclude those who cannot traverse the whole of it, nor render useless the one who falls short of accomplishing his purpose.

Moreover, to praise she who in every respect is beyond 2
nature is itself beyond our nature, for it is impossible for those who attempt this to accomplish it through the genres either of history or encomium. This is because it is not possible for someone to include all things, or even most of them, which is the task of history; nor is it possible to speak with loftiness about the things which are included, which is the task of encomium. Far from it, since one must necessarily employ neither of these genres equally, but also depart from both, even though paradoxically the two genres are conversely predicable. This is because the historian praises his subject by referring to things that are outside the genre of an encomium, while the encomiast offers historical details that are not only unsupported by evidence but also insufficient, ignoring a great many things. So too, for me, it is not necessary to include all the details, neither is it required to elevate those that are included to the level of encomiastic loftiness, and I will thus include only things that are of greater importance and more notable, and for which there exists an abundance of ancient and illustrious witnesses, though they are unknown to most people even now.

By touching on these things in cursory fashion and wherever possible, I will render what is both reasonable for our festal assembly and seasonable for those who yearn for history, along with our gifts of gratitude to the Virgin, who is

Μητρὶ καὶ Δεσποίνῃ κοινῇ πληρωτέον τὰ χαριστήρια. Εἰ δὲ μετὰ πολλοὺς καὶ ἄλλους τῷ γράφειν ἐπεχειρήσαμεν, οὐ μέμψεως, εἰ μὴ καὶ ἀποδοχῆς ἄξιοι, ὅτε γὰρ πόθος οὐδενὸς τῶν ἄλλων λειπόμενος, ἀλλ'—εἰ καὶ τολμηρὸν εἰπεῖν—καὶ τῷ μετὰ πάντας ἐπιχειροῦντι ἀνάγκη καὶ τὰ πάντων καὶ εἴ τι πλέον τῶν πάντων εἰπεῖν. Συνείλεκται δὲ καὶ ἡμῖν οὐ μόνον ὅσα παρὰ τῶν εὐαγγελιστῶν τὲ καὶ προφητῶν, ἀλλὰ καὶ ὅσα παρ' αὐτῶν τῶν ἀποκρύφων ἀνελεξάμεθα, σύμφωνα καὶ ταῦτα δηλαδὴ καὶ ἀκόλουθα τοῖς εὐαγγελισταῖς καὶ προφήταις καὶ τοῖς μεγάλοις καὶ θεολήπτοις πατράσι καὶ διδασκάλοις· εἴσεται δὲ πάντως ὅ γε δίκαιος ἀκροατὴς καὶ κριτής. Εἰ δ' ἔστιν οὗ καὶ τὰ τοῦ ταύτης υἱοῦ συμπαραληψόμεθα, τοῦτο μὴ τῆς ἀνάγκης ἔστω τοῦ λόγου μόνον—ἐπεὶ καὶ δι' ὅλου ταῦτα συνῆπται σχεδόν—ἀλλὰ καὶ τῆς δόξης αὐτῆς ταύτης τῆς αὐτοῦ μητρός. Ἔστι μὲν γὰρ καὶ ἄλλως δόξα ταῖς μητράσι πάντα τὰ τῶν υἱῶν, μάλιστα δὲ τὰ τούτου καὶ ταύτῃ, τοῦ μὲν ὡς φύσει θεῖά τε καὶ ἐκ Θεοῦ, τῇ δὲ ὡς μόνῃ καὶ ὑπὲρ πάσας μόνην τὴν τοῦ υἱοῦ δόξαν, δόξαν ἐχούσῃ καὶ ἀγαλλίασιν.

Κἀκεῖνο δὲ πρὸ πάντων μικροῦ καὶ διὰ πάντων θεωρητέον, ὅπως οὐ μόνον κατὰ βίου καὶ λόγου παντός, ἀλλὰ καὶ κατ' αὐτῆς τῆς φύσεως ἔχει τὰ νικητήρια, καὶ ὅπως, ὥσπερ ἐν λύρᾳ, μία διὰ πάντων εὐαρμοστία καὶ συμφωνία, τὸ γένος, ἡ ἐπαγγελία, ἡ γέννησις, ἡ κλῆσις, ἡ ἀφιέρωσις, ἡ φύσις ψυχῆς ὁμοῦ τὲ καὶ σώματος, ἡ τροφὴ καὶ διαγωγή

the Mother of God and the Queen of all. And though I undertake to write after many others, this is not worthy of condemnation, but should be seen rather as a mark of approbation, since my desire is not inferior to that of my predecessors. Indeed—and though it may be a bold thing to say—someone who attempts such a feat after so many others, must necessarily say everything that they have said along with something more. I have thus collected material not only from the evangelists and prophets, but also from apocryphal works, for even these are in agreement with and follow the evangelists, the prophets, and the great and inspired fathers and teachers, as any impartial listener and judge will easily perceive. And if, in places, I include things that concern her son, this is not imposed on me solely by the exigencies of the discourse—since these things have been more or less included throughout—but is rather also done for the glory of his own mother. This is because things pertaining to sons generally bring glory to their mothers, and this is especially the case with this son in relation to this mother, for the simple reason that what pertains to him is divine by its very nature and from God, while she alone, beyond all other mothers, possesses the glory and exultation of her son.

Beyond anything else, one should also always consider briefly how not only with respect to her entire life and speech but also with respect to nature itself, she takes the prize of victory, and how, just as in the case of a lyre, all things concerning her resound in a single harmony and agreement. By this I mean her ancestry, the promise concerning her, her birth, her calling, her dedication in the temple, the nature of her soul and body, her nourishment,

τε καὶ ἀγωγή, καὶ τὰ τούτων ἔτι πάλιν θειότερα, καὶ τοῦ κόσμου παντὸς σωτήρια, ἡ θεία σύλληψις, ἡ κύησις καὶ ἡ γέννησις, ὅσα τὲ ἄλλα περὶ αὐτὴν τοῦ θείου τόκου καὶ ἐνθεέστατα καὶ φρικτότατα καὶ αὖθις ὅσα περὶ τὸν θεῖον τόκον περιπαθέστατα διηγήματα, οἷα δὲ καὶ μετὰ τὴν εἰς οὐρανοὺς ἀνάληψιν τοῦ υἱοῦ ταύτῃ τὰ πολιτεύματα καὶ πέρας, ὃ δὴ καὶ πάντων τῶν περὶ αὐτὴν μυστηρίων πέρας καὶ ὃ καὶ ἡμεῖς πανηγυρίζομεν σήμερον, ἐπίγεια καὶ οὐράνια, μεθ' οἵας δόξης τὲ καὶ λαμπρότητος πρὸς οὐρανὸν καὶ αὐτὴ καὶ τὸν υἱὸν καὶ Θεὸν ἑαυτῆς ἐξεδήμησεν ἢ ἀνέλυσε καὶ ἀπολιποῦσα τὴν γῆν καὶ τὸν τῇδε κόσμον οὐκ ἔλιπε.

Γέννησις

3 Πόθεν οὖν πόθεν ἀρκτέον τοῦ λόγου; ἢ δῆλον ὅθεν κἀκείνη τοῦ βίου, τοῦ γένους φημί, καὶ ὅπως οὔτε τοῦτο τοῖς ἄλλοις αὐτῇ παραπλήσιον οὔτε δὲ τῆς μελλούσης αὐτῇ θείας συλλήψεως καὶ οἰκονομίας ἀσύμβολον καὶ ἀνεπισήμαντον; Ἀλλὰ πρῶτον μὲν τοῦ βασιλικωτάτου καὶ προφητικωτάτου καὶ θειοτάτου γένους τοῦ Ἰούδα τὲ καὶ Δαβίδ (ἀμφότερα γὰρ ὁ θεοπάτωρ καὶ εἴπερ τις ἐπιφανὴς καὶ ἀμφότερα καὶ προφήτης καὶ βασιλεύς, καὶ ὅσοι μετὰ τοῦτον ἐκ τούτου καὶ προφῆται καὶ βασιλεῖς), ἔπειτα καὶ τῷ ἰουδαϊκῷ τοῦ λευϊτικοῦ, εἴτ' οὖν τοῦ ἱερατικοῦ τῷ βασιλικῷ συμπλακέντος· οὕτω γὰρ ἄμφω καὶ Ἰωακεὶμ ὁ πατὴρ καὶ Ἰωσὴφ ὁ μνηστὴρ ἱστορεῖται, μικτοί τινες τὰς

formation and education. Also things still more divine than these that are salvific for the whole world, namely, her divine conception, her pregnancy, her birth-giving, and the other exceedingly divine and awe-inspiring things concerning her which have to do with her divine offspring, and again the deeply moving accounts of her divine offspring himself. And then, after her son's ascension into heaven, there is her conduct and the completion of her life which is indeed the completion of all the mysteries concerning her and the very event that we are celebrating today, both on earth and in heaven, with such glory and splendor as is appropriate for her departure to heaven and to her son and God—whether we call this her departure or death—for though she left this earth, she did not abandon this world.

Birth

Where, oh where, should I begin my discourse? Where 3
else than with the place where she herself began her life? By this I mean her family, which, as with other things, nothing could equal, and which did not fail to contribute to or confer distinction on her divine conception and the dispensation of salvation. In the first place, she was descended from the most royal, prophetic, and divine race of Judah and David. (To be sure, David, the ancestor of God, was illustrious on both sides, for he was both a prophet and a king, and all who trace their lineage back to him were prophets and kings.) With the tribe of Judah she was also of the tribe of Levi, that is, the priestly line was mingled with the royal line. Thus it is recorded in the historical account that both her father, Joachim, and her betrothed, Joseph, were of

φυλὰς κατά τινα περιπέτειαν, εἰ καὶ κατ' ἐπικράτειαν τοῦ κρείττονος ὠνομάζοντο ἐξ οἴκου καὶ πατριᾶς Δαβίδ. Τοῦτο μὲν γὰρ ἦν αὐτοῖς κατὰ φύσιν, ἐκεῖνο δὲ κατὰ νόμον, ὡς τῶν μὲν ὄντες, τῶν δὲ δοκοῦντες, τῷ δὲ πατρῴῳ γένει καὶ τὸ μητρῷον ἐφάμιλον ἢ ἀνάλογον.

Τοῖς δὲ πατράσι καὶ αἱ πατρίδες Ἰουδαία καὶ Γαλιλαία, Βηθλεέμ τε καὶ Ναζαρέτ, τῶν μὲν γὰρ κατὰ φύσιν ἦσαν, τὰς δὲ κατὰ περίστασιν ᾤκουν, ἵνα καὶ προχωρῇ διὰ πάντων ἡ κρᾶσις, οὐ μόνον ὅτι καὶ ὁ ἐξ αὐτῆς ἱερεύς τε καὶ βασιλεύς, ἀλλὰ καὶ ἄνθρωπος καὶ Θεός, ὧν τὸ μὲν τὸ ἱερατικόν, τὸ δὲ τὸ βασιλικὸν ἐτύπου γένος, καὶ τὸ μὲν Βηθλεέμ, τὸ δὲ Ναζαρέτ, ἣν καὶ Ναθαναὴλ ὡς χείρονα καὶ τοῦ χείρονος οἶδε τύπον, καὶ ἀδύνατον εἶναι *λέγει τὸ ἀγαθὸν ἐξ αὐτῆς*, ὡς οὐκ ἐνὸν διὰ τὴν ἀκαρπίαν τῆς φύσεως. Οὕτως ἐκ τριπλόκου σειρᾶς καθάπερ τριπλόκου ῥίζης τουτὶ παγὲν τὸ φυτὸν ἢ τὸ ἔρνος—ἢ καὶ τὸ κάλλος—ἐκ τριῶν τῶν καλλίστων, ἱερατείας καὶ προφητείας καὶ βασιλείας, ἵν' ᾖ καὶ αὐτὸς ὁ ἀριθμὸς τοῦ ἀριθμοῦ τύπος, ὡς ἕνα μὲν τέκοι καὶ αὐτὴ τῆς Τριάδος, οὐκ ἄνευ δὲ τῶν λοιπῶν (ἀμέριστος γάρ), ἀλλ' *εὐδοκίᾳ μὲν τοῦ Πατρός, συνεργίᾳ δὲ καὶ τοῦ Πνεύματος*. Καὶ ὅπως τοὺς ἐν μέσῳ προγόνους αὐτῆς, τοὺς μετὰ τὸν Ἰούδαν τὲ καὶ Δαβίδ, Λευῒ τε καὶ Ἀαρών, παραδράμωμεν ἐκ τῶν αὐτῶν, εἰ καὶ μὴ κατὰ τὸν αὐτὸν τούτοις ἐκλάμψαντας χρόνον ἢ τρόπον, ἀλλ' ἐπὶ τοὺς ταύτης γεννήτορας ἐλθεῖν ὁ λόγος ἐπείγεται

mixed descent from these tribes due to an unexpected event, though due to the predominance of the superior they were named as being from the house and lineage of David. The one was given to them by nature, while the other was given by law, so that they descended from the one but are also said to be part of the other, because the maternal line was equal and equivalent to the paternal.

Their fatherlands were consistent with the fathers: Judea and Galilee, Bethlehem and Nazareth. They hailed from the former by birth, but by circumstance they lived in the latter, in order for the mixing to spread through everything, so that the one born from her would be not only priest and king, but also man and God, of which the one was a figure of the priestly nation, while the other was a figure of the royal. Moreover, the one corresponds to Bethlehem and the other to Nazareth, which Nathanael considered the worse of the two, and a figure of what was even worse, *saying* that it was impossible for *anything good to come from it,* since such a thing was not possible given the barrenness of its nature. So, from a triple-stranded chain, as though sprouting forth from a threefold root, this plant or young sprout—or indeed this beauty—emerged from three most beautiful things, I mean from the priesthood, prophecy, and royalty, so that even the number might be a figure of the number of the Trinity, since she would give birth to one of the Trinity, not without the others (for its members are indivisible), but by *the goodwill of the Father and the cooperation of the Spirit.* But allow me to omit her intermediary ancestors, those, I mean, who lived after Judah and David, as well as after Levi and Aaron, even though they did not flourish at the same time or in the same manner as them, because my discourse must hasten to speak

καὶ τῶν καλῶν περὶ ταύτης ἀγωνισμάτων ἢ καὶ περὶ ταύτην ἅμα θαυμάτων ἅψασθαι.

4 Ἰωακεὶμ ἐνταῦθα καὶ Ἄννα τὸ μέγα τῆς Παλαιᾶς διήγημα καὶ καλλώπισμα, τὸ μεῖζον τῆς Νέας αὔχημα, μᾶλλον δέ, εἰ δεῖ τἀληθὲς εἰπεῖν, τὸ παντὸς τοῦ γένους ἔρεισμά τε ὁμοῦ καὶ παράδειγμα, καθάπερ ἡ θυγάτηρ τῆς παρθενίας, οὕτω καὶ οὗτοι τῆς εὐγαμίας ὥσπερ καὶ τῆς εὐτεκνίας ὕστερον· οἱ καὶ τῆς φύσεως ἑκατέρας ὅροι καὶ νόμοι τῆς ἀρετῆς, οἱ πρῶτοι τῶν ἄλλων, ἢ καὶ μόνοι διαφερόντως τὰς κλήσεις τοῖς τρόποις ἢ μᾶλλον ταῖς κλήσεσι τοὺς τρόπους ἁρμόσαντες. Ὁ μὲν ἄνωθεν καὶ παρὰ τοῦ Θεοῦ τῶν ἀνδρῶν δοθεὶς κόσμος, ἡ δὲ χάρις τῶν γυναικῶν· τὸ χρυσοῦν καὶ ὁμόζυγον καὶ ὁμόψυχον πάντα τὰ καλὰ ζεῦγος, οἱ δύο καὶ μεγάλοι φωστῆρες καὶ μηδὲν ἀλλήλων λειπόμενοι, οἱ πάντα μὲν πάντων τῶν ἄλλων κρατοῦντες, μόνης δὲ τῆς θυγατρὸς ἡττώμενοι. Τί δεῖ τὰ πολλὰ λέγειν; Οἱ πατέρες τῆς τοῦ Θεοῦ καὶ κοινῆς Μητρός τε καὶ σωτηρίας, οἱ τοῦ Θεοῦ μητροπάτορες, οὓς τίς οὐκ οἶδε, μᾶλλον δὲ ὧν τίς οὐ πεπείραται καὶ διηνεκῶς πρὸς αὐτοὺς καταφεύγων καὶ τῶν δεήσεων οὐκ ἀποτυγχάνων, ἀλλὰ καὶ τῶν κατ' αὐτοὺς ἀπολαύων χαρίτων καὶ μεσίταις πρὸς τὴν κοινὴν μεσῖτιν καὶ δεσπότιν χρώμενος; Ἀλλ' οὗτοι καὶ τοιοῦτοι τότε τυγχάνοντες καὶ οὕτω πρός τε τοὺς ἄλλους καὶ πρὸς ἀλλήλους καὶ πρὸς αὐτὸν τὸν Θεὸν ἔχοντες, οἵαν

of her parents and the noble struggles they undertook on her behalf, and at the same time touch on the miracles surrounding her.

Joachim and Anna are the great story and glory of the Old Covenant, and they are the greatest boast of the New Covenant, or rather, if one must speak the truth, they are the pillar and paradigm of the whole human race; and just as their daughter is the pillar and paradigm of virginity, her parents are the same for happy marriages, as they also later became for childbearing. They are likewise the definitions and standards of virtue for male and female nature, because compared to all the others they were the first, or rather the only, ones who preeminently united their calling with their manner of life, or rather their way of life with their calling. Joachim was the adornment of men, which was given by God from above, while Anna was the beauty of women. Together, these two great and shining lamps constitute a golden couple, unified in soul and yoked together for all good things, so that neither was in any way inferior to the other, and together they were superior in every way to all other couples, being surpassed only by their daughter. But why discuss the matter at length? The parents of the Mother of God—the common mother of our salvation—are the grandparents of God and are known to all. Who does not know them, or rather who does not have experience of them and has been disappointed in his petitions when continually seeking refuge in them? For when doing so, he has the benefit of their very own gifts of grace, and avails himself of them as mediators to the Virgin who is our common mediator and sovereign. But despite all of this and the relationship they had with others and with each other, as well as with God 4

εἶχον καὶ παρὰ Θεοῦ τὴν δοκιμασίαν, εἴτε καὶ τὴν ἑτοιμασίαν, τῇ ἀπαιδίᾳ πρὸς εὐπαιδίαν πολὺν ἐξεταζόμενοι χρόνον, ἐξ αὐτοῦ τοῦ γάμου μέχρι καὶ βαθυτάτου τοῦ γήρως, ὥστε μὴ τὴν φύσιν μόνον, ἀλλ' ἤδη καὶ τὴν ἡλικίαν ἀδύνατον εἶναι πρὸς τὴν τεκνογονίαν.

Ἐπειδὴ καὶ φιλεῖ πως τὸ θεῖον τὰς ἄκρας εὐθυμίας ἐξ ἄκρας ἀθυμίας ἀεὶ χαρίζεσθαι, τὸ μὲν ἵνα μὴ δῶρον ἁπλῶς, ἀλλὰ καὶ ἆθλον ἢ πυρώσεως ἢ δεήσεως τὸ δωρούμενον, τὸ δ' ἵνα καὶ χαριέστερον ὡς ποθεινότερον ἢ καὶ ἀνελπιστότερον, τὸ δὲ τρίτον ἵνα καὶ θαυμαστότερον μετὰ τὴν ἀπόγνωσιν, ὥσπερ καὶ τούτοις μετὰ τὴν ἄκραν καὶ τοῦ χρόνου καὶ τῆς φύσεως ἐναντίωσιν· ὃ δὲ μάλιστα τοὺς τῆς χαρᾶς ἐλύπει γεννήτορας, ὅτι μὴ μόνον οὕτω τὸ τοῦ γάμου καλὸν ὁμοίως ἔν τε αὐτοῖς καὶ τῷ Θεῷ διασῴζοντες τῶν τοῦ γάμου καλῶν ὁμοίως τοῖς ἄλλοις οὐ μετελάμβανον, ἀλλ' ὅτι μηδὲ τῆς εὐλογίας ἧς ἐκ τοῦ νόμου τότε μετεῖχον αἱ γόνιμοι· προσῆν δὲ καὶ τρίτον οὐχ' ἧττον, ἡ πονηρὰ καὶ ἀκόλαστος τῶν γειτόνων γλῶσσα καὶ τῶν ἐχθρῶν αὐτῶν βαρυτέρων φίλων καὶ φυλετῶν—πρᾶγμα πάντων ἀφορητότατον—οὐχ ὡς ἀτυχίαν ὀνειδίζουσα μόνον τὴν ἀκαρπίαν, ἀλλ' οἷα καὶ τῷ Ἰὼβ ἐπιτιμίαν παρὰ Θεοῦ πολλῶν καὶ μεγάλων ἀδικημάτων οὓς καὶ *παρακλήτορας κακῶν* λίαν ἐκεῖνος ὀνομάζει καλῶς.

Ἔμελλε δὲ ἄρα τὸ τεχθησόμενον οὐκ αὐτῶν μόνων, ἀλλὰ καὶ παντὸς τοῦ γένους τὸ ὄνειδος ἐξελεῖν, μᾶλλον δὲ

himself, they endured examination by God, which was also a preparation, inasmuch as they were tested for many years by their inability to bear children, from the very moment of their marriage until their great old age, so that it was not only because of nature but already because of their age that they were incapable of childbearing.

God somehow always delights in bestowing the greatest joys after the greatest sorrows. He does this so that what he gives will not, on the one hand, simply be a gift but also the prize for a fiery ordeal or a prayerful appeal, and, on the other, so that it will be all the more delightful, being greatly longed for and beyond what was hoped for; and, third, so that it will be even more marvelous after the experience of despair, as it was in the case of Joachim and Anna, after the extreme opposition they faced from both time and nature. But what saddened the parents of joy more than anything else was not only that, while they had preserved the good things of marriage for themselves and God, they were not able to share those good things with others, but also that they did not share in the blessing which the law at that time gave only to parents. To this there was added a third and not less significant cause for their sorrow: the evil and unbridled tongues of their neighbors, friends, and fellow tribesmen, who were harsher than enemies to them—which is the hardest thing of all—since their words not only reproached the misfortune of their inability to bear children, but argued that, like Job, their misfortune was a punishment from God for numerous and great misdeeds, which is why Job very rightly called such friends *miserable comforters.*

But the child to be born was destined to take away the shame not only of her parents but also of the entire human

καὶ εἰς αὐτὴν ἄκραν ἀναγαγεῖν τὴν δόξαν τὲ καὶ λαμπρότητα, τοῦτο μὲν διὰ τοῦ ἑαυτῆς παραδόξου τόκου καὶ παραδοξοτέρου βίου τὲ καὶ φρονήματος, τοῦτο δέ (ὃ καὶ μᾶλλον) διὰ τοῦ ἐξ αὐτῆς παραδοξοτάτου τόκου καὶ θεανδρικοῦ γεννήματος· μιμεῖται τοίνυν τὰ τῆς Ἄννης ἡ Ἄννα, τῆς τῷ χρόνῳ πρεσβυτέρας ἡ τὴν ἀξίαν πολλῷ προτέρα, ἡ μήτηρ τῆς τοῦ Δεσπότου καὶ προφητευομένου μητρὸς τῆς τοῦ δούλου τὲ καὶ προφήτου—τῆς τοῦ Σαμουὴλ ἡ τῆς τοῦ Ἐμμανουήλ· καὶ ἡ μὲν πρὸς τὸν ναὸν ἀποτρέχει καὶ τῇ φύσει δοῦναι καρπὸν τὸν καὶ τῆς φύσεως αἰτεῖται δημιουργὸν ἅμα καὶ γεωργόν, τὸ δὲ δῶρον Θεοῦ γενέσθαι καὶ δῶρον Θεῷ καὶ προσαναθεῖναι τῷ χαρισαμένῳ τὸ χάρισμα· οὐ μὴν οὐδὲ ὁ πατὴρ ἠμέλει τοῦ γενέσθαι πατήρ, ἀλλὰ κἀνταῦθα τῇ Ἄννῃ σύζυγος ἦν, νῦν μὲν κατὰ τὸ ὄρος, νῦν δὲ καὶ κατὰ τὸν ναὸν νηστεύων καὶ δακρύων καὶ προσευχόμενος καὶ ὁμοίως δοῦναι τὸ δοθησόμενον ὑπισχνούμενος.

Νεύει τοίνυν ὁ Καρποδότης τὸ δῶρον καὶ δοῦναί τε καὶ λαβεῖν· ἀλλ' ὅρα Θεοῦ σοφίαν καὶ δικαιοσύνην ὁμοῦ καὶ φιλανθρωπίαν, καὶ ὅπως τοῖς διπλῆν μὲν τὴν εὐχὴν ποιουμένοις οἰκονομεῖ διπλᾶ καὶ τὰ εὐαγγέλια. Προτίθησι δὲ κἀνταῦθα τὸν ἄνδρα, καίτοι τῆς Ἄννης θερμότερον ὅτι μάλιστα προσκειμένης ὅσον οὐ τεκοῦσαι μόνον πατέρων μητέρες φιλοτεκνότεραι, ἀλλὰ καὶ αὐτοῦ τοῦ τίκτειν ἐφετικώτεραι, καὶ ἀποκλεισθεῖσαι δὲ τοῦ τίκτειν ἀφορητότεραι, οὐ διὰ τὴν ἐκ τῆς ἀπαιδίας ἀδοξίαν μόνον τὲ καὶ τὸ ὄνειδος, ἀλλὰ καὶ διὰ τὴν ἐκ τῆς εὐπαιδίας δόξαν καὶ

race, and indeed to be raised to the pinnacle of glory and splendor, and this on account of her paradoxical birth and even more paradoxical life and way of thinking, and also (and perhaps more so) on account her supremely paradoxical child and offspring, who was both divine and human. Thus Anna imitates the things of Hannah, and the one who is far superior in worthiness imitates the one who has mere seniority in time; the mother of the mother of the prophesied Master imitates the mother of the slave and prophet—the mother of Emmanuel imitates the mother of Samuel. And she runs quickly to the temple and asks the creator and cultivator of nature to make nature fruitful, so that the child would be a gift from God, and a gift given to God, so that the gracious gift would be dedicated to the God who gave it. Neither was the father indifferent to becoming a father, but even in this he was the husband of Anna, now on the mountain and now in the temple, fasting and weeping and praying and vowing to make a gift of what would be given to him.

So it was that the Giver of Fruit deigned both to give and receive his own gift. Behold the wisdom and righteousness as well as the love of God for mankind, and how to those who make a double vow he dispenses a double reward of good tidings. Even here he preferred to give these first to the man, though Anna was more ardently disposed to the matter at hand, for certainly mothers not only love the children to whom they give birth more than fathers do, but they are also moved by the very desire to bring forth children, so that it becomes unbearable for them to be excluded from the process of childbirth, not only because of the ignominy and shame of being childless, but also on account of the glory

αὐτὴν τὴν ὥσπερ ἀφ' ἑαυτῶν τοῦ ἀνθρώπου παραγωγήν—*χαρᾷ χαίρουσαι* κατὰ τὸν Δεσποτικὸν λόγον διὰ τὴν προσθήκην τοῦ πλάσματος.

Ὁ μὲν οὖν ἐνταῦθα πρὸς αὐτῷ τῷ ναῷ καὶ τῇ προσευχῇ τῆς ἄνωθεν ἀκούει φωνῆς, ἡ δὲ φωνή· "Τέξεις παιδίον ὃ μὴ σοὶ δόξα μόνον, ἀλλὰ καὶ τῷ κόσμῳ παντὶ δόξα τὲ καὶ σωτήριον." Ἡ δὲ καίτοι τοῦ ἀνδρὸς λαβοῦσα τὰ εὐαγγέλια (φιλοῦσι γὰρ οἱ λίαν τινῶν ἐρωτικῶς ἔχοντες οὐ μόνον ἐξ ἄκρας περιχαρείας εἰς ἀπιστίαν ἐμπίπτειν, ἀλλὰ καὶ πολλάκις τὰ αὐτὰ ποθεῖν περὶ τῶν αὐτῶν ἀκούειν) παντοδαπή τις ἦν, ἔχαιρεν, ἤσχαλεν, ἐδάκρυεν, ἠγωνία, διεμερίζετο, τοῦτο μὲν ἠπίστει, τοῦτο δὲ ἀπιστεῖν οὐκ εἶχεν, ἠρεμεῖν οὐκ ἠδύνατο, εἰ μὴ καὶ αὐτὴ λάβοι τι σύμβολον ἄνωθεν τῆς συλλήψεως. Λαμβάνει τοίνυν, καὶ τόπος τῆς ἐπαγγελίας ὁ κῆπος, ἐν τούτῳ γὰρ καὶ ἡ Ἄννα τὸ δεύτερον *στεναγμοῖς ἀλαλήτοις* διεκαρτέρει τῷ Φυτουργῷ τοῦ γένους προσεντυγχάνουσα, αὐτόθεν εὐαγγελιζόμενος ὡς ἀποδώσει τῷ γένει παντὶ καὶ τὴν Ἐδὲμ τὸ τικτόμενον καὶ ὅτι *Ξύλον Ζωῆς* τὸ ταύτῃ φυτευθησόμενον. Οὕτως οὖν σὺν χαρᾷ τὴν κοινὴν χαρὰν καὶ κυρίαν καὶ συλλαβοῦσά τε καὶ τεκοῦσα Μαριὰμ ὀνομάζει καὶ κηρύττει καὶ ἄμφω ταῦτα δι' ἑνὸς τοῦ ὀνόματος. Τίς ἂν ἐφίκοιτο λόγος τῆς κατασχούσης τότε τοὺς γεννήτορας ἡδονῆς; Τίς τῆς ἑορτῆς; Τίς τοῦ περιλαβόντος πάντας θαύματος καὶ ἐκπλήξεως,

of being blessed with a child and the ability to bring a human being into existence, so to speak, from themselves. Thus, they *rejoiced greatly,* according to the word of the Lord, by the addition of a child.

It was then that Joachim, attending to the temple and to prayer, heard a voice from on high, saying: "You will beget a child, who will not only bring you glory, but will also bring glory and salvation to the whole world." Anna, on the other hand, when she had heard the good tidings from her husband (because those who greatly desire something are likely to disbelieve it when it happens, not only because of their excessive joy, but because they want to hear the good tidings affirmed repeatedly), experienced a range of reactions. She rejoiced, she was distressed, she wept, she was in suspense, she felt divided, at one moment she could not believe it, at another she could not but believe it, and she was unable to compose herself until she herself had received from on high a sign of the conception. And she received what she desired, and the place of the promise was a garden. There, for a second time, Anna waited patiently, and with *unutterable sighs* entreated the Planter of the human race. At once, an angel proclaimed the good news that the child would restore even Eden itself to the entire human race, and that what would be planted within her would be the *Tree of Life.* Thus, having joyfully conceived and given birth to the universal joy and sovereign lady, Anna named the child Mary, through which she proclaimed her two qualities with one name. What words could describe the pleasure which at that time possessed the parents? What words the celebration? What words the amazement and astonishment that took hold of

καὶ ὅπως ἀντιπεριΐστατο τῇ Ἄννῃ τὸ ὄνειδος εἰς ὑπερβολὴν δόξης, ἅμα δὲ καὶ ἀπορίας, ὅτι τοῦτο τὸ παιδίον γένοιτο; Τοιαῦτα τῆς Θείας Πύλης ἡμῖν τὰ προπύλαια, καὶ τοῦ προοιμίου τῆς δόξης τὰ τοῦ βίου προοίμια.

Τὰ Ἅγια τῶν Ἁγίων

5 Ἀλλ’ ἐπειδὴ καὶ ἔξω θηλῆς ἦν ἡ ὅσον οὔπω τοῦ Θεοῦ θηλή, ἐντὸς ἄγουσι καὶ τοῦ ναοῦ—τὸν ὅσον οὔπω μείζω καὶ κρείττω τοῦ Θεοῦ ναόν—καὶ τῷ Θεῷ διδόασιν ἀφιέρωμα τὸ μετ’ ὀλίγον ἐκείνου σκήνωμα· καὶ διεδέχετο τὴν μὲν θαυμαστὴν οὕτω σύλληψιν ἡ χαριεστέρα γονή, τὴν δὲ γονὴν ἡ τερπνοτέρα πρὸς τὸ ἱερὸν εἰσαγωγὴ τῆς Παρθένου καὶ προπομπὴ τῶν παρθένων, προγονικῇ καὶ αὕτη καὶ προφητικῇ καὶ βασιλικῇ προτυπωθεῖσα φωνῇ· *ἀπενεχθήσονται τῷ βασιλεῖ παρθένοι ὀπίσω αὐτῆς, αἱ πλησίον αὐτῆς ἀπενεχθήσονται*· πάντως μὲν καὶ διὰ τὰς τότε παρθένους οὐ προπορευομένας μόνον, ἀλλὰ δὴ καὶ ἐφεπομένας καὶ πάντοθεν περιεπομένας πρὸς τὸν ναόν, οἷα καὶ κατ’ οὐρανὸν ἀστέρων φαιδρῶν πολλῷ φαιδροτέραν τὴν σελήνην παραπεμπόντων· τάχα δὲ καὶ διὰ τὰς ὕστερον ἐπακολουθούσας παρθένους καὶ ὄπισθεν πάσας ὁμοῦ κινουμένας, τοῦτο μὲν διὰ τὸν χρόνον, τοῦτο δὲ καὶ πλέον διὰ τὸν τρόπον, ὡς καὶ μιμουμένας ἅμα καὶ λειπομένας, οὐκ αὐτὰς δὲ μόνον, ἀλλὰ καὶ τὰς *πλησίον αὐτῆς ἀπενεχθήσεσθαι*· καὶ τότε μὲν συγγενεῖς, νυνὶ δὲ καὶ ἄλλως ἐμφερεῖς ὅσαι ψυχαὶ

everyone, and how Anna's former shame had been replaced by the best and noblest kind of glory, along with her perplexity, that she would give birth to this child? These things, then, were for us the outer gateway of the Divine Gate and the prelude of her life was the prelude of the glory to come.

The Holy of Holies

When she who would soon nurse God had passed the 5
age of nursing, they led her into the temple—she who would soon be a far better and greater temple of God—and there they offered as a dedication to God the one who would soon be his habitation. In this way the marvelous conception was followed by a more beautiful birth, and the birth was followed by the more delightful entry of the Virgin into the sanctuary, preceded by an escort of virgins as was prefigured by the prophetic and royal voice of her ancestor: *Virgins behind her will be brought to the king; her companions will be brought forward.* This was certainly said with respect to those virgins who at that time not only preceded her, but who also followed her and were escorting her to the temple from every direction, just as bright stars in the sky reflect the much brighter moon. And it was perhaps also said with respect to those virgins who would subsequently follow her, and who would all take their place together behind her, partly because they would appear later in time, but even more so because of their way of life, since they imitate her but remain inferior to her, something that is true not only of them but also of those who were *her companions who were brought forward.* At that time, the virgins were her relatives, but now they are related to her in a different way, for they

καθαραὶ καὶ μετὰ τὸν γάμον ἢ καὶ σὺν τῷ γάμῳ παρθενικῶς αὐτῇ πλησιάζουσαι, ἃς καὶ αὐτὰς προσάγειν τῷ βασιλεῖ δι' αὐτῆς ὁ λόγος βούλεται καὶ εἰς τὰ ἐκεῖθεν τῶν Ἁγίων Ἅγια συνεισέρχεσθαι, ὅπου καθάπερ ὁ ταύτης υἱὸς *ὑπὲρ ἡμῶν πρόδρομος,* οὕτω καὶ αὕτη πρώτη τῶν πρὸ αὐτῆς καὶ κατ' αὐτήν τε καὶ μετ' αὐτὴν ὑπὲρ ἡμῶν εἰσελήλυθεν.

6 Ἀλλ' οὐκ ἔχω πῶς ποτε ἀποσπάσω τὴν ἀκοὴν ἢ τὴν ὄψιν τοῦ ἡδίστου τούτου θεάματος ἢ ἀκούσματος. Μικρὸν οὖν ἄνωθεν ἀναθεωρητέον οἵαν ἡμῖν καὶ τὴν θεωρίαν ὁ προφήτης καὶ βασιλεὺς καὶ προπάτωρ τῇ βασιλίδι καὶ θυγατρὶ καὶ τοῦ Θεοῦ μητρὶ περιΐστησι καὶ συμπληρωτέον καὶ αὐτοὺς ταύτῃ καὶ συνιστέον τὰ εἰσιτήρια· καὶ ὅπως εὐτάκτως ἐξ ἀρχῆς τοῦ ταύτης υἱοῦ προθεὶς τὰ πλεονεκτήματα ἢ γνωρίσματα, *τὴν ὡραιότητα* λέγω καὶ *τὸ κάλλος*—ὁπότερον βούλει—καὶ τὴν τῶν λόγων χύσιν καὶ τὴν *χάριν* καὶ τὴν σοφίαν, τὴν χρίσιν, τὴν πανοπλίαν, τὴν δύναμιν, τὴν ῥάβδον καὶ *τὴν ῥομφαίαν,* ἣν καὶ περὶ *τὸν μηρὸν περιεζῶσθαι* λέγει—τὸ σύμβολον, οἶμαι, τῆς αὐτοῦ σαρκώσεως—καὶ ἣν *ἀλήθειαν* λέγει καὶ *πραότητα* καὶ εὐθύτητα *καὶ δικαιοσύνην,* καὶ τέλος τὴν ἐκ τούτων ἢ μετὰ τούτων ἀκατάλυτον εὐτονίαν καὶ εὐπραγίαν καὶ βασιλείαν, εὐθὺς καὶ τὰ ταύτης ὑποτίθησι καλλωπίσματα, καθάπερ νυμφίου καὶ νύμφης ᾄδων ἐπιθαλάμια, κἂν τισιν ἔδοξε μὴ περὶ ταύτης μᾶλλον, ἀλλὰ καὶ περὶ τῆς Ἐκκλησίας ὁ λόγος, οὐδὲν γὰρ τῷ λόγῳ τὸ λυμαινόμενον.

are all those pure souls who after marriage or even in marriage approach her in a virginal manner. The prophetic saying wishes that these virginal souls might also be brought to the king through her, and enter into the Holy of Holies there with her, so that just as where her son *was a forerunner on our behalf,* she too might also enter on our behalf as the first of those before her, and with her, and after her.

I do not seem to be able to turn my ears or eyes away 6
from this most pleasant sight and sound. Let us therefore briefly consider from the beginning what kind of contemplation the prophet, king, and forefather framed for the queen and daughter and mother of God. And let us, in our turn, complete this contemplation by adding to it events related to her entry into the temple, seeing how, from the very beginning, the prophet described in an orderly manner the superior qualities or characteristic marks of her son, I mean his *bloom and his beauty*—whichever of the two you prefer—and the effusion of his words, and his *grace,* his wisdom, his anointing, the full array of his armor, his power, his scepter, and *his sword,* which, he says, is *girded about his thigh*—which is the symbol, as it seems to me, of his becoming flesh—and that *truth* which he mentions, *and gentleness,* uprightness, *and justice.* Finally there is his indissoluble vigor, prosperity, and kingdom, which arose out of these things or rather with them, after which the prophet immediately presents the adornments of his mother, just as if he were singing wedding songs to a bridegroom and a bride. And even if some have thought that this prophetic saying was not about her but rather about the Church, this in no way dishonors the word of the prophet.

7 Ἀλλ' ὅρα μοι καὶ ὅπως ἐπιμελῶς διαγράφει καὶ φιλοπόνως μὴ μόνον τὴν πρὸς τὸν ναὸν ταύτης προσαγωγήν τε καὶ κατοικίαν, ἀλλὰ καὶ τὴν ἄλλην πᾶσαν εὐμορφίαν τῆς ἀρετῆς, ἐπειδὴ πρὸς ταύτην ἀπηξίου καὶ τὴν τοῦ σώματος· *παρέστη ἡ βασίλισσα ἐκ δεξιῶν σου,* τὴν νῦν λέγων ἄντικρυς παράστασιν ἐκ δεξιῶν τοῦ θυσιαστηρίου καὶ τὰ τῶν Ἁγίων Ἅγια, καὶ ὧν οὐδὲν αὐτῷ δεξιώτερον· εἶτα καὶ τὸν τῶν ἀρετῶν κόσμον καὶ ὅπως πάγκαλόν τι χρῆμα καὶ πολὺ καὶ ποικίλον, οὐ γὰρ ἐν ἱματίῳ, φησίν, ἀλλὰ καὶ *ἐν ἱματισμῷ,* τὸ πλῆθος δηλῶν, οὐδὲ ἁπλῶς *περιβεβλημένη,* ἀλλὰ καὶ *πεποικιλμένη,* καὶ ὅτι πολλὰ μὲν αὐτῇ, μᾶλλον δὲ καὶ πάντα τὰ τῆς ἀρετῆς εἴδη καὶ καθ' ἑαυτὸ δὲ τούτων ἕκαστον πεποίκιλται τοῖς διαφόροις χρώμασί τε καὶ κάλλεσιν· ὥσπερ καὶ ἡ κατ' οὐρανὸν ἶρις, μία μὲν καθ' ὑπόστασιν ἢ καὶ ἔμφασιν, πολλὴ δὲ καὶ μυρία τοῖς ἀπαυγάσμασιν.

8 Ἀλλὰ τίνα καὶ τὰ ἐπὶ τούτοις ὡς λίαν σχετικά τε καὶ παραινετικά; *Ἄκουσον θύγατερ* τῶν λογίων τοῦ Πνεύματος ἢ τῶν πάλαι περὶ σοῦ προφητευμάτων τὲ καὶ ᾀσμάτων ἢ καὶ τῶν ἔναγχος τῶν πατρῴων διηγημάτων—τὸ γῆρας, τὴν στείρωσιν, τὴν εὐχήν, τὴν ἐπαγγελίαν, τὴν γέννησιν—*καὶ ἴδε* τὴν νῦν προέλευσιν, τὴν τιμήν, τὴν τοῦ ναοῦ κατοίκησιν, ἀλλὰ καὶ τὴν ἐν αὐτοῖς τοῖς τῶν Ἁγίων Ἁγίοις δίαιταν καὶ διαγωγήν, καὶ τὸν ἐξ οὐρανοῦ τροφέα καὶ τὴν τροφήν· *καὶ κλῖνον τὸ οὖς σου* πρὸς ἑτοιμασίαν καὶ πίστιν τοῦ ἀσπασμοῦ καὶ ὑποδοχὴν τοῦ Λόγου τὲ καὶ Θεοῦ καὶ μηδὲν ἔτι κατὰ τὸν σὸν *λαὸν* τὸν Ἰουδαϊκόν, μηδὲ κατὰ *τὸν οἶκον τὸν πατρικόν,* ἀλλὰ πάντων *ἐπιλαθομένη* τῶν κάτω

See how diligently and painstakingly he describes not only her introduction to and habitation in the temple, but also all the other beautiful forms of her virtue, since he deemed the beauty of her body as unworthy in comparison to this. *The queen stood at your right hand,* referring directly to her present position at the right of the altar and the Holy of Holies, compared to which nothing is closer to God's right hand. He then speaks of the adornment of her virtues, and how this was something of great beauty and embroidered in different colors, for he says she was clothed not in a garment but in *sumptuous apparel,* signifying the multitude of her virtues. And neither was she simply *clothed* but also *arrayed with embroidery of colors,* for her virtues were many, or rather every kind of virtue was manifested in her, and each one was embroidered with different colors and adornments, just like the rainbow in the sky, which is one according to its substance or outward appearance yet multiple and innumerable in its effulgence. 7

But what are the things he says after this, which are exceedingly appropriate and instructive? *Hear, O daughter,* the words of the Spirit, or the ancient prophecies and hymns concerning you, or the more recent narratives concerning your parents—their old age, their barrenness, their prayer, the promise made to them, and your birth—*and see* now your entry into the temple, the honor bestowed upon you, your habitation in the temple, and not least your way of life and instruction in the Holy of Holies, and the one from heaven who fed you, and your food. *And incline your ear* in preparation and faith for the embrace and the reception of the Word who is also God; *incline your ear* no longer to your Jewish *people* nor to *the house of your father,* and *forget* all the 8

τύπων καινήν τινα μεγαλοφροσύνην ἀναλαβοῦ καὶ ἐλπίδα. Τοῦτον γὰρ ἐπανῃρημένη τὸν τρόπον καὶ αὐτὸν ἐπιπλέον ἐπισπάσῃ τὸν βασιλέα ὡς συνεξομοιουμένη τὸ κάλλος αὐτῷ *καὶ ἐπιθυμήσει τοῦ κάλλους σου,* ὥστε διὰ τὴν κατὰ πνεῦμα συγγένειαν καὶ τοῦ κατὰ σάρκα μήτηρ αὐτῷ καταξιωθήσῃ γενέσθαι. Φιλοκαλῶν δὲ καὶ ἔτι τὴν θεωρίαν καὶ τὴν τῶν πλουσίων ἐπάγει προπομπήν τε καὶ λιτανείαν· *τὸ πρόσωπόν σου λιτανεύσουσιν οἱ πλούσιοι τοῦ λαοῦ·* καὶ τότε μὲν οἱ ἐπιφανέστεροι, νυνὶ δὲ τῶν ἄλλων οἱ κατ' ἀρετὴν ἢ ἀξίαν προέχοντες, εἶθ' ὥσπερ συγκρίνων καὶ αὐτὴν πρὸς ἑαυτὴν καὶ λαμπρὰ μὲν ἡγούμενος τὰ ὁρώμενα—εἴτε τὰ σωματικὰ ταῦτα εἴτε καὶ τὰ πνευματικὰ μὲν ταύτης καὶ διαφαινόμενα—πολλῷ δὲ λαμπρότερα τὰ κρυπτόμενα· καὶ τοσοῦτον, ὡς μηδὲν ἐκεῖνα ποιεῖν, *πᾶσαν* λέγει *τὴν δόξαν τῆς θυγατρὸς τοῦ βασιλέως ἔσωθεν,* οὐ τῶν ἀρετῶν λέγων μόνον τὴν ἔνδον λανθάνουσαν ὡραιότητα, ἀλλὰ καὶ τῶν παντοδαπῶν τοῦ Πνεύματος χαρισμάτων τὸ πλῆθος ἢ καὶ τὸ κάλλος, ὧν δηλῶν καὶ τὴν ἕνωσιν ἅμα καὶ τὴν διαίρεσιν εἰς παραβολὴν τὴν τῶν χρυσῶν ἐπάγει κροσσωτῶν περιβολήν τε καὶ ποικιλίαν· ὡς γὰρ ἐκεῖνα, φησί, καὶ διῄρηνται καὶ συνάπτονται, τὸ μὲν ἕκαστον καὶ καθεαυτό, τὸ δὲ τῷ ὅλῳ καὶ ἀφ' οὗπερ ἐξήρτηνται—τοῦ γὰρ αὐτοῦ πάντως ἐνδύματος αἰωρήματα—οὕτω καὶ ταῦτα διάφορα μέν, τοῦ αὐτοῦ δὲ Πνεύματος ἐνεργήματα.

9 Τοιαῦτα τῇ Παρθένῳ τὰ εἰσιτήρια, καὶ ὅσα τὰ ἐπὶ τούτοις οὐχ ἧττον εὐφροσύνης τὲ καὶ ἀγαλλιάσεως· οἷα δὲ καὶ

lowly prefigurations, and receive instead a new confidence and a new hope. Taking up this manner of life, you will make yourself even more attractive to the king himself, and, insofar as you assimilate his beauty, he will *desire your beauty,* so that, through your spiritual kinship with him, you will also be deemed worthy to become his mother according to the flesh. Adorning his contemplation still further, the prophet mentions her escort and supplication by the rich: *the rich among the people will make supplication before your face.* At that time, the more distinguished of the people were present, but present now are those who surpass others in virtue or worthiness. After this, as if comparing her external honor with her interior honor, and considering how splendid were the things visible to the eyes—whether these were her physical qualities or her manifest spiritual qualities—and how much more splendid were the things concealed from sight, as if these external things meant nothing, he says: *all the glory of the daughter of the king is within.* Here he is speaking not only of the beauty of her hidden, interior virtues, but also of the multitude of the manifold gifts of the Spirit, or of their beauty as well, of which he indicates both their union and division by comparing them figuratively to her clothing with its golden tassels and embroidery in different colors; for just as tassels, he says, are divided and conjoined, each particular one being distinct in itself, while at the same time conjoined with the whole garment to which they are attached—inasmuch as they are all hanging from the same garment—so too the gifts of the Spirit are different, but nonetheless of the same Spirit.

Such were the things that took place during the Virgin's 9
entry into the temple, and all the things that follow from it

τὰ κατοικέσια καὶ οἵαν ἡ Ἐπουράνιος Κλίμαξ καὶ ἡμῖν τὴν κλίμακα τῶν αὐτῆς ἢ καὶ περὶ αὐτὴν θαυμάτων ἀνίστησιν ἀεὶ τοῦ προτέρου τῷ δευτέρῳ τὸ πρωτεῖον παραδιδόντος; Μετὰ γὰρ τὴν καινὴν οὕτω πάλιν προπομπὴν καὶ εἰσαγωγὴν καὶ ἡ καινοτέρα μετελάμβανε ταύτην τῶν ἀδύτων καὶ ἀθεάτων διαγωγή· ταύτην δὲ ἡ καινοτάτη τροφή, τὴν δὲ τροφὴν ἡ κρείττων τῆς ψυχῆς ἀγωγή τε καὶ πλάσις· τρέφεται γὰρ ἡ μὲν οὐρανία σχεδὸν σὰρξ καὶ οὐρανίᾳ τροφῇ καὶ ἀγγέλου ἢ καὶ ἀρχαγγέλου χειρί, πλάττεται δὲ καὶ ἡ θεία ψυχὴ καὶ μυεῖται τὰ τελεώτερα παρ' αὐτοῦ τοῦ ἀγγέλου, μᾶλλον δὲ παρ' αὐτῆς τῆς Τριάδος—τά τε ἄλλα καὶ ὅσα τὰ τῆς Τριάδος—καὶ οὕτως ἀναλόγως αὔξεται καὶ τὸ σῶμα καὶ τὴν ψυχήν, ὥσπερ καὶ ὁ ταύτης υἱὸς *ἡλικίᾳ καὶ χάριτι,* τὸ μὲν ὡς ἐκ τοιαύτης πηγνυμένη τροφῆς, τὸ δὲ καὶ ὡς ἐκ τοιούτων ἀγομένη καὶ πλαττομένη τῶν διδασκάλων. Ἐχρῆν γὰρ πάντως τὴν οὕτως οὐσιωδῶς οὐ μόνον χώρημα τῆς θείας ὅλης φύσεως χρηματίσουσαν, ἀλλὰ καὶ ἀνάκραμα δι' αὐτῆς ὅλης τῆς ἀνθρωπίνης φύσεως, οὕτω καὶ αὐτὴν συμπαγῆναι τὴν ὅλην φύσιν διὰ τοιαύτης ἕξεως. Ἀλλ' ὢ πῶς ἄν, καὶ τὰ λίαν μικρὰ δοκοῦντα ταύτης παραλιπών, μὴ λίαν μεγάλα ζημιῶσαι δόξω τοὺς ταύτης φίλους καὶ φιλοκάλους, μηδὲ παραλεῖψαι τὰ καίρια; Λεγέσθω γοῦν καὶ ὅσα παρὰ τῶν ἀποκρύφων—οἷα παρὰ μετάλλων τὰ ψήγματα—ἐπειδὴ μὴ τὰ μέγιστα μόνον τῶν δεσποτῶν, ἀλλὰ καὶ τὰ ἐλάχιστα λόγου πλείστου τοῖς φιλοδεσπότοις

provide no less joy and exultation. What can one say about her habitation in the temple and how she, who was the Heavenly Ladder, raised up for us the ladder of her miracles, or the miracles concerning her, the former always giving first place to the latter? Her novel entrance and introduction into the temple were followed by her more novel way of life in the hidden and innermost recesses of the Holy of Holies. This was followed by her utterly novel nourishment, and her nourishment in turn by the superior training and formation of her soul; for her all but heavenly flesh was nourished by heavenly nourishment received from the hand of an angel or even an archangel, while her sacred soul was formed and initiated into higher mysteries by the same angel, or, rather, by the Trinity itself—both the other mysteries and all those related to the Trinity—and thus the growth of her body and soul advanced in parallel, just as that of her son later did, *in stature and grace,* the former from such solid food, the latter from being trained and formed by such teachings. It was absolutely necessary that she essentially should become, not only a receptacle of the whole divine nature but also a blending, through herself, of that nature and the whole of human nature. In this way, the whole of nature was compounded within her through the special disposition of her soul and body. But how should I not appear to be occasioning a great loss for those who love her and love what is beautiful, or to be overlooking what is important, were I even to omit what is of minor importance concerning her? Let us hear, then, from the apocryphal writings—which are like the shavings found next to ground metals—because those who love their sovereigns are not interested only in the greatest things concerning them, but also in things that

ἄξια, οἵαν μὲν αὐτὴν ἡ ἱστορία καὶ τὴν ἐκτὸς ὥραν λέγει τοῦ σώματος, οἵαν δὲ καὶ τὸ ἦθος καὶ τὸ ἐντὸς κάλλος καὶ τὴν ὅλην ἕξιν τοῦ πνεύματος, καὶ ὅπως οὕτω διὰ πάντων τὸ κατὰ πάντων ἔσχε κράτος τῆς φύσεως, ὥστε μὴ μόνον ὅρον εἶναι πάσης τῆς νῦν, ἀλλὰ καὶ τῆς πρὶν ἀνθρωπίνης φύσεως, τῶν ἀγαθῶν ἁπάντων ψυχῆς ὁμοῦ τὲ καὶ σώματος, καθάπερ τὴν πρώτην Εὔαν, οὕτω καὶ ταύτην χειρὶ Θεοῦ πλασθεῖσαν, ἐκείνης ἀντίθετον, ὥσπερ καὶ τὸν ταύτης υἱὸν τοῦ Ἀδάμ.

Ταῦτα μὲν οὖν παραλειπτέον, ὡς καὶ λόγου κρείττονα· ἐκεῖνα δέ· ἦν μὲν γάρ, ὥς φησιν ἡ ἱστορία, καὶ φιλομαθεστάτη μὲν καὶ εὐμαθεστάτη τὴν φύσιν, τὸν δὲ λόγον ἀστειοτάτη· ἐμπειροτάτη μὲν τῶν λογίων, εὐσυνετωτάτη δὲ καὶ σοφωτάτη τὴν γνῶσιν, εὐγνωμονεστάτη δὲ καὶ τὴν κρίσιν ἡ ὅσον οὔπω τοῦ Λόγου καὶ τῆς Σοφίας μήτηρ· ἐμμελεστάτη μὲν τὴν φωνὴν καὶ ἡδυτάτη τὴν γλῶτταν, *διήνοιξε τὸ στόμα αὐτῆς προσεχόντως καὶ τάξιν ἐστείλατο τῇ γλώττῃ αὐτῆς*· εὐτεχνοτάτη δὲ καὶ φιλεργοτάτη τὰς χεῖρας, ἣν καὶ Σολομῶν ἐγκωμιάζει πόρρωθεν, οὐ διὰ τὴν *ἀνδρείαν* μόνον, ἀλλὰ καὶ τὴν εὐμηχανίαν τὲ καὶ τὴν φρόνησιν· καὶ ζητεῖ μέν, ἀπορεῖ δὲ καὶ θαυμάζει διὰ τὸ σπάνιον, *τιμιωτέραν* μὲν οὖσαν *λίθων πολυτελῶν,* ἐργαζομένην δὲ καὶ πάντα πλοῦτον καὶ λίθους πολυτελεῖς. Καὶ *θαρσεῖν* μὲν λέγων *ἐπ' αὐτῆς τοῦ ἀνδρὸς αὐτῆς,* εἴτ' οὖν υἱοῦ τὲ καὶ πατρός, *τὴν καρδίαν,* τὸ μὲν διὰ τὴν φιλεργίαν, τὸ δὲ καὶ διὰ τὴν φιλανδρίαν ἅμα καὶ φιλοπαρθενίαν καὶ ἀεὶ μὲν *οὐκ ἀποροῦσαν σκύλων, ἐνεργοῦσαν δὲ καὶ τῷ ἀνδρὶ αὐτῆς ἀγαθὰ*

are seemingly small. I am referring on the one hand to the historical account of her life before she reached the bloom of youth, and, on the other, to what is said about her character, her inner beauty, and the entire disposition of her spirit, and how in and through all things, she possessed mastery over her nature, so that she is not only a rule or standard regarding all the good things of both soul and body for the current condition of human nature, but also for all prior human nature, just like the first Eve, who likewise was fashioned by the hand of God, though she was the antithesis of Mary, just as her son is the antithesis of Adam.

These things, then, must be omitted, insofar as they are 10
beyond words. As far as the other things are concerned, she was by nature, according to the historical account, very eager for knowledge, quick at learning, and most refined and charming in her speech. She was fully acquainted with the scriptures, extremely quick of apprehension, most wise with respect to knowledge, and very sensible in her judgment as the soon-to-be mother of the Word and Wisdom. Her voice was most melodious, and her speech was incomparably sweet: *she opened her mouth carefully and imposed order on her speech.* She was most skillful and industrious with her hands, and thus from the distant past Solomon praised her, not only for her *courage* but also for her skill and prudence. And he seeks her, but is at a loss to explain and marvels at her rarity, for she is *more valuable than precious stones,* since she labors to produce all kinds of wealth and precious stones. And thus he says that, *the heart of her husband,* that is, her son and father, *trusts in her,* both because of her skill at labor and her wifely affection as well as her love for virginity. And she shall *never be in need of fine spoils, for she works always for her*

πάντα τὸν χρόνον, ὡς ἀεὶ μὲν κατὰ τῶν νοητῶν ἀνδραγαθιζομένην ἐχθρῶν καὶ σκυλεύουσαν, ἀεὶ δὲ καὶ τὰς τῶν ἀγαθῶν ἐργασίας προσάγουσαν τῷ υἱῷ, εὑρομένην *ἔρια καὶ λῖνον,* τοὺς παχυτέρους μέν, καθαροὺς δὲ ὅμως τῶν πρακτικῶν λογισμοὺς καὶ λεπτοτέρους τῶν θεωρητικῶν, καὶ δι᾽ ἀμφοτέρων ἐργαζομένην *εὔχρηστα* τῷ ἀνδρὶ αὐτῆς, *ὡσεὶ ναῦν ἐμπορευομένην μακρόθεν* καὶ *συνάγουσαν* ἑαυτῇ πλοῦτον.

Τίνα τρόπον; Εἴτε πρότερον τῶν παλαιῶν καὶ ἀγαθῶν βίων τὲ καὶ διηγημάτων, καὶ πάντων ἅμα τῶν μέχρις αὐτῆς τοῦ Θεοῦ θαυμασίων τὴν γνῶσιν ὁμοῦ καὶ μίμησιν, εἴτε καὶ ὕστερον τῶν Ἐθνῶν τὴν προσαγωγὴν καὶ τὴν πίστιν ἢ καὶ τῶν ἄλλως μακρόθεν Θεοῦ τὴν ἐπιστροφὴν καὶ ἐπίγνωσιν· ἀνισταμένη *μὲν ἐκ* μέσων *νυκτῶν* ὡς ἐπαγρυπνοῦσα καὶ διδοῦσα *βρώματα,* τοὺς θρεπτικοὺς λογισμούς τε καὶ θεωρητικούς, *τῷ οἴκῳ* τῆς ψυχῆς αὐτῆς, *ἔργα* δὲ *ταῖς θεραπαίναις,* ταῖς λοιπαῖς ἀγαθαῖς ὑπουργοῖς τοῦ λόγου καὶ πρακτικαῖς ἀρεταῖς, *γεώργια* μὲν ὠνουμένη ὡς καὶ τὰ τῶν ἄλλων καλὰ δι᾽ ἀγάπης παρακερδαίνουσα ἢ καὶ πάντας ὁμοῦ τοὺς ὑπὸ Θεοῦ γεωργουμένους κτωμένη, αὐτὴ δὲ ταῖς ἑαυτῆς χερσὶ *καταφυτεύουσα* ἀμπελῶνας ἀγαθῶν πράξεων καὶ λειμῶνας ἢ καὶ ἀναζωννυμένη *τὴν ὀσφῦν ἰσχυρῶς,* ὡς οὐ τὸ ἐπιθυμητικὸν μόνον εἴπερ τις ἀνθρώπων δι᾽ ἐγκρατείας σφίγγουσα, ἀλλὰ καὶ τὴν τοῦ θήλεος εἰς ἀνδρείαν μεταβαλοῦσα, μᾶλλον δὲ καὶ αὐτὴν τὴν τῶν ἀνδρῶν πᾶσαν νικῶσα φύσιν. *Καὶ οὐκ ἀποσβεννυμένη τὸν λύχνον*—ὁπότερον βούλει—κἂν μὴ τὸν αἰσθητόν, ἀλλὰ τόν γε πάντως τοῦ νοὸς φωτισμὸν ἢ καὶ τὸν τοῦ νόμου

husband's good, that is, she always acts courageously against spiritual enemies and despoils them, and she always offers the produce of her good labors to her son, finding *wool and flax,* that is, the coarser, though pure, thoughts concerning the practical life, and the more subtle thoughts concerning contemplation. Through both she *makes them useful* to her husband, *like a ship trading afar and procuring* wealth for herself.

In what manner did she do this? First, through knowledge and imitation of the lives and narratives of ancient and good personages, and indeed of all God's wonders that took place down to her own time. Second, through the calling of the Gentiles and their faith, or through the return to and knowledge of God on the part of those who were in some other way far off from him. And she rises in the *middle of the night,* as if she were keeping vigil, *and gives food,* that is, nutritious and contemplative thoughts, *to the household* of her soul, *appointing tasks to her maidens,* that is, the rest of her good servants who assist reason and the practical virtues. She purchases cultivated *fields,* inasmuch as she generates profits from the good things cultivated by others through love, or she acquires all those who have been cultivated by God, and with her own hands *plants* vineyards and meadows of good deeds, or *strongly girds her loins,* not only binding tightly her desire more than any human being might do through self-control, but also transforming the feminine into the masculine, or rather triumphing over the entire nature of men. *And she does not extinguish her lamp,* which does not refer to physical light, but certainly—and here you may choose whichever one you wish—to the light of the mind or

πληρωτικὸν Λόγον, ἐπειδὴ καὶ *λύχνος ὁ νόμος, ἐρείδουσα* μὲν *τοὺς βραχίονας αὐτῆς εἰς ἔργον* καὶ πάλιν ἐκτείνουσα *τὰς χεῖρας ἐπὶ τὰ συμφέροντα,* διὰ μὲν ἐκείνων τὴν εὐπραγίαν, ἐπειδὴ καὶ τῆς πρακτικῆς δυνάμεως ὁ βραχίων σύμβολον, διὰ δὲ τούτων καὶ τὴν εὐποιΐαν προσάπτουσα· τοῦτο γὰρ πάντως αὐτῇ τῶν χειρῶν ἡ ἔκτασις· ἐρείδουσα δὲ πάλιν καὶ *τοὺς πήχεις εἰς ἄτρακτον,* ὥσπερ ἔναγχος καὶ *τοὺς βραχίονας εἰς ἔργον,* ἐπειδὴ καὶ μὴ ταῖς ἐργασίαις ἁπλῶς, ἀλλὰ καὶ ταῖς τῶν εὐχῶν ἀσχολίαις τοὺς στερροτέρους ἐπιστηρίζουσα λογισμοὺς καὶ τὴν παρασκευὴν ἐντεῦθεν τῶν νοητῶν στολῶν διαπλέκουσα.

Ἐντεῦθεν καὶ τοῖς ἄλλοις διδάσκαλος καὶ χορηγὸς τῶν τοιούτων γίνεται, καὶ διανοίγει μὲν χεῖρα τῷ *πένητι* τῶν τοιούτων, *καρπὸν δὲ* ἐκτείνει *τῷ πτωχῷ,* τῷ ταπεινῷ καὶ κάτω, πρὸς θεωρίαν ἅμα καὶ πρᾶξιν ἐπαίρουσα. Ἐντεῦθεν καὶ *οὐδὲ φροντίζει τῶν ἐν οἴκῳ*—δῆλον *ὁ ἀνὴρ αὐτῆς*—ὡς καὶ τῆς ὅλης Ἐκκλησίας αὐτῆς προστατούσης καὶ ἐνδυούσης τὸν ἱματισμὸν τῆς πίστεως ὁμοῦ καὶ πράξεως ἢ καὶ *δισσὰς* μὲν *στολάς, δισσὰς δὲ* καὶ *χλαίνας ἐποίησε τῷ ἀνδρὶ αὐτῆς, ἐκ βύσσου δὲ καὶ πορφύρας ἑαυτῇ ἐνδύματα,* εἴτε διὰ τὰς τότε τῶν ἱερέων οὐκ ὀλίγας στολὰς καὶ περιβολάς, οἳ καὶ τύποι τοῦ καθ' ἡμᾶς *ἀρχιερέως* Χριστοῦ, καὶ τὴν βύσσον καὶ τὴν πορφύραν, ἃ καὶ τότε νήθουσα ἡ Παρθένος ἦν καὶ ὑπερβάλλουσα πάσας τὰς κατ' αὐτὴν καὶ πρὸ αὐτῆς νεάνιδας, εἴτε καὶ οἷς τὸ μὲν ἑαυτῇ ὡς ἐκ βύσσου καὶ πορφύρας—ἤγουν λόγου καὶ θεωρίας—ἢ καὶ διὰ σώματος καὶ ψυχῆς τὰ τοῦ Πνεύματος περιτέθεικε περιβόλαια· τὸ δὲ καὶ τῷ ἑαυτῆς υἱῷ, τὸ μὲν ἑαυτῆς τὸ σῶμα καὶ τὴν ψυχὴν

perhaps the Word who fulfills the law, for *the law is a lamp.* And she *strengthens her arms for work,* and again stretches forth *her hands to profitable labor.* With the former she lays hold of good works, for the arm is a symbol of the practical power of the soul, while with the latter she dispenses beneficence, for surely this is what is meant by the stretching out of her hands. *She applies her forearms to the spindle* in the same way that just now she stretched out *her arms for work,* since it is not only by means of external labors but also by her occupation with prayer that she supports more stable thoughts in preparation for the weaving together of noetic garments.

As a result, she becomes a teacher of others and provides them with things such as these; and she opens her hand and offers these things *to the needy, and* extends *fruit to the poor,* that is, to the humble and lowly, raising them up to contemplation and practice. As a result, *he*—obviously *her husband—is not anxious about things in the house,* because she protects and clothes the whole of the Church in the apparel of faith and good works, or in *two sets of clothes,* for *she made for her husband two robes, and garments for herself of fine linen and scarlet.* This refers either to the many clothes and vestments of the priests at that time, who are figures of Christ, who is our *high priest,* as well as with respect to the linen and scarlet which at that time the Virgin was spinning, and by means of which she surpassed all the maidens who were with her and who preceded her. Or else it refers, on the one hand, to the vestments of the Spirit, which, as if woven from linen and scarlet—that is, from reason and contemplation—she wrapped around herself on all sides or indeed throughout her own body and soul; or, on the other, it refers to her

ὡς στολὴν καὶ χλαῖναν προκατεστήσατο, τὸ δὲ κἀκείνῳ τὴν ἡμετέραν φύσιν ὅλην περιεβάλετο, καθάπερ καὶ βασιλεῖ στολὴν μὲν τὴν ψυχήν, χλαῖναν δὲ τὴν σάρκα περιθεμένη. Τί γὰρ καὶ ἕτερον βούλοιτ' ἂν τῷ Σολομῶντι τῶν στολῶν καὶ χλαινῶν ἡ ἐπαναδίπλωσις;

Διὸ καὶ *περίβλεπτος ἐν πύλαις ὁ ἀνὴρ αὐτῆς* καὶ υἱός, ὅταν κάθηται μετὰ τῶν Ἰουδαϊκῶν πρεσβυτέρων *ἐν ἱερῷ* τὲ καὶ *συνεδρίῳ*, ἀλλὰ καὶ πάντων τῶν *κατοίκων τῆς γῆς*, ὡς ἀπορουμένων πάντων καὶ θαυμαζόντων πῶς ἄνθρωπος μὲν τὴν φύσιν καὶ κομιδῇ τὴν ἡλικίαν παῖς, Θεὸς δὲ τὴν σοφίαν τὲ καὶ τὴν δύναμιν, ἢ καὶ ἄνθρωπος μὲν τὸ φαινόμενον, Θεὸς δὲ τὸ νοούμενον. Ἀλλὰ καὶ ἀποδιδομένη *τοῖς Φοίνιξι* μὲν *σινδόνας, περιζώματα δὲ τοῖς Χαναναίοις*. Πῶς; ὡς καὶ διαλλακτὴς καὶ μεσῖτις καὶ λαμβάνουσα μὲν εἰς τιμὴν τὴν πίστιν ἢ καὶ τὴν μεταβολήν, καὶ τοῖς μὲν ἀπίστοις τὰ τῆς αἰσχύνης περικαλύμματα ἢ τὴν τοῦ λουτροῦ καὶ τοῦ σταυροῦ περιζωννῦσα δύναμιν, τοῖς δὲ πεπιστευκόσι μέν, φοινικοῖς δὲ τὴν ἁμαρτίαν ἢ καὶ ἄλλως πάσης γυμνοῖς ἀγαθοεργίας καὶ θεωρίας τὴν ἑαυτῆς λευκότητα τῆς καθάρσεως ἢ καὶ λεπτότητα τῆς γνώσεως περιβάλλουσα. Διὸ καὶ ἀνίσταται *τὰ τέκνα αὐτῆς* αἰνέσαι αὐτήν, καὶ οὐ ταῦτα μόνον, ἀλλὰ *καὶ ὁ ἀνὴρ αὐτῆς*, ὡς τὴν τῶν πιστευόντων ἢ μεταβαλλομένων σωτηρίαν ἀποδεχόμενος.

Αὕτη καὶ *ἰσχὺν καὶ εὐπρέπειαν ἐνεδύσατο* διὰ τὸν ἐξ αὐτῆς *εὐπρέπειαν* ἐνδυσάμενον *καὶ* περιζωσάμενον *δύναμιν*. Ἀλλὰ καὶ *εὐφράνθη ἐν ἡμέραις ἐσχάταις* αὐτῆς, ὡς καὶ πάντων κρατήσασα καὶ ἔτι κρατήσουσα τῶν περάτων, καὶ τὰ Ἔθνη προῖκα τῷ ἑαυτῆς ἀνδρὶ προσάγουσα ἢ καὶ

own son, for whom she prepared her own body and soul as clothing and robe, and whom she invested in the whole of our nature, and, as is fitting for a king, wrapped a human soul around him like clothing and a robe of flesh. For what else does Solomon mean by the doubling of robes and raiments?

For this reason, *her husband* and son *is distinguished in the gates,* when he sits with the Jewish elders in *the sanctuary* and the *council,* but also with all *the inhabitants of the earth,* all of whom were both puzzled and amazed at how a man according to nature, and entirely a child in age, was God in his wisdom and power, or how he was visibly a man but invisibly God. But she also sells *sheets to the Phoenicians and cinctures to the Canaanites.* How? Because as a conciliator and a mediator she also receives faith or conversion as a gift of honor, and gives coverings of shame to the faithless or girds them with the power of baptism and the cross. The faithful, however, who are dyed purple in sin, or who are entirely stripped of good works and contemplation, she covers with the whiteness of her own purification or with subtlety of knowledge. Thus, *her children* arise to praise her, and not only them but also *her husband,* who approves the salvation of those who believe or convert.

She also *puts on strength and honor,* thanks to the one who put on *honor* and clothed himself in *power.* And *she will rejoice at the end of* her *days,* for she has authority over all people, and authority over the ends of the earth, and she offers the Gentiles as a dowry to her husband, with whom she reigns,

συμβασιλεύουσα καὶ ἔτι μᾶλλον ἐπ' ἐσχάτων μετὰ τὴν τῶν ἐνταῦθα πάντων κατάλυσιν συμβασιλεύσουσα τῷ ἑαυτῆς υἱῷ βασιλείαν τὴν ἀκατάλυτον ἅμα καὶ ἀκατάληπτον.

11 Καλὸν κἀκεῖνα προσθήσειν αὐτῇ καὶ λίαν κατὰ καιρὸν ὡς καὶ οἰκειότερα τῶν ἄλλων πάντων, μάλιστα τὰ ἀκροτελεύτια· *πολλαὶ θυγατέρες ἐκτήσαντο* κάλλος εἴτε ψυχῆς εἴτε σώματος, *πολλαὶ* θυγατέρες *ἐποίησαν* ἢ ἐγέννησαν δύναμιν, ἀλλὰ σὺ *πάσας ὑπέρκεισαι* κατά τε φύσιν καὶ γνώμην καὶ *πάσας ὑπερῆρας* κατά τε τὴν θείαν χάριν καὶ γέννησιν. Ταῦτα κἂν παρεκβατικώτερα, ἀλλά γε τῶν ἄλλων πάντως οὐκ ἐνδεέστερα πρὸς ἡδονὴν ὁμοῦ καὶ ὠφέλειαν τοῖς γε φιλομαθεστέροις καὶ φιλοκάλοις. Ἐπὶ γοῦν τὴν ἱστορίαν ἀπὸ τῆς θεωρίας ταύτης ἀνακαμπτέον, ὅτι καθάπερ τἄλλα πάντα οὕτω καὶ τὸ ἦθος αὐτὸ δυσμίμητος ἢ ἀμίμητος, χαριεστάτη μὲν ἰδεῖν καὶ αὐτόχρημα χάρις ἢ μᾶλλον καὶ ὑπὲρ πᾶσαν χάριν, σεμνοτάτη δὲ καὶ προσιδεῖν τὲ καὶ προσειπεῖν, σύννους τὰ πολλὰ καὶ εἴσω συννενευκυῖα, ταραχῆς τὲ καὶ διαχύσεως, ὀργῆς τὲ καὶ ἀστειολογίας ὁμοίως ἀπέχουσα, ἧς καὶ τὸ μειδίαμα—καθάπερ ἥδυσμα—πρὸς ὀλίγον καὶ ἐπ' ὀλίγοις, εὐόμιλος, εὐπρόσιτος, εὐπροσήγορος· ἐξαισιωτάτη μὲν τὸ κάλλος καὶ ἀναλογωτάτη τὸ μέγεθος, οὕτω δὲ καὶ τὸ ἐντὸς ὑποφαίνουσα κάλλος, καὶ ἀναλογωτέρα τὸ τῶν ἀρετῶν πλῆθος ἢ καὶ τὸ μέγεθος, ὡς ἐκεῖνα μὲν ἀποκρύπτειν, πρὸς δὲ ταῦτα μόνα τὸν θεατὴν

and with whom even more in the end she will reign after the destruction of all the things of this life, reigning together with her son in a kingdom that is both indestructible and incomprehensible.

It will be good also to add these proverbial sayings to her, 11
since they are most appropriate to the occasion, and more appropriate to her than anyone else, especially the words that appear toward the end: *Many daughters have obtained* beauty either of soul or body, and *many* daughters *have wrought* or brought forth power, but you *have surpassed them all* in nature and in the inclination of your will, and *you have exceeded them all* in divine grace and birth. Even though these things were uttered more by way of a digression, they are by no means lacking in either pleasure or profit for the more diligent lovers of learning and beauty. Let us now leave aside our contemplation and return to the historical account, for just as with all the other things, so too in her manner of life she was difficult and indeed impossible to imitate. She was most gracious to behold, and in very deed grace, or rather she transcended every grace, being exceptionally modest in appearance and conversation. She possessed deep understanding and was inclined to inwardness, keeping herself far removed from disorder and confusion and equally from wrath and levity; and her smile—like seasoning—was used only rarely and in the presence of few people. She was sociable, approachable, and affable. She was extraordinarily beautiful and perfectly proportioned in stature, and at the same time gave subtle indications of her inner beauty and, in still greater proportion, of the multitude or magnitude of her virtues, so that she would conceal the former and turn the viewer solely to the latter, even then making it impossi-

ἐπιστρέφειν, καὶ αὐτῶν τούτων ἄπορον εἶναι κρῖναι ποτέρῳ καλλίων ἐκείνη· τὸν δὲ νοῦν οὕτως ἁγνοτάτη καὶ παρθένος αὐτόχρημα, ὡς μηδὲ λογισμὸν ὑπελθεῖν αὐτήν ποτε ῥυπαρὸν καὶ φθορέα τοῦ πνεύματος.

12 Πρὸ δὲ πάντων, φιλανθρωποτάτη τὴν ψυχὴν ἐξ ἀρχῆς, καὶ τούτῳ γε μάλιστα πάντων ἐμφερεστάτη τῷ ἑαυτῆς υἱῷ· καὶ ἐπὶ πᾶσι μετριοφρονεστάτη τὸν τρόπον κἂν τοσούτῳ κάλλει τῶν ἀρετῶν καὶ πλεονεξίᾳ τῶν χαρισμάτων, ὡς βασιλὶς μὲν ἐξ ἀρχῆς πάσης ὑπερκειμένη φύσεως κατά τε φύσιν καὶ γνώμην, ὡς δὲ καὶ τοῦ ὄντως βασιλέως ἐσομένη μήτηρ καὶ τοσοῦτον πτωχεύσαντος καὶ ταπεινωθέντος καὶ ὑπακούσαντος δι' ἡμᾶς, πτωχὴ καὶ ταπεινὴ καὶ αὐτὴ τῷ πνεύματι. Καὶ πᾶσι τοῖς ἱερεῦσιν ὑπήκοος καὶ διάκονος, αἰδοία τὲ ἅμα καὶ αἰδουμένη, τιμῶσα καὶ τιμωμένη πάντας καὶ παρὰ πάντων καὶ ὑπὲρ ἅπαντας, ὥστ' εἴ τις καὶ ταύτην λόχευμα λέγοι θεῖον—τὴν μετ' ὀλίγον τὸν Θεὸν Λόγον λοχεύουσαν—οὐ πόρρω ἂν εἴη τῆς ἀληθείας. Οὕτω θεία τις δύναμις ἦν ἀτεχνῶς ἡ ταύτην ἐξ ἀρχῆς τὴν φύσιν ἐξοργανώσασα καὶ ἐξωραΐσασα, καὶ ἀναλόγως μὲν τῇ ψυχῇ τὸ σῶμα, ἀναλόγως δὲ τῷ σώματι καὶ τὸ ἦθος κατ' ἄκραν ἁρμονίαν ἁρμοσαμένη, ὥστε καὶ τὸν λόγον οὕτω σῴζεσθαι, καθάπερ ἐν ἀριθμοῖς ἢ γραμμαῖς. Ὥσπερ γὰρ οὐθ' ἑτέραν τινὰ ψυχὴν τοιαύτην ἔχειν ἐχρῆν φύσιν τὲ καὶ μορφὴν καὶ οὐθ' ἑτέραν μορφὴν καὶ φύσιν τοιαύτην ψυχήν, οὕτως οὐθ' ἑτέραν τινὰ γυναικὸς τὸ συναμφότερον φύσιν τὸν ὑπὲρ φύσιν χωρῆσαι τόκον· οὔκουν οὐδὲ

ble to say whether she was superior in one virtue or another. Her mind was most pure and in very deed virgin since she never granted entry to any kind of impure thought that might have corrupted her spirit.

But more than anything else, her soul from the beginning 12
was extremely compassionate toward mankind, and in this she most certainly, and more than anyone else, resembled her son. To everyone she was incomparably modest in her manner, even though she possessed such beauty from her virtues and an abundance of spiritual gifts, because she was a queen from the very beginning, and by her nature and the inclination of her will she transcended all nature, and would become the mother of the true king, and to the extent that he made himself poor, and humbled himself, and became obedient for our sake, she too was poor and humble in spirit. She was obedient and a servant to all the priests; she was both reverential and revered, a woman of honor who honored others, and who was honored by all and above all, so much so that if someone were to say that she was born of God—she who herself would presently give birth to God the Word—he would not be far from the truth. Thus from the beginning a certain divine power ingeniously arranged and adorned her nature so that her body was in perfect proportion to her soul, and, according to a supreme harmony harmonized her conduct of life in proportion to her body, so that the proportion between them was preserved, just as we observe in numbers and geometrical figures. For just as no other soul would have need of such a nature and form, and just as no other form or nature would have need of such a soul, so too no other woman's nature, as a combination of body and soul, would need to contain a child who was

ἐχώρησεν οὐθ' ἕτερόν τινα τόκον τοιαύτην φύσιν ἀποτεκεῖν, οὔκουν οὐδὲ ἀπέτεκεν, ἀλλ' ἐκεῖνον μόνον, ὃς καὶ αὐτὴν οὐκ ἀδιάφθορον διαφυλάξαι μόνον, ἀλλὰ καὶ ἐκθεῶσαι καὶ βασιλίδα πάντων ἀποτελέσαι δυνατὸς ἦν, καὶ δι' οὗπερ ἔμελλε τῷ Θεῷ καὶ Πατρὶ τὸν υἱὸν κοινὸν ἕξειν καὶ συμμερίσασθαι· ἀλλ' ἡ μὲν οὕτως ἀνέκειτο τῷ ναῷ, θεῖον ὄντως καὶ ἔμπνουν ἄγαλμα καὶ ἀνάθημα, δαίμοσι μὲν φοβερόν, ἀγγέλοις δὲ ποθεινόν, μᾶλλον δὲ καὶ ἀγγέλοις μὲν φοβερὸν ὁμοῦ καὶ τερπνόν, τῷ δὲ υἱῷ καὶ Θεῷ ποθεινόν.

13 Πάλαι καὶ ταῦτα καθάπερ τὰ πρὸ τούτου τῷ θείῳ Δαβίδ, οὕτω καὶ τῷ τούτου παιδὶ καὶ τοῖς ἄλλοις προφήταις προτεθεωρημένα, κάλλος ἄσυλον, κάλλος ἄφραστον, *κῆπος ἄβατος*, φρέαρ ἀνόρυκτον καὶ ἀείρρυτον καὶ οὐκ ἴδιον μόνον, ἀλλὰ καὶ ἄξιον τοῦ ποιήσαντος, *βιβλίον ἐσφραγισμένον*, περὶ οὗ πᾶσαι βίβλοι καὶ ἐν ᾧ Λόγος ἄγραφος καὶ ἀΐδιος, *κλίνη τοῦ* βασιλέως, ἣν καὶ *δυνατοὶ* κυκλοῦσιν *ἑξήκοντα*—οἵτινές ποτε οἱ δυνατοὶ οὗτοι, πάντα ὁμοῦ τὰ ἐν αὐτοῖς τοῖς τῶν Ἁγίων Ἁγίοις ἄψυχά τε καὶ σύμβολα· ἔμψυχος αὐτὴ καὶ ἀλήθεια· *λυχνία χρυσῆ*, *ῥάβδος* ἱερατικὴ καὶ βασιλικὴ καὶ ἀειθαλής· *στάμνος τὸ μάννα* κρύπτουσα, *τράπεζα* τὸν ἄρτον ἔχουσα, *πλάκες τῆς διαθήκης*, κιβωτὸς αὐτὴ *πάντοθεν χρυσίῳ περικεκαλυμμένη*, τῷ Ἁγίῳ Πνεύματι, πάντα ὁμοῦ καὶ αὐτὸν φέρουσα τὸν τὰ πάντα φέροντα.

Τὴν μὲν οὖν ἐν τῷ ναῷ λέγειν τῆς Παρθένου διατριβὴν καὶ ὅσα τὰ ἐκεῖ ταύτῃ καὶ ἀγωνίσματα παρ' ἡλικίαν—ἔδει γὰρ πάντως κἀνταῦθα τὴν φύσιν νικᾶν—ἀλλὰ καὶ θεάματα καὶ ἀκούσματα, καὶ δι' ὅσων κατ' ὀλίγον ἤγγιζε τῷ

beyond nature; and no such nature would contain or give birth to any other kind of child, nor would it have given birth to such but him alone who would not only preserve her virginity but also be able to deify her and establish her as queen of all, for he would be a common son possessed and shared between her and God the Father. And thus, she was dedicated to the temple as truly a divine, living, and pleasing gift and offering, at once frightful to demons and desired by angels, or rather to angels both fearsome and delightful, but desired by her son and God.

These things, just as the things before them, had long ago 13
been foreseen by the divine David, just as they had likewise been foreseen by his son Solomon and the other prophets, namely, beauty inviolate, beauty ineffable, a *garden* inaccessible, an ever-flowing spring produced without digging, not merely unique in itself but worthy of its creator; a *sealed book,* to which all books point, and which contains the eternal and unwritten Word; the king's *couch with sixty strong men* surrounding it—whoever these strong men might be; all things in the Holy of Holies were lifeless and symbolic whereas she is the living truth; the *lampstand of gold,* the royal and priestly evergreen *rod, the urn* concealing the divine *manna, the table* bearing the bread, *the tablets of the law,* the ark *covered on all sides with gold,* that is, the Holy Spirit, for she bears everything as well as him who bears all things.

To speak of the Virgin's way of life in the temple, and of all her contests there despite her youthful age—for it was absolutely necessary that even there she conquer nature—and to describe the things that she saw and heard, and the things by means of which she gradually drew near to the one

ἐγγίζοντι, καὶ ταύτην μνηστευομένῳ πολλὴν ἡγοῦμαι τῷ λόγῳ διατριβήν. Διατί; Διὰ τὸ καὶ πλήθει μὲν εἶναι πολλά, μεγέθει δὲ μηδὲ τῇ φύσει πιστά, εἰ καὶ ὅτι μάλιστα δι' ἀλλήλων ὁ λόγος καὶ ἀποδεικνὺς ὁμοῦ καὶ ἀποδεικνύμενος· ἥ τε γὰρ ἐσομένη τοσούτου μυστηρίου διάκονος καὶ τοσαύτης ὕστερον ἀξιωθησομένη τῆς χάριτος, οὐκ ἀπὸ πίστεως, εἰ καὶ τοσαύτης ἀρετῆς παρ' ἡλικίαν καὶ φύσιν κατέστη κύριος· ἥ τε τοσαύτης ἀρετῆς ἐξ ἀρχῆς καταστᾶσα κύριος, οὐκ ἀπὸ τρόπου δήπουθεν, εἰ καὶ τοσαύταις συνανεστράφη θεωρίαις καὶ ὀπτασίαις· ἥ τε καὶ ἄμφω ταῦτα καὶ οὕτως ἐκλεχθεῖσα τῷ Πατρὶ καὶ προπαρασκευασθεῖσα τῷ Πνεύματι, οὐκ ἄπο λόγου πάντως, εἰ καὶ τὸν ἀχώρητον καὶ ἀχώριστον τούτων οὐσιωδῶς ὑπεδέξατο Λόγον.

14 Ταῦτα μὲν οὖν ἐατέον· ὃ δὲ καὶ πάντων μεῖζον καὶ τῶν κατὰ τὸν ναὸν ἄθλων ἔπαθλον ἅμα καὶ τῶν μετ' ὀλίγον εὐαγγελίων ὥσπερ προευαγγέλιον· οὕτω διαλαμπούσης αὐτῆς καὶ τοσούτοις ἔργοις ἀρετῇ καὶ σοφίᾳ καὶ νηστείᾳ καὶ προσευχῇ, ὥστε μὴ παρθένων μόνον ἀλλὰ καὶ γυναικῶν εἶναι τὴν μικρὰν καὶ μεγάλην Μαρίαν καὶ λόγου καὶ βίου καὶ λόγῳ καὶ βίῳ διδάσκαλον, καὶ ἐτῶν οὔσης ὡσεὶ δύο καὶ δέκα, μέσων νυκτῶν παρὰ τὰς θύρας προσευχομένης τοῦ θυσιαστηρίου—ὢ τοῦ μεγάλου καὶ φρικτοῦ καὶ θεάματος καὶ ἀκούσματος—φῶς μὲν περιαστράπτει τὸν ναὸν ὅλον, οὕτω λαμπρὸν ὡς μηδὲν εἶναι μήδ' αὐτὸν τὸν ἡλιακὸν κύκλον κατ' αὐτὸ τῆς μεσημβρίας τὸ ἀκμαιότατον, φωνὴ δὲ πρὸς αὐτὴν παρὰ τοῦ ἱλαστηρίου· "Τέξεις

who was drawing near to her, and to whom she would be betrothed, would, I think, require an extensive discourse. Why? Because the multitude of these things is great, and their magnitude is by nature incredible, even if the discourse certainly both proves the truth of these things and is in turn proven by them. For she who would become the minister of such a great mystery, and who would subsequently become worthy of such grace, did not achieve this by faith, even if despite her age and nature she became the master of such great virtue, or, even if she did become the master of such great virtue from the beginning, she presumably did not do so unfittingly, seeing that she was occupied with so many contemplations and visions. And that she should experience both and thus be chosen by the Father and prepared in advance by the Holy Spirit was not in any way unreasonable, if she also received essentially the immeasurable Word who is inseparable from them.

We must therefore leave these things, but the greatest 14
achievement of all her contests in the temple, and at the same time a kind of evocation of her forthcoming annunciation, was this: she was distinguished brilliantly by so many great works of virtue, wisdom, fasting, and prayer, that by means of her speech and life, Mary, who was small and great, became the teacher of speech and life not only of virgins but also of all women. And when she was twelve years old, while she was standing by the doors of the sanctuary at midnight and praying—oh, the great and awesome sight and sound of it!—a light shone forth brilliantly throughout the whole temple; a light brighter than anything, brighter even than the sun shining at midday in its full strength. At the same time, a voice came forth from the altar of sacrifice and spoke

τὸν υἱόν μου.” Ταύτην ἡ Μαρία τὴν φωνὴν δεξαμένη οὔτε κατὰ παῖδας διεταράχθη οὔτε μὴν ὑπὸ περιχαρείας πάλιν ἐπήρθη καὶ ἐξελάλησεν, ἀλλ’ οὔτε μὴν ἠλλοίωσέ τι τοῦ σχήματος ἢ φρονήματος, ἀλλὰ κατεπλάγη μὲν ὡς εἰκός, ἔκρυψε δὲ ὅμως παρ’ ἑαυτῇ τὸ *μυστήριον,* τὸ ὄντως μέγα καὶ προαιώνιον *καὶ ἀγγέλοις ἄγνωστον,* ἕως οὗ καὶ τὸ πέρας εἶδεν τῶν περὶ αὐτὴν μυστηρίων, τὸν υἱὸν ἀνιστάμενον καὶ εἰς οὐρανοὺς ἀναλαμβανόμενον.

Μνηστεία

Ἀλλὰ τί τὰ ἐντεῦθεν; ἥπτετο μὲν ἡ Παρθένος ἤδη καὶ τῆς μείζονος ἡλικίας, ἔτος αὐτῇ που τέταρτον καὶ δέκατον ἦν, ὅτε καὶ καθ’ ὥραν καὶ νόμον ὁ γάμος ἦν· ἀπορία δὲ λοιπὸν τοῖς ἱερεῦσι περὶ αὐτῆς πολλή· οὔτε γὰρ ἀφαιρεῖν εἶχον ἐκ τοῦ ναοῦ τοῦ Θεοῦ τὸ ἀνάθημα, μᾶλλον δὲ καὶ ἀποσυλᾶν τῶν ἀναθημάτων τὸ κάλλιστον, ἀλλ’ οὔτε δὲ ὑπὸ ζυγὸν ἄγειν ἀνδρὸς τὴν ἐλευθέραν ἢ καὶ ἀνατεθειμένην Θεῷ καὶ τὸν ἐκείνου μόνον ἕλκειν ζυγὸν προεπηγγελμένην· οὔτε δὲ πάλιν ἐντὸς τοῦ ναοῦ κατέχειν, ὁπότε μηδὲ ἀνδρῶν μέσον, μηδὲ ἐν ἀγοραῖς ἢ οἰκίαις, μήτιγε καὶ ἱερέων καὶ ἀνακτόρων ἀναστρέφεσθαι παρθένους εὐπρεπὲς ἦν, ἄλλως θ’ ὁπότε καὶ ὁ νόμος διαρρήδην κωλύων ἦν. Τίς οὖν ἡ λύσις; Ἐνθύμησίς τις αὐτοῖς ἐκ Θεοῦ καὶ τὸ πρέπον διατηρῆσαι καὶ τὸν νόμον διαφυλάξαι καὶ τὸν γάμον διαφυγεῖν· ἀντὶ μὲν ἀνδρὸς μνηστῆρα, ἀντὶ δὲ πρὸς γάμον ὡραίου μὴ μόνον ἔξωρον καὶ εἰς ἔσχατον ἤδη γῆρως, ἀλλὰ

to her, saying: "You will give birth to my son." Mary heard and received this voice but was not frightened on account of her youth, neither did she become proud through excessive joy or speak out inappropriately, nor did she alter anything in her behavior or way of thinking, though of course she was amazed, but she concealed the *mystery* within herself, one that was truly great and preeternal and *unknown even to the angels,* until the time when she saw the end of the mysteries concerning her, that is, her son rising from the dead and being received into heaven.

Betrothal

What happened after this? The Virgin had already at- 15
tained a greater age, for she was fourteen years old, when it was time for marriage, according to both her age and the law. The priests, however, were at a great loss what to do about her. On the one hand, they could not remove from the temple one who had been dedicated to God, which would have despoiled the most beautiful of the temple's dedications. On the other hand, they could not place her under the yoke of a man since she was free or rather dedicated to God and had been promised to live under his yoke alone. But neither could they keep her within the temple at an age when it was not proper for a virgin to live among men, nor in the public squares or houses, not even of priests or temples, for in any case the law itself expressly prohibited this. What then was the solution? An idea sent to them by God enabled them to maintain what was proper, observe the law, and avoid marriage. Instead of choosing a husband, they opted for a suitor; and instead of selecting some youth ripe for mar-

καὶ εἰς ἄκρον ἀρετῆς ἀπολεξαμένοις, οἷα καὶ φύλακα μόνον τῆς παρθενίας ἐπ' ὀνόματι τῆς μνηστείας. Θεὸς δὲ ἦν ἄρα ὁ καὶ τούτων τι μεῖζον τρίτον οἰκονομῶν· καὶ καθάπερ αὐτὸς τῷ προβλήματι τῆς σαρκὸς ἀποκρύπτων αὐτοῦ τὴν θεότητα, οὕτω καὶ ἐπὶ τῆς αὐτοῦ μητρὸς τῷ τοῦ γάμου παραπετάσματι τὴν παρθενίαν ἐπισκιάζων, ἵνα λάθῃ δι' ἧς καὶ καθ' ὃν μέλλει καιρὸν ὁμιλεῖν ἡμῖν διὰ σώματος, καὶ οὕτω πρὸς συμπλοκὴν προκαλέσηται τὸν Ἀντίπαλον, εὖ εἰδότα καὶ αὐτὸν τὴν διὰ παρθένου καὶ μετὰ σαρκὸς αὐτοῦ παρουσίαν, ὡς καὶ αὐτῶν τῶν Ἡσαΐου καὶ τῶν ἄλλων προφητικῶν φωνῶν ἐπακροασάμενον.

16 Οὕτω τοῖς ἱερεῦσιν δόξαν, οὐδ' οὕτως ἑαυτοῖς ἐπιτρέπουσι τὴν ἐπιλογήν, ἀλλὰ μιμοῦνται καὶ ἄμφω τοὺς πρὸ αὐτῶν καὶ τοὺς μετ' αὐτούς, τὸ μὲν τοὺς κατὰ Μωσέα περὶ τῶν ἀρχιερέων καταστασιαζόμενον καὶ Θεῷ τὴν κρίσιν ἀνατιθέντα καὶ διὰ τῶν ῥάβδων δεχόμενον τὴν ἀπόφασιν· τὸ δὲ τοὺς κατὰ Πέτρον καὶ τοὺς ἄλλους μαθητὰς ὕστερον τὴν τοῦ προδότου χώραν ἀναπληροῦντας καὶ προσευχομένους καὶ κληρουμένους. Ἵστανται γοῦν καὶ οὗτοι πρὸς προσευχήν· παρῆν δὲ ἄρα καὶ Ζαχαρίας ὁ μέγας καὶ τοῦ μεγίστου πατὴρ Ἰωάννου, θειοτέρᾳ πάντως οἰκονομίᾳ μὴ τὴν ἀρχιερατείαν τότε μόνον λαχὼν τοῦ ἐνιαυτοῦ, ἀλλὰ καὶ τὴν ἐφημερίαν ποιούμενος, ἵνα καθάπερ ὁ τούτου υἱὸς πρὸς τὸ βάπτισμα τῷ ταύτης υἱῷ, οὕτω καὶ ὁ πατὴρ τῇ μητρὶ πρὸς τὴν μνηστείαν διακονήσηται, καὶ ἅμα μάρτυς ᾖ καὶ αὐτὸς τῇ Παρθένῳ τῶν κατὰ τὸν ναὸν αὐτῆς ἀγωνισμάτων τὲ καὶ πολιτευμάτων· συγγενὴς δὲ ὁ Ζαχαρίας

riage, they chose a man not only unsuitable for marriage on account of his already extremely advanced age but who was also of the highest virtue, and who would serve only as a guardian of her virginity under the name of betrothal. And so, it seems, it was God who arranged for a third solution, greater than the others; and just as he concealed his divinity beneath the covering of the flesh, so too, in the case of his mother, he used the veil of marriage to conceal her virginity, so that the woman through whom, and the time when, he would converse with us in the body might elude observation and thus incite his Opponent to fight him, because the latter had a good idea of his advent in the flesh through a virgin, having heard the prophetic words of Isaiah and the other prophets.

As the priests were thus considering this matter, they did 16
not entrust to themselves the choice of a suitor, but they imitated both their predecessors and their successors. On the one hand, they imitated what Moses did when there was dissension concerning the high priests, when he placed the decision before God and received the judgment through the rods. On the other hand, they imitated what Peter and the other disciples later did when they filled the place of the traitor by praying and casting lots. Thus the priests likewise stood in prayer. Present with them was the great Zacharias, the father of the incomparably great John the Baptist, and it was certainly due to a more divine dispensation that not only did it fall to him by lot to be high priest that year, but it was also his turn to serve, so that, just as his son would serve at the baptism of her son, so too would he, the father, serve at the betrothal of the mother, and at the same time be a witness of the Virgin's contests and way of life in the temple. This was because Zacharias was related not only to Joseph

οὐ τῷ Ἰωσὴφ μόνον, ἀλλὰ καὶ τῇ Μαρίᾳ, οὐδὲ ὡς ἐκ τῆς αὐτῆς φυλῆς μόνον διὰ τὴν ἐπιμιξίαν, ὡς ὁ λόγος φθάσας ἐδήλωσε τῆς ἱερατικῆς καὶ βασιλικῆς, ἀλλὰ καὶ διὰ τὴν ἐπιγαμίαν τῆς Ἐλισάβετ αὐτῇ προσήκων—ὃ μὴ μόνον παρὰ τῆς ἱστορίας, ὅτι καὶ ἀδελφόπαιδες ἄμφω, ἀλλὰ καὶ παρ' αὐτοῦ τοῦ ἀγγέλου καὶ τῶν εὐαγγελίων ἐστὶν ἀκούειν· *Καὶ ἰδοὺ Ἐλισάβετ ἡ συγγενής σου.* Γίνεται γοῦν τὰ κατὰ τὸν πρόγονον τῷ Ζαχαρίᾳ πρὸς νοῦν καὶ δώδεκα ῥάβδους ἱερέων γερόντων λογάδων ἀλλὰ καὶ συγγενῶν τῆς Παρθένου λαβὼν ἀνατίθησι τῷ θυσιαστηρίῳ· καὶ αὐτός τε καὶ οἱ λοιποὶ προσκαρτεροῦσιν εὐχαῖς τὲ καὶ δάκρυσι καὶ σημεῖον αἰτοῦσιν, ὃ δὴ καὶ γίνεται· καὶ ἡ ῥάβδος τοῦ Ἰωσὴφ κατὰ τὴν πάλαι τοῦ Ἀαρὼν ἀνθεῖ καὶ βλαστάνει, καὶ οὕτω λοιπὸν Ἰωσὴφ κρίσει Θεοῦ καὶ ἀνθρώπων παρὰ τοῦ Ζαχαρίου καὶ τῶν λοιπῶν ἁρμόζεται καὶ ἐγχειρίζεται τὴν Παρθένον, φύλαξ μόνον καὶ μνηστὴρ διὰ τέλους.

17 Εἰ δὲ δεῖ μηδὲ τὰ τούτου παραδραμεῖν ἀνδρὸς οὕτως ὁσίου, καὶ μὴ μόνον τηλικούτου τὴν ἀρετήν, ἀλλὰ καὶ τηλικούτῳ μυστηρίῳ καὶ τοσούτοις ὑπηρετησαμένου πράγμασί τε καὶ θαύμασι, λέγεται μὲν οὗτος ὁ Ἰωσὴφ ἔτη τότε καὶ ὑπὲρ ἑβδομήκοντα γεγονέναι, ὃ καὶ παντελῶς τῆς τῶν γάμων αὐτὸν ὑπονοίας πρὸς τὴν Παρθένον ἀπάγει. Πένης δὲ τὴν περιουσίαν, ἵνα κἀν τούτῳ πτωχεύσῃ δι' ἡμᾶς πάντως ὁ πάντα πτωχεύσας καὶ πλουτίσας ἡμᾶς θεότητα, τέκτων δὲ τὴν τέχνην καὶ τὴν εὐτεχνίαν, μακρῷ τῶν τότε πάντων διαφορώτατος—οὐκ ἄπο καὶ τοῦτο, κἂν μικρὸν ᾖ, τῆς πάντα συμβιβαζούσης ἁρμονίας καὶ ἀρχιτεκτονίας τοῦ Πνεύματος, ἀλλ' ἵνα καὶ μέχρι τούτου σῴζηται τὰ τῆς

but also to Mary, not only because he was of the same tribe on account of the union of the priestly and royal tribes mentioned a moment ago, but also through marriage to his wife Elizabeth—and not only because this is noted in the historical account, namely, that they were the children of two sisters, but also because we hear this from the angel and in the Gospels: *And behold your kinswoman Elizabeth.* It was then that Zacharias called to mind the things that his ancestor had done, and, taking twelve rods from select elderly priests who were also related to the Virgin, he placed them on the table of sacrifice. And he, together with the others, stood in prayer and tears seeking a sign, which indeed took place. The rod of Joseph blossomed and bloomed as Aaron's had before it. Thus was Joseph by the judgment of God and men, through Zacharias and the other priests, betrothed to and entrusted to be the guardian of the Virgin only, as one permanently betrothed to her.

But we should not hurry past this righteous man, who 17
was not only so extremely virtuous, but who was also called upon to serve such a great mystery and so many matters and miracles. They say that, at the time, Joseph was more than seventy years old, so that he was absolutely removed from any suspicion of marital union with the Virgin. In terms of his resources, he was a poor man, so that the one who made himself poor for our sake might be impoverished, and make us rich through his divinity. He was a carpenter by trade and a highly skilled one at that, more highly distinguished than all the others of his day—and even this, though it be but a small thing, would not fall outside the universally reconciling harmony and architecture of the Spirit, but so that the likeness is maintained even to this degree, even the appar-

ὁμοιώσεως καὶ ὁ δοκῶν πατὴρ τύπος τοῦ ὄντος ᾖ, τοῦ σοφοῦ πάντων δημιουργοῦ τὲ καὶ ἀρχιτέκτονος. Οὕτω δὲ τῇ εὐτεχνίᾳ νικῶν, οὐδὲν ἧττον καὶ τῇ δικαιοπραγίᾳ τοὺς τότε πάντας ὑπερβάλλων ἦν πλὴν τῶν τῆς Παρθένου καθάπερ εἴρηται γεννητόρων. Καὶ τί δεῖ λέγειν οὗ τὴν δικαιοσύνην ἐμαρτύρει μὲν ὁ κρίνας Θεός, ἐμαρτύρουν δὲ καὶ οἱ κατ' αὐτὸν πάντες; Μαρτυρεῖ δὲ διαρρήδην καὶ Ματθαῖος οὑτωσὶ λέγων· *Ἰωσὴφ δὲ ὁ ἀνὴρ αὐτῆς δίκαιος ὤν*. Οὗτος μὲν οὖν οὕτως ἐξ Ἱερουσαλήμ τε καὶ τῆς Σιὼν καὶ τῆς Ἰουδαίας εἰς Γαλιλαίαν καὶ Ναζαρὲτ τὴν κώμην τὴν Μαρίαν κατάγει. Τάχα καὶ τοῦτο τύπος τῆς ἐκ τῆς νοητῆς καὶ ὑψηλῆς Ἱερουσαλὴμ καὶ τῶν ἀδύτων καὶ ἀθεάτων καὶ τῶν ἀρρήτων ἁγίων ἐκείνων καὶ τῆς βασιλικῆς χώρας εἴτε καὶ πόλεως πρὸς ἡμᾶς τοῦ Λόγου συγκαταβάσεως.

18 Ὁ δὲ Φαραὼ πρὸς τὸν Ἰωσὴφ πρότερον ὁρῶν αὐτοῦ τὸ κάλλος τοῦ πνεύματος, τοῦτο καὶ ὁ νῦν Ἰωσὴφ ἐπεπόνθει πρὸς τὴν Μαρίαν· μᾶλλον δὲ ὅπερ αὐτὸς ἐῴκει γεγονέναι πρὸς τὴν Μαρίαν—μνηστὴρ ὁμοῦ καὶ πατήρ—τοῦτο καὶ τὴν Μαρίαν πρὸς τὰς αὐτοῦ θυγατέρας, καίτοι τὴν ἡλικίαν προηκούσας, ἐπεποιήκει, φύλακα καὶ διδάσκαλον καὶ παιδαγωγὸν καὶ πάντα ὁμοῦ, μητέρα τὲ καὶ κυρίαν τοῦ *σοφίσαι* καὶ *συνετίσαι* κατὰ τὸ γεγραμμένον, ταύτας ὡς ἑαυτήν. Ἡ δὲ καθάπερ ὠδίνουσα τὸν Λόγον καὶ πρὸ τοῦ Λόγου καὶ καθ' ἑαυτὴν στρέφουσα τὸ μυστήριον, οὐ μόνον τῶν κρυφίων τούτων ἀκοινώνητος ἦν ὁμοῦ πᾶσιν, ἀλλὰ καὶ ἀπρόσμικτος τὰ λοιπὰ καὶ τὰ πολλὰ ἀπρόϊτος, ἑαυτῇ μόνῃ προσλαλοῦσα καὶ τῷ Θεῷ καὶ ταῖς εὐχαῖς ἐπι-

ent father is a figure of the true one, the wise architect and creator of all. Having become a master of his craft, he was no less accomplished in his works of righteousness, and in this he surpassed all of his contemporaries, except, as they say, the parents of the Virgin. And why is it necessary to say more about him whose righteousness was attested by God's judgment, as well as by all those close to him? Even Matthew clearly witnesses to this, saying: *Joseph, her husband, was a righteous man.* Thus it was he who led Mary forth from Jerusalem, Zion, and Judea, down to Galilee and the village of Nazareth. And perhaps even this was a figure of the descent of the Word to us from the spiritual and sublime Jerusalem, and from those hidden, invisible, and ineffable holy places, and from the place of his royal abode.

The beauty that Pharaoh saw long ago in the spirit of 18
Joseph, this Joseph experienced with respect to Mary. Or rather, the very thing that he in all probability became in relation to Mary—namely, both betrothed and father—Mary herself became in relation to his daughters. Even though they were older, Mary became all at once their guardian, teacher, instructor, and mother, as well as their sovereign lady, in order *to teach them wisdom* and *to instruct them,* as it is written, making them like herself. And just as when she was giving birth to the Word, even before the Word she kept her reflections on the mystery to herself, and she not only did not communicate these hidden things to anyone, but also refrained from communicating the rest of these matters, and was reserved with respect to most things, since she conversed only with herself and God, devoting herself to daily

διδοῦσα καθ' ἑκάστην καὶ ταῖς νηστείαις. Ἀλλ' ὅρα μοι Θεοῦ μυστήρια· ἅμα τὲ γὰρ αὕτη ἀφίστατο τοῦ ναοῦ καὶ ἐφίσταται μὲν τὰ ἐγκαίνια τῆς Σκηνοπηγίας, ἐφίσταται δὲ καὶ τῆς Κιβωτοῦ τὰ καταπαυστήρια. Μὴν δὲ οὗτος αὐτοῖς ἕβδομος ἀπὸ τοῦ πρώτου καθ' ὃν ἀριθμεῖν τοῦτο τὸ γένος τοὺς μῆνας εἰώθασι. Καὶ Ζαχαρίας ὁ μέγας εἰς τὰ Ἅγια τῶν Ἁγίων εἰσέρχεται καὶ τὸν Ἰωάννην εὐαγγελίζεται, οὐχ ὅτι μόνον ἐχρῆν καὶ τοῦ μὲν φωτὸς τὸν λύχνον, τοῦ δὲ ἡλίου τὸν ὄρθρον, τὴν δὲ φωνὴν τοῦ Λόγου, *τοῦ δὲ νυμφίου τὸν φίλον,* τὸν δὲ στρατιώτην καὶ δορυφόρον προτρέχειν τοῦ βασιλέως, ἀλλὰ καὶ τὸ θαῦμα τοῦ θαύματος, τὸ ἔλαττον τοῦ πολλῷ μείζονος, τὸ κατὰ τὴν στεῖραν τοῦ κατὰ τὴν Παρθένον καὶ ἅμα καθαπερεὶ πρὸς παρασκευὴν εἶναι καὶ πίστιν, μὴ τῇ Παρθένῳ μόνον, ἀλλὰ καὶ τοῖς ἄλλοις πᾶσι, τοῦ τόκου τὸν τοκετόν· οὕτω γοῦν καὶ ὁ ἀρχάγγελος τὸ ῥῆμα καὶ τὸ θαῦμα πιστούμενος φαίνεται· *Καὶ ἰδοὺ Ἐλισάβετ ἡ συγγενής σου καὶ αὕτη συνειληφυῖα υἱόν.*

Εὐαγγελισμός

19 Οὐ πολὺς ὁ ἐν μέσῳ χρόνος—ἕκτος γὰρ οὗτος μήν—καὶ αὐτόθι πρὸς τῷ οἴκῳ τοῦ Ἰωσὴφ πέμπεται Γαβριήλ, καὶ δέχεται μυστικῶς ἡ Παρθένος ἅμα καὶ τὰ εὐαγγέλια καὶ τῶν εὐαγγελίων τὴν ἀποπλήρωσιν, τὴν θείαν ἐκείνην καὶ ἀπόρρητον καὶ ἀκατανόητον καὶ πάντων τῶν καλῶν ὄντως σύλληψιν. Οἷος δὲ ταύτῃ καὶ ὁ καιρὸς καὶ ὁ χρόνος, καὶ ὁ τόπος τὲ καὶ ὁ τρόπος; Νηστευούσῃ γάρ, φασί, καὶ

prayers and fasts. But consider with me the mysteries of God: at the very same time she left the temple, the feast of Tabernacles and the resting of the Ark was at hand. And it was the seventh month after the first month, according to the customary numbering of the months among the Jews. And the great Zacharias entered the Holy of Holies, and the birth of his son John was announced to him, not only because it was necessary that the lamp should precede the light, and that the dawn precede the sun, and the voice precede the Word, and the friend arrive *before the bridegroom,* and the soldier and spearman before the king, but also, and this is the wonder of wonders, the lesser should precede that which is much greater, that is, the conception of the barren woman should precede the conception of the Virgin and, at the same time, just as this took place for the preparation and assurance not only of the Virgin but also for all the others, the giving birth should precede the one being born. Thus even the archangel seems to confirm the word and the miracle by saying: *Behold, Elizabeth, your kinswoman, also has conceived a son.*

ANNUNCIATION

After that, not much time had passed—for it was now 19
the sixth month—and Gabriel was sent to the house of Joseph, and the Virgin mystically accepted both the good tidings as well as their fulfillment, that is, the divine, ineffable, and incomprehensible conception, which is truly the source of all good things. What was the season, the time, the place, and the manner of this event? They say that the Virgin was

προσευχομένῃ καὶ πλησίον πηγῆς, ὅτι καὶ *πηγὴν* τέκοι *ζωῆς,* καὶ τῷ πρώτῳ μηνὶ καθ' ὃν καὶ ὁ Θεὸς τὸν πάντα κόσμον δημιουργεῖ, δηλῶν ὅτι καὶ νῦν καινουργεῖ, καὶ κατὰ τὴν πρώτη ἡμέραν τῆς ἑβδομάδος, καθ' ἣν καὶ τὸ πρωτόγονον μὲν ἠλάθη *σκότος,* τὸ δὲ πρωτόκτιστον ἐδημιουργήθη *φῶς,* καὶ καθ' ἣν καὶ ὁ ταύτης υἱὸς ἀνίσταται μὲν τοῦ μνήματος, συνανιστᾶ δὲ καὶ τὸ πᾶν τοῦ πλάσματος. Καὶ οὐ τῶν ἡμερῶν ἡ πρώτη μόνον, ἀλλὰ καὶ τῶν ὡρῶν. Ἔδει γὰρ συντρέχειν καὶ *τὸ πρὸς πρωῒ πρωΐ,* καὶ ἀρχὴν τοῦ καθ' ἡμᾶς φωτὸς εἶναι τὴν ἀρχὴν τῆς τοῦδε γεννήσεως.

Οἷα δὲ καὶ τὰ τοῦ ἀρχαγγέλου ῥήματα καὶ ὅσων καὶ ἡλίκων νοημάτων σπέρματα καὶ ὅπως ἀντίθετα τοῖς πάλαι τὰ νῦν· "*Χαῖρε*" καὶ "*κεχαριτωμένη*·" ἐκεῖνο διὰ τὴν πάλαι τῶν τέκνων λύπην καὶ τὴν λύσιν τῆς ἀποφάσεως, ἀλλὰ καὶ τὴν εὐδοξίαν καὶ χάριν τοῦ ἐπαγγέλματος· τοῦτο διὰ τὸν τῶν ἀρετῶν αὐτῇ πλοῦτον καὶ τῶν χαρισμάτων τοῦ Πνεύματος· καὶ τὸ μὲν οἱονεὶ μνῆστρον τοῦ νυμφίου καὶ ἀρραβών, τὸ δὲ τῆς νύμφης ὁ πλοῦτος· ἀμφότερα γὰρ ὁ ἄγγελος, τὰ μὲν ἐπαγγέλλεται, τὰ δὲ μαρτυρεῖ. Τὸ δὲ καὶ "*ὁ Κύριος μετὰ σοῦ*" πᾶς ὁ τοῦ νυμφίου πλοῦτος, αὐτὸ τῆς ἐπαγγελίας τὸ τέλος· αὐτὸς ὁ νυμφίος εὐλόγως ὡς Λόγος διὰ λόγου καὶ σὺν τῷ λόγῳ καὶ ὑπὲρ λόγον τὴν ἕνωσιν ἐργαζόμενος, καὶ νυμφίος ὁ αὐτὸς ὁμοῦ καὶ πατὴρ καὶ υἱὸς γινόμενος, ὡς αὐτὸς μὲν σπείρων, αὐτὸς δὲ σπειρόμενος, μᾶλλον δὲ καὶ δημιουργικῶς, ἀλλ' οὐ σπερματικῶς

fasting and praying near a fountain, because she was about to conceive the *fountain of life.* And this took place during the first month, when God also created the entire world, showing us that he is now renewing it. It was also on the first day of the week, when the primeval *darkness* was dispelled and the primordial *light* was created; and this was also the day on which her son rose from the tomb, raising the whole of creation together with himself. And it was not only the first of days but also the first hour, for it was necessary that the *morning* should hasten *toward morning,* and that the beginning of the physical light coincide with the beginning of his birth.

The words of the archangel were like seeds containing ex- 20
traordinarily great meanings contrasting the things of the present with those of the past, namely, "*Rejoice,*" and, "*O favored one.*" The first was said regarding the pain long associated with childbirth and the removal of the condemnation against us, but also on account of the honor and the grace of the promise. The second was in regard to the Virgin's wealth of virtues and the gifts of the Spirit. The former was like a dowry and engagement provided by the bridegroom, the latter was the wealth of the bride; the angel referred to both, promising the one and bearing witness to the other. The angel's subsequent words, "*the Lord is with you,*" comprise the entire wealth of the bridegroom, the very fulfillment of the promise. It was through this word, and with this word, and in a manner beyond words, that the same bridegroom, as the Word, reasonably brought about the union, so that one and the same Word became at once bridegroom, father, and son. He was both the sower and the one sown, or rather, acting as creator not by seed or like fig juice stirred into milk,

ἢ ὥσπερ ὀπὸς γάλα, τὴν ὅλην φύσιν κινῶν καὶ ἑαυτῷ περιπλάττων καὶ ὑφιστάμενος· τὸ αὐτὸ δὲ τοῦτο καὶ τῆς πρὶν κατάρας ἀντίρροπον ὅτι καὶ κύριος τῆς γυναικὸς ὁ ἀνὴρ καὶ τῆς γυναικὸς *ἡ ἀποστροφὴ πρὸς τὸν ἄνδρα*, ὥστε κύκλον εἶναι τῶν λυπηρῶν καὶ μήτε τῆς δουλείας μήτε τῶν ὀδυνῶν εἶναι λύσιν, ὡς ἀεὶ μὲν τῷ ἀνδρὶ συνεζευγμένης τῆς γυναικός, ἀεὶ δὲ τῇ γυναικὶ τοῦ γάμου καὶ τῆς δουλείας, καὶ τοῖς μὲν τοκετοῖς τῶν ὠδίνων, τῷ δὲ γάμῳ τῶν τοκετῶν· "οὐκέτι," γοῦν φησιν, "ὁ ἀνὴρ κατὰ σοῦ," ἀλλ' "*ὁ Κύριος μετὰ σοῦ,*" πάντως μὲν καὶ διὰ ταύτην ὡς μόνην οὕτω καὶ ὑπὲρ πάσας παρθένον, πάντως δὲ καὶ διὰ τὰς ἄλλας τὰς μετ' αὐτὴν ὡς δεδομένης καὶ ταύταις ἐξουσίας τοῦ παρθενεύειν.

21 Οἷον δὲ καὶ τὸ ἀκροτελεύτιον ὡς πληρέστατόν τε ἅμα καὶ συντομώτατον· "*Εὐλογημένη σὺ ἐν γυναιξί,*" παρὰ πάσας ὁμοῦ δηλαδὴ τὰς γυναῖκας, ἀλλὰ καὶ εὐλογημέναι πάντως ἐν σοὶ αἱ γυναῖκες, καθάπερ καὶ οἱ ἄνδρες ἐν τῷ υἱῷ, μᾶλλον δὲ καὶ ἐν ἀμφοτέροις ἀμφότεροι, καθάπερ διὰ μιᾶς καὶ ἑνὸς τῆς ἀρᾶς καὶ λύπης γυναικὸς καὶ ἀνδρός, οὕτω καὶ νῦν διὰ μιᾶς καὶ ἑνὸς τῆς εὐλογίας τὲ καὶ χαρᾶς καὶ τοῖς ἄλλοις πᾶσι διαδοθείσης. Ἀλλ' ὅρα μοι καὶ τῆς Παρθένου τὴν καθαρὰν καὶ σοφὴν καὶ ψυχὴν ὁμοῦ καὶ φωνήν· οὔτε φανερῶς ἀντιπίπτει διὰ τὴν ἀπιστίαν, οὔτε μὴν παντελῶς εὐθὺς ὑποπίπτει διὰ τὴν εὐκολίαν, ἀλλ' ἐπίσης ἐκφεύγουσα καὶ τὴν εὐπείθειαν τῆς Εὔας ἢ καὶ εὐπάθειαν καὶ τοῦ Ζαχαρίου δὲ τὴν ἀπείθειαν, μέσην χωρεῖ διὰ τὴν ἀσφάλειαν· καὶ διαταράττεται μὲν ὡς εἰκός, οὐ διὰ τὰ

he moved the whole of human nature and shaped it around himself, giving it subsistence. The same words were also a counterpoise to the ancient curse, since the man was made master of the woman, and the woman *had recourse to the man,* producing a cycle of pain with no end to their servitude or travail, because the woman was forever bound to the man, and marriage and servitude were forever bound to women, and pain was bound to childbirth, and childbirth to marriage. Thus the angel says: "No longer is man against you, but *the Lord is with you,*" for truly she alone is a virgin exalted above all other virgins, and has been given virginal authority over all the virgins who would come after her.

How complete and concise is the conclusion of the an- 21
gel's words: "*Blessed are you among women,*" that is, with respect to all women, though in you all women are certainly blessed, just as men are blessed in your son, or rather both are blessed in both, for just as the curse and sorrow came through one woman and one man, so too blessings and joy are now given to all through one woman and one man. Consider with me the purity and wisdom of the Virgin's soul as well as her response, for neither did she openly resist the angel's words due to any lack of belief, nor did she immediately accept them completely due to expediency. At the same time, she also avoided both the gullibility of Eve, or rather her passivity, and the incredulity of Zacharias, keeping instead to a middle path safely between the two. She was greatly troubled, as was only natural, not by the sight of the

ὁρώμενα μᾶλλον—τοσοῦτον αὐτῇ τὸ παράστημα ἅλλωστε καὶ τούτων οὖσα τῶν θεαμάτων ἤδη συνήθης—ἀλλὰ διὰ τὰ λεγόμενα· ταῦτά τοι καὶ οὐ τῇ θεωρίᾳ μᾶλλον ὁ εὐαγγελιστής, ἀλλὰ τῇ ἐπαγγελίᾳ τὸν τάραχον ἀποδίδωσιν· *ἡ δὲ* ἰδοῦσα *διεταράχθη ἐπὶ τῷ λόγῳ* αὐτοῦ *καὶ διελογίζετο ποταπὸς εἴη ὁ ἀσπασμὸς οὗτος*, οὐχ ὁ τοκετός. Ἔτι γὰρ ἠγνόει τοῦ μυστηρίου τὸ μέγεθος, ἀλλ' ὅμως ἐδεδοίκει καὶ ἔτρεμε τὴν θείαν ὁμιλίαν καὶ κοινωνίαν καὶ καθ' ἑαυτὴν ἠπόρει τὸ ποταπή τις αὕτη καὶ ὅπως, ἀλλὰ καὶ ὅπως ὁ χαροποιὸς νυμφαγωγός τε καὶ νυμφοστόλος ἀρχάγγελος, καὶ ταύτης μηδὲν εἰρηκυίας, οἷα νοῦς τῆς Παρθένου τὸν νοῦν ὁρῶν, οὐκ ἐκβάλλει μόνον τὸν φόβον, ἀλλὰ καὶ πᾶσαν ἀντεισάγει χαράν τε καὶ ἀγαλλίασιν καὶ διερμηνεύει τὸν ἄφραστον τόκον· "*Μὴ φοβοῦ*," φησί, "*Μαριάμ*·" οὐδὲν γὰρ δεινὸν οὐδὲ φοβερόν, ἀλλὰ καὶ τοὐναντίον χαρᾶς ὅλα καὶ χάριτος· "*εὗρες γὰρ χάριν παρὰ τῷ Θεῷ*," χάρισμα καλῶν ἄντικρυς τὸ ἀξίωμα τῆς θεοτοκίας.

22 Ἀλλὰ περιστησώμεθα καὶ ἡμεῖς τὴν παστάδα καὶ περιαθρήσωμεν τοῦ νυμφίου καὶ τῆς νύμφης τὸ κάλλος καὶ τῶν ὑμεναίων ἢ καὶ γαμικῶν συμφώνων ἢ καὶ αὐτῶν τῶν υἱϊκῶν ἐπαγγελιῶν ἀκούσωμεν, καὶ ὅπως αὐτὰ καὶ συντομώτατα καὶ σαφέστατα καὶ ἀκριβέστατα παρατίθησι καὶ διέξεισιν ὁ ἀρχάγγελος· "*Καὶ ἰδού*"—τὸ τάχος καὶ τὸ νῦν δηλῶν, ἵνα καὶ διὰ τούτου τὴν διὰ λόγου καὶ σὺν τῷ Λόγῳ δηλώσῃ σύλληψιν—"*συλλήψῃ* καὶ *ἐν γαστρὶ καὶ τέξεις υἱόν*·" ἔστι γὰρ καὶ *ἐν γαστρί*, κατὰ τὸν προφήτην, τῇ γε πνευματικῶς νοουμένῃ πνεῦμα συλλαβέσθαι Θεοῦ καὶ

angel—for she was a woman of great courage and was already accustomed to these sights—but rather by the things he said. To be sure, according to the evangelist, it was not the sight of the messenger but the message that troubled her, *for,* seeing this, *she was greatly troubled by* his *saying and considered what sort of greeting this might be,* not by the prospect of childbirth. This was because she was still unaware of the magnitude of the mystery, and she was afraid and trembled at the divine conversation and the encounter, and within herself was at a loss to understand what sort of greeting this was, and how it came about, or how the archangel, who was the bride's gladdening groomsman and escort, perceived, as if he were a mind, the state of her mind, without her saying anything; and how he not only removed her fear but also introduced in its place complete joy and exultation, explaining to her the ineffable childbirth, saying: "*Fear not, Mary,*" for there is nothing here that is terrible or frightening, but to the contrary everything is joy and grace, "*for you have found favor with God,*" this favor obviously being the honor of becoming the Theotokos.

But let us now gather around the bridal chamber and be- 22
hold the beauty of the bride and bridegroom; and let us hear the pledges of wedlock and union, and indeed the very promises concerning the son, and how the archangel presented them and set them forth most concisely, wisely, and with the greatest precision. "*And behold,*" he says—indicating the rapidity and immediacy of the event, revealing through this that the conception will take place through the Word and with a word—"*you will conceive in your womb and bear a son.*" According to the prophet, *in your womb,* in a spiritual manner, you will conceive the spirit of God, and bring

φόβον καὶ *πνεῦμα σωτηρίας* ἀποτεκεῖν. Ἀλλὰ σὺ "*καὶ τέξεις υἱὸν καὶ καλέσεις τὸ ὄνομα αὐτοῦ Ἰησοῦν·*" οὐ γὰρ ὁ πατήρ· ἀπάτωρ γὰρ τό γε κατὰ *τὴν κάτω γέννησιν,* ὥσπερ καὶ ἀμήτωρ κατὰ *τὴν ἄνω.* Κἀκεῖνος γὰρ μετ' οὐ πολὺ καλῶν, οὐ νῦν, ἀλλ' ὃ δὴ καὶ ἐξ ἀρχῆς αὐτὸν κέκληκεν, ἀγαπητὸν καλέσει υἱόν, οὐχ ὡς οὕτω γεννώμενον καθ' ἡμᾶς, ἀλλ' ὡς τῆς αὐτῆς αὐτῷ φύσεως προερχόμενον. Ἰησοῦς δὲ "Σωτήρ," οὐ γὰρ ὅσον οὐδὲν αὐτή, φησίν, ἐξ ἀνδρὸς ἢ τοῦ τόκου πείσῃ δεινὸν ἢ πικρόν, ἀλλὰ καὶ ὁ τόκος ἔσται τῷ κόσμῳ παντὶ σωτήριος, καὶ τὸ ἔργον δῆλον ἐκ τοῦ ὀνόματος· ἐπεὶ δὲ κοινὸν αὐτῷ τοῦτο καὶ πρὸς τὸν αὐτοῦ τύπον, τὸν στρατηγὸν καὶ δημαγωγὸν καὶ πρὸς τὴν τῆς ἐπαγγελίας γῆν ὁδηγόν, οὐ κατ' ἐκεῖνον, φησίν οὗτος, ἀλλ' *οὗτος ἔσται μέγας,* τὸ ἀνθρώπινον ὑποβάλλων, ὡς γὰρ Θεὸς καὶ ὑπὲρ "τὸ μέγα" καὶ οὕτω *μέγας, ὥστε καὶ Υἱὸς Ὑψίστου κληθήσεται,* οὐ διὰ τὴν καθ' ὑπόστασιν καὶ ἄκραν ἕνωσιν μόνον, ἀλλὰ καὶ τῶν ὀνομάτων τὴν ἀντιπεριχώρησιν. Σὺ μὲν γὰρ *καλέσεις αὐτὸν Ἰησοῦν,* παρ' αὐτῶν δὲ τῶν πραγμάτων καὶ τῶν θαυμάτων ἢ καὶ παρ' αὐτοῦ τοῦ Πατρός, *καὶ Υἱὸς Ὑψίστου κληθήσεται,* διὸ *καὶ δώσει Κύριος αὐτῷ τὸν θρόνον Δαβὶδ τοῦ πατρὸς αὐτοῦ,* καθὰ καὶ ἀνθρώπῳ, καὶ ὡς ἐντεῦθεν ἀρχομένῳ τῆς βασιλείας διὰ τῶν πιστευόντων, οὓς καὶ "οἶκον" καὶ "θρόνον" ὀνομάζει Δαβίδ τε καὶ Ἰακώβ. Καὶ τῆς βασιλείας αὐτοῦ οὐκ ἔσται τέλος· οὐ καθὸ Θεὸς μόνον, ἀλλὰ καθὸ καὶ ἄνθρωπος, καὶ ὡς οὐ κατὰ φύσιν μόνον, ἀλλὰ βασιλεύσων καὶ κατὰ γνώμην· καὶ νῦν μὲν πολλῶν, ἐπ' ἐσχάτων δὲ καὶ πάντων, ἡνίκα *καὶ*

forth fear and *the spirit of salvation.* And "*you shall bear a son and call his name Jesus.*" Here there is no father, because according to *his earthly birth* he is *fatherless,* just as he is *motherless* according to *his heavenly birth.* Not at this time, but very soon his Father will call him what he called him from the beginning, his beloved son, not because he was born as we are, but because he came forth from the same nature as God. The name Jesus means "Savior," because, the angel says, you will experience no suffering or sorrow from man or through childbirth, but the child will be the salvation of the whole world, and his work will be made known by his name. And since he holds this name in common with the general and leader who prefigured him, and who was the guide to the promised land, the angel does not say he will be like him, but rather, *he will be great,* referring to his human nature, for inasmuch as he is also God, he is beyond "great," and thus so great that *he will be called the Son of the Most High,* not only on account of the utter extreme of the hypostatic union, but also because of the exchange of idioms. And thus *you will call him Jesus,* by virtue of the facts themselves, and his miracles, or by virtue of the Father himself. *And he will be called the Son of the Most High,* because *the Lord will give him the throne of his father David,* inasmuch as he is man, from whence he inaugurates the kingdom through the faithful, whom both David and Jacob call a "house" and "throne." And of his kingdom there will be no end, not only because he is God but also because he is man, but not by virtue of his human nature alone, for he shall now also rule by virtue of the inclination of his will; and now he will rule over many, but at the end of time he will rule over all, when all things will be subjected to him, with the exception *of the one who*

ὑποταγήσεται αὐτῷ τὰ πάντα χωρὶς τοῦ ὑποτάξαντος αὐτῷ τὰ πάντα· καὶ αὐτὸς ὑποταγήσεται τῷ Θεῷ καὶ Πατρὶ διὰ τῆς ἡμετέρας πάντως γνώμης καὶ φύσεως, ὡς οἰκειοποιούμενος τὰ ἡμέτερα.

23 Τί οὖν ἡ Παρθένος; Ὅρα μοι σοφίας καὶ φιλοπαρθενίας ὑπερβολήν· δέχεται μὲν τὴν σύλληψιν, ἀπορεῖ δὲ καὶ διερωτᾷ τὸν τῆς συλλήψεως τρόπον· "*Πῶς ἔσται* μοι *τοῦτο* τὸ θεῖον οὕτω καὶ θαυμαστόν τε καὶ ἀπερινόητον; Καὶ οὐ ταῦτα μόνον, ἀλλὰ καὶ ἀνακόλουθον· τό τε γὰρ *ἄνδρα* με γνῶναι καθάπαξ Θεῷ καθιερωθεῖσαν τῶν ἀμηχάνων, καὶ τὸ χωρὶς ἀνδρὸς καὶ συλλαβεῖν καὶ τεκεῖν τῶν ἀδυνάτων·" ᾧ δὴ καὶ ἐδεδοίκει μᾶλλον τὸν γάμον, τῇ παρθενίᾳ μᾶλλον ἢ τῇ ἐπαγγελίᾳ καὶ τῇ ἀξιοπιστίᾳ τοῦ ἀρχαγγέλου προσφυομένη. *Ἐπεὶ ἄνδρα οὐ γινώσκω*, πάντως μὲν καὶ πρὸς τὸν Ἰωσὴφ ἀναφέρουσα, ὡς μέχρι μνηστείας μόνον εἰδυῖα τὸν αὐτοῦ γάμον καὶ ὡς οὐ νῦν μόνον, ἀλλὰ καὶ διὰ τέλους ἄχραντος ἐγνωκυῖα μένειν ἀνδρός, οἷα καὶ θεῖον καὶ ἄψαυστον ἀφιέρωμα, πάντως δὲ κἀκεῖνον βεβαιοῦσα τὸν λόγον, ὡς ἐκ πατέρων ἥκει πολλῶν καὶ σοφῶν, ὅτι μὴ τὴν πεῖραν τοῦ γάμου μόνον, ἀλλὰ καὶ τὴν ἔφεσιν ἡ Παρθένος ἠγνόησεν, οἷα καὶ ἐξ ἀρχῆς ἐξ ἁγνοῦ τὲ καὶ ἱεροῦ συμπαγεῖσα καὶ τραφεῖσα πνεύματός τε καὶ σώματος. *Ἄνδρα οὐ γινώσκω*· "οὐκ ἔγνωκα," φησίν, "ἐπιθυμίαν ἀνδρός, οὐκ ἔχω θέλημα τῆς σαρκός," ὃ δὴ πάλιν καὶ κατὰ πάσης αὐτῇ τῆς γυναικείας καὶ ἀνθρωπείας ἐξαίρετον φύσεως, ὅτι καὶ ὑπὲρ πάσας καὶ πάντας αὐτῇ καὶ ἐκ γνώμης ὅλως ἀνεπιδέκτου τῆς τοιαύτης κακίας ἡ σωφροσύνη. Τούτοις καὶ ὁ

subjected all things to him, and he himself will be subjected to God the Father, of course through the submission of the inclination of our will and nature, inasmuch as he has made the things of our nature his own.

What was the Virgin's response? Consider with me her 23
superabundance of wisdom and love of virginity. On the one hand, she accepted the conception, but on the other she was perplexed and questioned the manner of it, saying, "*How can this* divine and wondrous and incomprehensible thing *be* happening to me? And not only this, but these things are also logically inconsistent, for I have been dedicated wholly to God, and that I should know *a man* is out of the question, and to conceive and bear a child without a man is impossible." This is why she had feared marriage, clinging more to her virginity than to the promise and trustworthiness of the archangel. In saying, "*I have not known a man,*" she was obviously referring to Joseph, knowing marriage to him only insofar as they were betrothed, and not only at that time but throughout her entire life she remained untouched by man, as an inviolable offering to God; and her words completely confirmed this, as have many wise fathers of the church, who affirm not simply that she had no experience of marriage, but that the Virgin had not even the desire for it, for from the very beginning she was confirmed and raised in purity and holiness of both spirit and body. *I have not known a man:* "I have not known," she is saying, "desire for a man; I have no carnal impulse within me," that is, again, she was exempt from the very thing which is common to the nature of women and indeed to all human nature, for she was above all women and men, and, in the inclination of her will, her purity of mind was wholly unsusceptible to this sort of vice.

μέγας καὶ ἔνθους τίθεται Διονύσιος, ὁ καὶ θεόπτης ἅμα καὶ αὐτόπτης τοῦ θεοδόχου σώματος, τά τε ἄλλα καὶ ὅτιπερ καὶ ὑπὲρ ἄνθρωπον τὰ ἀνθρώπινα πράττουσα ἦν. Ὅρα δὲ ὅπως αὐτῇ λύει τὴν ἀπορίαν καὶ διερμηνεύει τὸν ἄφραστον τόκον καὶ ἀκατάληπτον τρόπον ὁ εὐαγγελιστὴς ὁμοῦ καὶ ἐξηγητής· "οὐ χρεία," φησίν, "ἀνδρός· οὐ γὰρ ὁμοίως ταῖς ἄλλαις τὰ σά, ὥσπερ οὐδὲ τὰ τοῦ υἱοῦ τοῖς υἱοῖς· οὐ γὰρ ἡ σὴ σύλληψις τῆς παρθενίας ἀφαίρεσις, ἀλλὰ καὶ τοὐναντίον σφραγὶς καὶ συντήρησις, μᾶλλον δὲ καὶ ἐπὶ πλέον κάθαρσίς τε καὶ θέωσις· οὐ γὰρ ἀνδρός, ἀλλ' Ἁγίου Πνεύματος ἡ ἐπέλευσις καὶ αὐτῆς τῆς τοῦ *Ὑψίστου* δυνάμεως ἡ ἐπισκίασις. Τὸ μὲν γὰρ οἷα νυμφαγωγός τε καὶ νυμφοστόλος προεπελεύσεται, προσκαθαῖρον καὶ προσκαλλωπίζον τὴν ἤδη προκεκαθαρμένην καὶ προκεκαλλωπισμένην καὶ ἁγιάζον τὴν σὴν μήτραν ἢ προσκιάζον τοὺς ἐμφερεῖς τῷ σῷ παιδὶ καὶ νυμφίῳ τύπους· αὐτὸς δὲ ὁ σὸς νυμφίος εἴτε καὶ παῖς, ἡ τοῦ *Ὑψίστου* δύναμις—*Χριστὸς γὰρ Θεοῦ δύναμις καὶ Θεοῦ σοφία*—καὶ ἐπισκιάσει *σοι* καθάπερ ἐσκιαγραφημένοις ἐπιβαλὼν χρώματα καὶ ὅλον ἑαυτὸν ὁλικῶς διαγράψας ἢ καὶ σκιοειδῶς μᾶλλον περιγραφήσεται καὶ τὴν παχύτητα τοῦ σώματος διαμορφωθήσεται καθάπερ χρώματος· ἢ τρίτον, καὶ αὐτὸ τὸ Ἀποσκίασμα τοῦ Πατρός—καθάπερ σώματος τὸ ἐκσφράγισμα—τὸ *Ἀπαύγασμα,* σὺν πάσαις αὐτοῦ ταῖς πατρικαῖς ἐμφερείαις καὶ ἐνεργείαις, οὐσιωδῶς ἐπισκιάσει σοι, Λόγος ἁπτὸς καὶ Θεὸς ὁρατὸς καὶ σὸς υἱός, ὁ καὶ τοῦ Θεοῦ καὶ Πατρὸς Υἱὸς γινόμενος καὶ καλούμενος, διὸ καὶ

This is affirmed by the great and divinely inspired Dionysios, who was both a divine visionary and an eyewitness of her God-bearing body, namely, that she did human things in a manner that transcended human nature. But see how the messenger, who was also an interpreter, resolved her dilemma and explained the ineffable birth and its incomprehensible manner: "There is no need of a man," he says, "for things with you are not like those with other women, just as things pertaining to your son are not like those pertaining to other sons. Your conception will not result in the loss of your virginity, but to the contrary shall seal and preserve it, or rather bring about its purification and deification. For not a man but the Holy Spirit shall come upon you, and you will be overshadowed by the very power of the *Most High.* Indeed the Spirit, like a bridal groomsman and escort, will arrive first and purify and adorn you in advance, though you are already completely pure and completely adorned. And he will sanctify your womb or rather foreshadow the figures that point to your son and bridegroom. Then your bridegroom and child himself shall come to you, the power of the *Most High*—for *Christ is the power and wisdom of God*—and he shall *overshadow you,* just as a painter adds color to a shadowy outline; and he will wholly inscribe himself within you, or rather he will be circumscribed in a shadowy, painterly manner, being transformed into the thickness of the body like a color; or, third, the very Shadow of the Father—just like the imprint of a body—the *Radiance,* together with all his paternal similitudes and energies, will overshadow you with his essence, the Word rendered tangible and God made visible, your own son who is called and truly is the son of God the Father, and who thus is common to both you and

κοινός σοι πρὸς τὸν Πατέρα· *τὸ γὰρ ὑπὸ σοῦ γεννώμενον* καὶ *Υἱὸς* τοῦ *Θεοῦ* καὶ ἔσται τὲ καὶ *κληθήσεται.*" Διατί δὲ οὐχ οὕτως, ἀλλ' ἁπλῶς *τὸ γεννώμενον;* Οἶδε γὰρ οὐκ ἀπὸ γυναικός, ἀλλ' ἀπὸ ἀνδρὸς κυρίως καὶ πρώτως τὴν γέννησιν· καὶ γεννᾷ μὲν ὁ πατήρ, ἡ δὲ μήτηρ διαδεχομένη τελεσφορεῖ καὶ προάγει τὴν γέννησιν, ἵν' οὖν μήτε ἀπὸ ταύτης ὅλον, μήτε δὲ καὶ ἀπὸ πατρός, ἀλλ' ἀφ' ἑαυτοῦ δείξῃ τὸ γέννημα καὶ γεννῶν ὁμοῦ καὶ γεννώμενον.

24 "Πίστις τῶνδε τῶν εὐαγγελίων καὶ ἕτερα εὐαγγέλια προσεμφερῆ καὶ ὑπερφυῆ καὶ δι' ἐμοῦ ταῦτα καὶ γινωσκόμενα καὶ γενόμενα· τούτων δέ σοι καὶ ἀμφοῖν παρὰ πολλῶν ἡ ἀπόδειξις, ἀπὸ τοῦ ὀνόματος, ἀπὸ τῆς συγγενείας, ἀπὸ τοῦ πράγματος, ἀπὸ τοῦ χρόνου, καὶ ἀπ' αὐτοῦ τοῦ θαύματος· *Ἰδοὺ* γὰρ *Ἐλισάβετ ἡ συγγενής σου, καὶ αὐτὴ συνειληφυῖα υἱὸν ἐν γήρει αὐτῆς καὶ οὗτος μὴν ἕκτος αὐτῇ τῇ καλουμένῃ στείρᾳ.*" Τοσοῦτον εἰς ἕξιν ἧκε τῆς ἀπαιδίας, ὥστε καὶ εἰς κλῆσιν αὐτῇ καὶ γνώρισμα τὸ ἀτύχημα, καὶ τὸ δὴ πλέον, ὅτι *οὐκ ἀδυνατήσει παρὰ τῷ Θεῷ πᾶν ῥῆμα·* οὐ γὰρ ὅσον, φησί, τὰ γενόμενά ποτε καὶ γενήσεται, ἀλλὰ καὶ τὰ ῥηθέντα καὶ ῥηθησόμενα. Προσθετέον δὲ πάντως καὶ τὰ νοηθέντα καὶ νοηθησόμενα καὶ ἃ μηδὲ λόγος εἰπεῖν μηδὲ νοῦς ἐννοῆσαι δύναται, βούλεται δὲ μόνον ἐκεῖνος. Ἀλλ' ὅρα μοι κἀνταῦθα τῆς Παρθένου τὸ ἦθος καὶ ὅσην εἶχεν ἐν νεαρῷ κομιδῇ τῷ σώματι καὶ φρονήματος ὁμοῦ καὶ πνεύματος τελειότητα· ἕως μὲν γὰρ ἀνδρὸς ὑπόληψις ἦν, τὴν σύλληψιν οὐκ ἐδέχετο, "ἀλλὰ κἂν ἀρχάγγελος ἦς,"

the Father; for *that which will be born* from you will be, and *will be called,* the *Son of God.*" Why, then, did he not say this, but simply: *that which will be born?* Because he knew that birth is not caused by the woman but principally and primarily by the man, for the father is the cause of birth while the mother, receiving what is given by the father, brings it to fruition and leads it to birth, so that what is born is neither entirely hers nor the father's, and this is to show that the child to be born is himself both the cause of birth and the one who is born.

"These good tidings are confirmed by other similar and 24
marvelous good tidings that have been made known and came about through me. The proof of both should be evident to you from many things: from the child's name, from the kinship, from the facts themselves, from the timing, and from the miracle itself, for *behold, Elizabeth your kinswoman has also conceived a son in her old age, and this is the sixth month for her who was called barren.*" So greatly had she become associated with the state of childlessness that this misfortune became her name and characteristic feature; and what is more, he says that *no word from God will be void of power,* referring not so much to things that have come about and that will come about, but to things that have been said and will be said. To this we can certainly add the things thought and the things that will be thought, as well as things that language cannot utter and which even the mind cannot conceive, but which God alone wishes to bring about. But consider with me once again the character of the Virgin, and the great perfection of mind and spirit she possessed in a young body. As long as there was some suspicion of contact with a man, she did not accept the news of the conception: "Even

φησί, "κἂν ὑπερφυῆ μοί τινα καὶ οὐράνια κομίζῃς τὰ εὐαγγέλια, ἀλλ' ἐμὲ καὶ ἀνδρὶ συνελθεῖν καὶ συλλαβεῖν καὶ τεκεῖν ἀμήχανον." Ἐπειδὴ δὲ καὶ τὴν παρουσίαν καὶ τὴν ἐνοίκησιν, τὴν μὲν τοῦ Πνεύματος, τὴν δὲ τοῦ Υἱοῦ προσευηγγελίσθη, πείθεται μὲν καὶ πιστεύει—μηδὲν γὰρ ἀδύνατον εἶναι Θεῷ—φυσᾶται δὲ καὶ ἐπαίρεται οὐδὲ οὕτως, ἀλλὰ καταπίπτει μᾶλλον καὶ ὑποστέλλεται καὶ *δούλην* μὲν ἑαυτὴν οὐκ ὀνομάζει μόνον, ἀλλὰ καὶ ὡς εἰκὸς ἑτοίμην εἶναι λέγει πρὸς τὸ ὑπούργημα· ὡς δὲ καὶ ὑπὲρ αὐτὴν ὄν, οὐ δέχεται μᾶλλον ἢ ἐπεύχεται τὸ ἐπάγγελμα· "*ἰδοὺ ἡ δούλη Κυρίου, γένοιτό μοι κατὰ τὸ ῥῆμά σου·*" ταῦτά τοι καὶ ἄπεισιν εὐθὺς *ἀπ' αὐτῆς ὁ ἄγγελος,* οὐ μόνον ἀπαρτίσας ὅπερ ἐβούλετο, ἀλλὰ καὶ ὑπερθαυμάσας τοῦ παρθενικοῦ κάλλους τὴν ὡραιότητα. Κρύπτει καὶ ταῦτα παρ' ἑαυτῇ ἡ Παρθένος, καὶ πολλῷ μᾶλλον σοφωτέρα γάρ, ὡς ἤδη καὶ τῆς Σοφίας μήτηρ, καθώς τινες τῶν παλαιῶν καὶ τὸ *οὐκ ἐγίνωσκεν αὐτὴν* Ἰωσὴφ *ἕως οὗ ἔτεκε* τὸν *υἱὸν* αὐτῆς τὸν πρωτότοκον ἡρμηνεύκασιν. Οὐκ ἐγίνωσκε τὰ κατ' αὐτήν, ἐπεὶ πῶς ἂν ἔγεμεν ὑποψίας, πῶς ᾐσχύνετο, πῶς ἐκβαλεῖν ἐπεχείρει, μέχρις αὐτῷ καὶ ἡ ἀποκάλυψις καὶ ἡ γέννησις, καὶ πάντα τὰ κατὰ τὴν γέννησιν, οἱ ποιμένες, ὁ ἀστήρ, οἱ Μάγοι, καὶ ἡ Παρθένος ἴσως ἐξεταζομένη τότε, καὶ μᾶλλον ἡ παρθενία μετὰ τὴν γέννησιν, καὶ πάλιν ὁ ἄγγελος, ὁ χρηματισμὸς ὁ πρὸ τῆς Αἰγύπτου, ὁ μετὰ τὴν Αἴγυπτον, φανερὸν καὶ αὐτὸ καθίστησι τὸ μυστήριον; Ἀλλὰ τοῖς μὲν ἄλλοις πᾶσιν ἀπόρρητα τῇ Παρθένῳ ταῦτα, τὰ δὲ πολλὰ

though you are an archangel," she said, "and bring me some marvelous and heavenly good tidings, it is nevertheless impossible for me to be joined to a man, and to conceive and give birth." But when the presence of the Spirit and the indwelling of the Son were proclaimed to her in advance, she was persuaded and believed—for nothing is impossible with God—though even this did not cause her to become prideful or haughty. Rather, she became more humble and more modest, calling herself not only a *handmaid,* but also, as was only proper, declaring herself ready to offer service; and as this was beyond her, she did not simply accept it as much as dedicate herself to the promise offered to her, and said: "*Behold, the handmaid of the Lord; be it unto me according to your word.*" When she said this, *the angel* immediately departed *from her,* not only having accomplished what he had set out to do, but also struck with amazement at the comeliness of her virginal beauty. But the Virgin hid all these things in her heart, and thus became even wiser, for she was already the mother of Wisdom, which is how some of the ancients interpreted the phrase, Joseph *did not know her until she gave birth* to her firstborn *son.* He did not know the mysteries concerning her, for how then could he have been filled with suspicion? How could he have felt ashamed? How could he have planned to divorce her until the revelation came to him, and before he saw all the things surrounding the birth? That is, the shepherds, the star, the Magi, and the way the Virgin came under examination at that time, to say nothing of her virginity after childbirth, another visit from the angel, the oracle before the flight into Egypt, which after Egypt plainly revealed the mystery. However, the Virgin did not speak to anyone of these things, most of which remained

καὶ ἀπρόϊτα, πρὸς δὲ τὴν Ἐλισάβετ ἀποτρέχει μόνην· τοῦτο μὲν εἰωθὸς αὐτῇ μὴ διὰ τὴν συγγένειαν μόνον, ἀλλὰ καὶ τὴν ἄλλην τοῦ τε ἤθους καὶ τοῦ τρόπου συνάφειαν, τοῦτο δὲ καὶ διὰ τὰ παρὰ τοῦ ἀγγέλου ῥηθέντα, καὶ παρ᾽ αὐτῆς ἐκείνης μαθεῖν βουλομένη καὶ ὀφθαλμοῖς αὐτοῖς θεασομένη τὰ προφητεύματα· τοῦτο δὲ ἦν ἀπὸ Ναζαρὲτ ἐπὶ Βηθλεέμ, τύπος ὂν τῆς ἐκεῖσε μετ᾽ ὀλίγον αὐτῇ γεννήσεως, ἣν καὶ διὰ τῆς ὀρεινῆς, ὡς ὑψηλοτέρας, ὁ Λουκᾶς αἰνίττεται· ἀλλ᾽ ὅτι καὶ ὥσπερ νῦν ἡ μήτηρ πρὸς τὴν μητέρα, ἡ τοῦ Δεσπότου πρὸς τὴν τοῦ δούλου, οὕτω μετὰ ταῦτα καὶ ὁ ταύτης Υἱὸς καὶ Δεσπότης πρὸς τὸν ταύτης υἱὸν καὶ δοῦλον ἐλεύσεται, καθαίρων ἅμα καὶ καθαιρόμενος. Ἄλλωσθ᾽ ὅτι καὶ ἐχρῆν ἄρα μὴ τὸν Δεσπότην μόνον, ἀλλὰ καὶ τὴν τούτου μητέρα τῇ μετριοφροσύνῃ κατὰ πάντων τῶν ἄλλων τοῦ υἱοῦ χωρὶς ἔχειν τὰ νικητήρια, καὶ τούτῳ αὐτῷ τὸ πρωτεῖον ἔχειν, τῷ τὸ δευτερεῖον πάντων καὶ πανταχοῦ ζητεῖν, ἀλλὰ καὶ τύπον εἶναι πᾶσι καθάπερ κἀκεῖνον τοῦ μετρίου καὶ τῆς ὑφέσεως.

Οὐ φθάνει γοῦν ἀσπασαμένη τὴν Ἐλισάβετ καὶ ἡ πρὸ τῆς Φωνῆς *φωνὴ* καὶ ὁ πρὸ τοῦ Φωτὸς προφήτης ὀξύτερον τῆς μητρὸς καὶ ὁρᾷ καὶ ἀκούει καὶ ἀσπάζεται τὸν προφητευόμενον· καὶ ἐπεὶ μὴ εἶχε τῷ δακτύλῳ μηδὲ τοῖς ῥήμασι, τοῖς ἅλμασιν αὐτὸν ποιεῖ δῆλον, οὐκ ἐκεῖνον μόνον, ἀλλὰ καὶ ἑαυτὸν τοῖς πράγμασι προφητεύων, ὅτι προφήτης ἐστί τε καὶ ἔσται τούτου καὶ πρόδρομος, ὃν καὶ προλέγων καὶ οὗ καὶ προτρέχων ἀπὸ γαστρὸς ἦν· ὥσπερ δὲ οὗτος ἐκείνου προφήτης, οὕτω καὶ τῆς μητρὸς ἡ μήτηρ,

hidden, though she ran to Elizabeth alone. This was partly because it was customary for her, not only on account of their relation but also because of Elizabeth's character and her manner of comportment; but also on account of the words spoken to her by the angel and because she wished to learn for herself and see with her own eyes, the things that had been prophesied. Thus she left Nazareth and went to Bethlehem, which prefigured her impending childbirth there, and Luke hints at this when he mentions the hill country, as it was more lofty. And just as now the mother went to meet the mother, that is, the mother of the Master went to the mother of the servant, so too, after these things came to pass, the former's Son and Master would come to the latter's son and servant, purifying him and at the same time being purified by him. It was also necessary not only for the Master alone but also for his mother, by her modesty, to take hold of the rewards of victory over all the others (except her son), and to attain first place by seeking everywhere and in all things to be in second place, and also to be, like himself, a model of moderation and lowliness.

No sooner had the Virgin embraced Elizabeth when the 25
voice who was before the Voice, the prophet who preceded the Light, saw and heard more acutely than his mother and greeted the one foretold in prophecy. But because he could make neither gestures nor sounds, he made him known by leaping in his mother's womb, and not just him but also himself, prophesying through his movements that he was himself a prophet and would be the forerunner of the Lord, speaking of him in advance and running before him even from his mother's womb. And just as he was the prophet of the son, so too was his mother the prophetess of the mother,

μήτερα γὰρ αὐτὴν *τοῦ Κυρίου* καλεῖ καὶ διαπορεῖται καθάπερ τοῦ ταύτης υἱοῦ πρὸς ἀνθρώπους, οὕτω δὴ καὶ αὐτῆς ταύτης πρὸς ἐκείνην τὴν συγκατάβασιν· οὐ ταῦτα δὲ μόνον, ἀλλὰ καὶ ὅπως αὐτῇ τούτων διδάσκαλος τὸ κυοφορούμενον ἐκ γαστρὸς σκιρτῶν καὶ τὸν ἐν γαστρὶ ταύτης προασπαζόμενον. Εἶτα πάντως καὶ πᾶσαν ἀκολούθως ἐξ ἀρχῆς μέχρι τέλους τὴν περὶ αὐτὴν καταλέγει τοῦ δράματος θαυματοποιΐαν, τὸν Ζαχαρίαν, τὴν ἱερατείαν, τὴν ὀπτασίαν, τὴν κώφευσιν, τὴν ἐξ ἐκείνου σύλληψιν, οὐ παρ' ἐκείνου μαθοῦσα—πῶς ἤδη σιγήσαντος;—ἀλλὰ τυχὸν μὲν καὶ γράψαντος, τυχὸν δὲ καὶ παρὰ τῆς σιωπῆς αὐτῆς. Οὐκ ἂν γὰρ οὗτος ἐσιώπα πάντως, εἰ μή τινων ἀθεάτων ἐγένετο θεατὴς καί τινων ἀρρήτων ἀκροατής, οὐδ' οὕτως εὐθὺς ἐξ ἐκείνου συνέδραμε καὶ ἡ παρ' ἡλικίαν καὶ φύσιν ἀμφοτέρων σύλληψις, εἰ μὴ καθάπερ τῷ Ἀβραὰμ καὶ τῇ Σάρρᾳ θεία τις ὑπόσχεσις καὶ χάρις ἦν· οὐ ταῦτα δὲ μόνον ἡ Ἐλισάβετ, ἀλλ' ὅτι καὶ ἄρρεν τὸ ἐν αὐτῇ παιδίον καὶ ὅσος ὁ τῆς συλλήψεως χρόνος. Ἀλλ' οἷον ἡμᾶς μικροῦ καὶ μεταξὺ τοῦ λόγου παρέδραμε· μητέρα μὲν γὰρ αὐτὴν *τοῦ Κυρίου* καὶ κυρίαν ἑαυτῆς παρὰ πάσας δὲ λέγει τὰς γυναῖκας εὐλογημένην, ἐκείνου δὲ πῶς καρπώσῃ τὴν ἔννοιαν ὅ γε φιλομαθής τε καὶ φιλεξεταστὴς τοῦ βάθους τοῦ Πνεύματος, τοῦ *εὐλογημένος ὁ καρπὸς τῆς κοιλίας σου,* ἢ δῆλον ὅτι μὴ τὴν σύλληψιν μόνον οἶδεν, ἀλλὰ δὴ καὶ τὴν δίχα σπορᾶς καὶ ἀνδρός, διὸ καὶ καρπὸν ἀφ' ἑαυτῆς μόνης καλεῖ τὸ κυοφορούμενον; Ἢ ὅτι καὶ "καρπὸς" ὄντως, ὡς

for Elizabeth calls her the mother *of the Lord,* and just as she was perplexed concerning the gracious condescension of Mary's son to human beings, so too was she perplexed concerning the mother's gracious condescension toward her. And not only these things, but the child leaping in her womb was also her teacher in these matters, greeting in advance the one carried in Mary's womb. After this, Elizabeth surely explained to Mary everything that had happened to her from the beginning of the entire marvelous drama to the end: Zacharias, the priesthood, the vision, the muteness, the conception by him, which she did not learn of from him—how could she since he had already been silenced?—though perhaps she learned of it through his writing, or perhaps from the silence itself. But he would not have been absolutely silent had he not become the seer of things that cannot be seen, or the hearer of words that cannot be spoken. Neither would the conception, which was contrary to the age and nature of the parents, also immediately have come about for him, had it not been the result of a divine promise and grace, just as it was in the case of Abraham and Sarah. And Elizabeth learned not only these things but also that the child in her womb was male along with the duration of the pregnancy. But there is something I almost overlooked in my discourse: Elizabeth calls her the mother *of the Lord,* and her own sovereign, and blessed beyond all other women. And how could one who loves learning and examining the depth of the Spirit bring to fruition the meaning of the words, *blessed is the fruit of your womb,* unless it was clear to Elizabeth not only from the Virgin's conception but also that this came about without seed or man, and that is why she calls the one in her womb the fruit of herself alone? Or

αὐτὸς ὢν ὁ τὸν κόσμον τρέφων καὶ ἔτι θρέψων τῷ σώματι καὶ τῷ αἵματι; Καὶ τὸ "εὐλογημένος" δὲ πρὸς τὸ "κατηραμένος" τὴν ἀντιδιαστολὴν ἔχον· ὁ μὲν γὰρ ἀραῖος ἡμῖν, ὡς ἀρᾶς αἴτιος ὁ τῆς γνώσεως, οὗτος δὲ ὁ καρπὸς εὐλογημένος, ὡς τῆς ζωῆς καὶ αὐτοζωή. Ἢ καὶ ὅτι τῶν μὲν ἄλλων οἱ καρποὶ πάντες ὑπὸ κατάραν, πάντες ὑπὸ τὴν ἁμαρτίαν—ἐκ γὰρ τοῦ πρώτου πεσόντος καὶ δι' ἁμαρτίας γάμου τὲ καὶ φθορᾶς καὶ ἐν ἁμαρτίαις—οὗτος δὲ μόνος εὐλογημένος ὡς οὔτε δι' ἀνδρὸς οὔτε δι' ἁμαρτίας, ἀλλὰ καὶ ἀναμάρτητος, εἰ καὶ ἄνθρωπος; Ὡς δὲ Θεός, οὐκ εὐλογημένος μόνον καὶ ἀναμάρτητος, ἀλλὰ δὴ καὶ εὐλογῶν καὶ *αἴρων τὴν ἁμαρτίαν τοῦ κόσμου.*

26 Τί δὲ καὶ ἡ θαυμαστὴ καὶ τὰ πάντα καινὴ Μαρία; Καθάπερ ὑπὲρ φύσιν καὶ τἆλλα μήτηρ καὶ παρθένος, οὕτω καὶ ταῦτα προφῆτις ὁμοῦ καὶ προφητευομένη, καθ' ἃ καὶ θεοφοροῦσα καὶ θεοφορουμένη, καὶ εὐχαριστοῦσα καὶ εὐχομένη καὶ θεολογοῦσα δείκνυται· οὐ γὰρ ἀλαζονευομένη ταῦτά γε—πολλοῦ γε καὶ δεῖ—ἥτις καὶ "*δούλην*" ἑαυτὴν καλεῖ καὶ *τὴν* "*ταπείνωσιν*" ὁμολογεῖ καὶ ἀπορεῖ τὴν ἐπ' αὐτῇ θείαν "*ἐπίβλεψιν·*" ἀλλὰ πρῶτον, τῷ Ἁγίῳ κινουμένη καὶ ὑπηρετοῦσα Πνεύματι, δεύτερον, καὶ βεβαιοῦσα τὴν πίστιν τῶν τὲ παρ' αὐτῆς τῆς Ἐλισάβετ αὐτῇ λεγομένων καὶ τῶν ἔναγχος παρὰ τοῦ ἀγγέλου λεχθέντων, ἃ καὶ μὴ παρ' ἑαυτῆς μᾶλλον, ἀλλὰ παρ' αὐτοῦ λέγει τοῦ Κυρίου ῥηθῆναι, καὶ διὰ τοῦτο μακαρίζουσα καὶ τὴν *πιστεύσασαν ὅτι ἔσται τελείωσις τοῖς λελαλημένοις αὐτῇ παρὰ Κυρίου,* τρίτον, καὶ *τὸν Κύριον μεγαλύνουσα* καὶ οὐδὲ

because the child in the womb is truly the "fruit" that nourishes the world, and which will nourish it by means of his body and blood? And that it is "blessed" in contrast to that "cursed" fruit, which had the opposite effect, for that was a curse since the fruit of knowledge was the cause of the curse, whereas this fruit is blessed since it is the fruit of life and life itself. Or also because, while the fruits of other women are under a curse and all under sin—for they are descended from the first fallen man, and from the sin of carnal marriage and corruption in sins—this fruit alone is blessed, since it was produced neither by a man nor through sin but indeed is sinless, even if the one born is man? But since he is also God, he is not simply blessed and sinless, but indeed blesses us and *takes away the sin of the world.*

What did the wondrous Mary, who was new in every way, 26
say in response to Elizabeth? Just as she surpassed nature and in other respects was both mother and virgin, so too, by virtue of these things, she was both a prophetess and the subject of prophecy, since she both bore God and was also borne about by God, and thus she appears as one who gives thanks, offers prayers, and speaks about God. And she was not boastful because of these things—far from it—since she called herself a "*handmaid,*" and acknowledged her "*humility,*" and was astounded at the divine "*regard*" for her. But first, she was moved by and became a servant of the Holy Spirit. Second, she confirmed the trustworthiness of the things said to her by Elizabeth, and the things recently said by the angel, or rather, it says, spoken not by her but by the Lord himself, and this is why she was blessed and believed that there would be a *fulfillment of those things spoken to her by the Lord.* Third, she *magnifies the Lord,* not with empty,

κενά τινα καὶ ὑπέρκομπα, ἀλλ' αὐτὰ ταῦτα προαγορεύουσα τὰ ἐσόμενα καὶ οὐ τὰ ἴδια μόνον, ἀλλὰ καὶ τὰ κοινὰ προθεσπίζουσα ὅτι τὲ αὐτὴ κατὰ πᾶσαν καὶ ὑπὸ πάσης μακαρισθήσεται γενεᾶς.

27 Ἀλλὰ σύ μοι πρόσθες καὶ τὰ ἑξῆς, ὅτι καὶ *τὸ ὄνομα αὐτοῦ καὶ τὸ ἔλεος αὐτοῦ*—τοῦτο δέ ἐστιν ὁ κοινὸς αὐτῆς τὲ καὶ τοῦ Πατρὸς Υἱός—ἅγιον εἴτ' οὖν ἔνδοξον ὁμοίως *εἰς γενεὰν καὶ γενεὰν πᾶσι τοῖς φοβουμένοις αὐτόν·* καὶ ὅτι *ἐποίησε κράτος ἐν βραχίονι αὐτοῦ* τῷ αὐτῷ Υἱῷ, καὶ τὸ μέλλον ὡς ἤδη παρελθόν· *διεσκόρπισε* γὰρ *ὑπερηφάνους διανοίας καρδίας αὐτῶν* καὶ *καθεῖλε* γὰρ *δυνάστας ἀπὸ θρόνων,* τοὺς τότε βίᾳ κρατοῦντας καὶ ἄρχοντας τοῦ κόσμου δαίμονας ἢ καὶ τοὺς τότε τυράννους καὶ βασιλεῖς.

28 *Καὶ ὕψωσε ταπεινούς,* ἀσήμους καὶ ἁλιεῖς καὶ πτωχοὺς καὶ *πεινῶντας* τὸν θεῖον λόγον καὶ ἀπαιδεύτους *ἐνέπλησεν ἀγαθῶν,* τῶν θείων θεωριῶν ἢ καὶ λογίων τοῦ Πνεύματος, καὶ *πλουτοῦντας* ἐν ἀπατηλοῖς λόγοις καὶ κόμποις Ἑλληνικοῖς *ἐξαπέστειλε κενούς,* ἀπελέγξας αὐτῶν ἢ ἐκφυσήσας τὴν ματαιότητα.

29 *Ἀντελάβετο* δὲ καὶ *Ἰσραὴλ παιδὸς αὐτοῦ,* τῶν εἰς αὐτὸν ὁρώντων καὶ πιστευόντων, καὶ δι' αὐτοῦ τοῦ Υἱοῦ καὶ αὐτῶν υἱοθετουμένων, καθὼς καὶ τοῖς πάλαι προφήταις καὶ πατριάρχαις ὁ λόγος καὶ ἡ ὑπόσχεσις. Τοσαῦτα ταύτῃ καὶ διὰ ταύτης πᾶσι καὶ τοῖς ἄλλοις ὁ *δυνατὸς* τὰ μεγαλεῖα πεποίηκεν. Οὐκ ἄλογος δὲ τῇ Ἐλισάβετ πάντως καὶ ἡ παραμονὴ τῆς Μαρίας ἐπὶ μῆνας τρεῖς, ἀλλὰ πρῶτον μὲν συνηδομένης τὰ τοιαῦτα μεγαλεῖα καὶ εὐαγγέλια, καὶ γὰρ ἐτύγχανε καὶ ἄλλως ὅσα καὶ μητρὶ τῇ Ἐλισάβετ χρωμένη

pretentious language, but by proclaiming in advance the very things that would come to be, not only with respect to herself, but also by establishing things that were true for all, namely, that she would be blessed everywhere by all generations.

But you should join with me in adding this, that his *name* 27
and his mercy—that is, the Son common both to her and to the Father—is holy and glorious in *generation from generation to all who fear him,* and that he *wrought strength with his arm,* that is, his Son, as if the future was already the past. *For he has scattered the proud in the imagination of their hearts,* and *he has put down the mighty from their thrones,* that is, the demons, who at that time were holding power by force and ruling the world, or perhaps the tyrants and kings of that time.

And he exalted the humble, the insignificant, and fishermen, 28
and the poor and those *who hunger* for the divine word, and *he filled* the uninstructed *with good things,* that is, divine contemplations or the sayings of the Spirit. And those who were *rich* in deceptive words and Greek pomposities *he sent away empty,* refuting them or rather deflating their folly.

But *he helped his servant Israel,* that is, those who looked to 29
him and believed in him, and who through his own Son became adopted children, just as the word and promise was made to the prophets and patriarchs of old. And by and through this promise, *he who is strong* did mighty things for all mankind. It was certainly not without reason that Mary remained with Elizabeth for three months. First so that together they might rejoice over these truly great and good tidings, and, as it happened, because after the death or departure of her own parents to God, Mary treated Elizabeth

μετὰ τὴν τῶν πατέρων πρὸς Θεὸν ἀποβίωσιν ἢ ἀνάλυσιν· δεύτερον δέ, ὃ καὶ οἴομαι, μᾶλλον καὶ τὰ ἑαυτῆς ἅμα καὶ τὰ τῆς Ἐλισάβετ βουλομένης καταμαθεῖν, ὅπως ἄρα προβήσεται τὰ ὑπὲρ φύσιν ταῦτα καὶ ἀμφοτέραις, ἐπεὶ δὲ καὶ ἡ μὲν ἤδη πρὸς αὐταῖς ταῖς ὠδῖσιν ἦν, καὶ ταύτῃ δὲ τῆς κυοφορίας προσῆν ἡ αἴσθησις. Δι᾽ ἄμφω ταῦτα, καὶ ὡς παρθένος αἰδουμένη τὸν τόκον τῆς Ἐλισάβετ καὶ ὡς ἔγκυος τὸν οἰκεῖον ὄγκον ὑπεξίσταται καὶ εἰς τὸν οἶκον Ἰωσὴφ ἐπανέρχεται, περικρυπτομένη καὶ λανθάνουσα μὲν καὶ ἔτι ἕως ἐξόν· ἐπεὶ δὲ καὶ οὐχ, ὡς τοῖς ἠλιθίοις ὑπόληψις, ἐξ ἀρχῆς τέλειον τὸ κυοφορούμενον, ἀλλὰ πάντως κατὰ νόμον κυήσεως καὶ ἡμέτερον *χωρὶς ἁμαρτίας*, ἐν ᾗ πάντως καὶ τὴν μετὰ σπορᾶς καὶ φθορᾶς συμπεριληπτέον σύλληψίν τε καὶ γέννησιν.

Οὕτω γοῦν κατ᾽ ὀλίγον καὶ τῆς γαστρὸς προϊούσης ὁρᾷ μὲν Ἰωσὴφ τὸ πρᾶγμα, τὸ δὲ τοῦ πράγματος ἀγνοῶν μυστήριον οὐκ εἶχεν ὅ,τι καὶ γένηται καὶ μάλιστα *δίκαιος ὤν*. Τοῦτο γὰρ αὐτῷ καὶ μᾶλλον ἐποίει δυσχερέστερον καὶ ἀμφίκρημνον τὸ ἐννόημα· τό τε γὰρ αὐτὴν ἔνδον κατέχειν παραβαίνειν τὸν νόμον, ἄλλωστε καὶ ὑποψίας ὁμοῦ γέμον ἦν, τό τε τῷ νόμῳ παραδιδόναι κολάζειν ἢ γοῦν θριαμβεύειν, ὅ ἐστι καὶ παραδειγματίζειν, οὐ κατὰ δίκαιον οὐδὲ φιλάνθρωπον ἦν. Ὁ δὲ πρὸς τὴν κόρην οἶκτος καὶ ἡ διὰ τὴν ἄλλην ἀρετὴν αἰδὼς αὐτῷ προσγενόμενα ἑτέραν ἐποίησε τὴν ῥοπήν, καὶ βουλεύεται φιλανθρωπότερα μᾶλλον ἢ δικαιότερα. Ἡ δὲ φιλανθρωπία καὶ ἀσφαλείας οὐχ ἧττον ἦν, μέση χωροῦσα τοῦ τε κατέχειν καὶ τοῦ κολάζειν, κρυφίως

as her own mother. Second, as I surmise, because she rather wished to learn about the things that had happened both to her and to Elizabeth, so that the things beyond nature might proceed within both of them, for the one was already approaching the time of her labor pains, while she herself would presently experience her own condition of pregnancy. For both of these reasons, she, as a virgin, praised the child of Elizabeth, and, as one already pregnant and carrying her own child, withdrew and returned to the house of Joseph in secret and avoiding notice as far as this was possible. Because contrary to what some foolish people think, the child in her womb was not fully formed from the very beginning, but assuredly developed according to the natural laws of pregnancy, though of course *without* the *sin* that always must accompany conception and birth which results from seed and corruption.

Thus it was not long before Joseph saw the growth of the 30
Virgin's womb, but being unaware of the mystery he did not know what to do, for truly he was *a just man,* which certainly made his grasp of the situation more difficult and more of a dilemma. If, on the one hand, he allowed her to remain in his home, he would be transgressing the law, and at the same time place himself under suspicion, but handing her over to be punished by the law, or at least to be publicly shamed, that is, to be made a public example, would be neither just nor compassionate. His compassion toward the young girl combined with his shame due to his other virtues disposed him differently and caused him to think in ways more compassionate and just. Yet his feeling of compassion did not eliminate his sense of caution, and thus, walking a middle path between keeping her at his home and punishing her, he

αὐτὴν ἀπολύειν. Οὐκ ἔφθη γοῦν ἀναβῆναι τοῦτο καλῶς αὐτῷ τὸ ἐνθύμημα καὶ φθάσας ὁ ἄγγελος διὰ νυκτερινῆς ὄψεως ἀπολύει τοῦτον καὶ τῆς ἀπορίας ταύτης καὶ τῆς οἰκονομίας· "*Ἰωσήφ, υἱὸς Δαβίδ*—τί τοῦτο λέγω;" φησίν "ἵνα καὶ σὺ μνησθῇς ὅτι καὶ ἐκ Δαβὶδ ὁ Χριστός—*μὴ φοβηθῇς*—μήτε τὸν Θεὸν μήτε τὸν νόμον, ὡς μοιχαλίδα κρύπτων—*παραλαβεῖν*—ἤδη γὰρ ἀπολέλυτο κατὰ τὴν αὐτοῦ γνώμην—*Μαριὰμ τὴν γυναῖκά σου,* κατὰ τὸ εἰωθός, τὴν μνηστήν." Καὶ οὐ διερμηνεύει μόνον φιλανθρώπως αὐτῷ τὴν αἰτίαν καὶ λύει τὴν ὑποψίαν, ἀλλὰ καὶ ἐπαίρει πρὸς τὴν Παρθένον καὶ πείθει κρείττονα φρονεῖν τὴν κυοφορίαν ἢ κατὰ ἄνθρωπον. *Τὸ γὰρ ἐν αὐτῇ γεννηθέν,* ὅ ἐστι συλληφθέν, σπαρέν, καθ' ὃν λόγον καὶ ὁ Πατὴρ γεννήτωρ—οὐχ ὥς τισιν ἔδοξεν ἀπαρτισθὲν ἐξ ἀρχῆς οὕτως ὥσπερ ἤδη γεννώμενον—*ἐκ Πνεύματός ἐστιν Ἁγίου·* οὐχ ὅσον, φησίν, ἐλεύθερός ἐστιν ἡ Παρθένος πάσης τοιαύτης παρανόμου σπορᾶς καὶ μίξεως, ἀλλὰ καὶ θείας ὅλη κοινωνίας καὶ ὁμιλίας, καὶ τὸ ἐν αὐτῇ καταβληθὲν ἐξ ἀρχῆς οἱονεὶ σπέρμα, τὸν Λόγον λέγων, ὃς καὶ τὸν τοῦ σπέρματος ἐπέχει λόγον, ἢ γοῦν καὶ τὸ ἐν αὐτῇ συμπαγὲν τῆς σαρκὸς ἀποκύημα, διὰ Πνεύματος καὶ ἐκ Πνεύματος ἐστὶν Ἁγίου, τῆς θείας φύσεως ἀποτέλεσμα, κατὰ τὸ κοινότερον, ἐπεὶ καὶ τὸ *Πνεῦμα,* φησίν, *ὁ Θεός,* ὥστε οὐ μόνον οὐχὶ φοβεῖσθαι, ἀλλὰ καὶ εὐφραίνεσθαι, μᾶλλον δὲ καὶ καθ' ἕτερον τρόπον ὑπὲρ αὐτῆς φοβεῖσθαι καὶ αὐτὴν φοβεῖσθαι χρὴ τὴν παρθένον, ὡς Πνεύματος Ἁγίου γέμουσαν καὶ ἄρρητον καὶ ἀκατάληπτον καὶ προαιώνιον τόκον κύουσαν.

decided to send her away in secret. However, this thought had hardly entered his mind when the angel appeared to him in a nocturnal vision, releasing him from both his perplexity and prudent handling of the matter, saying, "*Joseph, son of David*—why do I refer to you in this manner? So that you too might recall that the Christ is descended from David—*do not fear*—either God or the law as though you were concealing an adulteress—*to take*—for he had already made up his mind to send her away—*Mary your wife,* according to custom, as one to whom you are betrothed." And he not only interprets the reason to him in a compassionate manner and removes his doubts, but he also disposes him favorably toward the Virgin, and persuades him to think about her pregnancy in a lofty manner, and not simply in human terms. *For that which is born in her,* that is, that which has been conceived in her, sown in her, whose begetter is the Father—was not, as some people think, fully formed from the beginning as if it was already born—*is of the Holy Spirit.* It is not simply the case, he says, that the Virgin is free of every kind of illicit sowing and coupling, but she has partaken of a wholly divine communion and union, and that which from the beginning has been planted in her like a seed, by which I mean the Word, has taken the place of human seed. Or, rather, that which has taken the solid form of flesh within her is the offspring through and from the Holy Spirit, or to state it in more common terms, it is the result of the work of the divine nature, because *the Spirit,* according to scripture, *is God,* so you should therefore not only not fear, but should even rejoice, or rather, in another manner, be fearful of her, and you need to be fearful of this virgin, for she is filled with the Holy Spirit, and is carrying in her womb an ineffable, incomprehensible, and preeternal child.

Χριστοῦ γέννησις

31 Εὔδρομος ἡμῖν καὶ σύντονος τὸ μέχρι τοῦδε παρὰ τῆς ἱστορίας καὶ τῶν εὐαγγελίων ὁ λόγος, τὰ δ' ἐντεῦθεν καὶ ἡ προφητεία συνεπιπλέκεται τὰ τῆς βασιλείας μετατιθεῖσα. Καὶ τότε παύσεσθαι τοὺς ἰουδαϊκοὺς ἄρχοντας καὶ ἡγεμόνας, "ἡγεμόνας" μὲν τοὺς ἐν ταῖς βασιλείαις καὶ στρατηγίαις τὲ καὶ νομοθεσίαις, "ἄρχοντας" δὲ καὶ τοὺς ἐν ταῖς λοιπαῖς ἀρχαῖς προσαγορεύουσα, ὅτε καὶ αὐτὸς ὁ πάντων βασιλεὺς Χριστὸς ἐξ αὐτῶν παραγένηται, ᾧ καὶ ἀπόκειται *προσδοκία τῶν ἐθνῶν,* ὅ ἐστιν ἐλπὶς καὶ καραδοκία, δῆλον δὲ ὅτι καὶ τῶν ἐξ Ἰσραήλ, ὡς καὶ αὐτῶν λοιπὸν τοῖς Ἔθνεσιν ὁμογνωμονησάντων καὶ συγκατειλεγμένων. Οὕτω γὰρ καὶ ὁ Συμεὼν ἀμφότερα συλλαμβάνων φαίνεται· *φῶς* μὲν *εἰς ἀποκάλυψιν τῶν ἐθνῶν, δόξαν* δὲ *τοῦ Ἰσραὴλ* τοῦ πεπιστευκότος—*οὐ γὰρ πάντες οἱ ἐξ Ἰσραὴλ οὗτοι Ἰσραήλ*· "*δόξαν*" δὲ καὶ διὰ τὴν κατὰ σάρκα συγγένειαν, καὶ συνελὼν παντὸς τοῦ κόσμου λέγει *σωτήριον* τὸ μέγα τοῦτο μυστήριον. Ἀλλὰ πῶς ἐκλιπεῖν τοὺς ἐξ Ἰούδα, φησί, βασιλεῖς τὲ καὶ ἡγεμόνας, ὁπότε καὶ αὐτὸς παραγενόμενος ἡγούμενος μάλιστα πάντων καὶ νομοθέτης καὶ βασιλεὺς καὶ ἐκ τῆς Ἰούδα φυλῆς ἦν; Ὅτι μὴ πρὸς τὰ πνευματικὰ καὶ νοούμενα μᾶλλον, ἀλλὰ πρὸς τὰ σωματικὰ καὶ ὁρώμενα τότε τέως τὸ προφήτευμα ἦν. Οὕτω γοῦν καὶ αὐτὸς ὁ Σωτήρ· "*ἡ βασιλεία ἡ ἐμὴ οὐκ ἔστιν ἐκ τοῦ κόσμου τούτου,*" κἂν ὕστερον Ῥωμαῖοι μὲν Ἰουδαίων, αὐτὸς δὲ καὶ Ῥωμαίων καὶ πάντων μικροῦ τῶν Ἐθνῶν ἐβασίλευσεν, οὐ τὴν κατὰ φύσιν λέγω βασίλειαν μόνον καθὸ Θεός, ἀλλὰ

The Birth of Christ

Until this point, the account given by the historical nar- 31
rative and the Gospels has unfolded smoothly and succinctly; in what follows, however, prophecy is also woven in concerning the transfer of kingship. At that time, it says, the Jewish rulers and leaders will cease. Here the prophecy calls "leaders" those who held positions of leadership in kingdoms, armies, and legislative bodies, and "rulers" those who governed in other areas, when Christ himself, the king of all, came forth from them, for in him resides *the expectation of the nations,* which evidently includes those from Israel who later were of one mind with the Gentiles and who were likewise selected. And thus even Simeon seems to encompass the two together, calling them *a light unto the revelation of* the *Gentiles* and *the glory of Israel* which believed in him—*for not all who are descended from Israel belong to Israel.* "*Glory*" through the kinship with our flesh and, because it embraces the entire world, he calls this great mystery *salvation.* But how can the prophecy say that kings and rulers will depart from Judah, when Christ himself has appeared as the ruler, and indeed the ruler of all, and as the lawgiver and king from the tribe of Judah? Because the prophecy was not uttered with a view toward spiritual or intelligible realities but with respect to corporeal and visible things. This is why the Savior himself says: "*My kingdom is not of this world,*" for even if afterward the Romans ruled over the Jews, it was not long before he came to rule over the Romans and indeed over all men, not simply by virtue of his natural kingship inasmuch as he is God, but by virtue of the voluntary submission of

καὶ τὴν κατὰ γνώμην τῶν πιστευόντων, καὶ ἓν καὶ καινὸν ἀφ' ἑαυτοῦ τοὺς βασιλευομένους πάντας κέκληκεν ὄνομα, "Χριστιανοὺς" καὶ εἶναι καὶ ὀνομάζεσθαι· ἤδη γοῦν ἐκλελοιπυίας μὲν πάσης τῆς Ἰουδαϊκῆς ἀρχῆς τὲ καὶ βασιλείας, ἄρτι δὲ τῆς Ῥωμαϊκῆς ἐπικρατείας οὐ τούτους μόνους, ἀλλὰ καὶ πᾶσαν τὴν οἰκουμένην σχεδὸν διαζωσαμένης, ὃ δὴ καὶ τὸ Ἱερὸν Εὐαγγέλιον ἀναγράφει, *πᾶσαν* λέγον τὸ *δόγμα Καίσαρος ἀπογράφεσθαι* κελεῦον *τὴν οἰκουμένην*. Τηνικαῦτα δὴ καὶ ὁ πάσης τῆς οἰκουμένης ἀληθῶς βασιλεὺς καὶ Σωτὴρ τίκτεται ἢ γοῦν πρὸς τὴν ἐκτὸς βασιλείαν τὴν τῆς Ἰουδαϊκῆς ἀρχῆς καὶ ἡγουμενείας ὑποληπτέον ἔκλειψιν ἢ ὅτι κἂν ἐξ Ἰούδα ὁ Χριστὸς ἦν, ἀλλ' ὅμως καὶ λύων μὲν πάντα τὰ Ἰουδαϊκά, πρὸς δὲ τὰ Ῥωμαϊκὰ μᾶλλον μετατιθεὶς τὰ πράγματα· καὶ τὴν σιδηρᾶν κατ' αὐτῶν ῥάβδον τουναντίον ἐγείρων καὶ ποιμαίνων ὁμοῦ καὶ συντρίβων, τοῦτο μὲν διὰ τὴν σφαγὴν καὶ τὴν ἅλωσιν καὶ τὸν ἀνδραποδισμὸν καὶ τὸν πανταχοῦ τῆς γῆς διασκεδασμόν, ἐκεῖνο δὲ διὰ τὴν δουλείαν τοῦ καταλείμματος· καὶ Ῥωμαίους μὲν βασιλεύων τῶν Ἰουδαίων, αὐτὸς δὲ καὶ Ῥωμαίων καὶ πάντων ὁμοῦ τῶν ἐθνῶν καὶ αὐτῶν δὲ τῶν ἐξ Ἰσραὴλ βασιλεὺς αἰώνιος ἀποκαθιστάμενος καὶ τοὺς φόρους ἤδη διὰ Ῥωμαίων πάσης τῆς γῆς δεχόμενος.

32 Ἀλλ' ὅπως καὶ ἡ ἀρχὴ τῆς ἀρχῆς, καὶ ἡ ἀπογραφὴ τῆς ἀπογραφῆς τύπος ἦν· ἡ μὲν γὰρ τὴν μοναρχίαν ἐδήλου τοῦ ἑνὸς πάντων Θεοῦ τὲ καὶ βασιλέως, ἡ δὲ καὶ τὴν ἑκούσιον ὑποταγὴν ἢ καὶ εἰς οὐρανοὺς ἀπογραφὴν πάντων τῶν βουλομένων καὶ ὅτι καθάπερ τὸ δόγμα, οὕτω δὴ καὶ τὸ Κήρυγμα πᾶσαν διαδραμεῖται τὴν οἰκουμένην. Οὐ μὴν

those who believed in him, and he has called all those ruled by him by the one and new designation of "Christian," which they are and which they are named. Indeed, the entire Jewish rule and kingdom had already come to an end, and the power of the Romans came to encompass not only the Jews but also almost the entire world, which the Holy Gospel refers to, saying, *a decree went forth from Caesar* ordering *that the entire world should be enrolled.* It was then that the true king and Savior of the whole world was born, when, we must suppose, whether with respect to outward kingship, Judaic rule and leadership declined, or in the sense that, even if Christ came from Judah, he brought an end to all things Judaic, transferring them to the Roman. And he raised up an iron rod against them, both shepherding them and destroying them, the latter through their slaughter, the conquest of Jerusalem, their captivity, and their dispersal throughout the entire world, and the former through the enslavement of the remnant. For whereas the Romans ruled over the Jews, Christ rules over the Romans and indeed all the nations, including those which came from Israel, having been established as an eternal king, which is why through the Romans he already receives tribute from the whole world.

But just as Roman rule was a figure of Christ's rule, so too 32
was the earthly enrollment a figure of the heavenly enrollment. The one made clear the monarchy of the one God and king of all, while the other made clear the voluntary submission, or rather the enrollment in heaven, of all those who wished to enroll, and that, just like the decree, the Gospel was likewise proclaimed throughout the entire world. Again,

ἀλλὰ καὶ τὸ πάντας εἰς τὰς οἰκείας πατριὰς ἀνατρέχειν τοῦ καὶ πάντας εἰς τὴν ἀρχαίαν ἡμῶν καὶ πρώτην ἀναστρέφειν πατρίδα καὶ πολιτείαν, ἀφ' ἧς ἄλλος ἀλλαχῇ καὶ τοῖς βίοις καὶ ταῖς ὁρμαῖς διεσπάρημεν· καὶ τὸ πάντας δὲ φόρους φέρειν τῷ Καίσαρι τοῦ καὶ πάντας ὀφείλειν καρποφορεῖν Θεῷ κατὰ τὸ ἐνόν, οὐ τὰ σωματικὰ μόνον δι' εὐποιΐας τὲ καὶ θυσίας, ἀλλὰ καὶ τὰ πνευματικὰ διὰ θεωρίας καὶ πράξεως. Ἀλλ' ἡ μὲν ἀπογραφὴ κατὰ θείαν πάντως οἰκονομίαν ὤθει καὶ τὸν Ἰωσὴφ εἰς τὴν οἰκείαν πατρίδα—χώρας χώραν καὶ πόλεως πόλιν—τῆς μὲν Γαλιλαίας τὴν Ἰουδαίαν, τῆς Ναζαρὲτ δὲ τὴν Βηθλεὲμ ἀλλαττόμενον, ἵνα καὶ ἡ προφητεία τῇ προφητείᾳ καὶ ἡ δόξα τῇ ἀληθείᾳ καὶ ἡ πατρὶς τῇ πατρίδι συμβῇ, ἡ μὲν λέγουσα ὅτι *Ναζωραῖος κληθήσεται*, ἡ δὲ ὅτι *ἀπὸ Βηθλεὲμ ὁ Χριστὸς ἔρχεται*, καὶ ἡ μὲν μερισαμένη τὴν σύλληψιν, ἡ δοκοῦσα, ἡ δὲ τὴν γέννησιν, ἡ καὶ οὖσα. Σὺ δέ μοι σκόπει καὶ ταῦτα τοῦ πάντα πτωχεύσαντος δι' ἡμᾶς· ἡ μὲν γὰρ κἂν ἰδίᾳ μετρία τὴν φύσιν, ἀλλὰ καὶ ἄδοξος τῷ μηδὲ προφήτην ἔχειν ἐξ αὐτῆς ἐγειρόμενον, ἡ δέ, εἰ καὶ διὰ τὴν προφητείαν ἔνδοξος, ἀλλὰ τἄλλα πάντα πενιχρὰ καὶ λυπρόγεως, ὃ καὶ ὁ προφήτης παραμυθούμενος *οὐδαμῶς ἐλαχίστην* αὐτὴν εἶναι, φησίν, *ἐν τοῖς ἡγεμόσιν Ἰούδα* διὰ τὴν ἐξ αὐτῆς τοῦ Σωτῆρος πρόοδον.

Ἀλλὰ Μαριὰμ μὲν διὰ Ἰωσήφ, Ἰωσὴφ δὲ πότε καὶ πῶς καίπερ ἐξ οἴκου καὶ πατριᾶς, ὅ ἐστιν συγγενείας Δαβίδ—τοῦτο δέ ἐστιν ἐξ Ἰουδαίας καὶ Βηθλεέμ—ὢν μετανάστης

that everyone running back to their families was also a figure of all those turning back to our ancient homeland and citizenship, from which each of us was scattered to a different place by our way of life and our impulses. And that everyone paying tribute to Caesar was a figure of being obligated to offer, as much as possible, our fruits to God, not only corporeal things through good works and sacrifices, but also spiritual things offered through contemplation and ascetic practice. Certainly, then, the enrollment, through divine intervention, compelled Joseph to go to his homeland—moving from one region to another, and from one city to another—that is, from Galilee to Judea, and from Nazareth to Bethlehem, so that the one prophecy might coincide with the other prophecy, and glory with truth, and the one homeland with the other homeland, and the one prophetic saying, *he will be called a Nazarene,* with the other, namely, that *the Christ comes from Bethlehem,* for his conception seemed to be assigned to Nazareth, whereas his birth was assigned to Bethlehem, where indeed it took place. Consider with me the things concerning Christ who in every way made himself poor for us, for Nazareth was an average city, but without glory because no prophet had ever arisen from it, whereas Bethlehem, even if it was glorious on account of the prophecy, was nonetheless in all other respects poor and wretched, which is why the prophet comforted it, saying, *you are not the least among the rulers of Judah,* since it was from there that the Savior would come forth.

Mary went to be enrolled on account of Joseph, but we do not now have the leisure to speak of when and how Joseph, even though he was of the house and fatherland that is kin to David—that is, even though he hailed from Judea and

καὶ Γαλιλαῖος καὶ Ναζωραῖος γέγονεν, οὐ νῦν σχολὴ λέγειν, πλὴν ὅτι κατὰ μὲν ἱστορίαν πολλαὶ τῶν ἀνθρώπων αἱ μεταβολαὶ καὶ ἀνάγκαι, δι' ἃς ἕκαστοι πολλάκις τὰς ἐνεγκούσας καταλιμπάνοντες ἐπὶ τὰς ἀλλοτρίας αὐτομολοῦσι, κατὰ δὲ θεωρίαν, ὡς ἐχρῆν πάντως, ἄρτι καὶ τοῦ κοινοῦ Δεσπότου δι' ἡμᾶς ἐκ τῶν ἰδίων καὶ τῶν οὐρανῶν ἀπανισταμένου καὶ ταπεινουμένου, μὴ μέχρι τῶν ἐπιγείων μόνον, ἀλλὰ καὶ αὐτοῦ σώματος καὶ σταυροῦ τὲ καὶ μνήματος, καὶ αὐτὸν ὡς ἐκείνου τύπον καὶ τοσούτῳ μυστηρίῳ διακονούμενον ἐκ τῆς ἰδίας εἰς τὴν ἀλλοτρίαν μεταφοιτᾶν, τῆς ὑψηλοτέρας εἰς τὴν ταπεινοτέραν, καὶ καθάπερ ἐκεῖνον τῆς νοητῆς Ἱερουσαλὴμ καὶ Σιών, οὕτω καὶ τοῦτον τῆς αἰσθητῆς ἐπὶ τὴν μακρῷ πόρρωθεν Ναζαρέτ.

33 Ἀλλὰ τὸν μὲν οὕτως ὁ νόμος, μᾶλλον δὲ καὶ ὁ προφητικὸς ἠνάγκαζε λόγος ἀνατρέχειν αὖθις εἰς Βηθλεὲμ τὴν ὑψηλοτέραν, ἵν' ὥσπερ ἐξ ὑπερδεξίων ἐκεῖθεν ἀνίσχῃ τὸ μέγα καὶ δημιουργικὸν φῶς, συνείπετο δὲ τούτῳ καὶ Μαριὰμ καίτοι πρὸς αὐτῷ τῷ τίκτειν οὖσα δι' ἀνάγκην καὶ ταῦτα διπλῆν· μίαν μέν, διὰ τὴν ἔναγχος τοῦ ἀγγέλου φωνὴν τὴν ταύτην παραλαμβάνειν καὶ μεθ' ἑαυτοῦ φυλάττειν ἀεὶ κελεύουσαν, ἑτέραν δέ, τὸ καὶ ταύτην ἔνθεν ὁ Ἰωσὴφ τυγχάνειν, *ἐξ οἴκου καὶ πατριᾶς Δαβίδ.* Ἔνθεν καὶ Ἰωσὴφ τὸν μὲν ἄλλον ὅλον οἶκον αὐτοῦ καὶ τοὺς υἱοὺς προπέμπων, αὐτὸς δὲ συνάμα τῇ Μαριὰμ καὶ ταῖς θυγατράσι σχολαιότερον πορευόμενος ἦν. Οὐ φθάνει γοῦν εἰς τὴν Ἱερουσαλὴμ ἀφικόμενος καὶ λύει τὰς ὠδῖνας ἡ

Bethlehem—had moved from one place to another and become a Galilean and a Nazarene, except to say that, as history demonstrates, human beings are subject to many vicissitudes and necessities, and thus are often forced to leave behind their homelands and exchange them for a foreign land. But when these things are seen according to contemplation, as one certainly must, it was in this same moment that our common Master departed for our sakes from the conditions that were proper to him, and from the heavens, and humbled himself, not only to the level of earthly things but even to that of the body, the cross, and the tomb. Thus Joseph was a figure of the incarnate Word, and became the minister of an exceedingly great mystery, moving as he did from his proper place to a foreign land, for he too descended from a higher place into a lowly one; and just as the Word descended from the intelligible Jerusalem and Zion, so too did he descend from the sensible Judea to faraway Nazareth.

But the law, or rather the prophetic word, compelled him 33
to return again to the higher Bethlehem, so that he might behold from that superior location that great and creative light, and Mary accompanied him, even though the time of her delivery was near, since the necessity for her to accompany him was twofold. First, the voice of the angel, which Joseph had so recently heard, and which ordered him to take Mary with him and to safeguard her continuously. Second, because Joseph also happened to be from the same place as Mary, that is, *from the house and homeland of David.* It was from there that Joseph sent the rest of his household and his sons in advance, while he, together with Mary and his daughters, traveled at a slower pace. But Mary did not reach Jerusalem before she did away with her birth pangs.

Μαριάμ· ἀληθέστερον δὲ εἰπεῖν, ἕτερόν τινα λύει τρόπον, ὡς οὐκ αὐτὴ μόνον ὑπερφυῶς καὶ ἀνωδίνως τὸν φρικτὸν τοῦτον τόκον προαγαγοῦσα, ἀλλὰ καὶ τοὺς κοινοὺς ἀνελοῦσα πόνους καὶ τὰς ὀδύνας. Καὶ πολλῶν προκαταλαβόντων τοὺς τόπους—ὢ τῆς δι' ἐμὲ στενοχωρίας καὶ ξενιτείας τοῦ διὰ πάντων χωροῦντος καὶ πᾶσαν τὴν κτίσιν ἐμπεριέχοντος!—οὐχ εὑρίσκει τόπον οὐδὲ κατάλυμα· ἐντεῦθεν οὐ μόνον ὁ ἀπερίγραπτος, ἀλλὰ καὶ ὁ ἀκατάληπτος ἐν σπηλαίῳ καὶ ὁ Λόγος *ἐν φάτνῃ* καὶ ὁ τοῦ κόσμου δημιουργὸς αὐτουργὸς καὶ τοῦ τόκου καὶ ὁδηγὸς τοῦ τόπου γίνεται, αὐτὸς μὲν μαιεύων, αὐτὸς δὲ μαιευόμενος καὶ τῇ μητρὶ τὸν θάλαμον χαριζόμενος. Ἐντεῦθεν καὶ ὁ πάντων συνοχεὺς ἐν σπαργάνοις καὶ ὁ πάντων τροφεὺς ἐν τοῖς γαλακτοτροφουμένοις καὶ ὁ πάντων ἀπογραφεὺς ἐν τοῖς ἀπογραφομένοις.

34 Οὐ μὴν οὐδ' ἐνταῦθα τῆς Μαρίας ἡ Ἐλισάβετ ἀπελιμπάνετο, ἀλλὰ καθάπερ τῆς κυοφορίας προφῆτις καὶ μάρτυς, οὕτω καὶ τῆς θεοτοκίας ὑπουργὸς καὶ διάκονος καὶ τῆς μετὰ τὸν τόκον παρθενίας αὐτόπτις ἦν· παρῆν γοῦν ἐπὶ τῇ Γεννήσει καὶ συνετέλει τὰ εἰκότα καὶ συνεώρταζε τὰ γενέθλια. Τί ἔτι; Λύεται καὶ τὰ διαφράγματα καὶ καταλύεται μὲν ἡ ἔχθρα, κοινὴ δὲ πάντα καταλαμβάνει καὶ εἰρήνη τὲ καὶ ἐπιμιξία· καὶ οὐ Θεὸς μόνον ἄνθρωπος γίνεται, ἀλλὰ καὶ οὐρανὸς τῇ γῇ μίγνυται, καὶ ἄγγελοι μὲν τοῖς ποιμέσιν ἐφίστανται, ποιμένες δὲ τοῖς ἀγγέλοις περιαστράπτονται καὶ τὸν μέγαν εὐαγγελίζονται καὶ πρῶτον ποιμένα καθάπερ ἀμνὸν ἐν σπηλαίῳ τικτόμενον, καὶ γῆ μὲν τὴν οὐράνιον δοξολογίαν διδάσκεται, οὐρανὸς δὲ *ἐπὶ* τῇ

To speak more truly, she loosed them in another manner, since she did not simply bring forth her awe-inspiring child supernaturally and painlessly, but she loosed the common pains and distress of childbirth. And because so many had already occupied these places—oh, what limitation and exile for my sake, on the part of him who fills all things and contains all creation!—she finds no room at the inn. Thus the one who is not only beyond circumscription but also beyond comprehension was born in a cave, and the Word was placed *in a manger,* and the creator of the world becomes the mover of his own birth and guide to his birthplace; the same one delivered himself and was delivered, and granted his mother a private chamber. Thus the one who holds all things together was bound in swaddling clothes; the one who nourishes all living things joined the ranks of those nourished by milk; and the one who enrolls all was found among those who were enrolled.

At this time, Elizabeth did not abandon Mary, but just as 34
she was a prophet and witness of her pregnancy, so too was she an attendant and servant of the godly birth, and an eyewitness of Mary's virginity after parturition, for she was present at the Nativity, assisted in the delivery, and celebrated the birth. What happened then? The dividing walls were removed and enmity brought to an end. All things were overtaken by a common peace and an intimate intermingling, and not only did God become man, but heaven was also mingled with the earth; and angels drew near to the shepherds, and the shepherds were illumined on all sides by the angels, who proclaimed to them that the great and first shepherd, had been born in a cave like a lamb; and the earth was taught a heavenly doxology, for heaven was delighted by

τῆς *γῆς* εἰρήνῃ καὶ εὐδοκίᾳ τέρπεται. Καὶ τὸ παράδοξον μὲν τοῦ θεάματος καὶ ἀκούσματος φρίκης αὐτοῖς καὶ ἀγωνίας μεγίστης πρόξενον, ἡ δὲ φρίκη χαρᾶς μείζονος αἰτία γίνεται· σαφέστερον γὰρ αὐτοῖς ὁ ἄγγελος οὐ λύει τὸν φόβον μόνον, ἀλλὰ καὶ ἐπιτείνει τὴν εὐφροσύνην· "*μὴ φοβεῖσθε,*" λέγων, "*ἰδοὺ γὰρ εὐαγγελίζομαι ὑμῖν* οὐ φόβον μέγαν, ἀλλὰ καὶ *χαρὰν μεγάλην ἥτις ἔσται* οὐ τῷ Ἰουδαϊκῷ μόνον, ἀλλὰ καὶ *παντὶ τῷ λαῷ.*" Καὶ τὸ αἴτιον τῆς χαρᾶς ὁ νέος καὶ καινὸς ὄντως τόκος, οὗτος δὲ δῆλος ἐκ τῶν ὀνομάτων αὐτῶν, "*ὅτι,*" φησίν, "*ἐτέχθη* ἡμῖν *σωτήρ, Χριστὸς Κύριος,*" ὧν τὸ μὲν τῆς ἐνεργείας, τὸ δὲ τῆς ἐξουσίας, τὸ δὲ μέσον τῆς φύσεως ἢ τῶν φύσεων, ἐπεὶ καὶ τοῦτο φύσει Χριστός, Θεὸς καὶ ἄνθρωπος· καὶ τὰ τεκμήρια καιρὸς καὶ τόπος· *σήμερον* καὶ *ἐν πόλει Δαβίδ.* Ταῦτα μὲν οὖν ἐξέστησάν τε ἅμα καὶ τῶν ποιμνίων ἀπανέστησαν τοὺς ποιμένας καὶ διήρχοντο μέχρι Βηθλεὲμ ἐν νυκτὶ τὸν φωστῆρα καὶ Σωτῆρα ζητοῦντες. Συνήρχοντο δὲ καὶ ἄλλοι τινὲς οὐκ ὀλίγοι τῶν γνωρίμων καὶ συγγενῶν καὶ ἐξίσταντο τῶν ποιμένων ἀκούοντες.

35 Ἀλλ' ὅπως ἢ τίνα <τρόπον> καὶ ἡ Μαρία ταῦτα *συμβάλλουσα,* τυχὸν μὲν καὶ συναθροίζουσα καὶ συντηροῦσα *ἐν τῇ καρδίᾳ αὐτῆς* ἦν, τυχὸν δὲ καὶ ἀντιπαραβάλλουσα ἄλλο πρὸς ἄλλο καὶ συμβιβάζουσα μὴ τὰ ὁρώμενα μόνον, ἀλλὰ καὶ τὰ λεγόμενα, τὰ ἐν τῷ ναῷ, τὰ μετὰ τὸν ναόν, τὰ παρὰ τοῦ ἀγγέλου, τὰ παρὰ τῶν ποιμένων, τὸ τελευταῖον, τὰ παρ' αὐτὸν τὸν τόκον καὶ τὰς ὠδῖνας, ὅτι μὴ μόνον αὐτὴ ταύτας λαθοῦσα καὶ μήτηρ φανεῖσα καὶ διαφυλαχθεῖσα παρθένος, ἀλλ' ὅτι καὶ ταύτην λαθὼν ὁ υἱὸς—ὦ θείων

the peace and goodwill *on earth.* The strange sight and sound caused the greatest fear and anguish in them, but their fear became the cause of greater joy, for the angel not only expressly dispelled their fear, but also increased their joy. "*Fear not,*" he said to them, "*for behold, I bring you good news,* not of great fear but *of great joy, which is* not only for the Jewish people but also *for all people.*" And the cause of this joy is the young and truly new child, which is clear from his titles themselves, "*for unto* us," he says, "*is born a savior, Christ the Lord.*" Now of these three, the first designates his activity, the third his authority, and the one in the middle his nature or rather of his natures, for this is what Christ is by nature, that is, God and man. And the signs of this are the time and the place, namely, *today* and *in the city of David.* These events astonished the shepherds and caused them to leave their flocks and make their way to Bethlehem, seeking in the night the light and their Savior. Gathered together with them were also others, including not a few of their acquaintances and relatives, and they were amazed hearing the words of the shepherds.

But however or in whatever manner, Mary *pondered* these 35
things, whether gathering them together and treasuring them *in her heart,* or perhaps comparing one with another, examining not only the things she had seen but also what she had heard, what took place in the temple, what took place after the temple, what transpired with the angel, and what transpired with the shepherds, and finally the things concerning her giving birth and her labor pains, because not only had she avoided those and become a mother and remained a virgin, but even her son eluded her—oh, the

πραγμάτων οἰκονομίαι καὶ καινοτομίαι φύσεων!—οὔτε τῆς προόδου παρέσχεν αἴσθησιν καὶ ἄφνω τῆς γαστρὸς ἔξω καὶ πρὸς τοῖς κόλποις αὐτῆς ἦν, ἵν', ὥσπερ συνελήφθη καὶ ἀσπόρως τὲ καὶ ἀγνώστως, οὕτω καὶ γεννηθῇ μὴ μόνον ἀφθόρως, ἀλλὰ δὴ καὶ ἀνεπαισθήτως, καὶ τοῦτο τοῦ τύπου σχῇ πλέον τῆς δρόσου καὶ τοῦ πόκου. Ἡ μὲν γὰρ αὐτομάτη μὲν καὶ ἀψοφητὶ πρὸς τὸν πόκον, οὐκ αὐτομάτη δὲ οὐδὲ ἄνευ χειρὸς ἐκ τοῦ πόκου· ὁ δὲ πρὸς τοῖς ἄλλοις καὶ αὐτὸν τὸν νοητὸν Πόκον ἐν τῇ συλλήψει λαθὼν καὶ αὐτὸ δὲ περιβαλόμενος ὅλον τὸ πάχος καὶ τὸ ἔριον ἐξ αὐτοῦ, μεθ' ὁμοίας προῆλθε τῆς εὐκολίας, οὐ κἀνταῦθα τοὺς ἄλλους μόνον, ἀλλὰ καὶ αὐτὴν τὴν τεκοῦσαν λαθών, ὥσπερ αὐτὸς ἑαυτὸν καὶ μαιεύσας, ἀλλὰ δὴ καὶ γεννήσας. Ἐξ ὧν πάντων μίαν εὕρισκες, ὦ μῆτερ Σοφίας, τὴν συμφωνίαν, ὅτι τὲ Θεὸς πάντως ὁ σὸς υἱὸς καὶ σὺ θαῦμα παρὰ πάντα ταῦτα καὶ παρὰ πάντων τούτων συντεθειμένον καὶ οὐρανῷ καὶ γῇ μὴ χωρούμενον, ἀλλὰ μηδὲ ἀξίως ὑμνολογούμενον.

36 Ἐντεῦθεν καὶ ἀστὴρ καὶ Μάγοι πρὸς ἓν συντρέχοντες, ὡς δηλοῦντες τὸν οὐράνιον ὁμοῦ καὶ ἐπίγειον· καὶ ὁ μὲν ὁδηγῶν, οἱ δὲ ὁδηγούμενοι, δηλῶν τοῖς ἐπὶ γῆς λοιπὸν τὴν ὁδηγίαν τοῦ κρείττονος. Καὶ ἀστὴρ οὐκ ἀστήρ—ἵνα καὶ ἀστρολογίαν ἀνέλῃ καὶ πᾶσαν τὴν περὶ τὰ τοιαῦτα καταλύσῃ πλάνην—ἀλλὰ θεία τις δύναμις, οἷα λαμπτὴρ τὸν σκότον μᾶλλον τῆς τοιαύτης ἀγνοίας καταφωτίζουσα, εἰ μὴ κἀνταῦθα καινοτομία φύσεως ἀστέρα, μὴ μόνον σχολῇ

dispensation of things divine and the innovations of natures! She did not even feel the passage of the child through her body, when suddenly he was found outside her womb lying at her bosom, so that, just as he was conceived without seed and in a manner beyond knowledge, so too he might be born not only without corruption but also in a manner beyond perception, and this to an even greater extent than the figure of the dew upon the fleece. For though, on the one hand, the dew fell upon the fleece by itself and without a sound, it was not collected from the fleece by itself or without a human hand. But when, on the other hand, Christ was conceived, he eluded the observation of others and even of the spiritual Fleece herself, while clothing himself in all its thickness and wool, from which he emerged without hindrance. Thus, he not only eluded the others but even his own mother, just as he himself served as his own midwife and brought himself to birth. In pondering all these things, mother of Wisdom, you found a single, harmonious accord, namely, that your son is none other than God himself, and that you are a miracle that transcends all these things and is composed of all these things, and which cannot be contained by heaven or earth or worthily praised by them.

After this, the movement of the star and the Magi con- 36
verged, pointing to him who is at once heavenly and earthly. The former served as the guide while the latter were guided, signaling to those on earth that henceforth they would be guided by what is superior. And the star was not a star—in order to abolish astrology and destroy all the deception that comes with such things—but a divine power, like a light shining in the darkness of great ignorance, unless it was an innovation of nature, for it did not travel at a leisurely pace

καὶ βάδην καὶ κατ' ἀνθρώπους πορεύεσθαι, ἀλλὰ καὶ πῇ μὲν πορεύεσθαι, πῇ δὲ ἵστασθαι, ποτὲ δὲ καὶ κρύπτεσθαι, καὶ πρὸς νότον ἀπὸ βορρᾶ φέρεσθαι, οὕτω γὰρ τῇ Περσίδι πρὸς Ἰουδαίαν ἡ θέσις, καὶ μηδὲ ὑψηλῶς, ἀλλὰ ταπεινῶς καὶ πρόσγειον φέρεσθαι, καὶ οὕτως ὥστε καὶ κώμην μικρὰν καὶ καλύβην χαρακτηρίζειν· καί, τὸ μεῖζον, μηδὲ ἐν νυκτὶ μόνον, ἀλλὰ καὶ ἐν ἡμέρᾳ τοσοῦτον καταλάμπειν, ὥστε καὶ αὐτὸν τὸν ἡλιακὸν ἀποκρύπτειν δίσκον καὶ ἐπὶ τοσοῦτον, ἐφ' ὅσον καὶ ἀπὸ Περσίδος οἱ Μάγοι πρὸς Ἱερουσαλὴμ καὶ Βηθλεὲμ χρόνον· καὶ τὸ δὴ πλέον, ὅτι μήπω μηδὲ τεχθέντος ἢ τικτομένου—ὃ καὶ αὐτὸ κἄν τις εἰπεῖν τολμήσοι τῶν γενεθλιαλογουμένων—ἀλλὰ καὶ πρὸ πολλοῦ τοὺς Μάγους κινοῦντος καὶ μονονουχὶ καθάπερ φωνῇ τῇ μορφῇ καὶ ὁρμῇ καὶ τοῖς σχήμασι καὶ τοῖς νεύμασιν ἐπισπεύδοντος καὶ καθάπερ τινὸς λογικοῦ, μᾶλλον δὲ καὶ προφήτου τὰ τούτων προειδότος κινήματα καὶ τῶν τόπων τὰ διαστήματα, καὶ συμμετρουμένου τὸν χρόνον, καθ' ὃν ἐπιστήσονται πρὸς αὐτῇ τῇ φάτνῃ τῷ τικτομένῳ. Ποίας ταῦτα φύσεως ἀλόγου τὲ καὶ ἀστρῴου; Ἀλλὰ δῆλον ὅτι λογική τις δύναμις ἦν ἕκαστα προειδυῖα καὶ διατάττουσα ἢ καὶ ὑπερφυὴς μὲν καὶ καινοφανὴς ἀστέρος φύσις, ὑπὸ λογικῆς δὲ δυνάμεως ἢ καὶ τῆς προνοίας αὐτῆς ἀγομένη καὶ ταττομένη καὶ τοῖς ἐκείνης ὑπηρετοῦσα νεύμασιν.

37 Οὐκ ἀνοικονόμητος δὲ οὐδὲ ἡ μέχρι τῆς Ἱερουσαλὴμ τοῦ ἀστέρος φαῦσις, εὐθὺς δὲ πρὸς ὀλίγον ἐπίκρυψις, ἀλλὰ διὰ δύο ταῦτα· ἓν μέν, ἵνα καὶ πᾶσι τοῖς ἄλλοις τοῖς

like people do, but sometimes it moved, and sometimes it stood still, and at other times it concealed itself, and moved from north to south, since this is the route from Persia to Judea, and it was not borne along at a great height, but remained low-lying and close to the earth, and thus came to mark a small village and hut. And, what was greatest of all, it shone not only at night but also during the day, and so greatly that it concealed the disk of the sun, and it did this throughout the entire period of time required for the Magi to reach Jerusalem and Bethlehem from Persia. What is more, it did so not when Christ was not yet born or in the hour of his delivery—even if one of the diviners of horoscopes might dare to say this—but it appeared long before this and all but set the Magi on their course, as if its shape and movement, and its forms and indications, were like a voice urging them onward, and, as if it were a kind of rational being, or rather a prophet knowing in advance their movements and the distance between places, it calculated the time when they needed to arrive at the manger and the child. How do these things accord with the nature of an ordinary star that is devoid of reason? To the contrary, it is clear that either it was a rational power that knew things in advance and was directing their steps; or it was the supernatural and newly appearing nature of a star that was under the control of a rational power; or again perhaps it was being led and directed by divine providence itself and was serving its will.

Neither was it apart from God's design that the light of 37
this star shone all the way to Jerusalem, and then suddenly was briefly concealed. This happened for two reasons. The first was so that the mystery might be made known to all the

κατὰ τὴν Ἱερουσαλὴμ φανερὸν γένηται τὸ μυστήριον τῶν Μάγων ἀπορουμένων καὶ διαπυνθανομένων, ἀλλὰ καὶ τὸ ἀξίωμα τοῦ τεχθέντος εὐθὺς συμπροβαλλομένων· "*ποῦ ἐστιν ὁ τεχθεὶς βασιλεὺς τῶν Ἰουδαίων;*" Ἐσείσθη γοῦν *πᾶσα ἡ πόλις*, ἀλλὰ καὶ *Ἡρώδης* οὐ φαύλως διεταράχθη. Ἕτερον δέ, ἵνα καὶ παρ' αὐτῶν τῶν ἐχθρῶν, γραμματέων λέγω καὶ Φαρισαίων, ὅ τε τόπος μαρτυρηθῇ καὶ ὁ χρόνος, καὶ ὁ προφήτης παραχθῇ μάρτυς, αὐτῆς τὲ τῆς τοῦ Χριστοῦ πατρίδος λέγων τὸ ὄνομα καὶ μηδὲ τὸ ἐλάττωμα κρύπτων, ἐπάγων δὲ καὶ τὸ πλεονέκτημα· ὅτι μηκέτι, φησίν, *ἐλαχίστη*, ἀλλὰ καὶ λίαν μεγίστη διὰ τὸ ἀξίωμα τοῦ *ἐκ σοῦ ἡγουμένου* τὲ καὶ ποιμένος *τοῦ Ἰσραήλ*· οἱ μὲν γὰρ ἄλλοι σχεδὸν πάντες ἄρχοντες μὲν καὶ ἡγούμενοι τῆς δόξης καὶ τῆς ἀρχῆς ἀπολάβοντες, οὐ ποιμένες δὲ τοῦ ποιμνίου προκάμνοντες καὶ προκινδυνεύοντες, οὗτος δὲ καὶ ποιμὴν τά τε ἄλλα πάντα καὶ αὐτὸ τὸ προκινδυνεύειν, ὡς καὶ *τὴν ἑαυτοῦ ψυχὴν* τιθεὶς *ὑπὲρ τῶν προβάτων*.

Ὅρα δὲ ὅπως καὶ ὁ χρόνος λεληθότως συμπροφητεύεται, μᾶλλον δὲ καὶ αἱ προφητεῖαι συνέρχονται καὶ τὰ παρὰ τῶν Μάγων συντρέχουσιν. Ἡ μὲν γάρ φησιν ὅτι ἀπὸ *Βηθλεὲμ ἐξελεύσεται*, ἡ δὲ ὅτι καὶ καθ' ὃν καιρὸν αἱ Ἰουδαϊκαὶ ἀρχαὶ καὶ ἡγουμενεῖαι παύσονται. Οἱ δὲ ταῦτά τε ἀναφανδὸν καίτοι μηδὲν τῶν προφητευμάτων τούτων ἀκούσαντες μαρτυροῦσι καὶ τὰ παρ' ἑαυτῶν προστιθοῦσι, *βασιλέα* τε γὰρ αὐτὸν *τῶν Ἰουδαίων* ἀριδήλως ὁμολογοῦσι καὶ ζητοῦσιν ἐπιμελῶς· καὶ ἵνα μὴ δόξωσι πλανᾶν τὲ καὶ πλανᾶσθαι, τὸν ἔλεγχον ἅμα τῆς ἀληθείας καὶ ὁδηγὸν τῆς ὁδοιπορίας ἐπάγουσι, τὸν ἀστέρα, καὶ παρ' ἑαυτῶν

other inhabitants of Jerusalem, because the Magi did not know the exact location of the child's birth, and, in seeking to ascertain it, they announced the royal dignity of the one who was born, saying, "*Where is he who has been born the king of the Jews?*" For the *entire* city was disturbed, and even *Herod* was not a little troubled. The second reason was so that even the enemies themselves, I mean the scribes and the Pharisees, would bear witness to the place and time of Christ's birth, and that the prophet himself would be brought forward as a witness of Christ's place of birth, revealing the name of the town, not at all concealing its shortcomings, but also introducing its advantage, namely, that you will no longer be called *least,* but very great on account of the worthiness of the *ruler and* shepherd *of Israel who will come forth from you.* For whereas virtually all the other rulers and leaders who received glory and power were not shepherds who labored or put themselves at risk for their flock, this one is a shepherd who in every respect places himself at risk by laying *down his own life for the sheep.*

See how even the time is also included in the prophecy, or rather how the prophecies come together, while the things concerning the Magi coincide with them. For the one prophecy says that Christ would *come* from *Bethlehem,* while the other says that he would come at the time when the rulers and leaders of Judah would cease. The Magi openly bore witness to these things, even though they had not heard any of these prophecies; and they added their own testimony, for they clearly confessed him to be *the king of the Jews,* and searched for him diligently. And that they might not seem to deceive or be deceived, they had adduced the star as a witness to the truth and the guide of their journey, and they

πιστοῦνται τὴν περὶ αὐτοῦ δόξαν—ὅτι *ἤλθομεν προσκυνῆσαι αὐτόν*—καίτοι μηδὲν ὁρῶντες βασιλικὸν μηδὲ τῆς μελλούσης τύχης ἐχέγγυον, ἀλλὰ σπάργανα καὶ καλύβην καὶ φάτνην καὶ μητέρα πτωχήν. Τοσαῦτα καὶ ἀνέχονται καὶ παρρησιάζονται καὶ μηδένα μήτε πόνον μήτε κίνδυνον ὑπολογισάμενοι μήτε τῆς ὁδοῦ τὸ μῆκος μήτε τοὺς ἀναμεταξὺ κινδύνους μήτε τὸν τοῦ δήμου θυμὸν μήτε τὴν τοῦ βασιλέως μανίαν μήτε δὲ κἂν γοῦν αὐτὸ τοῦτο, τὰς κατὰ τοῦ παιδὸς ἐπιβουλὰς καὶ τοὺς φθόνους καὶ ὅτι μυρίοις αὐτὸν περιβαλοῦσι κακοῖς, ἀλλὰ πάντα πιστεύσαντες καὶ θαρρήσαντες τῷ Θεῷ αὐτοῦ τοῦ Θεοῦ καὶ τὸ πρῶτον οὕτως αὐτοὺς κινήσαντος καὶ νῦν ῥώσαντος τὴν ψυχὴν καὶ πάντα πείθεσθαι καὶ θαρρεῖν αὐτῷ πείσαντος. Ἀλλ᾽ οὗτοι μὲν οὕτω διὰ σχήματος ἀστέρος τοῦ συνήθους αὐτοῖς θεάματος, καθάπερ διὰ γλώττης γνωριμωτέρας, ὁδηγοῦνται πρὸς τὴν ἀλήθειαν.

Ποιμένες δὲ δι᾽ ἀγγέλων αὐτῶν καὶ *φυλακὰς φυλάσσοντες τῆς νυκτός*· τί κἀνταῦθα τοῦ λόγου τυποῦντος ἢ ὅτι καὶ ἡμῖν ἐπὶ τοιούτων τῶν φυλακῶν ἱσταμένοις καὶ ἑαυτῶν ἢ καὶ τῶν ἀδελφῶν καὶ πάντων τῶν λογικῶν ὑπεραγρυπνοῦσι θρεμμάτων, θεία τις ἐπιφοιτᾷ καὶ περιαστράπτει καὶ τὰ μὲν συμμαχεῖ, τὰ δὲ καὶ ἀνακαλύπτει δύναμις;

38 Ἀλλ᾽ ἐντεῦθεν μὲν Ἡρώδης διαταράττεται σφόδρα φίλαρχος ὢν καὶ παρὰ τῶν γραμματέων καὶ Φαρισαίων διαπυνθάνεται· οἱ δὲ λίαν κακούργως τὸ μὲν ὁμολογοῦσι, τὸ δὲ κρύπτουσι· τὸ μὲν γὰρ ἐκ Βηθλεὲμ τὸν Χριστὸν ἔρχεσθαι καὶ πάνυ σοφῶς παρὰ τοῦ προφήτου διερμηνεύουσι, τὸ δὲ *καὶ αἱ ἔξοδοι αὐτοῦ ἀπ᾽ ἀρχῆς αἰῶνος* οὐ προστιθοῦσιν,

confirmed Christ's glory by themselves—*we have come to worship* him—even though they had seen nothing royal nor anything that would assure such a destiny, but to the contrary, swaddling clothes, a manger, and a poor mother. They endured so many things and spoke openly, having no thought for toil or danger, nor for the length of the journey, the perils along the way, the anger of the people, nor the rage of the king, and not even his plots and jealousy against the child, and that there were a thousand evils surrounding him. Instead, they believed and took courage in the God of this God, who first set them on their journey and was now giving strength to their souls, enabling them to be completely persuaded and to take courage in the one who was persuading them. Thus, through the form of a star, a sight they were accustomed to observe, as if through a language they were more familiar with, they were led to the truth.

The shepherds, along with the angels themselves, were *watchers keeping watch at night.* What can scripture mean by this, if not that when we too are standing and keeping watch and holding vigil for ourselves or for the brethren as well, and for all the rational sheep, a divine power visits us and shines its brilliant light upon us, both fighting alongside us in our struggles and revealing to us its mysteries?

After this, Herod was deeply troubled, being a lover of 38
power, and so he questioned the scribes and Pharisees. They most wickedly both revealed something and concealed something, on the one hand that the Christ comes from Bethlehem, quite wisely interpreting the words of the prophet, but at the same time, however, they failed to disclose the second half of the verse: and *his goings forth are from the beginning of eternity.* It seems to me that they did this not

οὐ τοσοῦτον ἐμοὶ δοκεῖν τῷ βασιλεῖ χαριζόμενοι, ὅσον καὶ τῷ Χριστῷ φθονοῦντες καὶ Θεὸν αὐτὸν λέγειν μὴ ἀνεχόμενοι· τοσοῦτον βασκαίνοντες ἐξ ἀρχῆς καὶ τοῖς ἑαυτῶν ἦσαν καλοῖς καὶ οὕτως οὐ τυφλώττοντες μόνον, ἀλλὰ καὶ ἐθελοκωφοῦντες πρὸς τὴν ἀλήθειαν. Ἡρώδην δὲ ἄνοια καὶ ἀπόνοια, δύο κακά, περιπετῆ τοῖς ἑαυτοῦ πεποιήκασι λογισμοῖς· καλεῖ μὲν γὰρ κρύφα τοὺς Μάγους καὶ πολυπραγμονεῖ περὶ τοῦ παιδὸς ὡς ἐπιβουλεύσων (ὅπερ εἰ καὶ μανικόν, ἀλλ᾿ ἀληθὲς ἦν), ὑπισχνεῖται δὲ προσκυνήσειν οὐχ᾿ ὡς βασιλέα δῆλον ἁπλῶς, ἀλλὰ καὶ βασιλέα βασιλέων, ὅπερ οὐ ψευδὲς μόνον, ἀλλὰ καὶ εὐφώρατον ἦν. Εἰ μὲν γὰρ ἐπιβουλεύεις, τί προσκυνεῖν ζητεῖς; Εἰ δὲ προσκυνεῖν ζητεῖς, τί κρύφα πολυπραγμονεῖς καὶ λανθάνειν ἐθέλεις; Ἐπεὶ γοῦν δι᾿ ἀλλήλων πάντες ἐμάνθανον τὸ τεχθέν—Ἰουδαῖοι μὲν διὰ τῶν Μάγων καὶ τοῦ ἀστέρος, Ἡρώδης δὲ δι᾿ ἀμφοῖν, Ἰουδαίων τὲ καὶ τῶν Μάγων, καὶ μὴν καὶ οἱ Μάγοι μάλιστα διὰ πάντων, διὰ τοῦ ἀστέρος, διὰ τῶν Ἰουδαίων, διὰ τοῦ προφήτου, δι᾿ αὐτοῦ τοῦ βασιλικοῦ φθόνου καὶ τῆς μανίας—ἐπιφαίνεται πάλιν μᾶλλον ὁ καινὸς ἀστὴρ ἢ καὶ ἄγγελος ἐγγύτερος καὶ λαμπρότερος, ὥσπερ οὐχ᾿ ὁδηγὸς μᾶλλον ἢ καὶ χειραγωγὸς ἐν ἡλίῳ μέσῳ πρὸς τὸν μέγαν καὶ πρῶτον Ἥλιον αὐτοὺς ἕλκων καὶ τοῦ ἡλίου δημιουργὸν καὶ ὥσπερ εἰς οὐρανὸν δεύτερον καὶ δίσκον τὴν Βηθλεὲμ ἄγων καὶ τὴν καλύβην.

39 Ἐπεὶ δὲ καὶ ἐπέστη πλησιεστέρᾳ καὶ λαμπροτέρᾳ τῇ ἀκτῖνι καθάπερ τῷ δακτύλῳ δεικνύς, αὐτόν τε τῆς ὁδηγίας κἀκείνους τῆς ὁδοιπορίας ἔστησε· διὸ καὶ χαίρουσι κἀκεῖνοι *χαρὰν μεγάλην,* τοῦτο μὲν ὡς τοὺς μακροὺς πόνους καὶ

so much to placate the king, but because they were envious of Christ, and refused to call him God; being so jealous from the beginning, they were thus not only blind to their own good, but voluntarily deaf to the truth as well. As far as Herod is concerned, the two evils of folly and madness made him stumble in his own calculations. For he secretly summoned the Magi and questioned them about the child, against whom he was plotting (which, even if it is madness, was nonetheless true), promising to worship him not simply as a king but as the king of kings, which was not only a lie but also easy to detect. For if, on the one hand, you are plotting against him, why do you seek to worship him? And if, on the other hand, you are seeking to worship him, why are you inquiring in secret, and seeking to conceal your actions? Thus, since everyone had learned about the child from everyone else—the Jews from the Magi and the star, Herod from both the Jews and the Magi, and, not least, the Magi from all of them: from the star, from the Jews, from the prophet, and from Herod's envy and rage—the new star or angel appeared again, but now even more closely and more brightly. This time, however, it was no longer a guide but a leader drawing them in the light of the sun to the great and primal Sun, who is the creator of the sun, and, as if to a second heaven and a second sun, it led them to the hut in Bethlehem.

When the ray of the star had come closer and grown 39
brighter, and like a finger pointed to the place, it ceased guiding them and their journey came to an end. And they rejoiced *with great joy* because they had completed their

δρόμους καταλελυκότες, τοῦτο δὲ καὶ τῷ θαύματι τῷ περὶ τὸν ἀστέρα, μᾶλλον δὲ καὶ τῷ διὰ τοσούτων πιστωθῆναι θαυμάτων, καὶ ὡς αὐτάγγελοι δὲ τῶν τοσούτων καὶ τηλικούτων καὶ τῇ οἰκείᾳ καὶ τοῖς ἄλλοις πᾶσι μέλλοντες ἔσεσθαι· τὸ δὲ πάντων μεῖζον, τὸ καὶ θεῖόν τι καὶ κρεῖττον ἢ κατὰ τὰς ἐλπίδας εὑρεῖν τὸ εὕρημα, τοῦτο δὲ μὴ παρὰ τῶν ἄλλων τῶν προτοῦ μόνον, ἀλλὰ καὶ παρ' αὐτοῦ πάντως ἐμάνθανον τοῦ παιδός· ἅμα τὲ γὰρ ἐθεῶντο, καὶ χάριτος ἐξ αὐτοῦ καὶ ἡδονῆς καὶ φωτὸς ἐπληροῦντο καὶ αὐτῆς ἐκείνης ἐγεμίζοντο τῆς μεγάλης χαρᾶς. Οὐ μὴν ἀλλὰ καὶ ἡ τῆς μητρὸς ὁμιλία καὶ θεωρία πᾶσαν ὑπερβάλλουσα χάριν τὲ καὶ σεμνότητα καὶ τὸ κατ' αὐτὴν ἦθος ὡς ὑπὲρ ἄνθρωπον, ἄλλωστε καὶ ὅτι μηδὲν αὐτῇ μηδὲ τῶν τικτουσῶν ἐπεσήμαινεν, ἀλλὰ καὶ φαιδροτέρα μᾶλλον μετὰ τὸν τόκον διαφανῶς πᾶσιν ἐδείκνυτο, καθὰ καὶ αὐτὴ τοῦ τεχθέντος ἐξ αὐτῆς ἀναπλησθεῖσα φωτὸς πᾶσαν μετὰ τῆς ἡδονῆς καὶ τὴν ἔκπληξιν προσετίθει. Ταῦτα τὲ ἅπαντα καὶ ὅτι πρῶτοι κατηξιώθησαν τῶν τοιούτων ὑπερχαίροντας καὶ ὥσπερ ἔνθους ὑφ' ἡδονῆς ἐποίουν, διὸ καὶ ὡς βασιλέα καὶ Θεὸν οὐ προσκυνοῦσι μόνον, ἀλλὰ καὶ δῶρα προσφέρουσιν αὐτά τε ταῦτα πιστούμενοι. Τούτων γὰρ τὸ μὲν ὁ *χρυσὸς* ἐδήλου, τὸ δὲ ὁ *λίβανος*, ἡ δὲ *σμύρνα* καὶ ὅτι δι' ἡμᾶς θνητός, ὥσπερ καὶ ἄνθρωπος, ἵν' ἐγὼ γένωμαι δι' ἐκείνου Θεὸς καὶ ἀθάνατος. Τοῦτο δὲ καὶ οὕτω κινούμενοι παρὰ τοῦ Ἁγίου Πνεύματος, ἵν' ὥσπερ τὰ ἄλλα πάντα, οὕτω καὶ οὗτοι τύποι τῶν τοιούτων καὶ πνευματικῶν ἡμῖν γένωνται προσφορῶν, τὸν μὲν κεκαθαρμένον λόγον ἢ

lengthy labors and travels, and because of the miracle concerning the star, or rather because they had been deemed worthy of so many miracles, and because they themselves would now become the heralds of so many and such great wonders, both to those in the dwelling and to all the others as well. But what was greater than all these things, being divine and superior, was the discovery of something beyond their expectations, which they did not learn from the others who were there before them but indeed from the very child himself. For as soon as they beheld him, they were suffused with the grace, pleasure, and light that came forth from him, and this filled them with great joy. And not only this, but the company and sight of the mother transcended all grace and dignity, and her manner was beyond human understanding, for, above all, nothing of the weariness of childbirth could be observed in her, but instead it was clear for all to see that she was even more radiant after the birth, because she too was filled with the light of the child, adding astonishment to her pleasure. All these things, as well as having been the first to be counted worthy of such wonders, made the Magi rejoice exceedingly, being inspired with divine pleasure. Thus, they did not only worship him as king and God, but in confirmation of these titles they also offered him gifts. Of these, the *gold* was obvious, but the *frankincense,* and the *myrrh* also indicate that he became mortal for our sake, inasmuch as he became man, so that through him I might become God and immortal. They were moved to offer these gifts by the Holy Spirit, so that, just as with all the other things, they might also become examples for our own spiritual offerings: our purified mind or way of life as gold; our

βίον ὥσπερ χρυσόν, τὴν δὲ θεωρίαν ὡς λίβανον, καὶ μὴν καὶ τὴν ἀπονέκρωσιν τῶν παθῶν, εἴτ' οὖν μελῶν, ὡς σμύρναν προσάγουσιν, ὃ καὶ ἀπάθειαν καὶ οὐρανῶν βασιλείαν ὁ λόγος ὁρίζεται. Συμπροσκυνεῖται δὲ πάντως καὶ ἡ τοῦ Λόγου μήτηρ καὶ δῶρα παρ' αὐτῶν δέχεται. Τοσαῦτά σοι καὶ ἔτι πλείω τὰ μεγαλεῖα, Παρθένε, παρὰ τοῦ δυνατοῦ αὐτοῦ τούτου, τοῦ σοῦ υἱοῦ, καὶ οὕτω σε μακαρίαν ἐξ αὐτῆς ἀρχῆς καὶ διὰ πάντων τέθεικε πάντα θειότερα συνδραμεῖν ποιήσας, ὡς καὶ πρὸς τὸ τέλος μακαριωτέραν ἀπεργασόμενος, καὶ τοῦτο τοῖς ἤδη φθάσασι προπιστούμενος.

40 Ἀλλὰ δωροφορήσωμεν καὶ ἡμεῖς τὸν λόγον τοῖς Μάγοις φιλοτιμότερον, τοῖς πρώτοις καὶ πατράσι τῆς πίστεως, τοῖς πρώτοις λατρευταῖς καὶ προσκυνηταῖς, τοῖς πρώτοις φιλοσόφοις καὶ θεολόγοις καὶ μάρτυσιν, οἷς τὸ μὲν αὐτὸν διὰ τῶν πόνων ἐτίμων καὶ διὰ τῶν δώρων ἐθεολόγουν, τὸ δὲ καὶ τῆς Ἰουδαϊκῆς μανίας καὶ τῆς τυραννικῆς ἀπονοίας κρείττους ἐγίνοντο, μᾶλλον δὲ καὶ κατέπαιζον, τὸ μὲν βασιλέα φανερῶς ἀνομολογοῦντες, τὸ δὲ καὶ ὡς Θεὸν ἢ καὶ Θεάνθρωπον προσκυνοῦντες, καὶ οὐ δωροφοροῦντες μόνον, ἀλλὰ τούτου μὲν πειθόμενοι καὶ τοῖς ὀνείρασιν, αὐτοῦ δὲ τοῦ τυράννου καὶ τῶν τούτου παρακλήσεων καταγελῶντες. Οὕτω μὲν οἱ Μάγοι καὶ τοιαῦτα δωροφοροῦσι, τά τε ἄλλα καὶ ἑαυτοὺς τῷ καὶ *ὑπὲρ ἡμῶν ἑαυτὸν* δῶρον δώσοντι καὶ *ἀντίλυτρον,* οὐδὲν δὲ ἧττον δωροφοροῦνται καὶ αὐτοὶ παρὰ τῶν Ἐθνῶν, καθάπερ ἀπαρχὰς καὶ αὐτῶν τῷ Χριστῷ κομιζόντων, τοὺς Μάγους, τῆς αὐτῶν πλάνης καὶ δεισιδαιμονίας τὰ ἀκροθίνια. Τοσούτου τὴν πτωχείαν

contemplation as frankincense; and, not least, the mortification of our passions, that is, our bodily members, as myrrh, which scripture defines as impassibility and the kingdom of heaven. To be sure, they also venerated the mother of the Word, who likewise received gifts from them. These, and things still more magnificent than these, were given to you, O Virgin, by the mighty one, your son, and thus from the very beginning, and through all things, he made you blessed, causing all these divine events to concur, just as in the end he will make you more blessed, something which he has assured through the things that have already taken place.

But let us, too, bestow upon the Magi a still more lavish 40
gift of our words, for they were the first fathers of the faith, the first to worship and venerate, the first philosophers, theologians, and witnesses. Through their labors they honored God, and through their gifts they taught theology; they also showed themselves superior to the madness of the Jews and the folly of the tyrant, whom indeed they tricked, openly proclaiming the child to be a king, though they themselves worshipped him as God, or rather as the Godman; and they did not only bear gifts, but being persuaded of his divinity by dreams, they mocked the tyrant and his deprecations. These, then, are the gifts that the Magi brought, but they also offered themselves to the one who gave ***himself for*** us as a gift and a *ransom*. And the Magi themselves were no less honored with gifts by the Gentiles, who offered the Magi to Christ as their own first fruits, that is, the spoils, as it were, of their delusion and superstition. My

τιμᾶται ὁ ἐμὸς Χριστὸς καὶ οὕτως αὐτὴν πανταχοῦ τιμῶν δι' ἑαυτοῦ πρῶτον τιμήσας φαίνεται, ἵνα τῇ μὲν καλύβῃ τὸν οὐρανόν, τῇ φάτνῃ δὲ τὸν ἀστέρα, τοῖς σπαργάνοις δὲ καὶ τοῖς φόροις τὰ τῶν Μάγων καὶ τῶν Ἐθνῶν ἀντιτιθεὶς δῶρα, μηδὲν ἐν τοῖς ταπεινοῖς ταπεινὸν φρονῇς, ἀλλὰ δι' αὐτῶν μὲν οὖν τούτων ἐλπίζῃς τὰ ὑψηλότερα. Τοιαῦτα ὁρῶσαν καὶ τὴν μητέρα τοῦ παιδὸς τὰ προοίμια, οἵας εἰκὸς ἔχειν ἐλπίδας καὶ περὶ τῶν μελλόντων.

41 Ἀλλ' ὅρα μοι καὶ πάλιν τὰ ταπεινότερα καὶ ἀνθρωπινώτερα· διαδέχεται γὰρ τὴν μὲν γέννησιν καὶ τὴν φάτνην ἡ ἀπογραφή, τὴν δὲ ἀπογραφὴν ἡ περιτομή, ἣν καὶ κατὰ τὴν ὀγδόην ἐτέλουν, ὡς τύπον τῆς ἐκεῖθεν μακαριότητος, ἣν καὶ ἡ ἐντεῦθεν προξενεῖ περιτομὴ τῆς σαρκὸς καὶ ἀπάθεια· τὴν δὲ περιτομὴν ὁ καθαρισμός, τεσσαρακονθήμερος μετὰ τὴν γέννησιν ὤν, ὡς καὶ τύπος τῆς τελειότητος, οἷα καὶ τοῦ τελείου τῶν ἀριθμῶν τῆς δεκάδος ἐπὶ τὴν τετρακτὺν ἀνακυκλουμένου τῶν ἀρετῶν. Ἀλλ' οὐκ ἄχαρι, μᾶλλον δὲ καὶ ἀναγκαῖον κἀνταῦθα καὶ τὴν ἐναντιολογίαν λῦσαι τῶν εὐαγγελιστῶν, εἰ καὶ παρεκβατικώτερος ὁ λόγος δόξειε. Πῶς γὰρ Ματθαῖος μὲν μετὰ τὴν γέννησιν εὐθὺς τὴν εἰς Αἴγυπτον ἱστορεῖ φυγαδείαν καὶ τὴν Ἡρώδου μανίαν τὲ καὶ παιδοφονίαν, Λουκᾶς δὲ τὴν εἰς Ἱερουσαλὴμ μᾶλλον ἐπιδημίαν καὶ τὰ κατὰ μόνον τοῦ πᾶσαν καθαίροντος ἡμῶν τὴν φύσιν καθάρσια; Ἢ δῆλον ὅτι Ματθαῖος μὲν ὑπερπηδήσας τὰ ἀναμεταξὺ τὰ μετὰ συχνὸν γενόμενα χρόνον, ἔτος που δεύτερον ἢ ὀλίγῳ πλέον ἢ ἔλαττον, ὥς φασι, τόν τε τοῦ Ἰωσὴφ ἐπισυνάπτει χρησμὸν καὶ τὴν εἰς Αἴγυπτον καὶ φυγὴν καὶ ἀναστροφήν—εἰωθὸς καὶ τοῦτο

Christ so greatly honors poverty and seems to honor it everywhere, having honored it first in his own life, so that by contrasting the hut with heaven, the manger with the star, and the swaddling clothes and the tributes with the gifts of the Magi and the Gentiles, you may perceive nothing among humble things to be ignoble, but through these very things you may hope for higher things. As the mother of the child was seeing these beginnings, what hopes she naturally must have had for the future as well!

But behold with me things still more humble and more 41
human, for the birth and the manger were followed by the enrollment, and the enrollment by the circumcision, which took place on the eighth day as a figure of the future blessedness, which may be conferred now by the circumcision of the flesh and freedom from the passions. The circumcision was followed by the purification, forty days after the birth as a figure of perfection, since it is the perfect number of the decad, which, in the form of the tetrad, recapitulates the four virtues. It would not be disagreeable, and at this point perhaps necessary, to explain the divergences among the evangelists, even though doing so might make my discourse appear rather digressive. For how is it that Matthew describes the flight into Egypt immediately after the birth of Christ, along with Herod's madness and slaughter of the infants, while Luke, on the other hand, describes the going up to Jerusalem and the purification of him who alone purifies our nature? It should be clear that Matthew passes over the intervening events which took place over a long period of time, perhaps more or less two years, as they say, and continues with Joseph's dream and the flight into Egypt and the return from there—for this is the custom of scripture in

πολλαχοῦ τῆς γραφῆς τὰ διεστῶτα καὶ μετὰ πολὺν γενόμενα χρόνον ἐπισυμπλέκειν—Λουκᾶς δὲ καὶ τὰ μετὰ τὸν Τόκον εὐθὺς καὶ ἃ τῷ Ματθαίῳ παρεῖται; Ἐπεὶ καὶ τοῦτο τοῖς εὐαγγελισταῖς σύνηθες, ἵνα μηδεὶς ᾖ περιττὸς ὡς μηδὲν ἔχων εἰπεῖν πλέον καὶ οὕτω *τὰ πᾶσι παρειμένα πᾶσι καὶ πεπλήρωνται.*

42 Ἀλλὰ τοῦτο μὲν οὕτω διαλυτέον, κἀκεῖνο δὲ πάντως προσεπαπορητέον ὡς ἀναγκαῖον· πῶς μὲν Ἡρώδης οὕτως εὐθὺς καὶ περιφανῶς ὑπὸ τῶν Μάγων ἐμπαίζεται μέν, οὐκ αἰσθάνεται δέ, ἢ καὶ συνίησι μέν, ἀνέχεται δὲ τὴν ἐπὶ τοσοῦτον χρόνον διατριβήν, κατέχει δὲ τὴν ὀργήν, καίτοι θυμικώτατος ἀνθρώπων γενόμενος καὶ ἀκρατέστατος, ὡς ἱστόρηται, καὶ οὐδὲ ἐννοούμενος μή που καὶ τὸν ἀναμεταξὺ λάθῃ χρόνον ὁ παῖς ἢ καὶ παρ᾽ αὐτῶν τῶν Μάγων ὑποκλαπεὶς μετὰ τῆς μητρός, οἷα καὶ συννενοηκότων αὐτοῦ τὸ βούλημα, ἢ καὶ ἄλλως ὑπεκτεθεὶς ἢ καὶ κατὰ τύχην τὸν τόπον ἀμείψας, οἷαι πολλαὶ τῶν ἀνθρώπων μεταβολαὶ καὶ μεταναστάσεις ἑκουσίως ἢ ἀκουσίως; Ἀλλὰ καὶ τούτου λύσις ἡ ἱστορία. Φασὶ γὰρ ὅτι κατ᾽ αὐτὰς ἐκείνας τὰς ἡμέρας αἷς οἱ Μάγοι μὲν ἐπεδήμουν καὶ ἐθρύλλουν τὰ περὶ τοῦ παιδός, Ἡρώδης δὲ κακὰ ῥάπτων ἦν καὶ ἐν σχήματι προσκυνήσεως τὸν τρόπον ἐπενόει τῆς ἀναιρέσεως, πόλεμος ἔνδοθεν αὐτῷ παρὰ τῶν οἰκείων ἀναρριπίζεται χαλεπός, ἐκ θειοτέρας πάντως οἰκονομίας ἀπασχολούσης αὐτὸν τοῦ παιδὸς παρά τε τῆς γυναικὸς αὐτῆς καὶ τῶν παίδων. Ἔνθεν καὶ τῶν καιριωτέρων γενόμενος, τὴν μὲν γυναῖκα παραυτίκα διαχειρίζεται, τῶν δὲ παίδων, ἐπεὶ μὴ ἐξῆν αὐτῷ χωρὶς Καίσαρος, φείδεται μὲν ἐπ᾽ ὀλίγον, τῆς

many places, namely, to weave together events separated by great periods of time—but Luke describes events after the Nativity which Matthew leaves out, since this is the custom of the evangelists, so that none of them would appear to be superfluous as having nothing more to say, and so *that which has been neglected by each, has been accomplished by all.*

But if this question must be resolved in the manner we 42
have suggested, the following is a quandary that needs to be addressed: How was it that Herod was immediately and famously deceived by the Magi, and yet did not perceive this? Or if he was aware of it, why did he remain inactive for a long period of time, and constrain his wrath, even though he was the most irascible of men lacking in self-control, as the history affirms, not considering that in the meantime the child might escape notice; or be stolen away by the Magi themselves together with his mother, since they had understood Herod's intention; or that the child would otherwise be taken to a place of safety, or even by chance change location, as people experience many changes and migrations willingly or unwillingly? The solution to this problem is found in the historical account. For they say that, in those days, during which the Magi were traveling around and speaking out about the child, and Herod, under the pretext of venerating the child, was wickedly weaving together a way to kill him, a fierce domestic war was being waged against him by the members of his household, though according, no doubt, to a more divine dispensation, he was more preoccupied with his wife and children than with the child. Then, at an opportune moment, he immediately killed his wife, but he spared his children for a little while, though he was fully raging against them, because he could

δὲ κατ' αὐτῶν ὁρμῆς ὅλως ὤν, ἐπὶ Ῥώμην ἀνέπλει τὴν ἐκεῖθεν ψῆφον ληψόμενος, ὃ δὴ καὶ γέγονε· καὶ τὴν αὐθεντίαν ἐκεῖθεν λαβὼν ἀποπνίγει καὶ τοὺς υἱούς.

43 Οὕτω τούτων ἐμφορηθεὶς ὁ ἡμιμανὴς ἐκεῖνος, μᾶλλον δὲ καὶ ὅλη δαιμονιώδης καὶ ἀνθρωποκτόνος ψυχή, καὶ ὥσπερ ἀνενεγκὼν καὶ ῥαΐσας εἰς δευτέραν ἐμπίπτει πολλῷ χαλεπωτέραν μανίαν. Τὸν γὰρ ἐντὸς πρότερον καταλελυκὼς πόλεμον καὶ ἐπὶ τὸν ἐκτὸς τρέπεται, περὶ τῆς ἀρχῆς ἀεὶ τρέμων ὁ φιληδονώτατος καὶ φιλοδοξότατος, καὶ τῶν Μάγων ὑπομιμνήσκεται καὶ τοῦ παιδὸς βασιλέως· καὶ ἐπεὶ φανερὸς ὁ ἐμπαιγμὸς ἦν, τοῦτο μὲν ἀσφαλείας ἕνεκα, τοῦτο δὲ καὶ τῆς τοῦ θυμοῦ καὶ φθόνου παραμυθίας—ὢ τῆς μανίας ἤ, τἀληθέστερον εἰπεῖν, τῆς θεομαχίας!—ἐπὶ τοὺς οὐδὲν ἠδικηκότας παῖδας ἀφίησι τὴν ὀργήν· τῷ γὰρ κοινῷ πάντως καὶ τὸν ἕνα που συμπεριλαβεῖν ᾤετο, καὶ πέμψας ἀποθερίζει πᾶσαν, οἴμοι, τὴν ἐν Βηθλεὲμ ἄωρον ἡλικίαν ὁ δείλαιος, τοιαῦτα δράσας εἰς λογικὰ καὶ τοσαῦτα καὶ οὕτω βρέφη κομιδῇ μικρά τε καὶ νεογνά, ἃ κἂν εἰς ἄλογα, κἂν εἰς ἄψυχα καὶ ἔρνη νεαρὰ καὶ καλὰ καὶ ἐλάττω πολλῷ δρᾶσαί τις κατηλέησεν, ὅ γε φιλοσυμπαθὴς καὶ φιλόκαλος, ἀλλ' οὐκ ἐκεῖνος· πῶς γὰρ ὅ γε μηδὲ τῶν οἰκείων υἱῶν, ἀνδρῶν ἤδη καὶ βασιλέων, διὰ τὴν βασιλείαν φεισάμενος; Ὡς ἀπόλοιτο καὶ ἄμφω φιλαρχία καὶ φθόνος, τὰ πρῶτα κεφάλαια τῶν κακῶν, ὧν ἡ μὲν ἐξ Ἑωσφόρου σκότος καὶ ἐξ ἀρχαγγέλου ἀρχέκακον καὶ ἐκ τῶν τοῦ Θεοῦ λειτουργῶν ἀντίθεον παρασκευάζει τὸν ἀποστάτην, ὁ δὲ τὸν αὐτὸν τοῦτον καὶ δι' αὐτοῦ τὸν δῆμον τὸν Ἰουδαϊκὸν

not kill them without the permission of Caesar; and thus he sailed to Rome, seeking to receive permission, which he received. After he received this authority, he strangled his sons.

After Herod, that half-mad man, or rather that entirely demonic and murderous soul, had sated himself with these actions, as if he had recovered and found renewed strength, he fell into a second act of madness more grievous than the first. Having first brought the internal war within his family to an end, he turned to an external war, and, because this lover of pleasure and glory was always fearful of losing his power, he remembered the Magi and the child king. And since it was obvious that he had been deceived, he acted partly for his own safety, and partly to sooth his anger and envy—oh, what madness, or, to speak more truly, what hostility toward God!—he unleashed his wrath on children who had done no wrong, for he was surely thinking that with this he would somehow include the child Jesus with the many, and the wretch issued the command, alas, for all children in Bethlehem under a certain age to be cut down. He did this to so many rational, tiny little infants and newborn babies, though any compassionate person and lover of goodness would show greater compassion in doing far less to charming baby animals, even if they are irrational and have no soul, but not Herod, for how could he when for the sake of his throne he did not spare his own sons, who were already men and princes? If only the love of power and envy, those first principals of evil, might cease to exist! Of these, the first turned the Morning Star into darkness, an archangel into the originator of evil, and God's minister into a godless apostate, while the second persuaded Herod, and through 43

οὐκ ἀνθρωποκτόνον μόνον, ἀλλὰ καὶ θεοκτόνον, τὸν δημιουργὸν καὶ Δεσπότην ἀλλὰ καὶ τοσούτων θαυμάτων καὶ εὐεργημάτων αὐτουργὸν αὐτοῖς ἀναιρεῖν πείθων. Οὐ θαυμαστὸν οὖν, εἰ καὶ ἄμφω συνελθόντα τὸν Ἡρώδην τότε καὶ τῆς ἰδίας καὶ τῆς κοινῆς ἐχθρὸν ἀπέδειξε φύσεως καὶ παιδοκτόνον μὲν τῶν ἰδίων, παιδοκτόνον δὲ καὶ τῶν τοσούτων καὶ ἀλλοτρίων, μᾶλλον δὲ καὶ αὐτοῦ τοῦ τῶν ὅλων δημιουργοῦ καὶ Δεσπότου, τό γε κατὰ τὴν αὐτοῦ γνώμην. Καίτοι, εἰ μὲν ψευδῆ τὰ παρὰ τῶν Μάγων παράφορε, τί δέδοικας; Εἰ δὲ καὶ ἀληθῆ, τί μέμηνας, θεομαχεῖν, μᾶλλον δὲ θεοκτονεῖν, ἄντικρυς ἐπαιρόμενος; Ἀλλὰ τοιοῦτον ὁ φθόνος, μὴ τοῖς ἄλλοις μόνον, ἀλλὰ καὶ αὐτὸς ἑαυτῷ μαχόμενος καὶ δι' ἑαυτοῦ φθειρόμενος. Ταῦτά τοι καὶ ἀμφοτέρων δικαίως ἀποτυγχάνεις καὶ τῆς ἀναιρέσεως· οὐ γὰρ ἀναιρεῖς τὴν Ζωὴν καὶ τῆς βασιλείας, μᾶλλον δὲ καὶ αὐτῆς τῆς ζωῆς, θεηλάτου πληγῆς, ὡς δέ τινες φασί, καὶ σκωλήκων ἔργον γενόμενος. Καὶ ἐνταῦθα μὲν φρικτὸν φανεὶς ὁμοῦ καὶ ἐλεεινὸν καὶ τοῖς τότε πᾶσι θέαμα καὶ παράδειγμα καὶ τοῖς μέχρι τοῦ νῦν διήγημα, κἀκεῖθεν τὰ πολλῷ χείρω τούτων καὶ αἰώνια δικαίως ὑποίσων δικαιωτήρια, τοσοῦτον ὑπερβάλλων καὶ τὸν *ἐν φλογὶ πλούσιον,* ὅσον ἐκεῖνος μὲν καθ' ἑαυτὸν ἦν μόνον τρυφῶν μὴ μεταδιδοὺς τῶν οἰκείων, αὐτὸς δὲ καὶ τοσούτων αἱμάτων ἀνοσίως ἐμφορηθεὶς καὶ κατατρυφήσας, ποίας ἂν ἢ πόσας ὑπέχων τὰς ἀξίας εἴης δίκας διδούς;

44 Τοῦτο τὸ πάθος οὐ μόνον τὴν Βηθλεὲμ καὶ πάντα τὰ περὶ τὴν Βηθλεὲμ ὥσπερ πῦρ κατέφλεξε καὶ διέθηκεν

him the Jewish mob, not only to become a killer of man but also a killer of God, and to slay our creator and Master, who had worked so many great miracles and gifts for them. It is thus unsurprising if, at that time, both of these evils came together in Herod and showed him to be the enemy of his own nature and of human nature as a whole, the slayer of his own children, and the slayer of the children of so many others, or rather those of the Master himself and creator of all things. And this was the result of his free choice. If, you madman, what the Magi told you was false, what were you afraid of? If, on the other hand, the things they said were true, why did you go out of your mind and fight God, or rather attempt to kill God outright? But envy is such that it fights not only others but also itself, and destroys itself in the process. Thus you rightly failed in both of these things, including your attempt to kill the child. For you did not destroy Life or the kingdom, but rather your own life, struck down by God, as some say, and you became food for maggots. And thus, in this life, you became a fearful and piteous sight and an example to those of your own era, and continue to be a byword for those today; and in the next life, you will justly endure far worse eternal punishments, exceeding even those of the *rich man in flames,* because inasmuch as he luxuriated merely by himself, failing to give to his neighbors, whereas you luxuriated in and were sated profanely with so much human blood, what sort of, and how many, punishments do you deserve to receive?

It was not only in Bethlehem and in all the districts sur- 44
rounding it, that this event raged like a fire, placing the

ὥσπερ ἑαλωκυῖαν καὶ πεπονθυῖαν, ἃ μηδὲ παρὰ τῶν πολεμίων, ἀλλὰ καὶ τὴν Ἰουδαίαν πᾶσαν κατέσεισε. Διὸ καὶ πάλαι καὶ πρόπαλαι προφητικῶν ἠξίωται θρήνων· *φωνὴ ἐν Ῥαμᾷ ἠκούσθη, θρῆνος καὶ κλαυθμὸς καὶ ὀδυρμὸς πολύς· Ῥαχὴλ κλαίουσα τὰ τέκνα αὐτῆς·* ἀπὸ τῶν γυναικῶν καὶ τῶν τάφων τοὺς τόπους ἀποκαλῶν καὶ ὡσπερεὶ ζώσας τὰς ἄρτι γυναῖκας καὶ ὀδυρομένας ποιῶν· *καὶ οὐκ ἤθελε παρακληθῆναι,* φησίν, *ὅτι οὐκ εἰσί·* μὴ γὰρ ἰάσιμον, φησίν, ἢ κἂν γοῦν μερικὸν τὸ κακόν; Μὴ γὰρ κἂν ἅλωσις καὶ ἀνδραποδισμός; Ἀφανισμὸς παντελὴς τῇ Ῥαχὴλ καὶ πάντων τῶν τέκνων.

Ἀλλὰ καὶ οὕτως ἡ Βηθλεὲμ οὐ παρὰ τῶν ἄλλων μόνον, ἀλλὰ καὶ παρ' αὐτοῦ τούτου σεμνύνεται καὶ τὸ Πάσχα τελεῖ καὶ τελεῖται, οὐχ' ἓν ἀρνίον ἄλογον θύουσα, εἰ καὶ ἄμωμον, ἀλλὰ τοσαῦτα καὶ λογικὰ καὶ ἀκίβδηλα, τοὺς ἄρτι τῶν ὠδίνων λυθέντας καὶ τὰς ὀδύνας τοῦ βίου λιπόντας, τοὺς ἄρτι τοῦ φωτὸς γευσαμένους καὶ ὑπὲρ τοῦ Φωτὸς διηγωνισμένους, τοὺς στρατιώτας καὶ ἀριστέας ὑπὲρ τῆς ἀληθείας καὶ πρὸ τῆς ἡλικίας, τοὺς ἡλικιώτας μὲν Χριστοῦ, πρώτους δὲ προδρόμους καὶ δορυφόρους καὶ μάρτυρας, τὰ ἀναθήματα καὶ θύματα καὶ προθύματα Χριστῷ καὶ πρὸ Χριστοῦ καὶ ὑπὲρ Χριστοῦ.

Ἐχρῆν γὰρ ἐχρῆν πάντως ἐπιφανέντος Χριστοῦ καὶ πᾶσαν εὐθὺς ἐμφυτευθῆναι τῷ βίῳ φιλοσοφίαν, καὶ μὴ τὴν παρθενίαν ὑπὲρ φύσιν ἐκλάμψαι διὰ τῆς μητρὸς μόνον, ἀλλὰ καὶ τὴν ἀνδρίαν παρ' ἡλικίαν διὰ τῶν παίδων, καὶ τὴν γῆν προκαθαρθῆναι τῶν λύθρων διὰ τῶν καθαρῶν καὶ

towns, as it were, under a siege and suffering of a kind not seen even during times of war, but it also shook all of Judea. This is why formerly and of old the region was accounted worthy of the prophetic lament: *A voice was heard in Ramah, mourning, weeping, and great lamentation; Rachel was weeping for her children,* naming this place from these women and the tombs, and making it seem as if these women were still alive and mourning. *And she would not be consoled,* he says, *for they were no longer;* for this was incurable, he says. Even if this was a partial evil? Or even if it was conquest or enslavement? To the contrary, it was the utter obliteration of Rachel and all her children.

And thus Bethlehem is also revered, not only on account of other things but also because of this, namely, that it both fulfills the Passover and constitutes its fulfillment. It did not sacrifice one irrational lamb, even if it was spotless, but so many rational and pure ones, infants who had just been freed from the travail and pangs of labor, and who were suddenly sent forth from the pains of life, who had just seen the light of day, and suddenly entered combat on behalf of the Light, who were soldiers and chieftains fighting on behalf of the truth at a tender age. They were the same age as Christ, his first forerunners, companions, and martyrs; they were sacrifices, offerings, and preparatory offerings for Christ, offered before Christ and on behalf of Christ.

For it was necessary, absolutely necessary, that when 45
Christ appeared and the true philosophy was planted in human life, not only should a virginity transcending nature shine forth from his mother, but also that courage beyond the measure of their age shine forth through the infants, and that the earth should be purified of the impure blood by

ὁσίων αἱμάτων, καὶ ὡσπερεὶ προοδοποιῆσαι ταῖς βασιλικαῖς ἐπὶ σταυροῦ ῥανίσι τὰ τούτων αἵματα. Σὲ δὲ κἀνταῦθα προσενθυμεῖσθαι τὰ κατὰ τὴν Παρθένον καὶ μητέρα δέον· ποίαν μὲν εἰκὸς ἔχειν αὐτὴν τότε ψυχήν, ποίας δὲ τὰς ἐλπίδας καὶ πόσας καὶ ὅπως ἐξ ἐναντίας ἀνθέλκεσθαί τε καὶ ταλαντεύεσθαι, τοῦτο μὲν τὰ κατὰ τὸν Ἡρώδην καὶ τοὺς παῖδας ἀκούουσαν, καὶ τούτου μὲν τὴν μανίαν, ἐκείνων δὲ τὴν τραγῳδίαν, καὶ τὸν μὲν μισοῦσαν, τὴν δὲ κατοικτείρουσαν ἅμα καὶ φρίττουσαν, τὸν δὲ ἑαυτῆς υἱὸν ἐκ μέσων ὁρῶσαν ἀνηρπασμένον τῶν φόνων, καὶ οὕτως ἐκ βρέφους τοσαύτης ἐπιμελείας καὶ φυλακῆς ἠξιωμένον παρὰ Θεοῦ, καὶ διὰ ταῦτα μὲν ὑπερχαίρουσαν, τὸν δὲ τοσοῦτον ἐκ προοιμίων πάλιν φθόνον μὴ φέρουσαν, ἀλλὰ καὶ περὶ τῶν μελλόντων ἀγωνιῶσαν, μήτε δὲ αὖθις καταπίπτουσαν ὑπὸ τῶν τοιούτων, οἷα ταῖς ἐλπίσιν ἐπαιρομένην καὶ πτερουμένην καὶ πάντα πρὸς τοῦτο συλλέγουσαν, ὅτι ὄντως οὗτος *μέγας καὶ Υἱὸς Ὑψίστου* κατὰ τὴν τοῦ ἀρχαγγέλου φωνὴν καὶ πρὸ τῆς συλλήψεως. Ὢ πόσαι σου τῆς ψυχῆς αἱ ῥομφαῖαι, Μῆτερ, καὶ πρὸ τοῦ Πάθους μυρίοις μεριζομένης τοῖς πάθεσιν.

Ἀλλ’ ἡμῖν γε καὶ αὖθις περὶ τὸν καθαρμὸν καὶ τὸν γλυκὺν Ἰησοῦν ἐνδιατριπτέον, ἐπεὶ καὶ ταῦτα τῆς τεκούσης ἐγκώμια, ἄλλωστε καὶ ὅτε τοῖς ἐκείνου καὶ τὰ ταύτης συμπεριέχεται καὶ οὐκ ἐνὸν διελεῖν τὰ κατὰ φύσιν ἡνωμένα τοῖς πράγμασι. Περιτέμνεται μὲν οὖν οὐ κατὰ τὴν ὀγδόην μόνον, ἀλλὰ τὴν αὐτὴν καὶ πρώτην καθ’ ἣν καὶ συλλαμβάνεται καὶ ἀνίσταται, καὶ καθάπερ ἐν περιτομῇ τὸ

means of their pure and righteous blood, just as if their blood was a precursor of the drops of royal blood that were shed on the cross. But you should now recall the things pertaining to the Virgin and mother: what was likely the disposition of her soul, what were her hopes, and how and to what extent was she swayed and pulled in different directions. For she had heard what Herod had done to the infants and learned both of the former's madness and the latter's tragedy, and whereas she hated the former, she was filled with compassion but at the same time was terrified by the latter, for she had seen her own son snatched away from the midst of those murders, and how, from his infancy, he was counted worthy of such great care and protection by God. On account of this, she rejoiced exceedingly, but she could not endure such great envy at the beginning of her son's life, and she was also anxious about the future, though she was not overcome by this, but was raised up and given wings by her hopes, and always remained concentrated on this, namely, that the child was truly *great and the son of the Most High,* according to the word of the archangel before the conception. But oh, how many swords passed through your soul, Mother, and even before the Passion you were cut in pieces by your innumerable sufferings.

But now we must turn to the purification and the sweet Jesus, for these things also redound to the praise of the one who gave him birth; and, from another point of view, and especially when matters concerning the child and the mother coincide, it is not fitting to separate what nature has united. And thus the child was circumcised not simply on the eighth day, but on what was also the first day, the same day as his conception and resurrection; and just as in

φυσικὸν ἀποτίθεται πάχος, καὶ καθ' ἣν ἀναστήσει πάντας πάλιν τὸ δεύτερον ἐνδοξότερον καὶ ἐξ οὐρανῶν ἐρχόμενος περιτέμνων τὴν ὕλην καὶ συντέμνων πᾶν τὸ ὁρώμενον. Καὶ ὀνομάζεται "Ἰησοῦς," ὅ ἐστι Σωτήρ, ὃ καὶ προηγόρευται.

Εἰς τὴν Ὑπαπαντήν

46 Καὶ οὕτω μετὰ τὴν συμπλήρωσιν τῶν ἡμερῶν ἀνάγεται πρὸς Ἱεροσόλυμα καὶ παρίσταται *τῷ Κυρίῳ* κατὰ τὸν νόμον *ὅτι πᾶν ἄρσεν διανοῖγον μήτραν ἅγιον τῷ Κυρίῳ κληθήσεται.* Καὶ τοῦτο μὲν ἐνταῦθα γνῶναι παντός, ὡς *αὐτὸς μὲν ὁ ἁγιάζων, αὐτὸς δὲ ὁ ἁγιαζόμενος,* ἐκεῖνο δὲ οὐ παντός, ὡς ἐλέγετο μὲν καὶ ἐτελεῖτο κοινῶς ὑπὲρ ἄρρενος καὶ πρώτου παντὸς αὐτοῦ τὲ τούτου προσαγομένου καὶ *ζεῦγος* ὑπὲρ αὐτοῦ *τρυγόνων ἢ καὶ δυεῖν περιστερῶν νεοσσῶν,* ἅτινα δὴ ταῦτα θεωρητέον. Οἶμαι δὲ διὰ μὲν τῶν τρυγόνων τὸ σῶφρον τὲ καὶ φιλέρημον, διὰ δὲ τῶν περιστερῶν τὸ πρᾶον τὲ καὶ ἀκέραιον. Ἀλλὰ τί δήποτε καὶ ἀπὸ μὲν τῶν τρυγόνων αὐτῶν τὸ ζεῦγος, ἀπὸ δὲ τῶν περιστερῶν οὐκ αὐτῶν, ἀλλὰ τῶν νεοσσῶν ἢ καὶ ὅτι βούλεται μὲν ὁ λόγος αἰνίττεσθαι τὴν ἀπάθειαν; Οἶδε δὲ ταῖς μὲν τρυγόσιν ἀεὶ τὸ σῶφρον καὶ φιλομόναχον, ταῖς δὲ περιστεραῖς τὸ μὲν ἄκακον καὶ ἀκέραιον ἀεί, τὸ δὲ ἀνέραστον οὐκ ἀεί, ἀλλὰ πολλὴν ὅτι μάλιστα ταύταις περὶ τὴν ἡλικίαν τὴν λύσσαν. Διὰ τοῦτο τούτων μὲν ἁπλῶς τὸ ζεῦγος ἐκλέγεται, ἐκείνων δὲ οὐχ ἁπλῶς, ἀλλὰ τῶν νεοσσῶν, ἃ καὶ τῆς ἀκεραιότητος ἅμα σύμβολα καὶ τοῦ ἔρωτος ἀνεπίδεκτα. Ἀλλ' οὕτω

circumcision the natural density of the flesh is put aside, so also on that day he will resurrect all human beings, coming a second time more gloriously from heaven, circumcising matter and cutting short all that is visible. And he is given the name "Jesus," which means Savior, which had also been foretold.

On the Presentation in the Temple

After the completion of the requisite days, the child was 46
taken up to Jerusalem and presented *to the Lord* according to the law *that every male that opens the womb shall be called holy to the Lord*. That he himself is the one who both *makes things holy and is made holy* is something known to all, but what is not known to all is that this law was established and commonly observed that *a pair of turtledoves or two young pigeons* should be offered on behalf of a male child, and first of all for him when he was brought forward. Now these things require interpretation. It seems to me that whereas the turtledoves symbolize temperance and love of solitude, the pigeons symbolize meekness and purity. And for what other reason do you suppose that for turtledoves a pair was specified, but for the pigeons nothing else was required except that they should be young, if scripture were not hinting at the state of dispassion? Scripture knows that turtledoves are characterized by temperance and love of solitude, whereas pigeons by guilelessness and purity, but not always by the absence of desire, since especially after a certain age they can be filled with raging love. This is why for the turtledoves simply a pair is prescribed, but the pigeons in addition had to be young, for they are then at once symbols of purity and

μὲν ὁ λόγος τὲ καὶ ὁ νόμος, νοούμενος μὲν κοινῶς καὶ τελούμενος, οὐ μὴν πρὸς ἀλήθειαν ὤν, ἀλλ' οἷα καὶ τἄλλα τῶν προφητικῶν τὰ πολλά, μᾶλλον δὲ τὰ πλεῖστα, σχεδὸν συνεσκιασμένα καὶ ἀγνοούμενα, οὕτω καὶ τοῦτο. Μήτε γὰρ πᾶν ἄρρεν καὶ πρωτότοκον "ἅγιον" καὶ μαρτυρεῖ Κάϊν τὲ καὶ Ῥουβὶμ καὶ Ἠσαῦ, καὶ ὅσους οὐ μόνον παρὰ τῆς ἱστορίας, ἀλλὰ καὶ παρὰ τῆς ἀληθείας αὐτῆς ἐφ' ἑκάστης ἰδεῖν ἔστι, μήτε δὲ "διανοῖγον" ἀφ' ἑαυτοῦ "τὴν μήτραν," ἀλλὰ τῆς παρθενίας ἤδη περιῃρημένης καὶ προηνεῳγμένης ἐξέρχεσθαι. Ποῦ δὲ θήσεις καὶ τὸ "*ἐν ἀνομίαις* συλληφθῆναι *καὶ* τὸ *ἐν ἁμαρτίαις* δὲ κισσηθῆναι," εἰ πᾶν πρωτότοκον "ἅγιον" ἐξ αὐτῆς γεννήσεως, ὅπου γε μὴ μόνον ἡ γέννησις, ἀλλὰ καὶ ἡ σύλληψις καὶ αὐτὴ δὲ τῆς σαρκὸς ἡ πρώτη κίνησις ἐναγὴς κατὰ φύσιν, εἰ καὶ ὁ νόμος δέδωκε τὴν συγχώρησιν;

47 Δῆλον οὖν ὡς ἐκεῖνο μόνον ἄρρεν τὲ καὶ πρωτότοκον ἅγιον, οὗ καὶ μὴ δίχα μόνον ἐπιθυμίας τὲ καὶ σπορᾶς, ἀλλὰ καὶ μεθ' ὅλης τῆς τοῦ Παναγίου Πνεύματος παρουσίας ἡ σύλληψις, οὗ δὲ μὴ δίχα μόνον φθορᾶς, ἀλλὰ καὶ ὅλης τῆς τοῦ Θεοῦ δυνάμεως καὶ σοφίας ἡ γέννησις. Καὶ ὃ καὶ τίκτεται μὲν ἄρσεν ἐκ τῆς προφήτιδος, οὐκ ἀνοίγεται δὲ αὐτῷ δι' ἑαυτοῦ μόνον ἡ μήτρα, ἀλλὰ καὶ πάλιν κλείεται κατὰ τὸν τῶν ἀθεάτων θεωρὸν Ἰεζεκιήλ· ὅτι "*αὕτη ἡ πύλη κεκλεισμένη καὶ οὐθεὶς οὐ μὴ διέλθῃ δι' αὐτῆς,* εἰ μὴ *Κύριος* μόνος *ὁ Θεὸς Ἰσραήλ·* αὐτὸς μόνος *εἰσελεύσεται* καὶ ἐξελεύσεται *δι' αὐτῆς καὶ ἔσται* ἡ πύλη *κεκλεισμένη.*" Οὐκοῦν ἀμφοτέρωθεν κέκλειστο καὶ μετὰ τὴν σύλληψιν καὶ μετὰ τὴν γέννησιν. Ἀλλὰ πῶς καὶ κέκλειστο καὶ ἠνέῳκτο; Κατὰ

exclude the idea of impassioned love. This is how scripture and the law are commonly understood and fulfilled, though not in truth but, as it is with many of the prophecies, or indeed I should say most of them, which are generally obscure and hard to grasp, so too is it also the case with this one. For not every firstborn male is "holy," as Cain, Reuben, and Esau bear witness, along with all those who may be observed not only in stories but also in life on a daily basis. Neither does every firstborn male "open the womb" by himself, but he only emerges after his mother's virginity has already been taken and her womb already open. And if every firstborn male is "holy" from the moment of his birth, what will you do with the words that say: "I was conceived *in transgressions, and* brought forth *in sins,*" when not only birth but also conception and the very first formation of the flesh according to nature is impure, even though the law granted it forgiveness?

From this it follows that Jesus alone is the firstborn male 47
who is holy, and his conception took place not only without sexual desire or seed, but also with the whole presence of the all-Holy Spirit, while his birth took place not only without corruption, but also with the whole power and wisdom of God. Thus, when the male child was born from the prophetess, her womb was not only opened by him for himself, but he also closed it behind himself, according to that visionary of invisible things, Ezekiel, who said: "*This gate will be closed, and no one will go forth through it,* except *the Lord God of Israel* alone. He alone *will enter in* and come out *through it, and* the gate *will be closed.*" Thus in both cases it was closed, that is, both before the conception and after the birth. But how was it both closed and open? It was closed according to the

μὲν τὴν φύσιν τῆς παρθενίας κέκλειστο, κατὰ δὲ τὴν δύναμιν τοῦ τικτομένου ἠνέῳκτο. Τίς οὖν ἄλλος ὁ μήτραν αὐτὸς καὶ διανοίξας ἑαυτῷ καὶ πάλιν κλείσας, εἰ μὴ μόνος αὐτὸς ὁ οὕτω καὶ συλλαμβανόμενος καὶ γεννώμενος; Σὺ δέ μοι σκόπει καὶ τοῦ προφητεύματος τὴν ἀκρίβειαν· οὐ γὰρ ἁπλῶς φησι *κληθήσεται, ἀλλὰ τῷ Κυρίῳ*. Ποίῳ δὲ καὶ τῶν ἄλλων παρ' αὐτῇ τῇ γεννήσει καὶ παρ' αὐτοῦ τοῦ Κυρίου τὸ ὄνομα ἢ ᾧ καὶ πρὸ τῆς γεννήσεως διὰ τοῦ ἀγγέλου μέν, παρὰ τοῦ Κυρίου δέ, οὐ τὸ τῆς ἁγιότητος μόνον, ἀλλὰ καὶ τὸ τῆς υἱότητος; Διὸ καὶ τὸ γεννώμενον *ἅγιον κληθήσεται* Υἱὸς Θεοῦ. Εἰ δὲ κοινῶς καὶ καθολικῶς ὅτι *πᾶν ἄρσεν*, οὐδὲ τοῦτο κενῶς, ἀλλ' ἵν' ἐν τῷ κοινῷ λάθῃ καὶ τὸ κατ' αὐτόν· μυστήριον γὰρ καὶ ἄλλως πάντων πλέον ἀπόκρυφον.

48 Ἀλλὰ μικρόν τι κἀνταῦθα προσδιατρίψωμεν, οὐ διὰ τὸν γλυκὺν Ἰησοῦν μόνον—οὗ τί μὲν ἡδύτερον καὶ λέγειν τὲ καὶ ἀκούειν, τί δὲ καὶ ὠφελιμώτερον;—ἀλλὰ καὶ τὴν τούτου μητέρα. Ποίας μὲν δέχεται καὶ παρὰ τοῦ Συμεὼν τὰς ἐπαγγελίας, οἵας δὲ καὶ τῶν μελλόντων αὐτῇ πειρασμῶν παρ' αὐτοῦ τὰς προαγορεύσεις; Ὃς ἔρχεται μὲν ἐν Πνεύματι, τῷ Ἁγίῳ δῆλον, πρὸς τὸ ἱερὸν δίκαιος ὤν, οὐ δυναμούμενος ἀθρόον ὑπὲρ ἡλικίαν καὶ φύσιν μόνον, ὡς πόρρω τῶν ἀνθρωπίνων ὅρων τῆς ἐνταῦθα ζωῆς ὤν, ἀλλὰ καὶ κινούμενος τὸν κεχρηματισμένον ἰδεῖν, καὶ λαβεῖν μὲν ἐν ἀγκάλαις καὶ ἀποδοῦναι τὴν εὐλογίαν, ἀπολαβεῖν δὲ παρ' αὐτοῦ τὴν ἐλευθερίαν. Διπλοῦς δὲ καὶ οὗτος ὁ Συμεὼν τύπος καὶ τῷ θεανθρώπῳ θεάνθρωπος. Ἢ μὲν γὰρ *Παλαιὸς Ἡμερῶν* καὶ ἐν ἀγκάλαις ὑπολαμβάνων καὶ εὐλογῶν

nature of virginity but opened according to the power of the one born. Who else is there, then, who opened for himself his mother's womb and then closed it again, if not the very one who was conceived and born in this way? Consider with me the precision of the prophecy, for it does not simply say, *he will be called,* but rather *by the Lord.* About whom else was it said that he received his name from his birth, and from the Lord himself except the one who had not only his holiness but also his sonship proclaimed by God through an angel even before he was born? Therefore the one who is born *holy will be called* the Son of God. For even if it was said generally and universally that *every male* would be called holy, this was not without a deeper purpose, but so that the particular things concerning Jesus would be concealed in the generality, for this mystery is truly more hidden than all the others.

But here let us briefly turn our attention, not only to 48
sweet Jesus—though what could be more pleasant to speak about or hear, or indeed be more beneficial?—but also to his mother. What sort of promises did she receive from Symeon, and what were the prophecies of her future trials that he pronounced? For he was a righteous man, and entered the temple inspired by the Spirit, clearly the Holy Spirit, not only because he was suddenly strengthened beyond his years and nature, since he was far beyond the limits of an ordinary human lifespan, but also because he was moved to see the promised child, and to receive him into his embrace and bless him, receiving from him his freedom in return. Symeon is thus a double figure, for he was a man like God for the God made man. For in truth he was an *Ancient of Days,* holding in his arms the Son, who is contained in the

τοῦ παλαιοῦ καὶ ἀχρόνου καὶ ἀϊδίου Πατρὸς καὶ ἐν κόλποις ἀεὶ κατέχοντος τὸν Υἱὸν καὶ εὐλογοῦντος αὐτὸν ἐρχόμενον, ἣ δὲ καὶ παρειμένος καὶ νῦν ῥωννύμενος καὶ κινούμενος, ἀλλὰ καὶ ἀγκαλιζόμενος ὁμοῦ καὶ τῆς τῆδε ζωῆς καὶ μοχθηρίας ἀπολυόμενος, τῆς γεγηρακυίας ἡμῶν ἤδη καὶ παρειμένης φύσεως, καὶ λαμβανούσης μὲν ἐν ἀγκάλαις τὸν ἐλευθερωτὴν ἢ λυτρωτήν, ἀπολυομένης δὲ τῆς παλαιᾶς σαρκικῆς τῶν παθῶν ἢ καὶ τυραννικῆς τῶν δαιμόνων δουλείας τὲ καὶ λατρείας, ἀλλὰ καὶ Πνεύματος Ἁγίου γεμιζομένης.

49 Δι᾽ ὧν κἀκεῖνος ὑπὸ τοῦ αὐτοῦ κινούμενος Πνεύματος, ἅμα δὲ καὶ αὐτοῦ τοῦ ἀγκαλισθέντος ὅλος τῆς θεοφορίας γενόμενος, πρῶτον μὲν ἀποδίδωσι τῷ Θεῷ τὴν εὐχαριστίαν ἅμα καὶ προφητείαν, ὅτι τὲ τοῦ σώματος ἀπολύεται καὶ τοῖς ὀφθαλμοῖς ἐθεάσατο, ὡς πρότερον δῆλον ὁρῶν καὶ τοῖς λογισμοῖς, *τὸ σωτήριον,* Ἰησοῦν, τὸ αὐτὸ καὶ πρᾶγμα καὶ ὄνομα, ὅπερ καὶ ἡτοίμαστο μὲν ἐξ ἀρχῆς καὶ πρὸ τῶν αἰώνων, κατακέκρυπτο δὲ καθὰ καὶ μυστήριον. Καὶ ἡτοίμαστο *κατὰ πρόσωπον* οὐχὶ τοῦ Ἰουδαϊκοῦ μόνον, ἀλλὰ καὶ *πάντων* ὁμοῦ *τῶν λαῶν.* Ἀλλὰ καὶ *φῶς* μὲν *εἰς ἀποκάλυψιν Ἐθνῶν, δόξαν* δὲ *λαοῦ σου Ἰσραὴλ* ἢ καὶ ὅτι τοῖς μὲν ἐν σκότει τῆς ἀγνοίας αὐτὸς μὲν ἦν ὁ ἀποκαλύπτων, αὐτὸς δὲ ὁ ἀποκαλυπτόμενος, ὡς αὐτὸς μὲν ὢν φῶς, αὐτὸς δὲ καὶ Θεός, καὶ αὐτὸς μὲν ὁρᾶν ποιῶν, αὐτὸς δὲ καὶ ὁρώμενος, ἐκείνοις δὲ τοῖς ὑπὸ νόμον τὲ καὶ θεογνωσίαν (διὸ καὶ ἐνδιαθέτως *λαοῦ σου δόξα*), τοῖς γε βουλομένοις, οὐχ ὡς ὑπ᾽ αὐτῶν λατρευόμενος μόνον, ἀλλὰ καὶ ὡς ἐξ αὐτῶν

bosom of the ancient, timeless, and eternal Father, who also blesses him as he comes into the world. Even though he was weak, he was now invigorated and divinely inspired, and at the same time that he was embracing the child, he was being set free from the toil of this earthly life, from our already aged and weak nature, which received in its embrace the liberator or rather redeemer, being freed from its ancient carnal bondage to the passions and the tyrannical enslavement to and worship of demons, but being filled with the Holy Spirit.

For these reasons, being moved by the Spirit itself, and at 49
the same time being wholly caught up in the inspiration of the one whom he bore in his embrace, Symeon first offered thanks to God along with a prophecy, for he was being released from his body and was seeing with his eyes what he had previously seen only in his thoughts, namely, his *salvation,* Jesus, who is salvation in both deed and name, a name which had been prepared from the very beginning and before all the ages, but until now had remained a hidden mystery. And this salvation was not prepared only *before the face* of the Jewish people, but also at the same time for *all peoples.* And, on the one hand, as a *light unto the revelation of the Gentiles,* but on the other, *unto the glory of your people Israel.* To the former, who were in the darkness of ignorance, he was both the revealer and the one revealed, for he himself is light, and he himself is God, just as he is the creator of sight and the one who is seen. But to the latter, those under the law, who wish for the knowledge of God (and thus innately for *the glory of your people*), he is not only someone they worshipped, but someone who arose from among them. And thus even

καταγόμενος. Οὕτως ὑπὲρ αὐτῶν καὶ Παῦλος ἐγκαλλωπίζεται, *ἐξ ὧν Χριστὸς τὸ κατὰ σάρκα,* εἰ καὶ ἄλλως ἀλληγορικώτερον· Ἔθνη μὲν οἱ ψευδεῖς περὶ τῶν ὄντων τὲ καὶ τοῦ Ὄντος ἢ ἐμπαθεῖς καὶ τῇ σαρκὶ λατρεύοντες λογισμοί, διὸ καὶ κατὰ πλῆθος, οἷα δὴ καὶ περὶ πολλὰς καὶ διαφόρους ἢ καὶ ἐναντίας ἀλλήλων σχιζόμενοι πλάνας καὶ φαντασίας. Ἰσραὴλ δὲ ὁ καθαρὸς καὶ διορατικὸς πάντων ἢ καὶ Θεοῦ αὐτοῦ καὶ τῶν θείων μόνων ἐπιθυμητικὸς νοῦς, διὸ καὶ εἷς ὡς ἀληθὴς καὶ περὶ τῶν αὐτῶν ὁ αὐτός, εἰ καὶ αὐτὸς ἑαυτοῦ πῇ μὲν κρείττων, πῇ δὲ καὶ ταπεινότερος κατὰ τὴν ἀναλογίαν τῆς καθάρσεως ἢ ἐλλάμψεως. Ἀμφοτέροις οὖν ὁ Χριστός, τοῖς μὲν φῶς ὡς ἐκ σκότους καὶ τῆς ἀγνοίας τῆς ἀληθείας νῦν ἀποκάλυψις, τοῖς δὲ δόξα ὡς καὶ ἀνάβασις καὶ προσθήκη τῆς θεωρίας τὲ καὶ θεώσεως. Τί δὲ καὶ τὸ *λαοῦ σου* (μηδὲ γὰρ τοῦτο παραλειπτέον τοῖς φιλεξεταστικωτέροις τὲ καὶ φιλοθεώροις) ἢ ὅτι κἂν εἷς καὶ πρὸς ἓν διὰ τὸ ἐξ ἑνὸς σκοποῦ καὶ πρὸς ἓν τείνειν πέρας, ἀλλὰ καὶ οὗτος ποικίλος τὲ καὶ πολύχους ταῖς κατὰ μέρος διαφοραῖς, ὥστε τὸ μὲν σύστημα καὶ τὸ γένος ἕν, ἀφ᾽ οὗπερ ἤρξατο καὶ πρὸς ὅπερ ἀνάγεται, τὰ δὲ κατὰ μέρος πολλά τε καὶ ἄπειρα; Διὰ τοῦτο "λαοὶ" μὲν ἐκεῖνοι, οὗτος δὲ καὶ "εἷς" καὶ "λαός." Ἀλλὰ ταῦτα μὲν οὕτω τῷ πρεσβύτῃ πεπροφήτευταί τε ὁμοῦ καὶ πεφιλοσόφηται.

Τί δὲ καὶ τὰ ἐπὶ τούτοις; Θαυμάζουσι μὲν καὶ ἀμφότεροι, σὺ δὲ ὅρα πῶς οὐδὲν ἧττον θαυμασίως καὶ ὁ εὐαγγελιστὴς νῦν πρῶτον ἀποδιϊστᾷ τὸν Ἰωσὴφ τῆς Παρθένου

Paul boasted on their behalf, saying: *from them, by physical ancestry, came Christ.* To take this more allegorically, we could say the following: the Gentiles are the false thoughts concerning things that exist and the One who exists, or impassioned thoughts worshipping the flesh, which is why they are referred to in the plural, since they are differentiated into a multiplicity of divided and mutually opposed delusions and fantasies. Israel, on the other hand, is the pure mind that sees all things clearly, and which desires God and divine realities alone, and thus is one because it is true and remains itself in relation to all things, even though at times it appears either superior or inferior to itself, relative to the degree of its purification or illumination. Yet Christ exists for both: to the Gentiles he is like light in the darkness, and now the revelation of their ignorance of the truth; but to Israel he is the glory, as well as the elevation and increase of contemplation and deification. And what is the meaning of the words *your people* (since this question must not be passed over by lovers of rigorous examination and contemplation)? What else could it mean except that, even though Israel is one, and is turned toward the one, and has one aim and reaches out toward one end, it is nonetheless manifold and diverse in its particular differences, so that it is one according to the composition and genus from which it began and to which it reverts, but the particulars are many and infinite? For this reason, the Gentiles are "peoples," but Israel is both "one" and "a people." This is how the elder's words are understood as prophecy and philosophy.

What happened after these things? Both Joseph and 50
Mary were filled with wonder, but observe how no less wondrously the evangelist for the first time separates Joseph

μετὰ τὴν Γέννησιν καὶ τὴν λύσιν τῆς ὑποψίας καὶ τὴν πληροφορίαν τοῦ θεῖον εἶναι τὸ γέννημα. *Ἰωσήφ*, φησί, *καὶ ἡ μήτηρ αὐτοῦ*, τὸν μὲν ἁπλῶς καλέσας ἐκ τοῦ ὀνόματος, ἅτε μήτε τοῦ παιδὸς πατέρα μήτε δὲ τῆς τοῦ παιδὸς μητρὸς ἄνδρα, τὴν δὲ κεχωρισμένως καὶ ἀπὸ μόνης μᾶλλον τῆς πρὸς αὐτὸν σχέσεως, "*καὶ ἡ μήτηρ αὐτοῦ*·" ᾧ καὶ Συμεὼν ὡσπερεὶ κατακολουθῶν καὶ ὁρῶν, οἷα καὶ πρὸ τῶν ἄλλων ἀποκαλυφθεὶς τὸ μυστήριον, *εὐλογεῖ μὲν καὶ ἀμφοτέρους*, οἷα καὶ τὸν Ἰωσὴφ εἰδὼς οὐ δίκαιον μόνον, ἀλλὰ καὶ ὑπουργὸν τὰ πολλὰ τούτου τοῦ μυστηρίου, πρὸς δὲ τὴν Μαρίαν ὅλον συμπεραίνει τὸν λόγον ὡς καὶ μόνην αὐτουργὸν τοῦ τηλικούτου θαύματος καὶ γεννήματος. Τίνα δὲ καὶ τὰ προφητεύματα; *Ἰδοὺ οὗτος κεῖται εἰς πτῶσιν καὶ ἀνάστασιν πολλῶν ἐν τῷ Ἰσραήλ.*

51 Ὅρα μοι τὴν ἀκρίβειαν τῆς διαφορᾶς· ἡ μὲν ἑτοιμασία τοῦ σωτηρίου *κατὰ πρόσωπον πάντων τῶν λαῶν*, ἡ δὲ *πτῶσις καὶ ἡ ἀνάστασις πολλῶν* καὶ μάλιστα *ἐν τῷ Ἰσραήλ*· ἡ μὲν γὰρ θεία βούλησις, ἡ πάντων σωτηρία καὶ θέωσις, ἡ δὲ πτῶσις καὶ ἡ ἀνάστασις ἐν τῇ τῶν πολλῶν γνώμῃ, πιστευόντων τὲ καὶ μὴ πιστευόντων. Ἀλλὰ τὸ μὲν τοὺς κειμένους, ὅπερ ἐστὶ τοὺς ἀπίστους, ἀνίστασθαι, κατὰ λόγον—πῶς δ' ἂν καὶ οἱ κείμενοι πέσοιεν;—ἢ πάντως ὅτι τὸ βαθύτερον αὐτοῖς τοῦ πτώματος ὑπαινίσσεται, ὡς οὐχ ὁμοίως κολασθησομένους πρὸ τῆς οἰκονομίας καὶ μετὰ τὴν οἰκονομίαν τὲ καὶ τὸ κήρυγμα. Τοῦτο γὰρ αὐτὸ βούλεται καὶ *τὸ κηρυχθῆναι τὸ Εὐαγγέλιον εἰς* μαρτύριον πᾶσι τοῖς Ἔθνεσιν, ὅ ἐστιν εἰς ἔλεγχον, εἰς κατάκρισιν, ὥστε

from the Virgin after the Nativity and the resolution of his doubts, and after his assurance that the child was indeed divine. This is why he first says *Joseph,* and then, *and* his *mother.* He identifies Joseph simply by name, since he was neither the child's father nor the husband of the child's mother; but he refers separately to the Virgin and without mentioning her relationship with Joseph, saying, "*and* his *mother.*" Symeon, as if he had been following and observing this, because the mystery had been revealed to him before the others, *blessed them both,* for he knew that Joseph was not only a righteous man but also a servant assisting in many things pertaining to the mystery. But it was to Mary that he addressed all his words, since she acted in her own right in the accomplishment of this great and miraculous birth. What, then, were the things he prophesied? *Behold, this child is appointed for the fall and rising of many in Israel.*

Observe with me the precision of the distinction here. 51
On the one hand, we have the preparation of salvation *before the face of all the peoples,* but on the other the *fall and rising of many,* especially *in Israel.* The former is the divine purpose, namely, the salvation and deification of all, while the falling and rising, in the opinion of most people, affects believers and unbelievers alike. But those who have already been laid low, by which I mean the unbelievers, will, in a manner of speaking, be raised—for how could those who are already laid low fall down?—but surely here the deeper sense of their fall is being hinted at, since they will not be punished in the same way after the incarnation and the proclamation of the Gospel as before the coming of Christ. For the same meaning is also intended by the phrase, *preaching the Gospel* as a testimony to all the Gentiles, namely, for reproof and

πλείονα μετὰ τὴν διαμαρτυρίαν τὴν καταδίκην δέξασθαι, ἐξαιρέτως δὲ τοῖς ἐξ Ἰσραήλ, ὡς οὐκ ἀρκέσον αὐτοῖς τὸ ἐπὶ τῶν αὐτῶν ἑστάναι μὴ δεχομένοις μηδὲ πιστεύουσιν, ἀλλ' ἀνάγκη καὶ τῶν προτέρων ἐκπεσεῖν καὶ δίκας ὑποσχεῖν πάντων τῶν Ἐθνῶν χείρους, ὅτι τὲ τὸν πάλαι παρ' αὐτοῖς προφητευόμενόν τε καὶ λατρευόμενον καὶ τὸν ἐξ αὐτῶν γεννώμενον οὐκ ἐδέξαντο καὶ ὅτι καὶ τὸν δίκαιον, μᾶλλον δὲ τὸν εὐεργέτην, ὡς κατάδικον ἐλογίσαντο καὶ κακοῦργον, καὶ μετὰ τῆς ἀπιστίας αὐτοὶ μόνοι καὶ τὴν θεοκτονίαν ἐτόλμησαν. Διὸ καὶ ἰδιαζόντως ἀπειλεῖται τούτοις ἡ πτῶσις, ὡς οὐ κἀκεῖθεν μόνον, ἀλλὰ καὶ ἐντεῦθεν τῆς τε πόλεως ἡ κατασκαφὴ καὶ τῶν ἐνοικούντων ὁ ἀνδραποδισμός τε καὶ ἡ σφαγὴ καὶ τῆς πολιτείας καὶ πάσης ἄλλης ἐλευθερίας καὶ παρρησίας ἡ διὰ τέλους ἔκπτωσις. Ἀλλὰ καὶ ἡ ἀνάστασις τοῖς πιστεύουσι τῇ μὲν ὡς κειμένοις ὑπὸ τὸν νόμον καὶ ἐλευθερουμένοις αὐτοῦ τῆς δουλείας καὶ τῆς βαρύτητος, τῇ δὲ καὶ ὡς συνθαπτομένοις μὲν τῷ Χριστῷ, συνανισταμένοις δέ, καὶ συμπάσχουσι μὲν καὶ συνδιωκομένοις, συνδοξαζομένοις δέ.

52 Οὐκ ἄχαρι δὲ καὶ τὸ *εἰς πτῶσιν καὶ ἀνάστασιν,* ὥς τισιν ἔδοξεν, οὐκ ἄλλων καὶ ἄλλων, ἀλλὰ τῶν αὐτῶν καὶ πιπτόντων μὲν καὶ ἀνισταμένων· πιπτόντων μὲν κατὰ τὸ χεῖρον, ἀνισταμένων δὲ κατὰ τὸ βέλτιον· τὸ μὲν κατὰ τὴν ἀπιστίαν ἢ ἀλογίαν, τὸ δὲ κατὰ τὴν πίστιν καὶ τὸν ἐν ἡμῖν διεγειρόμενόν τε ὁμοῦ καὶ διεγείροντα λόγον, καθὼς καὶ Παῦλος ἀσθενεῖ τὲ ὁμοῦ καὶ δύναται, τὸ μὲν τῷ σώματι, τὸ δὲ τῷ πνεύματι. Καὶ τὸ θαυμαστότερον, ὅτι καὶ δι'

condemnation, so that after the testimony they would be subject to an even greater sentence, especially those from Israel. This is because it was not right that they remain in the same situation after they did not accept or believe him, but rather that they should be worse off than they were before and suffer worse punishments than all the Gentiles, since they did not accept him who of old was proclaimed to them and worshipped, and who was born in their midst, but to the contrary they condemned the righteous one, or rather their benefactor, as a convicted criminal and an evildoer, and together with their unbelief they alone dared to become killers of God. This is why the threat of falling is directed to them in particular, and not just then, but afterward the destruction of their city, the enslavement and slaughter of its residents, and in the end their exclusion from citizenship, liberty, and freedom of speech. But the faithful will rise, on the one hand, from having been laid low by the law, being freed from its slavery and weight, and, on the other, insofar as they have been buried with Christ, being resurrected with him, and, having suffered and experienced persecution for his sake, likewise being glorified with him.

Thus there is nothing disagreeable, as some people think, 52
in the words, *for the fall and rising,* since it does not refer to the fall of some and the rising of others, but rather the falling and the rising of the same individuals, who fall because of what is evil or rise because of what is better. The former is on account of disbelief or irrational thinking, the latter is on account of faith as well as our power of reason when it awakens within us and awakens us, just as Paul is both weak and strong, being weak in body but strong in spirit. And what is more marvelous is that he is strong through his weakness,

αὐτοῦ τοῦ ἀσθενεῖν δύναται, καθάπερ ἐπὶ πλάστιγγος καὶ ἀμφοῖν ἀντιταλαντευομένων ἀλλήλοις. Οὕτω γοῦν καὶ ἡ κατὰ Χριστὸν δύναμις δι' αὐτοῦ τοῦ πίπτειν καὶ τὸ ἀνίστασθαι περιποιουμένη τοῖς πολλοῖς, δηλαδὴ τοῖς πιστεύουσιν, ἀλλὰ πίπτειν μὲν ἐκ τῆς προτέρας στάσεως τῆς κατὰ τὴν ἁμαρτίαν, ἀνίστασθαι δὲ ἐκ τῆς προτέρας πτώσεως τῆς κατὰ τὴν δικαιοσύνην. *Καὶ εἰς σημεῖον ἀντιλεγόμενον,* τὸν σταυρόν· μίγνυσι γὰρ τῇ δόξῃ καὶ τὸν ὀνειδισμὸν καὶ δείκνυσι δι' οὗ καὶ ἡ δόξα. Τοῦτο γὰρ ἡμῖν τοῖς ἀπὸ Χριστοῦ τὸ σημεῖον, τὸ γνώρισμα, ἡ σφραγίς. *Ἀντιλεγόμενον* δὲ ὡς τοῖς μὲν πρὸς τὸ χεῖρον, τοῖς δὲ πρὸς τὸ κρεῖττον ἐκλαμβανόμενον, καὶ τοῖς μὲν γελώμενον, μᾶλλον δὲ καὶ μισούμενον, τοῖς δὲ καὶ λίαν τιμώμενον. Τυχὸν δὲ καὶ αὐτὸν τὸν Χριστὸν *σημεῖον,* ὡς ὑπὲρ φύσιν καὶ τῶν σημείων δημιουργόν, *ἀντιλεγόμενον* δὲ διὰ τὸ τοῖς μὲν ἐκ τοῦ Ἐναντίου, τοῖς δὲ τοῦ ἐν αὐτῷ καὶ Ἁγίου Πνεύματος ἐκτελεῖσθαι λέγεσθαι τὰ τεράστια, ἢ καὶ ὅτι πολλὰ τὰ περὶ τοῦ Χριστοῦ ζυγομαχούμενα τοῖς πολλοῖς, κατ' αὐτόν τε ἐκεῖνον καὶ ὕστερον μᾶλλον ἐπιφυόμενα τοῦ πονηροῦ γεωργοῦ σπέρματα ἢ καὶ *ζιζάνια.* Οἱ μὲν γὰρ αὐτοῦ τὴν ἐπιδημίαν ἀσώματον, οἱ δὲ φαντασίαν τινὰ σώματος, οἱ δὲ καὶ σῶμα μέν, ἄλογον δὲ καὶ ἄνουν ἀνοήτως λίαν καὶ ἀλογίστως, οἱ δὲ καὶ ταῦτα μέν, οὐράνιον δὲ σῶμα καὶ ὡς διὰ σωλῆνος καὶ ὅτι τέλειον ἐξ ἀρχῆς τὸ κυοφορούμενον καὶ τοιαῦτά τινα τοῖς ὀρθῶς λεγομένοις καὶ πεπραγμένοις καὶ ἀντιλέγοντες οὐκ ἐπαύσαντο. Εἴτε γοῦν διὰ ταῦτα εἴτε καὶ δι' ἐκεῖνα εἰς *σημεῖον ἀντιλεγόμενον.* Ταῦτα δὲ πάντως περὶ

like a scale on which each side balances the other. In the same way, the power of Christ through this falling brings about a rising for many, that is, the faithful, who fall from their former state on account of sin, but rise from their former fall on account of righteousness. *And a sign that is disputed,* which is the cross, for it mingles reproach with glory and through itself reveals glory. For to us who believe in Christ, the cross is the sign, the token, and the seal. It is *disputed* because some have taken it in a worse sense and others in a better; among the former it is an object of ridicule, or rather of hatred, but among the latter an object held in great honor. And perhaps Christ himself is the *sign,* since in a manner beyond nature he is the creator of signs; and he is a *sign that is disputed* by those who are opposed to him, because some believe that he worked these great signs through the Opponent, while others believe that he worked them through the Holy Spirit working within him; or perhaps also because the many things about Christ that have been disputed by many people, both during his own lifetime and even more so afterward, were the seeds or rather the *weeds* grown by the wicked farmer. For some said his coming into the world took place without a body, while others said his body was illusory, and others again that if he had a human body it was without human reason or mind, as they so irrationally and mindlessly argued. Others also said he had a celestial body claiming that he passed through the Virgin as if through a tube, and that from the beginning the child in her womb was fully formed, and they did not stop propounding such ideas in response to those who spoke and acted correctly. So, either on account of these or the other things he is *a sign that is disputed.* These things were clearly said about

τοῦ υἱοῦ μέν, κοινὰ δὲ ὅμως καὶ πρὸς τὴν αὐτοῦ μητέρα τὰ προφητεύματα, πάντα τὰ τοῦ παιδός ἑαυτῆς ποιουμένην, ἐν ᾧ καὶ συνεκινδύνευε καὶ συνεδοξάζετο.

53 Ὅρα δὲ ὅπως οὐ τὰ χρηστότερα ταύτῃ μόνα προσαγορεύεται, ἀλλὰ καὶ τὰ σκυθρωπώτερα, ἵν' αὐτὸ τοῦτο μᾶλλον ἀσφαλεστέραν ἐργάσηται τὴν Παρθένον οὐκ ἀπαράσκευον οὖσαν, καὶ ὅπως οὐ τἄλλα μόνον τὰ περὶ τὸ τοῦ ταύτης υἱοῦ πάθος, ἀλλὰ καὶ αὐτὸ τοῦτο τὸ ἑαυτῆς περὶ αὐτὸ προειδῇ πάθος, ὥστε καὶ ἐν ᾧ παθαίνεται, αὐτῷ τούτῳ τῆς περὶ αὐτὴν προφητείας ἀναμιμνήσκεσθαι καὶ παραμυθίαν τοῦ πάθους δέχεσθαι. *Καὶ σοῦ δὲ αὐτῆς* κατ' ἐξοχὴν ὁ λόγος· οὐ γὰρ τῶν ἄλλων μόνον, φησί, παρὰ τὸν καιρὸν τοῦ Πάθους ἅψεταί τις δισταγμός, διακριτικὸς λογισμὸς καὶ σάλος—καὶ ὡς ὁ Δεσποτικός φησι λόγος, πάντες σκανδαλισθήσονται—ἀλλὰ *καὶ σοῦ αὐτῆς,* τῆς οὕτω βεβηκυίας καὶ σταθηρᾶς ἢ τῆς τοσαύτην πληροφορίαν ἔκ τε τῶν περὶ σὲ μυστηρίων ἔκ τε τῶν περὶ τὸν σὸν υἱὸν καὶ παρ' αὐτοῦ τοῦ σοῦ υἱοῦ θαυμασίων λαβούσης τοῦ Θεὸν εἶναι καὶ Θεοῦ Υἱόν, *τὴν ψυχὴν διελεύσεται ῥομφαία,* μερισμός, ἀμφιβολία τῶν λογισμῶν, διάκρισις, ὅπως τὲ καὶ Θεός ἐστι καὶ θνητός, καὶ ἀπαθὴς καὶ τοσαῦτα πάσχων, ἢ καὶ εἰ τοσαῦτα πάσχων ὄντως ἐστὶ Θεός, ἢ καὶ εἰ αὐτοῦ τοῦ θανάτου κρείττων ἔσται, καθάπερ καὶ τῶν λοιπῶν. Ἡ *ῥομφαία* καὶ αὐτὸ τὸ περιὸν τῆς ὀδύνης καὶ ἀκμαιότατον καὶ ὀξύτατον, ἥτις αὐτῆς τὴν ψυχὴν διῆλθε κατὰ τὸν καιρὸν τοῦ Πάθους, εἰ καὶ μὴ τὴν ἀνάστασιν ἀπεγίνωσκε, μονονουχὶ λέγων ὅτι διχοτομήσει σοῦ τὴν ψυχὴν ἡ περὶ τὸν υἱὸν περιωδυνία, *ὅπως ἂν ἀποκαλυφθῶσιν ἐκ πολλῶν*

the son, but the prophecies nevertheless also speak of his mother, who was taking care of everything regarding her child, with whom she was also both subject to danger and glorified.

See how Symeon speaks to her not only of the more joy- 53
ous things but also of the more sorrowful. He did this so that the Virgin would be more steadfast, though she was not unprepared for what was to come, and so that she might know in advance not only about the suffering of her son but also about her own suffering, so that when these things befell her she would remember this from the prophecy about her and find consolation for her suffering. But his most significant words to her are *you yourself,* for at the time of the Passion, he says, not only will others be assailed by doubt, divisive thoughts, and confusion—just as the Lord said, you will all fall away—but also *you yourself.* Even though at present you are confident and composed because you have been assured from the mysteries concerning you and your son, and from the marvels concerning and occasioned by him, that he is God and the Son of God, nevertheless *a sword shall pierce your soul,* that is, division, uncertainty in your thoughts, and doubt, when you see that he is both God and mortal man, both free from suffering and suffering so greatly; and you will wonder whether one who is suffering so greatly can truly be God, and if he will be superior to his own death, as he also was about other things. The *sword* is the extreme and most severe and acute experience of pain that pierced her soul at the time of the Passion, for even if she did not abandon hope in the resurrection, Symeon is all but saying that the intolerable pain concerning your son will cut your soul in two, *so that thoughts from many hearts may be revealed.* That

καρδιῶν διαλογισμοὶ πρὸς πάντα τὰ προειρημένα καθολικῶς, ἀλλ' οὐκ αἰτιολογικῶς οὐδὲ μερικῶς πρὸς μόνα τὰ πρὸς τὴν Παρθένον ἔναγχος εἰρημένα, ὅτι τούτων πάντων οὕτω συμβαινόντων τῶν οὕτω περιπαθῶν καὶ ἐκπληκτικῶν καὶ σοὶ δὲ λίαν ὀδυνηρῶν καὶ *πολλῶν καρδιῶν* ἀποκαλυφθήσονται *διαλογισμοί,* καὶ ἀποβατικῶς, ἀλλ' οὐκ αἰτιολογικῶς. Ὁ μὲν γὰρ σταυρὸς καὶ τἄλλα τῶν Παθημάτων δι' ἄλλα, συμβέβηκε δὲ ὅμως πολλοῖς καὶ ἡ τῶν ἐν αὐτοῖς λογισμῶν ἀποκάλυψις οἵαν εἶχον περὶ τὸν Χριστὸν καὶ τὴν σχέσιν τὲ καὶ τὴν δόξαν. Οἱ μὲν γὰρ φανερῶς καὶ ἐπέχαιρον καὶ ἐτώθαζον, οὐ τῶν φανερῶς ἐχθρῶν μόνον, ἀλλὰ πολλοὶ καὶ τῶν προτοῦ φιλίαν ὑποκρινομένων καὶ νῦν διὰ τὸν καιρὸν τὰ τῆς γνώμης ἀνακαλυπτομένων, οἱ δὲ ὡς εἰκὸς ἐσκυθρώπαζον καὶ συνέπασχον. Καὶ οἱ μὲν καὶ ἐπὶ σταυροῦ Θεὸν ὡμολόγουν, ὥσπερ οὐκ ἄλλοι μόνον, ἀλλὰ καὶ αὐτὸς ὁ συσταυρωθείς, οἱ δὲ οὐδ' οὕτω τὴν ἔχθραν καὶ τὰς συκοφαντίας κατέλυον, ἀλλὰ καὶ πλάνον καὶ κακοῦργον ἐκάλουν. Ἢ καὶ ἐλλειπτικῶς, ὅπως ἂν κατὰ τὸν καιρὸν τοῦ Πάθους *ἀποκαλυφθῶσιν ἐκ πολλῶν καρδιῶν διαλογισμοὶ* καὶ διορθωθῶσιν διὰ τῆς ἀναστάσεως· ταχεῖα γὰρ αὐτοῖς μετὰ τὸν σκανδαλισμὸν ἡ βεβαίωσις, εἰ μὴ καὶ αὐτὸ τοῦτο τὴν ἀποκάλυψιν καθ' αὑτὸ φωτισμόν τις ἡγεῖται κατὰ τὸ εἰωθὸς τῆς γραφῆς.

54 Ἀλλ' ἡμῖν γε τῆς ἀκολουθίας καὶ πάλιν ἑκτέον. Οὕτω μὲν Ἰωσὴφ μετὰ τὸν καθαρισμὸν δέχεται τὸν χρησμὸν καὶ τὴν *εἰς Αἴγυπτον* φυγαδείαν αὐτὸς οἰκονομῶν, αὐτὸς καὶ ἀνέχεται ὁ πάντα πληρῶν Ἰησοῦς συνάμα τῇ μητρὶ καὶ τῷ

is, revealed generally with respect to all the things that were said, but not causally nor specifically with respect to what was just now said about the Virgin, because when the *thoughts* about all these events, which were so heartrending and astonishing, and which caused you such great pain were revealed *out of many hearts,* it came about consequentially but not causally. In other words, the cross and the other events of the Passion took place for other reasons, but at the same time they also happened to reveal the thoughts many people had concerning Christ, his relationship to God and man and his glory. For some openly gloated and mocked him, and not only those who had openly been his enemies, but also many who had formerly pretended to be his friends, whose attitude was now revealed at this critical moment, while others, as was only natural, lamented and suffered together with him. Some confessed him to be God even while he was on the cross, and not simply others but even the thief who was crucified with him, but others even then did not cease from their enmity and slanders, calling him a deceiver and a criminal. Or else these things took place elliptically, so that during the time of the Passion, *thoughts might be revealed from many hearts* and might be corrected by the resurrection, for not long after the scandal of the cross they received confirmation, unless one considers this very fact, namely, that the revelation is itself the illumination, as is customary with scripture.

But now we must return to the sequence of the narrative. 54
When Joseph received the oracle after the purification, it was Jesus, who fills all things, who arranged the flight *into Egypt,* and who endured this trial together with his mother and presumptive father, but it was Herod who unleashed

δοκοῦντι πατρί, τὴν δὲ μιαιφονίαν Ἡρώδης ἐτέλει. Ἔμελλε δὲ ἄρα πάντως καὶ Ἰωάννης ὁ μέγας—ὁ πρὸ τοῦ φωτὸς ἐκ γαστρὸς ἔτι καὶ ἐν γαστρὶ τὸ Φῶς ὁρῶν, ὁ πρὸ τοῦ τόκου σκιρτῶν, ὁ πρὸ τῆς φωνῆς κῆρυξ, ὁ πρὸ τοῦ λόγου τοῦ Λόγου μάρτυς—κἀνταῦθα καὶ προτυθῆναι καὶ προδραμεῖν τοῦ καινοῦ καὶ πρώτου καὶ μεγάλου θύματος μετὰ τῶν ἡλικιωτῶν, μετὰ τῶν συναθλητῶν. Τό τε γὰρ γένος καὶ τὸν τόκον καὶ αὐτὸς Βηθλεεμίτης καὶ τὸν χρόνον ὀλίγῳ προήκων ἦν. Ἐν γὰρ τοῖς ἀμφιβόλοις καὶ τοὺς ὑπὲρ τὴν διετίαν ἀνῄρουν προτιμῶντες τοῦ φιλανθρωποτέρου τὸ ἀσφαλέστερον καὶ κρεῖττον ἡγούμενοι τὸ καί τινας τῶν ἐκτὸς τοῦ χρόνου περιλαβεῖν ἢ καί τινα παραλιπεῖν τῶν ἐντός. Οὕτως ἐφιλοτιμοῦντο ταῖς μιαιφονίαις οἱ δείλαιοι. Θεὸς δὲ ἦν ἄρα ὁ καὶ τούτου φύλαξ, αὐτὸς ὁ ζητούμενος καὶ φυγαδευόμενος, ὥστε μὴ τὰ γενέθλια μόνον ἔχειν αὐτοῦ τηλικούτους ἀθλητάς τε καὶ σφάγια, ἀλλὰ καὶ τὰ πολιτεύματα μάρτυράς τε καὶ κήρυκας, καὶ τὰ ἐπ' ἐσχάτων δὲ ἐπιτάφια προθύματα καὶ μέχρις Ἅιδου τὰ προοδοποιήματα. Οὗτος καὶ τὴν Ἐλισάβετ καὶ τὸν υἱὸν ἐκ μέσων αὐτῶν ἀναρπάζει τῶν φόνων, ἔνθεν καὶ διωκομένη πρὸς τὴν ἔρημον ὑπεξέρχεται καὶ ὑπεκτίθεται τὸν υἱόν. Τὰ δ' ἐντεῦθεν ἄρρητα τοῦ μεγάλου καὶ ἀκατάληπτα, καθάπερ τῷ Ἡλίῳ καὶ Βασιλεῖ καὶ Νυμφίῳ καὶ ἡ σύλληψις καὶ ἡ γέννησις, οὕτω καὶ τῷ τούτου λύχνῳ καὶ φίλῳ καὶ στρατιώτῃ καὶ ἡ ἀναστροφὴ καὶ ἡ δίαιτα. Διὸ καὶ τῆς Ἐλισάβετ καὶ τοῦ παιδὸς ἀποτυχόντες οἱ δήμιοι, κατὰ τοῦ Ζαχαρίου

the bloody slaughter. But of course, the great John the Baptist—who saw the Light before he saw the light of day and while he was still in the womb, who leaped before he was born, who was a preacher before he had a voice, and a witness to the Word before he could speak a word—was here too ordained to be the first offering and to run ahead of the new, first, and great sacrificial victim, together with the other infants who were his comrades in age and combat. For by family and birth, John too was from Bethlehem, and was born shortly before Jesus. For when they were in doubt, Herod's men were killing even those infants who were older than two years, preferring the safer option to the humane one, considering it better to include some that would fall outside the designated age rather than miss some within it. This is how those wretches reveled in their slaughter. But God was John's protector, the same God who was then being sought and was fleeing into Egypt, and as a result, not only was John's birthday accompanied by such great contestants and sacrificial victims, but also his way of life was a witness and herald, and the funeral laments at his death were preparatory offerings and progressive steps even to Hades. It was this same God who snatched up Elizabeth and her son from the midst of the murderers; forced to flee secretly into the wilderness, she brought her son to a place of safety. The subsequent life of this great man was ineffable and incomprehensible, for just as the conception and birth of the Sun, King, and Bridegroom were ineffable and incomprehensible, so too was the upbringing and way of life of the one who was his lamp, friend, and soldier. This is why, when the executioners failed to capture Elizabeth and her son, they unleashed, as the story goes, their rage on Zacharias,

τὸν θυμὸν ἀφιᾶσιν, ὡς λόγος, καὶ πρὸς αὐτῷ τῷ θυσιαστηρίῳ λειτουργοῦντα καὶ θύοντα τῷ Θεῷ θύουσι καὶ ἀναμιγνύουσι τὸ αἷμα τῷ αἵματι. Καὶ ταῦτα μὲν ταύτην ἐδέχοντο τὴν οἰκονομίαν.

Τί δὲ καὶ ἡ πρὸς Αἴγυπτον τοῦ παιδὸς φυγή; Φυγὴ τῶν δαιμόνων ἐξ Αἰγύπτου γίνεται καὶ διωγμὸς τῆς πλάνης ἡ τοῦ Λόγου κατὰ τῆς πλάνης δίωξις· ἐπεὶ γὰρ δύο ταῦτα δεισιδαιμονέστατα καὶ κακοτεχνότατα καὶ οἰκειότατα τῷ Ἐχθρῷ τῶν Ἐθνῶν, Μάγοι τὲ καὶ Αἰγύπτιοι. Καὶ περιττοὶ μὲν τὴν ἔνυλον καὶ κάτω λατρείαν Αἰγύπτιοι, καὶ περὶ τὰς τῶν ἑρπετῶν καὶ κνωδάλων τιμὰς φιλότιμοι, περιττοὶ δὲ τὴν ἀέριον τῶν δαιμόνων οἱ Μάγοι, οὐ μὴν ἀλλὰ καὶ περὶ τὰς τούτων μὲν ἐπικλήσεις, τὰς δὲ παρατηρήσεις τῶν οὐρανίων ἐσχολακότες καὶ τὰ μαντεύματα. Ἀμφοτέρους ὁ Χριστὸς ἐξ ἀρχῆς αὐτῆς προνομεύει, ἵνα μηδὲ περὶ τῶν ἄλλων ὁ Ἐχθρὸς ἔχῃ θαρρεῖν, ἀφαιρεθεὶς ἐκ πρώτης τὰ κράτιστα, ἀλλά, τοὺς μὲν εὐθὺς γεννηθεὶς καὶ ὡς Θεὸς ἐξ οὐρανῶν καλῶν πᾶσαν καὶ τὴν ἀέριον δεισιδαιμονίαν καὶ τὴν οὐράνιον τερατολογίαν καὶ γενεθλιαλογίαν δι’ αὐτῆς αὐτοῦ τῆς γεννήσεως ἀνατρέπων, τοὺς δὲ μετὰ χρόνον καὶ ὡς ἄνθρωπος ἐπιδημῶν διὰ γῆς, ὡς καὶ τὴν ἀσέβειαν ἥττους ἢ παχυτέρους, καὶ πᾶσαν καὶ τὴν Αἰγύπτιον ἀκαθαρσίαν ἢ ἀλογίαν ἀποκαθαίρων καὶ τοὺς Αἰγυπτίους ἀπελαύνων ὄφεις τὲ καὶ σκορπίους, ἢ καὶ τοὺς μὲν πρότερον ὡς καὶ πρότερον ἀποστάντας καὶ παρ’ αὐτὸν τὸν τοῦ ἡλίου καὶ τῶν ὅλων δημιουργὸν τῷ ἡλίῳ καὶ πυρὶ λατρεύσαντας, τοὺς δὲ ὕστερον καὶ πρὸς αὐτοὺς ἐρχόμενος, ὡς καὶ ὕστερον παρ’ αὐτῶν διὰ τοῦ Ἰσραὴλ διωκόμενος, καὶ

and when he was performing service before the altar of sacrifice and offering sacrifices to God, they sacrificed him, mingling blood with blood. And these things were not outside God's dispensation.

But what was the reason for the child's flight into Egypt? 55
The Word's pursuit of deception resulted in the flight of the demons of Egypt and drove out their deception. For among the Gentiles, two nations were the most superstitious, the most wickedly artful, and the most closely bound to the Enemy, namely, the Magi and the Egyptians. The Egyptians were excessive in their material and lowly worship, and lavish in their devotion to reptiles and beasts. The Magi, on the other hand, were excessive in their devotion to the demons of the air: they not only invoked their names, but also observed the movements of celestial bodies, and divined the future. But from the very beginning Christ plundered them both, so that the Enemy might not be emboldened against the other nations, having been stripped at the outset of the most powerful. At the moment he was born, God called the Magi from heaven, and through his birth overthrew all their aerial superstitions, celestial fables, and casting of horoscopes. Not long afterward, when he became a man living on earth, seeing that the Egyptians were worse or more material in their impiety, he purged away all their impurity and irrationality, and drove out the Egyptian serpents and scorpions. Or perhaps he called the Magi first, inasmuch as they were the first to fall away, worshipping the sun and fire rather than the creator of the sun and of all things. But he came later to the Egyptians, since it was later that he was persecuted by them in the figure of Israel, but now is

νῦν τῆς ἐπιβουλῆς ῥυόμενος, ὡς καὶ πρότερον παρ' αὐτῶν ἐπιβουλευόμενος, ἵνα τὰ ἐναντία διὰ τῶν ἐναντίων ἰάσηται. Καὶ βρεφοκτονεῖ μὲν Ἡρώδης, ὁ ζωογονεῖν ἑαυτὸν τάξας τὰ οἰκεῖα τοῦ γένους σπέρματα, ζωογονεῖ δὲ Φαραώ, ὁ πρὶν ἀναιρεῖν κελεύσας τὰ Ἰουδαίων νήπια. Τοιούτοις λόγοις ὁ Λόγος ἦν πελαγίζων καὶ καθαίρων τὴν Αἴγυπτον καὶ καταπνίγων τοὺς ἐμφωλεύοντας αὐτῇ λεγεῶνας. Ἡ δὲ πηγὴ τῆς ζωῆς, ἡ μήτηρ, ὡς τοὺς μὲν φίλους ἐχθρούς, τοὺς δὲ ἐχθροὺς φίλους εὑροῦσα, καὶ τὸν μὲν τῆς πατρίδος ναὸν ὡς εὐάλωτον, τὸν δὲ ἐπὶ τῆς Αἰγύπτου κατοικισμὸν ὡς ἄσυλον ἱερόν, τὸν μὲν ἀπολιποῦσα, τὸν δὲ καταβαλοῦσα, ἥδιστον εἶχεν Αἴγυπτον ἐνδιαίτημα καὶ Αἰγυπτίοις θέαμα. Συμπεριῄει δὲ καὶ αὐτὴ καινὸν ὁμοῦ καὶ φρικτὸν Αἰγυπτίοις θαῦμά τε καὶ διήγημα· ἃ γὰρ ἐπὶ τῶν μύθων ἀνέπλαττον, ταῦτ' ἐπὶ τῶν πραγμάτων ἑώρων, μητέρα καινὴν Θεοῦ καὶ Θεὸν μετὰ σαρκὸς ὁμοῦ καὶ μητρός. Οὐκ ἄλογος δὲ οὐδὲ ὁ διετὴς τῷ Λόγῳ παρὰ τοῖς Αἰγυπτίοις χρόνος, ἀλλ' ἵνα καὶ τὸ διπλοῦν αὐτοῖς ἐνδείξηται τῆς ἰάσεως, τοῦ λόγου τὲ καὶ τῆς πράξεως, ἢ καὶ τὸ διπλοῦν αὐτοῖς τῆς ἑαυτοῦ παραστήσῃ φύσεως.

Ὥσπερ δὲ ὑπὸ χρηματισμῷ πρὸς Αἴγυπτον, οὕτω καὶ ἐξ Αἰγύπτου πάλιν ὑπὸ χρησμῷ μετὰ τοῦ παιδὸς καὶ τῆς μητρὸς ὁ Ἰωσὴφ ἐπανέρχεται, καὶ οὐχ ὑπὸ χρηματισμῷ μόνον, ἀλλὰ καὶ προφητικοῖς χρησμοῖς. Ἔνθεν μὲν γὰρ ὅτι "*ἰδοὺ κύριος κάθηται ἐπὶ νεφέλης κούφης καὶ ἥξει εἰς Αἴγυπτον,*" ἐκεῖθεν δὲ ὅτι καὶ "*ἐξ Αἰγύπτου ἐκάλεσα τὸν υἱόν μου.*" Καὶ οὐ ταῦτα μόνον, ἀλλὰ καὶ ἡ τῆς Ἰουδαίας ἀπόλειψις καὶ ἡ πρὸς Ναζαρὲτ ἄφιξις, ὥς φησι Ματθαῖος,

delivered from their plot, just as formerly he was plotted against by them, so that he might heal opposites by opposites. Herod, who had resolved to preserve the seeds of his nation, massacred the innocents, whereas Pharaoh, who had formerly given orders to kill the Jewish infants, preserved them. This is why the Word was inundating and purifying Egypt, drowning the legions of demons concealed within it. But his mother, who is the fountain of life, found her friends to be enemies, and her enemies to be friends, and whereas the temple in her own homeland was easily captured, her dwelling in Egypt was like an inviolable sanctuary. Thus she abandoned the former but embraced the latter, finding Egypt to be a sweet habitation and a pleasant sight for the Egyptians. She thus became part of a new and awesome marvel and report spread among the Egyptians, for what they had invented in their myths they were now seeing in reality: a new mother of God, and God in the flesh, together with his mother. The Word's two-year residence in Egypt was also not without reason, since he wished to show them the twofold character of his healing, consisting of word and deed, or perhaps to reveal to them the twofold character of his nature.

And in the same way that he went to Egypt by virtue of an oracular revelation, so too Joseph left Egypt, with the child and his mother, by virtue of an oracle; but not because of a mere oracle, but through prophetic oracles. These say in one place, "*Behold the Lord is sitting upon a swift cloud and is coming to Egypt,*" and in another, "*Out of Egypt have I called my son.*" And not only this, but their departure from Judea as well as their arrival in Nazareth was also disclosed, as

ὑπὸ χρηματισμῷ καὶ χρησμῷ. Τὸν μὲν γὰρ παρὰ τοῦ ἀγγέλου δέχεται, τὸν δὲ παρὰ τοῦ προφήτου μανθάνει τὴν τοῦ Ναζωραίου κλῆσιν προαγορεύοντα.

56 Καὶ μὴν καὶ ὁ Λουκᾶς αὐτὸν οὔ φησιν κατὰ χρηματισμόν, ἀλλὰ μετὰ τὸν καθαρισμὸν εὐθὺς ἐπανελθεῖν πρὸς τὴν Ναζαρέτ, οὐκ ἐναντιοφωνῶν, ἀλλὰ τὸν πρὸ τῆς καθόδου τῆς εἰς Αἴγυπτον χρόνον δηλῶν· ἐπειδὴ γὰρ ἕνεκα τῆς ἀπογραφῆς μόνον ἡ πρὸς Ἰουδαίαν ἐπάνοδος ἦν, ἐφ' ᾧπερ ἧκον διαπραξάμενοι καὶ ἅμα συνάψαντες τὰ περὶ τὸν καθαρισμόν. Οὕτω γὰρ καὶ τὸ κατὰ νόμον ἅμα καὶ λόγον καὶ χρείαν συνέβαινεν, ἅμα τὲ τὴν ἀπογραφὴν ποιουμένοις καὶ μετὰ τοῦ νεογνοῦ διαναπαυομένοις ἐπὶ μικρὸν καὶ συμπληρωμένων τῶν ἡμερῶν τοῦ καθαρισμοῦ. Ταῦτα γοῦν ἐχομένως οὕτω διοικονομησάμενοι, μᾶλλον δὲ παρ' αὐτοῦ τοῦ τεχθέντος διοικονομηθέντες, αὐθαιρέτως ὡς ἐμφιλοχωροῦντες τῇ πατρίδι λοιπόν, πρὸς Ναζαρὲτ ἐπανήεσαν καὶ ὁ διετὴς οὕτως αὐτοῖς ἐτρίβετο χρόνος, ὡς παρὰ τῶν ἀρχαιοτέρων ἐστὶ μανθάνειν, μεθ' ὃν αὐτοῖς καὶ ἡ εἰς Αἴγυπτον ἐχρηματίσθη φυγή. Νυνὶ δὲ πάλιν τὴν ὑποστροφὴν τῷ Ἰωσὴφ κελεύων ἄγγελος ἐπιφαίνεται, καὶ τὴν ἀπὸ τῆς Ἰουδαίας ἐπὶ τὴν Γαλιλαίαν καὶ τὴν Ναζαρὲτ μᾶλλον ἐπιστροφήν.

57 Σὺ δέ μοι πρὸ πάντων καὶ διὰ πάντων ἐκεῖνο σκόπει, τὴν θαυμασίαν διαπλοκὴν τῆς προνοίας, καὶ ὅπως κἀνταῦθα δι' ὅλου μίγνυσι τοῖς ταπεινοῖς ὑψηλὰ καὶ τοῖς λυπηροῖς τὰ χρηστὰ καὶ ἀνάπαλιν, πῇ μὲν ἀνιεῖσα τῶν πόνων τὴν Παρθένον τὲ καὶ μητέρα, πῇ δὲ καὶ πρὸς ὑψηλοτέρους

Matthew says, through an oracular revelation and an oracle. For Joseph received the former from the angel, but the latter he learned from the prophet who predicted that the child would be called a Nazarene.

To be sure, Luke does not say that Joseph acted in re- 56
sponse to an oracle, but that after the purification in the temple they returned immediately to Nazareth. However, he does not say this to contradict Matthew, but rather is speaking of the time before they fled to Egypt. Since they returned to Judea only on account of the enrollment, they completed this and then returned, combining with it at the same time things related to the purification. In this manner, they acted according to the requirements of the law, logic, and need; they thus completed the enrollment, and, at the same time, together with the newborn child, rested for a short time until they had completed the forty days required for the purification. This, then, is how they arranged these things in sequence, or rather how they were arranged by the child himself, and, after choosing to remain in their native land, they returned to Nazareth, where they stayed for two years, as one may learn from the more ancient writers, after which the flight to Egypt was announced by the oracle. It was at this point that the angel once again appeared to Joseph and ordered their return and their move from Judea to Galilee and indeed to Nazareth.

But above all these things, and through them all, consider 57
with me the wondrous interweaving of providence, and how, even here, it wholly mixes together sublime things with what is lowly, and the good with the sorrowful and vice versa, on the one hand allowing the Virgin and mother to experience affliction, and on the other raising her mind to-

λόγους ἐπαίρουσα καὶ δοξάζουσα καὶ τοῦ θεῖον εἶναι τὸν τόκον πείθουσα, καὶ ἵνα μικρὸν ἄνωθεν ἀναλάβωμεν. Μετὰ γὰρ τὴν θαυμαστὴν ἐκείνην σύλληψιν καὶ κυοφορίαν, καὶ τῆς τοσαύτης χάριτος ἢ καὶ θαύματος τὴν πληροφορίαν καὶ τὸ σκίρτημα τὸ προφητικόν τε καὶ ὑποφητικόν, τὸ φανερὸν ὁμοῦ καὶ κρυπτόν, καὶ τὴν δευτέραν τῆς Ἐλισάβετ μαρτυρίαν τὲ καὶ θεολογίαν, καὶ αὐτῆς δὲ ταύτης τὴν εὐχαριστίαν καὶ προφητείαν καὶ τῶν μακαρισμῶν τὴν μεγαλειότητα, φόβοι καὶ ὑποψίαι καὶ περὶ τῶν ἐσχάτων συκοφαντίαι καὶ κίνδυνοι. Λύεται ταῦτα. Μαρτυρίαι γὰρ ἄνωθεν θεῖαι καὶ τοῦ μὴ μόνον ἄχραντον, ἀλλὰ καὶ ἔμπλεων τοῦ Παναγίου Πνεύματος τὴν Παρθένον εἶναι καὶ ἔνθεον τὸν τόκον πληροφορίαι. Καὶ πάλιν ξενιτεῖαι τὲ καὶ ἀποδημίαι, καὶ Γαλιλαία μὲν ἀφιεμένη, καταλαμβανομένη δὲ Ἰουδαία μετὰ τοῦ χρυσοῦ φόρτου καὶ τὴν φέρουσαν τάχα φέροντος, ἀπορίαι τὲ καὶ στενοχωρίαι, αἱ μὲν πρὸς ταῖς ἀνωδύνοις ὠδῖσιν, αἱ δὲ μετὰ τὴν καλὴν καὶ γλυκεῖαν ὠδίνων λύσιν. Ἐντεῦθεν οὐδ᾽ ἔχει ποῦ χωρηθῆναι διὰ τὸν ἀχώρητον ἴσως οὐδὲ προσανακλιθῆναι καὶ προσανακλῖναί πως τὸν ἀσώματον, ἀλλὰ σπηλαίῳ τὸν καὶ λῃστὰς σῴζοντα καὶ θηριωδίας ἡμᾶς ἀπαλλάττοντα καὶ φάτνῃ τὸν αἰσθητῶς ἅμα καὶ νοητῶς πάντας τρέφοντα. Ἀλλὰ μῖξον πάλιν καὶ τοῖς ταπεινοῖς ὑψηλὰ ὁ διπλοῦς, ἀεὶ δὲ καὶ τἀναντία κιρνῶν, καὶ δι᾽ ἀδοξίας δοξάζων ἅμα καὶ δοξαζόμενος· ἀγγέλων ἐντεῦθεν ἐπιστασίαι καὶ δοξολογίαι, καὶ ποιμένων δρόμοι καὶ Μάγων, καὶ ἀστέρων δορυφορίαι τὲ καὶ δωροφορίαι.

ward sublime thoughts, glorifying her, and persuading her that her child was divine, as we can see if we return briefly to an earlier moment in the narrative. After the wondrous conception and pregnancy and the assurance of such great grace, or rather of such a great miracle; after the prophetic and inspired leaping, which was both manifest and hidden; and after the subsequent testimony and theology of Elizabeth, as well as her gratitude and prophecy, and the magnificence of the blessings she pronounced—after these things, I say, there were fears and suspicions, and, toward the end, calumnies and danger. Yet all of these were dispelled. Divine testimonies from above assured not only that the Virgin was undefiled but that she was also filled with the all-Holy Spirit, and that her child was indeed divine. But once again this was followed by exiles and long journeys, her departure from Galilee, her settling in Judea with the golden freight, when she was bearing the one who in a way bore her, and once again by doubts and worries. The former were occasioned by her painless pangs of labor, the latter after the beautiful and sweet deliverance from the labor pangs. And though there was nowhere he could be contained, being uncontainable, nor, equally, anywhere he could be laid down or lie down, being incorporeal, the one who saved thieves and freed us from our bestial nature was placed in a cave, and the one who nourishes everyone, physically and spiritually, was placed in a manger. But intermingle again, you who are twofold, sublime things with the lowly, since you are forever mixing together things that are contrary, glorifying and being glorified through things lacking in glory. This was followed by the ministrations and praises of angels, journeys of shepherds and Magi, the accompaniment of stars, and the donation of gifts.

58 Καὶ πάλιν τῇ μητρὶ καὶ παρθένῳ τὰ πειρατήρια· Ἡρώδου μανίαι τὲ καὶ παιδοφονίαι, καὶ ψυχὴ ζητουμένη τοῦ τὴν βασιλικὴν ἐπιζητοῦντος εἰκόνα καὶ τὴν δραχμήν, καὶ φυγαδεῖαι πρὸς Αἴγυπτον τοῦ φυγάδα ποτὲ τὸν λαὸν καὶ δι' αὐτοῦ τὸν νῦν διώκτην ἐξ Αἰγύπτου σώσαντος· καὶ χρόνον οὐκ ὀλίγον ἐπ' ἀλλοτρίαις διατριβαὶ τοῦ πᾶσαν τὴν κτίσιν οἰκείαν ἔχοντος, καὶ πάλιν μετασκηνώσεις τὲ καὶ μεταναστάσεις καὶ δρόμοι πρὸς τόπους ἐκ τόπων στρατοπεδείαις μᾶλλον ἢ γυναικείαις ἀσθενείαις μετὰ καὶ παιδίου κομιδῇ νηπίου πρέποντες. Ταῦτα δὲ μὴ τῆς οὕτω πάντα πλεκούσης καὶ ἡμᾶς οὕτω παρασκευαζούσης μόνον, ἀλλὰ καὶ τῆς παρθενικῆς ἀνδρείας ἔστω καὶ καρτερίας τεκμήρια, καθάπερ καὶ τὰ προτοῦ τῆς σοφίας τὲ καὶ τῆς σωφροσύνης.

59 Ἀλλὰ τίνα σοι καὶ τὰ μετὰ τὴν ἐπάνοδον, ὦ Θεοῦ Μῆτερ καὶ τὰ πάντα σύναθλε καὶ καλλίνικε; Βλέπεις μὲν καὶ ἀπολαμβάνεις, κατὰ τὴν ἐπαγγελίαν, τὴν γλυκεῖαν σοῦ τὲ καὶ τοῦ σοῦ παιδὸς καὶ πάντων πατρὸς πατρίδα, τὴν τῆς ἐπαγγελίας, τὴν ὄντως μέλι καὶ γάλα, τὸν σὸν Υἱὸν καὶ τὸ σὸν γάλα, ῥεύσασαν. Εὑρίσκεις δὲ καὶ τὸν τὴν ψυχὴν ἀπολέσαι τοῦ παιδίου ἐπιζητοῦντα, δικαίως μὲν αὐτὸν παρ' ἑαυτοῦ καὶ γυναῖκα καὶ τέκνα καὶ πᾶν ἀπολωλεκότα τὸ γένος, δικαιότερον δὲ καὶ αὐτὸν συναπολωλότα καὶ τὸ σῶμα καὶ τὴν ψυχήν, καὶ εἰς τετραρχίας ὑποβεβηκυῖαν καὶ καταμεμερισμένην τὴν βασιλείαν. Ἀλλὰ καὶ οὕτω λείψανα τῶν προτέρων κακῶν, Ἀρχέλαον βασιλεύοντα, τὴν ἥττω δηλαδὴ πολὺ τῆς πρὶν βασιλείας, καὶ ἡ διαστολὴ πρὸς τὸν

And again there were further trials for the mother and virgin, namely, Herod's rage and infanticide, his seeking the life of the one who came to seek the royal image and the coin; the flight into Egypt for the one who once led the flight of his people out of Egypt, and through which he saved the one who was now pursuing him; and no small amount of time on foreign soil, by the one who possesses all creation as his own; and, once again, relocations and migrations, and moving about from place to place, which would be more appropriate for military encampments than for a weary mother with a recently newborn child. Let all these things, which were brought about by divine providence, not only weave everything together and prepare us, but also let them be sure signs of the Virgin's courage and perseverance, just as the things that happened earlier were signs of her wisdom and chastity. 58

But what happened to you after your return from Egypt, Mother of God, as you struggled in all things and emerged victorious? On the one hand, according to the promise, you beheld and enjoyed the fatherland that is sweet both to you and your son, who is the father of all, I mean the promised land, flowing with the true honey and milk, that is, your Son and your milk. But on the other hand, you discovered that the man who sought to destroy the life of your child, who by his own hand had fittingly destroyed his wife and children and his entire family, had thus even more fittingly destroyed himself along with them in body and soul, and his kingdom was degraded and divided into four provinces. But remnants of his former evils survived, I mean Archelaos, whose kingdom was greatly inferior to the one that preceded it, and was distinct from that of his brother Herod, 59

ἀδελφὸν Ἡρώδην *ἀντὶ Ἡρώδου τοῦ πατρὸς αὐτοῦ.* Διὸ καὶ τὴν Ἰουδαίαν μὲν Ἰωσὴφ ἀπολείπει, πρὸς δὲ τὴν Ναζαρὲτ ἀποκλίνει πάλιν, ὃ καὶ αὐτὸ προειδὼς ἢ καὶ προοικονομῶν ὁ ἄγγελος οὐκ "ἀπόστρεφε πρὸς γῆν Ἰουδαίαν," φησίν, ἀλλὰ "πρὸς *γῆν Ἰσραήλ,*" ἵν' ἅμα συμβῇ καὶ τὴν προφητείαν συμβῆναι καὶ τὴν παραγγελίαν· τὴν μὲν προφητείαν τῷ Ναζωραῖον κληθῆναι, τὴν δὲ παραγγελίαν τῷ μὴ τὴν Ἰουδαίαν ὡρισμένως, ἀλλ' ἁπλῶς εἰπεῖν *εἰς γῆν Ἰσραήλ·* ταύτῃ γὰρ καὶ ἡ Γαλιλαία συμπεριείχετο. Πολλὴν ἀπορίαν παρέσχετο καὶ τὸ πῶς ἐν ταὐτῷ τῆς Ἰουδαίας καὶ Ἀρχέλαον βασιλεύειν καὶ Πιλάτον ἡγεμονεύειν ἦν· τό τε γὰρ λέγειν ὡς ἔναγχος τῆς Ἡρώδου τελευτῆς γενομένης καὶ μήπω τῆς βασιλείας διῃρημένης μηδὲ τῆς Ῥωμαϊκῆς καταπεμπομένης ἀρχῆς Ἀρχέλαος τῷ τέως ἦρχεν, ἕωλον καὶ αὐτόθεν ἔχον τὸν ἔλεγχον· ἰδοὺ γὰρ καὶ πρὸ τελευτῆς Ἡρώδου καὶ μετὰ τελευτήν, ὡς τὸ μὲν παρὰ τῆς ἱστορίας, τὸ δὲ καὶ παρὰ τῶν εὐαγγελιστῶν ἔστιν ἀκούειν, πάλαι τὲ Ἀριστόβουλος καὶ πάλιν ἕτερος ἦρχεν Ἡρώδης καὶ Πιλάτος συνῆρχεν, ὁ μὲν ἡγεμονεύων, ὁ δὲ βασιλεύων. Τί γοῦν ἔστιν εἰπεῖν ἢ ὅτι κατὰ τὴν ἐπιδημίαν Χριστοῦ καὶ ὀλίγον τι πρὸ τῆς ἐπιδημίας τῆς αὐτοκράτορος τῶν Ἰουδαίων καὶ ἀρχιερατείας καὶ βασιλείας ὑπὸ Ῥωμαίων κατὰ τὴν προφητείαν καθαιρεθείσης, ἡνίκα καὶ Ἀριστόβουλος μὲν ὁ ἀρχιερεύς τε καὶ βασιλεὺς καὶ Ὑρκανὸς ὁ τούτου ἀδελφός, ἐχθρὸς δὲ διαφερόντως καὶ νεωτεροποιός, ὁ μὲν δέσμιος ὑπὸ Πομπηίου πρὸς Ῥώμην ἀπήχθη καὶ ἀπολυθεὶς φόρους ἐτάχθη τελεῖν, ὁ δὲ ἀρχιερεὺς ἐχειροτονήθη καὶ μετ' αὐτὸν Ἡρώδης οὐκ ὀλίγαις θεραπείαις καὶ στρατεύμασί τε

was *ruling in place of his father Herod.* This is why Joseph departed from Judea, and once again made his way to Nazareth, which the angel knew or arranged in advance, for he did not say "return to Judea," but "to *the land of Israel,*" so that his words might agree, and the prophecy might coincide with the angel's command. For the prophecy said he would be called a Nazarene, while the angel's command did not mention Judea specifically, but simply directed him *to the land of Israel,* for this includes the region of Galilee. Now considerable uncertainty has arisen over the question of how Archelaos was reigning and Pilate was ruling in Judea at the same time. To say that Archelaos was in power for a short period of time because Herod's death had only recently taken place, the kingdom had not yet been divided, and the Romans had not yet appointed a ruler, is an anachronistic and self-contradictory solution. Consider instead the things that took place both before and after the death of Herod, which may be confirmed from the historical account and the evangelists: Aristoboulos in the past and again another Herod held power at the same time as Pilate was in power, the former reigning and the latter ruling. In other words, at the time of Christ's advent and a little before the advent of the emperor (when the high priesthood and kingship of the Jews were abolished by the Romans, in accord with the prophecy), Aristoboulos was both high priest and king having as his chief adversary his rebellious brother Hyrcanus. The former was taken prisoner by Pompey and dragged off to Rome, and upon being released was ordered to collect tribute for Rome, but Hyrcanus, on the other hand, was ordained high priest, and it was after him that Herod, through many services, military alliances, and ex-

καὶ ἀναλώμασι παρὰ Καίσαρος Αὐγούστου βασιλεὺς κατέστη τῆς Ἰουδαίας. Ὀνόματι μὲν "βασιλεία τῶν Ἰουδαίων" ἦν, πράγματι δὲ δουλεία Ῥωμαίων, ἐκεῖθεν αὐτοῖς τῶν βασιλέων καὶ χειροτονουμένων καὶ οἰκονομουμένων, καὶ δῆλος αὐτὸς Ἡρώδης μηδὲ τῶν οἰκείων παίδων ἔχων τὴν αὐθεντίαν, εἰ μὴ παρὰ τῆς Ῥωμαίων λάβοι βουλῆς τὲ καὶ βασιλείας· ἐντεῦθεν αὐτοῖς καὶ φρούραρχοι καὶ φρουραὶ καὶ ἔφοροι τῆς χώρας καὶ τῆς ἀρχῆς, οἷα καὶ τὰ πολλὰ καταστασιαζόντων καὶ καταστασιαζομένων ὑπ' ἀλλήλων καὶ πρὸς ἀλλήλους, ἔστι δὲ ὅτε καὶ πρὸς Ῥωμαίους. Ἡ γοῦν μεγίστη τῶν ἐφορειῶν καὶ πάντων κυρεία καὶ ἡγεμονία παρὰ Ῥωμαίοις ἦν, ὑφ' ᾗ καὶ τὸ στρατιωτικόν, ἡ δὲ βασιλεία παρὰ Ἰουδαίοις μέν, οὐκ αὐτοκρατὴς δέ, ἀλλὰ τὰ πολλὰ Ῥωμαίων κατήκοος. Οὕτως οὐκ Ἀρχέλαος καὶ Πιλάτος μόνον, ἀλλὰ καὶ Πιλάτος ὕστερον καὶ Ἡρώδης, ὁ μὲν ἡγεμόνευεν, ὁ δὲ ἐβασίλευε, καὶ ἦν ὥσπερ ὑπὸ βασιλείαν, μᾶλλον δὲ καὶ ἡγεμονίαν τῆς βασιλείας ἡ βασιλεία.

60 Ἡμῖν δὲ καὶ πάλιν πρὸς τὴν ἀκολουθίαν ἰτέον. Τὰ μὲν οὖν λοιπὰ τοῦ παιδὸς παρὰ τῶν Εὐαγγελίων μάνθανε, τὴν αὔξησιν, τὴν κραταίωσιν, τὴν προκοπὴν τῆς ἡλικίας ἅμα καὶ χάριτος, τὴν τῆς σοφίας πλήρωσιν, οὐχ ὡς Θεοῦ ταῦτα, (τί γὰρ τοῦ ἐξ ἀρχῆς ὑπερτελείου καὶ ὑπερκραταίου καὶ ὑπερπλήρους πάντων τῶν ἀγαθῶν τελειότερον ἢ κραταιότερον ἢ πληρέστερον;) ἀλλ' ὡς ἀνθρώπου μὲν αὔξοντος καὶ προκόπτοντος, τὰ δ' ἄλλα διοριστέον, τὴν κραταίωσιν, τὴν ἑτέραν προκοπὴν τῆς χάριτος, τῆς σοφίας τὴν πλήρωσιν· οὔτε γὰρ ὡς Θεοῦ ταῦτα, ἀλλ' οὔτε δὲ ὡς ἀνθρώπου

penditures, was made king of Judea by Augustus Caesar. In name he was the "king of the Judeans," but in reality he was a slave of the Romans, since it was at their pleasure that kings were appointed and controlled, and it is clear that, without the consent and authority of the Romans, Herod himself did not have authority even over his own children, and that the Romans also had authority over the garrisons and their commanders, and the magistrates of the region and its government, which explains the strife between opposing factions both among themselves and against each other, and, at times, against the Romans. Thus, the greatest power and authority over the magistrates and over everything lay with the Romans, who controlled the army, while the Jews retained their kingdom, which was not independent, but for the most part subordinate to Rome. Thus it was not only with Archelaos and Pilate, but also with Pilate and afterward Herod, that one reigned and the other ruled, and it was as if the ruling power was subject to a ruling power or rather the reign of a ruling power.

But we must return once again to the sequence of our 60
discourse. You may learn about the child's subsequent activities from the Gospels, which speak of his increase, his strength, his progress in stature and grace, and the fullness of his wisdom. These things were not said of him insofar as he is God (for what could be more perfect or have more strength or be more complete than the one who from the beginning is transcendently perfect, powerful, and completely filled with all good things?) but they were said insofar as he was a human being subject to increase and progress. But one must distinguish the other things, namely, his strength, the other progression in grace, and the fullness of wisdom, for neither as God or man was he growing stronger

πλεῖον κραταιουμένου παρὰ τοῦ ἐνοικοῦντος Πνεύματος ἢ προχωροῦντος ἢ πληρουμένου παρὰ τὰ ἐξ ἀρχῆς, ἐφ' οὗπερ ἐξ αὐτῆς ἑνώσεως *πᾶν τὸ πλήρωμα* κατῴκησε *τῆς θεότητος,* ἀλλ' ὡς κατὰ μικρὸν παραφαινομένης αὐτῷ τῆς θείας χάριτος καὶ δυνάμεως, ἢ καὶ ὥσπερ ὀργάνῳ τῷ σώματι κατ' ὀλίγον χωροῦντι πρὸς τὴν ἐνέργειαν συναπαρτίζεσθαι, καὶ τῆς τοῦ τεχνίτου νομιζομένης κατ' ὀλίγον τέχνης ἢ ἐπιστήμης. Ἀλλ' οὐδὲ ἡ ἐπίδειξις αὐτῷ τῆς σοφίας παρ' ἡλικίαν, ἀλλὰ καθ' ὃν χρόνον καὶ ἡμῖν ὁ λόγος εἴωθεν ἤδη συμπληροῦσθαι τῆς διακρίσεως, ὁ τῆς δωδεκαετίας.

61 Καὶ ὁ καιρὸς ὁ τῆς ἑορτῆς, καθ' ὃν ἔμελλε καὶ μετὰ πολὺν χρόνον αὖθις αὐτοὺς εἰς φθόνον προαγαγεῖν καὶ αὐτὸς ὑπὲρ ἡμῶν παθεῖν, ὡσπερεὶ πόρρωθεν προτυπῶν τὸν φθόνον τὲ καὶ τὸ πάθος, ἀλλὰ καὶ ὑπομένων εἰς Ἱεροσόλυμα καὶ τρεῖς ἡμέρας ἀφανὴς ὢν καὶ ζητούμενος καὶ ὕστερον εὑρισκόμενος, ἵνα καὶ τὴν ταφὴν καὶ τὴν ἀνάστασιν προτυπώσῃ, κἀν τούτῳ κρυπτόμενος καὶ ποθούμενος καὶ τριήμερος ἀνιστάμενος, ὑπομένων δὲ λάθρα καὶ μηδὲ τοῖς γονεῦσιν αὐτοῖς γινωσκόμενος, ἵνα μηδ' ἕτερον ἢ φανερὸς γενόμενος κωλυθῇ ἢ καὶ ἀπειθῇ κωλυόμενος. Ἀλλ' οὐδὲ προπετῶς διδάσκων οὔτε τοὺς διδασκάλους οὔτε τοὺς ἱερεῖς, καίτοι μόνος αὐτὸς αὐτόχρημα Σοφία καὶ Λόγος ὤν, μᾶλλον δὲ καὶ τοῖς ἄλλοις πᾶσι λόγου καὶ σοφίας αὐτὸς ὁ χορηγὸς ὤν. Ἀλλὰ διὰ ταῦτα μὲν οὖν ταῦτα μέτρα καὶ ἡλικίας καὶ ἀξίας αὐτός τε καλῶς εἰδὼς καὶ τοῖς ἄλλοις ὁρίζων, καὶ τοῖς μὲν ἱερεῦσι καὶ διδασκάλοις τοῦ διδάσκειν παραχωρῶν, αὐτὸς δὲ καὶ ἐρωτῶν λογικῶς καὶ

by means of the indwelling Spirit, or progressing, or being more greatly filled than what he was at the beginning, for from the very moment of the union *the entire fullness of the divinity* dwelt within him. Nonetheless, divine grace and power appeared in him slowly, as if his body were a kind of instrument that gradually came to contain the full measure of the Spirit's activity, along with the art or knowledge properly belonging to the artisan. And neither was the demonstration of his wisdom inappropriate to his age, but was manifested at the time when human reason is usually fully able to discriminate, that is, at the age of twelve.

And this took place at the time of the feast, the same 61
feast on which, many years later, he was going to be betrayed out of envy, and suffer on our account, as if he were now prefiguring from afar both the envy and the suffering he would experience. And thus, he remained in Jerusalem and was not seen for three days, and though he was sought for and later found, so that he might prefigure both his burial and resurrection at which time he was also concealed, desired, and resurrected on the third day, he eluded those who were looking for him, and his whereabouts were unknown even to his parents, so that he would neither be prevented from staying had they found him, nor be disobedient if he was prevented. And while he was teaching, he showed no rashness to either the teachers or the priests, even though he alone is Wisdom and Reason itself, or rather the source of reason and wisdom for all others. On account of these things, he knew well the measure of age and respect, and determined the limits for others, and thus allowed the teachers and priests to teach, while he intelligently asked them questions, listening with

ἀκροώμενος συνετῶς καὶ ἀποκρινόμενος συνετώτερον, ὃ καὶ τὸ θαῦμα πολλῷ μεῖζον ἐποίει τῆς ἀκροάσεως. Ἡ δὲ τῆς εὐταξίας σοφία πάλιν τῆς Σοφίας οὐχ ἥττων, καὶ οὐ ταῦτα κατώρθου μόνον, ἀλλὰ καὶ τὸ τῆς μητρὸς διωρθοῦτο πάθος καὶ τὴν διάλεξιν· ἐπεὶ γὰρ ὡς μήτηρ ἐκείνη πάντα ὁμοῦ καὶ παρρησιαστικώτερον καὶ ἀνθρωπινώτερον καὶ περιπαθέστερον διελέγετο· "*τί τοῦτο, τέκνον, ἐποίησας ἡμῖν;*" καὶ ὅτι· "*ἰδοὺ ἐγὼ καὶ ὁ πατήρ σου ὀδυνώμενοι ἐζητοῦμέν σε.*" Καὶ αὐτὸς πάντα λύων, ὅτι καὶ ἕτερος ὁ πατὴρ αὐτῷ καὶ ὅτι οὐχ ὡς ἀνθρώπῳ ψιλῷ, ἀλλ' ὡς καὶ Θεῷ καὶ τὴν μητέρα προσεκτέον αὐτῷ καὶ ὅτι *ὁ τοῦ Πατρὸς οἶκος*, ὁ ναὸς δῆλον, οἶκός ἐστι καὶ αὐτοῦ, καθάπερ καὶ τὰ ἄλλα πάντα τὰ τοῦ Πατρός, ἀλλ' ὅτι καὶ αὐτοῖς ἐγκλητέον μᾶλλον ἀγνοοῦσι ταῦτα καὶ ἔτι χαμαὶ βαίνουσι, καὶ μηδὲν μήτε λαλοῦσι μήτε φρονοῦσι τῶν πρὸς ἀλήθειαν. "*Τί ὅτι,*" φησίν, "*ἐζητεῖτέ με; Οὐκ οἴδατε ὅτι ἐν τοῖς τοῦ Πατρός μου δεῖ εἶναί με;*" Ἐνταῦθα πρώτως ἀνδρικώτερον ἢ μᾶλλον εἰπεῖν θειότερον πρὸς τοὺς οἰκείους διαλεγόμενος καὶ πρώτως τοῦ ἀληθῶς Πατρὸς φανερώτερον μνημονεύων καὶ παραγυμνῶν αὐτοῦ τὴν θεότητα· εἴ γε Πατὴρ μὲν αὐτῷ ὁ Θεός, ἀνάγκη δὲ τὸν Υἱὸν τῆς αὐτῆς εἶναι τῷ Πατρὶ φύσεως, ὥσπερ καὶ τῷ Υἱῷ τὸν Πατέρα. "*Ὁ γὰρ ἑωρακὼς ἐμέ,*" φησίν, "*ἑώρακε τὸν Πατέρα·*" οὕτω γοῦν καὶ ὁ τὸν Πατέρα ἑωρακὼς ἑώρακε τὸν Υἱόν. Τίς καὶ τοῦτό φησιν; Αὐτὸς ὁ Υἱός· "*εἰ τὸν Πατέρα μου ᾔδειτε, κἀμὲ πάντως ἐγνώκατε ἄν.*"

understanding, and responding with even greater understanding, which was a miracle far greater than anything they had heard. The wisdom of his well-ordered behavior was not inferior to his divine Wisdom, and not only did he accomplish this correctly but he also corrected his mother's emotion and speech. For as his mother, she always spoke to him with greater boldness of speech, and with greater human feeling, and with deeper emotion, saying, "*Child, why have you done this to us?*" and, "*Behold, your father and I have been looking for you in great distress.*" But he resolved everything, stating that another was his father, and that his mother must not consider him as an ordinary human being but also as God; and that *the house of the Father,* that is, the temple, is also his house, just as are all the other things of the Father, and that they were not at fault but rather did not know these things and were still on an earthly level, neither speaking nor thinking anything with a view toward the truth. "*Why were you looking for me?*" he says. "*Did* you *not* know *that it is necessary for me to be in my Father's house?*" Here, for the first time, he spoke to his family more boldly, or rather I should say more divinely, and for the first time he mentioned more openly his true Father, and laid bare his divinity. For if God is his Father, then the Son must be of the same nature as the Father, just as the Father is of the Son. This is why he says: "*Whoever has seen me,*" he says, "*has seen the Father,*" from which it follows that whoever has seen the Father has also seen the Son. And who said this? The Son himself. "*If you have known the Father, then you clearly know me too.*"

62 Τοῦτο πρῶτον δεῖγμα τῆς τοῦ παιδὸς Ἰησοῦ σοφίας τὲ καὶ δυνάμεως. *Τὰ γὰρ καλούμενα Παιδικὰ* μὴ παιδαριώδους μόνον, ἀλλὰ καὶ δαιμονιώδους τιθώμεθα γνώμης καὶ προαιρέσεως, οὐ μόνον ὡς τῶν ἡμετέρων λογίων τὲ καὶ Εὐαγγελίων παρέγγραπτα, ἀλλὰ καὶ λίαν κακοτέχνου τινὸς κατὰ τῆς ἀληθείας ἐπινοήματα, διαβάλλειν ἐκ τούτων τῶν μυθευμάτων ἐπιχειροῦντος καὶ τἄλλα τῶν ἡμετέρων· πλὴν εἰ μόνα τις ἐκεῖνα προσδέχεσθαι βούλοιτο, παρὰ πολλῶν λεγόμενά τε καὶ πιστευόμενα, ἃ μήτε τοῖς ἄλλοις τῶν ἡμετέρων ἐναντιούμενα, πρὸς δὲ καὶ τοῖς προφητικοῖς σύμφωνα, ὅτι καὶ τὴν ὥραν τοῦ σώματος *ὡραῖος κάλλει παρὰ τοὺς υἱοὺς τῶν ἀνθρώπων,* καὶ ὅτι τῆς μητρὸς ἐμφερὴς καὶ τὸ ἦθος ἐπιτερπής, τῷ δὲ κάλλει τὴν ἡλικίαν ἀνάλογος καὶ ἰδεῖν μὲν χαριέστατος ὁμοῦ καὶ σεμνότατος, καὶ ὁμιλῆσαι γλυκύτατος ἅμα καὶ εὐγλωττότατος, ἐπιστρεφὴς δὲ πρὸς ἑαυτὸν καὶ ἐπὶ συννοίαις τὰ πολλὰ φαινόμενος, οἷα καὶ γέμων φρονήματος ἢ καὶ Πνεύματος καὶ συνελόντα φάναι καθάπερ ἐν πᾶσι τοῖς ἄλλοις, οὕτω καὶ τῆς ἀνθρωπίνης ὁμιλίας καὶ καταστάσεως, εἰ καὶ ὑπὲρ ἄνθρωπον ὅρος καὶ λόγος, ἡ δὲ πραότης αὐτῷ τὸ ἐπίσημον, καὶ ὅτι μήποτε μήτε ξυρὸς ἀνῆλθεν ἐπὶ τῆς αὐτοῦ κεφαλῆς μήτε δὲ χεὶρ ἀνθρώπου, πλὴν τῆς αὐτοῦ μητρός.

63 Ἀλλ' οὕτω τότε καὶ τὸν πατέρα καὶ τὴν μητέρα καὶ τὸ Συνέδριον καὶ πάντας τοὺς παρόντας ἐκπλήξας ὁμοῦ καὶ διορθωσάμενος κάτεισι μετ' αὐτῶν εἰς Ναζαρέτ. Καὶ πᾶσαν αὐτοῦ τὴν ἀναμεταξὺ μέχρι τοῦ βαπτίσματος καὶ τῆς ἀναδείξεως ἡλικίαν ὡς ἄνευ ἐπιφανοῦς τινος καὶ δημοσίου θαυματοποιΐας τὲ καὶ διδασκαλίας ὁ εὐαγγελιστὴς ἑνὶ

This was the first example of the wisdom and power of the child Jesus. As for the book known as *The Infancy of Jesus,* we regard it not only as infantile but also as demonic in intention and purpose, since it not only falsifies our own scriptural sayings and Gospels, but also contains contrivances of someone very skilled in evil that are contrary to the truth, endeavoring to discredit our own doctrines with these myths. Unless, of course, someone is willing to accept from this book only those things that are said and believed by many, and which do not contradict our doctrines, and which are in accord with the prophets, such as, for example, that in the maturity of his body Jesus *was more beautiful than the sons of men;* that he resembled his mother and was pleasant in his manner; that his beauty was proportionate to his age; that he was most graceful to look at and exceedingly reverent; that he was sweet and eloquent in his speech, and in general was inwardly attentive and deeply thoughtful; that he was filled with prudence or rather with the Spirit, and to put it briefly, he was the same in his human speech and behavior as he was in all other things, and even though he transcended human nature and reason, his distinctive characteristic was his meekness; and that no razor ever came upon his head, nor any human hand, except that of his mother. 62

After he had thus astonished and corrected his father and his mother, together with the Sanhedrin and all who were present at that time, he traveled with them down to Nazareth. As for the entire intervening period of time until his baptism and public ministry, since it was without any kind of conspicuous or public miracle and teaching, the 63

ῥήματι συνελὼν ἑτέραν αὐτῷ μαρτυρεῖ πολιτείαν ὁμοῦ καὶ νομοθεσίαν. Πῇ μὲν γὰρ τῷ λόγῳ νομοθετῶν πρότερον, δεύτερον αὐτὸς ὡς ὡρᾶτο τῷ βίῳ τοῦτο βεβαιῶν καὶ καταπραττόμενος, ὡς τὸ *μηδεὶς ζητείτω τὸ ἑαυτοῦ* καὶ τὸ τοῦ καλοῦ ποιμένος τοῦ τιθέντος *τὴν ψυχὴν ὑπὲρ τῶν προβάτων*· αὐτὸς γὰρ μετ᾽ οὐ πολὺ φαίνεται τὴν ἡμετέραν σωτηρίαν ἐπιζητῶν καὶ τὴν ἑαυτοῦ ψυχὴν προϊέμενος. Πῇ δὲ τῷ βίῳ πρότερον παραδεικνὺς τὸ παράδειγμα, δεύτερον καὶ διὰ τοῦ λόγου προὐτίθει τὸ νομοθέτημα, καθάπερ τὸ μὴ ἐπιθυμεῖν μηδὲ ὀμνύειν μηδὲ ὀργίζεσθαι καὶ τἄλλα τῶν ἐντολῶν· αὐτὰ γὰρ αὐτὸς ταῦτα πρότερον πάντα καὶ διὰ παντὸς τοῦ βίου φυλάξας, οὕτω καὶ τοῖς ἄλλοις ἐπιτάξας φαίνεται, ὥστε πῇ μὲν προηγεῖσθαι τὸν νόμον τοῦ τρόπου, πῇ δὲ τὸν τρόπον τοῦ νόμου, ὥσπερ κἀνταῦθα τρία ταῦτα πρὸ τῶν ἄλλων νομοθετήσας ἢ καὶ νομοθετῆσαι μέλλων, τό τε τὸν Θεὸν ἀγαπᾶν καὶ τοὺς γονεῖς τιμᾶν, τὸν δὲ Θεὸν καὶ αὐτῶν τούτων προτιμᾶν τῶν γονέων καὶ τοῦ φυσικοῦ τὸ θεῖον καὶ τοῦ καλοῦ προτιθέναι φίλτρον.

Ὅρα πῶς αὐτὸς προλαβὼν οὐ τούτους φυλάττει τοὺς νόμους μόνον, ἀλλὰ καὶ τῶν νόμων τὴν τάξιν καὶ τὴν προτίμησιν, πρότερον μὲν τὸν αὐτοῦ τιμῶν Πατέρα τὲ καὶ Θεὸν καὶ ἐν τοῖς αὐτοῦ τὰ αὐτοῦ ποιῶν ἐν τῷ ἱερῷ τῶν ἱερῶν λογίων καὶ ἀκροώμενος καὶ διαλεγόμενος, οὐ μὴν ἀλλὰ καὶ παρὰ τῶν γονέων ἐπεγκαλούμενος ὑπερτιθεὶς καὶ ἀντεγκαλῶν καὶ δευτέρου λόγου τἄλλα ποιούμενος, ἔπειτα καὶ τοῖς γονεῦσι διὰ τέλους ὑποτασσόμενος. Ἡ δὲ μήτηρ πάλιν μαθήτρια γίνεται τοῦ παιδός, ἡ ὄντως τῆς

evangelist summarizes this in a single remark, testifying that he lived another kind of life and by another law. For sometimes he taught this law first through his spoken word, and then he himself was subsequently seen to confirm and practice it in his life; as, for example, with the precept, *no one should seek his own good,* and that of the good shepherd laying down *his life for his sheep,* for not long afterward he himself appeared seeking our salvation and giving up his own life. At other times he first presented his own life as the example, and then subsequently brought forward its legal principle, such as to not covet, or swear oaths, or be angry, or the rest of the commandments. By first keeping all these commandments himself throughout his life, he was obviously commanding that others keep them, so that sometimes he placed the legal injunction before its manner of observation, and other times the manner of observation before the injunction, so that he established, or would come to establish, these three laws above all, namely, to love God and honor one's parents, and to prefer God over one's own parents, and to choose divine love over natural beauty.

See how he himself from the start observed not only these laws but also their arrangement and order of importance. First, he honors his Father and God, and in his Father's house undertakes his Father's business by listening to and uttering the words of sacred scripture in the temple. And not just this, but when he is criticized by his parents, he places himself on a higher level, responds with a countercriticism, and considers the other matters of secondary importance, but after that he was completely submissive to his parents. And his mother, moreover, became the disciple of her own child, for she was truly the mother of Wisdom as

Σοφίας μήτηρ καὶ τῆς Σοφίας θυγάτηρ. Οὐ γὰρ κατὰ παῖδας, μᾶλλον δὲ οὐδὲ κατ' ἄνδρας ἢ ἄνθρωπον ὅλως, ἀλλ' ὡς Θεῷ προσεῖχε λοιπὸν καὶ θείας πράξεις τὲ καὶ φωνὰς τὰς ἐκείνου φωνὰς ἡγεῖτο καὶ πράξεις· ᾧ δὴ καὶ μηδὲν αὐτὴν τῶν ὑπ' ἐκείνου λεγομένων ἢ πραττομένων ἐξέπιπτεν, ἀλλὰ καθάπερ τὸν Λόγον αὐτὸν ἐν τοῖς λαγόσι τὸ πρότερον, οὕτω καὶ νῦν τοὺς αὐτοῦ λόγους καὶ τρόπους καὶ πάντα τὰ πολιτεύματα συλλαμβάνουσα καὶ ὡσπερεὶ τρέφουσα *ἐν τῇ καρδίᾳ αὐτῆς*. Τοῦτο μὲν καθ' ἑαυτὴν διαπλάττουσα καὶ ἀνασκοποῦσα, τά τε εἴδη καὶ κάλλη καὶ τὰς δυνάμεις, τοῦτο δὲ καὶ τὸν καιρὸν ἀναμένουσα τῆς πάντων τούτων ἐκδηλοτέρας ἀποκαλύψεως, καὶ τοῦτο μὲν ὡς τύποις καὶ νόμοις κατὰ παντὸς τοῦ βίου χρωμένη, τοῦτο δὲ καὶ ὡς τεκμηρίοις τῶν μελλόντων περὶ αὐτὴν καὶ τὸν ταύτης υἱὸν ἀπορρήτων μυστηρίων καὶ τῶν θαυμάτων.

Ἀλλ' ἵνα τὰ ἐν μέσῳ παραδράμωμεν πάντα, ἃ δὴ καὶ τὸ Εὐαγγέλιον καὶ ἅπερ αὐτὸς ὁ Θεὸς Λόγος ἑαυτὸν ἐπικρύπτων καὶ μὴ φανερῶν αὐτοῦ τὴν δύναμιν τῆς θεότητος, ἵνα καὶ τὸ πλῆρες ἀπολάβῃ τῆς ἡλικίας καὶ *τὸ* τῆς οἰκονομίας συνάψῃ *σῶμα* τοῖς θαύμασι καὶ τοῖς δόγμασι καὶ τοῖς πάθεσι *συναρμολογούμενον*, ἀλλὰ μὴ διεσπασμένον ἢ καθάπερ διερριμμένον τοῖς μέλεσιν, ἄλλωστε καὶ ἵν' αὐτὰς παρ' ἑαυτῶν τὰς αἰτίας ἔχῃ τῶν ἀποβάσεων, εἴ γε τὰ μὲν θαύματα προοδοποιὰ καὶ βεβαιωτικὰ τῶν δογμάτων, τὰ δὲ δόγματα τῶν θαυμάτων· δι' ἀλλήλων γὰρ πιστούμενα καὶ ἑκάτερα, δι' ἀμφοτέρων δὲ τὰ τῶν ὄχλων ῥεύματα, πῇ μὲν λεγόντων "*οὐδέποτέ τις οὕτως ἐλάλησε*," πῇ δὲ "οὐδέποτέ

well as the daughter of Wisdom. For she no longer saw him as if he were a child, or rather not as a man, or even a human being at all, but as God, and she considered his words and deeds as divine deeds and words. And this is the reason why she did not forget any of the things he said or did, but just as she had formerly held the Word in her womb, so too now she held within herself his words, mannerisms, and his entire manner of living, as though cherishing them *in her heart.* She would often turn these things over in her mind and consider their form, beauty, and qualities; at other times, she awaited the moment when all these things would be more clearly revealed. Moreover, she made use of the former as a pattern and rule throughout her life, and the latter as testimonies to the ineffable mysteries and wonders concerning herself and her son that were to come.

But here we must omit everything that happened after this, which the Gospel and indeed God the Word himself concealed, choosing not to reveal the power of his divinity, so that he might attain the fullness of his human stature, and *join his body,* which he assumed in the divine economy of salvation, in a *fitting manner* to his miracles, teachings, and sufferings. He did this so that his constitutive members would not be broken or scattered but would have the causes of their principles within themselves, so that his miracles would prepare the way for and confirm his teachings, and his teachings his miracles. For since each is confirmed through the others, it was on account of both that crowds of people streamed toward him, sometimes saying, "No man *has ever spoken like this,*" and at other times, "No one has ever

τις οὕτως ἐποίησεν ὡς οὗτος ὁ ἄνθρωπος." Διὰ δὲ τὸν ὄχλον ὁ φθόνος, διὰ δὲ τὸν φθόνον τὸ μῖσος, διὰ δὲ τὸ μῖσος τὸ Πάθος καὶ ὅσα λοιπὸν τοῦ Πάθους ἐπέκεινα.

Θεοφάνια

64 Ἵν' οὖν παραλίπωμεν τὰ παραλειπόμενα, συναναφανῇ δὲ καὶ τοῖς Θεοφανίοις ὁ Λόγος. Ὁ μὲν οὖν τριακονταέτης, ὁ δὲ Ἰωάννης καὶ μικρόν τι πρός· ὁ μὲν ἐπὶ τὸ βαπτίζεσθαι, ὁ δὲ ἐπὶ τὸ βαπτίζειν ἔρχεται, καὶ οὐ τοῦτο μόνον παρόμοιον, ἀλλ' ὅρα μοι Θεοῦ μυστήρια. Ἐπεὶ γὰρ τῷ μὲν δοκεῖν ὑψηλότερος ὁ ἐρημικός, τὸ δ' ἀληθὲς ὁ πολιτικὸς βίος καὶ δυσχερέστερός τε καὶ ἐνδοξότερος, ὁ μὲν ἐνδοξότερόν τε καὶ χαλεπώτερον ἑαυτῷ, ὁ δὲ δεύτερόν τε καὶ εὐχερέστερον, Ἰωάννῃ τῷ δούλῳ καὶ φίλῳ τὸν ἐρημικὸν ἐγχειρίζει βίον. Ἐπεὶ δὲ καὶ τῷ φαινομένῳ προσέχοντες οἱ πολλοί—μᾶλλον δὲ σχεδὸν πάντες—καὶ διὰ τὴν ἡλικίαν καὶ διὰ τὴν πολιτείαν ὡς ὑπὲρ ἄνθρωπον πολλῷ κρείττω τὸν Ἰωάννην ἐνόμιζον· καὶ ἐκείνῳ μὲν τὸ βαπτίζειν, ἑαυτῷ δὲ τὸ βαπτίζεσθαι, ἄλλωστε καὶ ἵνα μὴ παρ' ἑαυτοῦ—καὶ γὰρ κομπαστικόν τε καὶ ἄλλως ὕποπτον—ἀλλὰ παρ' αὐτοῦ τούτου μαρτυρηθῇ, παρ' οὗ καὶ τἄλλα τῶν μαρτυριῶν εἶχον τὸ ἀξιόπιστον καὶ παρ' οὗ καὶ αὐτὸ τὸ βάπτισμα καὶ τὰς παραγγελίας ἐδέχοντο. Καὶ ἐμαθητεύοντο δὲ οὐκ ὀλίγοι καὶ ἀδιασπάστως εἴχοντο, καθάπερ Ἀνδρέας τὲ καὶ Πέτρος καὶ Ἰωάννης ὁ ταῦτα γράφων αὐτός.

65 Οὕτω γοῦν καὶ ἀπὸ τῆς πολιτείας καὶ ἀπὸ τῆς διαίτης, καὶ ἀπὸ τῆς στολῆς καὶ ἀπὸ τῆς μορφῆς αὐτῆς, καὶ ἀπ'

done the things that this man has done." And it was because of the crowds that envy arose against him, and because of the envy, hatred arose, and because of the hatred, the Passion, and all the things that followed after the Passion.

Theophany

Passing over, then, as we must, what has been omitted, the 64
Word was made manifest at the Theophany. He was thirty years old, and John the Baptist was a little older. The former came to be baptized, the latter to baptize, and since this was not the only similarity, consider with me the mysteries of God. Whereas the ascetic way of life may seem loftier, the truth is that public life is both more difficult and more glorious. The one is more glorious and more difficult in and of itself, while the other comes second and is easier, and this is why John, the Word's servant and friend, was entrusted with the solitary way of life. Now because most people pay attention to outward appearances—or perhaps nearly all people—they thought that John, on account of his stature and way of life, which surpassed human nature, was far superior. And while it was John's part to baptize, it was the Lord's to be baptized so that he would not be testified to by himself—which would have been immodest and at all events suspect—but rather by John, whose other testimonies had proved trustworthy, and whose baptism and promises were being accepted. And not a few people became John's disciples and followed him closely, such as Andrew, Peter, and John, who himself wrote these things down.

Thus it was that, because of his way of life and his pecu- 65
liar diet, as well as his attire and indeed his very appearance

αὐτῆς δὲ τῆς παρρησίας, ἀνηρτήσατο τὸν ὄχλον καὶ μετὰ τοσούτου παραστήματος καὶ φρονήματος, ὥστε καὶ ὁ Χριστὸς δοκεῖν εἶναι καὶ πέμποντας ἐρωτᾶν, ἵνα καὶ πάλιν ἄμφω μαρτυρηθῇ ὅτι τὲ αὐτὸς ὁ Χριστὸς οὐκ ἔστι καὶ ὅτι μετ᾽ αὐτὸν εὐθὺς ὁ Χριστός. Διὸ καὶ ὁ Χριστὸς ἐκείνου μὲν ἀνέσχε τὰ θαύματα, ἑαυτῷ δὲ κατέλιπεν, ἵνα τούτῳ γοῦν ἑαυτῷ μὲν ἐπιστρέψῃ τὸν ὄχλον, ἐκείνου δὲ ἀποσπάσῃ. Ἀλλὰ πῶς ὅτι καὶ *ὀπίσω μου ἔρχεται* καὶ *μέσος ὑμῶν* ἢ ὅτι καὶ *ὀπίσω* μὲν *ἔρχεται* τῷ κηρύγματι καὶ τῇ ἀναδείξει τοῦ ἀξιώματος, εἰ καὶ *ἔμπροσθεν* πάλιν τῷ ἀξιώματι; Μετὰ γὰρ τὸν δορυφόρον ὁ βασιλεύς. *Μέσος* δὲ καὶ νῦν ἔστηκε τῷ σώματι καὶ ὅτι μετὰ τῶν ἄλλων ὁμοίως πρόσεισι τῷ βαπτίσματι. Καὶ οὐ τοῖς ῥήμασι μαρτυρεῖ μόνον, ἀλλὰ καὶ αὐτῷ τῷ δεικτικῷ τοῦ δακτύλου σχήματι· βλέπων γὰρ καὶ αὐτὸν μετὰ τῶν ἄλλων ἐρχόμενον ὡς καθαρθησόμενον, "*ἴδε,*" φησίν, "*ὁ Ἀμνὸς τοῦ Θεοῦ ὁ αἴρων τὴν ἁμαρτίαν τοῦ κόσμου.*" Οὐ γὰρ ὅσον, φησίν, αὐτὸς οὐκ ἐστι καθαρσίων δεόμενος, ἀλλὰ καὶ παντὸς τοῦ κόσμου καθάρσιον. Ὁ μὲν οὖν οὕτως ἡμᾶς καθαίρει καὶ ἡμῖν καθαίρεται καὶ εὐθέως ἀνέρχεται ἐκ τοῦ ὕδατος, ὥσπερ καὶ μετ᾽ ὀλίγον τοῦ μνήματος, ἐκεῖνο μὲν ὡς ἁμαρτίας ἐλεύθερος, τοῦτο δὲ ὡς καὶ διαφθορᾶς ἀνεπίδεκτος, ἤδη δὲ καὶ ὡς αὐτῆς τῆς φθορᾶς ἀλλότριος, αὐτῇ τῇ φθορᾷ φθορὰ διὰ τῆς φθορᾶς γενόμενος· ἢ καὶ ἐκεῖνο μὲν ὡς ἑαυτῷ τοῦ κάτω βίου τὸν κόσμον συναναφέρων, τοῦτο δὲ ὡς καὶ τοῦ θανάτου συναφθαρτίζων ἑαυτῷ καὶ συνυιοθετούμενος. Καὶ ὁ μὲν ἀνέρχεται, τὸ δὲ Πνεῦμα κατέρχεται· ἐχρῆν γὰρ κἀντούτῳ τυπωθῆναι τὴν θείαν καὶ ἀνθρωπίνην ἕνωσιν, καὶ ἡμῶν μὲν τὴν

and boldness of speech, the crowds clung to him, and such was his standing and loftiness of mind that they thought he was the Christ; and they sent others to ask him if he was, so that in response he might also testify that he himself was not the Christ, but that the Christ was coming immediately after him. This is why, while Christ consented to his miracles, he also reserved miracles for himself, so that the crowds would leave John and turn to him. But how can John say that Christ is *coming after me* and is *already among you?* Or that he is *coming after* in terms of my preaching and in the recognition of his honor if he is again *before* me in honor? Because the imperial escort comes after the emperor. And he now stands *among you* in body and because he likewise comes forward for baptism with others. And John bore witness to him not only with his words but also gestured to him with his finger, for when he saw him in the crowd coming with the others as though seeking purification, he said, "*Behold the Lamb of God, who takes away the sin of the world.*" It is not, he said, the case that he is in need of purification but rather that he is the purification of the whole world. Thus he both purifies us and is purified by us, and he immediately arose from the water just as he would soon rise from the tomb. From the former he came forth as one free of sin, and from the latter as one precluding destruction; and even then he was a stranger to corruption itself, becoming the very corruption of corruption by means of corruption. Or by means of his baptism he raises up, together with himself, the world from its lower life, just as by means of his death he makes us incorruptible and adopted sons together with himself. And as he ascends from the water, the Spirit descends, for even here it was necessary to express the union of the divine and

ἀνάβασιν, ἐκείνου δὲ τὴν κατάβασιν, ἀλλ' ἡμῶν μὲν τὴν ὀλίγην, ἐκείνου δὲ τὴν πολλήν τε καὶ ἄπειρον συγκατάβασιν.

66 Οὐ κατερχόμενον δὲ μόνον, ἀλλὰ καὶ μένον ἐπ' αὐτόν, οὐχ ὡς νῦν μένον, ὥσπερ οὐδ' ὡς νῦν κατερχόμενον, πῶς γάρ, ἐφ' ὃν ἐξ ἀρχῆς *πᾶν τὸ πλήρωμα* κατῴκησε *τῆς θεότητος;* Ἀλλ' ἵν', ὅπερ ἦν, τοῦτο φανῇ καὶ τοῖς ἄλλοις, ὅλος Θεοῦ καὶ Θεός. Οἶμαι δὲ ὅτι καὶ καθάπερ τὰ πλεῖστα τῶν ἄλλων, οὕτω δὲ καὶ τοῦτο τύπον εἶναι τῆς ἐφ' ἡμᾶς μετὰ τὴν κάθαρσιν ἐπιδημίας τοῦ Πνεύματος. Οὕτω μὲν οὖν τὸ Πνεῦμα συντρέχει, συνέλκει δὲ καὶ τὴν φωνὴν ἅμα ἑαυτό τε πιστούμενον ὅτι Πνεῦμα Θεοῦ. Καὶ τίνος ἕνεκεν ἡ φωνή; Καὶ ὅτι καὶ οὗτος Υἱὸς Θεοῦ, ᾧ καὶ ὅτι Πατὴρ ἐκεῖνος συναναφαίνεται, καὶ οὕτως ἡ Τριὰς ἑνουμένη τὲ ἅμα καὶ διαιρουμένη γνωρίζεται, τὸ μὲν τῷ ἰδίως ἕκαστον ὀνομάζεσθαι, τὸ δὲ τῷ καὶ ἅμα συντρέχειν τὲ καὶ συναναφαίνεσθαι. Οὐ μὴν ἀλλὰ καὶ τῷ μίαν εἶναι τὴν ὑπόστασιν τοῦ Χριστοῦ ἀνθρώπου τὲ καὶ Θεοῦ, καὶ τοσοῦτον ἄνθρωπον τὸν Θεόν, ὅσον καὶ Θεὸν τὸν ἄνθρωπον, εἴ γε τὸν αὐτὸν καὶ συναμφότερον ὁ Πατὴρ *Υἱὸν* καλεῖ καὶ *ἀγαπητόν.* Ἀλλὰ τῆς μὲν τοῦ Πνεύματος θεωρίας Ἰωάννης ἠξιοῦτο μόνος, τῆς δὲ τοῦ Πατρὸς φωνῆς τὲ καὶ μαρτυρίας καὶ πᾶς ὁ λαός, ὥσπερ καὶ πρότερον ἐπὶ τοῦ ὄρους ἡνίκα τῷ Μωϋσῇ Θεὸς ἐχρημάτιζε. Μωϋσῆς μὲν ἑώρα μόνος, ἤκουον δὲ καὶ πάντες, οὐχ οἱ περιεστηκότες μόνον, ἀλλὰ καὶ οἱ πόρρωθεν ἑστηκότες, κατὰ τὴν ἀναλογίαν τῆς στάσεως ἢ τῆς τάξεως, πλὴν εἰ τις ἀνάξιος καὶ τῆς ἀκοῆς, ὡς κἀν τοῖς ἄλλοις ἀνήκοος καὶ μηδὲν τῷ θείῳ νόμῳ

the human, and whereas the ascent is ours, the descent is his, but while our accommodation to him is small, his to us is rich and boundless.

And not only did the Spirit descend upon him but it also 66
remained upon him, though it did not remain upon him only in that moment or descend upon him only then, for how could such a thing be possible when in him, from the beginning, dwelled *the entire fullness of the deity?* But this happened so that he, who is wholly from God and is himself God, might be revealed to others. And I also think that, just as with the majority of other things, this too was a figure of the coming of the Spirit upon us after our purification. This is why the Spirit appeared with him, drawing down the divine voice, which at the same time confirmed that this was the Spirit of God. And why was this voice heard? To declare that he is the Son of God, and that the Father is manifested together with him, and thus the Trinity is made known as simultaneously united and distinguished, the latter insofar as each of the three persons may be individually named, and the former inasmuch as they act and appear as one. And not only this, but by virtue of the single hypostasis of Christ as man and God, and because he is as much man as he is God, and as much God as he is man, God called both together his *beloved Son.* But, while John alone was deemed worthy of the vision of the Spirit, the people were deemed worthy of the voice and testimony of the Father, just as long ago when God spoke to Moses on the mountain. Moses alone saw the vision, but the voice was heard by all, and not only by those who were present, but also by those standing far off, in proportion to their position or rank, except those who were unworthy of hearing, as they were disobedient in other things

πειθόμενος. Ἀμφότερα γοῦν συμφερόντως καὶ ἐπὶ τοῦ βαπτίσματος ᾠκονόμητο· εἴ τε γὰρ ἄμφω, καὶ ὁ λαὸς καὶ ὁ Ἰωάννης, ἀμφοῖν ἠξιώθησαν, οὐδὲν ἂν τῷ Βαπτιστῇ καὶ διδασκάλῳ περιεγένετο, ἀλλὰ κοινὸν ἂν καὶ τὸ φρικτὸν τοῦ Πνεύματος ἐλογίζετο· εἴ τε δὲ καὶ τῆς φωνῆς ἀπεκέκλειντο, ἀμάρτυρα μὲν τὰ κατὰ τὸν Χριστόν, ὕποπτα δὲ καὶ τὰ κατὰ τὸν Ἰωάννην ὡς μαρτυροῦντα πρὸς χάριν· νυνὶ δὲ τὸ κατὰ τὴν φωνὴν πιστὸν ἐποίει καὶ τὸ κατὰ τὴν ὄψιν.

67 Ἐπεὶ δὲ βαπτίζεται, τὸν Βαπτιστὴν διαδέχεται καὶ τοῦ Ἰορδάνου τὴν ἔρημον ἀνταλλάττεται, ἅμα τὲ καὶ τῷ πολιτικῷ καὶ τὸν ἐρημικὸν βίον συμπλέκων, καὶ τῷ τόπῳ πρὸς τὴν πάλην τὸν Ἀντίπαλον ἐκκαλούμενος, καὶ ἡμῖν μετὰ τὴν κάθαρσιν τοῦ βαπτίσματος καὶ τὴν δι' ἐγκρατείας νομοθετῶν κάθαρσιν καὶ τὴν παρασκευὴν τὴν πρὸς τοὺς ἀγῶνας. Τοιγαροῦν νηστεύει, πειράζεται διὰ πάντων, νικᾷ διὰ πάντων, διακονεῖται μετὰ τὴν νίκην καὶ τοῖς ἀγγέλοις, τύπος καὶ ἡμῖν διὰ πάντων γίνεται, μετὰ τὴν πίστιν καὶ τὴν τάξιν παραδιδοὺς καὶ τῶν ἄθλων καὶ τῶν ἐπάθλων. Πάλιν κατέρχεται πρὸς τὸν Βαπτιστήν, πάλιν μαρτυρεῖται τοῖς αὐτοῖς ῥήμασι, τῷ αὐτῷ τοῦ δακτύλου σχήματι, πάλιν ἀναχωρεῖ, πάλιν ἐπιφαίνεται, μαρτυρεῖται πάλιν τῇ αὐτῇ φωνῇ, τῇ αὐτῇ χειρί. Διπλοῦς γὰρ ἦν—καὶ Λόγος νοούμενος καὶ λεγόμενος καὶ ἄνθρωπος ὁρώμενος καὶ δεικνύμενος—ὁσάκις κρείττων ὡς Θεὸς τοῦ ἀντιθέου γίνεται, τοσαυτάκις καὶ περὶ Ἰωάννου τὴν μαρτυρίαν δέχεται. Προσδέχεται καὶ τοὺς αὐτοῦ μαθητάς, ἐπεὶ καὶ τὴν μαθητείαν ὅλην τοῦ κόσμου· Ἀνδρέας οὗτος καὶ Ἰωάννης ἦν, τὰ

and disregarded the divine law. It was thus fitting that both of these things took place at the baptism of Christ, for if the people and John had been deemed worthy of both, then nothing greater would have remained for the Baptist and teacher, since the awe-inspiring manifestation of the Spirit would have been considered as common to all. But if, on the other hand, the voice was not heard, then the things concerning Christ would have remained without testimony, and John's testimony would have been suspect, as if it were given in order to please. But as it happened, the voice also confirmed what was seen.

Having been baptized, he became the Baptist's successor, 67
and exchanged the Jordan for the desert, weaving together public life with life in the wilderness, and calling his Opponent to battle in that place. And he established a law for us that after our purification in baptism there is also purification through self-control and preparation for ascetic struggles. Thus, he fasted, was tested in all things, and triumphed in all things, and after his victory he was ministered to by angels, in all things becoming an example for us, and teaching us, after faith and order, about spiritual contests and their prizes. After this he returned once again to the Baptist, and once again he was testified to with the same words and with the same gesture of the finger, and again he departed, and once again he appeared, and again was testified to by the same voice and by the same hand. For he was double—both understood to be and being called the Word of God, and equally a human being who could be seen and to whom one could gesture—and as many times as God is superior to what is not God, the same number of times he received the testimony of John. And he received John's disciples, and thereafter the discipleship of the whole world.

πρῶτα τῶν ἀρετῶν, ὁ μὲν γὰρ τῆς ἀνδρείας, ὁ δὲ τῆς παρθενίας γνώρισμα. Ἄγει καὶ τὸν Πέτρον Ἀνδρέας, τὴν σαρκικὴν ἀναστρέφων γέννησιν καὶ πρῶτος ὁ δεύτερος ἐπὶ τὴν πνευματικὴν ἀναγέννησιν καθηγούμενος, ἅμα τὲ τοῦτο τυπῶν καὶ ἵνα μὴ τὰ πάντα πρῶτος ὁ Πέτρος ᾖ, ἀλλ' ἔστιν οὗ καὶ τὸ δευτερεῖον, εἰ δεῖ, φέρειν καὶ περικόπτῃ τὴν ἔπαρσιν. Οὕτω παραδίδωσι μὲν Ἰωάννης τῷ Δεσπότῃ καὶ τοὺς μαθητὰς καὶ τὸ κήρυγμα, αὐτὸς δὲ παραδίδοται τῷ Ἡρώδῃ· σπεύδει γὰρ καὶ ἄνωθεν προλαβεῖν τῷ πάθει τὸ Πάθος καὶ κάτωθεν τὴν ἔλευσιν τῷ κηρύγματι. Καὶ Γαλιλαία μὲν πρώτη τὸν Ἰησοῦν σὺν τοῖς μαθηταῖς ὁρᾷ παρρησιαζόμενον καὶ διδάσκοντα, καὶ Φίλιππον καὶ Ναθαναὴλ προστίθησι τῷ πληρώματι.

68 Τρίτη μετὰ ταύτην καὶ ὁ *γάμος* ὁ *ἐν Κανᾷ* καὶ ἡ τῶν θαυμασίων ἀρχή, τοῦ ὕδατος ἡ πρὸς οἶνον μεταβολή. Παρῆν δὲ καὶ ἡ μήτηρ, καὶ τῶν θαυμάτων καὶ τῶν δογμάτων αὐτόπτις τὲ καὶ αὐτήκοος. Μέγα μὲν οὖν καὶ τοῦ θαύματος τὸ φαινόμενον, πολὺ δὲ μεῖζον τὸ κρυπτόμενον καὶ νοούμενον, τῆς ἀνθρωπίνης, οἶμαι, φύσεως ἡ πρὸς τὴν θείαν ἕνωσις καὶ τῶν καθαρῶν καὶ ἀμιάντων ψυχῶν ὁ καθαρώτατος πολλῷ Δεσπότης τὲ καὶ Νυμφίος· ἐν ᾧ καὶ ἡ τοῦ ἀτιμοτέρου καὶ ὑγροτέρου βίου πρὸς τὸ κρεῖττον μεταβολὴ ἢ καὶ τοῦ ἐξιτήλου καὶ ὑδατώδους καὶ Παλαιοῦ Δόγματος πρὸς τὸν ἡδὺν καὶ συνεστηκότα μᾶλλον καὶ ὠφελιμώτερον λόγον, τὸν Εὐαγγελικόν, ὃν καὶ ἐκστατικὸν ὁ λόγος οἶδε, τὴν ἀμείνω καὶ θειοτέραν ἔκστασιν, ὃν καὶ κρατῆρα κιρνᾶν τὴν Σοφίαν βούλεται, ὡς καὶ τοῦ

These were Andrew and John, the chiefs of virtue, Andrew being the symbol of courage and John of virginity. Andrew brought Peter, reversing the order of their carnal birth, so that the second became the first leader by virtue of his spiritual rebirth, though at the same time this indicated that Peter would not be first in all things, but there would be a time when he would be second when it was necessary to curb his pride. Thus, John surrendered both his disciples and his preaching to the Lord, while he himself was surrendered to Herod, for while he was still on earth, he hastened to anticipate the Passion by his passion, and to proclaim the advent of Christ to those below the earth. And it was Galilee which first saw Jesus speaking boldly with his disciples and teaching, and it was there that Philip and Nathanael became disciples.

On the third day after this, the *wedding at Cana* took 68
place, and the beginning of his wonders, namely, the transformation of the water into wine. His mother was also present, and she was both an eyewitness of his miracles and a direct hearer of his teachings. Great was the outward impression made by this miracle, but what it concealed, which is available only to thought, was far greater, and in my opinion this is the union of human nature with the divine nature, and that he is by far the purest Master and Bridegroom of pure and undefiled souls. In this miracle, we also see the transformation of our self-indulgent and dishonorable life into something superior, as well as the transformation of the weak and watery Old Testament into the sweet, solidified, and beneficial word of the Gospel, which scripture knows to be ecstatic, inducing a superior and more divine state of ecstasy, which Wisdom herself desires to mix in

παλαιοῦ τι παραμιγνῦσαν πρὸς ἠπιωτέραν καὶ κεκερασμένην εὖ τὴν κατάποσιν. Ἡ δὲ μεσῖτις τῶνδε τῶν ἀγαθῶν καὶ τοῦ τύπου μεσῖτις γίνεται. Καὶ ὅρα πῶς καὶ φιλοτιμουμένη καθὰ καὶ γυνή τε καὶ μήτηρ ἐπὶ ταῖς τοῦ υἱοῦ θαυματοποιΐαις καὶ ἀνεπαχθῆ ποιουμένη τὴν ἀφορμήν. Οὔτε γὰρ ἐπιτάσσει τοῦ θαύματος τὴν ἐπίδειξιν, οὔτε δὲ πάλιν δέεται· τὸ μὲν γὰρ οἶδε τραχὺ λίαν, τὸ δὲ ταπεινόν, ἀμφότερα δὲ φορτικά, ἄλλωστε καὶ ὅτι τὸ μὲν ἐπιτυγχάνειν οὕτω λυπεῖ, τῷ δὲ ἀποτυγχάνειν λυπεῖται. Τί οὖν ποιεῖ; Μερίζεται καὶ ἁρμόζεται πρὸς ἑκάτερα καὶ ὡς μὲν μήτηρ θαρρεῖ, ὡς δὲ δούλη καὶ ὑποστέλλεται, καὶ ὑποβάλλει μὲν τὴν χρείαν, ἅμα δὲ καὶ τὴν ταύτης ἐπιθυμίαν, καὶ ὡς ἐρᾷ τὴν τοῦ παιδὸς ἀνακαλυφθῆναι καὶ δημοσιευθῆναι δύναμιν. Οἶδε γὰρ ὡς οὐ μόνον ταύτης υἱός, ἀλλὰ καὶ τῶν ὅλων δημιουργὸς καὶ καινουργὸς καὶ μεταβολεὺς τῶν ἁπάντων, ὅτε καὶ βούλεται· τά τε ἄλλα καὶ ἐξ ὧν αὐτῆς οὔτε τὴν μήτραν ἀνέῳξε καὶ τὴν γαστέρα κατῴκησε, καὶ πάλιν οὔτε τὴν παρθενίαν διέφθειρε καὶ τὴν μήτραν ἀνέῳξε καὶ τῆς γαστρὸς ἐξώλισθε καὶ κεκλεισμένην ταύτην κατέλιπε· διὸ καὶ ἐλπίζει καὶ οὐκ ἐπιτάσσει τὸ θαῦμα, τὸ μὲν διὰ τὴν ἐκείνου δύναμιν, τὸ δὲ διὰ τὴν οἰκείαν ὕφεσιν. Ταύτῃ τοι κἀκεῖνος καὶ τὸ φιλότιμον ἅμα ταύτης ἀποκρουόμενος καὶ τὸ κατ' ἶσον ταῖς λοιπαῖς μητράσι καὶ ταύτην παρρησιάζεσθαι ἐπικόπτει καὶ διορθοῦται· διὸ καὶ οὐδὲ "μητέρα," ἀλλ' ἁπλῶς "γυναῖκα" καλεῖ, ὑπακούει δὲ ὅμως καὶ ὡς μητέρα

a mixing bowl so that by mingling it with the old she might make the drink milder and well blended. And the mediator of these good things also became the mediator of this symbol. And observe her generosity, which is fitting for a woman and a mother, in view of her son's miraculous works, and how, without being irksome, she creates the opportunity for the miracle. She did not order the performance of a miracle, nor again did she beg for it, because she knew that the former would have been extremely irritating, while the latter would have been demeaning, and both would have been tiresome; and had she succeeded in this manner, she would have caused sorrow, whereas failing would have caused her to sorrow. What then did she do? She divided her efforts and adapted them to each, so that, on the one hand, she acted boldly as a mother and, on the other hand, as a servant, she drew back and called attention to the need for wine, but at the same time expressed her own desire, inasmuch as she longed to see her son's divine power revealed and made public. For she knew that he was not only her son but also the creator, renewer, and transformer of all things, whenever he chooses. And she knew, among other things, that though he dwelt in her womb, he did not open her uterus, nor did he despoil her virginity when he opened her uterus, came forth from her womb, and then left it closed behind him. This is why she hoped for but did not demand the miracle: the former because of his power, the latter because of her own modesty. Yet the Lord rebuffed her and her generosity, and cut off and corrected her boldness of speech, though this is a prerogative of other mothers. He thus addressed her not as "mother" but simply as "woman," but he nevertheless obeyed her, honoring her as his mother, or

ταύτην τιμῶν καὶ τῆς προαιρέσεως μᾶλλον ἀποδεχόμενος, ὁμοῦ δὲ καὶ τὸν κεκληκότα τῆς προθέσεως ἀμειβόμενος. Ἡ δὲ καθάπερ τῆς τοῦ παιδὸς δυναστείας αὐτάγγελος, διδάσκαλος καὶ τοῖς διακόνοις τοῦ πρακτέου γίνεται· "*ὅ,τι ἂν λέγῃ ὑμῖν* ποιεῖν ποιεῖτε." Ἡ δὲ τοῦ οἴνου μεταβολὴ καὶ τοῦ κεκληκότος μεταβολὴ γίνεται, καὶ τὸν γάμον καὶ τὸν οἶκον καταλιπὼν ὁ νυμφίος τῷ φίλῳ καὶ θαυματοποιῷ καὶ νυμφίῳ καὶ νυμφαγωγῷ τῶν καθαρῶν ψυχῶν μαθητεύεται, καὶ ἡ νύμφη δὲ τῇ μητρί, ἵνα μὴ τὸ ὕδωρ εἰς οἶνον μόνον, ἀλλὰ καὶ τὸν γάμον εἰς τὸ κρεῖττον, τὴν παρθενίαν, φανῇ μεταβάλλων· καὶ ὁ μὲν τῶν ἀνδρῶν, ἡ δὲ τῶν γυναικῶν ᾖ τύπος τὲ καὶ διδάσκαλος, μᾶλλον δὲ καὶ ἀμφοτέρων ἀμφότεροι. Οὕτω διηνεκῶς ἡ μήτηρ αὐτῷ συνῆν καὶ πανταχοῦ περιϊόντι συνεπορεύετο, τοῦτο ζωὴν ἔχουσα μόνον καὶ πνοὴν καὶ λόγον καὶ φῶς, ὅπερ ἐκείνῳ συνέζη τὲ καὶ συνέπνει καὶ ὃ συνωμίλει καὶ ὅπερ ἐκεῖνον ἔβλεπεν.

69 Ἀμέλει καὶ εἰς Βηθσαϊδὰ παρελθόντι καὶ Πέτρου τὴν πενθερὰν θεραπεύσαντι (ἐχρῆν γὰρ ἀπὸ τῶν οἰκειοτάτων τῶν θαυμάτων ἄρξασθαι καὶ μάλιστα Πέτρου τοῦ τιμιωτάτου τῶν μαθητῶν καὶ κορυφαιοτάτου), συνῆν μὲν ἡ μήτηρ, συμμερίζεται δὲ τῷ υἱῷ καὶ τὰς μαθητρίας, αὐτήν τε τὴν ἰαθεῖσαν σὺν τῇ θυγατρὶ καὶ τῇ γυναικὶ Πέτρου, διακουούσας μὲν καὶ τῶν τοῦ Ἰησοῦ λόγων, τὰ δὲ πλεῖστα τῇ Θεοτόκῳ καὶ συνούσας καὶ ὁμιλούσας. Ἐκεῖθεν πάλιν εἰς Ναζαρέτ· ἤδη γὰρ καὶ Ἰωσήφ, ὁ ταύτης μνηστήρ, πλήρης

rather accepting her wish, and at the same time rewarding the one who prompted her eagerness. And she, as the herald of her son's authority, also became the teacher of the stewards and told them what to do: "*Whatever he tells you* to do, do it." And the transformation of the wine also brought about the transformation of the host, for the bridegroom abandoned the wedding and his home and became a disciple of Christ, who is the friend, miracle worker, bridegroom, and bridal escort of pure souls. The bride, on the other hand, followed Christ's mother, so that not only would the water be transformed into wine, but that the marriage might also be seen to have been transformed into what is superior, namely, virginity. This took place so that Christ might be the example and teacher of men, and his mother the example and teacher of women, or rather that both should become teachers of both. In this way, the mother of the Lord remained with him continually, and she traveled together with him wherever he went, for she had this alone as her life, breath, word, and light, namely, to live with him, to breathe together with him, to speak with him, and to see him.

And indeed when the Lord was in Bethsaida and healed 69
Peter's mother-in-law (for it was necessary that his miracles begin with those to whom he was closest, and indeed with Peter, who was the most honored and chief of the disciples), his own mother was there with him, sharing the female disciples with her son, as was the woman herself who was healed together with her daughter and Peter's wife, who were listening to Jesus's words, but for the most part spent their time with the Theotokos and conversed with her. From there, they went again to Nazareth, because Joseph, who was Mary's betrothed, was already full of days, that is,

μὲν ἡμερῶν καὶ τῶν τοῦ βίου καὶ τῶν τοῦ Πνεύματος, πλήρης δὲ καὶ τῶν περὶ αὐτὴν μυστηρίων καὶ τῶν τοῦ ταύτης υἱοῦ τεραστίων, ἐτελεύτα, δέκα, φασί, πρὸς τοῖς ἑκατὸν γεγονὼς ἔτη καὶ ποθῶν τὴν ἀνάλυσιν. Καὶ ὁ μὲν οὕτως ἄνω πρὸς τὸν ὄντως Πατέρα, μᾶλλον δὲ πρὸς ὅλην ὁμοῦ τὴν Τριάδα, οἱ δὲ υἱοὶ—οὗτοι δὲ Ἰάκωβος καὶ Ἰούδας ἦν—τῷ υἱῷ κάτω συνηκολούθησαν καὶ αἱ θυγατέρες δὲ τῇ μητρί, μαθηταὶ γενόμενοι καὶ μαθήτριαι. Καὶ οὕτω πορευομένῳ κατὰ πᾶσαν χώραν καὶ πόλιν καὶ ἰωμένῳ πᾶσαν νόσον καὶ πᾶσαν μαλακίαν, συνεπορεύοντο μὲν πάντες καὶ πᾶσαι, καὶ θεαταὶ τῶν θαυμάτων καὶ ἀκροαταὶ τῶν διδαγμάτων καὶ δογμάτων ἐγίνοντο. Ἡ δὲ μήτηρ κἀνταῦθα πάντων ἐκράτει καὶ πάντων προστάτις καὶ μεσῖτις ἢ καὶ δεσπότις ἦν.

Τί ἔτι; Ζεβεδὴ καὶ Γενησαρέτ, ἡ μὲν κώμη, ἡ δὲ λίμνη—πάγκαλόν τι καὶ πάμφορον τῆς Γαλιλαίας χρῆμα καὶ θέαμα, “φιάλη” μὲν καλουμένη διὰ τὸ περιφερὲς τοῦ σχήματος, οὕτω γὰρ καθ᾽ Ἑβραΐδα γλῶτταν ἡ Γενησαρὲτ ἑρμηνεύεται, βύσσου δὲ καὶ βαλσάμου κυκλόθεν μήτηρ, τροφὸς δὲ παντοδαπῶν καὶ ἡδίστων ἰχθύων. Τὸ δὲ ὕδωρ οὕτω μὲν κοῦφον καὶ διαυγές, ὡς ἀέρι σχεδὸν παραβάλλειν, οὕτω δὲ καὶ πότιμον καὶ τρόφιμον καὶ ἡδύ, ὡς μηδὲν παραβάλλειν ἢ καὶ τοὺς ἰχθύας αὐτοὺς ἐν ταῖς πόσεσιν ὑπερβάλλειν ἢ ταῖς τροφαῖς ἐκείνους. Οὕτω δὲ οὖσα καὶ τὸ κάλλος καλλίστη καὶ τὴν χρείαν ἡδίστη καὶ ὠφελιμωτάτη, οὕτω τυγχάνει καὶ μεγίστη, μᾶλλον δὲ ἀναλογωτάτη τὸ μέγεθος, ὡς οὐκ ὀλίγῳ πλεῖον ἢ πεντήκοντα σταδίων πάντοθεν τὴν

the days of his life and the Spirit, and also of the mysteries concerning her and the wondrous signs of her son. He was, they say, one hundred and ten years old and longing for his departure. And thus he began his journey heavenward to the true Father, or rather to the entire Trinity, while his sons on earth—James and Jude—followed the son, just as his daughters followed the mother, becoming male and female disciples. And as the Lord traveled through every region and city, healing every illness and every infirmity, all these men and women accompanied him, witnessing his miracles and listening to his teachings and precepts. At this time, his mother led them all, and was their protector, mediator, and sovereign.

What more can we say? Zebedee and Gennesaret, the former a village, the latter a lake—that exceedingly beautiful and productive location and sight of Galilee, called a "bowl" on account of its round shape, for this is what Gennesaret means in Hebrew. The lake is the mother of the flax and balsam that surrounds it, and the nurse of every variety of delectable fish. Her water is both buoyant and clear, almost comparable to the quality of air, and also potable, nourishing, and sweet, and in this regard is beyond comparison, other than to say that the fish themselves indulge more in drinking than eating. The lake, which is thus stunningly beautiful, and both exceedingly pleasant and most beneficial in providing for human needs, is also very large, or, rather, well proportioned in size, being well over fifty *stadia*

διάμετρον ἔχειν διὰ τὸ καὶ εἰς κύκλον ὥσπερ ἀποτορνεύεσθαι. Ἡ δὲ περὶ τὸν κύκλον πᾶσα δενδρῖτις, ὥσπερ στέφανος περικειμένη τῇ λίμνῃ καὶ ποικιλλομένη τοῖς φύλλοις τὲ καὶ τοῖς ἄνθεσιν, ἄλλοις τὲ πολλοῖς κάλεσι καὶ μεγέθεσι τῶν ἀκροδρύων βρύουσα, καὶ μάλιστα τῶν ἐλαιώνων καὶ ἀμπελώνων, ὑπερπληθέσι μὲν τὸ πλῆθος, ὑπερφυέσι δὲ τὴν φοράν, κατά τε κάλλος ἅμα καὶ γεῦσιν καὶ μέγεθος, ὥστε μετὰ τῶν ἄλλων καὶ αὐτοῦ τοῦ ὕδατος καὶ αὐτὰ τὰ κάλλιστα τῶν καλλίστων καθ' ὑπερβολὴν αὐτὴν λαχεῖν, τὸν οἶνον τὲ καὶ τὸ ἔλαιον. Ἐν ταύτῃ καλλίστην καὶ μεγίστην τὴν ἄγραν καὶ ὁ Ἰησοῦς ποιεῖται, μετὰ καί τινων ἄλλων καὶ αὐτοὺς τοὺς περιβοήτους τῶν μαθητῶν Ἰάκωβον ἀγρεύσας καὶ Ἰωάννην, μετὰ τῆς μητρὸς εἰς τὸν οἶκον τοῦ πατρὸς αὐτῶν εἰσελθὼν Ζεβεδαίου, ὅτε καὶ ἡ μήτηρ τῶν ὅσον οὔπω τῆς *βροντῆς υἱῶν* τὴν ἐπαγγελομένην αὐτοῖς βασιλείαν οὐκ οὐράνιον, ἀλλ' ἐπίγειον εἶναι μᾶλλον νομίσασα, καὶ ταπεινὰ καὶ αὐτὴ φρονήσασα καὶ ἐπίγεια τὴν προεδρίαν αὐτῆς τοῖς υἱοῖς ἐξαιτεῖται, ἧς ὁ Χριστὸς τὴν ὑφεδρίαν μᾶλλον καὶ πάντων διακονίαν οἶδε καὶ διδάσκει πρόξενον.

70 Μετὰ τὴν Γενησαρὲτ ἡ Καπερναούμ, ὅπου τὸ μέγα θαῦμα καὶ αἴνιγμα τῆς ἡμετέρας φύσεως, ὁ παράλυτος· ὁ μὲν σφιγγόμενος καὶ ῥωννύμενος καὶ εἰς τὸν οἶκον ἀπέρχεσθαι κελευόμενος, ἡ δὲ καὶ αὐτὴ μὴ μόνον τὰ ἑαυτῆς ἐπισυνάγουσα μέλη, τὰ Ἔθνη, καὶ ἑνοποιουμένη διὰ Χριστοῦ καὶ αὐτὴ ἑαυτῇ καὶ συναπτομένη τοῖς ἄκροις ἔθεσί τε καὶ σπέρμασιν, ὥστε πάντας ἓν εἶναι σῶμα καὶ μίαν ἔχειν κεφαλήν, τὸν Χριστόν, ἀλλὰ καὶ ῥωννυμένη

in diameter in each direction, and rounded off, as it were, into a circle. Its entire shoreline is wooded, as if the lake were wearing a crown, elegantly embellished with leaves and flowers, and bursting with many other large and beautiful fruit trees, especially olives and vines, which are superabundant in number and supernatural in their productiveness, in terms of their beauty, taste, and size, so that together with the other things and the water itself, it possesses in abundance the finest of the finest products, by which I mean wine and olive oil. It was in this vast and beautiful lake that Jesus did his fishing, together with some others, and where he caught his celebrated disciples James and John, at which time, in the company of his mother, he entered into the house of their father Zebedee. This was when the mother of the men who would soon be his *sons of thunder* thought the kingdom promised to her sons was not a heavenly place but an earthly one, and in her lowly and earthly mind, she asked that her sons preside over it, though Christ knew and taught that the kingdom was rather the incentive for ministry and service to all.

After Gennesaret comes Capernaum, where the great 70
miracle and mystery of our nature took place: the healing of the paralytic. For he was straightened, strengthened, and instructed to return to his home. At the same time, our nature not only gathered together its own members, that is, the Gentiles, but was also unified with itself through Christ, and was conjoined with the extremes of their different customs and origins, making them all one body and having one head, namely, Christ. And our nature was so greatly

τοσοῦτον, καίτοι παρειμένη τοσοῦτον τὲ καὶ ἐπὶ τοσοῦτον, ὥστε καὶ τὴν οἰκείαν συναναφέρειν κλίνην, τὴν ὕλην αὐτὴν τοῦ σώματος, ὅτι μάλιστα συνεξαίρουσα καὶ εἰς τὴν ἀρχαίαν ἐπαναγομένη πατρίδα τὲ καὶ οἰκίαν, ἀφ' ἧς ἐξέπεσεν.

Ἐντεῦθεν, ὥσπερ σημείου δοθέντος ἢ καὶ πελάγους ἀναχεθέντος, ἥ τε συνδρομὴ τῶν ὄχλων καὶ τὰ συνεχῆ καὶ ἀμύθητα ῥεύματα τῶν θαυμάτων, ἃ καὶ τοῖς εὐαγγελισταῖς παρεῖται καὶ οὐδὲ χωρητὰ λέγεται τῷ κόσμῳ, μὴ διὰ τὸ πλῆθος μᾶλλον ἢ καὶ τὸ μέγεθος, ὡς οὐ χωροῦντος τοῦ κατὰ τὸν κόσμον ἀνθρώπου τὴν τούτων δύναμιν ἢ διάκρισιν. Ἀλλ' ὁ μὲν Ἰησοῦς ἐδίδασκε καὶ ἐθεράπευε μόνον σώματά τε ὁμοῦ καὶ πνεύματα, οἱ δὲ μαθηταὶ τοὺς μαθητευομένους ἢ καὶ θεραπευομένους παραλαμβάνοντες κατήχουν τὲ καὶ ἐβάπτιζον, ἀφ' οὗ δῆλον ὅτι καθάπερ ἐπὶ τῶν ἄλλων πάντων ὁ Χριστός, τῶν μὲν ἦν τέλος, τῶν δὲ ἀρχή, τὰ μὲν παλαιὰ πληρῶν, τὰ δ' ἑαυτοῦ καὶ τυπῶν ὁμοῦ καὶ πληρῶν, ἵν' ἅμα καὶ τὸν νόμον ὁμοῦ φανῇ τηρῶν, καὶ καινοτομῶν ὁμοῦ, καὶ φυλάττων ὁμοῦ τὴν ἀκρίβειαν. Οὕτω καὶ ἐπὶ τοῦ βαπτίσματος, τὸ μὲν γὰρ αὐτὸς ἐβαπτίσατο, τὸ τοῦ Ἰωάννου διὰ τοῦ ὕδατος, τὸ δὲ αὐτὸς ἐβάπτισέ τε καὶ ἐβαπτίσατο, τὸ δι' ἑαυτοῦ καὶ διὰ τοῦ Πνεύματος.

Ἐντεῦθεν καὶ θνήσκων μὲν Ζεβεδαῖος, οἱ δὲ υἱοὶ θάπτειν μὲν ἐφιέμενοι καὶ δεόμενοι, μὴ συγχωρούμενοι δέ, μὴ καὶ τὸ πάθος ἅμα καὶ ὁ πόθος ὁ τοῦ συνδούλου κατακρατήσῃ τοῦ θείου τὲ καὶ δεσποτικοῦ, καὶ ἡ φύσις τῆς χάριτος, ἀλλὰ τότε μὲν οὕτω τοῦ φυσικοῦ πάθους ἢ

strengthened, even though it had been so weak for so long, that it was able to carry its own bed, that is, the very matter of the body, and, rising up together with it, it returned to its ancient homeland and house from which it had fallen.

Then, as if a sign had been given, or as if an ocean had overflowed, the crowds began to gather and there appeared constant and indescribable waves of miracles, which even the evangelists passed over, and which, it is said, the world itself could not contain, not so much because of their great number but rather their magnitude, since no man in this world could comprehend their power and the discernment with which they were performed. While Jesus was teaching and healing only bodies and souls, his disciples were catechizing and baptizing those who had accepted to become disciples and to be healed. From this it is clear that Christ, as in all other things, was the end of some things and the beginning of others, fulfilling the things of old, and both figuring and fulfilling the things concerning himself, so that he might be seen both to maintain the law and change it, while at the same time preserving strict conformity to it. This is what happened at his baptism: he himself was baptized in water by John, yet he also both baptized and was baptized, through himself and through the Spirit.

After this, when Zebedee died and his sons sought and entreated to bury him, they were not permitted to do so, lest the suffering and longing for a fellow servant should prevail over their desire for the divine and lordly, and nature prevail over grace. At that time they were thus deterred

θελήματος ἀποτρέπονται, μετ' ὀλίγον δὲ συγχωροῦνται λόγῳ πάντα ποιεῖν τῷ Λόγῳ τυπούμενοι, καὶ οὕτω τελέσαντες τὰ ἐξόδια καὶ εὐχαριστήρια, καὶ τὴν μητέρα τῇ μητρὶ προσάγουσι τοῦ Δεσπότου καὶ Διδασκάλου μαθήτριαν καὶ διακονήτριαν πάντα τὸν ἑξῆς αὐτῆς χρόνον. Ὥσπερ δὲ τὴν γεννησαμένην, οὕτω καὶ τὴν θρεψαμένην οἰκίαν καὶ κτῆσιν οὐ φαύλην οὖσαν οὐδὲ ὀλίγην οἰκονομεῖν καὶ ταύτην παρὰ τοῦ Λόγου μαθόντες, τὴν μὲν τοῖς πενομένοις, τὴν δὲ τοῖς συμμαθητευομένοις, τὴν δὲ καὶ ἀπεμπολήσαντες εἰς τὸν ἐπὶ τῆς Σιὼν οἶκον ἢ ἀγρὸν καταβάλλονται, τῇ τοῦ Θεοῦ σκηνῇ καὶ μητρὶ σκήνωμα διὰ τέλους ἐσόμενον μετὰ τὸν τοῦ παιδὸς σταυρόν τε καὶ τὴν ἀνάληψιν, εἰς ὃν καὶ παρὰ τοῦ σταυρωθέντος ὁ μαθητὴς αὐτὴν ὡς μητέρα παραλαμβάνει, καθώς φησιν αὐτός, *εἰς τὰ ἴδια.*

Μετὰ τὴν Γαλιλαίαν καὶ ἡ Ἰουδαία τῶν θαυμάτων καὶ τῶν δογμάτων, ἅμα δὲ καὶ τῶν βαπτισμάτων, ἀναπίμπλαται τοῦ Χριστοῦ. Καὶ ἡ μήτηρ πανταχοῦ συνέκδημος καὶ θεατὴς καὶ ἀκροατὴς τῶν λεγομένων καὶ πραττομένων, καὶ διδάσκαλος καὶ δεσπότις καὶ μαθητριῶν τὲ καὶ διακόνων, ὅτε καὶ σὺν ἄλλαις οὐκ ὀλίγαις *καὶ Ἰωάννα,* γυνή τις λίαν εὐγενὴς καὶ ἐπιφανὴς τόν τε πλοῦτον καὶ τὴν προαίρεσιν, ἀκούσασα τοῦ παραγγέλματος, "*ἐάν μη τις ἀποτάξηται πᾶσι,*" πᾶσιν ἀποταξαμένη, καὶ ἀνδρὶ καὶ παισὶ σὺν ἅμα καὶ ἀγροῖς καὶ οἰκίαις καὶ χρήμασί τε καὶ σώμασι, καὶ τὸν σταυρὸν ἀραμένη καὶ πρὸ τοῦ σταυροῦ, τῷ δι' ἡμᾶς σταυρωθησομένῳ καὶ τῇ αὐτοῦ μητρὶ πάντα τὸν ἑξῆς συνηκολούθησε χρόνον.

from their natural passion or will, but later they were permitted by word to do all the things taught to them by the Word, and thus after they performed the customary funeral rites and thank offerings they brought their mother to the mother of the Master, whose disciple and minister she became for the rest of her life. Since the house in which they were born and raised, as well as their family wealth and possessions, were by no means meager or insignificant, as they had been taught by the Word, they distributed part of it to the poor, part of it to their fellow disciples, and part of it they sold and bought the house in Zion or its farm, which, after the crucifixion and ascension of her child would be the dwelling place for God's dwelling place and mother for the rest of her life. It was there that the disciple took her, as he himself says, *to his own home,* after he received her from the Lord on the cross.

After Galilee, Judea was filled with the miracles, teachings, and baptisms of Christ. And his mother went everywhere with him, seeing and listening to all he said and did, and serving as the teacher and leader of the female disciples and ministers. Among them, for they were not a few in number, was *Joanna,* a very noble woman and distinguished in terms of her wealth and conduct, who when she heard the command of the Lord, "*unless one renounces all that one has,*" renounced everything, including her husband, children, land, houses, belongings, and slaves, and took up her cross even before the cross, and followed the one who was going to be crucified for us, together with his mother, all the rest of her life.

71 Ἐνταῦθα καὶ ὁ τῆς μεγάλης ἑορτῆς καιρὸς τῆς Σκηνοπηγίας, ὅτε μετὰ πολλῶν καὶ ἄλλων νοσημάτων τὲ καὶ πνευμάτων καὶ τοῦ ἱεροῦ τοὺς κερματιστάς τε καὶ κολυβιστὰς καὶ καπήλους ἀπήλασε φραγέλλιον πλέξας, οὐ τὸ φαινόμενον μόνον, ἀλλὰ καὶ τὸ νοούμενον, καὶ τὸν παλαιὸν καὶ καινὸν νόμον ἢ τῷ λόγῳ τὲ καὶ τοῖς θαύμασιν. Οὕτω τὴν Ἰουδαίαν κύκλῳ περιελθὼν ἐπανέρχεται πάλιν πρὸς Γαλιλαίαν, τάς τε ἄλλας κώμας καὶ πόλεις περιϊὼν καὶ Μαγδαλᾶ πόλιν, ἀφ' ἧς καὶ Μαγδαληνὴ Μαρία, τοσοῦτον σχεδὸν καὶ ὑπερβάλλουσα τὰς ἄλλας τῷ τε περὶ αὐτὸν καὶ τῷ περὶ τὴν τεκοῦσαν πόθῳ καθ' ὅσον ἐκείνη καὶ ταύτην. Αὕτη γένει μὲν καὶ ὥρᾳ καὶ πλούτῳ περίβλεπτος, οὐχ' ἧττον δὲ καὶ διὰ τὸ περὶ αὐτὴν πάθος διαβόητος πᾶσι καὶ πάντας ἐφελκομένη πρὸς ἔλεον τὴν κοινὴν τῆς ἀνθρωπείας φύσεως ἰδίαν ἔχουσα συμφοράν, ὅλοις ἑπτὰ τῆς πονηρίας ἐλαυνομένη πνεύμασιν, ἃ καὶ τῆς εὐσεβείας ἀντίθετα. Ἀλλὰ καὶ αὕτη τυχοῦσα τοῦ πᾶσαν ἡμῶν τὴν φύσιν πάσης κακίας ἀποκαθαίροντος καὶ πᾶσαν νόσον καὶ μαλακίαν ἐκθεραπεύοντος, οὐ μόνον ὅλων καὶ ὅλως ἀπηλλάγη τῶν δαιμονίων, ἀλλὰ καὶ ὅλων ἐνεπλήσθη τῶν χαρισμάτων τοῦ Πνεύματος, θερμοτάτη φανεῖσα καὶ τὴν πίστιν καὶ τὴν πρᾶξιν καὶ τὴν προαίρεσιν, οὐ μόνον ἀκόλουθος διὰ βίου παντὸς καὶ μαθήτρια καὶ διάκονος καὶ σύνοικος τῇ κοινῇ Δεσποίνῃ καὶ ὑπηρέτις καὶ διὰ πάντων σύναθλος, ἀλλὰ καὶ ὕστερον ἀπόστολος καὶ ἀπόδημος ὑπὲρ Χριστοῦ καὶ μάρτυς καὶ ἀθλητὴς μέχρις αἵματος και, συνελόντα εἰπεῖν, τοῦτο καὶ αὕτη ἐν γυναιξίν, ὅπερ

After this it was time for the great feast of Tabernacles, 71
when, along with healing all sorts of infirmities and casting out evil spirits, the Lord plaited a whip and drove away the moneychangers, merchants, and hucksters who were in the temple. This was not only a visible whip but also a spiritual one, formed of the old and the new law, or by his teaching and miracles. Having traveled round about Judea, the Lord returned to Galilee, and visited the villages and towns, including the town of Magdala, from where Mary Magdalene hailed, she who almost surpassed all the other women followers in her desire for the Lord and his mother to the same extent that the latter surpassed her. She was distinguished by her birth, her bloom of youth, and her wealth, though she was no less well known to all for her affliction, and she moved everyone to compassion for her affliction with the plight common to human nature, since she was plagued by all seven spirits of wickedness, which are opposed to piety. But she found him who purifies our whole nature from every evil, and who heals every sickness and weakness, and thus she was not only completely delivered from the demons but also filled with the gifts of the Spirit. She subsequently became wholly ardent in faith, works, and disposition, and not only did she become throughout her entire life a follower, disciple, servant, and intimate associate with our common Lady, serving her and struggling alongside her in everything, but also later became an apostle and exile for the sake of Christ, and a martyr and contestant to the point of shedding her blood. To state the matter briefly, among women she became exactly what Peter was among men. But

καὶ ἐν ἀνδράσιν ὁ Πέτρος. Ἀλλὰ τὰ ταύτης μὲν καὶ αὖθις ἀναληπτέον κατὰ καιρὸν καὶ μάλισθ' ὅτε κατὰ τὸν σταυρὸν γενώμεθα.

72 Νυνὶ δὲ πάλιν ἐπὶ τὸν σκοπὸν ἰτέον καὶ τὰ ἐπίλοιπα παραληπτέον τῆς τοῦ Θεοῦ μητρὸς καὶ ἡμετέρας Δεσποίνης θαύματά τε καὶ πάθη καὶ πολιτεύματα, ὅσα μὲν σὺν τῷ υἱῷ, ὅσα δὲ καὶ καθ' ἑαυτήν, συγγνώμονας εἶναι παραιτησαμένοις τῷ μήκει τοῦ λόγου τοὺς ἐπιγνώμονας, εἰδότας ὅτι περὶ τοσούτων οἱ λόγοι καὶ τηλικούτων, περὶ ὧν πᾶσα μὲν γλῶσσα, πᾶσα δὲ τέχνη (προσθήσω δ' ὅτι καὶ χάρις καὶ δύναμις, ἅπας δὲ χρόνος ἐξ ἀρχῆς αἰώνων καὶ μέχρι τοῦ νῦν καὶ ὄντων καὶ γενομένων καὶ ἐσομένων), κεκίνηται μὲν καὶ ἀεὶ κινεῖται καὶ κινηθήσεται, νενίκηται δὲ καὶ ἀνάλωται καὶ ἀεὶ νικηθήσεται καὶ ἀναλωθήσεται, καὶ οὐδὲν μὲν οὐδέποτε τῶν μυστηρίων τούτων τοσοῦτον ῥηθήσεται (οὐδὲ παρ' αὐτῶν τῶν ἄνω δυνάμεων), ὅσον ἄξιον, ἀλλ' ὅμως ἀεὶ καὶ διηγηθήσεται καὶ δοξασθήσεται κατὰ δύναμιν.

Ἐκεῖνο μὲν οὖν ἀποδεῖξαι διὰ πάντων ἡμῖν ὁ σκοπός, ὅτι καθάπερ ἡ σκιὰ τῷ σώματι (μᾶλλον δὲ καθάπερ ὁ τοῦ Θεοῦ Λόγος καὶ ταύτης υἱός, ἀφ' οὗπερ ἐξ ἀρχῆς τὴν ἡμετέραν ἐνεδύσατο φύσιν, οὐδ' ὁπωσοῦν οὐδαμοῦ ταύτης διῄρητο καθ' ὑπόστασιν, εἰ καὶ ἰδίως ἑκατέρας τῶν φύσεων ἐδείκνυ τὰς ἰδιότητας), οὕτω σχεδὸν οὐδὲ αὕτη τοῦ ταύτης υἱοῦ μετὰ τὴν ἐξ αὐτῆς πρόοδον κατὰ πᾶσαν πρᾶξιν καὶ σχέσιν τὲ καὶ προαίρεσιν (εἰ καὶ τοὐναντίον κεχώριστο καθ' ὑπόστασιν), ἀλλὰ καὶ ἀποδημοῦντι συνείπετο καὶ θαυματουργοῦντι καθάπερ καὶ αὐτὴ

the things concerning her will be taken up again at the appropriate time, certainly when we come to the crucifixion.

But now we must return to the object of our discourse, 72
and take up the remaining marvels, sufferings, and way of life of God's mother and our Lady, touching on those things that took place in conjunction with her son and on those that concern her alone, asking that I be forgiven by my discerning listeners for the length of our discourse, knowing that it concerns such great mysteries. For, with respect to these, though every tongue and every art (to which I will add every grace and power, and every period of time from the beginning of the ages until now, past, present, and future), which has been set in motion, is forever moved, and which will be moved, has been vanquished and destroyed, and always will be vanquished and destroyed, will never be capable of saying anything concerning these mysteries that is worthy of the Virgin (for not even the celestial powers are able to do this), these glorious events will nonetheless always be recounted and celebrated to the extent that this is possible.

But what I aim to demonstrate in all these things is that, just as a shadow is inseparable from a body (or rather just as the Word of God, who is also her son, from the very moment he clothed himself in our nature, was never in any way separated from that nature according to his hypostasis, even if he distinctly manifested the unique properties of each of the natures), she too, after he came forth from her womb, was virtually never separated from her son in her every deed, relationship, and disposition (even if they were separate according to hypostasis), so that when he traveled she followed him, and when he worked miracles, she also worked

συνθαυματουργοῦσα μετεῖχε τῆς δόξης καὶ ἐπηγάλλετο. Καὶ προδιδομένῳ δὲ καὶ ἑλκομένῳ καὶ κρινομένῳ καὶ πάσχοντι οὐ συμπαρῆν πανταχοῦ μόνον, καὶ τότε πλεῖον συνεπεφύκει μάλιστα, ἀλλὰ καὶ συνέπασχε, μᾶλλον δέ, εἰ καὶ μὴ τολμηρὸν εἰπεῖν, καὶ πλεῖον ἤπερ ἐκεῖνος ἔπασχεν. Ὁ μὲν γὰρ Θεὸς ὢν καὶ ἑκὼν ἢ καὶ ποθῶν, αὕτη δὲ καὶ μετὰ τῆς ἀνθρωπίνης ἀσθενείας καὶ γυναικείας καὶ τῶν μητρικῶν καὶ τοιούτων καὶ ἐπὶ τοιούτῳ παιδὶ σπλάγχνων καὶ σφόδρα διακοπτομένη καὶ αὐτὴ μυριάκις εὐχομένη τὰ τοιαῦτα παθεῖν μᾶλλον ἢ τὸν υἱὸν πάσχοντα θεωρεῖν.

Τὰ Ἅγια Πάθη

73 Ἧκει δὲ λοιπὸν πρὸς αὐτὴν τὴν ἀκμὴν τῶν ἄθλων ὁ λόγος καὶ οὐχ ἧττον ἀγὼν αὐτῷ περὶ τῶν κατ’ αὐτὴν ἀγώνων διεξελθεῖν. Ἐπειδὴ γὰρ τὰ μὲν τῶν θαυμάτων καὶ τῶν δογμάτων καὶ τῶν ἄλλων αὐτοῦ πολιτευμάτων τῷ Χριστῷ πέρας εἶχεν, ἐλείπετο δὲ μόνον τὸ μέγα τῆς οἰκονομίας τέλος ὁμοῦ καὶ κεφάλαιον, ὁ σταυρὸς καὶ ὁ τάφος καὶ ἡ ἀνάστασις, ἐνταῦθά μοι λοιπὸν καὶ τὰ κρείττω λόγου καὶ διανοίας τῆς Παρθένου πάθη καὶ πειρατήρια καὶ ὅσον πρὸς τοὺς ἄλλους πάντας αὐτῇ τὸ διάφορον. Καθάπερ γὰρ πῦρ ὁ τοῦ Πάθους ἐπελθὼν τότε καιρός, πάσης διακριτικὸς τῆς ὕλης, τῶν μὲν ἄλλων πάντων ἀναλωτικὸς ἐφάνη γενόμενος, ἑνὸς δὲ μόνου καθάπερ χρυσοῦ φεισάμενος, τῆς μητρός, ὅτι μὴ καὶ καθαρωτέραν μᾶλλον καὶ δοκιμωτέραν ἀπεργασάμενος· ἤ, τἀληθέστερον εἰπεῖν, ὁ

miracles with him, sharing in his glory and exulting in him. And when he was betrayed, dragged off to trial, judged, and suffered, she was not only everywhere present with him, but in those moments especially she also became even more united to him in nature, and thus she also suffered together with him, and indeed, if it is not too daring a thing to say, she suffered more than he did. For whereas he was God and acted voluntarily and even with longing, she possessed the frailty of being human and a woman, together with extraordinary maternal compassion for such an extraordinary child, and so she was utterly torn in two, and prayed a thousand times to suffer these things rather than see her son suffering.

The Holy Passion

My discourse has finally arrived at the culmination of its 73
contests, and no less a struggle will be required to recount in detail the struggles of the Mother of God. Since the miracles, teachings, and other activities of Christ had reached their end, there remained only the great crowning goal of the divine dispensation, namely, the cross, the tomb, and the resurrection, and thus what remains for me is to recount the sufferings and trials of the Virgin, which are beyond speech and thought, and the extent to which these distinguished her from all the others. For the time of the Passion arrived like a fire, which was able to differentiate between all material, and while it consumed all the others, it spared only the mother, who emerged like gold, though now it also made her purer and more thoroughly tested. Or to say what is even more true, just as her son and God had shown her to

ταύτης υἱὸς καὶ Θεός, ὥσπερ ἐν τῷ τίκτειν μητέρα καὶ παρθένον, οὕτω καὶ νῦν ἐν τῷ Πάθει τὴν αὐτὴν ἀπαθεστάτην τὲ ὁμοῦ καὶ συμπαθεστάτην ἀπέδειξε, τὸ μὲν διὰ τὴν φύσιν, μᾶλλον δὲ καὶ τὸ μεῖζον ἢ κατὰ τὴν φύσιν φιλότεκνον, τὸ δὲ διὰ τὴν χάριν καὶ τὸ σφόδρα ὑπὲρ φύσιν φιλόσοφον, μᾶλλον δὲ καθ' ὅσον αὐτῇ τὸ φιλόστοργον, τοσοῦτον ἀναλόγως καὶ τὸ φιλότολμον διαφλεγομένῃ τὰ σπλάγχνα, καὶ οὐ συγκινδυνεύειν μόνον, ἀλλὰ καὶ προκινδυνεύειν ὑπὲρ τοῦ παιδὸς αἱρουμένῃ.

74 Ταῦτ' οὖν πρὸ τῶν ἄλλων λεγέσθω καὶ οὗτος ὁ καιρὸς τὸ ἀνδρωδέστατον αὐτὸ τῆς ἀνανδροτάτης ἐπιδεικνύτω. Μικρὸν δὲ ἀνωτέρω τὸν λόγον ἀναληπτέον, ὅτι συνῆν μέν, ὡς ὁ λόγος ἀπέδειξε, κατὰ πᾶσαν ὁδὸν καὶ πρᾶξιν καὶ αὐτὴ τῷ υἱῷ, συνῆν δὲ οὐχ ὡς θεωμένη καὶ πάντων συναπολαύουσα μόνον, ἀλλ' ὡς καὶ τὴν προστασίαν καὶ τὴν ἀρχὴν συμμεριζομένη, καθάπερ τῶν ἀνδρῶν καὶ τῶν μαθητῶν ἐκεῖνος, οὕτω καὶ αὕτη τῶν γυναικῶν καὶ μαθητριῶν.

Ταῦτά τοι καὶ ὅτε τὸ μυστικὸν καὶ καινὸν ἐτελεῖτο δεῖπνον· οὐ γὰρ δὴ καὶ τὸ νομικόν, ὥς τινες ὑπειλήφασιν· οὐδὲ γὰρ ἂν ἀνόμως τὸν νόμον ἐπλήρου οὐδ' ἂν πρὸ τῆς νενομισμένης ἡμέρας τὲ καὶ τῆς ὥρας ἐτέλει τὴν ἑορτήν· οὐ γὰρ ἐξῆν, ὥσπερ καὶ μετὰ τὴν ἑορτὴν μέχρι τῆς μεγάλης καλουμένης ἡμέρας τῆς Πεντηκοστῆς, ἀλλ' οὐδ' ἂν ἔθυεν· οὐδὲ γὰρ ἂν Ἰούδας τὸν ἄρνα παραδραμὼν τὸν ἄρτον ἐδείκνυ, καὶ τὸ μεῖζον τῶν ἐγκλημάτων ἀφείς, τὴν

be a mother and a virgin at the time of his birth, so also now, at the time of his Passion, he showed her to be completely free of passion and completely filled with compassion. The latter was on account of nature, or rather on account of a mother's love for her child, which is greater than nature, and the former on account of grace, and also because of her love of wisdom, which utterly transcended nature, or rather her tender loving affection, which was in proportion to her maternal boldness, and burned her insides like fire, so that she chose not only to subject herself to danger along with her child, but even to brave the danger on his behalf.

Let these things be stated before the others and let this 74
moment demonstrate the supreme manliness of this woman who never knew a man. But my discourse must return briefly to what we said a moment ago, namely, that she was inseparable from her son throughout all his travels and in all that he did. And she was inseparable from him not only as an observer who shared in the enjoyment of all these things, but also as someone who shared a role in leadership and authority, for just as the Lord had this over the men and the male disciples, so too she had this over the women and female disciples.

This was also the case when the mystical and new supper took place, though this was not the Passover prescribed by the law as some have supposed. For the Lord did not fulfill the law unlawfully nor did he observe the feast before its appointed day and hour. Such a thing was forbidden, just as it was forbidden after the feast, and he would have not made sacrifice until the great day known as Pentecost. Nor would Judas have ignored the lamb and gestured toward the bread, and thus ignored the greater crime, namely, the transgres-

τοῦ Πάσχα παρανομίαν, ἐπὶ τὴν ἐλάττω τοῦ μυστικοῦ δείπνου συκοφαντίαν ἐχώρει, οὐδ' ἂν Ἰουδαῖοι τοῦ μὲν τὸ Σάββατον λύειν αὐτὸν ᾐτιῶντο, τοῦ δὲ τὴν τηλικαύτην παραλύειν τῶν ἑορτῶν ἠφίεσαν· ταῦτά τοι καὶ οὐδὲ θῦσαι τὸ Ἱερὸν αὐτὸν ἱστόρησεν Εὐαγγέλιον, ἀλλ' αὐτὸς ἑαυτὸν ὥσπερ ἱερεὺς ἅμα καὶ ἱερεῖον, ἐσθίων καὶ ἐσθιώμενος, παρατιθεὶς καὶ παρατιθέμενος. Αὐτὸς μὲν οὖν τοῖς ἀνδράσι καὶ μαθηταῖς παρεδίδου τὰ ὑψηλότερα, τοῦ θειοτέρου Πάσχα τὰ σύμβολα, τὸ μὲν σῶμα καὶ αἷμα διὰ τοῦ ἄρτου τὲ καὶ τοῦ πόματος, τὴν δὲ ἀνωτάτω δόξαν καὶ τὸ ἀξίωμα διὰ τῆς ἐσχάτης διακονίας καὶ ὑποπτώσεως, οὐ τὰ ἑαυτοῦ Πάθη προτυπῶν μόνον καὶ τὴν διὰ τούτων δόξαν τὲ καὶ ἀνάστασιν, οὐδὲ τοὺς μαθητὰς προπαρασκευάζων ἅμα δὲ καὶ παραμυθούμενος, ἀλλὰ καὶ ἡμῖν πᾶσι τὸ ἀληθινὸν ὑποδεικνύων ὁμοῦ καὶ νομοθετῶν Πάσχα, τὸ διὰ μαρτυρίου καὶ ταπεινώσεως. Ὁ μὲν οὖν ἐκείνοις συνανεκλίνετο καὶ τῷ μὲν σώματι καὶ τῷ αἵματι καὶ τὸ σῶμα καὶ τὴν ψυχὴν ἔτρεφε, ταῖς δὲ χερσὶ τοὺς πόδας ὑπένιπτεν, οὐχ, ὅπερ ἔφην, διδάσκων μόνον, ἀλλὰ καὶ ἐκείνῳ μὲν ῥωννύων, τούτῳ δὲ καὶ πρὸς δρόμον τοὺς μαθητὰς εὐτρεπίζων καὶ ἐξωραΐζων μετὰ τοῦ τάχους τὰ διαβήματα. Τῇ δὲ μητρὶ τὰς γυναῖκας ἐπέτρεπε καὶ τὸ εὐπρεπὲς ἅμα φυλάττων καὶ τὴν μὲν τιμῶν, τὰς δὲ καὶ διὰ ταύτης παιδεύων, ἤδη δὲ καὶ φιλοφρονούμενος καὶ τοῦ πόθου καὶ τῆς διακονίας αὐτὰς ἀμειβόμενος.

75 Ἐπεὶ δὲ καὶ ὁ δαιτυμών—φεῦ τῆς ἀγνωμοσύνης—προδότης καὶ ὁ μαθητὴς αὐτοῦ τοῦ διδασκάλου λῃστής, καὶ ὁ τοὺς πόδας νιφθεὶς καὶ τρώγων αὐτοῦ τὸ σῶμα καὶ πίνων

sion of the law regarding Passover, and proceeded instead with the lesser accusation regarding the mystical supper; nor would the Jews have accused Jesus of failing to observe the Sabbath while ignoring the fact that he failed to observe such a great feast. For these reasons, the Holy Gospel itself does not record that he celebrated the Passover sacrifice, but rather that he was a priest and at the same time the sacrificial victim, both eating and being eaten, offering and being offered. To the men and disciples who were present, he himself conveyed the exalted symbols of the more divine Passover. Through the bread and the wine, he gave them his body and blood, and through his uttermost humble service and submission, he revealed his lofty glory and honor, not only foreshadowing his own Passion, and through it his glory and resurrection, nor preparing and at the same time consoling his disciples, but also revealing to us and establishing the true Passover, that of martyrdom and humility. While he was reclining with his disciples, he nourished their souls and bodies by means of his body and blood, and with his hands he washed their feet, not only, as I said a moment ago, to teach them humility, but also with the former to strengthen them, and with the latter to prepare them for the road ahead and beautify their steps with speed. To his mother, on the other hand, he entrusted the women disciples, safeguarding their dignity and at the same time honoring her, and instructing them through her, already rewarding them, in his kindness, for their desire and devotion.

After that, his dinner companion—oh, the ingratitude!— 75
became a traitor, the disciple robbed his teacher, and the one whose feet were washed, and who ate his body and

τὸ αἷμα, τοῖς μὲν ἀπέτρεχε καὶ πάλιν ἐπέτρεχε κατ' αὐτοῦ, τὸ δέ—ὢ τίνος ἂν εἴποιμι μᾶλλον τῆς θηριωδίας ἢ τῆς φιλαργυρίας;—ἐπίπρασκε καὶ ἐξέχεεν· αὐτὸς δέ, Δαυϊτικῶς εἰπεῖν, παραδιδόμενος μέν, οὐκ ἐκπορευόμενος δέ, καὶ ἐκκλίνων καὶ ὡς ἀμνὸς οὐκ ἐρίζων οὐδὲ κραυγάζων, ἀλλὰ καὶ σφόδρα βουλόμενος καὶ ἕλκων τὸ Πάθος ἤπερ αὐτὸς ἑλκόμενος. Ἐπεὶ ταῦτα καὶ αὐτὸς καθ' ἑαυτοῦ τὴν ψῆφον ὁ Κριτὴς ἐξετίθετο καὶ τῇ μητρὶ γνωστὰ τὰ τῆς κρίσεως, ἐνταῦθά μοι σκόπει καθάπερ τῆς ἁγνείας οὕτω καὶ τῆς φιλοστοργίας καὶ τῆς ἀνδρείας αὐτῆς τὴν ὑπερβολήν. Οἱ μὲν γὰρ ἄλλοι πάντες καὶ πᾶσαι, καὶ μαθηταὶ καὶ μαθήτριαι, καὶ γνωστοί τε καὶ ἀδελφοί, καὶ ἔνορκοι καὶ ἀνώμοτοι, οἱ μὲν μικροῦ καὶ θᾶττον αὐτὸν ἢ συλληφθῆναι δρόμῳ καταλιμπάνουσιν, οἱ δὲ τέως ἀφίστανται καί, κατὰ τὸν προφήτην, "*οἱ φίλοι καὶ οἱ πλησίον ἐξ ἐναντίας* ἵστανται," οἱ δὲ βραχὺν μέν, σφόδρα βραχύν, ἀντέχουσι χρόνον, ἀρνοῦνται δὲ ταχύτερον ἢ συντίθενται καὶ βεβαιότερον ἢ τὸ πρότερον ἰσχυρίζονται. Αὕτη δὲ ἡ ὄντως ἐκείνου μήτηρ καὶ τὴν ἀνδρείαν θυγάτηρ καὶ πιστουμένη τὸ γένος, οὐχ' ὅσον ἐκ φύσεως, ἀλλὰ καὶ τῆς κατ' ἀρετὴν ὁμοιώσεως, ὥσπερ οὐ κατὰ τῶν τότε μόνον ἀνδρῶν τὲ καὶ γυναικῶν, ἀλλὰ καὶ κατὰ πάσης ὁμοῦ καὶ τῆς γυναικείας καὶ τῆς ἀνδρείας φύσεως, ὥσπερ κἀν τοῖς ἄλλοις πᾶσιν, οὕτω κἀνταῦθα τὸ μεγαλεῖον ἐνδεικνυμένη καὶ μόνη καὶ γυνὴ καὶ παρθένος καὶ ἄλλως αἰδημονεστάτη.

76 Καὶ ἥκιστα συνήθης ὄχλων καὶ ἀρρένων, μήτιγε καὶ λῃστῶν καὶ πολεμίων ἐνόπλων ὄψεσιν, οὐ μόνον οὐκ

drank his blood, ran off with those same feet and hastened to betray him, and—how could anyone describe such savagery and greed?—sold that body and spilled that blood! But the Lord, in the words of David, was handed over but did not go forth, and like a sheep did not resist or cry out, but went most willingly and drew the Passion to himself rather than being dragged toward it. After this the Judge pronounced the verdict against himself, and as the details of the judgment became known to his mother, consider with me how the extraordinary degree of her affection for her child and her courage matched the extraordinary degree of her purity. For considering all the other men and women, the male disciples and the female disciples, acquaintances and family members, those bound to him by an oath and those not bound, some abandoned him on the street even more quickly than he was arrested, while others kept their distance for a while, as the prophet says, "*My friends and neighbors* stood *at a distance,*" while others again remained with him for a short time, indeed a very short time, denying him more speedily than they supported him, and acting with greater conviction in the former than the latter. But she, on the other hand, truly being his mother and in terms of her courage his daughter, and the guarantor of the human race, not so much by her nature, but by her assimilation to virtue, not only in comparison to the men and women who were alive at that time, but to the whole of womanly and manly nature, so that just as in all other things, here too she has her greatness revealed as a unique woman and a virgin along with her great modesty.

Though she was not at all accustomed to crowds of 76
people and men, and to the faces of criminals and armed

ἀφίστατο, ἀλλὰ καὶ ἐν χρῷ γενομένη τότε μάλιστα τοῦ υἱοῦ οὐδ' ὅσον οἷον διεχωρίζετο, ἀλλὰ καθάπερ καὶ αὐτὴ συνεδέδετο καὶ τὸ σῶμα τῷ σώματι καὶ τῇ ψυχῇ τὴν ψυχήν. Διὸ καὶ ὡς ἐξ ἀρχῆς καὶ μέχρι τέλους αὐτῷ παρακολουθήσασαν εἰκὸς αὐτὴν καὶ τὰ πλεῖστα καὶ τῶν πρὸ τοῦ σταυροῦ καὶ τῶν μετὰ τὸν σταυρὸν καὶ τοῖς εὐαγγελισταῖς καὶ τοῖς ἄλλοις μαθηταῖς ἀναθεῖναι. Αὕτη καὶ πρὸς Ἄνναν καὶ Καϊάφαν συνήρχετο καὶ ἐβιάζετο μὲν καὶ συμπαρίστασθαι κρινομένῳ καὶ προκατακρίνεσθαι κατακρινομένου· ἐπεὶ δὲ τοῖς μιαροῖς ἐκείνοις ἐξωθεῖτο καὶ ἀπεκρούετο, κάτω μένουσα καὶ λανθάνουσα τῶν ἐξετάσεων ἠκροᾶτο, τί μὲν οὐ πάσχουσα, τί δὲ οὐ δρῶσα καί, ὥσπερ ἐκκρεμαμένη τῆς ἐκείνου κρίσεως, τίνος δὲ καὶ οὐκ ἀκροωμένη, τῶν ἐχθρῶν, τῶν φίλων, τῶν ἀνιόντων, τῶν κατιόντων; Καὶ τὰς εἰσόδους καὶ τὰς ἐξόδους παρατηροῦσα τῶν εἰσιόντων ἢ ἐξιόντων, τίνος δὲ καὶ οὐ πυνθανομένη τῶν ἐπιεικεστέρων ἢ καὶ γνωριμωτέρων πρὸς τὰς ἁπάντων γλώσσας, ἤδη δὲ καὶ τὰ σχήματα καὶ τὰ νεύματα καὶ τὴν ἀκοὴν καὶ τὴν ὄψιν μεριζομένη; Τίνες οἱ κατασκυθρωπάζοντες καὶ φιλίως ἔχοντες, εἴπερ τινὲς ἦσαν, καὶ τοὺς μὲν ἄλλους λανθάνειν σπεύδοντες, αὐτῇ δὲ δῆλοι γενόμενοι, τίνες οἱ πολεμίως καὶ ἐπιχαίροντες, τίνες τί φράσοιεν ἢ τίνες τί μάθοιεν περὶ τῶν κρίσεων, τῶν ψήφων, τῶν ἀποφάσεων; Ἆρά τις ἐστὶ καὶ μεμφόμενος ἢ *πάντες ἐξέκλιναν,* πάντες ἔκφρονες εἶπον οὐ τῇ *καρδίᾳ* μόνον, ἀλλὰ καὶ τοῖς στόμασιν· "*οὐκ ἔστι Θεὸς* ὁ Θεός, ἀλλὰ καὶ ἀντίθεος;"

soldiers, she not only did not keep herself at a distance but would not be separated from her son for any reason whatsoever, and it was as though she was bound to him, body to body and soul to soul. And because she followed him closely from the beginning until the end, it seems likely that it was she who reported to the evangelists and the other disciples the majority of the events that took place both before and after the crucifixion. She even came before Annas and Caiaphas, and exerted herself forcefully to be at his side when he was being judged, and to be condemned in his place prior to his condemnation. However, since those vile men did not allow her to enter and drove her away, she remained below, where, avoiding detection, she listened to the trial. What did she not suffer? What did she not do? And, just as if her own life were hanging on the outcome of her son's trial, whom did she not listen to among friends, enemies, and those going up and coming down from the scene of the trial? And as she observed the comings and goings of those entering and exiting the scene, from whom, among those who were kinder or better known to her, did she not try to gain information with regard to what everyone was saying, as she analyzed their bearing, their gestures, their words and their faces? And looking for any who were downcast or sympathetic, if any were, and who were hastening to avoid the others, did it become clear to her which ones were hostile and rejoicing, and which ones might report or tell something about the trial, the votes, and the sentence? Was there anyone who objected to the trial or *had all turned away,* and had all lost their minds saying, not only *in their hearts* but also with their mouths, that "this God *is no God,* but is even

Διεφθάρησαν καὶ ἐβδελύχθησαν ἐν οἷς ἐβδελύξαντο καὶ διέφθειραν. Εἶπον· "*δεῦτε καὶ ἀποκτείνωμεν ἄνδρα δίκαιον*, δεῦτε καὶ τὸν Χριστὸν ἡμῶν ὡς *δύσχρηστον* ἐκ ποδῶν ποιησώμεθα."

Οἱ μὲν οὖν οὕτω πάντες κενὰ μελετῶντες καὶ φρυαττόμενοι, ἡ δὲ καθάπερ ἐν μέσῳ τοσούτων ὄφεων ἢ θηρίων ὄρνις ἢ δάμαλις, ἄκακος μέν, εὐσύνετος δέ, περιϊπταμένη σοφῶς καὶ λαθραίως ἢ περιτρέχουσα καὶ ὑπ' αὐτοῦ σκεπομένη τοῦ νεοσσοῦ καὶ ποιμένος, καὶ τῇ μὲν ὄψει καὶ τῇ αἰσθήσει τῆς ἁπάντων, ὡς εἰπεῖν, κατ' αὐτὸ καὶ γλώττης καὶ θέας ἐξηρτημένη, τῇ δὲ διανοίᾳ τὸ πλεῖον καὶ τῇ ζέσει τῷ υἱῷ συμπαρισταμένη καὶ τὰς κατ' αὐτοῦ ψήφους καθ' ἑαυτῆς δεχομένη.

77 Ἐπεὶ δέ, βαβαὶ τοῦ τολμήματος! εἰς ὅσον ἧκον ἀπονοίας καὶ ἀσεβείας οἱ θεομάχοι, πάντες ἑνὸς φρονήματος! ὦ φθόνε, πάντων τῶν κακῶν ἀρχηγὲ καὶ περιεκτικὲ καὶ τέλος, ὃς καὶ τὸν πρῶτον ἀποστάτην ἀνθρωποκτονεῖν καὶ κατὰ Θεοῦ φρονεῖν καὶ τὸν δεύτερον, Κάϊν, ἀδελφοκτονεῖν καὶ νῦν τοὺς Ἰουδαίους θεοκτονεῖν ἐδίδαξας, ἡ Δικαιοσύνη παρὰ τῶν ἀδίκων κατεδικάζετο, καὶ ἡ πάντων Ζωὴ καὶ τὸ Φῶς ἐκ τοῦ κόσμου παντὸς καὶ τοῦ φωτὸς ἀπηλαύνετο καὶ πρὸς θάνατον παρεδίδετο, καὶ ὁ τῇ χειρὶ περιδεδραγμένος τῶν ὅλων συνελαμβάνετο, καὶ ὁ ἀπερίληπτος ἐδεσμεῖτο καὶ περιήγετο, συμπεριήγετο κἀκείνη καθάπερ δάμαλις ἢ ἀμνάς, οὐ προηγουμένη μᾶλλον, ἀλλ' ἑλκομένου τοῦ γεννήματος ἑπομένη καὶ συσταυρουμένη τῇ προαιρέσει, μᾶλλον δὲ καὶ μυρίους αἱρουμένη καὶ οἰομένη

opposed to God"? Thus, they were corrupted and became abominable by what they had made abominable and had corrupted. They said: "*Come, let us kill the righteous* man; come, and let us get our *inconvenient* Messiah out of the way."

And while all of them thus raged and plotted in vain, she was there in their midst like a bird among serpents or a young heifer among wild beasts, innocent, but quick to learn, fluttering about wisely and discretely, or darting about being protected by her son, who was both a nestling and a shepherd. Thus her gaze and awareness were attached, so to speak, to the words and appearance of everyone, but at the same time, in her mind and her ardor she stood beside her son, receiving the judgments against him as if they had been pronounced against her.

Oh, what a daring and shameless deed! To what a degree 77
of madness and impiety did these godfighters come, all being of one mind! Envy, you are the originator, sustainer, and end of all evils; you taught the first apostate to commit homicide and to think in a manner contrary to God; and you taught the second, Cain, to commit fratricide, and now you have taught the Jews to commit deicide! For after this, when Righteousness itself was condemned by unrighteous men; when the Life and Light of all was driven away from the whole world and from the light of day, and handed over to death; when the one who holds all things in his hand was seized by human hands; and when the one who cannot be grasped was bound by fetters and led about, his mother too was led about like a heifer or a ewe lamb, not leading the way, but by following her child as he was dragged away and being voluntarily crucified together with him, or rather considering and choosing ten thousand deaths over life without

θανάτους τὴν δίχα τοῦ ζωοδότου τέκνου ζωήν. Ὦ πόσοι σου, δεσποτικὴ ψυχὴ καὶ ἀπαθεστάτη, διὰ τὸν σὸν υἱὸν καὶ Δεσπότην οἱ ἀγῶνες καὶ τὰ παθήματα! Τίς μὲν ἧς ἐκεῖνον ὁρῶσα τὸν λυτρωτὴν τὰς χεῖρας ὄπισθεν ὡς κακοῦργον περιαγκωνιζόμενον, τὸν ἐλευθερωτὴν ὑπὸ δούλου καὶ μιαρᾶς χειρὸς ῥαπιζόμενον, τὸν ὑπὸ μυριάδων ἀγγέλων εὐφημούμενόν τε καὶ προσκυνούμενον ὑπὸ πλήθους στρατιωτῶν ὑβριζόμενόν τε καὶ ἐμπαιζόμενον, τὸ φωτοποιὸν ἐκεῖνο πρόσωπον ἐμπτυόμενον, τὸ ζωοποιὸν σῶμα πρὸς θάνατον μαστιζόμενον. Ὦ τῆς σῆς μεγαλοψυχίας ἢ τῆς τοῦ πάσχοντος ἀνεξικακίας εἴτε καὶ φιλανθρωπίας ἢ καὶ ἀμφότερα! *Πορφύραν* χλεύης τὸν ἀληθῆ τὴν θέωσιν ἐνδύσαντά με περιβαλλόμενον, *στέφανον ἀκανθῶν* τὸν βασιλέα τῶν ὅλων κἀμὲ βασιλεύσαντα τῶν ὁρωμένων πάντων περιτιθέμενον, ἐκεῖθεν ἔνθεν σὺν ὕβρει περιαγόμενον τὸν οὐρανοὺς περιάγοντα καὶ εἰσέτι καὶ νῦν περιάγοντα, καθειργνύμενόν τε καὶ φυλαττόμενον, τὸν θάλασσαν μὲν τῇ χέρσῳ, χέρσον δὲ τῇ ἀβύσσῳ, ἄβυσσον δὲ τῷ μηδενὶ περικλείοντα. Πῶς ποτε ἄρα τότε τὴν ψυχὴν διετίθου καὶ τί ποτε ἐνενόεις; Εἴτε καὶ τῶν ὑψηλῶν τούτων τί κατενόεις, εἴτε καὶ ὡς πρὸς υἱὸν ἁπλῶς οὕτω διετίθου ψιλόν, καλὸν δὲ ὅμως οὕτω καὶ ἀγαθόν τε καὶ θαυμαστόν, καὶ τὴν φύσιν εἶχες ἐνοχλοῦσαν μόνον (ἀλλ' οὐχὶ καὶ τὴν ὑπόληψιν), ἤδη δὲ καὶ τῶν ὧν εἶχες ἐλπίδων τὴν ἐναντίωσιν, εἴτε καὶ ἀμφότερα μᾶλλον ἐπολιόρκει τότε τὴν σὴν ψυχήν, καὶ ἡ κατὰ φύσιν ἢ ὑπὲρ φύσιν σχέσις· ὡς γὰρ ὁ τόκος, οὕτω δηλαδὴ καὶ ὁ πόθος ὑπερφυής, καὶ ἡ παρὰ φύσιν τοῦ

her life-giving child. Oh, lordly and most dispassionate soul, how many were the struggles and sufferings you endured for the sake of your son and Lord! What did you experience when you saw the redeemer's hands bound behind him like a criminal, the liberator struck by the foul hand of a slave, the one who is praised and worshipped by myriads of angels insulted and mocked by a mob of soldiers, his luminous face spat upon, and his life-giving body beaten almost to death? Oh, your greatness of soul! Or should I say the patient forbearance and love for humanity of the one who suffered, or both of these things at once! A *purple robe* was wrapped in mockery around the one who clothed me in deification; *a crown of thorns* was placed on the king of all, who made me a king over all visible things; this way and that, the one who makes the heavens turn round, and continues to do so even now, was led around in insolence; and the one who confined the sea by the dry land, the dry land by the abyss, and the abyss by nothing, was confined in a prison and kept under guard. What was the state of your soul throughout this, Virgin, and what were you thinking? Perhaps you understood something from among these lofty things, or perhaps you were simply disposed as a mother toward her defenseless son, but still noble in this state, and good, and wondrous, and it was your nature alone that was troubling you (but not your character), though you were already facing the contradiction of all the hopes you held; or perhaps it was both of these which at that time besieged your soul, along with your natural or supernatural relation to your son, for just as your birth-giving transcended nature, so too did your longing for him, and the outrage directed against him in his suffering was also contrary to nature, and, third, also beyond

πάσχοντος ὕβρις, καί, τρίτον, ἡ τῆς ἀνεξικακίας ὑπερβολὴ καὶ κατάπληξις.

78 Προστιθῶ σου, Μῆτερ, καὶ τὰ τούτων ἐπέκεινα. Ἐπεὶ γὰρ καὶ ὁ τῶν μειζόνων ἢ τῶν μεγίστων ἀγώνων ἐπέστη καιρός, ἔστη τὲ ὁ σταυρός. Ὢ πῶς ἤνεγκεν ἡ γῆ τὸν σταυρὸν πηγνύμενον; Ὢ πῶς ἀὴρ τὸν Θεὸν κρεμάμενον; Πῶς ὁ οὐρανὸς αὐτὸς ἐπὶ ξύλου κάτω καὶ μετὰ τῶν κακούργων σταυρούμενον τὸν ὑπὲρ τὸν οὐρανὸν ἄνω καὶ αὐτὸν τὸν οὐρανὸν τοῦ οὐρανοῦ καὶ ἐπὶ θρόνου ὑψηλοῦ καὶ ἐπηρμένου καὶ φοβεροῦ καὶ μετὰ τοῦ Πατρὸς συγκαθήμενον; Ἐπεὶ γοῦν ταῦτα καὶ κέκριτο καὶ ἡτοίμαστο καὶ ὁ σταυρωθησόμενος ηὐτρεπίζετο, πῶς ἤνεγκας ἐκεῖνον ὁρᾶν οὕτως ὠμῶς τοῖς μιαιφόνοις ἀπογυμνούμενον, τὸν *φῶς ἀναβαλλόμενον ὡς ἱμάτιον,* τὸν μηδὲ τοῖς σεραφὶμ τρανῶς ἀποκαλυπτόμενον, ἅπερ αὐτὴ ταῖς σαῖς χερσὶ κατεσκεύασας περιβόλαια καὶ ἄχραντα τῷ ἀχράντῳ περιετίθεις σώματι, ταῦτα κλήροις ἀνοσίοις καὶ χερσὶν αἵματος ὅλαις διακληρούμενά τε καὶ μεριζόμενα; Πῶς ἥλοις τὰς ἡλιακὰς ἐκείνας σάρκας καὶ παλάμας διαπειρόμενον τὸν ἀοράτῳ τινὶ δυνάμει πᾶσαν τήνδε διαπεραίνοντα καὶ περικρατοῦντα τὴν κτίσιν; Πάντως *καὶ σοῦ τὴν ψυχὴν ἡ ῥομφαία τότε διήρχετο,* ὅτε καὶ κατὰ τῶν σῶν μᾶλλον ὠθεῖτο μελῶν καὶ σαρκῶν ἢ καὶ μέσης τῆς καρδίας αὐτῆς ἢ τῶν ἐκείνου χειρῶν καὶ ποδῶν τὰ κεντήματα. Ἐνίκας καὶ τὸν υἱόν, εἰ μὴ τολμηρὸν εἰπεῖν, ἐν τοῖς πάθεσιν. Ὁ μὲν γὰρ προαιρετῶς καὶ εἰδὼς ἅπερ ἔπασχεν, ἀλλὰ καὶ τοσαῦτα καὶ ἐπὶ τοσοῦτον πάσχων, ὅσα καὶ ἐφ᾽ ὅσον ἠβούλετο, αὕτη δὲ

nature was the excess of your patient forbearance and consternation.

And I will add, Mother, things that go beyond even these, 78
for the time has come for the greater or rather the greatest contests, namely, the cross. Oh, how did the earth bear to have the cross fixed within it? How did the air endure God suspended in its midst? How indeed did heaven itself endure seeing him crucified on earth below with the evildoers, when on high he is above the heavens, beyond the very heaven of heavens, seated upon a sublime, lofty, and awesome throne together with the Father? And when the one to be crucified was condemned, prepared, and arrayed, how did you endure the sight of him violently stripped naked of his garments by those vile men, he who *clothes himself with light as with a garment,* and who cannot be fully revealed even by the seraphim? How did you endure seeing those pure garments, which you wove with your own hands and wrapped around his pure body, being divided by profane lots and distributed by men's hands all covered with blood? How did you endure the sight of him, who by means of an invisible power completely encompasses and holds together all of creation, being pierced by nails in his flesh and hands, which shone like the sun? There can be no question that *a sword pierced through your own soul* when the nails that pierced his hands were also being pushed into the members of your own body and into your own flesh, or even into the very center of your heart. If it is not too bold a thing to say, you surpassed your son in your sufferings. For he suffered voluntarily and knew exactly what he would suffer, and also the things he suffered, and the extent of his suffering were as many and as much as he wished. But his mother, on the other hand, was

καὶ σφόδρα σπαραττομένη καὶ τὸν τοῦ πάθους ἀγνοοῦσα λόγον καὶ τοσαῦτα παθεῖν βουλομένη καὶ μέντοι καὶ πάσχουσα, ὅσα καὶ παθῶν καὶ ἀλγηδόνων εἰσὶν εἴδη—καὶ αὐτὸ τοῦτο πάθος ἔχουσα, τὸ μὴ ταὐτὰ παθεῖν τῷ υἱῷ, μᾶλλον δὲ τὸ μὴ καὶ πολλῷ χείρω παθεῖν ὑπὲρ τοῦ υἱοῦ. Ὁ μὲν τὰς χεῖράς τε καὶ τοὺς πόδας, αὕτη δὲ καὶ πάσας καθηλοῦτο τὰς σάρκας καὶ αὐτὴν τὴν ψυχήν· ὁ μὲν αἱμάτων, αὕτη δὲ καὶ πολλῷ δριμυτέρων ἔρρει δακρύων ῥεύματα. Πῶς ἤνεγκεν ἢ τοὺς ταῦτα δρῶντας ὁρᾶν ἢ τὸν υἱὸν οὕτω πρὸς αὐτοὺς ὁρῶντα καὶ οὕτω παρ' αὐτῶν πάσχοντα;

79 Ὁ μὲν ἑώρα πρὸς αὐτοὺς μαλακόν τε καὶ ἥμερον, οἱ δὲ πρὸς αὐτὸν βλοσυρόν τε καὶ φόνιον· ὁ μὲν ἠπίᾳ καὶ πρὸ τοῦ σταυροῦ διελέγετο τῇ φωνῇ καὶ μετὰ τὸν σταυρὸν ἠπιωτέρῳ πρὸς αὐτοὺς ἐχρῆτο τῷ σχήματι, οἱ δὲ καὶ πρὸ τοῦ σταυροῦ βρύχοντες τοὺς ὀδόντας καὶ διαστρέφοντες ὀφθαλμοὺς καὶ ἐν αὐτῷ τῷ σταυρῷ τῶν ἥλων μᾶλλον τὴν λύσσαν θήγοντες καὶ μετὰ τὸν σταυρὸν καθάπερ κύνες ἢ θῆρες ἐπιόντες τὲ καὶ προσεπεμβαίνοντες, ὡς καὶ αὐτῶν ἅψασθαι τῶν σαρκῶν, εἰ οἷόν τε καὶ ἐμφορηθῆναι τοῦ αἵματος. Ἐῶ τὰ τῶν διαχλευαζόντων, τὰ τῶν διαγελώντων, τὰ τῶν ὀνειδιζόντων καὶ κωμῳδούντων, τῶν παραπορευομένων, τῶν παρισταμένων, τῶν περιϊσταμένων αὐτὸν σκώμματα καὶ μυκτηρίσματα· ὅτι γὰρ πάντες ὁμοῦ καὶ οὐ ῥήμασι μόνον, ἀλλὰ καὶ σχήμασι καὶ νεύμασι καὶ κινήμασιν ἐξευτέλιζον καὶ ὠνείδιζον καὶ ἐξεμυκτήριζον καὶ μυρίας κατ' αὐτοῦ τὰς ὕβρεις διέπλεκον. Δηλοῖ μὲν πάλαι καὶ ὁ προφήτης πῇ μὲν λέγων· "*ἐγὼ δέ εἰμι σκώληξ καὶ οὐκ*

brutally torn to pieces and, though she did not know the reason for the suffering, was still willing to suffer so much and, indeed, suffered every form of suffering and pain there is—and experienced this very suffering, namely, that she was unable to suffer the same things as her son, or rather was unable to suffer even much greater things for him. His hands and feet were pierced by nails, but her entire body and her soul itself were pierced; he shed blood, but she shed streams of tears that were far more bitter. How did she bear to look upon the men who did these things, or to see her son seeing them in this way and in this way suffering so greatly at their hands?

He looked upon them with soft and temperate eyes, but 79
they looked at him with fierce and murderous glances. Before he was crucified, he spoke to them in a gentle voice, and after he was crucified, he gestured to them more gently still. But they, on the other hand, before he was crucified, gnashed their teeth and rolled their eyes; while he was being crucified they whetted their rage until it became sharper than the nails; and after he was crucified, they came against him and lunged at him like dogs or wild beasts, as if to take hold of his very flesh and drink their fill of his blood. Permit me to leave aside the jests and the sneering of those who mocked him, ridiculed him, reproached him, and made sport of him, those, I mean, who were passing by or standing by round about him. For all alike disparaged him not only with their words but with their postures, gestures, and movements, and they sneered and scoffed at him and hurled a thousand abuses at him. The prophet makes this clear of old when he says in one place: "*I am a worm and no man*"—for

ἄνθρωπος"—τί γὰρ σκώληκος εὐτελέστερον;—"*ὄνειδος ἀνθρώπων καὶ ἐξουθένημα λαῶν*," πῇ δὲ ὅτι "*πάντες οἱ θεωροῦντές με*," καὶ οὐχ' "οἱ μέν, οἱ δ' οὔ," καὶ οὐκ "ἐμυκτήριζον," ἀλλὰ καὶ "ἐξεμυκτήριζον," ὃ πολλῷ πλέον, "*ἐλάλησαν ἐν χείλεσιν, ἐκίνησαν κεφαλήν·*" δηλοῖ δὲ καὶ τὰ Εὐαγγέλια· πολλοὶ δὲ καὶ *κινοῦντες τὰς κεφαλὰς αὐτῶν*. Καὶ ὅσα καὶ οἷα τὰ τῆς ἀνοίας αὐτῶν ἢ ἀπονοίας ῥήματα καὶ παραληρήματα, ἃ πικρότερον αὐτὴν ἐκέντει μᾶλλον ἢ τὰ παθήματα, αὐτοῦ τοῦ συσταυρωθέντος τὰς δυσφημίας, ὡς καὶ αὐτὴν λίαν οἰκείως εἰπεῖν ἔχειν τὰ τοῦ Δαβίδ· *οἱ ὀνειδισμοὶ τῶν ὀνειδιζόντων σε ἐπέπεσον ἐπ' ἐμέ*. Ὅτι γὰρ πάντες, οἱ μὲν καὶ ἐπετώθαζον καὶ ἐπέχαιρον, οἱ δὲ καὶ ἐν χάριτι τὸ μὴ κακῶς ποιεῖν ἐποιοῦντο, πάλαι δηλῶν ὁ προφήτης, "*καὶ ὑπέμεινα*," φησί, "*συλλυπούμενον καὶ οὐχ' ὑπῆρξε, καὶ παρακαλοῦντα καὶ οὐχ' εὗρον*." Ἀλλ' εἰπέ, προφῆτα, καὶ τί τῶν παρακλήσεων ἀντεισφέρουσι; "*Καὶ ἔδωκαν εἰς τὸ βρῶμά μου χολὴν καὶ εἰς τὴν δίψαν μου ἐπότισάν με ὄξος*."

Ταῦτα τοῦ σταυροῦ καὶ τοῦ πάθους καὶ τῷ υἱῷ καὶ τῇ μητρὶ τούτου τὰ παραμύθια. Τοῖς μὲν λόγοις αὐτῶν ὥσπερ βέλεσι, τοῖς δὲ τοῦ παιδὸς ἥλοις ὥσπερ λόγχαις κατετιτρώσκετο, καὶ οὐ μιᾷ μόνον, ἀλλὰ καὶ μυρίαις καθ' ἕκαστον πάντοθεν καὶ κατ' αὐτὸ διεπερονᾶτο ῥομφαίαις. Τί δ' ἂν ἔπαθε μήτηρ καὶ τοιαύτη καὶ οὕτως ἔχουσα, ὁπότε καὶ ἡ ἔμψυχος πᾶσα καὶ ἡ ἄψυχος ἐκλονεῖτο κτίσις, καὶ ἡ γῆ μὲν ἐσείετο, ὁ δὲ Ἅιδης κάτωθεν ἀνερρήγνυτο, καὶ ὁ οὐρανὸς ἄνωθεν ἐσκοτίζετο; Ἐπεὶ γὰρ καὶ οὗτος οὐκ εἶχε

what could be more wretched than a worm?—"*I have become a reproach among men and an object of contempt among the* peoples"; and in another place that: "*All those who looked upon me*"—he does not say "some and not others" but "all," and not just "laughed" but even "laughed scornfully," which is much worse, and "*spoke with their lips and shook their heads.*" This is also made clear in the Gospels, where it says there were many *who wagged their heads.* Permit me also to leave aside the number and kind of their foolish or rather deranged words and nonsense, and the slanders of the thief who was crucified with him, which pierced her more bitterly than the physical sufferings, so that the words of David would most properly apply to her: *The reproaches of those who reproached you fell upon me.* For concerning both those who jeered and exulted over him and those who were grateful to him and thus were not doing him any harm, the prophet makes clear of old: "*I waited for one to grieve with me, but there was none, and for one to comfort me, but I found none.*" But tell us, prophet, what did they give him instead of comfort? "*They gave me gall as my food, and for my thirst they gave me vinegar to drink.*"

Such were the consolations of the cross and the passion for the son and his mother. The words of the crucifiers wounded her like arrows, and the nails in her child pierced her like spears, and not just once but each one that struck her was like a thousand swords passing through her from every side. What would such a mother in such a state have endured when the entire animate and inanimate creation shook violently, when the earth quaked, when Hades below was torn open, and when heaven above was darkened? For when heaven was not able through its agitation to bring

διὰ τοῦ κλόνου παρέχειν τοῖς ἀνθρώποις τὴν αἴσθησιν, διὰ τοῦ σκότου τὸ ἐπὶ τῷ Δεσποτικῷ πάθει πάθος ἐδήλου, μελανειμονῶν καὶ ὥσπερ πενθῶν καὶ αὐτὸς τῷ σχήματι. Ἀλλ᾽ ἡ μὲν κτίσις οὕτως ὅλη καθάπερ συναυλίαν ὀδυρομένη καὶ τῇ μητρὶ τὸν θρῆνον συνερανίζουσα, καὶ αἱ ὑπὲρ τὸν οὐρανὸν δὲ δυνάμεις πᾶσαι διεταράσσοντο, καὶ πολλαὶ μὲν τὸν οὐρανὸν ὑπερκύπτουσαι, πολλαὶ δὲ καὶ κατὰ τοῦ ἀέρος χεόμεναι, πλεῖσται δὲ καὶ αὐτὸν τὸν τοῦ Κρανίου Τόπον περιϊπτάμεναι, τοῦτο μὲν τὴν ὑπερβολὴν τῆς τόλμης τῶν ταῦτα δρώντων, τοῦτο δὲ καὶ τὴν ἀνοχὴν τοῦ πάσχοντος κατεπλήττοντο, καί, ὡς εἰκός, κατὰ τοιούτων πάλιν ἀποστατῶν καὶ πονηρῶν κτισμάτων καὶ ὁμοδούλων πολεμίων συνεκινοῦντο καὶ ἠπείγοντο πάντα καταβαλεῖν καὶ αὐτῇ καταχῶσαι τῇ κτίσει τοὺς θεοκτόνους—ὢ πῶς οὐκ ἀνετράπη καὶ διελύθη, πῶς οὐ συνεχύθη τὰ πάντα τότε καὶ τάφος ὁ κόσμος εἷς ἑαυτῷ καὶ πᾶσι τοῖς ἐν τῷ κόσμῳ γέγονεν;—ἀλλ᾽ ἐπείχοντο δηλαδὴ παρ᾽ αὐτοῦ τοῦ πάσχοντος. Τίς γὰρ ἂν καὶ ἕτερος καὶ τὴν ὁρατὴν ἅμα καὶ τὴν ἀόρατον οὕτως ὀργῶσαν καὶ φερομένην ἀνεχαίτιζε κτίσιν, ὡς μήτε καθ᾽ ἑαυτῆς πρὸς διάλυσιν, μήτε δὲ καθ᾽ ὅλου τοῦ τῶν ἀνθρώπων γένους ὁρμῆσαι πρὸς τὴν ἐκδίκησιν, εἰ μὴ αὐτὸς οὗτος ὁ ταῦτα πάσχων καὶ δι᾽ ὃν οὕτω συνεταράττοντο; Εἰκότως δὲ καὶ ὁ οὐρανὸς καὶ ἡ γῆ μᾶλλον ὑπὲρ τοῦ πάσχοντος ἐπαθαίνοντο, καὶ οὐχὶ τὴν θεοκτονίαν μόνον, ἀλλὰ καὶ τὴν παρανομίαν φέρειν οὐκ εἶχον. Ἐπεὶ γὰρ καὶ διὰ Μωϋσέως τούτους ὡς ἐναργεῖς τὲ καὶ διαρκεῖς καὶ αἰωνίους μάρτυρας ἐμαρτύρατο—*καταβὰς διαμάρτυραί μοι*

men to their senses, it displayed its suffering at the Lord's Passion through darkness and cladding itself, as it were, in the black robes and guise of mourning. In this way, all of creation, like a grieving chorus, joined its lament to that of the mother. And all the angelic powers above the heavens were thrown into confusion: many of them peered over the edge of heaven, many poured out into the air below, while most of them flew around the Place of the Skull, astounded partly at the extreme daring of those who were doing these things, and partly at the forbearance of the one who was suffering. As was only natural, again, they were deeply stirred up against those rebels, those wicked creatures and hostile fellow servants, and they hastened in every way to strike down the killers of God and bury them under the earth—oh, how was it that everything then was not overthrown and broken asunder? How was everything not confounded and the world not become a single grave containing itself and all things in the world?—but they were restrained by the one himself who was suffering. For who else could have held back visible and invisible creation when it was thus enraged and carried away, and prevented it from hurtling toward its own destruction, and inflicting punishment on the entire human race, if not the very one who himself was suffering the things described above, and on account of whom all creation was troubled? It seems that heaven and earth suffered more than the one who was suffering, and not only because of the deicide, but also because they were unable to endure this transgression. For since also, through Moses, the Lord bore witness to these visible, enduring, and eternal witnesses—*when you go down, call heaven and earth to testify on my*

τὸν οὐρανὸν καὶ τὴν γῆν—κἀκεῖνος δὲ οὕτω τῆς διαμαρτυρίας ἤρξατο· "*πρόσεχε οὐρανὲ καὶ λαλήσω, καὶ ἀκουέτω γῆ τῶν ῥημάτων μου.*" Καὶ διὰ Ἱερεμίου δὲ πολλὰ κατηγορήσας αὐτῶν ἐπὶ τούτοις καὶ τὴν τῶν οὐρανῶν ἔκστασιν καὶ τὴν φρίκην παραλαμβάνει τῆς γῆς, "*ἐξέστη*" λέγων "*ἐπὶ τούτῳ ὁ οὐρανὸς καὶ ἔφριξεν ἐπὶ πλέον ἡ γῆ, λέγει Κύριος.*" Ἀλλὰ καὶ δι' οὐρανοῦ καὶ γῆς καὶ τῶν μυρίων αὐτοὺς ἐνέπλησεν εὐεργετημάτων καὶ τεραστίων, ἐτάζων Αἴγυπτον, ἐξάγων αὐτοὺς ἐν νεφέλῃ καὶ στύλῳ πυρός, θάλασσαν τέμνων, ἄρτον ὕων καὶ βρέχων σάρκας, ὕδωρ ἐκ πέτρας καὶ μέλι βλύζων, ἥλιον ἐπέχων ἢ ἀντιστρέφων, ποταμοὺς ἀνακόπτων, τἆλλα τερατουργῶν, καρπῶν αὐτοὺς καὶ στεάτων καὶ τῶν παντοδαπῶν ἀγαθῶν κατὰ τὴν Παλαιστίνην ἀναπιμπλῶν. Εὐλόγως οὖν καὶ νῦν ταῦτα τὰ στοιχεῖα καὶ ὡς μάρτυρες καὶ ὡς διάκονοι τῶν πρὸς αὐτοὺς εὐεργεσιῶν, καὶ τῆς ἀχαριστίας αὐτῶν καὶ τῆς ἀσεβείας ἐναργεῖς ἔλεγχοι καὶ κήρυκες καθειστήκεισαν, καὶ ὥσπερ διά τινος στόματος αὐτοῦ τοῦ κινήματος τοῦ σχήματος κατεμαρτύρουν καὶ κατεβόων.

Ἀλλὰ ταῦτα μὲν οὕτω καὶ κατηγόρουν ἅμα καὶ ἀπωδύροντο, ἡ δὲ μήτηρ ὑπὸ πάντων ὁμοῦ καὶ τῶν ἀνθρώπων καὶ τῶν στοιχείων καὶ ἑαυτῆς, ἀνεβράσσετο μὲν τὰ σπλάγχνα καὶ διεκόπτετο καὶ πάντοθεν ἐμερίζετο· πρὸς ἓν μόνον ἑώρα καθάπερ ἐν ἀσελήνῳ νυκτί, μᾶλλον δὲ καὶ νυκτομαχίᾳ, λύχνον, καὶ ὑπὸ μιᾶς ἤρτητο τῆς ἐλπίδος, τοῦ Θεὸν εἶναι καὶ ἑκουσίως ταῦτα πάσχειν τὸν πάσχοντα, ᾧ δὲ μᾶλλον ἐνεπίμπρατο τὴν ψυχήν, ὅτι ἐφλέγετο μὲν

behalf—and thus Moses began his testimony, saying: "*Hear, heaven, and I will speak, and let the earth hear my words.*" And through Jeremiah, after the Lord reproached them for these things, he associates with himself the astonishment that would overtake the heavens and the terror that would grip the earth, by saying: "*Heaven was astonished by this, and* the earth *trembled, says the Lord.*" Yet it was through the same heaven and earth that he also lavished innumerable mercies and wondrous signs upon these people, striking Egypt, leading them by a cloud and a pillar of fire, dividing the sea, raining down bread and showering them with meat, making water and honey flow from the rock, arresting the movement of the sun or causing it to move backward, driving back the course of rivers, and the other wondrous signs; giving them their full measure of fruit, meat, and every manner of good thing in Palestine. Thus, it was only natural that the elements of creation, as witnesses and ministers of the good things these people had received, should now have become open accusers and heralds of their ingratitude and impiety, as if they were all denouncing them and bearing witness against them in the very disruption of the form of the world as if speaking through one mouth.

But while all creation was simultaneously condemning 80
and lamenting these things, the mother was seething inwardly because of all the people, all the elements of creation, and herself, and she was cut in two, and divided into pieces from every direction. As if it were a moonless night, or rather a battle taking place in the dark, she looked to one source of light alone, and clung to one source of hope, namely, that the one who was suffering was God, and that his suffering was voluntary. Yet this inflamed her soul even

προσεγγίσαι τῷ υἱῷ καὶ συμπαθεῖν οὕτω πάσχοντι καὶ προσάψασθαι καὶ προσφθέγξασθαι καί τινος καὶ ἀκοῦσαι φωνῆς, τὰ τελευταῖα δὴ ταῦτα καὶ τοῦ Πάθους καὶ τοῦ θανάτου λοιπὸν παραμύθια· ἀπεστρέφετο δέ—περιεκύκλουν γὰρ *κύνες πολλοί* τὴν ἀναίδειαν, οὐ τὴν φιλοδεσποτείαν, καθάπερ θήραν περιϊστάμενοι καὶ τῆς σφαγῆς ἀπολαύοντες ἢ καὶ αὐτοῦ τοῦ αἵματος ἀπολάπτοντες, καὶ *μόσχοι πολλοὶ καὶ ταῦροι πίονες* περιεῖχον διὰ τὸ περιὸν τῆς τρυφῆς καὶ τῆς ἀπειθείας, καὶ αὐτὸ τοῦτο τὸ κατὰ τοῦ Δεσπότου νεανιεύεσθαι, ἐπεὶ καὶ *νεῦρον αὐτῶν ὁ τράχηλος σιδηροῦν*. Καὶ ὁ μὲν ἱλαρὸν αὐτὴν πόρρωθεν ἀπεβλέπετο, ἡ δὲ καθάπερ ἀγκίστροις εἴτε τισὶν ἄλλοις δεσμοῖς ἀφύκτοις ἑλκομένη τοῖς ἐκείνου βλέμμασιν, ὤρεγε μὲν τὰς χεῖρας καὶ περιεπλέκετο πόρρωθεν καὶ ὥσπερ ἐπέρριπτεν ἑαυτὴν τῷ υἱῷ, εἰργομένη δὲ ὅμως ἀντέβλεπε λίαν οἰκτρὸν περιπαθέσιν ἅμα καὶ ὥσπερ ἐγκαλοῦσι τοῖς ὀφθαλμοῖς, οἷα παρὰ τῶν μιαιφόνων αὐτός τε πάσχει καθάπερ τῶν μιαιφόνων ὁ χείριστος, ὁ πάντων εὐεργέτης καὶ λυτρωτής. Καὶ αὐτὴ δὲ οὐδὲν ἧττον, εἰ μὴ καὶ μᾶλλον, συμπάσχουσα πρὸς τούτῳ καὶ τῶν ἑαυτῆς ἀποχωρίζεται σπλάγχνων.

Ἐπεὶ δὲ καὶ πάντα μὲν ἐπενοήθη κατὰ τοῦ σταυρωθέντος τοῖς σταυρωταῖς τὰ καὶ αὐτοῦ τοῦ σταυροῦ χείρονα, πάντα δὲ ἐπληρώθη, καὶ πᾶς μὲν ἀπηλάθη τῶν φίλων καὶ τῶν γνωρίμων, καὶ αὐτῶν δὲ τῶν Θεοκτόνων ἀπελύθη τὸ πλεῖστον, ὡς ἤδη κεκρατηκότων καὶ προβάσης τῆς ἀναιρέσεως εὐωχηθησομένων ὡς τὸ εἰκὸς καὶ ἑορτασόντων καὶ παιωνιζόντων τὰ ἐπινίκια, τηνικαῦτα λοιπὸν καὶ τὰ τῆς

more for she was burning to draw near to her son, to suffer with him in his suffering, to touch him, and speak to him, and hear his voice, these being the final remaining consolations of his Passion and death. But she turned away, for *many dogs* now surrounded him in their shamelessness, devoid of love for their master, as if encircling their prey and relishing the slaughter, or rather greedily lapping up blood; and they were the *many young bulls and strong bulls* surrounding him, on account of the excess of their depravity and disobedience, and their youthful insolence against their Master was because *the sinews of* their *necks* were *iron.* But he looked at her from afar with a cheerful countenance, while she, as if she were caught on hooks or held fast by other inescapable bonds, was drawn toward his gaze, and stretched forth her hands and embraced him from afar, as if she were throwing herself at her son, but, being kept away, she could only look on in a most pitiful way, with her eyes expressing her emotion and at the same time bringing accusations for what he was suffering at the hands of these murderers, as if he, who was in fact the benefactor and redeemer of all, was the worst of murderers. And she was suffering along with him, no less and even more, and was not separated from him in her own feelings.

When all things had been contrived by the crucifiers against the one who was crucified, including things even worse than the cross, and all things were now fulfilled, and he had been deprived of all his friends and acquaintances, most of the God killers themselves dispersed, since they had already succeeded in their aim, and were probably feasting over his imminent death, and celebrating by singing songs of triumph. At that same time, the soldiers neglected

φυλακῆς ἠμελεῖτο τοῖς στρατιώταις καὶ οὕτως ἡ μήτηρ ἠρέμα καὶ κατ' ὀλίγον ἐγγίσασα, ὥστε καὶ λέγειν τι καὶ τῶν λεγομένων ἐπαΐειν δύνασθαι, μετ' ὀλίγον καὶ ὅλη προσελθοῦσά τε καὶ προσψαύσασα, τί μὲν οὐκ ἔλεγε, τί δὲ οὐκ ἔπασχε, τί δὲ οὐκ ἔπραττε, τοῖς ὀφθαλμοῖς μὲν θερμότερα τὰ ῥεύματα καταχέουσα, τῷ στόματι δὲ τοὺς ἥλους καὶ τοὺς πόδας καταφιλοῦσα, μᾶλλον δὲ καὶ αὐτοὺς τοὺς ἥλους, εἰ οἷόν τε καταπίνειν ἐφιεμένη καὶ μέντοι καὶ τῶν αἱμάτων τι σπῶσα καὶ καταπίνουσα; Κατέψα μὲν τὰς πληγὰς παρειαῖς ἅμα καὶ ὀφθαλμοῖς, ἐκίρνα δὲ τοῖς αἵμασι δάκρυα, μᾶλλον δὲ καὶ αὐτοὺς τοὺς ὀφθαλμοὺς καὶ τὰς παρειὰς συνεπεφύκει τοῖς ἥλοις καὶ ταῖς πληγαῖς. Ἐφιλονείκει πρὸς αὐτῷ τῷ σταυρῷ καὶ τὸ φῶς ἀφεῖναι καὶ τὴν ψυχήν· τοῦτο μέν ποτε καὶ τοῖς ἤδη κενωθεῖσιν ἐκ τῶν δακρύων ὄμμασι περιπαθέστερον πρὸς αὐτὸν ἀφεώρα, τοῦτο δὲ καὶ ῥήμασιν ὠλοφύρετο καὶ τοῖς σχήμασι, καὶ σὺν τῷ φιλοστόργῳ πανταχοῦ τὸ φιλόσοφον, ὡς μηδέν τι πρᾶξαι τῶν ἀγεννῶν καὶ τοῦ υἱοῦ καὶ ἑαυτῆς ἀναξίων. Ἐποικίλλετο καὶ τοῖς πάθεσι, τὸ μὲν πάθος τῆς ὑπερβολῆς ἀπωδύρετο, τὸν δὲ πάσχοντα τῆς ἀνοχῆς κατεπλήττετο, τοὺς δὲ θεοκτόνους ᾐτιᾶτο τῆς τόλμης ἢ τάχα μᾶλλον καὶ αὐτοὺς ἀπεκλαίετο.

81 "Τί ταῦτα," λέγουσα, "Δέσποτα καὶ υἱὲ καὶ Θεέ μου, τίς ἡ τοσαύτη σου τῆς μακροθυμίας ὑπερβολή; Μὴ ὄναρ, οὐχ ὕπαρ μοι τὰ ὁρώμενα; Μετὰ τῶν ἀνόμων ὁ ἀναμάρτητος, μᾶλλον δὲ καὶ ὁ *αἴρων τὴν ἁμαρτίαν τοῦ κόσμου,* μετὰ τῶν καταδίκων ὁ δικαστής. Τί τὸ τῆς συγκαταβάσεως τοῦτο βάθος; Τί τὸ τῆς ἀνεξικακίας ἢ φιλανθρωπίας πέλαγος;

the duties of their watch, and thus the mother was able to draw near, quietly and by degrees, so as to be able to speak and to hear some of the things that were being said, and, after a while, she was able to approach completely and touch the body of her son. What words did she not utter, what did she not suffer, what did she not do? With her eyes she was shedding hot tears, with her mouth she was kissing the nails and his feet, or rather she longed to be able to consume the nails themselves and, indeed, to suck in what she could of the blood and swallow it. She caressed his wounds with her cheeks and eyes, mingling her tears with his blood, or rather she united her eyes themselves and her cheeks with the nails and wounds. She was striving to leave even her life and soul on the very cross. At one moment, with her eyes already emptied of their tears, she would gaze at him with a heart-rending glance, at another she was animated by words and gestures of mourning, though her affection was tempered in every way by philosophical restraint, so that she did nothing improper or unworthy of herself or her son. She experienced a range of emotions: she lamented the extremity of his suffering, she was astonished by the forbearance of the sufferer, and she condemned the audacity of the God murderers, or rather she probably mourned for them as well.

Speaking to him, she said: "What are these things, my 81
Master, son, and God? What is the nature of your extreme forbearance? Is what I am seeing taking place in a dream and not when I am awake? The sinless one, or rather *the one who takes away the sin of the world,* is being counted among transgressors, and the judge among the condemned. What is the depth of your gracious condescension? How great is the ocean of your forbearance and love for mankind? Was it not

Οὐκ ἤρκει σοι τὸ Θεὸν ὄντα γενέσθαι δι᾽ ἡμᾶς τοὺς ἀνθρώπους ἄνθρωπον; Οὐκ ἤρκει σοι τὸ τοσούτους ὑπὲρ ἡμῶν ἐκ βρέφους ὑπομεῖναι τοὺς πειρασμούς, ἐπιβουλάς, διωγμούς, μεταναστάσεις, φυγάς, φθόνους, ὕβρεις, συκοφαντίας, ἐπιδρομάς, ἀπαγωγάς, λιθασμούς, τἄλλα, ἀλλὰ καὶ μέχρι σταυροῦ καὶ μέχρι τοσούτων παθῶν τὸ κατὰ σοῦ τῶν Ἰουδαίων τόλμημα; Τοῦτό σοι τῆς μεγάλης οἰκονομίας περὶ ἡμᾶς καὶ τῆς τοσαύτης εὐσπλαγχνίας τὸ ἀνταπόδομα; Ταῦτα τῶν πρὸς αὐτοὺς εὐεργετημάτων τὰ χαριστήρια καὶ τῶν παλαιῶν ὁμοῦ καὶ νέων;

"Μάστιξιν ἐτάζουσι καὶ καταξαίνουσι ταῖς πληγαῖς τὸν μαστίγων αὐτοὺς αἰγυπτιακῶν ῥυσάμενον, τὸν τοσαύταις πληγαῖς ἐτάσαντα δι᾽ αὐτοὺς τὴν Αἴγυπτον. Χλαῖναν καὶ πορφύραν χλεύης ἐνδύουσιν, οὓς καὶ πάλαι φωτοειδεῖ νεφέλῃ περιεκάλυψας, οὓς ἐσκέπασας ἐν ἡμέρᾳ πολέμων καὶ ὡς πατὴρ ἐν ἡμέρᾳ γάμων υἱὸν καὶ νυμφίον περιεκόσμησας. Καὶ πάλαι μὲν *ὡς ἀετὸς* νεοσσοὺς ἐπὶ τῶν πτερύγων ἐφύλαξας *καὶ ἐπὶ τῶν μεταφρένων* ἀνέλαβες, καὶ νῦν δὲ ὡς Θεὸς Θεοὺς ἑαυτῷ περιέθηκας καὶ αὐτοὺς ἑαυτὸν ἐνέδυσας. Ἀκάνθαις στεφανοῦσι τὸν εὐλογίαις αὐτοὺς στεφανώσαντα, οὓς *δόξῃ καὶ τιμῇ ἐστεφάνωσας,* οὓς στεφάνῳ χαρίτων καὶ *εὐδοκίας* ὅπλῳ περιετείχισας. Καλάμῳ παίουσιν οὓς ῥάβδῳ πλήξας τὴν θάλασσαν διεπέρασας, τοὺς δὲ ἐχθροὺς αὐτῶν ἐκάλυψε θάλασσα. Κατὰ τοῦ σοῦ προσώπου, τέκνον, ἐμπτύσματα, κατὰ τῶν σῶν παρειῶν ῥαπίσματα, τοῦ σημειώσαντος *ἐφ᾽ ἡμᾶς τὸ φῶς τοῦ προσώπου σου,* τοῦ τὸ πρόσωπον Μωσέως πάλαι δοξάσαντος, τοῦ πτύσαντος καὶ τὸν τυφλὸν ὀμματώσαντος. Κατὰ τῶν

enough for you, being God, to become a human being for the sake of us human beings? Was it not enough for you to have endured, from your childhood, for our sake so many trials, plots, persecutions, wanderings, exiles, envy, insolence, false accusations, attacks, assaults, stonings, and all the rest, and now this shameless treatment by the Jews which extends even to the cross and to so many sufferings? Is this the recompense for your great dispensation for our salvation and your great compassion? Are these the expressions of their gratitude for your acts of kindness to them, old and new?

"They have afflicted you with scourging and lacerated you with wounds, though you were the one who delivered them from the scourges of the Egyptians, and who for their sake inflicted great plagues on Egypt. They dressed you in a purple robe of mockery, though of old you enveloped them with a luminous cloud, and covered them in a day of war, like a father adorning his son and bridegroom on the day of his wedding. Long ago, *like an eagle* you protected them like nestlings under your wings, and bore them aloft *on your back,* and now, as God, you have placed them around yourself as Gods and clothed them with yourself. They placed on you a crown of thorns, though you crowned them with blessings, for you *crowned* them *with glory and honor,* and encircled them with a crown of graces and *a shield of favor.* They have struck you with a reed, on whose behalf you struck the sea and allowed them to cross, while the sea covered their enemies. They have spat in your face, my child, and struck your cheeks, you who manifested *the light of your face upon us,* who of old glorified the face of Moses, and with your spittle opened the eyes of a blind man. They pressed iron nails

σῶν χειρῶν ἧλοι, κατὰ τῶν σῶν ποδῶν σίδηρος, ὃς καὶ πάλαι τῆς αἰγυπτιακῆς αὐτοὺς δουλείας καὶ τῶν δεσμῶν καὶ νῦν τῆς ἐν ξύλῳ κατάρας καὶ τῶν δαιμόνων ἔλυσας *καὶ τὰς χεῖρας* αὐτῶν καὶ τοὺς πόδας *παρειμένας* ἔρρωσας. Ἀντὶ τῶν καθαρθέντων λεπρῶν τραυματίζουσιν, ἀντὶ τῶν ἐγερθέντων νεκρῶν θανατοῦσιν, ἀντὶ τῶν φωτισθέντων τυφλῶν—οἴμοι τῶν ἐμῶν ὀφθαλμῶν φῶς—τοὺς σοὺς ὀφθαλμοὺς τῷ σκότῳ παραδιδόασι. Διὰ σέ, τέκνον, καὶ Βαραββᾶν, οἴμοι, σῴζουσιν, ἐπίσης ἐξαιτοῦνται τὴν ζωὴν ἐκείνου καὶ σοῦ τὴν σφαγήν.

"Ὢ πῶς σείεται μόνον, ἀλλ' οὐ πρὸς Ἅιδην χωρεῖ γῆ; Ὢ πῶς σκοτίζονται μόνον, ἀλλ' οὐ πίπτουσιν οἱ φωστῆρες; Ὢ πῶς ὁ οὐρανὸς ἀλλοιοῦται μέν, ἵσταται δέ; Πῶς καὶ οἱ ἄγγελοι φρίττουσι μέν, φέρουσι δὲ ὅμως καὶ τὸ πᾶν οὐ συγχέουσιν; Ἢ δῆλον ὅτι σὰ καὶ ταῦτα, Θεέ μου καὶ υἱέ, τεράστια, τοῦ καὶ δι' αὐτοὺς πάλαι τὰ στοιχεῖα πολλάκις μεταβαλόντος, καὶ νῦν πάλιν ὑπὲρ αὐτῶν τούτων τῶν σφαγέων κατὰ χώραν κρατοῦντος, καὶ σὺ ταῦτα σφίγγεις ὁ τὰς χεῖρας ἁπλῶν. Εἴθε, τέκνον, τῶν σῶν ὑπερήθλουν ἐγὼ μελῶν, εἴθε τῶν σῶν παθῶν ὑπερέπασχον. Νῦν δέ μοι τοῦτο—τοῦτο, τὸ πάντων παθῶν καὶ θανάτων ἀφορητότερον—ὅτι μὴ δέχομαι τὰς πληγὰς ἐγώ, ὅτι μὴ τοῦ σοῦ θανάτου πολλοὺς ὑπεραποθνήσκω θανάτους ἢ καὶ τὸ δεύτερον προαποθνήσκω σοῦ θνήσκοντος. Ἀλλὰ φθέγξαι τι μικρὸν τῇ σῇ μητρὶ παραμύθιον, ἄφες τι ῥῆμα τῆς σῆς κατ' αὐτῶν καὶ τοῦ θανάτου νίκης ἐχέγγυον, διάθου τὰ περὶ

through your hands and feet, though of old you freed them from their slavery and bondage in Egypt, and now have freed them from the curse of the tree, and from the demons, and you gave strength to their *weakened hands* and feet. In return for cleansing the lepers, they have inflicted wounds upon you; in return for raising the dead, they have put you to death; in return for restoring light to the eyes of the blind—alas, you who are the light of my eyes!—they have delivered your eyes to the darkness. Instead of you, my child, they have even, alas, spared Barabbas, and demanded that he live and you be slaughtered.

"Oh, how is it that the earth is only trembling but not collapsing into Hades? How is it that the stars are only darkened but have not fallen from the sky? How has the sky been so strangely altered yet still remains in place? How are the angels shuddering in fear and yet enduring and not confounding the universe? But it is clear, my God and my son, that these portents are yours, you who of old often changed the elements of creation for their sake, and who now again, for the sake of these murderers, is holding the elements in their places, and grasping them tightly though your hands are stretched out. Oh, how I wish, my child, that the members of my body were contending in place of your limbs, and that I could have suffered in place of your suffering. Now there remains for me only this—this, which is more unbearable than all sufferings and every death—that I cannot take your wounds upon myself; that I cannot die many deaths in the place of your death, or at the least that I cannot die before you. But speak to me, your mother, and give me a small word of consolation, a pledge of your victory over them and over death; take thought for the situation of your mother,

τῆς μητρός, ὑπόθου τὰ γενησόμενα. Τίς γένωμαι, πρὸς τίνα, τέκνον, ἀποστραφήσομαι, τίνι λοιπὸν κοινωνήσω λόγων, στέγης, διατριβῆς; Πῶς ἐν μέσῳ τοσούτων θηρῶν μόνη καὶ γυνὴ καὶ σοῦ γυμνὴ διαζήσομαι; Ἀπόδος τῇ σῇ μητρὶ τὰ συντακτήριά τε ἅμα καὶ εὐαγγέλια, ἀκοῦσαι μὲν ἥδιστα, ἐλπίσαι δὲ ἀσφαλέστατα. Πότε σὲ καὶ πάλιν, τέκνον, τὸ ἐμόν, θεάσομαι φῶς; Πότε περιβαλοῦμαι τὰ ἐμὰ φίλτατα μέλη ζῶντα καὶ κατασπάσομαι; Πότε τῆς ἡδίστης ἀκούσω γλώττης καὶ ζωογονούσης νεκρούς, καὶ πρὸ πάντων ἐμέ, τὴν μητέρα, τῷ περὶ σὲ πόθῳ θνήσκουσαν; Πλὴν ὅσον τῶν ἐπὶ σοὶ πόνων οὕτω σφοδρῶς αἰσθάνεσθαι, οὐ φέρω σου τὰς ὠδίνας, τέκνον, ἃς ἐν τῷ σῷ τόκῳ διέφυγον. Εἶδον, ὥσπερ ἔφης, τὸ σὸν πάθος, ἴδοιμι καὶ τὴν ἀνάστασιν καὶ τὴν δόξαν, ὡς πολλάκις εὐηγγελίσω μοι."

82 Οὕτω τῆς μητρὸς ὀλοφυρομένης καὶ προσκειμένης, αὐτὸς ἥμερον πρῶτον καὶ συμπαθὲς αὐτὴν ἀπιδών, πρὸς δὲ καὶ τὸν ἠγαπηκότα καὶ ἠγαπημένον συμπαριστάμενον μαθητὴν μικρὰ τὰ χείλη διακινήσας, ἡ Αὐτοσοφία, βραχέα καὶ πάντα φθέγγεται, καὶ διατιθέμενος ἅμα καὶ παρακατατιθέμενος· "*γύναι, ἴδε ὁ υἱός σου·*" παρθένῳ μητρὶ παρθένον καὶ πάλιν υἱὸν χαριζόμενος καὶ ἀντιτιθεὶς ἑαυτῷ, οὐκ αὐτὸς τὴν πρόνοιαν τῆς μητρὸς ἀπαρνούμενος—ἄπαγε—ἀλλ' ὁμοῦ καὶ τοῖς αἰσθητοῖς τὸ σφοδρὸν τοῦ πάθους τῆς μητρὸς προσπαραμυθούμενος καὶ τὸν μαθητὴν τοῦ περὶ ἄμφω φίλτρου καὶ τῆς ἀρετῆς, ἤδη δὲ καὶ αὐτῆς ἕνεκα τῆς ἐν τῷ Πάθει παραμονῆς ἀμειβόμενος, ὡς καὶ εἰς τὴν ἑαυτοῦ τάξιν αὐτὸν ἀντικαθιστᾶν καὶ τοσοῦτον αὐτῷ

explain to me the things that shall happen after this. What shall become of me? To what child shall I turn? With whom shall I share my words, my house, my time? How will I, a woman, alone and without you, survive among so many wild beasts? Provide your mother with your final arrangements as well as with tidings of joy, which are sweet to hear and provide a most certain hope. When will I see you again, my child, you who are my light? When will I again embrace these living limbs which are so dear to me and kiss them? When will I hear your sweet voice, which brings life to the dead, and above all to me, your mother, who is dying in her longing for you? Though I have such strong feelings for your sufferings, I cannot relieve you of the travail, my child, from which I myself escaped at your birth. I have seen your passion, as you said I would, so too may I see your resurrection and your glory, as you have often promised me."

While his mother was caught up in her mourning and 82
lamentation, he looked upon her peacefully and with compassion. To the loving and beloved disciple, who was also standing there, the very Wisdom of God moved his lips ever so softly and in a few words said everything, making a bequest and at the same time entrusting her to him: "*Woman, behold your son!*" And thus to his virgin mother he once again gave a virgin son, giving him to her in place of himself, not because he refused to care for his mother—by no means!—but by perceptible things he consoled his mother's excessive grief and rewarded the disciple for his affection to them both, and for his excellence of character, as well as for his standing beside her during the time of the Passion, and thus he substituted the beloved disciple for himself, and established him in his own place, and bestowed upon him such a

περιτιθέναι ἀξίωμα· καὶ οὐ ταῦτα μόνον ποιῶν, ἀλλὰ καὶ ἡμῖν νομοθετῶν τὴν μέχρι τέλους τῶν γονέων πρόνοιαν καὶ κηδεμονίαν, καίτοι κἂν τοῖς ἄλλοις σφοδρότερον αὐτῇ προφερόμενος· "*τί ἐμοὶ καὶ σοί, γύναι;*" Καὶ πάλιν· "*τίς ἐστιν ἡ μήτηρ μου;*" Καὶ· "*μήτηρ μου καὶ ἀδελφοί μου* οὗτοι εἰσίν." Ἀλλ' ἐνταῦθα φανερῶς καὶ διαφερόντως ἀπηρτισμένην αὐτῇ δείκνυσι τὴν φιλοστοργίαν, τὴν ἑαυτοῦ σχεδὸν πᾶσαν εἰς τὸν μαθητὴν προστασίαν μετατιθείς, εἶθ' ἵνα μὴ νομίσῃ διὰ προστασίαν μόνην τὴν υἱοθεσίαν ἐγχειρίζεσθαι τῆς αὐτοῦ μητρός, ἀλλὰ καὶ διὰ τὴν πρὸς αὐτὸν ἀγάπην τὲ καὶ τιμήν, κἀκεῖνον προσβλέψας, "*ἴδε,*" φησίν, "*ἡ μήτηρ σου,*" μονονουχὶ κἀκείνῳ ταύτην προστάτιν καὶ κυρίαν ἀντιδιδοὺς καὶ τὴν ὀρφανίαν αὐτῷ καὶ τὴν ἐρημίαν παραμυθούμενος, καὶ ὁμοῦ μὲν ὑποτάττων αὐτῇ τοῦτον, ὁμοῦ δὲ καὶ πρὸς ἀγάπην συνάπτων καὶ ἓν ἄμφω ποιῶν. Τούτῳ καὶ ὁ μαθητὴς ὑπακούσας *εἰς τὰ ἴδια,* τὸν τῆς Σιὼν οἶκον, παραλαμβάνει ταύτην, ὃν καὶ φθάσας ὁ λόγος ἐδήλωσεν.

83 Ἐπεὶ τοίνυν τοῖς σταυρωταῖς ὅσαπερ εἰς νοῦν ἦκε πεπλήρωτο, δεικνύων ὁ σταυρωθεὶς ὡς εἴ τι καὶ χεῖρον εἶχον πρὸς ὕβριν τὲ καὶ ὀδύνην ἐπιλογίσασθαι, οὐκ ἂν οὐδὲ τοῦτο παρῆκαν, "*διψῶ,*" λέγει· καὶ αὐτίκα καθάπερ αὐτοὶ διψῶντες μᾶλλον τὴν τοιαύτην κατ' αὐτοῦ μανίαν ἐπινοήσασθαι, ὄξος, οἴμοι, καὶ χολὴν τῷ γλυκασμῷ τῆς ζωῆς, τῇ πηγῇ τῆς ἀθανασίας ὀξέως προσφέρουσιν, εἰκόνα τῆς ἑαυτῶν κακίας, ἐγκερασάμενοι τὸ πικρότατον καὶ δριμύτατον, ἵνα μηδὲν τῶν περὶ αὐτοῦ προφητευθέντων παραλειφθῇ. Οὐχ' ὅτι δὲ πεπροφήτευτο, διὰ τοῦτο καὶ πεπλήρωτο, ἀλλ' ὅτι πεπλήρωτο, διὰ τοῦτο καὶ πεπροφήτευτο·

great honor. But this was not all he did, for he also established as a principle for us to care for and support our parents until their death, even if at other times he strongly reproached his mother, saying, "*Woman, what have you to do with me?*" And again, "*Who is my mother?*" and "*My mother and my brothers* are these." But now, however, quite clearly and distinctly, he shows her the completeness of his tender affection for her, transferring essentially all of her care to his beloved disciple. And then, so that the disciple would not think that this adoption was bestowed on him solely to care for the Lord's mother, but that it was also because of his own love and honor for him, the Lord looked at him and said, "*Behold your mother!*" all but giving her to him as his protector and sovereign, comforting him in his orphanhood and abandonment, both subjecting him to her and uniting them in love and making them both one. Being obedient to the Lord, the disciple took her *into his home,* that is, to his house in Zion, which my discourse will touch on presently.

When those who crucified him fulfilled everything they 83
had thought of, the one they crucified showed them that there was one more outrage and torment they could inflict on him, and they would not let this pass unnoticed; and thus he said: "*I thirst.*" And immediately, as if they were themselves thirsting to contrive such madness against him, they rushed, alas, to give vinegar and gall to he who is the sweetness of life and the fountain of immortality, thereby producing an image of their own evil, mixing together the most bitter with the most acrid, so that none of the things prophesied about him would be left out. But this did not take place because it was prophesied, but rather was prophesied

οὐ γὰρ ἡ προφητεία τῆς τόλμης, ἀλλὰ τῆς προφητείας ἡ τόλμα μᾶλλον αἰτία. Καὶ ταῦτα τολμῶσιν οἱ ὠμότατοι καὶ ἀχαριστότατοι, μήτε τοῦ πάλαι διαστρέψαντος δι᾽ αὐτοὺς ἐν Αἰγύπτῳ πρὸς αἷμα τὰ ὀμβρήματα καὶ τὰ νάματα, μήτε τοὐναντίον εἰς πόμα γλυκὺ τὰ πικρὰ τῆς Μερρᾶς ὕδατα, μήτε τοῦ πολλάκις κορέσαντος αὐτοὺς ἐν δίψει καύματος, ἐν ἀνύδρῳ, τοῦ ἡδίστου πόματος, μήτε τοῦ *μέλι* θηλάσαντος αὐτοῖς καὶ θηλάζοντος *ἐκ πνευματικῆς ἀκολουθούσης πέτρας*, μήτε δὲ τοῦ νῦν ἔναγχος τὸ ὕδωρ αὐτῶν εἰς οἶνον μεταβαλόντος ἐπιμνησθέντες, ἀλλ᾽ ὄντως αὐτῶν ὁ βότρυς *βότρυς πικρίας* καὶ ἡ *σταφυλὴ σταφυλὴ χολῆς* καὶ *θυμὸς δρακόντων ὁ οἶνος*. Ἐπὶ τούτοις καὶ τοῦτο λογίζεσθαι δέον, οἵα καὶ πάλιν τὴν μητέρα κατελάμβανεν ἡ πικρία καὶ οἷον καὶ αὐτῇ κιρνᾶται παρ᾽ αὐτῶν τὸ ἀψίνθιον· ὁμοῦ μὲν τῇ φωνῇ διακινουμένην τὰ σπλάγχνα καὶ περιθέουσαν καὶ διψῶσαν καὶ ταύτην καὶ φλεγομένην διαπυρώτερον, ὅπως κἂν τὴν ἐσχάτην γοῦν διαναψύξῃ τῷ παιδὶ φλόγα, καὶ τοῦτο μὲν τῶν παρόντων δεομένην, τοῦτο δὲ καὶ αὐτὴν ἐπισπεύδουσαν, ἀπωθουμένην δὲ ὅμως παρὰ τῶν μιαιφόνων καὶ μὴ ἐώντων μήτε ταύτην μήτε τινὰ τῶν ἄλλων φιλανθρωπότερον τῷ κρεμαμένῳ χρήσασθαι, ἀλλὰ καὶ προσπαροινούντων εἰς αὐτὸν ἔτι καὶ τὸ ὄξος καὶ τὴν χολὴν ἀντιδιδόντων τοῦ ὕδατος. Ἐν ἀρχῇ μὲν οὖν τὸν *ἐσμυρνισμένον* ἐπεδίδοσαν *οἶνον*, ὁ δὲ οὐκ ἤθελεν, ἵνα μὴ ὁ θᾶττον αὐτοῦ καὶ παραδόξαν θάνατος οὐ τοῦ θελήματος αὐτοῦ μᾶλλον, ἀλλὰ καὶ τῆς τοῦ φαρμάκου νομισθῇ δυνάμεως. Ἐπεὶ δέ ποτε καὶ ἀφορμὴν τὴν ἐκείνου φωνὴν εἰλήφεσαν, τὴν οἰκείαν ἀποπληροῦσι μανίαν.

because it took place, for the prophecy was not the cause of their audacity, but rather their audacity was the cause of the prophecy. And these most savage and ungrateful men audaciously dared to do such things because they failed to remember that in Egypt it was he who turned the rain and the streams into blood for them; that it was he who, in the opposite manner, made the bitter waters of Marah sweet and potable; that it was he who countless times slaked their thirst in a waterless place in the heat of the day by giving them the sweetest of drinks; that it was he who had suckled them *with honey* and still suckled them *from the spiritual rock that accompanied them;* and that it was he who had now recently changed water into wine for them. But in truth, their grapes *are the grapes of bitterness,* their *cluster of grapes is a cluster of gall,* and *their wine is the wrath of dragons.* In addition to these things, it is also necessary for us to consider what bitterness once again seized his mother, as if those people had also mixed wormwood for her. For when she heard her son's voice, she was moved in the deepest parts of her being, and she rushed about, thirsting herself and burning even more fiercely, as if she might thus cool the extreme flame burning in her child. At one moment she was begging those who were there to slake his thirst, and at the next she herself was hastening to do this, but she was pushed away by those murderers who allowed neither her nor anyone else to show any compassion to the one hanging there but instead they continued to insult him, and gave him vinegar and gall instead of water. In the beginning, they offered him *wine mixed with myrrh,* but he did not want it, so that no one would attribute his sudden and unusual death to the strength of the drug and not to his own will. But when they took his cry as an excuse, they satisfied their frenzy against him.

84 Ἀλλὰ τὰς μὲν ἐκείνης καθ' ἕκαστον λέγειν ὀδύνας οὐ τῆς ἡμετέρας, ἀλλ' οὐδ' ἄλλης ἡστινοσοῦν δυνάμεως, πλὴν ὅσον ὅτι καθάπερ ὑπὲρ λόγον ἔτικτεν, οὕτω καὶ ὑπὲρ λόγον ἔπασχε, καὶ οὐδ' αὐτῆς ταύτης, εἰ καὶ τολμηρὸν εἰπεῖν, ὁ λόγος ἂν ἐξισωθείη τοῖς πράγμασιν. Ἀλλ' οἶδε μὲν ταῦτα μᾶλλον τῶν ἄλλων ἐκ τῆς πείρας αὐτῆς, μόνου δὲ τοῦ ἐξ αὐτῆς Λόγου τὸ καὶ εἰδέναι ταῦτα καὶ ἐξειπεῖν κατὰ λόγον. Ἐπεὶ δὲ καὶ τὴν *μεγάλην* ἐκείνην καὶ φρικτὴν *ἀφῆκε φωνὴν* ὁ Λόγος καὶ *κλίνας τὴν κεφαλὴν* καὶ τῷ θανάτῳ νεύσας, ἡ πάντων κεφαλὴ καὶ αὐτοῦ τοῦ θανάτου Κύριος, *ἀφῆκε καὶ τὴν πνοὴν* ἡ πάντων Ζωή. Ὢ μακαρίας ἐκείνης καὶ ἀδαμαντίνης ψυχῆς! Πῶς οὐχὶ καὶ αὐτὴ τῇ τοῦ παιδὸς συναπέπτη; Πῶς οὐ διερράγη τὰ σπλάγχνα μᾶλλον ἤπερ ἡ γῆ τὰς πέτρας ἢ πῶς οὐ διεσχίσθη μέση καθάπερ τὸ καταπέτασμα; Ἢ δῆλον καὶ πάλιν ὡς αὐτὸς ὁ καθηλωμένος, αὐτὸς ὁ τὴν πνοὴν ἀφείς, αὐτὸς καὶ ταύτης τὴν πνοὴν ἐκράτει, καὶ ὥσπερ μὴ βουλομένην καθήλου τὴν ψυχὴν τῷ σώματι, καὶ δι' ὅλων ἐτήρει τῶν ἄθλων μυρίαθλον, ὥσπερ αὐτὸς ἑαυτόν, οὕτω καὶ τὴν τεκοῦσαν μᾶλλον ἀπεργαζόμενος. Ἐπέχει μου τὴν γλῶτταν ἡ φρίκη πρὸς τὰ πρόσω προβῆναι βιαζομένην, καὶ γίνομαι τοῦ Πάθους μετὰ ταύτης ὅλος κἀγὼ καὶ τῶν λογισμῶν ἐκφέρομαι, ἀλλά με τὸ δριμύτατον ὁμοῦ καὶ γλυκύτατον τοῦ σοῦ Πάθους, ὦ Δέσποτα, τιτρώσκει καὶ ἀντεγείρει βέλος, καὶ οὐκ ἔχω πῶς ἀποσπασθῶ τοῦ πικροτάτου τὲ ἅμα καὶ ἡδίστου μοι διηγήματος.

But to describe each of her torments is not within my power, nor is it within anyone else's power, except to say that, just as she gave birth in a manner beyond comprehension, so too did she suffer in a manner beyond comprehension, and, if it is not too daring a thing to say, her own power of comprehension would not have been equal to these matters. But she understood these things better than anyone else on the basis of her own experience, yet to know these things and describe them in a manner consistent with reason belongs only to the Word who came forth from her. But when the Word *cried out* with that *loud* and fearsome *voice, inclined his head* and nodded to death, then, though he is the head of all and the Lord of death itself, the Life of all *yielded up his spirit.* Oh, how blessed and unbreakable was her soul! How did it not fly away together with that of her son? How did her heart not split apart as the earth split the rocks? How was she not torn in two like the veil of the temple? Once again it is clear that the one nailed to the cross, who yielded up his spirit, was the one who sustained her spirit, and despite her wish, kept her soul as though nailed to her body. In all these trials he made her, just as he made himself, the victor ten thousand times over, and thus brought to perfection the one who had brought him to birth. Terror holds back my tongue and constrains it from advancing any further, and together with her, I too am wholly drawn into the Passion, and am swept away by my thoughts. But, Master, I have been wounded by the exceedingly sharp but also very sweet arrow of your Passion, and this raises me up, and I am thus unable to tear myself away from my narrative, which likewise is both exceedingly bitter and very pleasant. 84

Οἷα γὰρ καὶ τὰ μετὰ θάνατον, ἐπεὶ *μηδὲ* οὕτως αὐτοῖς ὁ τῆς κακίας *τρυγίας* διὰ τῆς χολῆς καὶ τοῦ ὄξους *ἐξεκενώθη*, οἷα τολμῶσιν οἱ καὶ θηρίων ὠμότεροι καὶ λίθων ἀναισθητότεροι θεοκτόνοι, οἷα τελοῦσι τῷ Δεσπότῃ τὰ ἐπικήδεια, οἷα προσάγουσι τὰ ἐντάφια, μήτε τῶν προφητικῶν ἀκούσαντες λόγων, *μὴ ἐπιξάνῃς τραύματα κεκαμωμένων ταῖς μάστιξι* (πολλῷ δὲ μᾶλλον νενεκρωμένων τοῖς πάθεσι), μήτε τὴν μητέρα κοπτομένην οὕτως οἰκτείροντες, ἣν κἂν ἐχθρὸς ἠλέησε καὶ πολέμιος ἢ κἂν θηρίον ἢ καὶ λίθος συνήλγησε, μήτε δὲ ὡς νεκρῷ τῷ ἐχθρῷ σπενδόμενοι, καθ' οὗπερ οὐκ ἔστι λοιπὸν οὐδὲ εἷς φθόνος οὐδὲ δυσμένεια, μήτε τὴν ἄψυχον γοῦν οὕτω πενθοῦσαν μιμούμενοι ἢ κἂν αἰδούμενοι κτίσιν. Ἀλλ' ὥσπερ αὐτὰ ταῦτα μᾶλλον τοῦ φθόνου καὶ τῆς κατ' αὐτοῦ μανίας ἔχοντες ὑπεκκαύματα, εἰ τοσαύτης ἠξίωται καὶ παρὰ τοῦ Θεοῦ τιμῆς καὶ παρὰ τῆς μητρὸς πένθους καὶ παρ' αὐτῆς τῆς κοινῆς κτίσεως θρήνων, ἁμιλλᾶσθαι διὰ τῶν ἐναντίων, τῶν ὕβρεων καὶ τῶν πληγῶν, ἐπεχείρουν. Καὶ ἐβούλοντο μὲν καὶ τὴν κοινὴν ὑπερβῆναι φύσιν καὶ μυρίους, εἰ οἷόν τε ἦν, ἑνὶ σώματι προσενεγκεῖν τοὺς θανάτους, ἐπεὶ δὲ μὴ ἠδύναντο καθάπερ ἐξαπορούμενοι—ὦ νόμοι καὶ ἔθη πατρῷα καὶ θεσμὰ φύσεως κοινῆς καὶ ὁσίας, ὦ δίκη καὶ ὀφθαλμοὶ Θεοῦ τοῦ ταῦτα καὶ ὁρῶντος ἅμα καὶ πάσχοντος—λόγχῃ τὴν πλευρὰν ὀρύττουσιν, ἵνα μηδὲν ἀπαθὲς

What sort of things took place after his death, since the 85
dregs of their wickedness had ***not yet been wholly poured out*** in the gall and vinegar! What things did those God murderers, who were more savage than wild beasts and more insensitive than stones, have the audacity to do! What preparations did they make for the burial of the Master! How did they conduct the obsequies! For they had never heard the prophetic words: *Do not chafe the wounds of those who have been scourged* (and how much more is that true of those who have died from sufferings). Neither did they take any pity on his mother, who was beating her breast, to whom even an enemy or hostile opponent would have shown mercy, and to whom even a beast or a stone would have shown sympathy. Nor did they make peace with their enemy now that he was dead, for whom one no longer harbors malice or ill will, nor indeed did they imitate or even show respect for inanimate creation which was in a state of mourning. But it was as if all these things were instead fuel for their envy and madness toward him, because even though the things that happened had been counted worthy of such honor by God, and by the mourning of the mother, and by the lamentations of all creation itself, these men chose instead to compete against them through contrary actions, namely, by imposing further insults and injuries on him. And they endeavored to surpass common human nature by inflicting, as if it were possible, a thousand deaths on a single body, and then, in a state of perplexity, when they were unable to do this—oh, paternal laws and customs and the principles of common and sacred nature! oh, the judgment and the eyes of God, who saw these things and at the same time suffered them!—they pierced his side with a lance, so that no part of his body would re-

παρέλθῃ τοῦ σώματος, ἀλλ' ἡ μὲν κεφαλὴ τὸν κάλαμον, αἱ δὲ παρειαὶ τὰ ῥαπίσματα, τὸ δὲ στόμα τὸ πόμα, τὸ δὲ πᾶν πρόσωπον τὰ ἐμπτύσματα, τὰ δὲ νῶτα τὰς μάστιγας καὶ τὰ λοιπὰ τοῦ σώματος, αἱ χεῖρες δὲ καὶ οἱ πόδες τοὺς ἥλους, ἡ δὲ πλευρὰ τὴν μεγάλην δέξηται λόγχην, ὡς καὶ πάλιν τὴν πρώτην ἡμῖν καὶ μεγάλην ἀπογεννήσῃ ζωήν, τὴν *δι' ὕδατος,* φημί, πηγὴν *καὶ* τοῦ *αἵματος,* εἶτ' οὖν Πνεύματος. Ἀλλὰ σύ μοι σκόπει καὶ πάλιν οἷα καὶ κατὰ τῶν τῆς μητρὸς σπλάγχνων διωθεῖτο ῥομφαία καὶ ὅπως διὰ πάντων σύναθλος ἢ μᾶλλον ὑπέραθλος ἦν· ὥσπερ γὰρ καὶ αὐτὴν ἀπονενεκρωμένην ἤδη τῷ Πάθει καὶ περὶ τῆς ταφῆς τοῦ υἱοῦ καὶ τῶν ἐνταφίων βουλευομένην, ἡ ἐκείνου λόγχη καὶ ταύτης νύξασα καὶ διαρρήξασα τὴν καρδίαν ἀνεζωπύρησεν αὖθις πρὸς τὰς καινὰς ὀδύνας, καὶ δάκρυα μὲν τῶν ὀφθαλμῶν ὥσπερ ὕδωρ, αἷμα δὲ τὴν ψυχὴν ἀποσταλάξαι πεποίηκεν, ὥστε καὶ αὐτὴν λέγειν· *ἐθερμάνθη ἡ καρδία μου καὶ τὸ ἄλγημά μου ἀνεκαινίσθη.* Καὶ προσδραμοῦσα πάλιν οὐκ αὐτόπτις μόνον, ἀλλὰ καὶ ὑποδέκτις καὶ κληρονόμος ἐκείνου τοῦ διπλοῦ πλούτου γίνεται, καὶ φιλοτίμως μὲν καὶ πανευλαβῶς τῆς νεκρᾶς ἐκείνης καὶ ζώσης καὶ ζωοδότου πλευρᾶς τὴν καινὴν ἀθανασίαν ἀπαρύεται καὶ ἀείρρυτον, καλῶς ἀπολαβοῦσα τῶν αἱμάτων αὐτῇ τὸ χρέος, ἐξ ὧν ἡ παναγία σὰρξ ἐκείνη συνεπάγη, διὰ τοῦ αἵματος καὶ τῶν ῥυέντων ἐπ' αὐτῇ δακρύων διὰ τοῦ ὕδατος.

86 Ὀλίγα δὲ καὶ πάλιν προσανακλαύσασα καὶ προσλαλήσασα τῷ υἱῷ, ὅτι μηδὲ νῦν οἱ μιαιφόνοι τῶν κατ' αὐτοῦ φόνων ἐλώφησαν, μηδὲ τῶν τοσούτων παθῶν καὶ αἱμάτων ἐνεφορήθησαν, ὅλη τῆς ταφῆς καὶ τοῦ τάφου γίνεται, μὴ

main without suffering. Thus his head endured the blows of the reed, his cheeks the slaps, his mouth the drink, his entire face their spitting, his back and the remaining parts of his body the scourge, his hands and feet the nails, but his side the blow of the great lance, so that it might once again give birth to our first and great life, I mean the fountain *of water and blood,* and thence of the Spirit. But consider with me once more what sort of sword pierced his mother's heart, and how she was a fellow contestant with him in all things, or rather was a superior contestant. For it was as if, when she had already been put to death by the Passion, and was contemplating her son's burial and obsequies, the lance that pierced him also pierced her, and, as it tore her heart asunder, it immediately rekindled new pains within her, and made tears stream from her eyes like water, and blood drip from her soul, so that she too would say: *My heart was enflamed within me, and my pain was renewed.* And she rushed forth again, not only as an eyewitness but also as a recipient and an heir of his double riches, and thus honorably and with all reverence she drew off the new and ever flowing immortality from his dead and living and life-giving side, having rightly received back through this blood the debt of blood that she was owed for that from which his all-holy flesh had been formed, and, through the water, for the tears which she had shed.

And after she had wept again and spoken briefly to her 86
son, for even now his murderers had not ceased from their slaughter nor had their fill, despite all the suffering and blood, she became wholly concerned with his burial and

φέρουσα μὲν ὁρᾶν αὐτὴ τὸν υἱὸν κρεμάμενον, μὴ φέρουσα δὲ τοὺς ἐχθροὺς καὶ ἔτι προσεπεμβαίνοντας καὶ νεκρὸν αἰκίζοντας, μὴ καί τι χεῖρον πρὸς ὕβριν ἐπινοήσωσιν, ὁρᾶν δὲ καὶ τοὺς παριόντας χλευάζοντας καὶ ὥσπερ κατὰ σκοποῦ πάντας βάλλοντας. Ἐπιθυμοῦσα δὲ καί τινα χῶρον καὶ τάφον εὑρεῖν, ἄξιον μὲν οὐδένα τοῦ θείου καὶ ζωοπαρόχου ἐκείνου σώματος, ὥσπερ καὶ τὸ ἑαυτῆς σῶμα τὸ θεοδόχον ἄξιον κατασκήνωμα τοῦ παντὸς πληρώματος *τῆς θεότητος*, ἄξιον δὲ ὅμως τοῦ ἑαυτῆς πόθου τὲ καὶ τῆς προθυμίας, ἐκπεριέρχεται γοῦν πάντα τὸν τοῦ Κρανίου Τόπον, ὥσπερ ὑπ' αὐτοῦ πτερουμένη τοῦ ζωοδότου νεκροῦ. Ἀλλ' ὁ μὲν δρόμος τοὺς πόδας εἶχεν, ἡ δὲ ψυχὴ οὐ μετέβαινε, καὶ ὁ μὲν τόπος ἠμείβετο, ὁ δὲ νοῦς πᾶς καὶ οἱ ὀφθαλμοὶ σχεδὸν τῷ κρεμαμένῳ συνήρτηντο, πυκνὰ καὶ πρὸς αὐτὸν ἐπιστρεφομένης καὶ ἀνακαλουμένης τὲ καὶ ἀνακλαιούσης. Εὑρίσκει γοῦν παρ' αὐτοῦ τούτου καὶ τὴν εὕρεσιν αἰτουμένη χωρίον ἔγγιστα μὲν τοῦ σταυροῦ. Τοῦτο γὰρ αὐτῇ μάλιστα καὶ καταθύμιον ἦν, ὥστε καὶ τὸν σταυρὸν ὁμοῦ βλέπειν καὶ τὸν τάφον ὀρύττειν, εἰ καὶ λύει τούτου τοῦ μόχθου ταύτην ὁ ἀνωδύνως ἐξ αὐτῆς τεχθείς, οὕτω καὶ ἀμόχθως παρ' αὐτῆς ταφείς. Εὑρίσκεται γὰρ πάγκαλον μέν τι καὶ παναρμόδιον καὶ τὴν θέσιν τὲ καὶ τὴν κρᾶσιν, εὖ μὲν ἔχον ὡρῶν, εὖ δὲ καὶ ἀέρος, εὖ δὲ καὶ ἀσφαλείας, πάντοθεν περιειλημμένον, ἄπονον δὲ καὶ προειργασμένον. Ἐν αὐτῷ μὲν γὰρ κῆπος εἰς ὥραν καὶ αὐτὸς πάντοθεν περιειργασμένος, ἐν δὲ τῷ κήπῳ τάφος ηὐτρεπισμένος καινὸς ὁμοῦ καὶ κενός, ἄρτι μὲν γὰρ *λελατομημένος ἐκ πέτρας*, ὥσπερ καὶ τὸ Ἱερὸν διέξεισιν Εὐαγγέλιον,

tomb, because she could not bear the sight of her son hanging there, she could not bear his enemies continuing to trample him down and torture him, even though he was dead, lest they contrive some still worse insult, and she could not bear the sight of those present mocking him as if they were still aiming to attack him. She wished to find a place and tomb that, while in no way worthy of that divine and life-giving body in the way that her own God-receiving body was a worthy dwelling place for the entire fullness *of the divinity,* would nonetheless be worthy of her desire and purpose; and so she searched the entire Place of the Skull, as if she had received wings from his life-giving corpse. And while her feet were moving forward, her soul did not move; and though the place was promising, her entire mind and, more often than not, her eyes remained fixed on the body hanging on the cross, for she was intensely focused on him, calling out to him and bursting into tears. Through him she found, after saying a prayer, a place near to the cross. To be sure, this was exactly what she had wished for, since from there she could both see his cross and dig his tomb, though she was relieved of this labor by the one who was born from her without pain, and so too would he now be buried by her without labor. For she found a most beautiful and suitable place, both in terms of its location and climate, mild in all seasons, having good air, secure, enclosed all around and already arranged and in need of no work. For there was a garden there in full bloom, richly cultivated, and in it was a new and empty tomb already prepared, recently *hewed from the rock,* just as the Holy Gospel informs us, and it had not yet

οὔπω δέ τινα δεξάμενος τῶν νεκρῶν, ἀλλὰ τὸν καινὸν μένων νεκρὸν ὁμοῦ καὶ Θεόν. Ταῦτα δὲ πάντα καὶ ᾠκονόμητο καὶ τετύπωτο· ὁ κενὸς διὰ τὴν ἀνάστασιν, ἵνα μή τινος ἑτέρου νομισθῇ τῶν κειμένων· ὁ ἐκκαινῆς διὰ τὸν νέον Ἀδάμ, τάχα δὲ καὶ διὰ τὸ ἀνεπίδεκτόν τε καὶ ἄθικτον πάσης ἀνθρωπίνης ἀσθενείας καὶ ἁμαρτίας· ὁ ἀσφαλὴς ἵνα μὴ καὶ κλαπῇ, μᾶλλον δὲ συκοφαντηθῇ τὴν κλοπήν, οὕτω πάντοθεν ἀνάλωτος ὤν· ἡ πέτρα διὰ τὸν *Λίθον,* ἡ λελατομημένη διὰ τὸν *Ἀκρογωνιαῖον,* ἡ ἐρριζωμένη διὰ τὸν Ἀρραγῆ, ἡ κατὰ γῆς διὰ τὸν Θεμέλιον· ὁ κῆπος ὑπὲρ τῆς Ἐδέμ, ὥσπερ καὶ ὁ τοῦ Κρανίου Τόπος ὑπὲρ τοῦ ἐν αὐτῷ πεσόντος Ἀδὰμ καὶ τὸ Πάθος κατὰ τοῦ πάθους καὶ κατὰ τοῦ θανάτου ὁ θάνατος.

87 Οὕτω καὶ τὸν χῶρον πλησίον τὲ καὶ ἀσφαλῆ καὶ περικαλλῆ, καὶ τὸν τάφον τερπνὸν ὁμοῦ καὶ καινὸν καὶ ἄχραντον τῷ ἀφθάρτῳ μάλιστα πρέποντα κατιδοῦσα, μαθοῦσα δὲ ὅτι καὶ οὐ φίλου μόνον ἁπλῶς ἀλλὰ καὶ μαθητοῦ, τἆλλα μὲν ἀγαθοῦ, *κεκρυμμένου δὲ* ὅμως *διὰ τὸν φόβον,* στέλλεται πρὸς αὐτὸν αὐτίκα καὶ λόγοις, οἷς ἔδει τὴν τοῦ ὄντως Λόγου καὶ τῆς Σοφίας μητέρα, οὐ περὶ τοῦ τάφου διαπρεσβεύεται μᾶλλον ἢ τῆς ταφῆς. Ἤιδει γὰρ ὅτι τοῦτον μὲν ἑτοίμως ἕξει παρ' αὐτοῦ, ῥᾷστον γὰρ αὐτῷ τοῦτο μᾶλλον καὶ ἥδιστον τῷ φίλῳ καὶ διδασκάλῳ χαρίσασθαι καὶ λυσιτελέστατον τὸ παρ' ἑαυτῷ τοιοῦτον ἔχειν τὸν θησαυρόν, ἐκεῖνο δὲ καὶ τόλμης μάλιστα δεόμενον καὶ πειθοῦς καὶ δαπάνης, τὸν δὲ Ἰωσὴφ πλούσιόν τε εἶναι καὶ τῷ Πιλάτῳ γνώριμόν τε καὶ τίμιον·

received any other body, but awaited the newly dead body of God. All these things were arranged and prefigured in advance. It was empty on account of the resurrection, so that no one would think that someone else had been buried there. It was new on account of the new Adam, and perhaps also because, having received no other body, it was thus untouched by any human fault or sin. It was secure so that no one could rob it, or rather falsely claim that it had been robbed, and thus it was impregnable on every side. It was made of rock on account of the *Stone,* and hewn from rock on account of the *Cornerstone.* It was solid on account of the Unbroken one; it was in the earth on account of the Foundation. It was a garden on account of Eden, just as it was the Place of the Skull on account of Adam who fell in that garden, with the Lord's Passion in opposition to his passion, and the Lord's death instead of his.

Thus she saw that the place was nearby, safe, and very 87
pleasant, and the tomb was beautiful, new, undefiled, and, most importantly, fitting for the burial of the incorruptible body. And when she learned that it belonged to someone who was not only a friend but also a disciple, and good in other respects, though *secretly out of fear,* she immediately sent word to him, as was fitting for the mother of the true Word and Wisdom, not to ask about the tomb but rather the burial. For she knew that he was eagerly disposed to do this, and that it was easy or rather highly desirable for him to offer his tomb to his friend and teacher, and that it would be the greatest advantage for him to acquire such a treasure; she also knew that this required boldness, persuasion, and expense, and that Joseph was a rich man and an acquaintance of Pilate, who held him in honor.

“Τῶν μὲν μιαιφόνων, ὦ φίλτατε,” λέγουσα, “καὶ δὴ πέρας ἔχει τὸ κατὰ τοῦ Θεοῦ καὶ Δεσπότου τόλμημα, καὶ τὸν πάντων ἐπονειδιστότατον αὐτῷ καὶ πικρότατον ἐπήγαγον θάνατον, πολλὰς καὶ πρὸ τοῦ θανάτου καὶ μετὰ θάνατον χείρους καὶ αὐτοῦ τοῦ θανάτου προσενεγκόντες τὰς ὕβρεις καὶ μηδὲ μίαν λιπόντες, μᾶλλον δὲ καὶ πάσης μανίας ὑπερβαλόντες ὑπερβολήν. Πλὴν ἀλλὰ καὶ ἔτι νῦν κρέμαται νεκρός, γυμνὸς ἐπὶ ξύλου, φρικτὸν ἐμοὶ καὶ πάσῃ τῇ κτίσει θέαμα, τὴν πλευρὰν διορωρυγμένος, ἀφ’ ἧς, καὶ ἔτι θαῦμα φρικτότερον, αἷμα καὶ ὕδωρ καὶ μετὰ θάνατον, ἀλλ’ οὐδὲ τοῦτο τοὺς θεοκτόνους ἵστησιν, ὦ γῆ καὶ ἥλιε, ὥσπερ οὐδὲ ἥλιος σκοτιζόμενος οὐδὲ γῆ κλονουμένη οὐδὲ πέτραι ῥηγνύμεναι, ἀλλὰ προβέβληται πᾶσιν οὐ θαυμαζόμενος διὰ ταῦτα μᾶλλον ἢ γοῦν ἐλεούμενος, ἀλλὰ καὶ γελώμενος καὶ εἰσέτι μισούμενος καὶ παρὰ πάντων βαλλόμενος, αἵματι ῥεόμενος, ἀτημέλητος. Ἀλλὰ σὺ νῦν ἐπίδειξαί τι καὶ τῆς σῆς εὐσεβείας, καὶ τῆς πρὸς τὸν κοινὸν διδάσκαλον καὶ Δεσπότην εὐνοίας, καὶ τῆς πρὸς ἐμὲ τὴν ἐν τοσούτοις πάθεσι συμπαθείας ἄξιον. Θαρρήσας αἴτησαι παρὰ Πιλάτου τὸ σῶμα περιφρονούμενον νῦν, οὐ φθονούμενον, καὶ ταφῇ παρ’ ἑαυτοῦ δὸς καὶ παρ’ ἑαυτῷ θάψον· κρύψον παρ’ ἑαυτῷ τοῦ κόσμου τὸν θησαυρόν, ὀλίγης τόλμης τὲ καὶ δαπάνης ὅλην ἅρπασαι καὶ παρ’ ἑαυτῷ κάτασχε τὴν Ζωήν, ὅλον παρ’ ἑαυτῷ μόνος τὸν κοινὸν συνάγαγε πλοῦτον. Δὸς χάριν σοὶ μὲν ἐλαχίστην, ἐμοὶ δὲ μεγίστην, τῷ δὲ σῷ καὶ κοινῷ διδασκάλῳ πρώτην ἅμα καὶ τελευταίαν ὡς ἀναγκαίαν καὶ ἐπιτάφιον. Γενοῦ νῦν τῶν ἄλλων μαθητῶν εὐθαρσέστερος, ἡμῖν καὶ ὠφελιμώτερος. Οἱ μὲν γὰρ καὶ

And speaking to him, she said: "O most cherished friend, the audacity of those murderers against our God and Master has reached its end. They subjected him to the most disgraceful and bitter of all deaths, and before his death and after his death they inflicted many insults upon on him that were worse than death itself, and they did not omit even one, but indeed went beyond every extreme in their fury. And even now his dead body is hanging naked on the cross, a sight dreadful to behold for me and all creation, with his side dug open, from which, an even more dreadful miracle, blood and water flowed though he was already dead. But, earth and sun, not even this stopped those killers of God, and likewise not even the sun being darkened, the earth shaken, or the rocks being split stopped them, but these things were ignored by all of them since they did not see him as someone to be wondered at on account of these things or indeed to be pitied, but rather to be mocked and even hated, and left unheeded as they all struck him and his blood flowed out of him. But you, now, show something of your piety and devotion to our common teacher and Master, as well as to me as I am worthy of compassion having undergone so many sufferings. Take courage and ask Pilate for the body which is now disrespected but no longer resented, and bury it yourself in your own tomb; conceal for yourself the treasure of the world, and through a little daring and expense, seize and secure for yourself the whole of Life, procuring for yourself alone the wealth that is common to all. Do yourself this small favor, which to me is great, and give him his funeral, which is the first and last necessity for the teacher who at once is yours and everyone's. Be braver now than the other disciples and more beneficial to me, because

τελέως ἀπέστησαν, οἱ δὲ ἀπὸ *μακρόθεν ἔστησαν*. Ἐγὼ δὲ γυνὴ καὶ μόνη καθὼς ὁρᾷς καὶ ξένη, σὺν ἑνὶ μόνῳ περιλειπομένη τῶν μαθητῶν, ἐν μέσῳ τοσούτων στρεφομένη θηρίων, καὶ πανταχόθεν ἄπορος καὶ ἀμήχανος καὶ τὰ πάντα σχεδὸν νεκρά, τοῦτο μόνον ζῶσα καὶ πλουτοῦσα, τὰ πάθη καὶ τὰς ὀδύνας. Οὕτω μοι στήσεις τὰς συμφοράς, οὕτω μοι παραιρήσεις τὰ δάκρυα· μὴ δείσῃς μηκέτι μηδέν· πέπαυται τῶν θεοκτόνων ἡ λύσσα, τὸ πλεῖστον αὐτῶν κεκένωται τῆς μανίας, ὅσαπερ βουλομένοις ἦν ἐξυβρίκασιν. Αὐτός σοι συμπαραστήσεται πάντως ὁ ἐμὸς υἱός, ὁ νεκρὸς οὗτος καὶ τοὺς νεκροὺς ἐγείρας Θεός, ὁ κλονήσας τὴν γῆν καὶ ῥήξας τὰς πέτρας καὶ ὅλην σκοτίσας καὶ ἀλλοιώσας τὴν κτίσιν. Τὰ μὲν οἶδας, τὰ δὲ εἴσῃ προβάς, τὰ μὲν ἰδὼν ὄψει, τὰ δὲ καὶ ἀκοῇ μαθών."

88 Οὕτως ἡ μεγαλοφρονεστάτη καὶ σοφωτάτη τῶν γυναικῶν τὸν Ἰωσὴφ ἐπιρρώσασα καὶ στομώσασα πρὸς Πιλάτον ἐκπέμπει, ῥήτορα καὶ πρεσβευτὴν εὐστομώτατον καὶ θερμότατον, ὃς καὶ παρ' αὐτοῦ τοῦ ζωοποιοῦ νεκροῦ, τοῦ Λόγου, λέγω, καὶ τῆς Ζωῆς, εὐγλωττότερος φανεὶς ἅμα καὶ εὐτολμότερος εἴσεισι πρὸς Πιλάτον καὶ θαρρούντως αἰτεῖ τὸ σῶμα, μηδὲν μήτε τούτου τὴν ἀξίαν μήτε τῶν Ἰουδαίων ὑποδειλιάσας ἢ κἂν ἐν λόγῳ θέμενος τὴν μανίαν. Διὰ τοῦτο καὶ οὐκ ἀποτυγχάνει τοῦ ἐγχειρήματος, ἀλλ' αἰτήσας λαμβάνει, καὶ ἀντικαταλλάττεται τῶν μὲν λόγων τὸν Λόγον, τοῦ δὲ κήπου τὸν οὐρανόν, τοῦ τάφου δὲ τὴν Ζωήν, τῆς δὲ πρὸς τὸν ἡγεμόνα πρεσβείας τὴν πρὸς τὸν κοινὸν Δεσπότην παρρησίαν· καὶ τὸ ἀξίωμα ὄντως οὐ πλούσιος μόνον, ἀλλὰ καὶ φρόνιμος, οὐ φρόνιμος μόνον,

some of them have completely abandoned him, *while others stood at a distance.* I, a woman alone and a stranger, as you can see, have remained with but one of the disciples, staying here in the midst of such savage beasts; and I am utterly helpless and powerless, and in all respects almost dead, my life and my wealth consisting only in my pain and sufferings. In this way, you will bring my misfortunes to an end, and in this way you will take away my tears. Henceforth do not be afraid of anything; the madness of the God killers has ceased; the major part of their rage has been spent, they have treated him with insolence as much as they wanted. My son himself, this dead man, who is also God who raises the dead, who confounded the earth and split the rocks and darkened and altered all creation, will always stand with you. Some of these things you know, the rest you will soon come to learn; some things you will see with your own eyes, other things you will learn by hearing."

Thus she who is the most prudent and wise among 88
women after strengthening and steeling Joseph, sent him to Pilate as an eloquent rhetor and ardent ambassador. Thanks to the life-giving corpse, by which I mean the Word and Life, he was more articulate and at the same time bolder, and courageously asked Pilate for the body, fearing neither Pilate's position nor the Jews, even if what he said might provoke their wrath. Thus he did not fail in his undertaking, but having asked, he received, and in exchange for his words he received the Word; for the garden he received heaven, for the tomb, Life, and for his request to the governor he received boldness of speech toward our common Master. And while he had the reputation of being not only rich but also prudent, he was not only prudent but also more prudent

ἀλλὰ κἀκείνου φρονιμώτερος τοῦ ἐμπόρου, καθότι μὴ πάντα δούς, ἀλλὰ τόλμαν ὀλίγην καὶ γῆν καὶ τάφον, τὸν τίμιον οὐκ ὠνήσατο μόνον, ἀλλὰ καὶ ἀσφαλῶς ἔκρυψε παρ' ἑαυτῷ μαργαρίτην, ἀντίθετος τῷ Ἰούδᾳ διὰ πάντων φανεὶς μαθητής. Ὁ μὲν γὰρ σπεύσας ἐκοινολογεῖτο κατ' αὐτοῦ τοῖς ἐχθροῖς, οὗτος δὲ σπεύσας ὑπὲρ αὐτοῦ πρὸς τοὺς ἐχθροὺς καὶ παραδόντας διεπρεσβεύετο· καὶ ὁ μὲν χρημάτων ὀλίγων προεδίδου τοῖς ἀναιροῦσιν, οὗτος δὲ καὶ λόγων καὶ χρημάτων πολλῶν καὶ ἀνῃρεῖτο παρὰ τῶν ἀνελόντων καὶ φιλοτίμως ἐνεταφίαζε· καὶ ὁ μὲν κατεφίλει δολίως, ἐφ' ᾧ πρὸς τὸ ξύλον ἀναγαγεῖν, οὗτος δὲ τοῦ ξύλου καταγαγὼν κατεφίλει σφόδρα φιλίως καὶ περιέβαλλε· καὶ ὁ μὲν μετὰ ξύλων συλλαμβάνων καὶ ὅπλων τῇ πικρᾷ συναγωγῇ παρεδίδου τῶν Ἰουδαίων, οὗτος δὲ τοῦ ξύλου καὶ τῶν ἥλων λύων τῇ γλυκείᾳ μητρὶ δῶρον ἐδίδου καὶ δῶρον γλυκύτατον, οὗ μηδὲν ἰσοστάσιον.

89 Ὅρα δέ μοι πάλιν τὴν μητέρα· πρὸς μὲν τὸν Πιλάτον ὥσπερ νεφέλῃ καλυπτομένην, καὶ λανθάνουσαν μέν, ἀκολουθοῦσαν δὲ κατόπιν τῷ Ἰωσὴφ καὶ παλλομένην τὴν καρδίαν περὶ τὴν αἴτησιν· πρὸς δὲ τὴν ἐπίνευσιν, ὥσπερ ὑπὸ πτεροῖς ἐρχομένην καὶ τὴν καταγωγήν, εἴτ' οὖν ἀποκαθήλωσιν, ἐπισπεύδουσαν. Ἀλλὰ καὶ πρὸς τὰ ἔργα καὶ τὰ πάθη μεριζομένην ἅμα καὶ ἑκάτερον τούτων μεταχειριζομένην εὐρύθμως, τῷ τε γὰρ πάθει συμμέτρως ἐκέχρητο καὶ τὰ μητέρων δεικνῦσα καὶ τὰ τῶν κοσμίων οὐχ ὑπερβαίνουσα, ἀλλὰ καὶ τοὺς τοῦ υἱοῦ πληροῦσα νόμους, ὃς ἐπὶ νεκρῷ φίλῳ καὶ τὸ πάθος ἅμα καὶ τὸν λόγον ἔδειξε, τὸ μὲν δακρύσας, τὸ δὲ τηρήσας τὸ μέτριον. Καὶ πρὸς τὰ

than the merchant, for Joseph did not give everything he had, but a handful of courage, earth, and a tomb, and he did not just purchase the precious pearl, but he securely buried it for himself, appearing as a disciple in every way opposite to Judas. For the latter hastened to conspire against the Lord with his enemies, whereas Joseph hastened to serve as envoy on his behalf to his enemies and betrayers. Judas for a small sum of money betrayed him to his killers, while Joseph, on the other hand, through many words and much money, took the body of Christ from those who had killed him, and buried him honorably. Judas kissed him treacherously to lead him up to the cross, but Joseph took him down from the cross and kissed him most devoutly and embraced him with affection. Judas came against him with clubs and swords and delivered him to the vindictive synagogue of the Jews; but Joseph released him from the nails and the cross and gave as a gift to the sweet mother the sweetest gift of which there is no equivalent.

Consider with me once again the mother. In front of Pi- 89
late, it was as if she was concealed by a cloud and eluded his sight as she followed behind Joseph, with her heart pounding as he made his request. When it was granted, it was as if she left there on wings, and rushed to attend to the deposition, or rather the unnailing, from the cross. She divided herself between the tasks at hand and her emotions, dealing gracefully with each at the same time, for she gave herself over to her emotions in suitable proportion, demonstrated the duties of a mother, and did not exceed the boundaries of appropriate behavior, but fulfilled the teachings of her son, who, when his friend died, demonstrated both emotion and reason, shedding tears but with moderation. To the tasks

ἔργα δὲ σπουδαίως καὶ ἡδέως ὑπούργει ταῖς χερσὶ διακονουμένη καὶ τὸν υἱὸν ἀγκαλιζομένη, καὶ τοὺς μὲν ἥλους ὑποδεχομένη τοῖς κόλποις, τὰς δὲ πληγὰς τῷ στόματι καὶ τὰ αἵματα τοῖς δάκρυσιν ἐκκαθαίρουσα, καταφιλοῦσα καθ' ἕκαστον τῶν μελῶν καὶ ἐπικλαίουσα καὶ τὰ ἐπιτάφια καταλέγουσα, χεῖρας ἐκείνας, πόδας ἐκείνους ἤ που τάχα καὶ στόμα καὶ ὀφθαλμούς. Ἐτόλμα γὰρ καὶ μέχρι τούτου τὸ φίλτρον καὶ τὸ πάθος ἔχον συνήγορον. Ἐπεὶ δὲ καὶ πρὸς τῇ γῇ τὸ ὑπερουράνιον ἐκεῖνο κατηνέχθη σῶμα καὶ ἀνεκλίθη, τότε καὶ ὅλη ὅλῳ περιχυθεῖσα τῷ σώματι, θερμοτέροις μὲν αὐτὸ κατέλουε δάκρυσιν, ἐνθεεστέροις δὲ καὶ τοῖς ῥήμασι τὸν κοινὸν κατέλεγεν ἐπιτάφιον:

"Ὢ φρικτοῦ," λέγουσα, "μυστηρίου πέρας, ὢ τοῦ πάλαι κεκρυμμένου καὶ μέχρι τοῦ νῦν φανέρωσις, ὢ καινῆς σαρκώσεως καινοτέρα νέκρωσις! Ἄπνους ὁ πᾶσι τῆς πνοῆς χορηγός; Νεκρὸς ὁ ζωῆς πάσης δημιουργός; Ἄφωνος ὁ τοῦ Πατρὸς Λόγος καὶ πάσης παρακτικὸς καὶ συνεκτικὸς τῆς λογικῆς φύσεως; Ἀκίνητος καὶ ἀόμματος ὁ πάντα κινῶν τῷ ῥήματι ἢ τῷ νεύματι; Ὁ πάντα βλέπων καὶ τήκων *ὄρη* τῷ ὄμματι; Ὁ *ἐπιβλέπων ἐπὶ τὴν γῆν καὶ ποιῶν αὐτὴν τρέμειν;* Ὁ ἐπιβλέπων ἐπὶ ἀνθρώπων *καρδίας καὶ* ἐμβατεύων *νεφρούς,* οὗ καὶ *τὰ βλέφαρα* ἐξετάζουσι *τοὺς υἱοὺς τῶν ἀνθρώπων;* Ὁ σοφίζων καὶ φωτίζων *τυφλούς,* ὡς τὸ μὲν τοὺς ἐντός, τὸ δὲ τοὺς ἐκτὸς ἰώμενος ὀφθαλμούς; Οἴμοι, ποῦ σοῦ τὸ κάλλος, υἱέ, ποῦ δὲ καὶ τὸ εἶδός τε καὶ τὸ ἦθος τοῦ ὡραίου τῷ *κάλλει παρὰ τοὺς υἱοὺς τῶν ἀνθρώπων,* τοῦ τὸν κόσμον εἰδοποιήσαντος, τοῦ πάντα θέλξαντος ἢ κινήσαντος καὶ τὰ ἄψυχα, πλὴν τούτων τῶν

before her she applied her hands earnestly and sweetly and embraced her son. She clutched the nails to her breast, and cleaned the wounds with her mouth and the blood with her tears; she kissed each of his limbs as she continued to weep and utter the funeral lamentations: those hands, those feet, and at times perhaps also his mouth and eyes. She ventured to do even this, having maternal affection and her suffering as her advocates. And when that transcendently heavenly body was taken down and placed on the earth, she embraced the whole of his body with her whole self, washing it in still more ardent tears, and with inspired words uttered the common funeral lament:

"Oh, what an end," she said, "to this awesome mystery! Oh, revelation of what had been hidden of old until now! Oh, more remarkable mortification of the remarkable incarnation! Is he who grants breath to all now without breath? Is the creator of all life dead? Is the Word of the Father silent, who creates and sustains all rational existence? Is the one who moves all things by his word and command, motionless and devoid of sight? The one who sees everything and melts *mountains* by his glance? *He who looks on the earth and makes it tremble,* He who looks into the *hearts* of men *and* frequents their emotions, whose *eyes* examine *the sons of men?* Who instructs and enlightens the *blind,* healing both their spiritual and physical eyes? Alas, where is your beauty, my son? Where is the shape and form of you who were *more beautiful than the sons of men,* which formed the world and attracts and moves all things, even those that are inanimate, except for those who killed you? Your whole

σφαγέων τῶν σῶν; Ἀλλὰ καὶ τετραυματισμένος ὅλος καὶ μεμωλωπισμένος, ὁ τὰ ἀνίατα τῆς φύσεως ἡμῶν ἐξιώμενος ἕλκη καὶ τὰ πρόσκαιρα καὶ τὰ χρόνια τραύματα καὶ τοὺς μώλωπας. Ἀλλὰ σὺ μέν, ὦ Δέσποτα, τετραυμάτισαι καὶ μεμωλώπισαι δι' ἡμᾶς, καὶ νῦν ἐπ' ὄψεσι πάντων τὰ τῆς οἰκονομίας τῆς σῆς καὶ τῆς ἀνοχῆς, μᾶλλον δὲ καὶ τὰ τῆς εὐσπλαγχνίας καὶ φιλανθρωπίας ἀποπεπλήρωται· ὑπὲρ γὰρ τούτων αὐτῶν πάσχεις, παρ' ὧν οὕτω καὶ πάσχεις. Δεῖξον δὴ καὶ τὰ τῆς δυναστείας, ἐλθὲ καὶ σπεῦσον εἰς τὸ σῶσαι ἡμᾶς. Οἶδα τοῦτο καλῶς ἐγώ, σὺ ἀναστὰς οἰκτειρήσεις πρώτην μὲν τὴν μητέρα, εἶτα καὶ ταύτην τὴν θεοκτόνον Ἱερουσαλὴμ ἢ Σιών, ἀφ' ἧς καὶ τὰ ἄλλα συλλέξεις πρόβατα, τὰ Ἔθνη καλῶν. Ἀλλ' εἴθε σου τῆς γλυκείας ἀκούσαιμι θᾶττον φωνῆς, εἴθε σου τῆς θείας καὶ θεοειδοῦς μορφῆς καὶ τῶν φιλτάτων μελῶν καὶ τῶν ἡδίστων ἀπολαύσαιμι πάλιν χαρίτων· εἴθε καθάπερ νυνὶ νεκρόν, οὕτω καὶ Θεὸν ἀληθῆ πᾶσι φανερὸν γενόμενον καὶ τοῖς ἄλλοις καὶ ζώντων καὶ νεκρῶν Κύριον κατασπάσαιμι."

90 Οὕτω καὶ λόγοις ἐπιθειάσασα καὶ χερσὶν οἰκείαις καὶ ἀχράντοις τὸ ἄχραντον ἐκεῖνο καὶ ζωοποιὸν σῶμα, συνάμα καὶ Ἰωσὴφ καὶ τῷ Νικοδήμῳ, σινδόνι καὶ μύροις ἐνταφιάσασα τῷ θεοδόχῳ μνήματι παραδίδωσιν. Ἀλλὰ ταῦτα μὲν οἱ περὶ τὸν Ἰωσὴφ καὶ Νικόδημον καταπράξαντες ἢ μᾶλλον ταύτῃ συγκαταπράξαντες ὑποχωροῦσι τοῦ μνήματος. Αὕτη δὲ ὑπομένει μόνη περιθυροῦσα καὶ ὄμμασιν ἀκοιμήτοις καὶ τῆς ψυχῆς καὶ τοῦ σώματος καὶ κλίσεσι γονάτων ἀδιαλείπτοις καὶ ἀσιγήτοις δοξολογίαις καὶ προσευχαῖς διακαρτεροῦσα καὶ ἐπικαλουμένη τὲ ἅμα καὶ

body has been wounded and covered with bruises, you who heal completely the incurable sores of our nature, as well as our temporary and chronic wounds and our welts. But you, Master, were wounded and bruised for our sake, and now the workings of your divine economy of salvation and your forbearance are evident to all, or rather the workings of your compassion and love for mankind have been fulfilled, because you suffered for the sake of the very ones who made you suffer. Show us, therefore, the things of your power, come in haste to save us. I know well that, when you have risen from the dead, you will first show compassion to me, your mother, and then to God-killing Jerusalem or Zion, from where you will gather the other sheep, summoning the Gentiles. But how I wish that I might quickly hear your sweet voice, and behold your divine and godlike form, and the beloved limbs of your body, and enjoy once again your most pleasant graces. How I wish that, just as I embrace you now that you are dead, so too when you reveal yourself to all as the true God, I may embrace you, with all the others, as Lord of the living and the dead."

When she had thus offered words of prayer, and had 90
wrapped the immaculate and life-giving body in a shroud with her own immaculate hands, together with Joseph and Nikodemos, and had anointed it with myrrh, they placed it in the God-receiving tomb. When those who were with Joseph and Nikodemos completed their service, or rather completed it together with her, they departed from the tomb. But she remained there alone keeping watch patiently at the entrance of the tomb with the unsleeping eyes of her soul and body, making ceaseless prostrations and incessant praises and prayers, and she called for and awaited

ἀπεκδεχομένη πότε τὸ γλυκὺ φῶς αὐτὴν περιαστράψει τῆς ἀναστάσεως.

91 Εἰ γὰρ καὶ *εἰστήκεισαν παρὰ τῷ σταυρῷ*, φησίν, οὐχ *ἡ μήτηρ* μόνον, ἀλλὰ καὶ αἱ ἄλλαι δύο Μαρίαι, μᾶλλον δὲ καὶ πορρωτέρω τὸν λόγον ἀγάγωμεν, ἵν' οὕτω ῥᾷον καὶ τὸ τοῖς πολλοῖς ἄπορον λύσωμεν. Πῶς γὰρ οἱ μὲν ἄλλοι τῶν εὐαγγελιστῶν πάντες συμφώνως *μακρόθεν* ἑστηκέναι, φασί, τὰς συνακολουθούσας γυναῖκας, οὗτος δὲ μόνος ὁ θεῖος καὶ θεολόγος παρ' αὐτῷ τῷ σταυρῷ μὴ τὴν μητέρα μόνον, ἀλλὰ καὶ τὰς ἑτέρας, τήν τε τοῦ Κλωπᾶ Μαρίαν καὶ τὴν Μαγδαληνήν; Ἢ δῆλον ὅτι καὶ ἄμφω συνέβη; Πολλὰς μὲν γὰρ ἐν ἐκείναις εἶναι καὶ ἄλλας, ἐν αὐταῖς δὲ καὶ αὐτὰς ταύτας· ἀλλ' ἐκεῖναι μὲν ἀτολμότεραί τε ἅμα καὶ ἀφανέστεραι, διὸ καὶ ἀορίστους αὐτὰς ὁ λόγος παρῆκε, ταύτας δὲ καὶ ἀπὸ τῶν ὀνομάτων καὶ ἀπὸ τῶν ἐπωνύμων ἢ τοῦ γένους ἐγνώρισεν. *Ἦσαν γὰρ ἐκεῖ γυναῖκες πολλαί*, φησὶν ὁ Ματθαῖος, *ἀπὸ μακρόθεν* ἱστάμεναι καὶ *θεωροῦσαι, ἐν αἷς* καὶ *Μαρία τὲ ἡ Μαγδαληνὴ καὶ Μαρία ἡ τοῦ Ἰακώβου καὶ Ἰωσῆ μήτηρ καὶ ἡ μήτηρ τῶν υἱῶν Ζεβεδαίου*. Ταύτας καὶ ὁ μὲν Μάρκος ὁμοίως κατ' ὄνομα, ὁ δὲ Λουκᾶς τῷ ἀορίστῳ συμπεριέλαβε. Τὰς μὲν οὖν ἄλλας μετὰ τὴν προδοσίαν μακρόθεν καὶ ἔστιν ὅτε ὅπη παρείκοι λαθραίως ἀκολουθούσας, εἰκὸς καὶ τότε λανθανούσας, ὡς οἷόν τε μακρόθεν καὶ κατὰ χώραν μένειν· τὴν δὲ Μαγδαληνὴν καὶ τὴν Ἰακώβου καὶ ἐξ ἀρχῆς τῷ τε περὶ τὸν διδάσκαλον φίλτρῳ καὶ τῷ περὶ τὴν τούτου μητέρα διαφερόντως ἐκπεφλεγμένας, ἅμα δὲ καὶ αὐτὴν ταύτας ἐχούσας τῆς ἀνδρείας ὑπόδειγμα καὶ διδάσκαλον, ὡς οὐχ' ὁμωνύμους μόνον,

the moment when the sweet light of the resurrection would shine on her.

Now if, as it says, *standing by the cross were* not only *his* 91
mother but also the two other Marys, we must extend our discourse somewhat further so that we might more easily resolve the difficulty concerning this question which presents itself to many. For how can it be that, whereas all the other evangelists are agreed in saying the women who had followed Jesus were looking on *from a distance,* John, the divine theologian, alone states that standing by the cross was not only his mother, but also other women, namely, Mary of Clopas and Mary Magdalene? Or is it clear that both happened? For among those who were looking on from a distance were many other women, including those who were standing by the cross. The former were not as bold and went largely unnoticed, which is why scripture leaves them unidentified, while the latter are mentioned by their names and surnames: For *there were also many women there,* Matthew says, *who were* standing and *looking on from afar, among whom were Mary Magdalene, Mary the mother of James and Joses, and the mother of the sons of Zebedee.* Mark also mentions them by name, but Luke groups them together without identifying them. As for these other women, after the betrayal they stood far off, and, whenever it seemed prudent to do so, they followed secretly, and it is likely that even then they escaped notice, as it was possible for them to remain at a distance and in their place. But Mary Magdalene and Mary the mother of James from the beginning were more ardent in their affection for the teacher, and were especially devoted to his mother, whom they had for themselves as an example of courage and a teacher, sharing not only the same name

ἀλλὰ καὶ ὁμοψύχους ἀλλήλαις τὲ καὶ αὐτῇ σχεδόν, ἐγγυτέρω τὲ ἀεὶ καὶ παραβολώτερον παρακολουθεῖν καὶ τὰ πολλὰ συνεῖναι, τὴν μὲν παραμυθουμένας, τὸν δὲ τιμώσας ἅμα καὶ τὸν περὶ αὐτὸν πόθον ἐνδεικνυμένας. Οὕτως οὖν καὶ τότε λαβομένας καιροῦ θαρραλεωτέρας φανῆναι τῶν ἄλλων καὶ ἀποχωρισθείσας αὐτῶν τῇ τοῦ Θεοῦ Μητρὶ προσδραμεῖν καὶ τῷ σταυρῷ προσελθεῖν, ὥστε καὶ ἐκείνῃ συγκαταλέγεσθαι, πῇ δὲ καὶ σὺν αὐτῇ λέγεσθαι τῷ σταυρῷ παρίστασθαι. Πλὴν ἀλλ᾽ εἰ καὶ τῶν ἄλλων διέφερον, ἀλλ᾽ ὅμως αὐτῆς ἐκείνης ἀπελιμπάνοντο, καὶ πολὺ πλέον ἢ ὅσονπερ αὐτῶν αἱ ἄλλαι. Διὰ τοῦτο καὶ τῇ μητρὶ μὲν εἰκὸς αὐτάς ποτε συνελθεῖν καὶ τῷ σταυρῷ προσελθεῖν, ὅτε καὶ καιρὸς ἦν, ἐπεὶ δέ ποτε καὶ κατὰ μέσον τὸν φόνον ἐκεῖνος "*διψῶ*" κράξας ἐπιδραμεῖν αἴφνης καὶ σὺν θορύβῳ τοὺς θεοκτόνους ἐποίησε, ταύτας μὲν διαθρυλληθῆναι καὶ ἀποδειλιᾶσαι καὶ ὑποστείλασθαι, τὴν δὲ καὶ οὕτω προσκαρτερεῖν δι᾽ αὐτό τε τοῦτο καὶ τὸ τὰ τολμώμενα θεωρεῖν. Ἀλλὰ μηδὲ κατὰ τὸν τοῦ ἐνταφιασμοῦ καιρὸν θαρρῆσαι καὶ προσελθεῖν αὐτὰς ἔτι κρατουμένας τῷ δέει, κατὰ δὲ τὸν τῆς καταθέσεως μόνον *ἀπέναντι* καθίσαι καὶ θεωρῆσαι, καθά φησι καὶ Ματθαῖος, ποῦ τίθεται. Πολλῷ δε μᾶλλον ἑσπέρας τῆς κουστωδίας ἐπιφανείσης καὶ σὺν ὄχλῳ τοῦ τάφου διασφραγιζομένου πλείονι τῷ φόβῳ κατασεισθείσας ὑποχωρῆσαι, διὸ καὶ καθάπαξ πρὸς ἀμφότερα μεριζόμεναι, τόν τε φόβον καὶ τὸν πόθον, συντόμως μὲν ἀνεχώρουν, συντόμως δὲ καὶ ἐπέτρεχον. Ὅρα γάρ· τῆς ἐπιούσης *ἐπιφωσκούσης* καὶ *ἔτι σκοτίας οὔσης* ἦλθον θεωρῆσαι τὸν τάφον καὶ ἀλεῖψαι τὸν Ἰησοῦν. Οὐκ ἂν δὲ ἦλθον, εἰ μὴ καὶ

with her and each other but also virtually the same soul, and so they always followed her closely and with greater boldness, and spent more time with her, comforting her, honoring her son, and at the same time demonstrating their desire for him. Thus, at that time, taking advantage of the moment, they exhibited greater courage than the other women, from whom they separated themselves, hastening to the Mother of God, and drawing near to the cross, so that thus they are mentioned with her, and are said to be standing together with her at the cross. But even though they differed in this from the other women, they nonetheless abandoned her, and even much more than the other women had. Therefore, it seems likely that at one point they accompanied the mother to the cross, but during the murder, when he cried out, "*I thirst!*" and caused the God killers to run about suddenly in an uproar, these women were stunned, became afraid and withdrew, but his mother remained even through this and witnessed what those men dared to do. And not even during the time of his preparation for burial did these women find the courage to come near but were still held back by fear, and, during his deposition from the cross, they only sat *opposite* and observed where he was placed, just as Matthew also says. And they were shaken by still greater fear when evening came, and the guard of soldiers appeared along with a crowd to seal the tomb, at which point they fled. Being divided in this way between fear and longing at the same time, at times they quickly withdrew, and at other times they quickly approached. For consider this: *as dawn was approaching,* and *while it was still dark,* they came to see the tomb and anoint Jesus. But they could not have come to

ἀπῆλθον πρότερον, ἀγοράζουσι δὲ καὶ ἀρώματα καθάπερ διχόθεν ἀπολογούμεναι διὰ τὴν ἀπόλειψιν, ἔκ τε τῆς πρὸς αὐτὸν ταχὺ ἐπαναδρομῆς καὶ τῆς περὶ αὐτὸν τιμῆς, ἔκ τε τῆς περὶ τὰ μύρα σπουδῆς τὲ καὶ ἀσχολίας.

Ἐπεὶ δὲ "Μαρίαν" οὐ τὴν Μαγδαληνὴν οὐδὲ τὴν τοῦ Κλωπᾶ μόνον, ἀλλὰ καὶ τὴν τοῦ Ἰωσῆ καὶ τὴν Ἰακώβου καταλέγει τὸ Εὐαγγέλιον, πῇ δὲ ἀορίστως ἄλλην Μαρίαν—*ἡ δὲ Μαγδαληνὴ καὶ* ἡ ἄλλη *Μαρία ἐθεώρουν ποῦ τίθεται*—τινὲς μὲν τὴν ἀόριστον διὰ τὸ ἀνερμήνευτον τὴν καινὴν ὑπειλήφασιν μητέρα τὲ καὶ Παρθένον καὶ Μητέρα Θεοῦ, τινὲς δὲ καὶ τὴν Ἰακώβου ταύτην εἶναι μᾶλλον ἢ τὴν αὐτὴν εἶναι καὶ τὴν Ἰωσῆ, ἣν ἀναφανδὸν ἑτέραν οὗτος λέγει παρὰ τὴν Ἰακώβου. Ἀλλὰ ταῦτα μὲν εἰκαῖα καὶ στοχασμῶν οὐκ εἰκαίων μόνον, ἀλλὰ καὶ ἀπιθάνων ἐπινοήματα. Πόθεν γὰρ αὐτοῖς ἡ πίστις ἢ τοῦ ἀναπλάσματος γοῦν ἡ πρόφασις, ὁπότε πανταχοῦ τῶν Εὐαγγελίων μετὰ τὴν ἀπόρρητον ταύτης κύησιν οὔτε πατρόθεν οὔτε μητρόθεν, ἀλλ᾽ οὐδὲ παρ᾽ αὐτοῦ τοῦ μνηστῆρος ὀνομαζομένην ἔστιν εὑρεῖν, ἀλλὰ τούτῳ μόνῳ παρατετηρημένως τῷ τῆς "μητρὸς" ὀνόματι καλουμένην; *Παράλαβε τὸ παιδίον* καὶ *τὴν μητέρα,* καὶ *ἦν ἡ μήτηρ τοῦ Ἰησοῦ ἐκεῖ,* καὶ *λέγει ἡ μήτηρ αὐτοῦ τοῖς διακόνοις,* καὶ ἐν αὐτοῖς δὲ τούτοις ὀλίγῳ πρότερον, *εἱστήκεισαν δὲ παρὰ τῷ σταυρῷ ἡ μήτηρ αὐτοῦ καὶ ἡ ἀδελφὴ τῆς μητρὸς αὐτοῦ.* Καὶ μακρὸν ἂν εἴη καταλέγειν τὰς μαρτυρίας οὐ τῶν Εὐαγγελίων μόνον, ἀλλὰ καὶ τῶν τοῦ εὐαγγελιστοῦ Λουκᾶ Πράξεων. Οὐδὲν γάρ ἐστιν ὅτι μὴ οὕτως ἔχει περὶ αὐτῆς, ἐπεὶ γὰρ οὐδὲ μία κλῆσις αὐτὴν οὕτως, ἀλλ᾽ οὔτε γένος οὔτε σχέσις ἐγνώριζεν, ἀλλὰ

the tomb had they not earlier gone away from it, and they purchased perfumes, just as they defended their desertion in both ways, that is, by their swift return to the tomb to honor the body, and their eagerness and concern for procuring the myrrh.

Because the Gospel mentions a "Mary" who is neither the Magdalene nor the wife of Clopas, but the mother of Joses and James, there was somewhere present there another, unidentified Mary—*Mary Magdalene and* the other *Mary who observed where he was laid*—and, in the absence of other explanations, some people have supposed that the unidentified Mary is the new mother and Virgin and Mother of God, while others say that she is the mother of James, or the same as the mother of Joses, who this clearly states is someone other than the mother of James. But these things are pointless speculations, and not only pointless but they are also implausible contrivances. For where is their proof or indeed the motive for their fabrication, when everywhere in the Gospels, after her ineffable conception, the Virgin is named neither from her father nor mother, nor even from her betrothed, but rather is carefully called only by the name of "mother"? *Take the child and his mother;* and, *the mother of Jesus was there;* and, *his mother spoke to the servants;* as well as the verse mentioned a moment ago, *standing by the cross were his mother and the sister of his mother.* And it would take a long time to recount not only the testimonies of the Gospels but also the Acts of the evangelist Luke. There is nothing that goes against this point about her, for she is thus not named even once, and neither is her family nor her relation characterized, but this distinctive term alone

τοῦτο μόνον αὐτῆς τὸ παράσημον, τὸ γνωριμώτατον καὶ ἐξαιρετώτατον, ἄλλωστε καὶ τὸ τιμιώτατον καὶ παραδοξότατον, εἰκότως ἀπὸ τούτου μόνου καὶ ὡς ἰδιωτάτου καὶ ὡς ἐνδοξοτάτου πανταχοῦ καὶ κεκλημένην ἐστὶν εὑρεῖν ὁμοῦ καὶ τετιμημένην. Ἔνθεν οὐδὲ αὐτῷ τῷ κυρίῳ πολλάκις ὀνόματι, ἀλλὰ τὰ πλεῖστα, μᾶλλον δὲ τὰ πάντα σχεδὸν μετὰ τὴν Γέννησιν, ὥσπερ ἔφην, τούτῳ μόνῳ γυμνῷ καὶ κυριωτέρως καὶ ἀληθεστέρως αὐτὴν καὶ καλεῖσθαί τε καὶ γνωρίζεσθαι. Ὃ δὲ μάλιστα τὸν ἔλεγχον δείκνυσιν, ὅτε ταύτην αὐτὸς οὗτος ὁ μαθητὴς ἐγγύς τε εἶναι καὶ σχεδὸν τοῦ σταυροῦ προσψαύειν καὶ τῷ μαθητῇ παρατίθεσθαι, τότε καὶ οἱ λοιποὶ συμφώνως αὐτήν τε τὴν Ἰακώβου καὶ τὴν Ἰωσῆ πρὸς τῇ Μαγδαληνῇ καὶ τῇ μητρὶ τῶν υἱῶν Ζεβεδαίου καὶ ἄλλαις πολλαῖς ἀπὸ μακρόθεν τὲ ἑστάναι καὶ θεωρεῖν, ἔφησαν, τὰ γινόμενα. Οὐκ ἂν οὖν ἅμα καὶ ἀπὸ μακρόθεν ἵστατο καὶ τῷ σταυρῷ παρίστατο, καὶ τῷ μαθητῇ παρεῖτο και τῷ μαθητῇ παρετίθετο. Ἀλλ' αἱ μὲν ἄλλαι τὸν καιρὸν ᾠκονόμουν καὶ ᾠκονομοῦντο κατὰ καιρόν, ἵν' ἄγγελοι καὶ διάκονοι τῶν γινομένων εἶεν τοῖς ἀποστόλοις ἐρχόμεναί τε καὶ ἀπερχόμεναι, καὶ τὰ μὲν παρ' ἑαυτῶν, τὰ δὲ πλεῖστα καὶ ἀκριβέστατα καὶ παρ' αὐτῆς μανθάνουσαι μόνης ἐκείνης, ἀπρὶξ αὐτῷ προσεδρευούσης καὶ ὥσπερ προσπεφυκυίας τῷ τάφῳ ἢ καὶ τῷ υἱῷ συγκατεχομένης, καὶ πάντα μὲν τὰ θαυματουργούμενα καταθεωρούσης, ἐχομένης δὲ τῆς ἐλπίδος καὶ καραδοκούσης τοῦ υἱοῦ καὶ Θεοῦ τὴν ἀνάστασιν.

identifies her, which is the most characteristic and the most exceptional, and at all events the most honorable and contrary to all expectation, which is likely why it is by means of this term only, which is the most appropriate and glorious, that one finds her everywhere called and likewise honored. Thus many times, indeed most times, her proper name is not even used; and virtually every time after the Nativity, as I said, it is by means of this unadorned term, which is both more accurate and true, that she is called and known. In particular, the proof of this is demonstrated when John himself was standing close to her and almost touching the cross, and she was placed in his care, for it is then that the other evangelists unanimously refer to Mary the mother of James and Joses, in addition to Mary Magdalene and Mary the mother of the sons of Zebedee, and many other women as standing there and observing the events from a distance. For it is not possible that at the same time she was standing both far off and beside the cross and was both abandoned by the disciple and was placed in the care of the disciple. But the other women were managing the circumstances and were themselves being managed according to the circumstances, so that as they were coming and going, they might serve as messengers and servants for the apostles concerning the events taking place. Some things they learned by themselves, but they learned of most things, and with great detail, solely from the Virgin, for she was close at his side, as if she were inseparable from the tomb or held fast by her son; and, beholding all the miraculous events that were taking place, she was filled with hope and awaited expectantly the resurrection of her son and her God.

Ἀνάστασις

92 Ἐκεῖναι μὲν οὖν τὸν λίθον ἀποκεκυλισμένον μόνον καὶ τὸν ἄγγελον ἐπ' αὐτῷ καθήμενον θεωροῦσιν, ὅτε δὲ καὶ ὅπως καὶ τἄλλα τὸ παράπαν οὐδέν. Αὕτη δὲ καὶ τὸν καιρὸν καὶ τὸν τρόπον καὶ τἄλλα τῶν πρὸ αὐτῶν καὶ τὰ μετ' αὐτά, τὸν σεισμόν, τὸν ἄγγελον τὸν ἐξ οὐρανῶν, τὴν ἀστραπήν, τοῦ ἀγγέλου τὴν καταφοίτησιν, τοῦ λίθου τὴν ἀποκύλισιν, τὴν τῶν φυλάκων νέκρωσιν καὶ αὖθις διαγρηγόρησιν, τὴν τινῶν αὐτῶν ὑποχώρησιν πρὸς τὴν πόλιν, ἃ τότε μὲν ἐξήγγειλεν οὐδαμῶς, μετὰ δὲ ταῦτα πρὸς ἀκρίβειαν καὶ τοῖς μαθηταῖς καὶ ταῖς μαθητρίαις ἀνατάττεται πάντα. Οἱ μὲν οὖν ἄλλοι τοσαῦτα μόνα περὶ τῶν γυναικῶν ἀναγράφουσιν, ὅσων δὴ καὶ ἠξίωνται, τήν τε τοῦ ἀγγέλου, καθάπερ ἔφην, πρὸς αὐτὰς ὀπτασίαν καὶ τὴν καθέδραν καὶ τὴν διάλεξιν. Μόνος δὲ Ματθαῖος καὶ τὰ πρὸ τῆς παρουσίας καὶ θεωρίας αὐτῶν, οἷον, εἰ καὶ τὰ αὐτὰ πάλιν ἐρῶ, τά τε περὶ τὸν καινὸν καὶ περιδέξιον ἐκεῖνον σεισμόν, ὃς τοὺς μὲν ἀπ' αἰῶνος νεκροὺς ἀφύπνισε, τοὺς δὲ ἐγρηγορότας ἐκοίμησε φύλακας, τήν τε τοῦ ἀγγέλου κατάβασιν καὶ τὴν τοῦ λίθου μετάθεσιν, καὶ εἴ τι ἄλλο τῆς τοιαύτης ἐστὶν ἀπορρήτου καὶ ἀκαταλήπτου καινοτομίας. Ἐπεὶ πῶς ἂν ἐν ταὐτῷ γυναῖκες ὑπὸ τοσούτου μὲν κατεχόμεναι πάθους, ὑπὸ τοσούτου δὲ καὶ καμάτου, ὑπὸ τοσαύτης δὲ καὶ ἀγρυπνίας καὶ νυκτοπορίας κατεργασμέναι, τοσοῦτον δὲ καὶ διάστημα τρέχειν ἀναγκαζόμεναι καὶ διηνεκῶς ἐπιφοιτῶσαι τὲ καὶ ἀποφοιτῶσαι καὶ διακονούμεναι τῇ μητρὶ καὶ τοῖς

Resurrection

The other women saw only the stone that had been rolled 92
away from the tomb and the angel sitting on it, but they saw nothing at all of when and how this and the other things took place. But the Virgin saw the entire sequence of events and the manner in which they unfolded, including the things that took place beforehand and those that took place afterward, I mean the earthquake, the appearance of the angel from heaven, the lightning flash, the descent of the angel, the rolling away of the stone, the way the guards became like dead men and their subsequent awakening, and the retreat of some of them to the city. At the time she spoke of none of these things, though later she related all of these events in detail to the male and female disciples. The other evangelists recount only the things that the other women were worthy of witnessing, namely, the appearance, as I said, of the angel to them, his sitting on the stone, and his words. It is only Matthew who records the events before their arrival at the tomb along with what they saw there, that is to say, to repeat what I have already said, about the remarkable and opportune earthquake, which both awakened those who had been long dead and put to sleep the wakeful guards; the descent of the angel and the moving of the stone, and whatever else was part of this ineffable and incomprehensible remarkable situation. For how could women who were in the grip of such great emotion, who were so weary, who were so exhausted from keeping such a vigil and traveling about at night, and who were required to run such great distances, and who were continually coming and going from the scene, conveying as intermediaries for the mother and the apostles

ἀποστόλοις ἅ τε παρ᾽ ἑαυτῶν καὶ ἃ παρ᾽ ἐκείνης μάθοιεν, ἅμα τὲ τούτοις πᾶσιν ὑπούργουν, καὶ τὰ ἐν συνεχείᾳ τοσαύτῃ καὶ παραδοξοποιΐᾳ γινόμενα πάντα κατὰ βραχὺ καὶ καθαρῶς καθεώρων, εἰ μὴ μόνης ἐκείνης ταῦτα τῆς οὕτω μὲν προσκαθεζομένης ἀκινήτως, εἰ δεῖ τι καὶ παραδοξοτέρως εἰπεῖν, ὥσπερ λίθου τῷ λίθῳ;

Οὕτω δὲ καὶ διεγρηγορυίας ἀκοιμήτως ὥσπερ ἀγγέλου, οὕτω δὲ καὶ διαπύρως διαφλεγομένης τὰ σπλάγχνα καὶ ὥσπερ ὑπὸ μυρίοις ὀφθαλμοῖς καὶ καθ᾽ ἓν καὶ πάντα κατοπτευούσης ὁμοῦ καὶ τὰ ἐν ἀκαρεῖ τοῦ χρόνου γινόμενα, ὡς εἰκὸς μητέρα καὶ τοιαύτην καὶ τοιούτου παιδός, ἀλλὰ καὶ ἐκ παιδὸς τὰ τοιαῦτα σεσοφισμένην μυστήρια καὶ πρὸς τοιαῦτα παρεσκευασμένην θαύματα καὶ επὶ πᾶσι τοιαῦτα προσδεχομένην καὶ πρὸς τοιαύτας ἀνεπτερωμένην ἐλπίδας, καὶ οὐκ ἀνεχομένην οὐδ᾽ ὅσον οἷον ἀποστῆναι τοῦ μνήματος, ἀλλὰ καὶ τῶν φυσικῶν ἀναγκῶν κρείττονα γινομένην, ὕπνου τὲ καὶ τροφῆς—ὧν πῶς ἂν καὶ εἰς μνήμην ἀφίκετο κατὰ τῆς φύσεως καὶ ἐξ ἀρχῆς οὕτω λαβοῦσα τὰ νικητήρια;—καὶ τότε καθάπερ ἔνθους ὑπὸ τοῦ Πάθους ὁμοῦ γινομένη καὶ τῆς ἐλπίδος, ἕως ἂν ὥσπερ καὶ αὐτὴ συναναστῇ τῷ υἱῷ καὶ μὴ ἀπολειφθῇ τῆς ζωηφόρου ταύτης ἐγέρσεως. Διὸ καὶ πρώτη τῶν λαμπροτάτων συμβόλων καὶ τῶν εὐαγγελίων τυγχάνει τῆς ἀναστάσεως, ἀλλὰ καὶ αὐτῆς τῆς θεοειδοῦς καὶ χαριεστάτης τοῦ υἱοῦ καὶ Θεοῦ μορφῆς ὡς ἐνὸν καὶ τῆς χαροποιοῦ φωνῆς, οὐχ᾽ ὡς μήτηρ μόνον καὶ τὰ τοιαῦτα πάντα τῆς οἰκονομίας ἐμπεπιστευμένη μυστήρια, καθάπερ τὰ τῆς σαρκώσεως οὕτω

whatever they might learn from themselves or from her—how, I ask, could they render service to all these people and, at the same time, see clearly and in such short time all the things that were happening in such a sequence and so miraculously, unless they were informed about them by the Virgin alone, who was sitting and watching everything without moving, and, if it is necessary to state this even more paradoxically, sitting there like a stone before a stone?

Thus she remained sleeplessly vigilant like an angel, with her maternal being burning intensely, and observing closely, as if she had a thousand eyes, each particular thing and all things, even those that took place in the briefest moment of time. This was natural for such a mother of such a child, and for someone who from her childhood had come to learn of such mysteries and had been prepared for such wonders, and who in all circumstances was expecting such wonders, and had been raised on the wings of such hopes, and thus she refused to distance herself from the tomb even for a little while, but overcame the necessities of nature, such as the need to sleep and eat—for how could they have even come to mind, when, from the start, she had been victorious over nature? She remained vigilant, then, inspired by the Passion and filled with hope, until she might rise up together with her son and not be deprived of his life-giving resurrection. And because of this, she was the first to experience the most radiant symbols and good news of the resurrection, as well as the godlike and delightful form of her son and God as much as possible, and be filled with joy at the sound of his voice. And this did not happen only because she was his mother and had been entrusted with all the mysteries of the divine economy of salvation, including those of the incarna-

καὶ τὰ τῆς ἀναστάσεως, ἀλλὰ καὶ ὡς μᾶλλον τῶν ἄλλων τῷ υἱῷ συγκακοπαθήσασα καὶ συννεκρωθεῖσα, καὶ διὰ τοῦτο μᾶλλον καὶ συζήσασα καὶ συνδοξασθεῖσα.

Ἀλλὰ ταύτην μὲν οὕτως ἀμέσως καὶ πρώτως ἡ τῆς ἐγέρσεως λαμπρότης καὶ δύναμις περιήστραψε, ταῖς μυροφόροις δὲ οὐχ ὁμοίως, ὡς μήτε ὁμοίως διακειμέναις μήτε δὲ χωρούσαις τὴν τοσαύτην δόξαν τὲ καὶ λαμπρότητα. Μήτε γὰρ ἀθρόον μήτε δὲ καθ' ἕνα τρόπον, ἀλλὰ καὶ κατ' ὀλίγον καὶ διὰ πολλῶν, τῇ μὲν γὰρ δι' ἀκοῆς καὶ τῆς τοῦ ἀγγέλου φωνῆς, τῇ δὲ καὶ δι' ὄψεως αὐτῆς τῆς τοῦ ἀγγέλου στολῆς καὶ μορφῆς, ἀλλὰ καὶ τῆς τοῦ λίθου μεταθέσεως ἀνακαλύπτονται τὴν ἀνάστασιν, καὶ οὕτω κατ' ὀλίγον προβιβασθείσαις αὐτὸς ἐκεῖνος, *ἡ Ζωὴ καὶ ἡ Ἀνάστασις*, ἐπιφαίνεται *λέγων· "χαίρετε."* Διὰ τούτων πρώτων καὶ τὴν λύπην ἐκβάλλων πάλιν καὶ τὸν φόβον τῆς Εὔας, καὶ οὐχ' ὥσπερ ἐπὶ τῆς συλλήψεως "χαῖρε," μόνῃ τῇ Παρθένῳ περιγράφων τὰ τῆς χαρᾶς, ἀλλὰ κοσμικὴν καὶ τοῦ γένους παντὸς ἐμφαίνων τὴν ἀγαλλίασιν. Ἀλλ' ἡ μὲν Αὐτοσοφία καὶ ἀμφότερα ταῦτα διῳκονόμει καλῶς. Εἴ τε γὰρ ἀθρόον κατήστραψεν, ἢ μὴ πιστευθεὶς ὑπερεξέπληξεν ἂν καὶ ὡς φάντασμα ἂν ἑαυτὸν παρέδειξεν, ὅπου γε καὶ τῶν ἀνδρῶν καὶ αὐτῶν τῶν μαθητῶν τινὰς ὕστερον οὕτω διέθηκεν, ἢ καὶ πιστευθεὶς εἰς ἀκάθεκτόν τινα χαρὰν οἷα καὶ θερμοτάτας ἐνέβαλε καὶ ἐξέστησε καὶ πᾶσαν αὐτὰς εὐταξίαν καὶ συμμετρίαν ὑπερβῆναι πεποίηκεν, ὅπου γε καὶ οὕτω

tion and the resurrection, but also because, more than the others, she had suffered together with her son and had been put to death together with him, and this is why she both lives and is glorified together with him.

Thus, it was around her, immediately and before anyone else, that the radiance and power of the resurrection flashed like lightning, but this did not happen in the same way to the myrrh-bearing women, for they were not disposed in the same way that she was, nor did they have the capacity for such glory and radiance. Neither was the resurrection revealed to them suddenly or in only one way, but little by little, and in many ways: to one through hearing the voice of the angel, to another through the vision of the angel's clothing and form, and also through the rolling away of the stone, and thus, after being led by stages, he who is himself *the Life and the Resurrection* appeared to them and *said, "Hail."* Thus it was first through them that Christ removed the pain and the fear of Eve again, for this was not like the "Hail" uttered at the conception, when the joyful news was limited only to the Virgin, but here he makes manifest the cosmic rejoicing of the entire human race. And Wisdom itself wonderfully arranged for both of these things. For if he had appeared suddenly in a flash of light, either they might not have believed it was him, since he would have exceedingly astounded them and would have seemed like an apparition to them, which indeed was the impression he later gave to some men and even some of his disciples; or else they would have believed it was him, and he would have astonished them and thrown those most ardent women into a state of uncontrollable joy, causing them to abandon all good order and due proportion, in which case, disposed in such a way,

διῳκονομημέναι διὰ τὸ τῆς χαρᾶς ὑπερβάλλον οὐχ᾽ οἷαί τε ἦσαν ἑαυτῶν κρατεῖν, ἀλλὰ καὶ περιβαλεῖν αὐτὸν ἠβούλοντο καὶ προσιέναι καθὼς τὸ πρότερον καὶ τῶν ποδῶν ἥπτοντο. Εἴ τε δὲ καὶ καθ᾽ ἕνα τρόπον καὶ δι᾽ ἀγγέλων μόνον, ἀλλὰ μὴ καὶ δι᾽ ἑαυτοῦ, τὰ τῆς ἀναστάσεως ἀπεκάλυψεν, οὐκ ἂν ἐβεβαίωσε τὴν ἀνάστασιν γυναιξὶ τὰ τοιαῦτα φύσει δυσπειθεστέραις καὶ ἀσθενέστερον ἔτι διακειμέναις.

Ἀλλ᾽ οὕτως μὲν οὕτως ὁ Λόγος πάντα κατὰ λόγον οἰκονομῶν· ὅρα δὲ καὶ τὴν τούτου μητέρα τὸν ἑαυτῆς υἱὸν μιμουμένην καὶ οὔτε ταῖς μυροφόροις οὔτε τοῖς ἀποστόλοις δι᾽ ἑαυτῆς ταῦτα προευαγγελιζομένην, ἵνα μὴ καὶ διὰ τὸ ὑπερβάλλον ἀπιστηθῇ καὶ διὰ τὸ πρὸς τὸν υἱὸν φίλτρον ὑποπτευθῇ, ἀλλ᾽ ἐνδιδοῦσαν ἐπὶ μικρὸν ὥστε καὶ αὐτοὺς ἐκείνους πρῶτον γενομένους αὐτόπτας, καὶ περὶ τοῦ κεφαλαίου τῶν ὅλων, τῆς ἀναστάσεως λέγω, βεβαιωθέντας, οὕτω καὶ τὰ παρ᾽ αὐτῆς ὕστερον μυστικώτερα ῥᾷον καὶ βεβαιότερον παραδέχεσθαι. Καὶ οὗτος ὁ τρόπος αὐτῆς οὐκ ἐνταῦθα μόνον, ἀλλὰ καὶ διὰ πάσης σχεδὸν τῆς οἰκονομίας, ἀναμένειν ἐκ τοῦ υἱοῦ καὶ Θεοῦ πρῶτον ἀνακαλύπτεσθαι τὰ μυστήρια τοῖς βουλομένοις ἢ καὶ ἀξιουμένοις, εἶθ᾽ οὕτω καὶ παρ᾽ ἑαυτῆς ἐκτίθεσθαι τὰ προεγνωσμένα, εἴτε τὸ ὕποπτον, ὥσπερ ἔφην, φυλαττομένη, εἴτε καὶ μὴ προπετεύεσθαι βουλομένη διὰ τὸ ἀφιλότιμόν τε καὶ μέτριον. Ἀλλ᾽ αὕτη μὲν καὶ ταῖς μυροφόροις καὶ τοῖς ἀποστόλοις ὕστερον πάντων διδάσκαλος τούτων γίνεται, *οὐχ ὡς* καὶ *ὑπὲρ ἀποστόλους καὶ μυροφόρους* μόνον, *ἀλλὰ καὶ* ὡς

they would not have been able to contain themselves on account of their overwhelming joy, but would have wanted to surround him and approach him, just as earlier when they had touched his feet. If, on the other hand, he revealed the things of the resurrection to them in only one way, and only through the angels and not through himself, he would not have confirmed the resurrection to women who, by nature are harder to convince of such things and weaker in disposition.

Thus, the Word arranged all things according to reason. Notice, too, how his mother imitates her son, and thus did not announce the good tidings of the resurrection either to the myrrh-bearing women or to the apostles, so that she would not be doubted on account of the extraordinary nature of her report and rendered suspect on account of her affection for her son. Instead, she gave them a short period of time so that they themselves, after first becoming eyewitnesses and being assured of the crowning act of all, I mean the resurrection, would thus later accept her more private testimony more easily and with greater confidence. And this was her manner of doing things, not only in this instance, but also throughout virtually the whole dispensation of salvation, that is, to wait for her son and God to first reveal the mysteries to those who wished to know them or who were worthy of them, and then to disclose what she herself had already known, either as a precaution, as I said, against coming under suspicion or because she did not want to act rashly, as she was unassuming and modest. But afterward, she herself became the teacher of all these things both to the myrrh-bearing women and the apostles, *not* only as *someone who was superior to the apostles and the myrrh bearers, but also as*

ὑπὲρ πᾶσαν ἀγγελικὴν καὶ νοερὰν μύησιν τὰ τοιαῦτα μεμνημένη θαύματα καὶ μυστήρια. Εἰ δὲ ταῦτα περὶ αὐτῆς οἱ εὐαγγελισταὶ καὶ θεολόγοι παρεσιώπησαν, καὶ τοῦτο τῆς κατ' αὐτοὺς σοφίας, καὶ τοῦτο τῆς οἰκονομίας τοῦ Πνεύματος. Πρῶτον μὲν γάρ, ὅπερ ἔφην, ὕποπτα ἂν οἷα καὶ μητρικὰ τὰ τῆς μαρτυρίας ἦν· ἔπειτα καὶ τὰ πρῶτα καὶ συνεκτικὰ πάντων τελευταῖα καθιστορήσαντες καὶ ὧν πολλοὶ μάρτυρες πίστιν καὶ τοῖς ἄλλοις τοῖς ἀνὰ μεταξὺ πᾶσι παρέσχον, ὥστε πρὸς τῷ ὑπόπτῳ καὶ περιττὸς ὁ λόγος ἂν ἦν, εἶτα καὶ περὶ αὐτῆς ἱστορῶν ἦν· τρίτον, ὅτι καὶ αὐτοὶ πρὸς χάριν ἂν αὐτῆς ταύτης συνθεῖναι τὴν ἱστορίαν, ἀλλὰ μὴ πρὸς ἀλήθειαν ἔδοξαν ἄν.

93 Νυνὶ δὲ τῶν περὶ αὐτῆς ἐγκωμίων ἀπαλλαγέντες καὶ πάσης τῆς τοιαύτης ἀπηλλάγησαν ὑποψίας· πλὴν ἀλλ' ἐκείνη πρώτη τῆς ἀστραπῆς οὕτω τοῦ παιδὸς ἀξιωθεῖσα καὶ τῆς φωνῆς, τῶν τε πρὸ τῆς ἀναστάσεως καὶ τῶν μετὰ τὴν ἀνάστασιν θειοτέρων ἀκουσμάτων καὶ θεαμάτων, σύνοικος τῷ ἠγαπημένῳ λοιπὸν μαθητῇ κατὰ τὴν τοῦ υἱοῦ φωνὴν ἦν συναπεκδεχομένη καὶ τὴν εἰς οὐρανοὺς ἀνάληψιν τοῦ υἱοῦ. Τοῦτο γὰρ ἦν τὸ κεφάλαιον τῆς ὅλης οἰκονομίας καὶ αὐτῆς δὲ τῆς μετὰ τὸ Πάθος ἐπαγγελίας τὸ τέλος. Ἐκείνῃ μὲν οὖν ἴσως ἐν ἀπορρήτῳ καὶ πάλιν, τοῖς δὲ μαθηταῖς κοινότερον ἐπιφαίνεται· τὸ μὲν οὖν ἐκείνης τοῖς εὐαγγελισταῖς παρεῖται, τὸ δὲ ἑαυτῶν ἀναγράφεται. Τὰ γὰρ ἐναργέστερα, καθάπερ ἔφην, καὶ ἐν πολλοῖς καὶ μᾶλλον ὁμολογούμενα πρὸς τὴν ἱστορίαν αὐτοῖς παρειλῆφθαι μᾶλλον διὰ τὸ εὐπαράδεκτον.

someone who, while recalling these great miracles and mysteries, *transcended every angelic and noetic initiation.* And if the evangelists and theologians remained silent about these things concerning her, this too was a sign of their wisdom, as well as the economy of the Spirit. For, in the first place, as I have already said, the content of her testimony would have been considered suspect and due to maternal bias. In addition, since the first and most essential things of all were recorded last, and since many witnesses had in the meantime shared their assurance concerning these things with all the others, then, in addition to being suspect, it would also have been superfluous to say more, even if it was also saying something about her. Third, they remained silent because they themselves would have been thought to have composed their accounts as a favor to her and not as a testimony to the truth.

Being thus freed at this point from praising her, they also 93
freed themselves from all suspicion. But she was, nevertheless, the first to be counted worthy of the lightning-like appearance of her child and to hear his voice, and of the even more divine instructions and visions both before and after the resurrection; and she was already living in the same house as the beloved disciple, as her son had directed them, and awaited eagerly her son's ascension into the heavens. For this was the summation of the entire economy of salvation, and, after the Passion, the completion of the promise. To her, he probably appeared again secretly, while to his disciples he appeared more publicly; so her own experience was omitted by the evangelists, but they recorded their own. For, as I said, the things that were more obvious, and which were acknowledged by many, were taken up by the evangelists in their account because they were easily received.

94 Ἀλλὰ καὶ συναυλίζεται πιστούμενος ὡς ἀτελεστέρους καὶ ἐξαγαγὼν εὐλογεῖ, ἐκείνης ἤδη τὴν εὐλογίαν κληρωσαμένης, ἀφ' οὗπερ *εὐλογημένη* τὲ ἤκουσε καὶ *κεχαριτωμένη*, ἀλλὰ καὶ τὴν Εὐλογίαν ἐκύησε καὶ εὐλογεῖν ἐτάχθη μᾶλλον τὰ πέρατα, κατάλληλα δὲ τίθησι τὰ φάρμακα καὶ ἀντίθετα. Ἐπεὶ γὰρ ἐξ ἀρχῆς μετὰ τὴν παρακοὴν τῶν μὲν γυναικῶν ἡ λύπη, τῶν δε ἀνδρῶν ἡ κατάρα, διὰ τοῦτο κἀνταῦθα ἐκείναις μὲν τὴν χαράν, τούτοις δὲ τὴν εὐλογίαν ἐπέθηκε, καὶ μικρῷ πρόσθεν ἐκείνοις μὲν τὴν παρουσίαν ἐπαγγέλεται τοῦ Ἁγίου Πνεύματος, ὡς ἐκείνης γεγεμισμένης ὅλης ἤδη τοῦ Πνεύματος καὶ ἐνδεδυμένης ὅλην τὴν *ἐξ ὕψους δύναμιν*, ἀφ' οὗπερ αὐτῇ καὶ *τὸ Πνεῦμα* μὲν ἐπῆλθε *τὸ Ἅγιον*, ἡ δὲ *τοῦ Ὑψίστου δύναμις ἐπεσκίασε* καὶ ἐνέδυσε δι' ὧν αὐτὴν ἐνεδύσατο. Καὶ ἐκείνῃ μὲν τὰ τῆς ἐπαγγελίας πάντα πεπλήρωτο καὶ τὸ βασίλειον τῶν οὐρανίων καὶ ἐπιγείων διάδημα περιέθετο, ἀφ' οὗπερ καὶ ὁ ταύτης υἱὸς οὐχ ὡς Θεὸς μόνον, ἀλλὰ καὶ ὡς ἄνθρωπος ἀναστὰς τὴν ἐν οὐρανῷ τὲ καὶ ἐπὶ γῆς καὶ αὐτοῦ τοῦ οὐρανοῦ καὶ τῆς γῆς ἐξουσίαν εἴληφεν, ὅπου γε καὶ ἐν ἡμῖν ταῖς ἀνάνδροις ἤδη μητράσιν ἔθος ἢ νόμος τὰ τῶν υἱῶν ἀξιώματα περιτίθεσθαι.

95 Ἀλλὰ τίνα ταύτης καὶ τὰ μετὰ ταῦτα; Ὡς λίαν ὑπερφυῆ τὲ καὶ ὑπερθαύμαστα καί, εἰ οἷόν τε πλέον εἰπεῖν, τῶν προλαβόντων ὑπερθαυμασιώτερα. Ἆρα γὰρ ἡ οὕτω μὲν συλληφθεῖσα καὶ γεννηθεῖσα, οὕτω δὲ καὶ ἐκ βρέφους ἁγιασθεῖσα, καὶ συλλαβοῦσα δὲ καὶ γεννήσασα τὴν ἀπόρρητον καὶ ἀκατάληπτον καὶ ἀγγέλοις σύλληψίν τε καὶ γέννησιν, τὸν βασιλέα τῶν ὅλων τὲ καὶ Θεόν, οὕτω δὲ δι' ὅλης

The Lord remained with his disciples, confirming their faith since they were not yet fully perfected, and blessing them before his departure, but she had already been in possession of his blessing from the moment she heard the words, *blessed are you, favored one,* and in truth she was pregnant with the Blessing and was appointed to bless the ends of the earth, administering the appropriate medicines and antidotes. For from the very beginning, immediately after the disobedience, women were subject to pain and men were under a curse, which is why the Lord bestowed joy on the former and a blessing on the latter, and a little later promised them the coming of the Holy Spirit, for she herself was already wholly filled with the Spirit, and clothed in the whole *power from on high,* from the moment the *Holy Spirit descended upon her,* and the *power of the Most High overshadowed her,* and clothed her in the things with which she was clothed. And the entirety of the promise was fulfilled for her, and she received the crown of the kingdom of heaven and earth from the time her son, not only as God but also as man, rose from the dead and received authority in heaven and on earth over heaven and earth itself, insofar as, among us it is a custom or law for husbandless mothers to have their sons' honors conferred upon them. 94

But what happened to her after this? Things quite extraordinary and wondrous, and, if it is appropriate to say more, far more wondrous than what happened to her before. For she who was conceived and born in such a manner, was also sanctified from her infancy, and conceived and gave birth to the king and God of all through a conception and birth-giving that was ineffable and incomprehensible even to angels. And thus, throughout all the days of her life, she 95

ἐξετασθεῖσα τῆς ζωῆς καὶ διὰ τοσούτων ἀγώνων τὲ καὶ πολέμων κατὰ τοῦ Ἀντιπάλου καὶ κατ' αὐτῆς δὲ τῆς φύσεως ἀνικήτους ἀραμένη νίκας, οὕτω δὲ ἐπὶ τέλει τῶν ἄθλων καὶ συναθλήσασα καὶ ὑπεραθλήσασα τοῦ υἱοῦ, καὶ διὰ πάντων τροπαιοφόρος καὶ μυρίους ἀναδησαμένη (μήτ' ἀριθμῆσαι ῥᾳδίους μήτε μετρῆσαι) στεφάνους, ἕνα δὲ τὸν πρῶτον καὶ μόνον καὶ μέγιστον, τὴν βασιλείαν ἐγκεχειρισμένη τῆς ὅλης ὁρωμένης καὶ νοουμένης κτίσεως. Ὁ δὲ αὐτῇ καὶ τῆς βασιλείας αὐτῆς μεῖζον, οὕτως ἰδοῦσα τὸν υἱὸν ἐκ τῶν τάφων τὲ ἐγειρόμενον, καὶ τῷ τοῦ Θεοῦ και Πατρὸς Λόγῳ τὲ και Θεῷ καὶ αὐτὸ τὸ ἐξ αὐτῆς πρόσλημμα συναποθεούμενον, καὶ μετὰ τοσαύτης δόξης είς οὐρανοὺς ἀναλαμβανόμενον καὶ ὑπὸ τῶν ἰδόντων καὶ ὑπ' αὐτῶν ὅσον οὔπω τῶν περάτων προσκυνούμενόν τε καὶ λατρευόμενον.

Ἆρ' οὖν ὡς ἤδη πάντα καὶ πόλεμον καταλύσασα καὶ ἀπολαβοῦσα στέφανον καὶ κατὰ πάντων καὶ διὰ πάντων σχοῦσα τὰ νικητήρια, τὸν ἄπονον αἱρεῖται λοιπὸν βίον καὶ περὶ τῶν ὅλων ἀφροντιστεῖ; Πολλοῦ γε καὶ δεῖ. Ἀλλὰ πρῶτον μὲν ὡς νῦν ἀρχομένη τῆς περὶ ταῦτα μελέτης καὶ τῆς ἀσκήσεως οὐκ ἀνίησιν ἑαυτὴν κατατρύχουσα νηστείαις καὶ ἀγρυπνίαις καὶ προσευχαῖς. Ὁ καὶ Λουκᾶς δηλοῖ μετὰ τὴν ἀπαρίθμησιν τῶν Χριστοῦ μαθητῶν, οὑτωσὶ λέγων· "*καὶ οὗτοι πάντες ἦσαν προσκαρτεροῦντες ὁμοθυμαδὸν τῇ προσευχῇ* καὶ τῇ δεήσει *σὺν γυναιξὶ καὶ Μαρίᾳ τῇ μητρὶ τοῦ Ἰησοῦ καὶ σὺν τοῖς ἀδελφοῖς αὐτοῦ,*" δυοῖν τούτοιν ἡμῖν παρέχων μαρτύριον, ὅτι τὲ πανταχοῦ μετὰ τῆς μητρικῆς σχέσεως, ἀλλ' οὐκ ἀπ' ἄλλου τινός, ὥς τινες ᾠήθησαν,

was tested, and, after so many trials and battles with the Opponent and indeed with nature itself, she attained unvanquished victories. And thus, upon the completion of her struggles, and after struggling together with and even surpassing her son in her struggles, she emerged victorious in everything and was adorned with myriad crowns (though they are not easily numbered or counted), of which the first, singular and greatest was being entrusted with the kingdom of all visible and intelligible creation. However, what for her was even greater than the kingdom itself was to have seen her son rising from the tomb, and the same human nature that was taken from her being deified together with the Divine Word of God the Father, and being taken up with such great glory into the heavens, and being venerated and worshipped by those who saw this, and soon by all the ends of the earth.

But, after having thus completely put an end to every battle, and receiving every crown, and seizing the spoils of victory from all and through all, was the rest of her life untroubled, and was she free from care in everything? Far from it! As if she were only now beginning her exercises and training in these matters, she did not spare herself the exhausting labor of fasts, vigils, and prayers. This is what Luke is describing when, after the gathering of Christ's disciples, he says, "*with one accord they all continued in prayer* and supplication, *along with the women and Mary the mother of Jesus, and his brothers.*" With this he provides us with a double testimony: that everywhere she is called by the term "mother" and not anything else, as certain people have supposed; and that she

ὀνομάζεται καὶ ὅτι οὐδαμοῦ τῶν ἄλλων ἀπελιμπάνετο, μᾶλλον δὲ καθάπερ ὁ ταύτης υἱὸς ἡγεμὼν τῶν καλλίστων πᾶσιν ἦν ἐπὶ γῆς ἔτι ὤν, οὕτω καὶ αὕτη μετὰ τὴν ἐκείνου πρὸς οὐρανοὺς ἀνάληψιν καὶ ἀνδράσι καὶ γυναιξί. Διὸ καὶ τότε τῆς νηστείας καὶ τῆς προσευχῆς ἔξαρχος ἦν, ὃ δὴ καὶ κατ' ἐξοχὴν αὐτὴν ὀνομασθῆναι πεποίηκεν. Ἔπειτα καὶ τῶν ἀποστόλων ὥσπερ στρατιωτῶν ἐνδυσαμένων ἤδη τὰ ὅπλα καὶ ἀναλαβομένων τὰ ξίφη, τὴν δύναμιν τοῦ Παναγίου Πνεύματος, καὶ κατὰ πάσης καὶ ὑπὲρ πάσης ὁρμώντων τῆς οἰκουμένης καὶ διαμεριζομένων καθάπερ στρατηγῶν τοῦ πολέμου τὰ μέρη, τὰς χώρας τὲ καὶ τὸ κήρυγμα, αὕτη καθάπερ ἔδει καὶ βασιλίδα τὸ μὲν μεσαίτατον κατέχει τῆς οἰκουμένης, τὴν Ἱερουσαλήμ, καὶ ταύτης τὸ καιριώτατον, τὴν Σιών, μετὰ τοῦ μαθητοῦ καὶ συμπαρθένου καὶ κατὰ θέσιν υἱοῦ, ἔνθα καὶ ὁ οἶκος αὐτοῖς ἦν καθάπερ στρατήγιον ἢ βασίλειον.

96 Ἐκείνους δὲ κυκλόθεν ἐκπέμπει καὶ πᾶσαν ὑποτίθησι τὴν ἀποστολὴν καὶ μόνη τὴν ὑπὲρ πάντων φροντίδα καὶ τὸν ὑπὲρ τοῦ υἱοῦ πάλιν ἀναδέχεται πόλεμον, περί τε τῶν ὅλων ἅμα διαγωνιζομένη ὑπὲρ αὐτοῦ καὶ πρὸς αὐτὸν διαπρεσβευομένη περὶ τῶν ὅλων, οὐχ ὑπὲρ τῶν ἄλλων μόνον, ἀλλὰ καὶ αὐτῶν τῶν ἐχθρῶν, ὥστε καὶ τοῖς σταυρωταῖς μὴ μόνον ἀφεῖναι, ἀλλὰ καὶ αὐτοὺς ἐπιγνῶναι ποιῆσαι καὶ τῶν ἀγαθῶν ἑαυτοῦ καὶ τῆς ζωῆς ἀξιῶσαι. Τοῦτο μὲν καὶ παρ' αὐτοῦ τούτου τοῦ υἱοῦ μαθοῦσα καὶ νομοθετήσαντος καὶ κατὰ τὸν σταυρὸν βοήσαντος· "*ἄφες αὐτοῖς, Πάτερ,*" τοῦτο δὲ καὶ παρ' ἑαυτῆς ὡς ἀγαθῆς ἤδη καὶ κοινῆς τὴν φιλανθρωπίαν. Τὸ γὰρ δὴ γένος ἐλάττονος αὐτῇ λόγου

certainly did not abandon the others, but rather, just as her son, when he was still on earth, was the guide for all people in terms of what is most noble and beautiful, so too was she the guide for men and women after his ascension into heaven. And thus, she led the way in fasting and prayer, practices for which she became widely renowned. Afterward, when the apostles like fellow soldiers were equipped with weapons and took up their swords, that is, the power of the all-Holy Spirit, and rushed headlong to fight against and on behalf of the whole world, and like generals in a war divided up the fields of battle, that is, the nations and their preaching, she, as was fitting for a queen, dwelled at the center of the whole world, that is, Jerusalem, and indeed in its most important place, Zion, together with the disciple and fellow virgin, her adopted son, such that their house was like a general's tent or the seat of a kingdom.

From there, she sent forth the apostles all around and in- 96
structed them on their entire mission, while she alone assumed responsibility once again for the care of everyone and for the battle on behalf of her son. She simultaneously struggled on behalf of all for his sake and interceded with him for all, not only for the other disciples but even for their very enemies, so that he would not only forgive those who crucified him but also might make them come to know him, and be counted worthy of his own goods things and his life. For this she had also learned from her son, who established it as a law and cried out on the cross: "*Father, forgive them.*" But she also knew this from herself, since she was already good and shared his love of mankind. Indeed, race held little

πάντως, ᾗ καὶ πᾶν ἤδη τὸ τῶν ἀνθρώπων γένος ἶσον τὲ καὶ οἰκεῖον οὐ διὰ τὴν φύσιν μόνον, ἀλλὰ καὶ τὴν ἐπίσης αὐτῶν Δεσποτείαν. Οὐ μὴν οὐδὲ τούτοις ἀρκεῖται, ἀλλὰ καὶ ἐπιτείνει τὴν ἀγωνίαν, μὴ ἀφισταμένη τοῦ μνήματος, ἀλλὰ καὶ οἶκον μὲν σχεδὸν ἐκεῖνον ποιησαμένη τὸν τάφον, κλίνην δὲ τὴν παρ' αὐτῷ κοίτην, προσκεφάλαιον δὲ τὸν λίθον, περιπάτους δὲ τὰς πρὸς τὸν υἱὸν νοερὰς ἐκδημίας, τράπεζαν δὲ τὰς δοξολογίας, ἡδύσματα δὲ τὰ κατ' αὐτὸν Πάθη καὶ διηγήματα, πόματα δὲ καὶ λουτρὰ τὰ δάκρυα, χορείας δὲ τὰς γονυκλισίας. Φασὶ γοῦν οἱ περὶ πλείστου τὰ ἐκείνης καὶ τὴν ἀλήθειαν ποιησάμενοι καὶ τύλους οὐ μετρίους, ἀλλ' οἷα γονάτων ταῖς ἀχράντοις ἐκείναις ἐντετυπῶσθαι χερσίν, αἷς καὶ τὸ πρότερον τὸν ἄσπορον ταύτης ἠγκαλίζετο καὶ νῦν ἐξευμενίζετο τόκον ἐκ τῆς συνεχοῦς τῷ λίθῳ καὶ τῷ ἐδάφει προσκλίσεως, ἅπερ, εἰ πρὸς ἀκρίβειαν καὶ νῦν ἡμῖν γράφειν βουλομένοις ἦν, ἄλλης ἂν ἐδέησεν ἱστορίας, καὶ οὐχ ἧττον ἂν ἦν τοῦ ἔργου τὸ πάρεργον. Ἐκεῖνα δὲ πάντως οὐ κατὰ πάρεργον, ἀλλὰ καὶ σφόδρα τῷ παρόντι λόγῳ καὶ τοῖς ἄλλοις τοῖς περὶ αὐτῆς διηγήμασιν ἀκόλουθα καὶ ἀναγκαιότατα, ὅτι, καθάπερ διάδοχος τοῦ υἱοῦ, προστάτις καὶ διδάσκαλος καὶ δεσπότις πάντων καταλειφθεῖσα, καὶ φίλων καὶ μαθητῶν καὶ ἀνδρῶν ἅμα καὶ γυναικῶν, οὕτω καὶ τὰς φροντίδας ἀνεδέχετο πάντων. Καὶ πρὸς ταύτην ἅπαντες ἀφορῶντες ἐκεῖνοι καὶ ἀντὶ τῆς σωματικῆς αὐτοῦ παρουσίας τὴν σωματικῶς αὐτὸν γεννησαμένην ἔχοντες ἅμα τὲ καθάπαξ τῆς ἀθυμίας ἐπελανθάνοντο καὶ τῆς πρὸς τοὺς ἀγῶνας προθυμίας ἐνεπιμπλῶντο.

meaning for her, since the entire human race for her was already equal and kindred not only on account of their common human nature, but also because of their common Lord. But she was not satisfied even with these things, and so increased her struggle, not departing from the tomb and virtually making the grave her home: the place where he lay became her bed, the stone became her pillow, the steps of her feet were the flights of her mind to her son, her hymns of praise served as her dining table, the delicacies upon it were her recollections of his Passion, her tears were her drink and her bath, and the bending of her knees in prayer was her dance. Those who have written extensively about her and who speak the truth say that her spotless hands, as if they were knees, were heavily calloused from her ceaseless prostrations on the stone floor, those same hands with which she had formerly embraced her child conceived without seed, whom now she was supplicating. And if we also wished even now to describe her prayers and prostrations in detail, it would be necessary to write another book, and the secondary work would not be inferior to the main work. But what is surely not secondary work, and which pertains greatly to this present discourse as well as to other accounts concerning her, and which follows necessarily, is that, because she was her son's successor, she assumed the role of protector, teacher, and sovereign of all, of his friends and disciples, and of both men and women, and thus she took upon herself the cares of all. And all of them, turning their eyes toward her, and having in place of the Lord's bodily presence the one who gave birth to his body, they all at once forgot their disheartenment and were filled with eagerness for their labors.

97 Καὶ πρὸς πᾶσαν καὶ αὐτοὶ τῶν ἄλλων ἐτυποῦντο διδασκαλίαν καὶ πολιτείαν, καὶ πρὸς πᾶσαν ἄθλησιν παρετάττοντο, ἡ δὲ καθάπερ κοινὸς ἀλείπτης καὶ παιδοτρίβης ἤλειφε μὲν καὶ πρὸς τοὺς ἀγῶνας καὶ ὑπετίθει τοὺς τρόπους τῶν παλαισμάτων, καὶ ἐγγύθεν καὶ πόρρωθεν, καὶ προὐξένει τὰς νίκας. Ὃ δὲ ταύτης ἐξαιρετώτατον ὅτι καὶ συνέπασχε πάλιν καθάπερ τῷ ταύτης υἱῷ, οὕτω καὶ τοῖς ἀπ᾽ ἐκείνου κήρυξί τε καὶ μαθηταῖς, τοῦτο μὲν μάλιστα καὶ διὰ τὸν ταύτης υἱὸν ὑπὲρ οὗ καὶ πᾶς ἦν ὁ λόγος αὐτοῖς καὶ ὁ πόνος, τοῦτο δὲ καὶ ὡς μήτηρ ἤδη κοινὴ καὶ ὑπὲρ πάντων διακαιομένη τὰ σπλάγχνα, οὐ τῶν πασχόντων μόνον, ἀλλὰ δὴ καὶ τῶν δρώντων, καὶ τάχα πολὺ πλέον τούτων ἤπερ ἐκείνων, ὅσῳ καὶ τοῖς μὲν οὐ κίνδυνος τὸ παθεῖν ἀλλὰ σωτηρία, τοῖς δὲ καὶ πολλῷ χείρων ὁ τῶν πασχόντων κίνδυνος. Οὕτω καὶ δεσμουμένοις συνεδεσμεῖτο καὶ μαστιγουμένοις συνεμαστίζετο καὶ πᾶσι τοῖς ἀθλοῦσι συνήθλει κατὰ προαίρεσιν ἐν ἑνὶ σώματι τοὺς ἁπάντων ἄθλους ὑπεραθλοῦσα καὶ προστιθεῖσα τοῖς μὲν ἄθλοις τοὺς λόγους, οἷς αὐτοὺς ἤλειφε τά τε ἄλλα καὶ αὐτὸ τὸ δεσποτικὸν αὐτοῖς παράγουσα Πάθος, ὑπὲρ οὗ τούτοις καὶ τὰ παθήματα, τοῖς δὲ λόγοις τὸν ἑαυτῆς βίον ὅλον ἐξ ἀρχῆς ἕως τέλους καὶ ἕνα καὶ μυρίους ὄντα τοὺς ἄθλους, τὸ μὲν διὰ τὴν συνέχειαν, τὸ δὲ διὰ τὸ πλῆθος καὶ τὴν ποικιλίαν τῶν παθημάτων. Οὕτω κατ᾽ αὐτὸν τὸν καιρὸν καὶ τὸν τόπον καὶ τῷ πρώτῳ τῶν μαθητῶν Πέτρῳ συλληφθέντι καὶ καθειρχθέντι τῇ διαθέσει συνελαμβάνετο καὶ συγκατεκλείετο καὶ αὐτή τε πρώτη προσηύχετο καὶ τὴν ἐκκλησίαν

And so while they prepared themselves with the teaching and conduct of everyone else, and readied themselves for every contest, she, as their common trainer and tutor, both anointed them for their bouts, those that were imminent and those that were far off, and taught them how to wrestle, thus securing their victories. But what was most remarkable about her was that, just as she had once suffered with her son, so too she suffered again with his heralds and disciples. To be sure, she did this for the sake of her son, for he was the focus of their every word and labor, and also because she was already their common mother, and because her maternal feelings for them all were on fire, not only for those who were suffering but also for those who were accomplishing things, and perhaps more for these than the others, since for the former, suffering brought not danger but salvation, while for the latter, the danger is much greater than that of those who suffer. Thus, when they were bound in chains, she was bound together with them; when they were whipped, she was whipped together with them, and in all their contests she contended voluntarily with them and in her one body she surpassed the contests of all. In their contests, for which she had trained them, she offered them words of encouragement, and, among other things, presented them with the example of the Lord's Passion, which was also the reason for which they were suffering; and to her words she offered the example of her entire life, which from beginning to end was both a single contest and countless contests, single for their continuity and infinite for the multitude and variety of the sufferings. Thus at that time and in that place, when Peter was the first to be arrested and imprisoned, she was arrested in spirit and shared his confinement and was the first to pray for him and directed the church to pray for 97

ἐκίνει πρὸς προσευχήν. Οὕτω καὶ πολὺ πρότερον τῷ Στεφάνῳ συλλιθοβολεῖται καὶ τῷ Ἰακώβῳ συγκαρατομεῖται καὶ τοῖς λοιποῖς τοῖς ὑπὲρ τοῦ Λόγου προκινδυνεύουσι, τοῖς μὲν συγκακοπαθεῖ, τοῖς δὲ καὶ συναποσφάττεται.

98 Ὡς δὲ λόγος, καὶ συναποδημεῖ ποτε μέχρι τινὸς τῷ ἀγαπητῷ καὶ κατὰ θέσιν υἱῷ πρὸς τὸ κήρυγμα, δεῖγμα τοῦ λόγου φασίν, αἱ μυροφόροι πρὸς Ἀσίαν μετ' αὐτῆς στελλόμεναι. Καὶ οὐδὲν ἄπιστον ἴσως, τὴν συνοικίαν αὐτῷ λαχοῦσαν καὶ τὴν συνεκδημίαν ἀσπάσασθαι, τοσαῦτα γινομένην αὐτῷ ὅσα δὲ καὶ μητέρα, κἀκείνου πάλιν αὐτῇ ὅσα δὴ καὶ υἱοῦ, καὶ ἐχομένους ἀλλήλων ἀδιασπάστως. Ἄλλως τὲ καὶ παράβασιν ἡγουμένους τῆς ἐντολῆς τοῦ παραθέντος οὕτως αὐτοὺς ἀλλήλοις ἐν τῷ σταυρῷ καὶ τοσαύτῃ συνδήσαντος τῇ ἀγάπῃ, ὅσῃ καὶ αὐτὸς μὲν τῇ μητρί, ἡ δὲ μήτηρ αὐτῷ συνεδέδετο. Ἀλλὰ ταύτην μὲν ὁ αὐτὸς ἀποστρέφει πάλιν υἱὸς δι' ἀποκαλύψεως, ἧς ἠβούλετο, προβᾶσαν ἐπὶ μικρόν, ἀμφότερα κατὰ τοὺς ἀρρήτους αὐτοῦ τῆς σοφίας λόγους, καὶ συγχωρήσας τὲ καὶ κωλύσας. Ἐκεῖνο μὲν διὰ τὴν πρόβασιν τοῦ κηρύγματος καὶ τὸ πλείονα λαβεῖν ἐξ αὐτῆς τὴν ἐπίτασιν, τάχα δὲ καθὼς ἱστορεῖται καὶ τοῦ ἠγαπημένου πρὸς τὴν λαχοῦσαν αὐτῷ μοῖραν οὐ πάνυ προθύμως ἔχοντος, ἀλλὰ μηδὲ ἀνασχετῶς πρὸς τὴν τῆς κατὰ θέσιν αὐτῷ μητρὸς διάζευξιν· ἵν' οὖν προθυμότερον καὶ αὐτὸ ἀπεργάσηται, συγχωρεῖ τὴν ἀρχὴν καὶ αὐτὴν καὶ δι' αὐτὴν ἅμα τὰς μυροφόρους. Ἐπειδὴ δὲ τῆς προθυμίας ὥσπερ ἱκανῶς ἐφωδίαστο καὶ πάντα τὸν

him. Long before this, she was struck in spirit by the stones that struck Stephen, and was beheaded along with James. As for the others, who for the sake of the Word were bearing the brunt of the battle, she suffered along with some, and was slain along with others.

As one account has it, she also traveled abroad some- 98
where at some time or other with the beloved disciple, her adopted son, as part of the preaching mission, but only for a short period of time; and as evidence of this, they say that the myrrh-bearing women were sent to Asia with her. And there is nothing implausible about this if, if it was her portion to dwell together with him, she was also happy to travel with him, so greatly had she become a mother to him, while he, in turn, became a son to her, such that they were inseparable from one another. And, to be sure, they would have considered it a transgression of the commandment of the one who, on the cross, united them to each other and bound them with such love that he was bound to the mother, and she to him. But through a revelation according to his will, the same son ordered her to turn back, after she had gone a little way, both permitting and hindering her according to the ineffable principles of his wisdom. He permitted her, for the advancement of the preaching of the Gospel, and so that its success might receive support from her, for perhaps, as it has been written, the beloved disciple was not entirely eager for the assignment allotted to him, nor could he endure being parted from his adopted mother. And so that he might be more eager for his work, the Lord permitted her to travel with him in the beginning, and for the myrrh-bearing women to accompany her. But, after the disciple had, as it were, sufficiently provisioned himself with eagerness, and

ὄκνον καὶ τὸν φόβον ἀπετινάξατο, ταύτην μὲν ἀνακαλεῖται, τὰς δὲ καὶ οὕτω καὶ τῆς ἀποστολῆς ὁμοῦ συνεργοὺς καὶ τῆς ἀποδημίας ὑπουργοὺς καὶ προθυμοποιοὺς ἅμα δίδωσι. Κατὰ τοιούτους μὲν ἴσως ἢ καὶ ἔγγιστα τούτων λόγους καὶ ἡ ὁρμὴ τῆς ἀποδημίας, ἡ δὲ ὑποστροφὴ διά τε τὸ πρέπον ἅμα γυναικὶ καὶ αὐτοῦ μητρί. Δεῖν γὰρ καὶ αὐτὴν πάντως τὸ οἰκεῖον σῴζειν ἀξίωμα, καὶ μὴ κοινοῦσθαι τοῖς ἀποστόλοις, ἀλλ' ἀποστέλλειν μᾶλλον ἢ ἀποστέλλεσθαι, καθάπερ δὴ καὶ αὐτόν, καὶ τὸ πολλῷ μᾶλλον καὶ τὰ ἐν Ἱεροσολύμοις πράγματα πλείονος ὅτι μάλιστα δεῖσθαι καὶ κρείττονος τῆς ἐπιστασίας, ἃ καὶ ῥίζα καὶ ἀρχὴ τοῦ κηρύγματος, ἣν Ἰάκωβος μὲν προστεταγμένος διϊθύνειν ἦν, αὐτὸς δὲ αὐτῇ προσέχειν καὶ παρ' αὐτῆς διϊθύνεσθαι, καὶ οἷα καὶ δεσποίνῃ πάντα κατακούειν καὶ καθυπηρετεῖσθαι.

Τὴν μὲν οὖν οὕτω καὶ τῷ βραχεῖ τῆς πορείας τὴν ὅλην γῆν εὐλογήσασαν καὶ καθαγιάσασαν πάλιν ὑπεδέχοντο τὰ Ἱεροσόλυμα καὶ ὁ τοῦ Ἰωάννου προειρημένος οἶκος, οὗ μὴ παρόντος Ἰάκωβος, ὁ τοῦ Ἰωσὴφ παῖς, τὴν ὅλην ἐπιμέλειαν ἀνεπλήρου, δι' ἣν καὶ εἰς τὴν τῶν Αἰλιέων ἐπισκοπὴν προκρίνεται. Αἱ δὲ μυροφόροι τῷ Θεολόγῳ συναπάρασαι καὶ τὴν Ἀσίαν καταλαβοῦσαι καὶ συναπόστολοι καὶ συναθλοφόροι γενόμεναι διὰ πάντων αὐτοῦ, καταλύουσι τὸν βίον καὶ πρὸς τὸν ποθούμενον ἀναλύουσιν, αἱ μὲν κατὰ προαίρεσιν, αἱ δὲ καὶ κατὰ πρᾶξιν αὐτὴν καὶ μέχρις αἵματος διηγωνισμέναι, καὶ τὸν ὑπ' αὐτῶν κηρυττόμενον τοῖς πάθεσι μιμησάμεναι. Καὶ ταύτης δὲ τῆς ἀποδημίας καὶ τῆς ὁρμῆς οὕτω τῇ τοῦ Θεοῦ Μητρὶ θαυμαστῆς γενομένης,

shaken off all hesitation and fear, she was called back, and at the same time she gave him the myrrh-bearing women as coworkers of his apostolic mission and eager ministers for his long journey. Reasons such as these, or ones similar to them, were perhaps the motivation behind setting off on a long journey, while her return from such a journey was appropriate both for a woman and his mother. For it was also absolutely necessary for her to preserve her proper honor, and not share it with the apostles, but rather for her to send out, not to be sent, just as she sent John, and for the more significant reason that affairs in Jerusalem were certainly in need of more and better oversight, since things there were the root and beginning of the preaching of the Gospel, which James was appointed to direct. He was also appointed to take care of her and be directed by her, and, as with a sovereign, to be subject to her and serve her.

Thus, when, despite the brevity of her journey, she had blessed and sanctified the whole earth, she was welcomed back to Jerusalem and to the aforementioned house of John. However, because John was not present there, James, the son of Joseph, assumed all care for her, on account of which he was chosen to be the bishop of Aelia. Meanwhile, the myrrh-bearing women set out together with the Theologian, and they took control of Asia, becoming fellow apostles and fellow victors with him in every respect, and they separated themselves from this life and departed for the one they desired, some dying the death of conscience, others in actual deed and ending their lives in the blood of martyrdom, imitating the sufferings of the one whom they preached. And if the departure and journey of the Mother of God happened in such wondrous fashion, we find her re-

θαυμασιωτέραν εὑρίσκομεν τὴν ἐπάνοδον καὶ τὴν ἐν Ἱεροσολύμοις μονὴν καὶ διατριβήν. Ἄρτι μὲν διὰ τὸν ἐπὶ Στεφάνῳ φόνον καὶ φόβον πάντων τῶν μαθητῶν διασκεδασθέντων, οὐ διὰ τὴν δειλίαν δὲ μᾶλλον, ἀλλὰ καὶ τὴν τῆς διδασκαλίας χρείαν καὶ τὴν τῆς ἀληθείας ἐπίδοσιν, ταύτην δὲ μόνην ἐννοοῦντες καθ' ἑαυτὴν ἀπολειπομένην καὶ πάσας καὶ πάντας πρὸς ἑαυτὴν ἀναδεξαμένην τὰς φροντίδας καὶ τοὺς κινδύνους, ἐν μέσῳ δὲ τοσούτων φονώντων οὐ διαζῶσαν μόνον, ἀλλὰ καὶ ἀντιπολιτευομένην καὶ πρὸς μυρίους καθ' ἑκάστην ἀνθοπλιζομένην τοὺς πολεμίους, ὥστε μηδὲν εἶναι μηδὲ τὰ κατὰ Παῦλον τοῖς τότε ταύτης ἀντιπαραβαλλόμενα.

99 Καὶ ἵνα τἄλλα παρῶμεν, τὰς οὐδένα διαλειπούσας καιρὸν τοῦ Εὐαγγελίου φροντίδας, τοὺς ὑπὲρ εὐσεβείας ἀγῶνας, τοὺς τῶν ἐκκλησιῶν πολέμους, τοὺς τῶν πιστῶν διωγμούς, τῶν χρημάτων τὰς ἁρπαγάς, τῶν μελῶν τὰς ἀποβολάς, τοὺς θανάτους, τῶν πανταχοῦ περιερχομένων κηρύκων τοὺς κινδύνους καὶ τὰς ἐπιβουλάς—ἃ πάντα καὶ πρὸς αὐτὴν ἀνεφέρετο καὶ ὑπὲρ πάντων ὠδυνᾶτο καὶ περὶ πάντων ἀντὶ τοῦ υἱοῦ διετάττετο καὶ πρὸς αὐτὸν τὸν υἱὸν ἐπρεσβεύετο. Ἀλλὰ ποῖος ἂν εἴποι λόγος ἢ καταλάβοι νοῦς τὰς τῶν ἔνδον καὶ ἐν αὐτοῖς τοῖς Ἱεροσολύμοις τῶν μιαιφόνων λεηλασίας, τὰς βίας, τὰς ἀπειλάς, τὰς σφαγάς; Ἃ τὰ μὲν καὶ ἐν ὄψει ταύτης τολμώμενα, τὰ δὲ καὶ δι' ἀκοῆς εἰς καρδίαν παραπεμπόμενα οὐ γενναίως ἔφερε μόνον, ἀλλὰ καὶ γενναιότερον διετίθετο πρὸς τὸ συμφερώτερον ἀποχρωμένη καὶ μεταβάλλουσα, καὶ οὕτως αὔξουσα πανταχόθεν τὴν δύναμιν τοῦ κηρύγματος· δι' ἅ μοι δοκεῖ

turn to Jerusalem and her dwelling and life there to be even more wondrous. For it was at that time that, with the killing of Stephen and the fear resulting from it, all the disciples were scattered, not because of cowardice, but because of the need to teach and convey the truth. But when we consider that she was left alone by herself, and had taken upon herself every care and danger, living not only in the midst of so many murderers but also being opposed by and having to defend herself against a myriad of enemies every day, then even the opposition Paul experienced was nothing compared to what she then faced.

Setting aside other matters, let us say that the unceasing 99
care for the preaching of the Gospel, the struggles on behalf of piety, the wars waged against the churches, the persecutions of the faithful, the seizure of property, the severing of limbs, and the deaths, dangers, and plots confronting itinerant preachers everywhere—all these were brought to her attention and she experienced pain for all of them, and, in place of her son, she gave detailed instructions concerning them all, and interceded with her son himself. But what speech could describe, or what mind could comprehend, the plundering, the violence, the threats, and the killings by those murderers that were taking place in Jerusalem itself? Some of these brazen attacks took place in her sight, others were brought to her hearing and entered her heart, and not only did she bear these nobly but also handled them still more nobly, making use of them and turning them into something more profitable, and thus everywhere she increased the power of the preaching. It certainly seems to me

πάντως καὶ ἐπὶ μήκιστον ἐλάσαι τοῦ τῆς ζωῆς χρόνου καὶ εἰς ἔσχατον ἐλθεῖν γήρως, ἵν' οὕτω τὰ τοῦ κηρύγματος ῥιζωθῇ τὲ ἅμα καὶ πλατυνθῇ καὶ μέχρι περάτων ἐλάσῃ γῆς ὑπὸ ταύτης, τὰ μὲν τελούμενα, τὰ δὲ καὶ οἰκονομούμενα. Καὶ ταύτην ἔχοντες οἱ ἀπόστολοι καὶ πάντες οἱ μαθηταὶ καθάπερ κέντρον ἢ ῥίζαν τὲ καὶ ψυχήν, ἀπ' αὐτῆς τὲ ὁρμῶνται τὴν ζωτικὴν λαμβάνοντες δύναμιν, καὶ αὖθις ἢ κατορθοῦντες ἢ καὶ ἐλλείποντες πρὸς αὐτὴν ἀνακάμπτουσι, καὶ πάλιν τυπούμενοι καὶ προθυμοποιούμενοί τε ἅμα καὶ διορθούμενοι τοῦ ἔργου τῆς ἀποστολῆς ἢ τῆς διακονίας ἔχονται. Φασὶ γοῦν μηδὲ καθάπαξ αὐτῆς ἔτι ζώσης ἀποστῆναι μηδένα τῶν ἀποστόλων μηδὲ καθολικὴν ἀναδέξασθαι τὴν ἀποδημίαν πλὴν Θωμᾶ τοῦ τὴν Ἰνδίαν λαχόντος, τοὺς δὲ λοιποὺς πάντας τῇ μὲν κηρύσσειν, τῇ δὲ καὶ πρὸς αὐτὴν ἐπιστρέφειν εἰς τὰ Ἱεροσόλυμα.

100 Ἀλλ' οἷα κἀκεῖνα καὶ ἅπερ ὁ λόγος μικροῦ παρέδραμεν, οἱ κατὰ τοῦ ταύτης υἱοῦ καὶ ἔτι ζέοντες τῶν θεοκτόνων θυμοί, τὰ κατὰ τῶν παθῶν ὀνείδη, τὰ κατὰ τοῦ θανάτου σκώμματα, τὰ κατ' αὐτῶν τῶν αὐτοῦ θαυματοποιϊῶν τοὐναντίον μᾶλλον αἰτιάματα καὶ ἀντικατηγορήματα, αἱ κατὰ τῆς ἀνθρωπότητος ὕβρεις, αἱ κατὰ τῆς θεότητος βλασφημίαι, οἱ καθ' ὅλης ὁμοῦ τῆς οἰκονομίας μυκτηρισμοί, οἱ κατ' αὐτῆς ἐκείνης ἐπιτωθασμοὶ καὶ διαβολαὶ καὶ συκοφαντίαι τῆς παρθενίας, καὶ τῆς θεοτοκίας αἱ εἰρωνεῖαι, τῆς ἀναστάσεως καὶ ἀναλήψεως οἱ διαχλευασμοί τε καὶ καταγέλωτες. Ἔτι πορρωτέρω, ταῦτα καὶ φορητότερα, οἱ προσιόντες ἐγγυτέρω καὶ ὑλακτοῦντες καὶ καθυβρίζοντες, ἔστι δὲ ὅτε καὶ καταλεύοντες οἱ τὸν οἶκον περιϊστάμενοι καὶ

that in this way she spent the greatest part of her life and arrived at the extremity of her old age, making sure that the preaching of the Gospel would thus take root and at the same time be spread and be carried by her to the ends of the earth, with some things brought to completion and others governed by divine dispensation. And all the apostles and disciples had her as the center or root of their souls, and it was from her that they received their vital power when they set out; and if they had accomplished something, or had failed in something, it was to her that they returned, and having been once again taught, encouraged, and at the same time corrected by her, they returned to the work of mission or service. Indeed, they say that, as long as she was alive, not once did she lose contact with any of the apostles, neither did she accept their permanent absence abroad, except for Thomas, who was assigned to India; with respect to all the others, they would spend time preaching, but then would return to her in Jerusalem.

But these were the sort of things that I almost omitted 100
from my discourse, namely, the still-burning rage of the God killers directed against her son; the reproaches against his sufferings; the jokes about his death; the accusations and recriminations made against his working of miracles; the insults to his humanity; the blasphemies against his divinity; the disdain directed against the whole of his divine economy; the mockeries and slanders and the calumnies directed against his mother's virginity, and the dissimulation over her divine birth giving; the jests and derision about the resurrection and ascension. In addition to these, but more bearable, were those who would approach her barking like dogs and hurling insults at her, and who sometimes surrounded her

καταβοῶντες καὶ προσαράσσοντες καὶ αὐτὴν αὐτῇ συνεμπιπρᾶν τῇ οἰκίᾳ φιλονεικοῦντες. Ταῦτα γὰρ πάντα φασὶν ἐν ἀρχῇ συμβαίνειν, ὡς δέ τινες ὅτι καὶ ἔργου ποτὲ διαφερόντως ἐκμανέντες εἴχοντο, καὶ τὸ πῦρ ἐπὶ χεῖρας καὶ οἱ λίθοι καὶ οἱ μοχλοί, καὶ τὰς ἑλεπόλεις προσῆγον, ἀλλὰ τὴν ἀπόρθητον καὶ ὑπὸ Θεοῦ πολιουχουμένην πόλιν οὐχ' εἷλον, εἰ μὴ καὶ στερροτέραν, ὅτι μάλιστα καὶ ἐνδοξοτέραν ταῖς προσβολαῖς ἀπειργάσαντο. Τὸ μὲν γὰρ πῦρ ἐφέρετο κατ' αὐτῶν, τὰ δὲ μηχανήματα διεστρέφετο καὶ οἱ λίθοι κατὰ τῶν ἀφιέντων ἀντεστρέφοντο, καὶ οὕτως αὐτοῖς τὸ ἐπιχείρημα διελύετο.

101 Ἀπιστήσει δὲ τούτοις πάντως οὐδεὶς ἢ ὅστις οὐκ οἶδε τὴν Ἰουδαίων μιαιφονίαν, μηδὲ τὴν κατ' αὐτοῦ τοῦ Σωτῆρος μανίαν, μηδὲ τὰ ἐξ ἀρχῆς μέχρι τοῦ νῦν ἀσεβήματα καὶ τολμήματα καὶ ἔτι πλέον τὴν κατ' αὐτοῦ τοῦ ζωοδόχου μνήματος ὕστερον ὕβριν, ὅπου γε καὶ τοσαυτάκις ἐπιχειρήσαντες καὶ τοσαυτάκις ἀνατραπέντες καὶ διὰ τοσούτων ἐπιστομισθέντες καὶ ἀπονεκρωθέντες θαυμάτων, οὐδὲ οὕτω νεκροῦ τοῦ σώματος ἀπέχεσθαι διὰ φθόνου καὶ μανίας ὑπερβολὴν ἠδύναντο. Ἀλλὰ ταῦτα μὲν μετ' ὀλίγον. Τίνα δὲ καὶ τὰ ἐπὶ τούτοις; Οὐκέτι λοιπὸν ἡ Παρθένος καὶ τοῦ Θεοῦ Μήτηρ εὐκαταφρόνητος, ἀλλ' αἰδοία καὶ φοβερὰ καὶ αὐτοῖς τοῖς λυττῶσι καὶ μιαιφόνοις κυσί, καὶ Ἰουδαίοις καὶ Ἕλλησιν, οὐ διὰ ταῦτα μόνον, ἀλλὰ καὶ δαίμονας μὲν ἀπελαύνουσα, νόσους δὲ ἀνιάτους ἐκθεραπεύουσα καὶ μυρία τερατουργοῦσα· πρὸς δὲ καὶ ἀπ' αὐτῆς ἐκείνης τῆς ὄψεως, οὐκ ὀλίγον φῶς καὶ δόξαν ὁμοῦ περιλάμπουσα καὶ πᾶσι προσβάλλουσα χάριν ἅμα καὶ φόβον, ὥστε

house, shouting and throwing stones at it, charging at it, and trying to set her on fire together with the house. They say that all these things happened in the beginning when there were some people who, being particularly out of their minds, wanted to engage in battle at some point, and they arrived with firebrands, stones, iron bars and siege engines, but were unable to take the impregnable and God-protected city; to the contrary they only made it stronger and more glorious by means of these attacks. For the fire was turned back against them, their siege machines were twisted out of shape, and the stones recoiled against those who had thrown them, and thus their attempt came to naught.

Absolutely no one would doubt these things except 101
someone unaware of the bloodthirstiness of the Jews, their frenzied opposition to the Savior, and their impieties and outrages from the very beginning until the present day, and indeed their subsequent assault upon the life-giving tomb of Christ, though as many times as they attempted to attack it, just as many times were they repelled, and through an abundance of miracles were silenced and benumbed; and not even when his body was dead were they able, out of envy, to restrain the excess of their madness. But this was for a short while. What happened to them afterward? The Virgin and Mother of God was no longer easily held in contempt by them but was revered and feared even among those rabid and bloodthirsty dogs, both Jews and Greeks, not only because of these things but also because she cast out demons, cured incurable diseases, and performed a multitude of other miracles. With respect to her face, great light and glory shone forth from it, transmitting grace and fear to all, so that, just as she was untouched by corruption, so too was

καθάπερ αὐτὴν φθορᾶς, οὕτω καὶ ὕβρεως καὶ βλασφημίας λοιπὸν ἀνέπαφον εἶναι, καὶ τὸν οἶκον αὐτῆς ἐχθροῖς ἀνεπίβατον, οὐ μόνον ἀλλὰ καὶ σεβαστόν τι καὶ ἱερὸν αὐτῇ τέμενος, ὥσπερ καὶ αὐτὴν τὴν Σιὼν τῷ ταύτης υἱῷ, ὃν καὶ Σιὼν τὸν αὐτὸν καὶ Γεθσημανῆ τὸν ἀγρὸν πάντες ἐκάλουν, τὸ μὲν κυρίως, τὸ δὲ ἐπιθέτως.

102 Ἡ δὲ καὶ τοσαύτης αἰδοῦς ἤδη καὶ τιμῆς κἀντεῦθεν παρὰ πάντων ἀξιουμένη καὶ εἰς βαθεῖαν τὴν πολιὰν οὐκ ὀλίγῳ πλεῖον ἢ ὀγδοηκοστὸν ἀναβιβαζομένη τὸ ἔτος, καὶ πάντων οὕτω καὶ νοητῶν καὶ ὁρατῶν πολεμίων κρατήσασα καὶ πάσης ὡς εἰπεῖν τῆς κτίσεως βασιλεύσασα, οὐδ' οὕτω τῆς ἀσκήσεως οὐδὲ τῆς τοῦ υἱοῦ καὶ Θεοῦ προσεδρείας ἠμέλει καὶ τῆς δεήσεως, ἀλλὰ καθάπερ ἁμιλλωμένη πρὸς ἑαυτήν, καὶ τοσοῦτον ἀεὶ τῇ συντονίᾳ προσέχειν, ὅσον καὶ τῇ ἀξίᾳ σπουδάζουσα, μικρὰ μὲν ἡγεῖτο τὰ προλαβόντα, μείζονα δὲ ἀεὶ τὰ δεύτερα τῆς ἀσκήσεως ἐπετήδευεν. Οὕτω γοῦν ἱστορεῖται περὶ αὐτῆς παρ' ἐκείνων ὧν καὶ οἱ ὀφθαλμοὶ μάρτυρες, ὧν εἷς καὶ Ἀνδρέας ὁ ἐξ Ἱεροσολύμων μέν, ἀρχιεπίσκοπος δὲ Κρήτης, οὕτω κατὰ λέξιν ἐκδιηγούμενος, ὅτι καὶ μέχρι τῶν αὐτοῦ χρόνων τὰ κοιλώματα τῶν γονάτων αὐτῆς ἐν τοῖς μαρμάροις τῆς ἁγίας Σιὼν δεικνύμενα καὶ ἡ ἀνάκλισις δὲ ἡ ἐπὶ τοῦ λίθου τετυπωμένη, ὅπου μικρὸν γοῦν τοῦ φυσικοῦ μετελάγχανεν ὕπνου. Προσῆν δὲ τούτοις πᾶσι καὶ ἡ ἀκτημοσύνη καὶ ἡ ἐλεημοσύνη νικῶσα καὶ τὴν ἀκτημοσύνην, τὸ χρυσοῦν ὄντως ζεῦγος καὶ ὑπ' ἀλλήλων βοηθούμενον πλέον καὶ θαυμαζόμενον, τὸ ἐν πενίᾳ πλούσιον καὶ τὸ ἐν ἀπορίᾳ μεγαλόψυχον ἢ καὶ πλέον εἰπεῖν μεγαλόδωρον. Ὃ δὲ τῆς

she henceforth untouched by insolence and blasphemy. Her home was inaccessible to her enemies, and not only this but it was also a venerable and sacred temple for her, as Zion itself was for her son, and everyone called her house Zion, while everyone called the field Gethsemane, the one being its proper name, the other an epithet.

From then on she was treated by everyone with great rev- 102
erence and honor and reached a ripe old age, living well beyond her eightieth year. Though she triumphed over all her invisible and visible foes and reigned, so to speak, as queen over all creation, she in no way relaxed her ascetic discipline or her devotion and supplication to her son and God, but rather lived as if she were competing with herself; and in the same way as she was always paying attention to the intensity of her practice, so too she was equally earnest to determine its value, reckoning her earlier sufferings to be of little account, while always striving harder at her later ascetic pursuits. It has thus been recorded concerning her by those who were eyewitnesses, one of whom is Andrew from Jerusalem, who later became the archbishop of Crete, who states explicitly that, up until his own day, the hollows made by her knees could be seen in the marble floor of her house in Zion, and the imprint of her reclining body could be seen on the stone where she took a small measure of bodily sleep. In addition to all these things, she possessed the virtue of poverty, and her generosity in almsgiving overcame poverty, that golden pair in which each is helped and admired by the other: wealth in poverty, and magnanimity, or I should rather say munificence, in penury. And the most beautiful

ἐλεημοσύνης τὸ κάλλιστον, ὅτι μὴ πρὸς τοὺς φίλους μόνον, μηδὲ πρὸς τοὺς οἰκείους, ἀλλὰ καὶ πρὸς τοὺς ἀλλοτρίους, ἀλλὰ καὶ πρὸς τοὺς ἐχθρούς. Μήτηρ γὰρ ἦν ὄντως ἐλέους, μήτηρ τοῦ Πατρὸς *τῶν οἰκτιρμῶν,* μήτηρ τοῦ *τὸν ἥλιον* ἀνατέλλοντος ὁμοίως *ἐπὶ πονηροὺς καὶ ἀγαθοὺς καὶ* βρέχοντος *ἐπὶ δικαίους καὶ ἀδίκους,* μᾶλλον δὲ καὶ μήτηρ ἐκείνου τοῦ σαρκωθέντος καὶ σταυρωθέντος ὑπὲρ ἡμῶν τῶν ἐχθρῶν, καὶ παρ' ἡμῶν αὐτῶν τῶν ἐχθρῶν, τοῦ πτωχοῦ καὶ πένητος δι' ἐμὲ καὶ πάντας πλουτίζοντος. Ἀλλ' ὁ μὲν τῶν περὶ αὐτῆς ὑπὲρ φύσιν ἐξ ἀρχῆς καὶ μέχρι τέλους ἀγώνων λόγος ὧδε καταπαύεσθω. Μόνον δὲ ἐκεῖνο καθάπερ σύντομον ἐπιφώνημα πρὸς ἐπὶ πᾶσι λεγέσθω, ὅτι καθάπερ ὑπὲρ φύσιν ἐγέννησεν, οὕτω καὶ ὑπὲρ φύσιν ἔζησε, καὶ πάντας τοὺς πρὸ αὐτῆς καὶ κατ' αὐτὴν ἐκείνην καὶ μετ' αὐτήν, τοὺς μὲν τῷ πλήθει, τοὺς δὲ καὶ τῷ μεγέθει τῶν παλαισμάτων νενίκηκε, μᾶλλον δὲ καὶ τῷ πλήθει πᾶν πλῆθος καὶ τῷ μεγέθει πᾶν μέγεθος ὑπερέβαλεν, ἐν συνεχείᾳ μὲν ἐξ ἀρχῆς οὐδ' ὅσον οἷον διαλείπουσα καὶ μέχρι τῆς τελευτῆς, ἐν ἀκριβείᾳ δὲ καὶ ὑπερβολῇ πᾶσαν ἄθλησιν διαθλήσασα, καὶ τοσοῦτον αὐτῆς καὶ πάντων ἐκείνων τὸ μέσον—οὐ κατὰ τὴν δόξαν λέγω μόνον καὶ τὴν ἀξίαν, ἧς μηδὲν ἢ τὸ τῆς Τριάδος ἐστὶν ὑψηλότερον, ἀλλὰ καὶ κατὰ τὴν πολιτείαν καὶ τῶν ἀθλήσεων τὴν ὑπερβολήν—ὅσον ἰδιώτου καὶ βασιλέως, ἡλίου τὲ καὶ ἀστέρος, εἰ δὲ καὶ μὴ τολμηρὸν εἰπεῖν, καὶ ἀνθρώπου τὲ καὶ Θεοῦ.

thing about her generosity was that she did not offer it only to her friends or to those of her household, but also to strangers and enemies. For she was truly the mother of mercy, the mother of the Father *of mercies,* the mother of the one who makes *the sun* to rise *on the evil and on the good alike, and* sends rain on *the just and the unjust,* and indeed she is the mother of the one who became incarnate and was crucified for our sake, though we were his enemies, and who for my sake made himself indigent and poor but made everyone rich. But let my discourse concerning her struggles, which from beginning to end were beyond nature, come to a conclusion here. But let this one thing yet be said in addition to everything, as a succinct finishing touch: just as she gave birth in a manner beyond nature, so too did she live her life in a manner beyond nature, and she surpassed all those who lived before her, all her contemporaries, and all those who came after her. Some she surpassed by the multitude of her struggles, others by their magnitude as well, or rather by their multitude she surpassed all multitudes, and by their great magnitude she surpassed all magnitude, having contended in all her struggles continuously from the beginning and without any pause whatsoever until the end of her life, but also with precision and rigor. As a result, the difference between her and all of them is as great—and I do not refer only to her reputation and her dignity, of which nothing but the Trinity is higher, but also to her way of life and the preeminence of her struggles—as the difference between a king and a private citizen, the sun and a star, and, if it is not too bold to say, God and man.

Περὶ τῆς Κοιμήσεως

103 Ταῦτα μὲν οὕτως ἔχει τὲ καὶ ἐχέτω, καὶ συγκεκλείσθω ταύτης τὰ ἐναγώνια. Τὰ δὲ νικητήρια, καὶ δὴ λεγέσθω καὶ προπεμπτήρια, δι' ἃ καὶ νῦν ἡ πανήγυρις, καὶ τὸ ταύτῃ τοῦ βίου πέρας καὶ τῶν ἀγώνων, πέρας ἔστω καὶ ἡμῖν τοῦ λόγου καὶ συγκαταλυέσθω τὰ ἀγωνίσματα. Ἐπειδὴ γὰρ ἔμελλεν ὁμοῦ πάντα καὶ τὴν φύσιν ἅμα πιστώσασθαι, καὶ τοῦτο τοῦ ταύτης υἱοῦ μιμήσασθαι, τὸ καὶ αὐτὴν ὁμοίως τοῦ θανάτου γεύσασθαι, καὶ τῶν ἀγώνων καὶ τῶν ἄθλων ποτὲ τὰ βραβεῖα δέξασθαι, καὶ μυρίαθλον καὶ στεφανηφόρον, *ἐν ἱματισμῷ διαχρύσῳ περιβεβλημένην πεποικιλμένην*, βασίλισσάν τε πάσης ἀναρρηθῆναι τῆς γεννητῆς φύσεως καὶ ἐκ δεξιῶν παραστῆναι τοῦ ταύτης υἱοῦ τὲ καὶ βασιλέως, ὅλης δὲ μᾶλλον εἰπεῖν τῆς Τριάδος, εἰσελθοῦσαν εἰς τὸ ἐνδοξότερον καὶ ἐνδότερον τοῦ καταπετάσματος, ἐπεὶ ταῦτα καὶ θανάτου ποτὲ μετασχεῖν ἢ μᾶλλον πρὸς τὴν Ζωὴν ἀπελθεῖν τὴν καὶ τῆς ὄντως Ζωῆς μητέρα ἐχρῆν, προαποκαλύπτεται μὲν οὐ πρὸ ὀλίγου τὴν ἰδίαν κλῆσίν τε καὶ μετάθεσιν, πέμπεται δὲ αὐτῇ μετὰ ταῦτα καὶ πάλιν ἀρχάγγελος τῶνδε τῶν εὐαγγελίων ἄγγελος. Κομίζεται δὲ καὶ τῆς κατὰ πάντων ἅμα νίκης αὐτῇ βραβεῖον καὶ τῆς ἀϊδίου ζωῆς σημεῖον, ὥσπερ καὶ τῷ ταύτης υἱῷ καὶ νικοποιῷ τῆς κατὰ τῶν παθῶν καὶ τοῦ θανάτου νίκης, φοίνικος ἀειζώου κλάδος.

104 Ὡς οὖν καὶ τὸ σύνθημα τῆς πρὸς τὸν υἱὸν αὐτῆς καὶ Θεὸν ἀποδημίας ἔμαθέ τε καὶ ἐθεάσατο, ποῖος ἂν ἐφίκοιτο λόγος εἴτε καὶ νοῦς τῆς ἡδονῆς ἐκείνης, ἥτις τὴν ψυχὴν

The Dormition

This is how things were, so let us leave them be and conclude the account of her contests. But let the memorials of her victory, which should also be called her funeral valedictions, and which are the occasion for this present celebration marking the end of her life and struggles, also mark the end of my discourse, and let them, at the same time, bring my rhetorical struggles to an end. For when she was about to confirm once and for all everything concerning her and her nature, and follow the example of her son and likewise taste death, and at last, as the hero of myriad contests and the bearer of the victor's crown, receive the prizes of her contests and struggles, and, *clothed in vesture wrought in gold and arrayed in diverse colors* be proclaimed queen of all created nature, and when she was about to take her place at the right hand of her son and king, or rather at the side of the whole Trinity, having entered into the more glorious and inner place behind the veil of the sanctuary, and since it was necessary that the mother of true Life partake of death, or rather depart to that Life, her calling and her translation were revealed to her well in advance and an archangel was again sent to her concerning these matters and as a messenger of the good news. And he brought her an evergreen palm branch as both the prize of her victory over all things and a sign of eternal life, just as it was of her victorious son's victory over sufferings and death. 103

What words or what mind could grasp the joy which overtook her soul when she learned of and saw the agreed-upon sign of her departure to her son and God? She hastened 104

αὐτῆς κατελάμβανεν; Ἀπέτρεχε πρὸς τὸ Ὄρος τῶν Ἐλαιῶν καθ' ἡσυχίαν προσάγειν τὰ εὐχαριστήριά τε ἅμα καὶ ἱκετήρια, τοῦτο μὲν ὑπὲρ ἑαυτῆς, τοῦτο δὲ καὶ ὑπὲρ τοῦ κόσμου παντός. Ἀπέβλεπε πρὸς τὸν οὐρανόν, ἔβλεπε δὲ καὶ τὸν ταύτης υἱόν. Γίνεται γοῦν, ὥς φασιν οἱ μυηθέντες τὰ μυστικώτερα, καὶ θαῦμά τι παραυτίκα, μήνυμα τῆς ἁπάντων ὑποταγῆς αὐτῇ καὶ τῆς προσκυνήσεως· ἡ μὲν γὰρ τὸν υἱόν, τὰ δὲ δένδρα τῶν ἐλαιῶν—ἀμφιλαφὲς δὲ τὸ ὄρος καὶ ἡδὺ καὶ κατάσκιον—εἰς γῆν ὑποκατακλινόμενα προσεκύνουν αὐτήν.

Οὕτως ἐκεῖθεν ἐμφορηθεῖσα τῶν προσευχῶν καὶ τῶν θεωριῶν ὁμοῦ καὶ τοῦ θαύματος ὑποστρέφει πρὸς τὴν Σιὼν ἔνθους ὅλη καὶ ὥσπερ αὐτὸν ἤδη περιπολοῦσα τὸν οὐρανὸν καὶ τὸν οἶκον εὐτρεπίζειν παρακελεύεται καὶ φῶτα καὶ μύρα τοῦτον κατέλαμπε καὶ κατευωδίαζε. Καὶ ἡ μὲν οὕτω κάτω τὸν οἶκον εὐτρεπίζεται τῷ υἱῷ καὶ οἷα παστάδι καλῇ τὸν καλὸν νυμφίον προσδέχεται, ὁ δὲ ἄνω τῇ μητρὶ καθὰ νύμφῃ καὶ βασιλίδι τὰ τῶν Ἁγίων Ἅγια, θάλαμον καὶ σκῆπτρα καὶ θρόνον. Καὶ κάτωθεν μὲν διὰ νεφελῶν ἦγε τοὺς ἀποστόλους, ἄνωθεν δὲ διὰ τοῦ αἰθέρος τὲ καὶ ἀέρος τοὺς ἀγγέλους κατῆγε. Συνήγετο δὲ καὶ πᾶν ὅσον γειτονικὸν καὶ συγγενικόν τε καὶ φίλιον, μετεκαλοῦντο καὶ τῶν ἀποστόλων καὶ τῶν ἄλλων μαθητῶν ὅσοι παρεπιδημοῦντες ἢ καὶ πλησίον περιπολοῦντες ἐτύγχανον. Οἱ γὰρ ἄλλοι διὰ νεφελῶν ὕστερον ἀνηρπάζοντο. Καὶ μὴν καὶ ἀφ' ἑαυτῶν οὐκ ὀλίγοι τῆς φήμης αὐτοὺς καλούσης, ἀλλὰ καὶ πᾶν ὅσον ἐν Ἱεροσολύμοις εὐσεβές τε καὶ ἔκκριτον, ὥστε καὶ τὴν παρεμβολὴν μεγάλην γενέσθαι

to the Mount of Olives to offer thanks and prayers in tranquility, both for herself and for the entire world. She looked toward heaven and beheld her son. And then, according to those who have been initiated into more mystical things, a miracle immediately took place, which was a sign that all things are subject to and venerate her, for as she was venerating her son, the olive trees—for the mountain was thickly wooded and pleasantly shaded—bent to the ground and venerated her.

Filled in this way with prayers and contemplations, and inspired by the miracle, she returned to Zion wholly absorbed in God, as if she were already traversing heaven itself. And she directed that her house be prepared so that it was lit with lamps and made fragrant with myrrh. While she was thus preparing her house on earth to receive her son, and was awaiting the beautiful bridegroom as if in a beautiful bridal chamber, he was at the same time preparing the Holy of Holies above, a radiant hall with a scepter and a throne, for his mother as for a bride and queen. On earth below, he brought together the apostles by means of clouds, while from heaven above he brought down the angels through the upper ether and the lower air. At the same time, he brought together all her neighbors, relatives, and friends, and called together as many of the apostles and other disciples who happened to be residing nearby or were in the region. The other apostles were carried there later by means of clouds. And not a few others came on their own, drawn there by reports of what was taking place, together with all the pious and eminent people in Jerusalem, so that an exceedingly great multitude formed. Some of them

σφόδρα, τῶν μὲν πόρρωθεν κυκλουμένων τὸν οἶκον, καθάπερ καὶ τὸ ὄρος πάλαι τοῦ Ἰσραήλ, τῶν δὲ πλησιαίτερον ἱσταμένων, τῶν δὲ καὶ εἰσαγομένων, ἄλλων δὲ καὶ περιϊσταμένων, ἑκάστων κατὰ τὴν ἀναλογίαν τῆς πρὸς αὐτὴν οἰκειότητος ἢ τῆς ἀξίας.

Ἔμελλε γὰρ καὶ πάλιν ὁ Θεὸς καταβαίνειν ἐπὶ *τὸ ὄρος τὸ ἐμφανὲς καὶ κατάσκιον,* εἴτ᾽ οὖν περίβλεπτον καὶ ἀρεταῖς κατάκομον, τὸ ὄρος τὸ ἀλατόμητον, ἀφ᾽ οὗπερ ὁ λίθος ὁ ἀκρογωνιαῖός τε καὶ ἀλάξευτος, τὸ ὄρος τὸ ὑπὲρ πᾶν ὄρος—ἐκεῖνο μὲν ὡς συνδέων τὰ διεστῶτα καὶ οὐ τὰ κάτω μόνον, ἀλλὰ καὶ τὰ ἐπίγεια καὶ τὰ οὐράνια, τοῦτο δὲ καὶ ὡς πᾶν συντρίβων ὕψος ἀξίας τὲ καὶ φρονήματος, ἀλλὰ καὶ πάντας ὑπερβαίνων ὅρους φύσεώς τε καὶ κτίσεως—*τὸ ὄρος ὃ εὐδόκησεν ὁ Θεὸς* οὐχ ἅπαξ κατοικῆσαι μόνον, ἀλλὰ καὶ *κατοικεῖν ἐν αὐτῷ.*

105 Τοιγαροῦν καὶ Μωσῆς πάλιν Ἰωάννης ἦν, ὁ μετὰ τὸν φύσει υἱὸν υἱός, ὁ καὶ τῆς νεφέλης εἴσω χωρῶν καὶ δεχόμενος πλάκας τῆς Παρθένου τὰς διαθήκας· ᾧ κἀκεῖνος μὲν ἀπιὼν τὴν Παρθένον, ἡ δὲ Παρθένος αὖθις πρὸς ἐκεῖνον ἐπαπιοῦσα τὰ μυστικώτερα τῶν θαυμάτων προσανατίθεται. Αἱ δὲ διαθῆκαι, τῆς ἀκτησίας ἅμα καὶ τῆς φιλανθρωπίας μαρτυρίαι τὲ ὁμοῦ καὶ νομοθεσίαι, καὶ τῆς παραδόξου δυάδος παρθενίας τὲ καὶ κυοφορίας σύμβολα, χιτωνίσκοι δύο. Ζώσῃ μὲν τῇ Μητρὶ καὶ Παρθένῳ σκέπη τὸν ἅπαντα χρόνον κατὰ διαδοχὴν τοῦ σώματος, ἀπιούσῃ δὲ γυναιξὶ κλῆρος χήραις καὶ μαθητρίαις, οὐ σκέπη μόνον,

surrounded the house at a distance, just as the Israelites once stood around the mountain, while others stood nearer, and still others took their places inside the house, while others stood around the Virgin, each one in a position determined by his familiarity with her, or according to his rank.

This took place because God was going to descend once again upon the *conspicuous and overshadowed mountain,* which is admired by all and richly adorned with virtues; that is, the unhewn mountain from which that stone, the unquarried cornerstone, was taken, the mountain higher than all mountains—and he would do this, on the one hand, in order to bind together the things that are separated, and not only lowly things but also heavenly and earthly things, and on the other hand to crush every peak of eminence and highmindedness, and indeed transcend all the boundaries of nature and creation—*the mountain upon which God is pleased* not simply to dwell once but *upon which he chooses to make his dwelling.*

The evangelist John, who after her son by nature was her 105
adopted son, accordingly became a new Moses. He entered into the cloud and received the tablets of the Virgin's testaments. It was to him that Christ entrusted the Virgin when he departed; and when in turn she was departing, she entrusted to John the deeper secrets of the miraculous things that had taken place. Her two legacies, which were at once testimonies and ordinances of her poverty and love of mankind, in addition to being symbols of the paradoxical dyad of her virginity and motherhood, were two small garments. When the Mother and Virgin was alive, these garments in turn covered her body all the time, but when she departed, they were given to two widowed female disciples, not simply

ἀλλὰ καὶ ἁγιασμὸς ψυχῆς ὁμοῦ τὲ καὶ σώματος, ἵνα μὴ παρθενία καὶ γέννησις μόνον, ἀλλὰ καὶ χηρεία δι' αὐτῶν πάντως ἁγιασθῇ, διάδοχος οὖσα τῆς παρθενίας καὶ τῆς γεννήσεως.

Οὕτω τῶν συμβόλων καὶ τῶν προοιμίων δοθέντων τῆς ἀναγεννήσεως καὶ τῆς ἀναλύσεως, ἔρρει μὲν ἀπὸ πάντων ὀφθαλμῶν ὡς εἰκὸς δάκρυα, ἀπὸ δὲ πάσης γλώσσης εὐφημίαι τὲ καὶ ἐγκώμια. Ἡ μὲν γὰρ μακαρίζεται μᾶλλον, ἀποκλαίεται δὲ πᾶν τὸ ὑπολειπόμενον—καὶ πῶς γὰρ οὐκ ἔμελλεν;—οὐ τὴν τοῦ Θεοῦ Μητέρα μόνον, ἀλλὰ καὶ τὴν κοινήν, μᾶλλον δὲ καὶ πολλῷ πλέον ἢ μητέρα τὰ πρὸς αὐτούς, καὶ καθάπερ ὑπὲρ φύσιν τὴν φύσιν, οὕτω καὶ τὴν πρὸς ἀνθρώπους σχέσιν τὲ καὶ προαίρεσιν, ὁρῶντες ἀφ' ἑαυτῶν μὲν αὐτὴν ἀφισταμένην, τοὺς δὲ κοινοὺς τῆς εὐσεβείας καὶ τῆς σωτηρίας ἐχθροὺς οὕτω πάντοθεν κινουμένους καὶ προσκειμένους, καὶ νῦν ἀκριβῆ μάλιστα τὴν ὀρφανίαν ὑφισταμένους, ὅσῳ τοῦ μὲν ταύτης υἱοῦ καὶ κοινοῦ Πατρὸς ἀπιόντος, αὕτη τὴν ἐκείνου τάξιν καὶ σχέσιν ὑπεισελθοῦσα καὶ μήτηρ ἁπάντων ὁμοῦ καὶ διδάσκαλος καὶ ποιμὴν καὶ στρατηγὸς ἦν, τοὺς μὲν ἀγκαλιζομένη, τοῖς δὲ ὑποτιθεμένη, τῶν δὲ προπολεμοῦσα, ὑπὲρ δὲ τῶν καὶ καταπολεμοῦσα τοὺς πολεμίους. Ἤδη δὲ καὶ ταύτης μετατιθεμένης, οὐδὲν λοιπὸν τὸ πρὸς σωτηρίαν ἢ παραμυθίαν ὑπολειπόμενον, εἰ καὶ διϊσταμένη σωματικῶς καθάπερ καὶ ὁ ταύτης υἱός, οὐδαμῶς οὐδαμῇ πνευματικῶς αὐτῶν ἐχωρίζετο.

Πρὸς οὓς ἐκείνη τοὺς παραμυθητικοὺς ὁμοῦ καὶ ἐξιτηρίους φθεγξαμένη τῶν λόγων, καὶ ἡ ἀφελοῦσα πᾶν

as coverings for the body but as sanctification for soul and body alike, so that, not only virginity and motherhood, but also widowhood might be honored through them as well, since it is the successor of virginity and motherhood.

As the Virgin was distributing the symbols and heralds of her rebirth and departure, it seemed that tears flowed from every eye, while praises and lamentations flowed from every tongue. For while the Virgin was being blessed, all those left behind were mourning—and how could they do otherwise?—when they saw the departure from their midst not only of the Mother of God, but also the common mother of all, who for them was indeed something even greater than a mother, for just as her nature is above nature, so too is her relationship and goodwill toward human beings. And as they also saw the common enemies of the true faith and salvation drawing near and moving about on all sides, they realized acutely how completely they were orphaned, insofar as after her son, the Son of their common Father, departed, she had assumed his position and role and became the mother of all, as well as their teacher, shepherd, and general, embracing and instructing some, defending others and also defeating their enemies. But, now that she was already in the process of being translated, it seemed that henceforth there would be no one left as their help and consolation, even if, despite being separated from them physically, she would, just like her son, never be separated from them spiritually.

The Virgin offered them words of consolation and farewell, and she who wiped away every tear from the face of the

δάκρυον ἀπὸ προσώπου τῆς γῆς, οὐδὲ τὰ ἐκείνων ἀφεῖσα τῆς ἀθυμίας δάκρυα, δεῖν γὰρ αὐτοὺς μὴ μόνον μὴ ἀνιᾶσθαι μηδὲ δακρύειν, ἀλλὰ καὶ χαίροντας καὶ εὐφημοῦντας προπέμπειν τήν τε διαδεξομένην αὐτὴν εἰδότας χαρὰν καὶ δόξαν καὶ βασιλείαν τὴν καὶ ἐκείνους δι' αὐτῆς καταληψομένην ὡς πλησίον νῦν μάλιστά τε τοῦ υἱοῦ γινομένης, καὶ ἀμέσως καὶ μετὰ πλείονος τῆς παρρησίας τοὺς ὑπὲρ αὐτῶν ποιουμένης λόγους, ἀλλ' "ὅπως καὶ τὸ ἐμόν," φησί, "σῶμα παραδῶτε ταφῇ κατὰ σχῆμα, ὃ ἂν ἐγὼ διάθωμαι ἐμαυτήν." Οὕτω πάντα διαθεμένη καλῶς ἐπὶ τοῦ σκίμποδος ἀνακλίνεται, ᾄδειν παρακελευσαμένη καὶ δὴ τὰ ἐξόδια. Τῶν δὲ μεταβαλλομένων ἔρρει καὶ πάλιν δάκρυα τῶν προτέρων ἀμείνω· τὰ μὲν γὰρ τῆς ἀθυμίας ἦν, ταῦτα δὲ τῆς πρὸς αὐτὴν ἱκετείας καὶ τῆς δεήσεως, ὥστε καὶ νῦν τῆς παρ' αὐτῆς εὐλογίας τυχεῖν καὶ ἀπελθούσης μὴ διαλιπεῖν τῆς ὑπὲρ αὐτῶν πρεσβείας καὶ προστασίας. Οἷς ἡ τοῦ φιλανθρώπου μήτηρ ἐκείνη καὶ πρὸς φιλίαν καὶ φιλανθρωπίαν ἑτοίμη, τὰ μὲν ἐπλήρου, τὰ δὲ ὑπισχνεῖτο.

106 Καὶ οὕτως εὐλογηθέντων ἀνάπτονται μὲν αἱ λαμπάδες, ἀνακαίονται δὲ τὰ λύχνα, καὶ τὰ μύρα δὲ προσευωδιάζονται. Καὶ ἰδοὺ νεφέλαι παρῆγον τοὺς ἀποστόλους καὶ οὕτω συνεπληροῦτο τῇ τοῦ Θεοῦ Μητρὶ καὶ Δεσποίνῃ κοινῇ τὸ τῆς ἐκδημίας θέατρον, πάντων ὁμοῦ τῶν μὲν ἐν Ἱεροσολύμοις παρόντων, τῶν δὲ αὐτοῦ που πλησίον συγκεκλημένων ἢ συνδεδραμηκότων, τῶν δὲ καὶ μακρὰν ἀφεστώτων ἀνηρπασμένων καὶ οὐδενὸς ἀπολειπομένου πλὴν Ἰακώβου, οὐχὶ τοῦ ἀδελφοῦ τοῦ Κυρίου, οὗτος μὲν γὰρ παρῆν, τοῦ ἀδελφοῦ δὲ Ἰωάννου, τῷ Ἡρώδῃ προανηρπασμένου

earth did not permit them to shed tears of despair, for it was not only right that they should not grieve and weep but should also bid her farewell with joy and praise, since they knew she was entering the joy and glory of the kingdom, and that, as she would be especially near to her son and speak to him on their behalf directly and with great boldness, it would be through her that they too would one day enter into the kingdom. "Place my body," she said, "in the tomb, in the position in which I myself shall arrange it." Having thus arranged all things well, she reclined on her bed and instructed them to sing funeral songs. However, when they began to sing, they started once again to weep, this time even more greatly than before, since the former were tears of despair whereas these were tears of prayer and supplication, entreating her in that moment for her blessing, and asking that after her departure she would never cease to intercede for them and protect them. In response to these requests, the mother of the one who loves mankind, who herself is always ready to show love and compassion, granted the former and promised the latter.

Having been blessed by her, the lights were lit and the 106
lamps kindled, and the fragrance of myrrh filled the house. And, lo and behold, the apostles arrived on clouds and thus the stage was set for the departure of the Mother of God and our common sovereign Lady, since all were now present: those from Jerusalem, those from nearby who were invited or had come together on their own, and those who had been far away and had been taken up by the clouds. And no one was absent, except for James, not the brother of the Lord, for he was present, but the brother of John, whom Herod

καὶ ἀναιρεθέντος μαχαίρᾳ. Οὐ χεῖρον δὲ οὐδὲ περιττὸν ἴσως ἐπιμνησθῆναι καὶ ἃ Διονυσίῳ τῷ Ἀρεοπαγίτῃ πρός τινα Τιμόθεον ἐπίσκοπον προσπεφώνηται, τῆς τῶν ἀποστόλων καὶ τῶν ἄλλων συνδρομῆς ἀπόδειξις ἐναργής τε καὶ ἀπαράγραπτος. Ἔστι μὲν γὰρ ὁ λόγος Ἱεροθέου τὲ πέρι καὶ τῆς ἱερᾶς εὐχῆς τὲ καὶ συγγραφῆς θεολογικῆς. Ἔχει δὲ κατὰ λέξιν οὕτως·

"Καίτοι καὶ τοῦθ' ἡμῖν ἐπιτετήρηται λίαν ἐπιμελῶς. . . . Ἐπεὶ καὶ παρ' αὐτοῖς τοῖς θεολήπτοις ἡμῶν ἱεράρχαις, ἡνίκα καὶ ἡμεῖς, ὡς οἶσθα, καὶ αὐτὸς καὶ πολλοὶ τῶν ἱερῶν ἡμῶν ἀδελφῶν ἐπὶ τὴν θέαν τοῦ ζωαρχικοῦ σώματος συνεληλύθαμεν, παρῆν δὲ καὶ Ἰάκωβος ὁ ἀδελφόθεος καὶ Πέτρος, ἡ κορυφαία καὶ πρεσβυτάτη τῶν θεολόγων ἀκρότης, εἶτα μετὰ τὴν θέαν ἐδόκει ὑμνῆσαι τοὺς ἱεράρχας ἅπαντας, ὡς ἕκαστος ἦν ἱκανός, τὴν ἀπειροδύναμον ἀγαθότητα τῆς θεαρχικῆς εὐσθενείας, πάντων ἐκράτει μετὰ τοὺς θεολόγους, ὡς οἶσθα, τῶν ἄλλων ἱερομυστῶν ὁ Ἱερόθεος, ὅλος ἐκδημῶν, ὅλος ἐξιστάμενος ἑαυτοῦ, καὶ τὴν πρὸς τὰ ὑμνούμενα κοινωνίαν πάσχων καὶ πρὸς πάντων, ὧν ἠκούετο καὶ ἑωρᾶτο καὶ ἐγινώσκετο (καὶ οὐκ ἐγινώσκετο), θεόληπτος εἶναι καὶ θεῖος ὑμνολόγος κρινόμενος. Καὶ τί ἂν σοι περὶ τῶν ἐκεῖ θεολογηθέντων λέγοιμι; Καὶ γάρ, εἰ μὴ καὶ ἐμαυτοῦ ἐπιλέλησμαι, πολλοὺς οἶδα παρὰ σοῦ καὶ μέλη τινὰ τῶν ἐνθεαστικῶν ἐκείνων ὑμνωδιῶν ἐπακούσας."

Ἃ μὲν οὖν ὁ ἱερὸς Διονύσιος τὴν τῆς εὐχῆς δύναμιν ἐξηγούμενος, ἀναγκαίως καὶ τῶν κατ' αὐτὴν εὐδοκιμησάντων καὶ διὰ τοῦτο καὶ ἑαυτοῦ τὲ καὶ Τιμοθέου καὶ Ἱεροθέου

had seized and put to death by the sword. It would perhaps be neither disagreeable nor superfluous to recount the things that Dionysios the Areopagite told his fellow bishop Timothy, since it constitutes a clear and irreproachable proof of the gathering of the apostles and others who were with them. I am referring to the discourse about Hierotheos and sacred prayer and the nature of theological writing. Here is the text:

"This is observed by us with great care . . . when our inspired hierarchs, at that moment when, as you know, we and you and many of our holy brethren had come together and were gathered at the viewing of that body which was the source of life, James, the brother of God, was there, and Peter, the head and most senior leader of the theologians. After the viewing, it was determined that each of the hierarchs, to the best of his ability, should sing praises to the infinitely powerful goodness of the supremely divine strength. It was then that, after the theologians, Hierotheos, as you know, surpassed all the other sacred initiators, wholly entering a state of ecstasy, wholly going outside himself, and experiencing communion with the realities being praised, so that everyone who heard him and saw him, and who knew him (or, rather, did not know him), considered him to be inspired and a divine singer of songs. And why should I say anything to you concerning the things there that were divinely spoken? For, if I do not forget myself, often have I heard from your mouth certain portions of those inspired songs of praise."

These are the things that Dionysios taught regarding the power of prayer. In explaining this power, it was necessary for him also to mention those who distinguished themselves in prayer. This is why he mentions himself, Timothy,

καὶ λοιπῶν θεολήπτων καὶ αὐτοῦ Πέτρου τοῦ κορυφαίου μέμνηται, ταῦτά ἐστιν. Ἀπορῆσαι δὲ ἄξιον, τί δήποτε μὴ καὶ Παύλου, καίτοι καὶ αὐτοῦ παρόντος ὡς ἔκ τε τῶν παρ' ἄλλοις ἱστορουμένων ἔστιν εὑρεῖν, καὶ αὐτῶν δὲ τῶν ἐξ ἐκείνου καὶ μέχρι τοῦ νῦν τοῖς γραφεῦσι κατὰ παράδοσιν διαγραφομένων. Καὶ αὐτὸς δὲ ὅλος ὁ λόγος αἱρεῖ τοσοῦτον καὶ τηλικοῦτον ἄνδρα τὴν ἀρετὴν ἅμα καὶ τὴν ἀποστολήν, καὶ πρῶτον καὶ αὐτὸν ἤδη καὶ κορυφαῖον, μᾶλλον δὲ καὶ ὑπὲρ τοὺς ἄλλους κεκοπιακότα, μὴ ἀπολειφθῆναι τῶν προπεμπτηρίων τοῦ θεοδόχου καὶ δεσποτικοῦ σώματος ἐκείνου καὶ τῆς ψυχῆς.

Τοσούτου πράγματος τί οὖν ἐστιν εἰπεῖν, ὡς ἡ αὐτὴ λύσις, ἣν καὶ περὶ ταύτης αὐτῆς ἐν τοῖς προλαβοῦσιν ἀνιστορήτου καταλειφθείσης ὁ λόγος εἴρηκεν, ὅτι διὰ τὴν πρὸς αὐτὸν σχέσιν τὲ καὶ οἰκείωσιν παρεῖται τὰ κατ' αὐτὸν τῷ Διονυσίῳ μαθητευσαμένῳ τὲ κατ' ἀρχὰς αὐτῷ καὶ παρηκολουθηκότι τὸν πλεῖστον αὐτοῦ χρόνον; Ὁ μὲν γὰρ ὕστερον, μετὰ τὴν εἰς οὐρανοὺς Ἀνάληψιν τοῦ Δεσπότου, χρόνοις, φασίν, ἓξ καὶ μικρόν τι πρός, ἐφ' οὓς ὅλους διώκτης ἦν, ἐξ αὐτοῦ τοῦ διωκομένου περιαστράπτεται καὶ βαπτίζεται. Καὶ εὐθὺς μὲν ἀνέρχεται πρὸς Ἱεροσόλυμα καὶ μερικῶς ἀντιλαμβάνεται τοῦ κηρύγματος, μετὰ δὲ τρία ἔτη καὶ τῆς καθολικῆς ἀποστολῆς ἀπάρχεται. Μετὰ δὲ τέσσαρα καὶ δέκα, καθὼς καὶ αὐτὸς ἱστορεῖ περὶ ἑαυτοῦ, κατὰ ἀποκάλυψιν πάλιν εἰς Ἱερουσαλὴμ ἐπανέρχεται, ἐφ' οὓς ὅλους αὐτῷ Διονύσιος ἀκόλουθος καὶ σύνοικος ἦν, καθάπερ καὶ Ἱερόθεος. Ἀλλ' ὁ μὲν Διονύσιος οὕτως εὐλαβεῖται τὸ περὶ αὐτοῦ λέγειν. Εἴτε γὰρ ἐμνήσθη ψιλῶς, οὐ

Hierotheos, and the other inspired hierarchs, as well as Peter, their head. You may be right to wonder why he does not also mention Paul, even though he too was there, a fact which can be ascertained from the accounts by other authors, and in the writings following this tradition of authors from his time down to the present. Indeed this entire body of work shows that a man so great in virtue and in his work as an apostle, who was himself the first and greatest of the apostles, who worked harder than the others, would not have been absent from the ceremony bidding farewell to that God-receiving, sovereign body and soul.

What sort of response can one give to such a significant matter, if not the same solution that my discourse set forth above regarding the Mother of God herself, that is, the relationship and attachment that Dionysios had with Paul, who from the beginning was his disciple and followed him for most of his life? After the Lord's Ascension into the heavens, Paul, they say, persecuted the Church for a little more than six years, but was then illumined by the very one whom he was persecuting, and was baptized. He immediately went up to Jerusalem, specifically took up the work of preaching the Gospel, and three years later, began his universal apostolic mission. After another fourteen years, according to his own testimony about himself, he was told in a revelation to return to Jerusalem. Throughout all of these years, Dionysios was his follower and companion, as was Hierotheos. But Dionysius is reticent in speaking about Paul. Had he simply mentioned his name, this would not have been

κατὰ μαθητήν, ἀλλ' οὐδὲ κατὰ Παῦλον ἂν ἦν, εἴτε μετ' ἐγκωμίων τῶν ἁρμοζόντων Παύλῳ, πάλιν φίλαυτος καὶ φιλοδιδάσκαλος ἔδοξεν ἄν, καὶ διὰ τοῦτο καὶ οὐ πάνυ πιστός. Διὰ τοῦτο τὸν περὶ αὐτοῦ λόγον τοῖς ἄλλοις ἀφίησιν, αὐτὸς δὲ τὰ περὶ τῶν ἄλλων ἱστορεῖ μᾶλλον.

Ἃ δέ τισιν ἀνδράσιν οὐ φαύλοις οὐδὲ ὀλίγοις ἱστορεῖται περὶ αὐτοῦ Παύλου καὶ τῆς κατὰ Παῦλον ἁρπαγῆς, ὡς ἡρπάγη μὲν διὰ νεφέλης ἀπὸ Ἐφέσου διὰ τὴν προκειμένην τῆς κοινῆς Δεσποίνης ἀπὸ γῆς εἰς οὐρανοὺς πρόοδον, ἡρπάγη δὲ κατὰ τὴν ἁρπαγήν, ἣν καὶ αὐτὸς ἡμῖν ἀπεκάλυψε, ταύτην δὲ διαφωνουμένην παρὰ πολλοῖς εἶναι. Τοῖς μὲν γὰρ *ἕως τρίτου οὐρανοῦ* τῆς κατ' οὐρανὸν ζώνης τῶν ἀστέρων ἔδοξε λέγειν, καθάπερ καὶ τῇ γραφῇ πολλαχοῦ φίλον "οὐρανὸν" τὸν "ἀέρα" καὶ πολλῷ μᾶλλον τὸν "αἰθέρα" καλεῖν, ὥσπερ καὶ "*τὰ πετεινὰ τοῦ οὐρανοῦ*" καὶ οἱ κατ' οὐρανὸν "ἀστέρες" τὲ καὶ "τὰ ἄστρα," ὧν τὰ μὲν ὑψηλότερα, οἱ δὲ ταπεινότεροι, καὶ τούτων αὐτῶν πάλιν ἄλλος ἄλλου ταπεινότερος ἢ ὑψηλότερος, ὧν καὶ τοῖς ἀποστήμασιν αἱ ζῶναι συνδιορίζονται, κἀκεῖθεν δὲ αὐτὸν κατοπτεῦσαι καὶ τὰ ὑπὲρ τὸν ὠκεανὸν ἢ πρὸς τῷ ὠκεανῷ πάντα καὶ αὐτὸν τὸν παράδεισον. Ἄλλοι δὲ "τρίτον οὐρανὸν" τὸν νοητὸν καὶ μετὰ τοὺς δύο τοὺς αἰσθητούς, ὧν ὁ μὲν καὶ τῇ ἐνεργείᾳ καὶ τῇ αἰσθήσει ληπτός, *τὸ στερέωμα,* ὁ δὲ κατὰ δύναμιν τῇ φύσει μὲν ὁρατός, ὁ πρῶτος, ἐπιπροσθούμενος δὲ ὅμως ὑπὸ τοῦ στερεώματος καὶ κρυπτός.

appropriate either for him, as his student, or for Paul; but had he praised Paul in a manner that was fitting, again he would have appeared boastful of himself and his teacher, and thus cast doubts on the objectivity of his testimony. This is why he leaves it to others to write about Paul, while he confines himself to writing about the other apostles.

Certain men, by no means insignificant in either intelligence or number, have written about Paul and his rapture, saying that he was caught up in a cloud from Ephesus so that he might be present at the departure of our common sovereign Lady from earth to heaven, and that this rapture was the same one he himself revealed to us, though this is contested by many. For some think that with the phrase, *as far as the third heaven,* Paul was referring to the sphere of the planets in the heavens, since scripture frequently likes to say "heaven" when it means "air" and especially "aether," as when it speaks of "the birds of heaven," or the "planets" or "fixed stars" of heaven, the stars being higher up and the planets lower. Of these latter, some are higher and lower than each other, their spheres being determined by their relative elevation. Those who hold these views conclude that Paul from there saw everything that lies beyond the ocean, or which is near the ocean, including paradise itself. Others believe that the "third heaven" is the intelligible heaven, which exists beyond the two sensible heavens, one of which, the *firmament,* may be grasped by the senses owing to its activities; whereas the other, the first one, is potentially visible by nature, but is concealed by the firmament and thus hidden from our sight.

Ὡς δὲ ἡμῖν ἔδοξε μᾶλλον, ὃ καὶ θεωρεῖν ὑψηλότερόν τε ἅμα καὶ οἰκειότερον καὶ τῆς κατὰ Παῦλον θεωρίας ἄξιον, ὁ "τρίτος οὐρανὸς" εἴη ἂν τὸ τρίτον τάγμα τῶν οὐρανίων, ἃ καὶ αὐτὰ πολλάκις "οὐρανοὺς" οἶδεν ἡ γραφὴ καλεῖν, εἰ δὲ καὶ μὴ τούτους αὐτούς, ἀλλά γε τὰς τάξεις αὐτῶν καὶ τὰς στάσεις, ὥσπερ καὶ τὰς παρ' ἡμῖν τῶν ἀστέρων ζώνας. Ἡ δὲ τάξις, ἀπὸ μὲν τῶν κάτωθεν ἀρχομένοις ἡ τῶν ἀρχῶν γένοιτο ἄν, ἀπὸ δὲ τῶν ἄνωθεν ἡ τῶν σεραφίμ· οἷς καὶ δι' ἀμφοτέρων γενόμενος τῶν ἀθεάτων τὲ θεατὴς καὶ τῶν ἀρρήτων ἀκροατὴς γίνεται. Εἶδέ τε γὰρ καὶ αὐτὸς τὸν Χριστὸν ἐν σαρκί, ἵνα μηδὲ τοῦτο τῶν ἄλλων ἀποστόλων ἀπολειφθῇ, καὶ τῶν ἀρρήτων ἐκείνων ἤκουσε παρ' αὐτοῦ ῥημάτων ἢ μυστηρίων· οὐ μόνον δέ, ἀλλὰ καὶ τῶν ἄλλων ἀπέλαυσε κατ' οὐρανὸν θεαμάτων καὶ ἀκουσμάτων, τῶν ἀγγελικῶν τὲ καὶ τῶν ἄλλων ταγμάτων καταμαθὼν τὴν εὐρυθμίαν καὶ τὴν ἀξίαν καὶ ὡραιότητα καὶ τῶν παρ' αὐτῶν δοξολογιῶν τὴν σοφίαν καὶ τὴν τερπνότητα. Ὧν καὶ τὰ πλεῖστα καὶ ὅσα γε καὶ γλώσσῃ ῥητὰ καὶ ἀκοῇ χωρητὰ δῆλός ἐστι τοῖς μαθηταῖς, Διονυσίῳ τὲ καὶ Ἱεροθέῳ παρακαταθέμενος, ὥσπερ καὶ αὐτὸς Διονύσιος ἀνομολογῶν περὶ ἑαυτοῦ τὲ καὶ Ἱεροθέου δείκνυται. Ἀλλὰ τὰ μὲν περὶ τῶν οὐρανῶν καὶ τῶν ἁρπαγῶν, εἴτε μία τις ἦν εἴτε καὶ ἄλλη μὲν ἐκείνη, ἄλλη δὲ αὕτη, καὶ ὁποία καὶ ὅπως ἑκατέρα, ἐχέτω ὅπῃ τις βούλεται πλὴν ὅτι καὶ οὗτος διὰ νεφέλης παρῆν, εἰ καὶ τῷ Διονυσίῳ δι' ἣν εἶπον αἰτίαν παρεῖται.

But what seems likelier to me, and which could also be considered both more sublime and more appropriate, and at the same time worthy of Paul's vision, is that the "third heaven" would be the third order of heavenly angels, which scripture often calls "heavens," though not so much the angels themselves as their ranks and positions, just as we call the spheres of stars the "heavens." The third rank, commencing from below, would be the principalities, but from above would be the seraphim. Being raised beyond the first two orders, Paul became a seer of things beyond vision, and a hearer of things beyond utterance. For he also saw Christ in the flesh, so that he would not be lacking anything with respect to the other apostles, and it was from Christ that he heard those ineffable words or mysteries. And this was not all, since he also enjoyed other heavenly visions and sounds, and he learned the harmonious arrangement, dignity, and beauty of the angelic and other heavenly orders, as well as the wisdom and delectation of their doxologies. It is obvious that Paul confided the greater part of these marvels, those, at least, which can be spoken by the tongue and heard by the ear, to his disciples Dionysios and Hierotheos, as Dionysios attests when speaking about himself and Hierotheos. But enough about heavens and raptures, and whether there was only one such rapture, or if the one described in scripture was different from this one, and of what sort they were and how they took place. Let it be as each one wants, since it is sufficient for us to acknowledge that Paul was present there, having been brought there on a cloud, even though, for the reasons given above, Dionysios is silent about this.

107 Οἷς ἡ τοῦ Θεοῦ μήτηρ ἤδη γινώσκουσι καὶ αὐτοῖς τὸ σύμβολον δείξασα τῆς ἀποδημίας, τὸ βραβεῖον τοῦ φοίνικος, ἀλλὰ καὶ εὐλογίας καὶ παραμυθίας μεταδοῦσα τῆς προσηκούσης καὶ προσειποῦσα τὰ ἐξιτήρια, πρὸς δὲ καὶ προθυμοποιήσασα πρὸς τὸ κήρυγμα καὶ ὑποθεμένη πᾶσαν αὐτοῖς ἐν βραχεῖ τῆς ἀποστολῆς τὴν οἰκονομίαν, εἶτα καὶ Πέτρον ἀσπασαμένη, μετὰ δὲ καὶ τοὺς ἄλλους, ἀλλὰ καὶ "Χαίρετε," φησίν, "ὦ τέκνα καὶ φίλοι καὶ μαθηταὶ τοῦ ἐμοῦ υἱοῦ καὶ Θεοῦ, καὶ μακαρίους ἑαυτοὺς ἡγεῖσθε, τοιούτου Δεσπότου καὶ διδασκάλου καὶ τοιούτοις ἀξιωθέντες διακονεῖν μυστηρίοις καὶ τῶν αὐτοῦ κοινωνεῖν διωγμῶν τὲ καὶ παθημάτων, ἵνα καὶ τῆς δόξης γένησθε κοινωνοὶ καὶ τῆς βασιλείας." Οὕτως αὐτοῖς εὐαγγελισαμένη τὰ τελευταῖα, ἐκείνοις μὲν ἐπιτάττει τὰ τῶν ἐξοδίων, αὕτη δὲ τῶν εὐχαριστηρίων ἤρχετο· "Εὐλογῶ σε," λέγουσα, "Δέσποτα καὶ Θεὲ καὶ Υἱὲ μὲν Θεοῦ τοῦ σοῦ προανάρχου Πατρός, υἱὲ δὲ διὰ φιλανθρωπίαν καὶ ἐμοῦ τῆς σῆς δούλης. Εὐλογῶ σε τὸν ῥυσάμενον τῆς κατάρας καὶ τὴν εὐλογίαν ἡμῖν χαρισάμενον. Εὐλογῶ σε τὸν αἴτιον ἡμῖν παντὸς ἀγαθοῦ, τῆς ζωῆς, τοῦ φωτός, τῆς εἰρήνης, αὐτοῦ τοῦ εἰδέναι σὲ καὶ τὸν σὸν Πατέρα καὶ τὸ συνάναρχον καὶ συζωοποιὸν Πνεῦμα. Εὐλογῶ σε Λόγε τὸν εὐλογήσαντα τὴν ἐμὴν γαστέρα καὶ ὑπὲρ λόγον ταύτην οἰκήσαντα. Εὐλογῶ σε τὸν οὕτως ἡμᾶς ἀγαπήσαντα, ὡς καὶ ὑπὲρ ἡμῶν σταυρωθῆναί τε καὶ ἀποθανεῖν. Εὐλογῶ σε τὸν μακαρίσαντα τὴν ἐμὴν κοιλίαν, καὶ πιστεύω ὅτι καὶ τοῖς ἄλλοις ἔσται τελείωσις τοῖς λελαλημένοις μοι παρὰ σοῦ."

The Mother of God showed the apostles that which they 107
already recognized, namely, the symbol of her departure, the prize of the palm branch. She also conveyed to them blessings and appropriate consolations, and, having spoken of her departure and encouraging them in their work of preaching, she briefly explained to them the meaning of the entire divine dispensation of their apostolic work. Then she embraced Peter and afterward the other apostles, saying: "Rejoice, my children, friends, and disciples of my son and God, and consider yourselves blessed to have been found worthy of such a great Master and teacher, and to be the ministers of such mysteries, and to partake in his persecutions and sufferings, so that you might also become partakers in the glory of his kingdom." Having thus proclaimed to them the good news of the end they would meet, she directed them concerning the details of her burial, after which she began to give thanks, and said: "I bless you, my Master and God, you who are both the Son of God your Father before all eternity, and the son of me, your handmaid, on account of your love of mankind. I bless you, who have delivered us from the curse and bestowed your blessing upon us. I bless you, who are the cause of every good thing for us, of life, of light, and of peace, and who have enabled us to know yourself, your Father, and your coeternal and life-creating Spirit. I bless you, Word, who blessed my womb and who dwelt in it in a manner beyond comprehension. I bless you, who so greatly loved us that you endured crucifixion and death for our sake. I bless you who blessed my womb, and I believe that the other things you promised me will be fulfilled."

108 Τούτοις καὶ ἡ παράδοξος εὐθὺς ἐπηκολούθει κάθοδος τοῦ ταύτης υἱοῦ, προφητῶν καὶ πατριαρχῶν καὶ πάντων δικαίων, ἤδη δὲ καὶ ἀγγέλων καὶ ἀρχαγγέλων καὶ τῶν ἄλλων δυνάμεων προερχομένων, καὶ οὕτω πληρουμένου μὲν τοῦ ἀέρος, πληρουμένου δὲ καὶ τοῦ οἴκου. Ἅπερ ἐκείνη μὲν πάντα καὶ προεγίνωσκε καὶ τότε φανερώτερον ἐθεᾶτο, τῶν δὲ ἄλλων ἄλλοι ἄλλα, ὅσοι τῶν τοιούτων θεαμάτων ἄξιοι. Καὶ οὕτως ἡ δευτέρα κατάβασις τῆς πρώτης ἐνδοξοτέρα τὲ καὶ φρικωδεστέρα καὶ τοῖς ὁρῶσι φανερωτέρα, οὐ τῶν ἄλλων μόνον ταγμάτων τὲ καὶ δυνάμεων, ἀλλὰ καὶ αὐτῶν τῶν σεραφὶμ καὶ χερουβίμ τε καὶ θρόνων ἐμφόβως τὲ καὶ εὐρύθμως κατὰ τάξιν παρισταμένων. Καὶ οὐχ ἧττον, εἰ μὴ καὶ μᾶλλον, εἰ μὴ μέγα εἰπεῖν, ἐκπληττομένων τὴν δευτέραν αὐτοῦ πάλιν κένωσιν ἢ συγκατάβασιν, ὅσῳ τότε μὲν ἕνεκα τοῦ παντὸς γένους, νυνὶ δὲ καὶ μιᾶς ἕνεκα ψυχῆς τὲ καὶ γυναικὸς τοσαύτην ἐνεδείκνυτο τὴν καινοτομίαν.

Ἀλλ’ ἡ μὲν προπομπὴ λαμπρὰ καὶ πολλὴ καὶ προσελεύσει Δεσπότου καὶ ἀπελεύσει Δεσποίνης πρέπουσα· ἡ δὲ θεωρία, καθάπερ ἔφην, μόνοις ὁρατὴ τοῖς κεκαθαρμένοις. Ἡ δὲ καὶ αὐτὴ τοῦ Δεσπότου παρουσία οὐδὲ αὐτοῖς χωρητὴ τοῖς Πνεύματος Ἁγίου χωρητικοῖς καὶ πεπληρωμένοις μαθηταῖς τὲ καὶ ἀποστόλοις. Ἀλλ’ ὁ μὲν ἐφίστατο μετὰ θεοειδεστέρου σώματός τε καὶ σχήματος, πλεῖον μὲν ἀστραπῆς καὶ τῆς ἐν τῷ Θαβωρίῳ καταλάμψας μορφῆς, ἔλαττον δὲ ὅμως ἢ κατὰ τὴν ἑαυτοῦ φύσιν· οἱ δὲ καὶ οὕτως ἔκειντο ὡσεὶ νεκροί. Καὶ ὁ μὲν ἔλεγεν εὐθὺς “*εἰρήνη ὑμῖν,*”

These words were followed immediately by the extraordinary descent of her son, accompanied by prophets, patriarchs, and all the righteous, preceded by angels, archangels, and the other heavenly powers; and with the air being filled in this way, the house was filled as well. The Virgin had known about all these things in advance but now she was seeing them clearly, whereas the others who were present saw them to the extent that they were worthy of such visions. Thus, the second descent was more glorious and awesome than the first, and plainer to those who saw it, not only the orders of angels and powers but also the very seraphim, cherubim, and thrones, who stood in reverent fear and in the order of their ranking. And they were no less struck, indeed, if it is not too much to say, they were even more greatly astonished by the Lord's second self-emptying or condescension, for what once took place for the sake of the whole human race was now taking place for one soul and for one woman. 108

Now the funeral procession was great and magnificent, as was fitting for the arrival of the Master and the departure of the Maiden. The sight of these things, as I said a moment ago, was visible only to those who were thoroughly purified. The very presence of the Master was incomprehensible even to the disciples and apostles, who had been able to receive and be filled with the Holy Spirit. The Lord was present among them in a more divine body and appearance, shining more brightly than lightning and more radiant than the brilliance that shone on Tabor, though it was less than his natural glory. And those who were present there nonetheless fell to the ground as if dead. But the Lord immediately said to them: "*Peace be with you,*" just as he had said to

οἷα καὶ πάλαι *τῶν θυρῶν κεκλεισμένων,* ἐπεὶ καὶ κατ' αὐτὸν ἐκεῖνον τὸν οἶκον πάλαι τὲ καὶ νῦν συνηγμένοις, τὸν Ἰωάννου, ὃς καὶ τότε *διὰ τὸν φόβον* αὐτοὺς κατεῖχε *τῶν Ἰουδαίων* καὶ νῦν διὰ τὴν τεκοῦσαν αὐτὸν συνῆγεν ἐν αὐτῷ συνδιαιτωμένην τῷ ἠγαπημένῳ μαθητῇ καὶ παρθένῳ καὶ δευτέρῳ κατὰ θέσιν υἱῷ· οἱ δὲ τῆς ἡδίστης καὶ φίλης ἀκούσαντες ἠρέμα φωνῆς εὐθὺς ἀνερρώννυντο καὶ τὸ σῶμά τε καὶ τὴν ψυχὴν καί, ὡς ἐνὸν ἦν, καθάπερ πρὸς δίσκον ἡλιακὸν ἐνητένιζον, μικρὸν κἀκείνου τῆς ὑπεραστραπτούσης ἀνέντος ἀνατολῆς καὶ ἡμερώτερον αὐτοὺς ἐπιλάμποντος.

109 Ἀλλὰ μικρόν τι κἀν τοῖς ἐπιθανατίοις ταύτης ὥσπερ κἀν τοῖς ἐπιθαλαμίοις ἐνδιατρίψωμεν, μᾶλλον δὲ ὥσπερ κἀν τῷ θανάτῳ τοῦ ταύτης υἱοῦ τὰ σκυθρωπότερα διαγγέλοντες, οὕτω καὶ πολλῷ μᾶλλον ἐν τῇ ταύτης Κοιμήσει τὰ χαριέστερα καὶ πάσης ἡδονῆς ὁμοῦ τὲ καὶ δόξης ἔμπλεα. Πῶς γὰρ αὐτὴν καὶ τότε πάλιν εἰκὸς ἔχειν καὶ πῶς ἐπαίρεσθαι τὴν ψυχήν, καὶ μονονουχὶ σκιρτᾶν καὶ προεξανίστασθαι, καὶ μηδ' ὅσον οἷον κατέχεσθαι καὶ σπεύδειν ἀποφοιτῆσαι τοῦ σώματος, ὥστε καὶ τῷ υἱῷ θᾶττον περιπλακῆναι καὶ εἰς χεῖρας ἐκείνου πεσεῖν καὶ συναπελθεῖν, ἢ πῶς ὑπέμεινε τὴν χαράν, καθάπερ κἀν τῷ Πάθει τὴν λύπην, καὶ εἰ μὴ καινὸν εἰπεῖν οὐχ ὑπ' αὐτῆς ἐκείνης ἐξέθανεν.

Ὅτι μὲν γὰρ ἔρρει δάκρυα καὶ πάλιν κρείττω δακρύων ὑφ' ἡδονῆς ἅμα καὶ τοῦ παραδόξου θεάματος φανερόν, ὁρῶσα σῶμα μὲν ἐκεῖνο τὸ πρὸ ὀλίγου περιελκόμενον καὶ καθυβριζόμενον καὶ μωλωπιζόμενον, ὑπὸ μὲν ἀγγέλων

them before, *when the doors were closed,* for in the past they were gathered together in the house of John, as they were now too, but then it was *because of the fear of the Jews,* whereas now it was because they were gathered together by the one who gave birth to the Lord, and who lived in it together with the disciple and virgin, her second son, whom she received through adoption. The apostles, upon hearing softly the sweet, beloved voice of the Lord, immediately received new strength in both body and soul, and, as much as they were able, gazed upon him as if looking into the face of the sun, while he reduced the overwhelming radiance of his dawning, and so shone upon them with a gentle light.

But let us linger for a while over what took place at her 109
death, just as we did with her nuptials, or rather, just as we proclaimed the more sorrowful aspects pertaining to the death of her son, let us now proclaim the much more joyful events surrounding her Dormition, which are replete with spiritual pleasure and glory. How she was now likely to have been as she was then, how she was in a state of exaltation, and all but leaping for joy and already rising up, unable to contain herself, and hastening to depart from her body, so that she might be embraced by her son, and fall into his hands and depart together with him. Let us also say how she endured such joy, just as she endured such sorrow during the time of the Passion, and, if it is not too novel a thing to say, how she did not simply die from her feeling of joy.

It was obvious that she was shedding tears, which were, again, superior to tears, due to her pleasure and the wonderful spectacle of seeing the body of her son, which not long ago was dragged about, insulted, severely beaten and

καὶ τοσούτων μυριάδων δορυφορούμενον, ὑπὸ δὲ τοσαύτης αἴγλης καὶ δόξης περιλαμπόμενον· πρόσωπον δὲ ἐκεῖνο καὶ σχῆμα τὸ πάλαι κατεμπαιζόμενον καὶ κατεμπτυόμενον καὶ χλαῖναν καὶ πορφύραν χλεύης περιβαλλόμενον εἰς τοσοῦτον νῦν περιελθὸν ἀξιώματος καὶ λαμπρότητος, *εἶδος* δὲ καὶ *κάλλος* ἐκλελοιπὸς ὑπὸ τοσούτου νῦν κάλλους καὶ καλλοποιοῦ καταστραπτόμενον τῆς θεότητος· ἀντὶ νεκροῦ καὶ καταδίκου καὶ ἀντιθέου, Θεὸν καὶ Βασιλέα καὶ Κριτὴν πάντων, ἀθάνατόν τε καὶ ἀκατάλυτον. Ὤ, πῶς ἐμερίζετο καὶ πάλιν τοῖς ἐναντίοις ἢ ἐν τῷ σταυρῷ πάθεσιν· ὑπερήδετο μὲν ὁρῶσα καὶ ἠγαλλιᾶτο τῷ πνεύματι, ὑπεστέλλετο δὲ ὅμως πρὸς τὴν ἐκεῖθεν ἐκπηδῶσαν αἴγλην καὶ ἀστραπήν.

Ἐμεγάλυνε δὲ πλέον ἢ τὸ προτοῦ τὸν οὕτως αὐτὴν μεγαλύναντα· ὑπερηύχετο δὲ τῶν ἀποστόλων καὶ τῶν παρόντων, ὑπερεδέετο δὲ καὶ τῶν ἁπανταχοῦ πιστῶν, μᾶλλον δὲ τοῦ κόσμου παντός, καὶ αὐτῶν τῶν ἐχθρῶν καὶ τῶν σταυρωτῶν. Ἠιτεῖτο δὲ δεσποτικόν τι ῥῆμα λαβεῖν ἢ νεῦμα τῆς σωτηρίας αὐτῶν ἐχέγγυον, χεῖρας ἐκείνας ἁπλοῦσα αἷς αὐτὸν τὸ πρότερον ἠγκαλίζετο, γλῶσσαν ἐκείνην καὶ χείλη κινοῦσα μεθ' ὧν αὐτὸν κατησπάζετο, θηλῆς ὑπομιμνήσκουσα καὶ τροφῆς, καὶ δάκρυα μεθ' ἡδονῆς καὶ σπουδῆς τῶν ὀφθαλμῶν καταρρέουσα, καὶ πάντα κινοῦσα καὶ μιγνῦσα τοῖς ἐξιτηρίοις τὰ ἱκετήρια. Εἶτα ὑμνοῦσι μὲν ἄγγελοι, καὶ πάντες οὐχ ὑπὸ τῆς φρίκης μᾶλλον ἢ καὶ τῆς ἡδονῆς μένουσιν ἐννεοί. Μετὰ δὲ ἀντιφωνοῦσι καὶ οἱ ἀπόστολοι καὶ οὕτω διάρασα τὸ πανάγιον αὐτῆς στόμα

bruised, now accompanied by so many myriads of angels, and shining all about with such great light and glory; of seeing that face and form, which only recently was ridiculed, spat upon, and clothed in the purple of mockery, now surrounded with such august dignity and splendor; of seeing the one who was deprived of all *form* and *beauty,* now shining brilliantly with such beauty of the divinity which produces beauty; of seeing instead of the one who was dead and condemned as an enemy of God, now God, and King, and Judge of all, immortal and invincible. Oh, how greatly divided she was again by emotions that were opposite to those she experienced at the cross! The sight of her son overtook her with pleasure, and she rejoiced in her spirit, but at the same time she held herself back in awe of the radiance and the overwhelming flashes of light that blazed forth from him.

She now magnified even more than before the one who 110
earlier had thus magnified her, and she prayed ardently for the apostles and those who were present, and ardently made entreaty on behalf of all the faithful, indeed for the entire world, and even for his enemies and crucifiers themselves. She asked to receive a word from the master or a sign from him that their salvation was assured, stretching forth those hands toward him with which she once held him, moving that mouth and lips with which she once kissed him, reminding him of the nourishment he had taken at her breast, and, with tears of joy and earnestness streaming from her eyes, moving her entire body and mingling her prayers together with her words of farewell. Then the angels sang their hymns, while all those present were rendered speechless not out of fear but joy. After the apostles had responded with their own hymns, opening her all-holy mouth, as if falling

καθάπερ ἐν ὕπνῳ γλυκεῖ τὸ ὑπεράγιον αὐτῆς πνεῦμα παρατίθησι τῷ ταύτης υἱῷ, παραπλησίως ὥσπερ τοῦ τόκου τὰς ὠδῖνας, οὕτω καὶ τοῦ θανάτου φυγοῦσα, μᾶλλον δὲ μεθ' ὁμοίας τῆς ἡδονῆς ἢ καὶ πλείονος· καὶ τότε τὸν υἱὸν αὐτῆς καὶ Θεὸν ἀπορρήτως ἀφ' ἑαυτῆς προελθόντα καὶ νῦν εἰς τὸν αὐτὸν ἑαυτὴν Θεὸν οὐ μόνον νοούμενον, ἀλλὰ καὶ φαινόμενον προελθοῦσαν ἰδοῦσα. Ἐπεκρότουν δὲ εὐθὺς καὶ πάντες οἱ ἄγγελοι καὶ εἴ τινες ἄλλαι δυνάμεις καὶ τῷ μὲν πνεύματι συνεξήρχετο ἡδεῖά τις ὀδμὴ καὶ πολλὴ καὶ ἀπόρρητος, τὸ δὲ σῶμα περιεχεῖτο φωτὶ πολλῷ τε καὶ ἀπροσίτῳ, ὥστε καὶ τὸν ἀέρα πληροῦσθαι μὲν ἤχων καὶ ἐμμελείας, πληροῦσθαι δὲ καὶ ἡδυτέρας τῆς εὐωδίας, τὸ δὲ σῶμα πανταχόθεν περιαστράπτεσθαι ὥστε μικροῦ καὶ ἀθέατον μένειν. Καὶ οὕτω λοιπὸν μερίζονται τὴν Παρθένον μαθηταὶ καὶ διδάσκαλος, ἐπίγεια καὶ οὐράνια, ὡς καὶ μετ' ὀλίγον οὐρανὸς καὶ παράδεισος. Ὁ μὲν τὸ πνεῦμα καὶ πάντα τὰ περὶ αὐτὸν λειτουργικὰ πνεύματα κύκλῳ περιϊπτάμενα, οἱ δὲ τὸ σῶμα λαμβάνουσι.

III Καὶ πάλιν τῶν ἀποστόλων ἱεραὶ μελῳδίαι τὲ καὶ θεολογίαι, καὶ κοιναὶ πάντων ὁμοῦ καὶ ἴδιαι καθ' ἕκαστον· καὶ Πέτρος καὶ Παῦλος ἀλλήλους ἐπὶ τὴν εὐχὴν προκαλούμενοι, καὶ ἁμιλλώμενοι μὲν πρὸς ἀλλήλους περὶ τῆς τάξεως, νικῶν δὲ ὅμως Παῦλος ἐν τῷ ἡττᾶσθαι καὶ πείθων τὸ πρωτεῖον ἔχειν Πέτρον καὶ τῆς εὐχῆς κατάρχεσθαι. Καὶ ὁ μὲν οὕτως ἐξῆρχεν οἷα καὶ τοῦ χοροῦ κορυφαῖος οὐ τῆς εὐχῆς μόνον, ἀλλὰ καὶ τῆς ᾠδῆς, συνεπήχει δὲ καὶ πᾶς ὁ λοιπὸς τῶν μαθητῶν χορός. Ἀλλ' οὗτος μὲν ὁ ὕμνος κοινός, ἦν δὲ καὶ ἑκάστου καθ' ἑαυτὸν ἴδιος. Καὶ πάντων πάλιν τῶν

into a sweet slumber, she entrusted her transcendently holy spirit to her son. And just as she had once escaped the pains of childbirth, so too she now escaped the pains of death, and indeed with the same or rather even greater spiritual pleasure. Then, her son and God ineffably came forth from her, but now she herself goes forth to him, as her God, seeing him not only spiritually but also visibly. Immediately, all the angels applauded together with the other heavenly powers, and, along with her spirit there arose a strong, sweet, and indescribable fragrance, while her body was suffused with an abundance of unapproachable light. As a result, the air around her was filled with graceful sounds and harmonies, and indeed with even sweeter fragrance, while her body was surrounded on all sides with dazzling light, so that for a short period of time it could not be seen. And thus the Virgin was shared by the disciples and their master, by things earthly and heavenly, and, before long, by heaven and paradise. The master, with all the ministering spirits that flew around him, received her spirit, while his disciples received her body.

Once again, the apostles sang their sacred melodies and 111
theologies, both all together and each individually. Peter and Paul each challenged each other to prayer and contended over who would yield first place to the other, but Paul prevailed by his own defeat since he had persuaded Peter to have primacy and begin the prayer. Thus Peter, as the chief of the choir, not only led the prayer but also the chant, while the rest of the choir of disciples joined in. They sang a common hymn, but each one also sang his own. And the holy

μετὰ τοὺς θεολόγους ἱεραρχῶν ὁ ἱερὸς κρατῶν Ἱερόθεος οὐ λόγῳ μόνον, ἀλλὰ καὶ λογισμῷ τῶν ἄλλων μᾶλλον αἰρόμενος καὶ ὅλος τῇ μεταστάσει συνεξιστάμενος.

Καὶ οὕτω μὲν εἶχεν εὐταξίας καὶ εὐρυθμίας τὰ ἐπικήδεια. Τίς δ' ἂν ἐφίκοιτο λόγος τοῦ κατασχόντος τότε πλήθους ἢ τοῦ πόθου τοὺς πλείονας ἢ τῆς τιμῆς ἢ τῶν δακρύων ἢ τῆς σπουδῆς ἢ τοῦ ἐπὶ πᾶσι τῶν θαυμάτων πλήθους καὶ τοῦ μεγέθους; Ἤγγιζον μὲν εὐθὺς οἱ ἀπόστολοι καὶ προσέψαυον καὶ τὸν σκίμποδα περιΐσταντο καὶ πᾶν μέλος ἄλλος ἄλλοθεν, πάντες δὲ ὅμως πανευλαβῶς κατησπάζοντο. Μετὰ δὲ καὶ τῶν ἄλλων μαθητῶν καὶ μαθητριῶν ἐκύκλουν οἱ κρείττονες. Ἕτερος τρίτος κύκλος ἀνδρῶν τὲ καὶ γυναικῶν καὶ πᾶν ὅσον οἰκειότερον τῶν λοιπῶν ἢ καὶ τῶν πολλῶν ἔκκριτον. Ἐπὶ δὲ τούτοις καὶ τὸ ἄλλο πᾶν ὅσον εὐσεβὲς καὶ ὁμόγνωμον καὶ ὁμόπιστον, καὶ οὐκ ὀλίγοι δὲ καὶ Ἑλλήνων καὶ Ἰουδαίων, οἱ μὲν ἐπιτωθάζοντες ἴσως, οἱ δὲ θαυμάζοντες. Οἱ μὲν ὥσπερ ποταμὸς εἷς ἐπὶ μίαν δεξαμενήν, τὴν κλίνην, συνέρρεον καὶ παρεβιάζοντο, ἀντωθούμενοι δὲ κύκλῳ περιειλίσσοντο καθάπερ εἰς λίμνην ἀναχεόμενοι ἢ μᾶλλον καὶ εἰς πέλαγος ἀνακυματούμενοι.

Καὶ οἱ μὲν ἀπόστολοι τῶν ἐπικηδείων ἢ προπεμπτηρίων εἴχοντο, κοινῇ δὲ πάντες τῶν πρὸς αὐτὴν ἱκετηρίων καὶ τῶν ᾀσμάτων. Συνανεκιρνᾶτο δὲ τοῖς ᾄσμασι καὶ τὰ θαύματα καὶ διὰ τοῦτο καὶ τοῖς δάκρυσι δάκρυα, τοῖς ἐξοδίοις τὰ τῆς χαρᾶς καὶ τοῖς προπεμπτηρίοις εὐχαριστήρια. Σπουδὴ μὲν γὰρ ἦν ἑκάστῳ τῶν ποθούντων ἢ καμνόντων ἢ καὶ ἀμφότερα μάλιστα μὲν ἅψασθαι τῶν ποδῶν τοῦ

Hierotheos prevailed again over all the hierarchs, after the theologians, not only by his words but also in his thoughts, being in a higher state of ecstasy than the others and becoming wholly a participant in the Virgin's translation.

In this way, the funeral chants were orderly and rhythmical. But what words could express the multitude of things that were going on then, the magnitude of the longing, or of the honor, or of the tears, or of the zeal, or the number and greatness of the miracles affecting everyone? The apostles immediately approached the bier and encircled it, each one embracing a different part of her body, but all with the greatest piety. After them, the more distinguished among the other disciples, male and female, gathered around the body. They were followed in turn by a third group of men and women, who were in every way better acquainted with her or chosen from the many. After them came all the pious, who were of the same mind and faith, along with not a few Greeks and Jews, some perhaps coming to jeer, but others to marvel. It was as if they all formed a single river, rushing forward and emptying into a single pool, that is, the Virgin's bier, pushing against each other and swirling around in a circle in contrary directions, as if they were pouring into a lake or rather swept into the sea.

The apostles were chanting dirges and funerary hymns, while all the others addressed their supplications and chants to her. Miracles were mixed together with the chants, and thus tears were mingled with tears, that is, tears of joy with tears of farewell, and tears of thanksgiving with tears for her departure. In each person, whether filled with longing or distress or both, there was above all a desire to touch the

ἀχράντου σώματος ἐκείνου· ποῦ γὰρ ἐτόλμων τῶν ἄλλων μελῶν καὶ ὡς ἐνὸν κατασπάσασθαι; Τὸ γοῦν δεύτερον, ἅψασθαι μόνον, ἢ μὴ τοῦ σώματος μόνον, ἀλλὰ καί τινος ἐπιβλήματος· εἰ δ' οὔ, καὶ τοῦ σκίμποδος. Οἱ δὲ καὶ πόρρωθεν ἠξιοῦντο τῆς θέας μόνης, οἱ δὲ καὶ τῆς προσκυνήσεως, ὡς ἂν ἕκαστος ἢ ἑκάστη παρ' αὐτῆς τῆς κειμένης ᾠκονομοῦντο. Ἡ δὲ ἁφή, πολλάκις δὲ καὶ ἡ θέα μόνη καὶ ἡ προσκύνησις, ἅμα τὲ τοῦ πόθου πλήρωσις καὶ πάθους παντὸς ἴασις οὐ σώματος μόνον, ἀλλὰ δὴ καὶ ψυχῆς. Ὀφθαλμοῖς μὲν τυφλῶν, ὠσὶ δὲ κωφῶν, ποσὶ δὲ χωλῶν, τοῖς δὲ λοιποῖς τῶν λοιπῶν, τοῖς δὲ καὶ πάντα παρειμένοις ἁπάντων· ἐπεχορήγει δὲ καὶ τοῖς τὰς ψυχὰς νοσοῦσι καὶ μὴ νοσοῦσιν ὁμοίως φιλοτιμότερον τὰς εὐεργεσίας, τοὺς μὲν ὑγιάζουσα, τοὺς δὲ καὶ καθαγιάζουσα. Καὶ ἄνθρωποι μὲν οὕτω τῆς μεταστάσεως τῆς κοινῆς Δεσποίνης ἀπήλαυον.

Τί δὲ καὶ ἡ ἄψυχος κτίσις; Ὥσπερ ἐπὶ τῷ ταύτης υἱῷ τὸ Πάθος οὐ φέρουσα συνεχέετο, οὕτω τοὐναντίον καὶ ἐπὶ ταύτῃ διεχεῖτο καὶ ὑπερέχαιρε. Καὶ ἀὴρ μὲν καὶ οὐρανὸς ἑαυτῶν λαμπρότεροι καὶ χαριέστεροι διεδείκνυντο, καὶ ὁ μὲν διΐστατο τῇ ἀφέσει καὶ τῇ ἀναβάσει τοῦ πνεύματος ἐπαγαλλιώμενος, ὁ δὲ πόρρωθεν διηνοίγετο τῇ ἐνοικήσει συναγαλλόμενος, καὶ ἀμφότεροι καθαγιαζόμενοι. Καὶ γῆ δὲ ὁμοίως οὐ τῷ οἰκείῳ μόνον γεννήματι, ἀλλὰ καὶ τῇ ταφῇ καὶ τῇ καταθέσει σεμνυνομένη καὶ γινομένη δοχεῖον τοῦ θεοδόχου σώματος. Οὐ μὴν οὐδὲ τὸ ὕδωρ ἐστερεῖτο

feet of that immaculate body, for how would they have dared to embrace her other limbs, and when possible kiss them? Those in the second group dared only to touch her, or not even her body but only some of the cloth that covered it; and, if not that, at least the bier. Those who were further away were worthy only of seeing her or venerating her in the measure that this was granted to each man or woman by she herself who was lying there. Even a mere touch, and often simply seeing and venerating her, was enough to satisfy one's longing and bring about the healing of every illness, not only of the body but also of the soul: the eyes of the blind, the ears of the deaf, the feet of the lame, the various ailing members of others, and everything in the case of those completely paralyzed. She similarly bestowed blessings even more abundantly on the souls of the sick and those who were healthy, healing the former and sanctifying the latter. And in this way human beings benefitted from the translation of our common sovereign Lady.

But what was the response of inanimate creation? Just as it was confounded when it was unable to endure the Passion of her son, now the very opposite occurred, for it was glad and rejoiced exceedingly. The air and heaven itself became brighter and lovelier. The former joyfully parted and opened a path for the release and ascent of her spirit, while from afar with equal joy the latter opened its gates as she came to dwell there, and both were sanctified by her presence. The earth in similar fashion was filled with joy and sanctified, not simply because the Virgin was its own offspring, but because it was being honored with her grave and burial, through which it would receive the God-receiving body. Neither was the water deprived of her blessing, for it was

τῆς εὐλογίας, ἀλλὰ καὶ τοῦτο περιχεόμενον ἡγιάζετο. Οὐ γὰρ ἐκεῖνό γε τὸ σῶμα καθαρσίων δεόμενον ἦν, ἀλλ' ὥσπερ ὁ ταύτης υἱὸς ἐκάθαιρε καθαιρόμενος, οὕτω καὶ τὸ ταύτης λουτρὸν οὐ μόνον αὐτὸ καθαρόν τε καὶ πάναγνον ἦν, ἀλλὰ καὶ ἑτέροις λουτήριον καὶ ἁγιαστικὸν ἦν.

Τί ἔτι; Σινδόσιν εἱλίσσεται καὶ μυρίζεται τὸ ταύτης σῶμα καθάπερ καὶ τοῦ ταύτης υἱοῦ, παρθενικῶν καὶ λίαν ἁγνῶν σωμάτων τὲ καὶ ψυχῶν ἐξυπηρετουμένων ταῦτα καὶ μυστικῶς τελούντων ἅμα καὶ τελουμένων. Καὶ οὕτω πάλιν *ἡ κλίνη* τοῦ βασιλέως τῇ κλίνῃ δίδοται, ἣν καὶ τότε κυκλοῦσιν οἱ *δυνατοί,* οὐχ *ἑξήκοντα* μόνον, ἀλλὰ καὶ πάντες οἱ χοροὶ τῶν ἀποστόλων τὲ καὶ μαθητῶν καὶ ἰσχυροὶ τῷ πνεύματι. Λαμπάδες ἐπὶ τούτοις καὶ μύρα τῇ κοινῇ λαμπάδι, τῇ χρυσῇ λυχνίᾳ, τῇ εὐωδίᾳ τοῦ γένους. Καὶ καταυγάζεται μὲν καὶ κατευωδιάζεται τούτοις ὁ οἶκος καὶ στενοχωρεῖται πάλιν τοῖς πλήθεσι, περιαστράπτεται δὲ μᾶλλον καὶ ὅλος ἓν πνεῦμα καὶ εὐωδία γίνεται παρὰ τῆς ἀπορρεούσης αἴγλης τὲ καὶ ὀδμῆς τοῦ σώματος, ἀγάλλεται δὲ πλέον τοῖς θαύμασι δοξαζόμενος, ὅτε καὶ οἱ μὴ μόνον τοῦ σώματος ἢ τοῦ σκίμποδος, ἀλλὰ καὶ αὐτῶν τῶν τοίχων τοῦ οἴκου ψαύοντες ἀδιστάκτως καὶ τῆς κειμένης τὴν δύναμιν ἱκετεύοντες ἀπελύοντο παντὸς πάθους τὲ καὶ νοσήματος.

Καὶ οὕτως αἴρεται τὸ ὑπερουράνιον ἐκεῖνο σῶμα καὶ βαστάσαν τὴν ἄστεκτον ἐκείνην φύσιν καὶ χωρῆσαν τὴν ἀπερίγραπτον, ἡ ἔμψυχος κιβωτός, οὐχ ἱερέων ὥσπερ

sanctified when it was poured over her body, not because her body was in need of purification, but just as her son purified the waters through his own purity, so too her own bath was not only itself pure and perfectly unpolluted, but became for others the cleansing water of sanctification.

What more happened besides this? Just like the body of her son, her own body was wrapped in a shroud and perfumed thanks to the assistance of those who possessed virginal and exceedingly pure bodies and souls, and who through their mystical assistance were themselves perfected. In this way, she who was *the couch* of the king was in turn placed upon a couch, and it was then that *powerful men* surrounded her, not merely *sixty* but all the choirs of apostles, disciples, and those who were powerful in spirit. In addition, lamps and sweet-smelling unguents were placed around her, our common lamp, the golden lampstand, the sweet fragrance of the human race. And thus the house was filled with light and fragrance and continued to be thronged by the crowds, or rather it was dazzling with light, wholly becoming one spirit and fragrance thanks to the splendor and fragrance emanating from her body. The house itself rejoiced even more at being glorified by the miracles, because healing was granted not only to those who touched her body or bier, but also to those who in supplication merely touched the walls of the house, unhesitatingly seeking the power of the one who was reposing therein, whereupon they were healed of every sickness and illness.

And thus the apostles took up that supercelestial body, which bore the nature that none can approach and contained the uncircumscribable God; the living ark was raised up, not by the hands of priests like the ark of old, but on the

ἐκείνη χερσίν, ἀλλ' ἱεραρχῶν καὶ ἀποστόλων ὤμοις τὲ καὶ βραχίοσιν, ἀνθρώπων μὲν κάτωθεν, ἀγγέλων δὲ ἄνωθεν ἐπᾳδόντων τὰ ἐπικήδεια, μᾶλλον δὲ τἀληθέστερον εἰπεῖν, νικητήρια καὶ ἐπιτάφια καὶ ἐπιθαλάμια, ὡς κατὰ πάσης μὲν τῆς φύσεως ἤδη τὴν νίκην λαβούσης, κατὰ δὲ πάσης βασιλευούσης τῆς κτίσεως· εἰς γῆν δὲ νόμῳ χωρούσης τῷ κοινῷ τῆς φύσεως καὶ μὴν καὶ ὑπὲρ τὴν φύσιν πρὸς τὸν υἱὸν αὐτῆς καὶ νυμφίον μεταχωρούσης εἰς τὸν ἐκεῖσε θάλαμον, τὸν θεῖον καὶ πᾶσι τοῖς ἄλλοις ἄβατον, παραπεμπόντων ἐπὶ τὸν τάφον, μετακαλουμένων ἐπὶ τὸν ἄνω θρόνον τὸν ἐν σαρκὶ τοῦ Θεοῦ θρόνον, ἐπὶ τὰ ἄνω βασίλεια τὴν κοινὴν βασίλισσαν, ᾀδόντων καὶ τὰ ἐγκαίνια, βαλλόντων ταῖς εὐφημίαις, κουφιζόντων τὴν κλίνην, περιπνεόντων εὐόδμοις καὶ ἀκηράτοις ἄσθμασι, περισκιαζόντων ταῖς πτέρυξι τὴν τῶν Ἁγίων Ἁγίαν, τὸ κοινὸν *ἱλαστήριον*, τὸ φρικτὸν μυστήριον, τὸ καινὸν τῆς θείας ἑνώσεως καὶ τῆς ἀνθρωπίνης ἀναπλάσεως ἐργαστήριον. Οὕτω τῆς θείας κιβωτοῦ μετατιθεμένης, ἧς τοσοῦτον ἐνδοξοτέρα καὶ ἡ μετάθεσις ὅσον τοῦ τύπου καὶ ἡ ἀλήθεια καὶ ὁ ἐν αὐτῇ κατοικήσας καὶ ἐξ αὐτῆς προελθὼν Θεὸς τῆς στάμνου καὶ τῆς ῥάβδου καὶ τῶν πλακῶν, γίνεταί τι καὶ τῷ Ὀζὰν παραπλήσιον, μᾶλλον δὲ καὶ πολλῷ χαλεπώτερόν τε καὶ ἰταμώτερον καὶ ἐξ ἐναντίας ἐκείνῳ τῆς γνώμης. Ὁ μὲν γὰρ περιτρεπομένην ἵστη τὴν κιβωτόν, οὗτος δὲ καλῶς περιφερομένην περιτρέπειν ἐφιλονείκει· καὶ ὅπως, ἄκουε.

shoulders and arms of hierarchs and apostles, while men on earth and angels above chanted funeral laments, or to speak more truly, they sang victory songs, funeral songs, and wedding songs all at once, for she had already been granted victory over the whole of nature and was ruling over all creation. And though she was subject to the common law of nature on earth, she was transported in a manner beyond nature to her son and bridegroom, unto his divine bridal chamber, which to all others is inaccessible. And as the apostles were conveying her to her tomb, the angels were summoning the throne of God in the flesh to her throne in heaven, and the common queen of all to the kingdom of heaven. They chanted hymns for her royal consecration, they offered her praises, they lifted up the bier, they breathed forth fragrant and undefiled songs, with their wings they covered her, for she is the Holy of the Holies, the common *mercy seat,* the awesome mystery, the new workshop of the divine union and of human reformation. Thus, when the divine ark was being transported, its movement was surpassingly glorious to the same degree that truth surpasses its prefiguration, indeed to the same degree that God, who dwelt in her and came forth from her, surpasses the urn, the rod of Aaron, and the tablets of the law. And so something similar happened here to what befell Uzzah, or indeed something much worse and far more reckless, and indeed contrary to what Uzzah intended, for whereas he sought merely to steady the ark when it was disturbed, this man sought to disturb the bier as it was being transported in an orderly procession. Listen to how this happened.

112 Πῶς γὰρ ἂν καὶ ἔφερε τὴν τοσαύτην δόξαν ὁ φθονερὸς καὶ τοῦ φθόνου δημιουργός, ὁ καὶ τῷ ταύτης υἱῷ μετὰ τὴν τοσαύτην τῶν ὄχλων τιμὴν καὶ τῶν παίδων ᾠδὴν καὶ τῆς βασιλείας ἀνάρρησιν σταυρὸν εὐτρεπίσας καὶ τοσαῦτα πάθη καὶ θάνατον; Εἰ καὶ καθ' ἑαυτοῦ ταῦτα κατασκευάζεται, ἀλλ' οὗτος καὶ κατ' αὐτῆς τὰ τοιαῦτα νεανιεύεται. Ἐκμαίνεταί τις τῶν Ἰουδαίων ἐπὶ τῷ τοσούτῳ πλήθει καὶ τῇ τοσαύτῃ δόξῃ τῆς ἐκφορᾶς καὶ τῇ λαμπρότητι, καὶ διασχίσας βίᾳ τὸ πλῆθος καὶ ἐπιδραμὼν καὶ ἐγγίσας, οἰκονομοῦντος καὶ τοῦτο πάντως ἢ παραχωροῦντος τοῦ ταύτης υἱοῦ καὶ αὐτῆς ἐκείνης, ἵν' οὕτω τῇ εὐεργετικῇ καὶ ἡ τιμωρητικὴ ταύτῃ συναναφανῇ δύναμις καὶ μάθωσιν Ἰουδαῖοι μὴ πάντα τολμᾶν, ἀλλὰ καὶ ὁ τούτων προστάτης, ὅπως ἀεὶ ταῖς ἰδίαις πάγαις καὶ τοῖς ἰδίοις πτεροῖς ἁλίσκεται.

113 Οὗτος οὖν ὁ πάντολμος ἐπιδραμών—ὢ ψυχῆς, ὢ χειρὸς ἀπονενοημένης καὶ λίθων ἀναισθητοτέρας ἅμα καὶ ἀκαθεκτοτέρας θηρίων—ψαύειν ἐπιχειρεῖ τῶν ἀψαύστων καὶ ὅπερ φρίττουσιν ἄγγελοι καὶ ᾧπερ ὀκνοῦσι προσεγγίσαι τὰ χερουβίμ, αὐτὸς κατασπᾶσαι πρὸς γῆν τὸ σῶμα παραβιάζεται· τοσοῦτον Ἰουδαῖοι κακόν! Ἀλλ' ἐμάνθανεν εὐθὺς τῆς νοητῆς καὶ ἀληθοῦς κιβωτοῦ κἂν τῷ σκίμποδι τὸ σεβάσμιον. Οὐ γὰρ ἐκείνης αἱ χεῖρες ἐφικνοῦντο μᾶλλον, ἀλλ' ἐκείνη τῶν χειρῶν ἀοράτως ἐπελαμβάνετο καὶ συνάμα καὶ βραχιόνων ἐκ τῶν ἀγκώνων εὐθὺς ἀπετέμνοντο. Πόσης τοῦτο τοῖς μὲν Ἰουδαίοις αἰσχύνης καὶ φρίκης, τοῖς δὲ πιστοῖς παρρησίας καὶ δόξης κατέστη πρόξενον, εἰ

How could the envious one, who is also the creator of envy, have endured the sight of such glory? For this was the same one who, after seeing the Virgin's son acclaimed by the crowds and praised by the children's hymn, and after hearing the proclamation of the kingdom, prepared a cross for him, along with such terrible sufferings and death. And even though he then unwittingly fell into his own snares, he once again ventured with wanton insolence to do the same to her. One of the Jews, having seen the multitudes and the magnificently brilliant procession, went out of his mind and pushed his way violently through the crowd, rushing toward the bier, and getting close to it. But this surely all happened according to a divine dispensation or with the permission of her son and the Virgin herself in order to demonstrate that God's power to punish is woven together with his power of benefaction, and so that the Jews might learn not always to be so reckless; also so that their patron would get his wings caught in his own snares, as he always does. 112

Thus when this totally shameless man rushed forward—oh, what a soul, what a reckless hand, more insensitive than a stone and more savage than a beast!—he tried to take hold of things that cannot be touched, things which cause angels to tremble, and which the cherubim hesitate to approach, and he attempted forcefully to throw her body to the ground, for such is the wickedness of the Jews! However, he immediately realized the hallowed character of the true, spiritual ark, even though she was lying on a bier. Though her hands could not move, she invisibly caught hold of the man's hands, and in that moment his arms were immediately cut off at the elbows. This caused great terror and shame among the Jews but was a source of courage and glory to the 113

κἀνταῦθα καὶ λύπης τι παρεμίγνυτο διὰ τὸ φιλάνθρωπον καὶ μάλιστα τοῦ παθόντος, εὐθὺς ὥσπερ οὐ τὴν μανίαν μόνον, ἀλλὰ καὶ τὴν ἄλλην πᾶσαν κακίαν ὁμοῦ συναποτμηθέντος καὶ τρέψαντος τὴν μὲν ὕβριν εἰς πίστιν, τὸν δὲ φθόνον εἰς φόβον ἢ πόθον, τὰ δὲ πρὶν κατ' αὐτῆς καὶ τοῦ ἐξ αὐτῆς σκώμματα καὶ συκοφαντίας εἰς εὐφημίας καὶ ἱκεσίας, τοὺς δὲ καταγέλωτας εἰς τὰ δάκρυα· ὃ δὲ μάλιστα τοῖς φιλανθρωποτέροις ἐλέους ἄξιον ὅτι μηδὲ χεῖρας εἶχε προτείνειν ἐφ' ἱκεσίᾳ, ἀλλὰ καὶ ταύτης περιαιρεθεὶς τῆς παραμυθίας ἢ βοηθείας δάκρυσι μόνον καὶ ῥήμασιν ὡς ἐνὸν ἐξεκαλεῖτο τὸν ἔλεον.

114 Ἡ δὲ πάσης αἰτία πᾶσι χαρᾶς οὐδὲ τούτῳ λυπηροῦ τινὸς αἰτία καθίσταται, ἀλλὰ καὶ παντὸς ἀγαθοῦ μᾶλλον, καθάπερ καὶ τῷ κόσμῳ παντὶ καὶ πάσῃ τῇ φύσει, πρόξενος, ἰασαμένη μὲν δι' ἑνὸς καὶ τοῦ ἐλάττονος πάθους πάντα τὰ τῆς ψυχῆς καὶ πολλῷ χείρονα, καὶ Χριστιανὸν αὐτὸν καὶ υἱὸν Θεοῦ κατὰ χάριν ἀντὶ ἐχθροῦ τὲ καὶ σταυρωτοῦ καὶ υἱοῦ τοῦ διαβόλου, κατὰ τὸν Δεσποτικὸν λόγον, δείξασα καὶ τὴν αὐτοῦ σωτηρίαν αὐτὴ μᾶλλον ἀντικερδήσασα, μετὰ δὲ ταῦτα καὶ αὐτὴν τὴν τούτων πάντων τῶν ἀγαθῶν πρόφασιν, τὸ πάθος, λύσασα καὶ ἀποκαταστήσασα τὰς χεῖρας αὐτῷ καὶ ῥωμαλεωτέρας ἅμα τῶν πρὶν καὶ σωφρονεστέρας. Ἵσταται μὲν γὰρ ἡ κλίνη Πέτρου τοῦτο κελεύσαντος, αἴρεται δὲ παρὰ πάντων πρὸς αὐτὴν βοή τε καὶ δέησις, ἄγεται δὲ θέαμα φρικτὸν καὶ ἐλεεινόν, καὶ ὁ πεπονθὼς ἐκεῖνος αἵμασι μὲν τῶν χειρῶν, δάκρυσι δὲ καὶ τῶν ὀφθαλμῶν τάς τε παρειὰς καὶ πᾶν τὸ σῶμα περιρρεόμενος καὶ οὕτω πάλιν προσψαύσας, οὐκέτι μεθ' ὁμοίας τῇ

faithful, even though these feelings were mixed with some sorrow on account of compassion, especially toward the man who had suffered. But not only was his madness immediately cut short, but also all his other wickedness, transforming his arrogance into faith, and his envy into holy fear and longing. His former jibes and slanders against her and her son became blessings and supplications, and his derisive laughter was transformed into tears. What was certainly worthy of pity among those who were more compassionate was that he no longer had hands to stretch forth in supplication, but being shorn of their consolation and support, he called out for mercy solely and as far as was possible by means of his tears and words.

But she who is the cause of every joy for all, did not make 114
herself a source of sorrow for him, but rather of every good, just as she is for the whole world and all of nature. Thus by healing this one lesser wound she also healed all the much worse wounds of his soul, showing that he was worthy to become a Christian and a son of God by grace, instead of an enemy and a crucifier and a son of the devil, according to the saying of the Lord, and instead gaining his salvation for herself. After this, she brought an end to the suffering that had been the pretext for these great blessings and restored his arms to him stronger and more prudent than they had been before. For Peter gave the order for the procession to stop, and all who were present raised cries and prayers to her. Then a spectacle that was both frightening and pitiful took place. The wounded man, with blood gushing from his arms, with tears streaming from his eyes and pouring over his cheeks and his whole body, once again reached out to touch

πρίν, ἀλλ' ἐξ ἐναντίας μᾶλλον τῆς γνώμης, ἁρμόζεται μὲν αὐτὸς αὐτῇ διὰ πίστεως καὶ τῷ ταύτης υἱῷ, ἁρμόζονται δὲ αἱ χεῖρες αὐτοῖς ἅμα βραχίοσι καὶ αὐτῷ. Καὶ οὐ μόνον οὐδεμία τῆς ὀδύνης, ἀλλ' οὐδὲ τῆς ἁρμογῆς αἴσθησις. Αὕτη κατὰ τὸν τότε τοῦ πλήθους σεισμὸν ἡ ἀθρόα καὶ δημοσία πληγή τε καὶ θεραπεία πολλοὺς μὲν καὶ τῶν ἀμφιβόλων πρὸς τὴν πίστιν ἐπέρρωσε, πολλοὺς δὲ καὶ τῶν Ἰουδαίων οὐκ ἐξέπληξε μόνον, ἀλλ'—ὃ καὶ παράδοξον καὶ πρὸ τοῦ γενέσθαι σχεδὸν ἄπιστον—αὐτήν τε Θεοτόκον καὶ τὸν ἐξ αὐτῆς τεχθέντα καὶ ὑπ' αὐτῶν σταυρωθέντα Θεὸν ὁμολογεῖν ἐποίησεν.

115 Οὕτω θαυμαστότερα τὰ πρὸς τῷ τέλει καὶ τῶν ἐξ ἀρχῆς, καὶ οὕτω λοιπὸν λαμπροτέρως πολλῷ λαμπροτέρα ὑπὸ πάσης οὐρανίου καὶ ἐπιγείου δορυφορουμένη καὶ δοξαζομένη τάξεως, ἀποστόλων μὲν χερσὶ καὶ ὤμοις ὁρατοῖς ἐποχουμένη διὰ τοῦ σκίμποδος, ἀγγέλων δὲ καὶ ἀρχαγγέλων ἀοράτως ὑποβασταζομένη καὶ περικυκλουμένη δυνάμεσι, καὶ πάντοθεν περιᾳδομένη καὶ ὑμνουμένη, τῶν μὲν κάτωθεν τὰ ἐξόδια μᾶλλον δὲ καὶ τὰ ὑπὲρ παντὸς τοῦ κόσμου σωτήριά τε καὶ ἱκετήρια, τῶν δὲ ἄνωθεν τὰ εἰσδεκτήρια καὶ ἐπιβατήρια καὶ ἀμφοτέρων τὰ ἐπινίκια καὶ βασιλευτήρια, τῇ Γεθσημανῇ καὶ τῷ τάφῳ δίδοται. Θαυμαστὸν δὲ οὐδὲν εἰ καὶ ἡ μήτηρ τῆς Ζωῆς θάπτεται, ὅπου γε καὶ αὐτὸς ὁ ταύτης υἱός, ἡ αὐτοζωή, ἡ πάντων καὶ αὐτῆς τῆς τεκούσης ζωὴ καὶ ἀθανασία, καὶ θνήσκει καὶ θάπτεται, εἰ καὶ δι' αὐτοῦ τοῦ θανάτου τῷ θανάτῳ θάνατος γίνεται, καθάπερ καὶ φῶς ὑπὸ τοῦ σκότους καταπινόμενον καὶ λῦον τῇ παρουσίᾳ τὸ σκότος.

her, though this time not with the same intention as before, but with its very opposite. Through faith, he attached himself to her and her son, and his hands were reattached to his arms and body, experiencing no pain or even sensing their rejoining. The sudden, public wounding and healing of this man created a commotion in the crowd, and strengthened many who harbored doubts concerning the faith. And it not only created astonishment among many of the Jews, but—in what prior to this would have been completely unexpected and virtually unbelievable—also made them acknowledge her as the Theotokos, and the one who was born from her and crucified by them as God.

These latter events, which took place toward the end of 115
the funeral, were far more marvelous than those that took place at its beginning, so that now it was with a glory still more magnificent, escorted and glorified by all the orders of heaven and earth, carried on a bier supported by the visible arms and shoulders of the apostles, and invisibly borne up by angels and archangels, surrounded by the singing of praises and hymns, with those on earth singing funeral dirges or rather songs for the salvation and supplication of the whole world, while those in heaven sang hymns of welcome and arrival, and both sang hymns of victory and royal triumph, her body was deposited in a tomb in Gethsemane. Let no one wonder that the mother of Life was buried in a tomb, since her son, who is life itself, and the immortal life of all human beings including his mother, also died and was buried in a tomb, even though by his death he put death to death, just as light swallowed by darkness dissolves darkness by its presence.

Οὐκ ἄξιον δὲ παραδραμεῖν οὐδὲ ὃ περὶ τὴν ταφὴν συμβαίνει ταύτης ἰδιαίτατόν τε ἅμα καὶ χαριέστατον. Τοὺς μὲν γὰρ ἄλλους μαθητάς τε καὶ μαθητρίας φόβος εἶχε καὶ τρόμος οὐ φαῦλος οὐδὲ μεμπτὸς ἅπτεσθαι τοῦ πανιέρου καὶ φοβεροῦ καὶ τοῖς ἀγγέλοις ἐκείνου σώματος, ἄλλως τὲ καὶ τὸ παράδειγμα λαβόντας ἐγγύθεν τὸν καὶ περὶ τὴν κλίνην προπετευσάμενον, εἰ καὶ τὸ τῶν ἐνταφίων ἀποσυλῆσαί τι μέρος τι τῶν οὐρανίων αὐτοῖς ἐδόκει καὶ κέρδος ἄσυλον καὶ ὑπέρτιμον καὶ φυλακτήριον ἀνυπέρβλητον ψυχῆς ὁμοῦ τὲ καὶ σώματος. Ηὐλαβεῖτο δὲ καὶ αὐτὸς ὁ πρῶτος τῶν ἀποστόλων χορὸς ὑπελθεῖν τὲ καὶ ἀμέσως αὐταῖς χερσὶν αὐτὸ τὸ πανάχραντον περιστέλλειν σῶμα, μάλιστα τὸ περιέχον αὐτὸ φῶς ὁρῶντες καὶ ὅπως ἡ Θεοφόρος ἐκείνη σὰρξ ὥσπερ τὴν χάριν ἀντιλαμβάνουσα καὶ θεοφορουμένη τότε πᾶσι περιφανῶς ἐφαίνετο.

116 Τί οὖν ἐπινοοῦνται; Πέτρῳ καὶ Παύλῳ πάλιν τὰ τῆς καταθέσεως ἐπιτρέπουσιν. Οἱ δὲ λίαν πανευλαβῶς οὐ τοῦ σώματος, ἀλλὰ τῆς περιεχούσης αὐτὸ σινδόνος καὶ ἠρτημένης ἑκατέρωθεν ἐφαψάμενοι καὶ οὕτως αὐτὸ τῆς κλίνης ἀπαιωρήσαντες αὐτῇ σινδόνι τῷ μνημείῳ παραδιδόασι. Καὶ θέα μοι κἀνταῦθα τὴν διὰ πάντων τῆς Μητρὸς καὶ Παρθένου πρὸς τὸν υἱὸν ἐμφέρειαν. Δίδοται μὲν γὰρ καὶ αὕτη παρομοίως ἐκείνῳ ταφῇ, φυλάττεται δὲ φυλακῇ καὶ ἀγγέλων ἅμα καὶ ἀποστόλων, τῶν μὲν λιγυρόν τι καὶ οὐ λόγῳ ῥητόν, ἀκουστὸν δὲ τοῖς ἀποστόλοις, ἄνωθεν ἐμπεριηχούντων καὶ περιχορευόντων τὸν τάφον, τῶν δὲ δι᾽ αὐτά τε ταῦτα παραμενόντων καὶ τιμῆς ἕνεκα τῆς κειμένης καὶ ὑμνῳδίας, ἴσως δὲ καὶ ἕνα τινὰ τῶν συναποστόλων

It would not be proper to pass over the most remarkable and beautiful things that occurred at the burial. All of the other disciples, both male and female, were stricken with a fear and trembling in a way that was both proper and justifiable, for they were reluctant to touch the body that was sacred and fearsome even to the angels, not least because they had seen what happened to the man who had rushed impetuously toward the bier, even though they believed that taking a piece of the burial linens would be like procuring a piece of heaven, a precious and inviolable blessing and an invincible safeguard for both body and soul alike. Indeed, even the first choir of the apostles was reluctant to lift her and cover her immaculate body directly with their hands, especially when they saw the light that surrounded it, and how it was manifestly evident to all that her God-bearing flesh had taken hold of grace, just as it had been taken hold of by God.

What, then, did the apostles decide to do? Once more, 116
they entrusted the deposition of the body to Peter and Paul. With the utmost piety and circumspection, they did not touch the body but instead took hold of the shroud in which it was wrapped and which hung down from both sides, and thus, lifting the body from the bier with the shroud, they placed it in the tomb. And consider with me how all things pertaining to the Mother and Virgin are in conformity with the son. Like him, she too is placed in a tomb, and is watched over by a guard of both angels and apostles. These angels surrounded the tomb and filled the air with a sweet and ineffable melody, audible only to the apostles. This was the reason why the apostles remained there, but they also stayed to honor her with their own hymns, and perhaps also to await

ἀπολειφθέντα παραμενόντων. Ὁ μὲν υἱὸς αὐτῇ μετὰ τρίτην ἀνίσταται, καὶ αὕτη δὲ μετὰ τοσαύτας εὐθὺς μετατίθεται ἢ γοῦν καὶ μετατεθεῖσα φανερὰ γίνεται· δῆλον δὲ καὶ τοῦτο τούτῳ καθίσταται.

117 Ἐπεὶ γὰρ ἀπολειφθεὶς ἐκεῖνος οὐ πρότερον ἧκεν ἢ μετὰ τρίτην ἡμέραν λόγῳ θειοτέρας πάντως οἰκονομίας, Θωμᾶς δέ φασιν οὗτος ἦν, ὅπως καὶ ἡ μετάστασις πιστευθῇ καὶ διὰ Θωμᾶ πάλιν ὥσπερ καὶ ἡ ἀνάστασις. Ἐπειδὴ οὖν ἐκεῖνος ἥκων ἠνιᾶτο πρὸς τὴν ἀπόλειψιν τῆς δεσποτικῆς ἐξόδου καὶ μάλιστα τοῦ ταύτης υἱοῦ καὶ Δεσπότου τὴν οὕτω φρικτὴν ἀκούσας κάθοδον καὶ τὴν τερπνὴν καὶ τὰ τοσαῦτα περὶ τὴν προπομπὴν θαύματα καὶ ἔτι καὶ νῦν τῶν ἀγγέλων περὶ τὸν τάφον ᾄσματα καὶ οὐδὲ φορητὸν ἡγεῖτο μὴ κἂν τὸ ζωηφόρον ἐκεῖνο σκήνωμα καὶ θεάσασθαι καὶ προσκυνῆσαι καὶ περιπτύξασθαι, βουλῇ καὶ γνώμῃ τῶν ἀποστόλων κοινῇ διαίρεται μὲν ὁ λίθος, ἀνοίγεται δὲ ὁ τάφος, εὑρίσκεται δὲ ὁ τῆς ζωῆς οἶκος, ὁ κοινὸς πλοῦτος, ἐντὸς οὐδαμῶς. Ὁ δὲ τρόπος τῆς πρὸς τὸν υἱὸν ἐμφερείας τοῦ θαύματος κἀν τοῖς ἐπιταφίοις· εὑρίσκεται γὰρ κἀκεῖνα μὴ μόνον σῶα καὶ μόνα, ἀλλὰ καὶ σῶος καὶ μόνος ὁ ἐν αὐτοῖς τοῦ σώματος τύπος, οἷα καὶ ἐπ' ἐκείνου σαφὴς τοῦ θαύματος ἄγγελος, ὥσπερ ἐπ' ἐκείνων ὅτι μή τινος κλοπῆς ἡ ὑπόληψις, οὕτω καὶ ἐπὶ τούτων ὅτι μὴ καθ' ἡμᾶς ἡ μετάθεσις. Ἀλλ' ἡ μὲν οὕτω πρὸς τὸν υἱὸν καὶ Θεὸν πᾶσα μεθίσταται σὺν αὐτῷ ζῆν τὲ καὶ βασιλεύειν, καὶ οὕτως οὐ

the arrival of one of their absent brethren. Her son rose from the dead on the third day, and she too, after an equal number of days, was translated, or rather it became obvious that she had been translated. And this is clearly established by the following.

By virtue of what was certainly a divine dispensation, one 117
of the apostles, who had been absent from these events, did not arrive until the third day. They say that this was Thomas, who was delayed so that the Virgin's translation might again be confirmed through him just as Christ's resurrection was. As soon as he arrived, he was distressed at missing the sovereign Virgin's departure, especially when he learned of the awesome descent of her son and Master, and of the delight and all the miracles that accompanied the funeral procession, and the songs of the angels heard around the tomb, which could still be heard down to that very moment. Since he did not think he would be able to endure not even seeing her life-bearing body and venerating and embracing it, with the apostles' common agreement and consent, the stone was removed and the tomb was opened. However, the house of life, the common treasure of mankind, was not found inside it. They found only the burial wrappings disposed miraculously in a manner similar to those of her son, for they were found not simply intact and by themselves, but preserving the imprint of her body on them, a clear messenger, as it were, of the miracle that took place, to demonstrate, just as in the case of the empty tomb of her son, that there was no suspicion of the body being stolen, and thus that the translation was not the result of human intervention. But she was in this way wholly translated to her son and God in order to live and reign with him, and thus it was not only

διὰ τοῦ ταύτης υἱοῦ μόνον, ἀλλὰ καὶ διὰ ταύτης αὐτῆς τὸ ἡμέτερον εἰς οὐρανοὺς ἀνάγεται φύραμα καὶ βασιλεύει πάντων καὶ ὁρωμένων καὶ ἀοράτων.

118 Οἱ δὲ χαρᾶς οὕτω καὶ πάλιν ἐμφορηθέντες ἀρρήτου σὺν τῷ Θωμᾷ καὶ ἀπορρήτου θεάματός τε καὶ θαύματος καὶ ἀπερινοήτου τῆς εὐωδίας καὶ χάριτος, ἀπέπνει γὰρ καὶ τῶν ἐνταφίων ἐξαίσιον οἷον καὶ ἀπέστιλβεν ὥσπερ τι φωτοειδὲς καὶ οὐράνιον, ἀσφαλίζονται μὲν τὸν τάφον, οὐ μὴν καὶ τὸ περὶ αὐτὸν συγκαλύπτουσι θαῦμα, ἀλλὰ καὶ τοῖς ἄλλοις συναποστόλοις καὶ πᾶσι μαθηταῖς τὲ καὶ μαθητρίαις παραδιδόασι, κἀκεῖνοι τοῖς ἄλλοις καὶ οὕτως παῖς παρὰ τοῦ πατρὸς ἐκδεχόμενος καὶ εἰς τοὺς ἔπειτα τὴν ἀκοὴν παραπέμπων καὶ μέχρι τοῦ νῦν εἰς ἡμᾶς διασῴζουσιν. Ἀλλ’ ὁ μὲν οὐρανὸς οὕτω καὶ τῷ πνεύματι καὶ τῷ σώματι ταύτης νῦν ἐπαγάλλεται, ἡ δὲ γῆ τῇ ταφῇ καὶ τοῖς ἐνταφίοις, ὁ δὲ ἀὴρ καὶ πᾶσα λοιπὸν ἡ κτίσις ταῖς ἀοράτοις ἐπιφοιτήσεσι καὶ ταῖς ἐνεργείαις, πᾶσα δὲ χώρα καὶ πόλις ταῖς ἀδιαλείπτοις εὐεργεσίαις. Ὅπως δὲ καὶ ἡ καθ’ ἡμᾶς ἔτι πρὸς τούτοις καὶ ταῖς καθ’ ἡμέραν ἐπισκιάσεσι καὶ τοῖς θαύμασιν ἀντὶ τῆς ταφῆς καὶ τῶν ἐνταφίων αὐτῆς ἐκείνης κατεκληρονόμησε τῆς ζώνης καὶ τῆς περιβολῆς, ὧν ἐκείνη καὶ ζῶσα τὴν μὲν περιεζώσατο, τὴν δὲ περιεβάλετο, ἐφ’ ᾗ καὶ πολλάκις τὴν πάντων ζωὴν καὶ τροφήν, τὸν ἑαυτῆς υἱὸν καὶ Θεόν, περιηγκαλίζετο καὶ μετεδίδου θηλῆς καὶ περιέθαλπε καὶ ἀνέτρεφεν, ὥστε καὶ ταῖς σταγόσιν αὐτὴν ἐκείνου περιηνθῆσθαι τοῦ καινοῦ καὶ παρθενικοῦ γάλακτος.

through her son but also through herself that the compound of our human nature has been raised to the heavens and reigns over all things, visible and invisible.

The apostles, together with Thomas, were again filled 118
with ineffable joy, seeing this inexpressible sight and miracle; and they were filled with an incomprehensible fragrance and grace, since even the burial wrappings were permeated by an extraordinary fragrance and were shining with light, as if they were some kind of radiant and celestial object. They thereupon securely closed the tomb, though they did not conceal the miracle concerning it but conveyed the news to their fellow apostles, and to all the male and female disciples, so that they in turn could convey the news to others, and thus son received the news from father and conveyed it to those who came after him, and thus it has been preserved for us down to the present day. Now heaven rejoices possessing both her spirit and her body, while the earth rejoices in her tomb and burial garments, and the air and all the rest of creation rejoices in her invisible interventions and actions, and every country and city enjoys her ceaseless benefactions. As for our city, in addition to these and her daily protection and miracles, it has inherited, instead of her tomb and burial garments, her belt and mantle, which she wore during her lifetime, girding herself with the former and covering herself with the latter. It was while wearing this covering that she often embraced her son, who is the life and the nourishment of the world, and offered him her breast, and cared for him and nourished him, so that the garment is now stained with drops of her new and virginal milk.

119 Καὶ ὅπως τὰ κατ' ἐκείνην μὲν τὴν παρθενικὴν καὶ νυμφικὴν ζώνην ἄλλως ᾠκονομήθη, ταύτην δὲ τὴν ἱερὰν ἐσθῆτα οἱ ἱεροὶ καὶ σοφοὶ Γάλβιός τε καὶ Κάνδιδος κατὰ τοὺς χρόνους Λέοντος τοῦ εὐσεβοῦς καὶ Μεγάλου παρὰ τῆς Παλαιστίνης ἐκ τῆς ἱερᾶς λαβόντες παρθένου τὲ καὶ πρεσβύτιδος καὶ κληρονόμου καὶ φύλακος τοῦ μεγάλου τούτου χρήματός τε καὶ κτήματος οὐ φαύλῃ σοφίᾳ καὶ τέχνῃ, μᾶλλον δὲ καὶ αὐτῆς ἐκείνης τῆς Θεομήτορος συνεργίᾳ καὶ γνώμῃ περιελθόντες τὸ γύναιον, εἰς τὴν ἡμετέραν ἀνακομίζουσιν, ἑαυτοῖς μὲν ὄντως μακάριον κλέμμα καὶ αὐτῆς ἄντικρυς τῆς τῶν οὐρανῶν βασιλείας ἅρπαγμα εἴτε σύλημα, ἡμῖν δὲ δώρημα καὶ θησαύρισμα παντὸς λόγου κρεῖττον καὶ διανοίας. Καὶ νῦν ἡ μεγαλόπολις αὕτη καὶ βασιλίς, ὥσπερ τι τεῖχος ἢ πανπευχίαν ἢ καὶ βασίλειον στέφος μᾶλλον ἢ ἁλουργίδα ταύτην περιθεμένη, τὴν ὥσπερ διάχρυσον καὶ πεποικιλμένην ἐσθῆτα τῆς πάντων βασιλίδος, καὶ ἑαυτῆς ἀγάλλεται μὲν ὡραϊζομένη ταῖς χάρισι καὶ τοῖς θαύμασιν, ἐπαίρεται δὲ σεμνυνομένη τοῖς κατὰ πάντων τροπαίοις καὶ περιβαλομένη τὴν ἐσθῆτα καὶ ἀναζωσαμένη τὴν ζώνην. Διὰ τούτων καὶ αὕτη κατὰ πάσης ἔχει τῆς οἰκουμένης τὰ νικητήρια ἡ βασίλεια. Καὶ ὡς αἱ τούτων ἡμῖν καὶ ἀμφοτέρων σοροὶ καὶ τῶν ἀγαθῶν πάντων ὄντως σοροὶ μὴ μόνον πάσης μὲν τῶν ἐθνῶν προσβολῆς, πάσης δὲ καὶ θεηλάτου πληγῆς καὶ παντὸς κινδύνου κοινοῦ τὴν πόλιν ἐλευθεροῦσαι, ἀλλὰ καὶ παντὸς ἄλλου πάθους ἰδίου καὶ τοῦ καθ' ἕκαστον καὶ σώματος καὶ ψυχῆς ἀπαλλάττουσαι πάντας τοὺς μετὰ σπουδῆς προσιόντας, πᾶσαν δὲ παρεχόμεναι καὶ καθ' ἑκάστην χάριν καὶ

And, as regards the events surrounding her virginal and bridal cincture, they came about through a different dispensation. These holy garments were acquired during the reign of the pious Leo the Great by the holy sages Galbius and Candidus, from an aged virgin in Palestine, who was the inheritor and guardian of this great treasure and possession. By means of a rather clever ruse and device, or rather with the agreement and cooperation of the Mother of God herself, they maneuvered the woman into allowing them to take the garment to our city. For them, it was a truly blessed theft, a capture and plundering of the kingdom of heaven from her, but for us it was a gift and a treasure surpassing every word and thought. And to this very day, this great and royal city is clothed in her garments as if they were a wall and a complete panoply of armor, or rather a royal crown and imperial purple robe, the clothing of the queen of all which is like a golden and richly woven garment. And so the city rejoices, being beautified by her grace and miracles, and it is elevated, being exalted by the trophies won from all, and being covered by her mantle and encompassed by her cincture. Through these, our city has triumphed over and rules the entire inhabited world. The caskets containing these two garments are for us receptacles of all good things: they have not only spared the city from every attack of the nations, every plague sent by God, and every public danger, but have also protected those who approach them in faith from every form of personal suffering and ailment of body and soul, continually and every day bestowing grace on them, 119

κοινὴν καὶ ἰδίαν καὶ βασιλεῦσι καὶ ἰδιώταις καὶ ἄρχουσι καὶ ἀρχομένοις καὶ πλουσίοις καὶ πένησι καὶ ἀνδράσι καὶ γυναιξὶ καὶ εἴ τι παραλέλειπται τούτων.

Ταῦτα μὲν οὖν ὡς οὐ τοῦ παρόντος οἰκεῖα καιροῦ καὶ ὡς ἰδίας καὶ οὐ τῆς τυχούσης ἱστορίας ἔργον καὶ ὡς οὐκ ὀλίγοις καὶ ἄλλοις καὶ πρὸ ἡμῶν παραδεδομένα παρείσθω. Πρὸς δὲ τὸ οἰκεῖον τέλος ὁ λόγος κατεπειγέσθω τῇ τοῦ Θεοῦ Μητρὶ καὶ Παρθένῳ προσάγων τὰ ἐπιτάφια καὶ ὡς ἐν κεφαλαίῳ δεικνύων ὅπως ἐπὶ ταύτης ἀεὶ τοῖς κατὰ φύσιν τὰ παρὰ φύσιν καὶ τὰ ἐναντία συμβαίνοντα, ἀφθορία καὶ σύλληψις, παρθενία καὶ γέννησις, ἀνωδυνία καὶ τόκος, καὶ ἐῶ πτωχείαν καὶ πλοῦτον, ἀδοξίαν καὶ δόξαν, ἀπορίας τὲ καὶ εὐροίας, κινδύνους καὶ νίκας, εὐπαθείας καὶ ἀπαθείας, φιλοστοργίαν καὶ φιλοσοφίαν ἐσχάτην, καὶ τὸ μηδ' ἕτερον διαφθεῖραι τῇ περὶ τὸ ἕτερον ἀμετρίᾳ μηδὲ ταῖς καθ' ἕκαστον τῶν καλῶν ὑπερβολαῖς ἢ ἐλλείψεσιν, ἀλλὰ καὶ νῦν θάνατος καὶ ζωή, διάζευξις καὶ ἡδονή, ταφὴ καὶ μετάθεσις. Θάπτεται γὰρ ὥσπερ βροτὸς καὶ βροτοῦ, μετατίθεται δὲ καὶ ὡς Θεὸς ἤδη κατὰ χάριν καὶ Μήτηρ Θεοῦ. Καὶ τῷ μὲν πιστοῦται μὴ τὴν οἰκείαν φύσιν μόνον, ἀλλὰ καὶ τὴν τοῦ ἐξ αὐτῆς προσληφθέντος, εἴγε καθάπερ οἱ φύντες τοὺς φύσαντας, οὕτω καὶ τοὺς φύντας δηλοῦσιν οἱ φύσαντες, τῷ δὲ μὴ τὴν τοῦ προσλαβόντος φύσιν μόνον μηδὲ τὴν τοῦ προσληφθέντος εἰς οὐρανοὺς ἔπαρσιν, ἀλλὰ καὶ τὴν ἡμετέραν ὕψωσιν καὶ τὴν ἀφθαρσίαν εἴτε καὶ θέωσιν. Ὥσπερ ἀφθόρως τίκτουσα, οὕτω καὶ νῦν ἀδιαφθόρως

generally and individually, to emperors and private citizens alike, rulers and ruled, rich and poor, men and women, and any other group one could mention.

Let these remarks suffice on these matters, inasmuch as 120
they do not pertain to the present time, and because they merit their own study rather than being a part of this one, and not least because they have already been treated in detail by many different writers before us. Instead, let my discourse hasten toward its proper end, namely, to offer to the Mother of God and Virgin a funeral oration and a summary account of how, in her, all things according to nature always unfolded in a manner beyond and even contrary to nature: bodily incorruption and conception, virginity and birth, painlessness and parturition, not to mention poverty and wealth, her obscurity and glory, penury and prosperity, perils and victories, sensitivity and dispassion, tenderness and perfect love of wisdom, and the fact that the way of one virtue was not negated by the boundless measure of another nor by the excesses of beauty or deficiency in each, so that even now we see even death and life, parting and pleasure, burial and translation. For she was buried like any mortal born of mortals, but was translated like someone who had already become God by grace and the Mother of God. With her burial, she guarantees the reality not only of her own human nature, but also of the nature he assumed from her, if indeed parents reveal the nature of their children and children manifest their parents' nature. With her translation, on the other hand, she guarantees not only the nature of the one who assumed it, or the rising of the one who assumed it into the heavens, but also our own exaltation, incorruptibility, and deification. Just as she gave birth without corrup-

θνήσκουσα, καὶ ὥσπερ λόγου καὶ τρόπου τότε, οὕτω καὶ χρόνου διαμένουσα νῦν κρείττων καὶ φύσεως. Καὶ τὸ παραδοξότερον, εἰς οὐρανοὺς ὑψουμένη καθάπερ τὸ πνεῦμα δίχα τοῦ σώματος, οὕτω καὶ νῦν τὸ σῶμα δίχα τοῦ πνεύματος, ἵνα καὶ τὸ πρὸς τὸν υἱὸν ὁμοῦ καὶ τὸ πρὸς τοὺς δούλους δείξῃ καὶ κοινὸν ὁμοῦ καὶ διάφορον, αἰρομένη μὲν εἰς οὐρανούς, ἀλλὰ καὶ ὅλη καὶ πρὸ τῆς ἀναστάσεως, καθάπερ ἡμεῖς μετὰ τὴν ἀνάστασιν, καὶ ὅλη μὲν καθάπερ καὶ ὁ ταύτης υἱός, ἀλλὰ διῃρημένη καὶ μετὰ τὴν διάλυσιν.

121 Οὕτως ἐγὼ καὶ τὴν φύσιν ἅμα καὶ τὴν χάριν ὁμολογῶ, καὶ οὔτε λίαν οὕτως εἰμὶ παρ᾽ ὃ χρὴ φιλοπάρθενος ὡς ἀθάνατον ταύτην καὶ ἀδιάλυτον, οὔτε λίαν ἢ καλῶς ἔχει φιλοσώματος ὡς εὐδιάλυτον τὸ ταύτης ὑπολαμβάνειν ὁμοίως τοῖς ἄλλοις σῶμα καὶ ἀμετάθετον, ἀλλὰ καὶ τὴν μετάστασιν κατὰ φύσιν ὁμολογῶ καὶ τὴν μετάθεσιν κατὰ χάριν διϊσχυρίζομαι. Καὶ τὴν μὲν τῇ ἀφθαρσίᾳ τιμῶν τὴν κατὰ φύσιν τοῦ θανάτου φθορὰν οὐκ ἀναίνομαι, τοῦ δὲ τὴν διάλυσιν συνιστῶν τῇ ἀκαταλυσίᾳ σεμνύνομαι. Καὶ οὕτω μᾶλλον ἐμαυτὸν δι᾽ ἀμφοτέρων τιμῶ· βροτὸς ἀληθῶς ἀληθῆ γεννήσας Θεόν, καὶ διὰ τοῦτο καὶ Θεὸς ἀληθῶς ἐκ βροτοῦ γενόμενος, οὔτε φαντάσας τὴν γέννησιν οὔτε φαντασθείς μοι τὴν ἀναγέννησιν, ἀλλ᾽ ἐπίσης καὶ μετ᾽ ἀληθείας καὶ τὴν φύσιν παρασχὼν καὶ τὴν χάριν ἀντιλαβών.

tion, so too does she now experience death incorruptibly, and just as then, when she remained superior to every principle and mode of operation, so too now she remains superior to time and nature. And what is even more paradoxical is that, just as her spirit without her body was exalted to the heavens, so too now her body without the spirit is now likewise exalted, so that she might manifest at the same time what she holds in common with, and how she differs from, both her son and his servants. She was thus raised up to the heavens, but wholly and before the resurrection, just as we will be raised after the resurrection. And she was raised in her entirety just as her son was, even though her soul and body were separated after their dissolution.

Thus, I confess together both nature and grace, for I am 121
not so excessively devoted to the Virgin as to declare her immortal and her soul and body inseparable, nor am I so excessively and altogether a friend of the body to think that her body was easily separated from the soul like the bodies of others, or that it was not capable of being transferred to heaven. To the contrary: I confess both her departure according to nature and affirm her translation according to grace. In honoring the soul for its incorruptibility, I am not denying the natural corruption of death; and while confirming the soul's separation from the body in death, I honor her body's exemption from dissolution. Thus, through both, I also honor myself, for a mortal human being truly gave birth to the true God, and for this reason God was truly born of a mortal human being, and his birth was neither an illusion nor does he offer me an illusory rebirth. Instead, he equally and truly submitted himself to nature and gave me divine grace in return.

Οὕτω μοι μὴ φθεῖρε τὰ τῆς ἀφθάρτου μηδὲ χραῖνε τὰ τῆς ἀχράντου δόγματα καὶ διδάγματα, μηδὲ προπετεύου περὶ τὴν τῶν νοημάτων ἔκτασιν, μήποτε καὶ σὺ τὰς χεῖρας καὶ τοὺς βραχίονας ἐκκοπῆς, ἣν ἔχεις ἀντιληπτικὴν τῶν θείων θεωρημάτων καὶ ἰσχυροτέραν τοῦ λόγου δύναμιν, καὶ ἴσως οὐδὲ ἐλεηθῇς αὐτοῦ τοῦ ὀργάνου τῆς μετανοίας ἀποκλεισθεὶς ἢ καὶ αὐτὴν ἀφαιρεθεὶς τὴν τοῦ ἐλέου πρόφασιν. Πολλά σοι καὶ ἄλλα καὶ τῶν ἀνεφίκτων χωρὶς τοῦδε τοῦ μυστηρίου τὰ θεωρήματα φαιδρότερά τε καὶ ἀσφαλέστερα, προσθήσω δὲ καὶ λυσιτελέστερα. Θεώρησον ὕλην εἰς οὐρανοὺς αἰρομένην καὶ νικωμένην ὑπὸ τοῦ κρείττονος, παρθενικὰς ψυχὰς ἢ παρθένους εἰς υἱϊκὰς ὁμοῦ καὶ δεσποτικὰς χεῖρας ἐναποτιθεμένας ἢ καὶ ὅλη τῇ παρθενικῇ καὶ βασιλικῇ Τριάδι, Λόγῳ μὲν ὡς υἱῷ καὶ νυμφίῳ, νῷ δὲ καὶ ὡς κηδεστῇ καὶ Πατρὶ τοῦ Λόγου τὲ καὶ νυμφίου, Πνεύματι δὲ καὶ ὡς ἁρμοστῇ τῆσδε τῆς καλῆς συναφείας, καὶ ὡς νυμφαγωγῷ τὲ καὶ νυμφοστόλῳ. Τοιαύτην οἶδα καὶ τῶν ἀζύγων τὴν συζυγίαν ἐγώ. Τά τε γὰρ ἄλλα πάντα πάντως ὁμόζυγες ὡς σύμμορφοι καὶ ὁμόφρονες καὶ ὅτι ὁμοίως ἄζυγες.

Ἅρπασον καὶ τὴν διὰ νεφελῶν τῶν μαθητῶν ἁρπαγὴν εἰς ἀπόδειξιν τῆς τελευταίας καὶ βεβαίας καὶ τῶν ἐσχάτων Χριστοῦ μαθητῶν ἐπὶ νεφελῶν ἁρπαγῆς, ἡνίκα κἂν οἱ ζῶντες ἁρπάζωνται, ἀλλ' ὅμως ὑπὸ τῶν τεθνηκότων φθάνονται, καὶ τὴν νῦν συνδρομὴν *εἰς* τὴν ἐκεῖθεν *ἀπάντησιν,* καὶ τὴν ἄνοδον εἰς τὴν ἀνάστασιν, κἂν σὺ βούλῃ παρθενικῶς καὶ νοερῶς μεταθέσθαι, μάθε καὶ τὴν μετάθεσιν.

Do not, then, corrupt the qualities of the incorruptible, do not defile the doctrines and teachings concerning the undefiled Virgin, do not be hasty in grasping at speculations concerning her, lest your own hands and arms be cut off, by which I mean the power of reason which is better able to grasp divine realities, and in case, perhaps, you should not find mercy, since you will be deprived of the very instrument of repentance or bereft of any pretext or excuse for mercy. For I will offer you many other brilliant, safer and more profitable contemplations from among those which are beyond understanding, without delving into this particular mystery. Contemplate, if you will, matter raised to the heavens and vanquished by what is superior, virginal souls or virgins placed in filial and lordly hands or given over to the entire virginal and royal Trinity, that is, to the Word as a son and bridegroom; to the Paternal Mind as to a father-in-law and Father of the Word and bride; and to the Spirit as the one who arranges this beautiful betrothal and union, and who is the groomsman and escort of the bride. Such is the wedlock that I see in the unwedded ones. For in all other respects, they are absolutely perfectly conjoined by their common form and mind, though they remain likewise unwedded.

Seize upon the rapture of the disciples into the clouds as proof of the final and assured rapture of the last of Christ's disciples into the clouds, when, even though the living will also be caught up, they will not precede those who were dead. You may also take this present gathering as proof of the *meeting there,* and this present ascension as proof of the future resurrection, and, if you wish to be translated virginally and spiritually, learn also the meaning of her translation.

Σύστειλον μὲν τὸ σῶμα τῆς ἔξω περιπλανήσεως, περίστειλον δὲ κοσμίως τὰς παρθένους αἰσθήσεις καὶ σώφρονας, πανηγύρισον δὲ τῶν παθῶν, τοῦ ἐν ἡμῖν φημι τάφου τὰ ἐπιτάφια, συγκάλεσον δὲ καὶ τὸ γειτονοῦν ἢ συγγενοῦν σοι, τὴν ἀρετήν, συλλαβέσθαι σοι τὰ ἐξόδια. Εἴθ' οὕτω καὶ μέλος ᾆσον ἢ τοῦ πνεύματος ἐπινίκια ἢ τοῦ σώματος προπεμπτήρια ἢ καὶ εἰσβατήρια τοῦ Ἁγίου Πνεύματος. Ἐντεῦθέν σοι καὶ ἀποστόλων—τῶν ἀποστολικῶν, φημί, χαρισμάτων—ἡ συνδρομὴ καὶ ἀγγέλων ἐπιδρομὴ συμμαχούντων τῷ κρείττονι καὶ τέλος ἡ φρικτὴ καὶ δεσποτικὴ προσέλευσις ὅλον ἀγκαλιζομένη τὸ σὸν πνεῦμα καὶ κολπουμένη, τὸν ὅλον οἰκειωθέντα διὰ τοῦ Πνεύματος. Τί ἔτι; Γεθσημανὴ μὲν ἱερωτάτη καταλαμβανομένη, τῶν προαιρετικῶν ἀπάθεια, καταλιμπανομένη δὲ καὶ αὕτη μετ' οὐ πολὺ καὶ ἡ ἀνωτέρα καταλιμπανομένη Σιών, μετατιθεμένης ὅλως τῆς φύσεως καὶ φυσιουμένης ὑπὸ τοῦ κρείττονος. Οὕτω σοι καὶ οὐρανὸς ἔσται βατὸς καὶ δεσποτικὸς ὁρατὸς θρόνος οἷς ἐκεῖνος βαίνεται καὶ οἷς οὗτος ὁρᾶται βήμασί τε καὶ θεωρήμασιν.

122 Εἰ δέ γε μὴ θεωρήματα μόνον, ἀλλὰ καί τινα τῆς ἡμέρας ταύτης αἰσθητὰ ποθεῖς θεατρίσματα καὶ φαιδρύματα, καὶ ταῦτά σοι τρυφᾶν ἐκ περιουσίας ἡ χαριεστάτη τῶν ἑορτῶν αὕτη δίδωσι, τὴν πασῶν τῶν ὡρῶν ὡραιοτέραν ἅμα καὶ ὠφελιμωτέραν προβαλλομένη καὶ ἣν οὐκ ἂν ἁμάρτοι τις ὥραν μόνην καὶ κυρίως εἰπών, ὡς καὶ μετὰ τῶν ἑαυτῆς ὡραίων οὐκ ἄνθεσιν ὡραϊζομένην, ἀλλὰ καὶ καρποῖς, οὐδὲ διὰ τὰς ἄλλας γεγενημένην, ἀλλὰ δι' ἣν αἱ ἄλλαι μᾶλλον καὶ εἰς ἣν πᾶσαι τείνουσι καὶ δουλεύουσι. Χειμὼν μὲν γὰρ

Summon back your body from its outward wanderings; decorously cover your virginal and chaste senses; celebrate the burial of your passions, I mean in the tomb that is within you; and call upon virtue, which is your neighbor and kin, to assist you with the funeral arrangements. After this, chant a melody: either victory songs for the spirit or farewell hymns for the body, or a hymn celebrating the entering in of the Holy Spirit. After this you will experience the gathering of the apostles—by which I mean the apostolic gifts—and the arrival of angels, allies in your fight for what is superior, and, finally, the fearsome advent of the Master, embracing the whole of your spirit and taking it to his bosom, assimilating your whole being through the Spirit. What then? The most sacred Gethsemane, the dispassion of human choices, will be taken up, but soon Gethsemane itself will be left behind, as well as the Zion which is above, since your nature will be wholly translated and exalted by what is superior. In this way, you too will be able to walk about in heaven, and behold the throne of the Master, for it is by these kinds of steps and this kind of vision that they become accessible and visible.

If, however, you long not only for contemplations but 122
also for some sensory spectacles and splendors proper to this day, this most gracious of feasts also offers you these to enjoy in abundance, as it proffers this most beautiful and useful season of the year, which one would not be mistaken in calling the only real season of the year, since, together with its own proper charms it is adorned not simply by flowers but also by fruits. Nor was this season made for the others, but the others were made for it, and they all tend toward it and serve it. Winter is a time for work, and spring an-

ἐργάζεται, ἔαρ δὲ ἐπαγγέλλεται θέρος δὲ καὶ μετόπωρον, ὧν καὶ ἀμφοτέρων αὕτη τοῦ μὲν τέλος τοῦ δὲ ἀρχή. Καὶ αὐτὰ δέχεται καὶ δίδωσι τὰ ἐπαγγελλόμενα, τὰ μὲν τὴν τῶν ἀνθρώπων ζωὴν συνέχοντα, τὰ δὲ καὶ πρὸς τρυφὴν χορηγοῦντα καὶ τέρψιν. Καὶ αὕτη φιλοτιμία φύσεως, μᾶλλον δὲ τοῦ δημιουργοῦ τῆς φύσεως, καὶ τῆς ἐν παραδείσῳ διαγωγῆς ὑπόμνησις, μὴ τῶν ἀναγκαίων μόνον, ἀλλὰ καὶ τῶν περιττῶν, μὴ τῶν πρὸς χρείαν μόνον, ἀλλὰ καὶ τῶν πρὸς ἀπόλαυσιν, καὶ οὕτως οὐ πολυφορωτάτη τῶν ἑορτῶν αὕτη μόνον, ἀλλὰ καὶ παμφορωτάτη, μὴ τῶν ἀπὸ γῆς μόνον, ἀλλὰ καὶ τῶν ἀπὸ θαλάσσης ἀγαθῶν καὶ ἀέρος. Οὕτω καὶ ταῦτα τὴν Παρθένον προπέμπουσι, μᾶλλον δὲ καὶ αὐτὴν ἡ κτίσις προσφέρει τῷ δημιουργῷ τὴν Παρθένον οἷά περ ὡραίων τὸ κάλλιστον ἢ καὶ αὐτὴν ὅλην τὴν ὥραν καὶ τὸ κάλλος τῆς ἡμετέρας φύσεως ἐν καιρῷ καὶ αὐτὴν τρυγωμένην καὶ εἰς τὰς θείας μετατιθεμένην αὐτῷ μονάς.

Τί μὲν γὰρ τῆς παρούσης ὥρας ἡδύτερον ἢ τοῖς ἀνθρώποις ὠφελιμώτερον ἢ πάσῃ τῇ κτίσει φιλοτιμότερον; Νῦν μὲν οὖν καὶ πλοῦτος ὥριος, νῦν δὲ καὶ ἀέριος ἡδονὴ καὶ νεογνῶν ἀκμὴ ζώων καὶ πᾶσα μὲν πτηνῶν, πᾶσα δὲ νηκτῶν, πᾶσα δὲ καὶ χερσαίων ἄγρα, καὶ ἅμα μελέται πολέμων καὶ τροπαίων εὐθηρίαι καὶ κυνηγέσια· νῦν καὶ κρᾶσις στοιχείων εὔκρατος καὶ ἀστέρων φαῦσις εὐθέατος καὶ ἄνεμοι ἐτήσιοι ἥδιστον πνέοντες καὶ ἥμερον ποταμοὶ ῥέοντες καὶ πηγαὶ καὶ κρῆναι δαψιλέστερον ἅμα καὶ διαφανέστερον νάουσαι καὶ κουφότερον. Ἡπλωμένη καὶ

nounces summer and also autumn, of which today's feast marks the end of one and the beginning of the other. And this season both receives and gives its promised fruits, some for the support of human life, some providing pleasure and delight. This abundance of nature, or rather of the creator of nature, is a reminder of life in paradise, which did not produce only what was necessary for life but also what was in excess; not only of what was useful but also of what brought joy. In the same way, this is not only the most prolific of the feasts but also the most abundant not only in the good things of the earth but also those of the sea and the sky as well. Thus these same things escort the Virgin, or rather creation offers the Virgin herself as the most beautiful product of the season, indeed as the whole ripeness and beauty of our nature, harvested in its proper season and translated to his divine mansions.

What is sweeter than this present season, or more useful to mankind, or more generous to all creation? Now we see seasonal riches, now the air is delightful, and there is an abundance of newly born animals, birds, fish, and land animals, all ready to be caught. At the same time, we see military exercises, and successes in winning trophies and hunting. Now the mixture of the elements is well tempered, the glimmer of the stars is easily seen, and the annual breezes blow sweetly; rivers run gently, springs and fountains flow more abundantly, clearly, and lightly. The smiling sea unfolds

προσγελῶσα θάλασσα καὶ παντοίως τὴν χέρσον ἐκθεραπεύουσα, προσπτυσσομένη μὲν μαλακῶς, ἀσφαλῶς δὲ καὶ ἡδέως παραπέμπουσα τοὺς ναυτίλους καὶ τοὺς ἐμπόρους ἐπιμιγνύσα καὶ φιλανθρωπίαν διδάσκουσα καὶ δωροφοροῦσα καὶ παρ' ἑαυτῆς καὶ παρ' ἀλλήλων ἀλλήλοις πᾶν ὅ,τιπερ ἀναγκαῖον εἴτε καὶ τίμιον. Νῦν καὶ χιὼν μάλιστα τηκομένη καὶ ἄμπελος δρεπωμένη καὶ φορολογουμένη μέλισσα καὶ ἡ μὲν ἀπολυομένη πρὸς ἄφθονον πόμα τὲ καὶ νηφάλιον, ἡ δὲ ἀποθλιβομένη πρὸς ἥδιστον κρᾶμά τε καὶ σωτήριον, ἡ δὲ καὶ δυοῖν τοῖν καλλίστοιν, μέλιτος καὶ φωτός, ἀνθρώποις παρέχουσα τὴν συντέλειαν καὶ τὸ μεμελημένον αὐτῇ σίμβλον ἑτέροις φιλοτιμουμένη πρὸς ἡδονὴν ὁμοῦ καὶ ὠφέλειαν. Νῦν καὶ ἄλση τερπνότατα καὶ εὐσκιώτατα καὶ περιηχέστατα καὶ ὀρνίθων οὐδὲν ἧττον ἐαρινῶν παντοδαπὰ μελίσματα καὶ ἀνθρώπων ᾄσματα καὶ κινήματα, στρατιωτῶν μὲν ἐπινίκια καὶ ἐνόπλια, γεωργῶν δὲ ἐπικάρπιά τε καὶ ἐπιλήνια, ὥσπερ καὶ μετ' ὀλίγον θαλύσια.

123 Καὶ ἵν' ἐῶμεν τὰ κάτω ταῦτα, λέγωμεν δέ τι καὶ ὑψηλότερον καὶ οἰκειότερον τῆς ἡμέρας. Νῦν ὅσον οὔπω καὶ νυκτὸς καὶ ἡμέρας ἰσομοιρίαι καὶ ἰσοδρομίαι φωστήρων, ἀνθρώπων οἶμαι καὶ ἀγγέλων, τυποῦσαι τὴν διὰ ταύτης ἰσοπολιτείαν ἢ καὶ πάντων ἰσονομίαν. Καὶ οὐρανὸς ἐπίσης ἡλίῳ καὶ ἄστρασι μεριζόμενος, ἐπεὶ καὶ Θεὸς αὐτὸς πᾶσιν ἑαυτὸν ἐπίσης παρέχων καὶ οἰκειούμενος. Ἥλιος ἀπὸ τοῦ κατ' οὐρανόν, ὥσπερ φασί, λαμπροτάτου καὶ βασιλικωτάτου τῶν ἀστέρων, Λέοντος, τῇ φαιδρᾷ καὶ σταχυηφόρῳ καὶ Παρθένῳ δίκῃ συνελθεῖν ἐπειγόμενος. Οὐκ ἄχαρι καὶ τοῦτο πρὸς τὰ νῦν θεωρεῖν τελούμενα ὅτι καὶ ὁ ταύτης

itself widely; it embraces the dry land and caresses it both gently and firmly, it sends forth sailors safely and sweetly, and brings them among merchants, teaching love for mankind, and bringing as gifts both from itself and in exchange with others whatever is necessary and precious. Now the snow has completely melted, the vine is harvested, and the bee pays her tribute; the snow has been resolved into an abundance of pure drinking water, while the grapes are pressed to give forth a sweet and salutary brew, while the bee provides us with the two loveliest things, honey and light, lavishing on others for both pleasure and profit the purpose and object of caring for her hive. Now also the groves are at their most delightful and well shaded, resounding no less than in spring with every kind of bird song, as well as the songs and dances of men: victory and martial songs of soldiers, farmers' songs of produce and the winepress, soon to be followed by songs of the harvest.

But so that we may set aside these lowly things, let us 123
speak instead of something more elevated and proper to the day. Now, very soon, the day and the night will be equally divided, and also running equal courses will be those shining stars, by which I mean human beings and angels, which are figures of the equality of rights and the equilibrium that came about through the Virgin. And heaven is equally shared between the sun and the stars, for God himself gives himself equally and intimately to all. The sun departs from what they say is the brightest and most royal constellation in heaven, Leo, and duly hastens to join the radiant and corn-bearing constellation of Virgo. It would not be disagreeable to consider this too, in relation to what is being celebrated on this day, namely, that her son departs from his

υἱὸς ἀπὸ τοῦ πάντων βασιλέως τὲ καὶ Πατρὸς ἐπὶ ταύτην νῦν συνερχόμενος τὴν πολλῷ φαιδροτέραν καὶ ἀληθῆ Παρθένον καὶ οὐ πάντων δικαιοτέραν μόνον, ἀλλὰ κἀμὲ δικαιοῦσαν ἐκ τῆς ἐλλάμψεως ἢ γεννήσεως ἢ τρίτον καὶ τῆς δεήσεως, οὐκ ἀμαυρουμένην ὥσπερ ἐκείνη διὰ τῆς συνελεύσεως, ἀλλὰ καὶ λαμπρυνομένην πλέον ὑπὸ τοῦ κρείττονος.

Ἔτι μικρὰ ταῦτα καὶ προσγειότερα κἂν ὑψηλὰ καὶ οὐράνια· νῦν ἡ ἐμὴ φύσις καὶ πάλιν εἰς οὐρανούς, πρώτη μὲν ὡς τὴν καθ' ἡμᾶς καὶ κοινήν, δευτέρα δὲ ὡς πρὸς τὴν καινὴν καὶ θεάνθρωπον, ἀνωτέρα καὶ θρόνων, φρικτοτέρα καὶ χερουβίμ, σοφώτερα καὶ σεραφίμ, μᾶλλον δὲ φοβερὰ καὶ θρόνοις, φρικτὴ καὶ τοῖς χερουβίμ, καὶ τοῖς σεραφὶμ ἀκατάληπτος, κοινὴ δὲ πάντων ὁμοῦ βασιλίς, βασιλείαν τὴν ἀκατάλυτον, μόνης αὐτῆς ἀποφερομένη τῆς βασιλικῆς Τριάδος τὰ δεύτερα, καὶ ταύτης αὐτῆς ἐμφορουμένη πρὸς κόρον, ὅλον τὸν βασιλικὸν περιβεβλημένη πλοῦτον, ἀποβλεπομένη καὶ προσκυνουμένη παντὶ καὶ τάγματι καὶ ὀνόματι καὶ ῥητῷ καὶ γνωστῷ καὶ ἡμῖν τῷ τέως ἀρρήτῳ τὲ καὶ ἀγνώστῳ. Ἃ δέ μοι μὴ λαμπρότερα μόνον, ἀλλὰ καὶ λυσιτελέστερα· νῦν δευτέρα μεσῖτις πρὸς τὸν πρῶτον μεσίτην, ἄνθρωπος θεοφόρος πρὸς ἀνθρωποφόρον Θεόν, ἀπαρχὴ τῷ Πατρὶ δευτέρα, τερπνὴ καὶ μετὰ τὴν πρώτην ἄμωμος. Ἀλλὰ ταῦτα μὲν ὑπὲρ πάντα λόγον τὲ καὶ καιρόν, καὶ οὐδὲ νοεῖν μήτιγε λέγειν τοῖς καθ' ἡμᾶς ἢ καὶ ὑπὲρ ἡμᾶς δώσομεν. Ἡμῖν δὲ τούτων μὲν ἀφεκτέος, πρὸς δὲ τὸ

Father, the king of all, and now joins the much brighter and true Virgin. And she is not only more just than all, but she even justifies me by her illumination, her birth giving, and, thirdly, by her intercession. The Virgin's brilliance, moreover, is never obscured by the arrival of the son, as is the constellation Virgo, but to the contrary is rendered brighter by the presence of what is superior.

Yet these are small things and rather earthly, even if they are lofty and celestial, because now my nature has once again ascended to the heavens. The first time was with the ascension of our common human nature in Christ; the second time was when our nature ascended toward the new and theanthropic nature, so that our nature is now above thrones, more fearsome than cherubim, wiser than seraphim, or rather formidable to thrones, striking fear even in the cherubim, and incomprehensible even to the seraphim, the common sovereign of all things; it is an indestructible kingdom, holding the second place only to the sovereign Trinity, and filled to completion with the Trinity itself, arrayed in the entirety of royal richness, admired and venerated by every rank and every name that can be uttered and known, as well as by every name which to us was hitherto ineffable and unknown. But that which is not only more splendid for me but also more profitable, is this: now we have a second mediator between us and the first mediator, a God-bearing human being between us and the man-bearing God; a second offering of our first fruit to the Father, an offering which, after the first one, is delightful and without blemish. But these things transcend all reason and every season, and we will allow neither ourselves nor those above us to think, let alone speak, about them. But while we must

πέρας ὁ λόγος ἤδη κατεπειγέσθω, βραχέα μὲν διὰ τὸ μῆκος, πολλὰ δὲ ὅμως διὰ τὴν χρείαν προσεπειπών. Ἔσται γὰρ ὁ αὐτὸς εὐχαριστήριός τε ἅμα καὶ προπεμπτήριος, ἤδη δὲ πάντως καὶ ἱκετήριος.

124 Εὐχαριστοῦμέν σοι, Δέσποτα καὶ οἰκονόμε πάντων τῶνδε τῶν μυστηρίων, τά τε ἄλλα καὶ ὅτι τοιαύτην ἡμῖν ἐξελέξω τῶν σῶν διάκονον μυστηρίων.

Εὐχαριστοῦμέν σοι τῆς ἀφάτου σοφίας καὶ δυνάμεως καὶ φιλανθρωπίας, ὅτι μὴ μόνον τὴν φύσιν ἡμῶν ἑαυτῷ συνέδησας καὶ ὁμοτίμως ἑαυτῷ συνεδόξασας καὶ ὁμοθέως ἐθέωσας, ἀλλὰ καὶ μητέρα σὴν ἐξ ἡμῶν γενέσθαι οὐκ ἀπηξίωσας, καὶ ταύτην βασιλίδα πάντων, οὐρανοῦ τὲ καὶ γῆς, ἀπέδειξας.

Εὐχαριστοῦμέν σοι, κοινὲ Πάτερ, ὅτι καὶ τὴν σὴν μητέρα κοινὴν ἡμῶν μητέρα γενέσθαι πεποίηκας, ἵνα μηδεὶς ἡμῖν λείπῃ τῶν γειναμένων καὶ δι' ἀμφοτέρων οὐ τῆς υἱοθεσίας μόνον, ἀλλὰ καὶ τῆς ἀδελφικῆς κλήσεώς τε καὶ σχέσεως κατηξίωσας.

Εὐχαριστοῦμέν σοι τῷ τοσαῦτα μὲν ὑπὲρ ἡμῶν δι' ἡμᾶς παθόντι, τοσαῦτα δὲ παθεῖν ὑπὲρ σοῦ καὶ ἡμῶν καὶ τὴν σὴν μητέρα παρασκευάσαντι, ὅπως μὴ μόνον τῶν παθῶν ἡ ὁμοτιμία καὶ τὴν κοινωνίαν αὐτῇ τῆς δόξης αὐτῆς ἐργάσηται, ἀλλὰ καὶ τὴν ὑπὲρ ἡμῶν οὕτως ἀεὶ μᾶλλον πραγματεύσηται σωτηρίαν μεμνημένη τῶν ἐφ' ἡμῖν ὠδίνων, καὶ τὸ φίλτρον ἔχῃ μὴ διὰ τὴν φύσιν μόνον, ἀλλὰ καὶ τὴν τῶν ὧν ἐσπούδασε παρ' ὅλον τὸν βίον ὑπὲρ ἡμῶν ὑπόμνησιν.

refrain from discourse about these matters, my own discourse is already nearing its end, so let me say a few additional words, brief on account of length, but many on account of necessity. May my discourse be at once an expression of my gratitude and one of farewell, or better, of supplication.

We thank you, Master and steward of all these mysteries, 124
for above all you have chosen the Virgin as the minister of your mysteries.

We give thanks to you for your ineffable wisdom, power, and love for mankind, for you not only joined our nature to yourself, glorified it with an honor equal to your own, and deified it, making it like God, but you also did not deem it unworthy for your mother to be chosen from among us, and you have established her as the queen of all things on heaven and earth.

We give thanks to you, our common Father, for you made your own mother our mother, so that none of us would lack parents, and through both you have made us worthy not only of adoption but to receive the name and relationship of brothers.

We give thanks to you who suffered so much for our sake, and who prepared your own mother to suffer so many things for you and for us, so that not only would her equal share of honor from the sufferings bring about our communion with your glory but would also always transact the business of our salvation, remembering her pain when she was with us, and that the love you have for us is due not only to human nature but also to the recollection of all that she strove to do for us throughout her life.

Εὐχαριστοῦμέν σοι τῷ δόντι μὲν ἑαυτὸν *λύτρον* ὑπὲρ ἡμῶν, δόντι δὲ μεθ' ἑαυτὸν καὶ τὴν σὴν μητέρα καθ' ἑκάστην λυτήριον, ἵνα ἅπαξ μὲν αὐτὸς ἀποθάνῃς ὑπὲρ ἡμῶν, αὕτη δὲ μυριάκις ἀποθνήσκει τῇ προαιρέσει διακαιομένη καθάπερ καὶ ἐπὶ σοὶ τὰ σπλάγχνα δι' οὕς, καθάπερ καὶ ὁ Πατήρ, οὕτω καὶ αὕτη τὸν υἱὸν αὐτῆς δέδωκεν ἢ καὶ ἐκδεδομένον εἶδε πρὸς θάνατον.

125 Εὐχαριστοῦμεν καὶ σοί, Δέσποινα, τῶν μέχρι τοῦ νῦν ὑπὲρ ἡμῶν καμάτων καὶ παθημάτων. Καὶ οὐ θρηνοῦμεν τὰ ἐπιτάφια, ἀλλὰ πανηγυρίζομεν τὰ ἐπιθαλάμια, οὐδὲ σχετλιάζομέν σου τὰ προπεμπτήρια, ἀλλὰ κροτοῦμεν τὰ εἰσβατήρια. Οὐδὲ γὰρ καταλείπεις ἡμῖν τὰ ἐπίγεια καταλαμβάνουσα τὰ οὐράνια, οὐδὲ τῶν ἐγκοσμίων ἀπολυθεῖσα μόχθων καὶ πρὸς τὴν ἀτελεύτητον ἅμα καὶ ἀνεκλάλητον μεταβᾶσα μακαριότητα, τῶν ἡμετέρων ἐπιλανθάνῃ κακῶν, ἀλλὰ νῦν μέμνησαι μᾶλλον καὶ ἀπολύεις τὰ χαλεπά, οὐδὲ τὴν ὀρφανίαν ἡμῖν διχόθεν κατέστησας, ἀλλὰ λύεις μᾶλλον τὴν ὀρφανίαν μεθ' ἑαυτῆς καὶ τὸν σὸν υἱὸν καὶ ἡμέτερον Πατέρα προσχαριζομένη καὶ διαλλάττουσα.

Νῦν ἕστηκας *ἡ βασίλισσα* τοῦ βασιλέως *ἐκ δεξιῶν* ὑπὸ πολλῶν καὶ ἄλλων δορυφορουμένη βασιλίδων λαμπρῶν, παρθενικῶν ψυχῶν καὶ βασιλικῶν, *ἐν ἱματισμῷ διαχρύσῳ* τοῦ Πνεύματος καὶ περιβολαίῳ τοῦ ἀξιώματος καὶ ποικιλίᾳ τῶν ἀρετῶν ἢ καὶ τῶν χαρισμάτων. Νῦν ἔχεις ἐκ χειρὸς τοῦ σοῦ υἱοῦ καὶ Θεοῦ τὸ διάδημα τῆς εὐπρεπείας καὶ τὸ σκῆπτρον τῆς βασιλείας καὶ τὴν ζώνην καὶ τὴν πορφύραν τῆς κατὰ πάντων ἐξουσίας καὶ τῆς περιχεθείσης σοι δι' ὅλου φωτοχυσίας καὶ τῆς θεώσεως. Ἀλλ' *ἄκουσον* καὶ νῦν

We give thanks to you who gave yourself as a *ransom* for us, and who subsequently gives us every day your own mother as a deliverance, so that, whereas you yourself died once and for all for us, she dies time and again voluntarily, her inner being consumed with fire as it also was for you, and for those for whom, like the Father, she also gave her son, or even saw him being given over to death.

We thank you also, sovereign Lady, for all the labors and 125
sufferings that you have endured for us down to this present day and hour. We are not mourning your death but celebrating with songs your wedding; nor are we singing songs of complaint about your departure, but applauding your entrance into heaven. For in obtaining heaven, you did not abandon us here on earth, and though you have been released from the toils of this earthly life and have been transferred to eternal and ineffable bliss, you have not forgotten our troubles and ills, but you remember us now even more and deliver us from hardships; you have not made us orphans a second time, but rather you deliver us from our orphanhood together with yourself, and you gratify your son and our Father and reconcile us to him.

Now you *stand as the queen at the right hand* of the king, accompanied by many radiant sovereigns, virginal and royal souls, clothed *in a golden robe* of the Spirit, and in a garment of honor and a variety of the virtues and graces. Now you have from the hand of your son and God a crown of august beauty, the scepter of the kingdom, the cincture and the purple robe of authority in every dominion, and the cascade of light and deification that has been wholly poured out upon you. *But hear* us now, *daughter: the rich among the people*

ἡμῶν, *θύγατερ· τὸ πρόσωπόν σου λιτανεύσουσιν οἱ πλούσιοι τοῦ λαοῦ,* πάντες οἱ κατ' ἀξίαν ἢ ἀρετὴν προέχοντες παρακλήτορες τῆς παρακαλούσης ὑπὲρ ἡμῶν γινόμενοι. Καὶ μὴ ἐπιλάθῃ *τοῦ λαοῦ σου καὶ τοῦ οἴκου τοῦ πατρός σου,* τοῦ ἀντιθέτου τῷ πρὶν λαῷ καὶ οἴκῳ. Καὶ ἐπιθυμήσει πάλιν *ὁ βασιλεὺς τοῦ κάλλους σου,* τῆς περὶ τὴν εἰκόνα καὶ κατ' ἐκείνην αὐτοῦ τὴν εἰκόνα φιλανθρωπίας, καθάπερ καὶ τῆς φιλοπαρθενίας ἢ παρθενίας τὸ πρότερον, μᾶλλον δὲ φιλανθρωπίας καὶ νῦν καὶ πρότερον.

126 Οὐ γὰρ ἀφιλάνθρωπον οἶδά ποτε τὴν Μητέρα τοῦ φιλανθρώπου. Πείθουσί με τοῦτο καὶ ζώσης ἔτι φιλοπτωχίαι τὲ καὶ ξενοτροφίαι καὶ προστασίαι καὶ θεραπεῖαι τῶν δεομένων καὶ ψυχῆς ἅμα καὶ σώματος, καὶ μεταστάσης αἱ καθ' ἡμέραν θαυματουργίαι καὶ μερικαὶ καὶ κοιναὶ καὶ πανταχοῦ καὶ παντοδαπαὶ καὶ λόγου κρείττονες καὶ ψάμμου πλείονες· ἃ δὲ πολλῷ κρείττω καὶ ὑψηλότερα, ἐγγύαι μὲν καὶ διαλλαγαὶ διηνεκεῖς τῶν ἁμαρτωλῶν, ὁδηγίαι δὲ καὶ φυλακαὶ τῶν δικαίων, καὶ συνελόντα φάναι, σωτηρίαι καὶ θεουργίαι καὶ κοιναὶ καὶ ἴδιαι τοῦ συγγενοῦς κράματος. Ὡς τάχα γε καὶ τούτου μᾶλλον ἑάλω τοῦ κάλλους ὁ βασιλεύς, τῆς περὶ τὴν φιλανθρωπίαν ἀπληστίας καὶ ἐμφερείας αὐτῷ, ἢ γὰρ τῶν ἄλλων, τῆς σωφροσύνης λέγω καὶ τῆς ἀνδρείας καὶ τῆς φρονήσεως καὶ ὅσα τῶν ταύτης καλῶν ὑπὲρ πᾶν κάλλος τῆς ἡμετέρας φύσεως. Καὶ οὕτως ὁ φιλανθρωπότατος ἑαυτοῦ πάλιν, εἰ οἷόν τε εἰπεῖν, φιλανθρωπότερος γίνεται, διὰ φιλανθρωπίαν καὶ ταύτην ἐκλεξάμενος, καὶ τὴν οὕτω καὶ φιλάνθρωπον οὐ μητέρα μόνον,

will make supplication before your face, that is, all those distinguished by their worthiness or virtue who have become intercessors with the one who intercedes for us. And do not forget *your people or the house of your father,* who are the opposite of the former people and their house; and *the king will* again greatly desire *your beauty,* that is, your great love of humanity, which relates to and reflects the image of God, just as he formerly desired your love of virginity or simply your virginity, or rather your love of humanity both now and then.

For I have never known the Mother of the one who loves 126
mankind to be without love for mankind. In this I am persuaded by all the examples, while she was living, of the way she loved the poor, gave hospitality to strangers, and offered protection and assistance to those in need, both in soul and body; and, after her translation, I am also persuaded by her daily miracles, both general and individual, in all places and of every kind, which are beyond reason and more numerous than the sand of the sea. And what is even greater and more sublime are the pledges to and constant reconciliations of sinners, the guidance and protection of the just, and, to speak succinctly, the miracles, both public and private, for the salvation of the human race. And perhaps the king has also been captivated by this particular beauty, namely, her insatiable love of mankind, which is his very likeness, more than all the other virtues, by which I mean her chastity, courage, prudence, and all the other beauteous things that surpass the beauty of our human nature. And thus the most compassionate king himself becomes, as it were, even more compassionate for having chosen her in his compassion, and wanting this compassionate Virgin to be not simply his

ἀλλὰ καὶ μεσῖτιν ἑαυτοῦ καὶ διαλλακτήν, ἵν' οὕτως ἑκατέρωθεν συνδεόμενος ἄφυκτον ἔχῃ καὶ ἀμετακίνητον τὴν πρὸς ἡμᾶς ῥοπὴν καὶ συμπάθειαν ὁ Παράκλητος τοῦ Πατρός, καὶ *ἄλλον* ἑαυτοῦ *παράκλητον* εὑρηκώς, ἀνατρέποντα μὲν καθεκάστην τοὺς δικαίους αὐτοῦ θυμούς, διαπορθμεύοντα δὲ πᾶσι τοὺς οἰκτιρμοὺς καὶ τὰς φιλοτιμίας ἐπιδαψιλευόμενον.

127 Ὢ πόσα τῇ Παρθένῳ καὶ ὑπὲρ φύσιν τὰ κατορθώματα, πόσα δὲ καὶ τῇ φύσει παρ' αὐτῆς τὰ φιλοτιμήματα! Ὑπερέβη τὴν φύσιν οὐ τῇ παρὰ φύσιν κυοφορίᾳ μόνον, ἀλλὰ καὶ τῇ παρὰ φύσιν φιλανθρωπίᾳ, καὶ ζῶσα καὶ θνήσκουσα. Ἔλυσε τὴν ἀράν, *τὴν ἔχθραν* κατέλυσεν, ὅλης με τῆς τιμωρίας ἀπέλυσεν, ὅλης με τῆς ἁμαρτίας νικητὴν ἀνέδειξε, δι' ἑαυτῆς ἐδίδαξε πρώτης νικᾶν τὸν πόλεμον, τὴν παρθενίαν φυτεύσασα, τὴν ἀνδρείαν παιδεύσασα, τὴν σοφίαν, τὴν μετριοφροσύνην, τῶν ἄλλων ἑκάστην καὶ μεθ' ὑπερβολῆς ὁρίσασα. Οὐχ ὅσον ἡττήμεθα νενικήκαμεν, ἀλλὰ καὶ πλέον ἢ ὅσον εἰπεῖν ἔχομεν· τὴν Ἐδὲμ ζημιωθέντες, τοὺς οὐρανοὺς ἐκερδήσαμεν ἢ καὶ ἀμφοῖν ἐκρατήσαμεν ἢ καὶ ὅλων ἐβασιλεύσαμεν· τὴν ἐντολὴν κλαπέντες, τὴν ἀρετὴν ἐχαρίσθημεν· τὸ τῆς Ζωῆς Ξύλον ἀφαιρεθέντες, αὐτὸν τὸν τοῦ Ξύλου δημιουργὸν ἐτύθημεν ἢ καὶ αὐτοῦ μᾶλλον ἐνεφορήθημεν· τὴν θείαν περιστολὴν ἀπογυμνωθέντες, τὸν Θεὸν αὐτὸν ἐνεδύθημεν ἢ ἐνεδύσαμεν ἤ, ὅπερ καὶ ἀληθέστερον, ἀνεκράθημεν καὶ ὅλως Θεοὶ γεγόναμεν.

mother but a mediator with himself and reconciler, so that the Intercessor to the Father, being supplicated on both sides, might be lovingly disposed toward us in a way that is inescapable and irrevocable, and find her to be *another intercessor,* who in every hour could overturn his just wrath, conveying mercies and lavishly bestowing munificence on all.

Oh, how many and how far above nature are the accom- 127
plishments of the Virgin, and how many generous gifts has she given to human nature! She has surpassed nature not only by her conception, which was contrary to the law of nature, but also by her love for mankind, which likewise transcends nature, both while she was alive and after her death. She removed the curse, she brought *the hostility* to an end, she delivered me from all punishment, she made me a victor over every sin, and through her own example first taught us to be victorious in war. She established virginity, she taught courage, and to a superlative degree she defined wisdom, moderation, and each of the other virtues. We have not been vanquished as much as we have been victorious, and we can say our victory is far greater than our defeat. Though we lost Eden, we have acquired heaven or rather we have kept both and indeed have become sovereigns wholly of both. Though we transgressed the commandment, we have been rewarded with virtue. Though we were deprived of the Tree of Life, we have won through sacrifice the creator of the Tree, or rather we are now filled with him. And though we were stripped naked of our divine covering, we have been clothed in God himself, or rather have clothed ourselves in God, or more truly, we have been mingled with God and have become wholly Gods.

Τοσαῦτά μοι καὶ ἔτι πλείω, Παρθένε καὶ Μῆτερ, χαρίζῃ καὶ ζῶσα καὶ θνήσκουσα· καὶ νῦν ζῶσα μᾶλλον ὅσῳ καὶ ζῶντι σύνει καὶ τῆς Τριάδος ἕνα τοῦτον ὁρᾷς τὸν ἐκ σοῦ γεννητόν, τὸν σοὶ χωρητὸν καὶ οὐρανῷ καὶ γῇ μὴ χωρούμενον· καὶ νῦν χαριζομένη μᾶλλον ὅσῳ καὶ τὸν χαριζόμενον ἐγγύτερον ἔχεις ἢ ἑτοιμότερον, μᾶλλον δὲ καὶ ἀφ' ἑαυτῆς ἤδη σχεδὸν τὸ πᾶν ἔχεις, ὅτε καὶ οἷς ἐθέλεις χαριζομένη καὶ τοῖς ἐθέλουσιν. Ὃ δέ μοι χαριέστατον ἅμα καὶ ἀσφαλέστατον, ὅτι μοι καὶ τούτων σφαλλομένῳ πολλάκις τῶν ἀγαθῶν, αὖθις ἀνόρθωσις καὶ ἀνάκλησις ἡ αὐτὴ καὶ τῆς ἐμῆς ἀεὶ σωτηρίας καὶ θεουργίας ἐπάνοδος οὐδέποτε παυομένη, ἀλλ' ἅπαξ μὲν τῷ γένει παντὶ γενομένη, ἀεὶ δὲ φυλαττομένη καὶ τῷ γένει καὶ τοῖς καθ' ἕκαστον, ἄνετος καὶ κοινὴ πᾶσι πύλη καὶ ἄκλειστος—τὴν νοητὴν γαστέρα, κἂν τὴν αἰσθητὴν κλειστὴν καὶ αὐτῷ τῷ διελθόντι καὶ διανοίξαντι.

128 Ἀλλ' ὦ κοινὴ καὶ καινὴ Μῆτερ, οὐχ ὡς τοῦ καινοῦ μόνον ἀνθρώπου τὲ καὶ Θεοῦ οὐδὲ ὡς καινῶς τὸν καινὸν γεννήσασα, ἀλλὰ καὶ ὡς ἡμῖν ὑπὲρ τὰς κοινὰς φανεῖσα μητέρας καὶ πᾶσιν ὁμοῦ καὶ ἑκάστῳ καὶ πολλῷ πλέον ἢ ἐκεῖναι καὶ οὐδ' ὅσον ἔστιν εἰπεῖν ἀγαπήσασα. Ὦ κρᾶμα καινῶν ἀρετῶν καὶ καινόν· ὦ σύστημα τῶν κατὰ φύσιν πάντων καλῶν καὶ τῶν ὑπὲρ φύσιν σύγκριμα· ὦ θείων χειρῶν καὶ θείων χαρίτων ἄγαλμα καὶ συμπλήρωμα· ὦ πάσης τῆς κτίσεως ἄνθος καὶ τῆς ἀνθρωπίνης φύσεως αὔχημα καὶ χαρὰ καὶ ζωὴ καὶ σωτηρία καὶ βραχίων καὶ δόξα καὶ εἰρήνη καὶ νίκη

Such, and many more, are the things that you have given us, Virgin and Mother, both when you were alive and after your death. And inasmuch as you now live all the more, since you are together with and see the one who lives, who is one of the Trinity, who was born from you, whom you contained though neither heaven nor earth can contain him, now also you grant us grace even more readily, inasmuch as you are closer to the giver of grace, or rather, since you yourself already possess everything, you give graciously to whomever you wish among those who themselves wish for your gifts. What is most lovely to me and at the same time most reassuring, is that no matter how many times I err with respect to these good things, you again are my reclamation and restitution, and you never cease being the one who constantly restores my salvation and deification, for having been born once for the whole human race you protect us forever, and, for both the whole human race and for each and every human being, you are a door that is always open and accessible to all—I speak of your spiritual womb, since your physical womb itself is closed, even to him who entered it and came forth from it.

O Mother, common and new! New not simply as one who 128
in a novel manner gave a new birth to the new man and God, but because you became our mother beyond our own mothers, both for all and for each; and much more than them, loving us more than we can say. O new mixture of new virtues! O amalgam of all the beautiful things of nature, and compound of all that transcends nature! O ornament and complement of divine hands and virtues! O flower of all creation, adornment of human nature, and joy, life, salvation, power, glory, peace, victory, wisdom, kingdom, deification,

καὶ σοφία καὶ βασιλεία καὶ θεουργία καὶ πάντων τῶν καλλίστων καὶ ὑπὲρ φύσιν ἄθροισμα καὶ ἡμῖν πρόξενε καὶ θησαυρέ, μήτε λόγῳ λεγόμενε, μήτε χρόνῳ κενούμενε, μήτε δὲ λογισμῷ καταλαμβανόμενε.

Ὦ Θεοῦ μὲν ἀνθρώποις, ἀνθρώπων δὲ Θεῷ, καὶ θεότητος μὲν ἀνθρώποις, ἀνθρωπότητος δὲ Θεῷ δώρημά τε καὶ δάνεισμα, Τριαδικῶν χαρίτων πλήρωμα, ὅλης καὶ ὅλη τῆς Τριάδος σκήνωμα καὶ μετὰ τὴν Τριάδα τῶν ὅλων Δέσποινα, στάμνε καὶ ῥάβδε καὶ λυχνία καὶ κλίνη καὶ τράπεζα καὶ οἶκε καὶ κιβωτὲ καὶ πηγὴ καὶ κῆπε καὶ νεφέλη καὶ στύλε καὶ δίσκε καὶ πύλη καὶ ὄρος, Ἐδέμ, οὐρανέ, θρόνε τὲ καὶ ναὲ καὶ εἴ τί σε ἄλλο συμβολικῶς οἱ θεόπται καὶ προφῆται καλοῦσι καὶ σοὶ προπάτορες. Σοῦ μὲν τίς τὴν πολυωνυμίαν, μᾶλλον δὲ τὴν μυριωνυμίαν ἀκούσας ἢ μηδ' ἀκοῦσαι δι' ὅλων ἰσχύσας τῶν κλήσεων ἄλλό τι πρὸ ταύτης ἐθαύμασε; Σοῦ δὲ τίς ἐννοήσας τὴν ἀπειρίαν ἢ μηδ' ἐννοῆσαι μᾶλλον ἰσχύσας τῶν ἀρετῶν ἢ μυστηρίων ἢ θαυματουργιῶν ἢ δυνάμεων οὐδ' ἐκείνην ἐθαύμασε; Καὶ σοῦ μέν τις τῶν ἀρχαιοτέρων ἀκούων οὐδέν τι καὶ τῶν νεωτέρων θαυματουργημάτων ἢ φιλανθρωπευμάτων ἐζήτησε· σοῦ δέ τις καὶ τὰ παρόντα βλέπων καθ' ἑκάστην θαυματουργήματα καὶ τὰ ἀεὶ νεώτερα καὶ καινότερα, οὐδέν τι καὶ τῶν παλαιοτέρων ἐδεήθη παραδοξολογημάτων. Οὕτω καὶ δι' ἀμφοῖν καὶ διὰ πάντων νικᾷς καὶ ἡβᾷς ἐς ἀεὶ τοῖς θαύμασιν.

129 Ἀλλὰ νῦν μᾶλλον εἴπερ ποτὲ τὸν σὸν ἐπισκέψοιο καὶ ἐπισκέπτοιο κλῆρον· νῦν τὸν σὸν περιέποις λαόν, τὸν σὸν κατὰ χάριν υἱὸν καὶ ἀγαπητόν, τὴν σὴν ποίμνην, ἣν καὶ ὁ

the gathering of all the most beautiful things transcending nature, and our patron and treasure: you, who cannot be uttered in speech, nor emptied by time, nor grasped by the mind.

O gift and loan of God to human beings, and of human beings to God, and of divinity to humanity, and of humanity to God, the fullness of the graces of the Trinity! You are the whole dwelling place of the whole Trinity, and after the Trinity the sovereign Lady of all; urn and rod and lampstand and couch and table and house and ark and fountain and garden and cloud and pillar and paten and gate and mountain; Eden, heaven, throne and temple, and everything else the divine visionaries and prophets and forefathers have symbolically called you. Who upon hearing your many names, or rather your myriad names, or even without being able to hear all your names, would marvel at anything else? Who upon comprehending your infinity, or rather being unable to comprehend your virtues, mysteries, miracles, and powers, would not also marvel at your infinity? Someone hearing only of your ancient marvels would not seek out any of your newer miracles and compassionate acts to mankind; but someone else, seeing the ever newer and ever more novel miracles that you work every day, would have no need of your ancient marvels. Thus, in both the past and the present and in all things, you prevail and thrive by your miracles.

And now, more than ever, visit and continue to visit your 129
inheritance! May you now treat your people graciously, which is your beloved son by grace, your flock, which your

σὸς υἱὸς τοῖς ἑαυτοῦ πάθεσί τε καὶ αἵμασι καὶ αὐτὴ τοῖς ἑαυτῆς μέχρι τοῦ νῦν ἀγωνίσμασι καὶ σπουδάσμασιν, ὁ μὲν ἐκτήσατο καί σοι προσεκτήσατο, σὺ δὲ περιεποιήσω καὶ υἱοθετήσω καὶ εἰσέτι καὶ νῦν θηλάζεις καὶ αὔξεις καὶ κοινῇ καὶ καθ' ἕκαστον, ὡς ἓν *σῶμα* καὶ ἕνα πάντας ἄνδρα γενέσθαι τῆς πνευματικῆς τελειότητος, μίαν κεφαλὴν τὸν σὸν υἱὸν ἔχοντας, τὸν Χριστόν. Ταύτην ἀνακαλοίης καὶ θεραπεύοις. Ὁρᾷς ὅπως ἔχουσαν καὶ ὅπως κάμνουσαν καὶ σώμασι καὶ χρήμασι καὶ ψυχαῖς, καὶ κοινοῖς καὶ ἰδίοις καὶ οἰκείοις καὶ ἀλλοτρίοις πολέμοις τὲ καὶ κακοῖς. Ὁρᾷς ὅπως καὶ καθ' ἑαυτῆς μαινομένην καὶ λυμαινομένην ὑφ' ἑαυτῆς καὶ οὐδὲ δεομένην θηρίων, ἀλλ' αὐτῶν μᾶλλον ἀντὶ προβάτων θηρίων καὶ τούτων παντοδαπῶν καὶ ἐναντίων ἀλλήλοις γεγενημένων καὶ οὐδὲ μάνδρᾳ περιεχομένων ὅσον ἐπὶ τῇ γνώμῃ ὡς εἴθε μὴ περιείχοντο, ἀλλ' ἐλευθερίαζον καὶ ἄλλος ἀλλαχοῦ διεσπείρετο, τὸ μετριώτερον τῶν κακῶν. Νῦν δὲ τοῦτο τὸ πάντων χαλεπώτατόν τε ἅμα καὶ ἀφυκτότατον, ὅτε τῷ μὲν τρόπῳ διΐστανται, τῷ δὲ τόπῳ συνέχονται, ὥστε μηδὲ τὰς κατ' ἀλλήλων ἐνὸν εἶναι φεύγειν ὁρμάς, ἀλλὰ περιπίπτειν ἀλλήλοις, καὶ μηδὲ ὑπεκκλίνειν ἀλλήλοις δύνασθαι, καὶ τὸ χείριστον, μηδὲ τοῖς ἀλλήλων κακοῖς παιδεύεσθαι, ἀλλὰ τοῖς ἀλλήλων κακοῖς κατ' ἀλλήλων μᾶλλον διερεθίζεσθαι.

Ἀλλὰ σὺ Μήτηρ ἡμῶν εἶ, καὶ ταῖς ἀδελφοκτονίαις καὶ ταῖς ἀσεβείαις ἡμῶν σὺ ἱλάσῃ, καὶ γένοιο νῦν μάλιστα διπλῆ καὶ ἡμῖν πρὸς ἀλλήλους καὶ κοινὴ πάντων πρὸς τὸν σὸν υἱὸν διαλλακτὴς καὶ μεσῖτις, οὐ μητρικαῖς παρρησίαις μόνον, ἀλλὰ καὶ ἱκετηρίαις καὶ δάκρυσιν, ὥσπερ καὶ τὸ

son acquired and won for you by means of his sufferings and his blood, and which you have kept safe until now by means of your struggles and labors, and which you have adopted, and which you even now nourish and increase both as a whole and individually, so that all may become *one body* and one man in spiritual perfection, having one head, Christ your son. May you remember this, your flock, and take care of it. May you see what a state it is in, how it is sick in body, in its affairs, in its soul, in public and private, how it is beset with domestic and foreign wars, and with disasters. May you see how it rages against itself and plunders itself without needing wild beasts to do so, since the sheep have turned into beasts of every kind, all of them hostile to each other. They are no longer contained within a sheepfold, inasmuch as they imagine they are not contained, but the flock is loose, scattered all over the place, and this is the lesser of the evils. But now the worst and most unavoidable evil of all is that, even though they are separated in this way, they are still gathered in one place, so they cannot evade each other's attacks, but one falls upon the other, and one is not able to avoid the other, and worst of all, no one learns anything from the evils befalling each other, but rather are provoked against each other by the evils befalling each other.

But you are our Mother, and so, may you forgive our acts of fratricide and impiety. May you be for us, especially at this time, a double and common reconciler and mediator between us and each other, and all of us to your son, not only through your maternal boldness of speech, but also by your supplications and tears, as you have done in the past with

πρὶν ἱδρῶσι καὶ κακουχίαις πολλαῖς καὶ θλίψεσιν ἀνακτωμένη τὴν σὴν ποίμνην καὶ συμβιβάζουσα, τοῦτο μὲν καὶ καθ' ἑαυτούς, τοῦτο δὲ καὶ ἀπὸ τῶν ἔξωθεν ληστῶν ἢ πολεμίων ἢ καὶ θηρῶν φυλάττουσα. Κἀνταῦθα μὲν ἀσφαλῶς καὶ εἰσάγουσα καὶ ἐξάγουσα καὶ ἐκτρέφουσα καὶ κατασκηνοῦσα τόποις χλόης καὶ ὕδασιν ἀναπαύσεως, κἀκεῖ δὲ πρὸς τὰς θείας μονὰς καὶ νομάς, εἴτ' οὖν τάξεις καὶ θεωρίας, ἀποκληροῦσα καὶ τῷ σῷ λαῷ τὸν σὸν λαὸν καὶ κλῆρον συμβασιλεύουσα.

Δέχοιο δὲ καὶ τόνδε τὸν λόγον δῶρον, ὃν καὶ ἤδη δῶρον αὐτὴ μετά γε καὶ πολλῶν ἄλλων τῷ νῦν δωρουμένῳ δεδώρησαι, οἴκοθεν ἀντιλαμβάνουσα οἴκαδε τῶν πολλῶν ὀλίγα, τῶν μεγάλων μικρά, καὶ αὐτὸ δὲ καὶ τὸ λαμβάνειν καὶ τὸ παρέχειν αὐτὴ παρέχουσα, καὶ ᾗ καὶ αὐτὸ τὸ διδόναι λαμβάνειν ἐστὶ καὶ πολυπλασιάζουσα τῷ χαριζομένῳ τὴν χάριν ἐν αὐτῷ Χριστῶ τῷ σῷ υἱῷ καὶ Θεῷ σὺν τῷ παναχράντῳ καὶ συνανάρχῳ αὐτοῦ Πατρὶ καὶ ζωοποιῷ καὶ συναϊδίῳ Πνεύματι, νῦν καὶ ἀεὶ καὶ εἰς τοὺς αἰῶνας τῶν αἰώνων. Ἀμήν.

your sweat and numerous hardships and your afflictions, defending your flock and bringing them together, in the latter case with each other, and in the former protecting them from thieves and enemies and savage beasts from without. May you do this here by leading them safely in and out, and by nourishing them and pasturing them in a place of green grass, by waters of rest; and there by assigning them to heavenly mansions and pastures, or, in fact, to orders and contemplations, and reigning over your people and your inheritance.

May you receive this discourse as a gift, which is already a gift from you, after so many other gifts that you have given to the one who is now giving it. From home to home, you receive little instead of much and small things instead of great, even though you are the one who grants both this very receiving and giving, and when you receive this very giving you also multiply the grace for the one who is being graced by Christ himself your son and God, together with his incorruptible and co-unoriginate Father, and his life-creating and coeternal Spirit, now and always and unto the ages of ages. Amen.

Abbreviations

ACO = E. Schwartz, ed., *Acta Conciliorum Oecumenicorum,* 4 vols. (Berlin, 1914)

GCS = *Die griechischen christlichen Schriftsteller der ersten drei Jahrhunderte*

GNO = Werner Jaeger, ed., *Gregorii Nysseni Opera,* 10 vols. (Leiden, 1960–)

ODB = Alexander P. Kazhdan, ed., *The Oxford Dictionary of Byzantium* (Oxford, 1991)

PG = Jacques-Paul Migne, *Patrologia cursus completus, series Graeca,* 161 vols. (Paris, 1857–1866)

Protevangelium = Harm Reinder Smid, *Protevangelium Jacobi: A Commentary,* trans. G. E. van Baaren-Pape (Assen, 1965)

SC = *Sources chrétiennes*

Note on the Text

The complete Greek text of Geometres's *Life of the Virgin* has long remained unpublished. In 1955, Antoine Wenger, *L'Assomption de la T. S. Vierge dans la tradition byzantine du VIe au Xe siècle* (Paris, 1955), 364–415, published the last part (the Dormition and the epilogue), together with a French translation. The complete text was edited by Anezoula Benia in a PhD dissertation submitted to the University of Athens in 2019.[1] The plans of earlier scholars, Martin Jugie, Wenger, and Michel-Jean van Esbroeck, to publish Geometres's text did not come to completion. Van Esbroeck's draft of chapters 1–102, which Fr. Maximos Constas recovered from Wenger's archives, was no more than a hasty transcription of Vaticanus gr. 504, along with an initial attempt to punctuate the text.[2] Some reference numbers in this draft may perhaps indicate endnotes with variant readings, but these notes are missing. Even the 1955 partial edition by Wenger (which corresponds to chapters 103–29 in our text) is marred by a large number of misreadings and typos, and we regret to say that all his attempts to intervene in the text, as recorded in his apparatus, were, in our view, mistaken or unnecessary.

The present edition is based on the following three manuscripts containing the full text of Geometres's *Life:*

V = Vatican City, Biblioteca Apostolica Vaticana, Vat. gr. 504, fols. 173v–94v, completed on July 6, 1105.[3] Manuscript V is a theological miscellany written by John Chaldos, "εὐτελὴς μοναχὸς καὶ πρεσβύτερος" (worthless monk and presbyter), a priest at the church of the Virgin and Saint Averkios at the Patriarchate in Constantinople.[4] The manuscript, 422 × 285 mm, is largely on paper, except for fols. 1–4, 116–56, and 191–97, which are on parchment. Because of a mistaken dating of P (below), V was for a long time thought by scholars to be the earliest by far and received high praise for the quality of its text.[5] Manuscript V was carefully collated against another source and corrected throughout, and consequently contains countless interlinear orthographical corrections or additions (for example, of an abbreviated δέ and καί, or an article written in smaller size and squeezed into insufficient space or written above the line). There are also many conjectures or variants noted in the margins as γρ (γράφεται or γράφε) readings.[6] In the Notes to the Text and the variant readings cited below, the following abbreviations have been used to indicate V's readings:

V^{ac} = V *ante correctionem,* meaning V before correction

V^{pc} = V *post correctionem,* meaning V after correction

$V^{\gamma\rho}$ = V γράφεται or γράφε, meaning V has a variant reading in the margin introduced by an abbreviated "it is written" or "write"

The same abbreviations have been used to report such readings in P (so P^{ac}, P^{pc}, $P^{\gamma\rho}$).

P = Paris, Bibliothèque nationale de France, Par. gr. 215, fols. A1–A10, pp. 1–268.[7] P has been dated to the thirteenth century but in fact belongs to the "typographic minuscule" script described and dated to the first half of the twelfth century by Georgi Parpulov, "Six Scribes of the Early Comnenian Period," *Estudios bizantinos* 5 (2017): 91–107.[8] Manuscript P is damaged at the beginning and the end: fols. A1–A10 lack half of each page, and pp. 255–68 are also badly damaged. Otherwise, like V, P is generally accurate and its testimony is extremely valuable, given the problems of G (below).

G = Genoa, Biblioteca Franzoniana, MS Urbanus 32, fols. 242r–309v, dated to 1321. The manuscript, 230 × 152 mm, on Western paper, is a miscellany, containing canonical, conciliar, and patristic texts. As already noted by Annaclara Cataldi Palau in her detailed description of the manuscript, the scribe of G makes orthographic mistakes, including several errors in breathings and accents, and many other mistakes.[9] The errors are countless and make this witness generally unreliable.[10] A few examples: ὅτι (for εἴ τι), ὑπέρ (for εἴπερ), τοῖς (for τῆς), αἰγόνιμον (for αἱ γόνιμοι), πρὸς ἣν (for προσῆν), εὐτεκνοτάτη (for εὐτεχνοτάτη), ἀντίθεον (for ἀντίθετον), λόγχευμα (for λόχευμα), πειρακτήρια (for πειρατήρια). The scribe also tends to accent both parts in compound words (for example, ὑπὲρηρμένη, συνεἰσενεγκῶν). Some of these mistakes could be explained if the scribe was writing at dictation and was hearing, or rather, mishearing words (instead of copying by eye). Yet although production by dictation cannot be excluded, it is also possible that these mistakes were made during the internal dictation by the scribe to himself (after he read and memorized portions of the text) and could be due to his indifference or insufficient training. As will be shown below, an ancestor of G was produced by collating at least two manuscripts. It is unfortunate that G's excessive errors undermine its credibility as a potential witness to an otherwise lost tradition.[11]

Our edition also takes into account the catena on the gospel of Luke by Niketas of Herakleia (abbreviated as Cat. below and in the Notes to the Text), an anthology of patristic comments perhaps compiled between 1105 and 1115. Niketas included forty-seven excerpts from Geometres's writings, primarily (if not exclusively) from the *Life of the Virgin* and the *Homily on the Annunciation*. The excerpts from the *Life* come from chapters 20–25, 32, 34–36, 38, 42–43, 46, 54, 60–63, and 86. Most of these excerpts have been edited by Angelo Mai from a very early manuscript, Vatican, Biblioteca Apostolica Vaticana, Vat. gr. 1611, dated to 1116/7,

which we consulted.[12] Following his usual method, Niketas often shortened and adapted Geometres's text in different ways, for example, by adding a sentence at the beginning of the excerpt or by changing participles to past tense verbs.[13] This creates problems for using such excerpts as secondary witnesses, but in a number of cases we are confident in reporting variant readings. Another problem is that several excerpts of the *Life* extant in this catena have been arbitrarily incorporated (within brackets) into the edition of the *Homily on the Annunciation* in *Patrologia Graeca* 106:811–48, which is not reliable, and this creates further confusion in identifying the catena excerpts from Geometres's works.

For this edition, we did not consult codex Milan, Bibliotheca Ambrosiana, E 100 sup. (gr. 307), fols. 135–70, of the thirteenth century, which contains the sections from the *Life* on the Passion and the Resurrection (chapters 73–102). It was thought that this manuscript transmitted an independent text, a homily *On Christ's Deposition from the Cross*, but Benia has shown that this text is identical to the corresponding section in the *Life*.[14] Benia adds that this manuscript, like G, has serious orthographical errors.[15] We also did not consider the manuscript Brussels, Bibliothèque des Bollandistes, 196, fols. 59r–182v, which is a copy of G made by the Jesuit Balthasar Cordier (1592–1650), who also provided a Latin translation.

Below we describe and explain some aspects of the copying history of this text, based on the three main manuscripts. We prefer not to draw a *stemma codicum* based on the information below, because this might give an oversimplified impression of the text's manuscript transmission, since all three manuscripts' production involved collation, incor-

porating many more copies than the witnesses such a stemma would present. In fact, it is very likely that earlier Byzantine editors of Geometres's *Life* had already collated various witnesses of the text by the time of our earliest extant manuscripts, and this could account for the generally high quality of the text's transmission. In any case, as will be shown, the two main manuscripts (V and P) were corrected through collation with additional manuscripts. Byzantine scribes and scholars were well aware of a single source's inevitable errors and aimed to produce a corrected copy by consulting additional exemplars. The copyist of the third manuscript (G), or more likely of its ancestor, which would not have had the innumerable orthographical problems of G, seems to have acquired his text from both V and P. In establishing the text of this edition, the readings of both V and P were treated on their own merits.

Manuscript V has its own errors and therefore cannot be the ancestor of P and G. Examples of these errors:

4	μόνοι V: μόνης PG
69	καὶ ἀμπελώνων *omitted* V: PG *have it*
84	πάθος V: πάθους PG
105	μὴ μόνον V: μὴ μόνον μὴ PG

Manuscript P in turn has its own errors, and may not be the ancestor of G. Examples of these errors:

4	θερμότερον *omitted* P: VG *have it*
8	τούτων P: τύπων VG
88	αἰτήματος P: ἐγχειρήματος VG
104	καὶ τὰ οὐράνια *omitted* P: VG *have it*
116	ἐμπεριεχόντων P: ἐμπεριηχούντων VG

Manuscript G shares some errors with V, but not all the errors of V. Similarly, it shares some errors with P, but not all the errors of P. This indicates that G's text (or one of its possible ancestors') draws on both V and P. Examples of where V (or one of its ancestors) appears to be the source:

8 διαφαινόμενα δὲ VG: καὶ διαφαινόμενα P

39 αὐτός VG: αὐτὸν P

79 διαμάρτυρέ VG: διαμάρτυραί P

91 ταύτην VG: ταύτας P

98 τῷ VG: τὸ P

105 τὴν φύσιν ὑπέρ φύσιν VG: ὑπὲρ φύσιν τὴν φύσιν V$^{\gamma\rho}$P

105 αὐτὴν μὲν ἀφ' ἑαυτῶν VG: ἀφ' ἑαυτῶν μὲν αὐτὴν V$^{\gamma\rho}$P

Examples where P (or its ancestors) may be the source:

15 προσκαλέσηται PGCat.: προκαλέσηται V

35 λεγόμενα . . . ὁρώμενα PGCat.: ὁρώμενα . . . λεγόμενα V

43 ᾤετο *omitted* PG: V *has it*

54 προτιμότερον PG: προτιμῶντες V

59 εὐαγγελίων PG: εὐαγγελιστῶν V

105 τῆς ἀναγεννήσεως *omitted* PG: τῆς ἀναγεννήσεως V

109 τοῦτον PG: τοσοῦτον V

The following errors appear in all three manuscripts, and thus they must have been made in a common ancestor of the three:

4 αὐτόθεν εὐαγγελιζόμενος: *a possible lacuna before or after* αὐτόθεν *detected by Alexakis*

35 τρόπον *Simelidis: omitted by the manuscripts*
128 ἄλλο τι: οὐκ *deleted by Constas and Simelidis before* ἄλλο

It is possible that some errors of this common ancestor were corrected in V by an able scholar, such as συνοιστέον (VP), corrected to συνιστέον in the margin of V, as a γρ variant, at chapter 6. Generally, V takes its corrections from P and/or G (or their possible ancestors), as well as from an additional source or an able scholar. Examples of some of the corrections for which there is another extant manuscript witness:

61 διελέγετο V$^{\gamma\rho}$PG: διαλεγομένη V
63 αὐτά V$^{\gamma\rho}$GCat.: αὐτός VP
63 τοῦ τρόπου V^{pc}P: τὸν τρόπον V^{ac}GCat.
105 ὑπὲρ φύσιν τὴν φύσιν V$^{\gamma\rho}$P: τὴν φύσιν ὑπέρ φύσιν VG
111 ἐκάθαιρε V$^{\gamma\rho}$G: ἐκκαθαίρει VP

Of course, not all of these corrections made in V are improvements, for example:

101 μνήματος V^{ac}P: σώματος V^{pc}G
113 τρέψαντος V^{ac}P: στρέψαντος V^{pc}G

It is impossible to know if the unique corrections or mistaken suggestions in V are taken from a different branch of the transmission or are conjectures and emendations by scribes and scholars:

17 κἀν V^{pc}: καὶ V^{ac}PG
36 νεύμασιν VPG: δόγμασιν V$^{\gamma\rho}$
46 τὰ πλεῖστα VPG: τὰ πλείονα V$^{\gamma\rho}$
88 μανίαν VPG: κακίαν V^{pc}

98 γινομένην VPG: γινομένη V^{pc}
111 κοινήν V^{pc}: καινὴν V^{ac}PG
114 πλήθους VPG: πάθους $V^{\gamma\rho}$
116 οὐ $V^{\gamma\rho}$: μηδὲ VPG
129 κακῶν VP: καλῶν $V^{\gamma\rho}$
129 ὑπεκκλίνειν P: ὑπ' ἐκκλίνειν V: ὑποκλίνειν $V^{\gamma\rho}$

Some of these readings seem to have been suggested as improvements of the text, for example, in chapter 16, οὐδὲ ὡς ἐκ τῆς VPG (οὐχ ὡς ἐκ τῆς $V^{\gamma\rho}$). Similarly, καθαρώτερος V^{pc} in 68 (καθαρώτατος V^{ac}PG) looks like a correction by a reader of V, made due to the πολλῷ that follows. It is a correct change from a grammatical point of view, though the superlative may be more appropriate here, given that the reference is to God. In any case, it is evident that V, and to a less extent P, were read carefully by later scribes, who made corrections based on collation with other manuscripts of Geometres's *Life* and possibly conjectures of their own. This is attested by the corrections in V mentioned above, but also by those found in P:

10 ἀναζωννυμένην P: ἀναζωννυμένη $P^{\gamma\rho}$V
33 ἀνωδίνως VP^{pc}: ἀνωδύνως P^{ac}G
51 σωτηρία $VP^{\gamma\rho}$G: θεωρία P
52 πεπραγμένοις $VP^{\gamma\rho}$: πραττομένοις P
87 μανίας $VP^{\gamma\rho}$G: μιαιοφονίας P
90 περιθυροῦσα VPG: περιθεωροῦσα P^{pc}
111 κτίσεως $VP^{\gamma\rho}$G: φύσεως P

Attentive scribes and scholars recognized problems in the text and endeavored to determine the correct reading or make conjectures of their own. Two examples will suffice. At

chapter 6, V and P have συνοιστέον, which has been rightly corrected to συνιστέον in V as a γρ variant (in the margin), where however a further (wrong) suggestion has also been made: an eta was written above iota (which is in fact the reading of G: συνηστέον). Awareness that συνιστέον comes from σύνοιδα must have led to the orthography συνοιστέον. Another example, where the puzzle is not grammatical but a matter of content, is found at chapter 10, where πατρὸς is offered by $V^{ac}G^{pc}$ and πνεύματος by $PV^{\gamma\rho}G^{ac}$. A later passage confirms that the correct reading is πατρὸς (chapter 20: καὶ νυμφίος ὁ αὐτὸς ὁμοῦ καὶ πατὴρ καὶ υἱὸς γινόμενος).

Our Notes to the Text are selective and do not include, for example, common and trivial scribal errors (such as several cases of *saut du même au même*), later additions or corrections to V, or the innumerable errors of G.

Some conventions used in this edition follow the accentuation of the manuscripts and not the rules generally used for the edition of classical texts. A clear trend in our manuscripts is that the particle τέ is accented when it follows a paroxytone and even (most of the times) a perispomenon.[16] However, we did not follow the manuscripts (and especially V) when they often do not treat the indefinite pronoun τίς as enclitic, because we wanted to avoid misleading readers into thinking that questions are implied.[17] Similarly, ἐστί and ποτέ are not always treated as enclitics in the manuscripts,[18] but V and P are not consistent or in agreement, and in these cases we follow the classical rules. We also avoided orthography that could be confusing today, such as the manuscripts' μὴ δὲ instead of μηδὲ.[19]

The punctuation adopted in this edition aims at clarifying the syntax of the text, which is often difficult to deci-

pher. The punctuation found in the manuscripts was often helpful in our work but has not been reproduced in this edition. The frequent commas, as well as high, middle, and low dots, were used by Byzantine scribes as a guide for reading aloud but would be confusing to the modern reader.

The division of Byzantine texts into chapters is largely arbitrary or subjective, but for ease of reference and study we have chosen to align (as much as possible) the chapter divisions of the original Greek text with those in the Georgian version, even though the editor of that version, Michel-Jean van Esbroeck, acknowledged that he did not closely follow the chapter divisions in the Georgian manuscripts.[20] We also opted to omit the subheadings that appear within many of the main sections (for example, ἐγκώμιον Ἰωσήφ, περὶ Ἡρώδου, περὶ τοῦ ἀστέρος, and so on), not only because they break up the text's rhetorical continuity but also and primarily because they are evidently later additions seemingly included to make the *Life* more navigable for readers. We are grateful to Thamar Otkhmezuri for confirming that the earliest Georgian manuscript (Tbilisi, National Center of Manuscripts, MS A-40, dated to around the year 1000) does not include any subheadings, but only the main section titles (with the exception of the Resurrection and the Conclusion).[21]

Notes

1 Anezoula Benia, "Ιωάννη Γεωμέτρη, Εξόδιος ή προπεμπτήριος εις την Κοίμησιν της υπερενδόξου Δεσποίνης ημών Θεοτόκου: Πρώτη έκδοση και μελέτη του κειμένου." Online access to the dissertation has been restricted by the author until November 2022, but an abstract is available at http://hdl.handle.net/10442/hedi/46340. It should be noted that our edition of Geometres's text was conducted independently of Benia's, and we

became aware of her dissertation only when our own work was at an advanced stage. In 2020, Christos Simelidis was briefly allowed to consult a hard copy of the dissertation at the National Documentation Centre in Athens.

2 See Maximos Constas, "The Story of an Edition: Antoine Wenger and John Geometres's *Life of the Virgin Mary,*" in *The Reception of the Virgin in Byzantium: Marian Narratives in Texts and Images,* ed. Thomas Arentzen and Mary B. Cunningham (Cambridge, 2019), 324–40.

3 The manuscript has been cataloged by Robert Devreesse, *Codices Vaticani Graeci,* vol. 2, *Codices 330–603* (Rome, 1937), 338–49. It is now available online at https://digi.vatlib.it/view/MSS_Vat.gr.504. For bibliography see the Pinakes database (https://pinakes.irht.cnrs.fr/notices/cote/67135).

4 This is according to the note on his other known manuscript, which was completed on April 21, 1086. For the identification of Ioannis as the same scribe, see Georgi Parpulov, "Six Scribes of the Early Comnenian Period," *Estudios bizantinos* 5 (2017): 91–107, at 93. Before this identification, scholars had tended to assume that the manuscript was written in the Athonite monastery of Chaldos. See, for example, Filippo Ronconi, "Nell' ἐργαστήριον di Ἰωάννης, monaco e presbitero: il Vat. gr. 504," in Filippo Ronconi, *I manoscritti greci miscellanei. Ricerche su esemplari dei secoli IX–XII* (Spoleto, 2007), 219–38.

5 Wenger, *L'Assomption,* 188.

6 For such variants, which could either report a reading found in another manuscript (γράφεται: it is written) or present such a reading or a scribe's or scholar's conjecture as a correction to be adopted (γράφε: write), see Nigel G. Wilson, "An Ambiguous Compendium," *Studi Italiani di Filologia Classica* 20 (2002): 242–43, and Nigel G. Wilson, "More about γράφεται Variants," *Acta Antiqua* 48 (2008): 79–81.

7 Available online at https://gallica.bnf.fr/ark:/12148/btv1b110002265. The only catalog available does not contain any helpful information: Henri Omont, *Inventaire sommaire des manuscrits grecs de la Bibliothèque nationale,* vol. 1 (Paris, 1886), 24.

8 We are thankful to Dr. Parpulov for discussing the date of this manuscript with us.

9 Annaclara Cataldi Palau, *Catalogo dei manoscritti greci della Biblioteca Franzoniana (Genova): (Urbani 21–40)* (Rome, 1996), 90–126.

10 For a similar conclusion reached by an editor of another text included

in the manuscript, see Alessandra Bucossi, ed., *Andronici Camateri Sacrum armamentarium,* Corpus Christianorum Series Graeca 75 (Turnhout, 2014), xlix.

11 One example will suffice: at 89 one would be tempted by G's παρεκτικός and prefer it over P's παρακτικός.

12 Angelo Mai, *Scriptorum Veterum Nova Collectio,* 10 vols. (Rome, 1825–1838), vol. 9, pp. 626–722. The manuscript is available online at https://digi.vatlib.it/view/MSS_Vat.gr.1611. For a study of this catena on the basis of a different manuscript, see Christos Krikonis, *Συναγωγὴ Πατέρων εἰς τὸ κατὰ Λουκᾶν Εὐαγγέλιον ὑπὸ Νικήτα Ἡρακλείας (κατὰ τὸν κώδικα Ἰβήρων 371)* (Thessaloniki, 1973). For Niketas's works see Bram Roosen, "The Works of Nicetas Heracleensis (ὁ) τοῦ Σερρῶν," *Byzantion* 69 (1999): 119–44.

13 On which see Krikonis, *Συναγωγὴ Πατέρων εἰς τὸ κατὰ Λουκᾶν,* 33.

14 Benia, "Ιωάννη Γεωμέτρη, Εξόδιος," 63. For a description of this manuscript and its contents, see Emidio Martini and Domenico Bassi, *Catalogus codicum graecorum Bibliothecae Ambrosianae,* 2 vols. (Milan, 1906), reprinted in one volume (Hildesheim and New York, 1978), 350–51; and the Pinakes database (https://pinakes.irht.cnrs.fr/notices/cote/42717).

15 Benia, "Ιωάννη Γεωμέτρη, Εξόδιος," 125.

16 On this feature see Jacques Noret, "L'accentuation de τε en grec byzantine," *Byzantion* 68 (1998): 516–18.

17 Compare Joseph A. Munitiz, *Nicephorus Blemmydes, Autobiographia (sive curriculum vitae) necnon epistula universalior,* Corpus Christianorum Series Graeca 13 (Turnhout, 1984), lx, at n. 113.

18 See Jacques Noret, "L'accentuation Byzantine: En quoi et pourquoi elle diffère de l'accentuation 'savante' actuelle, parfois absurd," in *The Language of Byzantine Learned Literature,* ed. Martin Hinterberger (Turnhout, 2014), 96–146, at 127, 130–31.

19 See Noret, "L'accentuation Byzantine," 113.

20 Michel-Jean van Esbroeck, *Maxime le Confesseur: Vie de la Vierge,* Corpus Scriptorum Christianorum Orientalium 478–79, Scriptores Iberici 21–22, 2 vols. (Leuven, 1986), vol. 1, p. xiv.

21 Thamar Otkhmezuri, personal correspondence with the authors, April 11, 2021.

Notes to the Text

title ἐξόδιος ἢ προπεμπτήριος εἰς τὴν κοίμησιν τῆς ὑπερενδόξου δεσποίνης ἡμῶν Θεοτόκου, τοῦ μακαρίου Ἰωάννου τοῦ Γεωμέτρου V: λόγος διαλαμβάνων σοφῶς καὶ <. . .> τῆς κυήσεως καὶ μέχρι καὶ αὐτ<. . .> ὑπεραγίας δεσποίνης ἡμῶν <. . .> ὅς: καὶ ἐξόδιος ἢ προπεμπτήριος P; τοῦ μακαριωτάτου Ἰωάννου Γεωμέτρου τοῦ Κυριώτου, ἐξόδιος ἢ προπεμπτήριος εἰς τὴν κοίμησιν τῆς ὑπερενδόξου δεσποίνης ἡμῶν Θεοτόκου, εὐλόγησον πάτερ G

1 δὴ V^{ac}: δὲ V^{pc}G; *omitted* P

τάξιν V: ἀξίαν G *(P's text is missing here)*

πολὺ V: καὶ κατὰ πολὺ G *(P's text is missing here, but the reading of G would not fit in P's space)*

ἄλλως θ' ὅτε PG (G: ἀλλ' ὡς θ' ὅτε): ἄλλωστε ὅτε V

ἐκείνην ἐστὶν PG: ἐστὶν ἐκείνην V

2 ποθοῦσι VG: παθοῦσι P

ἑαυτῆς VG: αὐτῆς P

ἔλιπε VP: κατέλιπε G

3 παραδράμωμεν VG: παρεδράμωμεν P

4 Ἰωακεὶμ ἐνταῦθα: ἐγκώμιον Ἰωακεὶμ καὶ Ἄννης *added by* VG *in the margin (title)*

μόνης PG: μόνοι V

κατ' αὐτοὺς V: καθ' αὑτοὺς PG

ὁμοῦ: τὲ *was added by* V

αὐτόθεν εὐαγγελιζόμενος: *Alexakis detected a possible lacuna somewhere here, as it is unclear precisely what* εὐαγγελιζόμενος *refers to, grammatically speaking. Euthymios has "the angel of God" as a subject.*

6 συνιστέον *(with an eta written above iota)* V^{γρ}, συνοιστέον VP, συνηστέον G

8 τύπων VG: τούτων P

αὐτῷ V^{pc}PG: αὐτοῦ V^{ac}

καὶ διαφαινόμενα P: διαφαινόμενα δὲ VG

9 παραλιπὼν VG: καταλιπὼν P

10 λέγων ἐπ' αὐτῆς V^{pc}P: ἐπ'αὐτῆς λέγων V^{ac}G

πατρὸς V^{ac}G^{pc}: πνεύματος PV^{γρ}G^{ac}; *compare 20,* καὶ νυμφίος ὁ αὐτὸς ὁμοῦ καὶ πατὴρ καὶ υἱὸς γινόμενος

λογισμοὺς V^{pc}PG: λογισμῶν V^{ac}

ἀναζωννυμένη P^{γρ}VG: ἀναζωννυμένην P

μεταβαλοῦσα V^{ac}PG: μεταβαλοῦσαν V^{pc}

νικῶσα V^{ac}PG: νικῶσαν V^{pc}

ἀποσβεννυμένη V^{ac}PG: ἀποσβεννυμένην V^{pc}

ἐρείδουσα V^{ac}PG: ἐρείδουσαν V^{pc}

ἐκτείνουσα V^{ac}PG: ἐκτείνουσαν V^{pc}

προσάπτουσα V^{ac}PG: προσάπτουσαν V^{pc}

ἐρείδουσα^{2} V^{ac}PG: ἐρείδουσαν V^{pc}

βύσσον VG: βύσσαν P

διαλλακτὴς VG: διαλλακτίς P

μεσῖτις V^{pc}PG: μεσίτης V^{ac}

12 ταύτην PG: ταύτη V

εἴη VG: ἴη P

διαφυλάξαι VG: φυλάξαι P

13 τοσούτου VG: τοιούτου P

τῆς V: *omitted* PG

15 ἀπολεξαμένοις VG: ἀποδεξαμένοις P

προκαλέσηται V: προσκαλέσηται PGCat.

16 οὐδὲ ὡς ἐκ τῆς VPG: οὐχ ὡς ἐκ τῆς V^{γρ}

17 Εἰ δὲ δεῖ μηδὲ τὰ τούτου: ἐγκώμιον Ἰωσὴφ *added by* P *in the margin (title)*

ὑπηρετησαμένου VPG: ὑπηρετήσαντι V^{ac}

κἂν V^{pc}: καὶ V^{ac}PG

ἁρμονίας VG: προνοίας P

οὗ V^{γρ} PG: ᾧ V

κώμην V^{pc}PG: πόλην V^{ac}

18 Ἀλλ' ὅρα μοι Θεοῦ μυστήρια: εὐαγγέλια Ζαχαρίου *added by* P *in the margin (title)*

πρὸς παρασκευὴν VPG: προπαρασκευὴν Cat.

19 Οὐ πολὺς ὁ ἐν μέσῳ χρόνος: εὐαγγέλια τῆς Θεοτόκου *added by* P *in the margin (title);* Τοῦ αὐτοῦ μακαρίου Ἰωάννου τοῦ Γεωμέτρου εἰς τὸν εὐαγγελισμὸν τῆς ὑπεραγίας Θεοτόκου *added by* V *in the margin (title)*

21 ἀμφότεροι PG: ἀμφότερα V

τὴν καθαρὰν καὶ σοφὴν καὶ ψυχὴν ὁμοῦ καὶ φωνήν VP^{ac}GCat.: τὴν καθαρὰν ὁμοῦ καὶ σοφὴν καὶ ψυχὴν καὶ φωνήν V^{pc}

22 δηλώσῃ VPG: ἐμφήνῃ Cat.

23 ᾧ V: ὃ P

24 ἀπαρτίσας PG: ἀπαρτήσας V

αὐτὸ V: αὐτῷ PG

θεασομένη VCat.: θεασαμένη PG

29 ἐξόν V: ἦν *added* P: ἐξῶν G

31 προσαγορεύουσα V: προαγορεύουσα PG

λέγει V: λέγων PG

32 λυπρογέως V^{pc}: λυπρόγειος VPG

33 διά *omitted* GP

ἀνωδίνως VP^{pc}: ἀνωδύνως P^{ac}G

35 τρόπον *after* τίνα *added Simelidis*

ὁρώμενα . . . λεγόμενα V: λεγόμενα . . . ὁρώμενα PGCat.

36 Ἐντεῦθεν καὶ ἀστὴρ: περὶ τοῦ ἀστέρος *added by* VP *in the margin (title);* ὁ ἀστὴρ *added by* G *in the margin (title)*

διατάττουσα VG: διαπράττουσα P, τάττουσα $P^{γρ}$

νεύμασιν VPG: δόγμασιν $V^{γρ}$

37 Ὅρα δὲ ὅπως καὶ ὁ χρόνος: περὶ τῶν μάγων *added by* VPG *in the margin (title)*

Ποιμένες δὲ δι' ἀγγέλων: περὶ τῶν ποιμένων *added by* V *interlinear, added by* P *in the margin (title);* σημείωσαι περὶ ποιμένων *added by* G *in the margin*

38 Ἀλλ' ἐντεῦθεν μὲν Ἡρώδης: περὶ Ἡρώδου *added by* V *interlinear, added by* PG *in the margin (title)*

39 αὐτὸν P: αὐτός VG

40 Ἀλλὰ δωροφορήσωμεν καὶ ἡμεῖς: ἐγκώμιον τῶν μάγων *added by* VPG *in the margin (title)*

42 πῶς μὲν Ἡρώδης: περὶ Ἡρώδου *added by* V *in the margin (title); omitted* PG

43 ᾤετο V: *omitted* PGCat.

ἦν V: *omitted* PG

44 Τοῦτο τὸ πάθος οὐ μόνον τὴν Βηθλεέμ: τὰ περὶ τῆς παιδοφονίας *added by* P *in the margin (title); omitted* VG

Ἀλλὰ καὶ οὕτως ἡ Βηθλεέμ: ἐγκώμιον τῶν νηπίων *added by* VP *in the margin (title);* ἐγκώμιον νηπίων *added by* G *in the margin (title)*

καὶ προθύματα: *omitted* P

45 Ἀλλ' ἡμῖν γε καὶ αὖθις: περὶ τῆς περιτομῆς *added by* V *in the margin (title);* σημείωσαι περιτομή *added by* G *in the margin (title); omitted* P

46 δυεῖν VG: δυοῖν P

τὰ πλεῖστα VPG: τὰ πλείονα V$^{\gamma\rho}$

47 οὗ δὲ P: οὐδὲ VG

51 σωτηρία V P$^{\gamma\rho}$G: θεωρία P

αὐτὸ V: αὐτῷ PG

52 μὲν V: δὲ P *(G misses this point)*

δημιουργόν VG: αὐτουργόν P

τοῦ VPG: τοῖς V *above the line*

σπέρματα ἢ καὶ ζι- V: τὰ σπέρματα ἢ ζι- P *(G misses this point)*

πεπραγμένοις VP$^{\gamma\rho}$: πραττομένοις P *(G misses this point)*

53 προσαγορεύεται VG: προαγορεύεται P

ἀμφιβολία τῶν λογισμῶν, διάκρισις VG: ἀμφιβολία λογισμῶν P

ἢ καὶ εἰ αὐτοῦ τοῦ θανάτου κρείττων: *after* εἰ V *added* καὶ *above the line*

ἀλλ' οὐκ αἰτιολογικῶς οὐδὲ V: ἀλλ' οὐ μερικῶς PG

54 Ἰωσὴφ μετὰ τὸν καθαρισμόν: περὶ τῆς εἰς Αἴγυπτον φυγῆς *added by* V *in the margin (title);* ἡ εἰς Αἴγυπτον φυγή *added by* PG *in the margin (title)*

Ἔμελλε δὲ ἄρα πάντως: περὶ Ἰωάννου τοῦ βαπτιστοῦ V *in the margin (title);* περὶ Ἰωάννου PG *in the margin (title)*

προτιμῶντες V: προτιμότερον PG

Οὕτως ἐφιλοτιμοῦντο: περὶ Ζαχαρίου *added by* V *in the margin (title)*

Διὸ καὶ τῆς Ἐλισάβετ: περὶ Ζαχαρίου *added by* PG *in the margin (title)*

55 κακοτεχνότατα VG: κακοτεχνέστατα P

Ὥσπερ δὲ ὑπὸ χρηματισμῷ: ἐπάνοδος ἐξ Αἰγύπτου *added by* P *in the margin (title); omitted* VG

ἰδοὺ κύριος κάθηται ἐπὶ νεφέλης κούφης καὶ ἥξει εἰς Αἴγυπτον: *omitted* P; φεύγει εἰς Αἴγυπτον G

58 προτοῦ VG: πρὸ τοῦ P

59 σοι καὶ τὰ: *combines the readings* σοὶ καὶ VG; σου καὶ τὰ P

εὐαγγελιστῶν V: εὐαγγελίων PG

60 Τὰ μὲν οὖν λοιπὰ τοῦ παιδὸς: περὶ τοῦ δωδεκαετοῦς καὶ τῆς διδασκαλίας τῆς εἰς τὸ ἱερόν *added by* P *in margin (title); omitted* VG

61 διελέγετο $V^{\gamma\rho}$PG: διαλεγομένη V

62 μόνα PGCat.: μόνον V

ἐπὶ συννοίαις P: ἐπισυννοίαις V, ἐπισυνοίαις G, ἐπὶ συννοίας Cat.

63 Ἀλλ᾽ οὕτω τότε καὶ τὸν πατέρα: ἀνατροφή *added by* VPG *in the margin (title)*

αὐτά $V^{\gamma\rho}$GCat.: αὐτός VP

τοῦ τρόπου V^{pc}P: τὸν τρόπον V^{ac} (GCat.: τοῦ νόμου τὸν τρόπον . . . τοῦ τρόπου τὸν νόμον)

μόνον VG: μᾶλλον P

Ἀλλ᾽ ἵνα τὰ ἐν μέσῳ παραδράμωμεν: θεοφάνια *added by* VPG *in the margin (we have transferred this title to the next paragraph)*

διερριμμένον V: διερρημμένον G, διερρηγμένον P

65 οὕτω γοῦν VPG: οὕτω γὰρ $V^{\gamma\rho}$

66 δὲ V^{pc}PG: δὴ V^{ac}

Θεὸν τὸν ἄνθρωπον V^{ac}P: τὸν Θεὸν ἄνθρωπον V^{pc}G

μαρτυρίας VPG: θεωρίας $V^{\gamma\rho}$

67 Ἐπεὶ δὲ βαπτίζεται: πειρασμός *added by* VPG *in the margin (title)*

68 Τρίτη μετὰ ταύτην: τὸ θαῦμα τὸ ἐν Κανᾷ *added by* VPG *in the margin (title)*

καθαρώτατος V^{ac}PG: καθαρώτερος V^{pc}

69 Τί ἔτι; Ζεβεδὴ καὶ Γενησαρέτ: περὶ τῆς Γενησαρὲτ *added by* VPG *in the margin (title)*

καὶ ἀμπελώνων PG: *omitted* V

71 Ἐνταῦθα καὶ ὁ τῆς μεγάλης ἑορτῆς: σκηνοπηγία *added by* G *in the margin (title)*

72 πᾶσαν PG: πᾶσιν V

74 Ταῦτά τοι καὶ ὅτε τὸ μυστικὸν: περὶ τοῦ δείπνου *added by* P *in the margin (title)*

ἐκείνῳ μὲν ῥωννύων, τούτῳ VG: ἐκεῖνο . . . τοῦτο P

75 Ἐπεὶ δὲ καὶ ὁ δαιτυμών: προδοσία *added by* P *in the margin (title)*

76 Αὕτη καὶ πρὸς Ἄνναν: Ὥρα Α′ *added by* V *in the margin*

δύσχρηστον PG: δύσχριστον V, *which would correspond better to* ἀντίθεος *above, if we understand* δύσχριστος *as meaning "enemy of Christ"; compare Theodore of Studios, Letter 407.29, ed. G. Fatouros, "Theodori Studitae Epistulae," vol. 2 (Berlin, 1992), 565. However, it is more likely that* δύσχρηστον *was suggested here from Wisdom 2:12.*

77 Ἐπεὶ δέ, βαβαὶ τοῦ τολμήματος!: τὰ ἅγια πάθη *added by* V *above the line, added by* P *in the margin (title);* Ὥρα Α′ τὰ ἅγια πάθη *added by* G *in the margin (title)*

ἀδίκων PV$^{ac?}$: καταδίκων VG

ὕβρει VG: ὕβρεσι P

79 διαμάρτυραί P: διαμάρτυρέ VG

80 τούτῳ PG: τοῦτο V

Ἐπεὶ δὲ καὶ πάντα: Ὥρα Γ′ *added by* VG *in the margin*

καταπίνειν VPG: πιεῖν V^{γρ}

81 σκότῳ V^{pc}PG: σκότει V^{ac}

83 Ἐπεὶ τοίνυν τοῖς σταυρωταῖς: Ὥρα ΣΤ′ *added by* VG *in the margin*

κἂν V^{ac}PG: *erased in* V^{pc}

παραδόξαν VG: παρὰ δόξαν P

84 Πάθους PG: πάθος V

85 κἂν V^{ac}PG: *erased in* V^{pc}

αὖθις VG: αὖ P

86 προσανακλαύσασα VG: προσκλαύσασα P

αὐτὴ VP^{ac}G: αὐτῇ P^{pc}

παναρμόδιον VPG: παναρμόνιον Cat.

μὲν γὰρ V: *omitted* P, γὰρ *omitted* GCat.

87 τἄλλα μὲν: γὰρ *added after* μὲν *in* P

μανίας VP^{γρ}G: μιαιοφονίας P

ἑαυτῷ VG: ἑαυτοῦ P

τελέως V: τελείως P, τελεῖος G

Θεός VG: υἱὸς PV^{γρ}

88 Οὕτως ἡ μεγαλοφρονεστάτη: Ὥρα Θ′ *added by* VG *in the margin*

μανίαν VPG: κακίαν V^{pc}

ἐγχειρήματος VG: αἰτήματος P

λόγων PG: αλόγων V *(as it seems breathing is missing)*

89 παρακτικὸς P: πρακτικὸς V, παρεκτικὸς G

90 Οὕτω καὶ λόγοις: ταφή *added by* VPG *in the margin (title)*

περιθυροῦσα VP^{ac}G: περιθεωροῦσα P^{pc}

91 ταύτας καὶ ὁ μὲν Μάρκος V^{pc}PG: ταύτας μὲν καὶ ὁ Μάρκος V^{ac}

ὅπη V^{pc}: ὅπου V^{ac}PG

ταύτας P: ταύτην VG

παρακολουθεῖν VG: ἀκολουθεῖν P

ἀποδειλιᾶσαι VG: ὑποδειλιᾶσαι P

92 ἀνάστασις VG: ἡ ἀνάστασις P

καινοτομίας V, P *in the margin:* οἰκονομίας P

διῳκονομημέναι PG: διοικονομημέναι V^{ac}, διῳκονομούμεναι V^{pc}

τὰ τοιαῦτα φύσει V^{ac}P: φύσει τὰ τοιαῦτα V^{pc}G

οὕτως V^{ac}: οὗτος V^{pc}PG

φυλαττομένη V: φυλαττομένην PG

βουλομένη V: βουλομένην PG

αὐτοὺς PG: αὐτοῦ V

93 ἐναργέστερα PG: ἐνεργέστερα V

94 συναυλίζεται VP: συναλίζεται G

πάντα πεπλήρωτο PG: πεπλήρωτο πάντα V

95 Ἀλλὰ τίνα ταύτης: τὰ μετὰ τὴν ἀνάστασιν *added by* P *in the margin (title)*

καὶ μετὰ τοσαύτης δόξης: ἡ ἀνάληψις *added by* V *in the margin (title)*

Παναγίου VG: ἁγίου P

96 γὰρ δὴ VG: δὴ *omitted* P

ἠγκαλίζετο VG: ἐνηγκαλίζετο P

ἐξευμενίζετο V: ἐξευμενίζεται P: ἐξηυμενίζετο G

98 Ὡς δὲ λόγος: σημείωσαι ὅτε συναπεδήμησε τῷ θεολόγῳ εἰς Ἀσίαν, εἶτα εἰς Ἱεροσόλυμα ἀπὸ τῆς Ἀσίας *added by* V *in the margin*

γινομένην V^{ac}PG: γινομένη V^{pc}

καὶ *omitted* PG

τὸ P: τῷ VG

καὶ *added after* καταλύουσι *in* VG

99 ἀνακάμπτουσι V: ἀνακάμπτωσι(ν) PG

ἔχονται V: ἔχωνται PG

100 πολιουχουμένην VG: πολιοχουμένην P

101 μνήματος V^{ac}P: σώματος V^{pc}G

102 καὶ *omitted* PG

103 περὶ τῆς Κοιμήσεως V *in the margin (title):* Κοίμησις G *in the margin (title)*

ταύτῃ PG: ταύτης V

ἅμα VG: ὁμοῦ P

μυρίαθλον καὶ στεφανηφόρον, ἐν ἱματισμῷ διαχρύσῳ περιβεβλημένην πεποικιλμένην, βασίλισσάν V^{pc}: μυρίαθλος καὶ στεφανηφόρος . . . περιβεβλημένη πεποικιλμένη βασίλισσά V^{ac}PG

ἐπεὶ ταῦτα καὶ θανάτου: ἡ ἀθάνατος κοίμησις τῆς θεοτόκου *added by* P *in the margin (title)*

104 ἥτις V: ἡ PG

Ἀπέτρεχε VG: ἀνέτρεχε P

ἔβλεπε δὲ V: ἔβλεπεν ἤδη PG

ἀφ' ἑαυτῶν V^{ac}PG: ἐφ' ἑαυτῶν V^{pc}

συνδέων PG: συνδέον V

105 ἐπαπιοῦσα VG: ἐπανιοῦσα P

ὑπὲρ φύσιν τὴν φύσιν $V^{\gamma\rho}P$: τὴν φύσιν ὑπὲρ φύσιν VG

ἀφ' ἑαυτῶν μὲν αὐτὴν $V^{\gamma\rho}P$: αὐτὴν μὲν ἀφ' ἑαυτῶν VG

τοῖς PG: τοὺς V

εἰ καὶ PG: καὶ V

φθεγξαμένη: λόγους *added after* φθεγξαμένη *by* V *and* G *(but* G *omits* τῶν λόγων *that follows). There is a reference sign at the end of* φθεγξαμένη *in* P, *but no actual note in the margin.*

μὴ μόνον μὴ PG: μὴ μόνον V

τὴν καὶ V: καὶ τὴν PG

106 συγκεκλημένων $P^{pc}G$: συγκεκλειμένων VP^{ac}

τοῦθ' ἡμῖν V: τοῦτο ἡμῖν PG

ἐπιτετήρηται λίαν ἐπιμελῶς V: ἐπιτηρεῖται λίαν ἐμμελῶς P, ἐπιτετήρηται λίαν ἐμμελῶς G

καὶ οὐκ ἐγινώσκετο *omitted* P

ὅλος: *omitted* PG

αἱρεῖ VP: ἐρεῖ G

δι' ἀμφοτέρων γενόμενος P: διὰ τῶν ἀμφοτέρων γενόμενος ἂν V, δι' ἀμφοτέρων γενόμενος ἂν G

τοῦτο VG: τούτῳ P

ἀπέλαυσε V: ἀπήλαυσε PG

107 Λόγε: *omitted* P

108 τῶν PG: τὸν V

109 ὑφ' ἡδονῆς VG: ἐφ' ἡδονῆς P

ἐκεῖνο PG: ἐκείνου V

τοσοῦτον V: τοῦτον PG

111 καὶ: *omitted* PG

ἐστερεῖτο VG: ὑστερεῖτο P

ἐκάθαιρε $V^{\gamma\rho}G$: ἐκκαθαίρει PV

κτίσεως $VP^{\gamma\rho}G$: φύσεως P

κοινήν V^{pc}: καινὴν $V^{ac}PG$

113 τρέψαντος $V^{ac}P$: στρέψαντος $V^{pc}G$

114 αὐτὴ P: αὐτῇ VG

πλήθους VPG: πάθους $V^{\gamma\rho}$

115 καὶ: *omitted* P

ἄλλους: ἄλλους καὶ VG

116 οὐ $V^{\gamma\rho}$: μηδὲ VPG

ἐμπεριηχούντων VG: ἐμπεριεχόντων P

παραμενόντων VG: προσμενόντων P

117 εὑρίσκεται *is added by* P *and* G *after* ἐπιταφίοις, *that is, the word is repeated twice in succession*

118 ὅπως δὲ καὶ ἡ καθ' ἡμᾶς: περὶ τῆς τιμίας ἐσθῆτος καὶ ζώνης *added by* P *in the margin (title)*

καὶ τῆς περιβολῆς: *from this point on* P *is damaged and lacks the second half of each page*

121 φαιδρότερα: *there is a lacuna in* P *(missing folios) after* δρό| *until* τοῦ νῦν ὑπὲρ ἡμῶν *in chapter 125*

πάντως V: πάντες G

καταλιμπανομένη $V^{\gamma\rho}$: καταλαμβανομένη VG

122 τί μὲν γὰρ $V^{\gamma\rho}$G: νῦν μὲν οὖν καὶ τί γὰρ V

123 σταχυηφόρῳ V^{pc}: ταχυηφόρῳ V^{ac}, σταχυοφόρῳ G

μήτιγε V: μήτε γε G

ἀφεκτέος V^{pc}G: ἀφεκτέον V

125 τοῦ νῦν: *at this point the testimony of* P *(p. 261) resumes*

τῆς *added* V *before* φιλανθρωπίας

127 ὁρίσασα: *there is a lacuna in* P *(missing folio) after this word until* ἄγαλμα *in chapter 128*

128 ἄγαλμα: *at this point the testimony of* P *(p. 263) resumes*

προφῆται καλοῦσι: *here ends the testimony of* G *(fol. 309v)*

ἄλλό τι: οὐκ *deleted by Constas and Simelidis before* ἄλλο

129 τὸν σὸν P: τῶν σῶν V

κακῶν VP: καλῶν $V^{\gamma\rho}$

ὑπεκκλίνειν P: ὑπ' ἐκκλίνειν V, ὑποκλίνειν $V^{\gamma\rho}$

διαλλακτὴς V: διαλλακτὶς P

ἢ: *omitted* P

φυλάττουσα: *here ends the testimony of* P

Notes to the Translation

1 *a tongue that transcended all speech*: The inability of language to offer adequate praise to the Mother of God is a common complaint voiced by Marian preachers; see, for example, pseudo-Modestos, *Encomium on the Dormition* 1 (PG 86:3277D–3279B); or Andrew of Crete, *On the Dormition* 1.1 (PG 98:1045C); and below, note to 72.

just as when . . . a single song: See below, 115. On the concurrence of human and angelic singing, see Gregory of Nyssa, *On the Inscriptions of the Psalms* 1.9 (GNO vol. 5, p. 66, lines 11–30); and Theodore of Stoudios, *On the Dormition* 5 (PG 99:728AB).

all the powers . . . above the earth: A phrase borrowed from Gregory of Nazianzus, *Oration* 39.14, ed. Claudio Moreschini and Paul Gallay, *Discours 38–41,* SC 358 (Paris, 1990), p. 178, lines 2–3.

The One who exists: See Exodus 3:14.

every knee will bend . . . and confess: See Philippians 2:10–11.

entirely lacking in worthiness: Geometres's acknowledgment of his unworthiness and inability is a modesty topos found in the prefaces of many Byzantine texts, especially hagiographical ones; see Thomas Pratsch, *Der hagiographische Topos* (Berlin, 2005), 22–34.

lacking in worthiness . . . subject to reproach: The contrast between "ability" (δύναμις) and "eagerness" (βούλησις) and between "irreproachable" (ἀνεύθυνον) and "reproachable" (ὑπεύθυνον) is taken from Gregory of Nazianzus, *Oration* 32.1, ed. Claudio Moreschini and Paul Gallay, *Discours 32–37,* SC 318 (Paris, 1985), p. 82, lines 3–8.

all people and every generation: See Luke 1:48, where the Virgin says, "Henceforth all generations shall praise and bless me."

hear and believe: See Romans 10:17, "faith comes from what is heard."

benefits to be gained . . . Mother of the Word: There is a wordplay in the Greek here on λόγῳ . . . Λόγου . . . λόγου, translated here as "discourse," "words," "Word"; it is further extended by the use of λογισμοῖς, "power of reason," in the following phrase.

2 *conversely predicable*: According to Aristotle, *Categories* 14b11, some properties or qualities can be "predicated conversely," so that each is predicable universally of the other; compare John of Damascus, *Dialectica,* ed. Boniface Kotter, *Das Schriften des Johannes von Damaskos,* 8 vols. (Berlin, 1969–), vol. 1, p. 85, lines 27–30: "A property is that which exists in one species and in the entire species, and which is always in it and is conversely predicable with it. Take, for example, the property of 'laughter': every man can laugh and everything that can laugh is a man."

apocryphal works . . . follow the evangelists: For a similar assessment of apocryphal sources, see, for example, Geometres, *On the Annunciation* 15 (PG 106:824D); and Epiphanios, *Life of the Theotokos,* ed. Albertus Rud Max Dressel, *Epiphanii monachi et presbyteri edita et inedita* (Paris and Leipzig, 1843), 14–15: "And even if we should take something from apocryphal or heretical works, let no one find fault with us, for 'the testimonies from enemies are worthy of greater trust,'" citing Basil, *On the Nativity of Christ* 5 (PG 31:1469C).

great and inspired fathers and teachers: On Geometres's sources, see the Introduction to this volume. Compare Epiphanios, *Life of the Theotokos,* ed. Dressel, *Epiphanii,* 14, which cites John of Thessaloniki, Andrew of Crete, Eusebius of Caesarea, and Cyril of Alexandria.

her nourishment: The Greek term τροφή, which also means "way of life," is likely here a reference to the angelic food the Virgin ate in the temple; see also *Protevangelium* 8.1; and below, 8.

she did not abandon this world: An allusion to the dismissal hymn *(apolytikion)* of the Feast of the Dormition, which is found in

the ninth- or tenth-century *Typikon of the Great Church* and the *Book of Ceremonies* compiled by Constantine VII, ed. Juan Mateos, *Le Typicon de la Grande Église,* vol. 1, *Le cycle des douze mois,* Orientalia Christiana Analecta 165 (Rome, 1962), p. 370, line 10. The scribe of G changes the Greek verb ἔλιπε to κατέλιπε (both meaning "abandoned"), most likely under the influence of this hymn.

3 *she was descended from . . . David*: The New Testament is silent about Mary's Davidic lineage, though legally she entered the House of David through her marriage with Joseph (Luke 1:27; compare Luke 2:4, Matthew 1:20). According to Luke, Mary was related to Elizabeth, who was of the House of Aaron (Luke 1:5, 1:36). The ambiguous Lucan phrase "of the House of David" (Luke 1:27) was also understood as a reference to Mary by some Church fathers, for example, John Chrysostom, *On the Nativity* 3 (PG 49:354). The *Protevangelium* 10.1 furnishes Mary with direct Davidic ancestry, a claim repeated by contemporary writers. Middle Byzantine writers also dealt with these questions at length; see, for example, the extensive remarks by Andrew of Crete, *On the Nativity of the Theotokos* 2.2–4 and 3 (PG 97:821C–828D, 844C–861A), and the elaborate genealogy presented by John of Damascus, *On the Orthodox Faith* 87 (4.14), ed. Kotter, *Schriften,* vol. 2, pp. 199–200, which was reproduced by Epiphanios, *Life of The Theotokos,* ed. Dressel, *Epiphanii,* 15–16. See further the helpful studies by Sebastian Brock, "The Genealogy of the Virgin in Sinai Syr. 16," *Scrinium* 2 (2006): 58–71; and Christophe Guignard, "Jesus' Family and Their Genealogy according to the Testimony of Julius Africanus," in *Infancy Gospels: Stories and Identities,* ed. Claire Clivaz, Andreas Dettwiler, Luc Devillers, and others (Tübingen, 2011), 67–93.

the priestly line . . . the royal line: See Andrew of Crete, *On the Nativity of the Theotokos* 1.3: "Today a virgin daughter comes forth out of Judah and David, tracing in outline form the kingship and priesthood of the one who made Aaron a priest 'after the order of Melchisedek'" (PG 97:812BC, quoting Psalms 109[110]:4).

the historical account: This is generally how Geometres refers to the *Protevangelium,* which in the manuscripts is described as a "history" or "historical account" (ἱστορία or λόγος ἱστορικός), while the work itself begins with a reference to a document called "the *Histories of the Twelve Tribes of Israel,*" implying that the author made use of Israelite historical sources; see *Protevangelium* 25.

Joachim, and . . . Joseph, were of mixed descent from these tribes: John of Damascus, *On the Orthodox Faith* 87 (4.14), ed. Kotter, *Schriften,* vol. 2, pp. 199–200, followed by Epiphanios, *Life of the Theotokos,* ed. Dressel, *Epiphanii,* 15, contends that Joachim and Joseph were related by marriage through their great-grandparents.

saying . . . anything good to come from it: See John 1:46.

triple-stranded chain: A phrase seemingly borrowed from Leontios, presbyter of Constantinople, Homily 14, ed. C. Datema and P. Allen, *Leontii presbyteri Constantinopolitani Homiliae,* Corpus Christianorum Series Graeca 17 (Turnhout, 1987), p. 447, line 346. Compare similar phrasing in Geometres, *Hymn* 2.3–4, ed. Jan Sajdak, *Ioannis Kyriotis Geometrae Hymni in SS. Deiparam* (Poznan, 1931), 64: Χαῖρέ μοι, ὦ Βασίλεια, παναγνοτάτης ἀπὸ ῥίζης / ἔρνος ἔφυς χαρίτων τρίπλοον ἐκ τριπλόου, "Rejoice, my Queen, a threefold shoot of grace coming from the purest threefold root."

goodwill of the Father and the cooperation of the Spirit: The phrase is found in many theological writings, notably in those of John of Damascus; see for example his *On the Orthodox Faith* 2 (1.2), ed. Kotter, *Schriften,* vol. 2, p. 9, lines 20–21.

4 *Joachim and Anna*: For more on Joachim and Anna, see Eirini Panou, "Mary's Parents in Homilies before and after James Kokkinobaphos," in *Wonderful Things: Byzantium Through Its Art,* ed. Antony Eastmond and Elizabeth James (Farnham and Burlington, 2013), 283–94.

Anna was the beauty of women: The Greek term χάρις, "beauty," can also mean "grace" or "favor," and thus is perhaps a complement to the idea here of Joachim as a gift from God.

our common mediator: See 1 Timothy 2:5, where the same term μεσίτης, "mediator," is used of Jesus. Geometres describes the Virgin as a mediator throughout the present work; see, in particular, 10, 68–69, and 123. In doing so he follows a tradition well established by his day, the term having perhaps first been applied to the Virgin in the fifth century by Basil of Seleucia, *On the Annunciation* 5 (PG 85:444A).

the prize for a fiery ordeal: The Greek word πύρωσις refers to "a trial" analogous to testing or assaying the purity and content of metals by fire. It draws on a number of Septuagint passages; see Jeremiah 6:27–30, Psalms 25(26):2, and Wisdom 3:5–6 (especially as cited by later Byzantines with ἐπύρωσεν for ἐπείρασεν at verse 5).

miserable comforters: Job 16:2; see also *Protevangelium* 1.2.

the things of Hannah: The story of Hannah and her conception of the prophet Samuel in answer to prayer is recorded in 1 Kings 1:2–2:21; see Eirini Panou, *The Cult of St Anna in Byzantium* (Abingdon, 2018), 49–50, who highlights the importance of Anna among Byzantine iconophiles, along with her links to Hannah.

she runs quickly to the temple: In the *Protevangelium* 2.4, Anna does not go to the temple, but to a garden outside her home.

the husband of Anna . . . in the temple: In the *Protevangelium* 1.4, Joachim retreats not to the temple but to the wilderness, where he receives the promise of a child, but middle Byzantine writers tend to relocate Joachim's vision to the temple; see, for example, Andrew of Crete, *On the Nativity of the Theotokos* 1.6 (PG 97:816C); and Mary B. Cunningham, "The *Life of the Virgin Mary* by Epiphanios Kallistratos: A Monastic Approach to an Apocryphal Story," in *The Reception of the Virgin in Byzantium: Marian Narratives in Texts and Images,* ed. Thomas Arentzen and Mary B. Cunningham (Cambridge, 2019), 14–15.

rejoiced greatly: John 3:29 uses the same phrase (χαρᾷ χαίρει), but Geometres likely has John 16:21 in mind here: "When a woman . . . is delivered of the child, she no longer remembers the anguish, for joy that a child is born into the world."

You will beget a child . . . salvation to the whole world: Geometres seems to be conflating the response to Joachim's prayer with the response to Anna's prayer; see *Protevangelium* 4.1–2.

the place of the promise was a garden: In the *Protevangelium,* the scene in the garden occurs before Joachim's return from the wilderness.

unutterable sighs: Romans 8:26.

the Tree of Life: Genesis 2:9, here understood as a figure of Mary, from whom Christ will blossom forth.

proclaimed her two qualities with one name: The English preserves the ambiguity of the Greek. Geometres may be alluding to a particular etymology of the name "Mary," such as that given by pseudo-Epiphanos, *In Praise of the Holy Theotokos:* "The name 'Mary' means 'sovereign lady' and 'hope,' for she gave birth to our sovereign Lord Christ, who is the hope of the world; and again her name means 'myrrh of the sea,' for she gave birth to Christ the Pearl in the sea of the world" (PG 43:488D–489A). Myrrh (σμύρνα) may have been associated with the "oil of gladness" and thus with "joy" on the basis of Psalms 44:8–9(45:7–8): "God has anointed you with the oil of gladness; myrrh and fragrant oil are exhaled from your garments."

the Divine Gate: See Ezekiel 44:2, a reference to the gate of the sanctuary that was understood as an Old Testament figure of Mary.

5 *they led her into the temple*: Euthymios, *The Life of the Virgin: Maximos the Confessor,* trans. Stephen Shoemaker (New Haven, 2012), 5, renders "they" as "her blessed parents" and, following *Protevangelium* 7.1–2, notes that Mary was three years old at the time; Epiphanios, *Life of the Theotokos,* ed. Dressel, *Epiphanii,* 16, says that she was seven.

the prophetic and royal voice of her ancestor: David, held to be the author of the Psalms.

Virgins behind her . . . will be brought forward: Psalms 44:15(45:14).

preceded her, but who also followed her: Some earlier writers, such as Germanos of Constantinople, *On the Entry of the Theotokos* 1.5 (PG 98:297A), refer only to virgins who precede the Virgin,

while others, such as Andrew of Crete, *On the Nativity of the Theotokos* 1.7 (PG 97:816D), and Peter of Argos, *On the Entry of the Theotokos* 2, ed. Konstantinos Kyriakopoulos, *Ἁγίου Πέτρου ἐπισκόπου Ἄργους βίος και λόγοι* (Athens, 1976), 152–54, describe them as both preceding and following her.

stars in the sky reflect: The basic meaning of the verb παραπέμπειν is "to escort," though we have opted for the less common reading of "reflect," on which see, for example, Marcus Aurelius, *Meditations* 8.57, ed. and trans. A. S. L. Farquharson, *The Meditations of the Emperor Marcus Aurelius,* vol. 1 (Oxford, 1944), 168–69: αὐτὸ γὰρ ἑαυτὸ στερήσει τῆς αὐγῆς τὸ μὴ παραπέμπον αὐτήν, "for that which does not reflect it will rob itself of the light."

was a forerunner on our behalf: Hebrews 6:20; see also 9:12.

6 *prophet, king, and forefather*: A further reference to David.

bloom and his beauty . . . and justice: This whole passage, studded with direct quotations, is a meditation on the content of Psalms 44:3–5(45:2–4).

And even if some have thought . . . word of the prophet: A number of patristic writers, such as Clement of Alexandria, *Stromateis* 6.11.92.1, ed. Otto Stählin and Ludwig Früchtel, *Clemens Alexandrinus: Stromata, Buch I–VI* (Berlin, 1985), 478, interpreted Psalm 44(45) as a type of the Church. Athanasius, *Letter to Marcellinus* (PG 27:16), understands the Psalm as referring to the Virgin, but the wider reception of this interpretation is not evident until the late sixth century. The association of Psalm 44 with ascetic virgins likely served as the transition from the ecclesial to the Marian interpretation.

7 *The queen stood . . . embroidery of colors*: This passage, which includes a number of direct quotations, is a meditation on Psalms 44:10(45:9).

embroidered with different colors: In Greek patristic literature, the virtues are frequently compared to colors added to the portrait of the soul; see, for example, Gregory of Nyssa, *On the Making of Man* 5 (PG 44:137A–B).

rainbow . . . innumerable in its effulgence: Geometres here reflects

an idea found in a letter by Gregory of Nyssa attributed to his brother Basil, *Letter* 38, trans. Roy J. Deferrari, *Basil: Letters,* vol. 1, *Letters 1–58,* Loeb Classical Library 190 (New York, 1926), 215: "The brilliance of the rainbow is both continuous with itself and separated, for though it is of many colors and multiform, it is intermingled with various hues, eluding from sight the point of mutual juncture of the various colors, for all the colors are seen as both distinct and yet extending into one another." The translation has been modified slightly. See also Cyril of Alexandria, *Paschal Homily* 27.3 (PG 77:936, lines 25–27).

8 *Hear, O Daughter . . . same Spirit*: See Psalms 44:11–13(45:10–12). In this paragraph, Geometres once again subjects three verses of the Psalm to an elaborate Marian exegesis, focusing minutely on each phrase and even word. He will do the same in chapter 10, below, with a passage from Proverbs.

the one from heaven who fed you: See *Protevangelium* 8.1, which states that the Virgin "received food (τροφή) from the hand of an angel," whom the later tradition would identify as the archangel Gabriel.

comparing her external honor with her interior honor: The text says simply "comparing her to herself," which we have rendered following the explanation given by Euthymios, *Life of the Virgin* 9: "Compare her deeds with each other and see in the external honor the higher and more glorious interior honor."

the gifts of the Spirit are different, but nonetheless of the same Spirit: See 1 Corinthians 12:4.

9 *Heavenly Ladder*: An allusion to Jacob's ladder (see Genesis 28:12), here understood, as in other Marian literature, as a figure of the Virgin. Compare Geometres, *Hymn* 1.15–16: Χαῖρε, κλίμαξ περόωσα καὶ οὐρανὸν ἀστερόεντα, / ἣ Θεὸν ἀνθρώποις, ἐς Θεὸν ἄνδρας ἄγεις, "Rejoice ladder, traversing even the starry heavens, who brings God to men and men to God." See also Geometres, *Poem* 143.3–4, ed. Emilie Marlène van Opstall, *Jean Géomètre: Poèmes en hexamètres et en distiques élégiaques* (Leiden, 2008), 332–34: σὺ δὲ θῆκας, Παρθένε, γῆθεν / ἄντυγος οὐρανίης εὐιέρην κλίμακα, "You, Virgin, set up a holy ladder that leads from earth to the vault of heaven."

in stature and grace: Luke 2:52.

blending: The Greek word ἀνάκραμα, rendered here as "blending," is a hapax. Geometres coined this word in place of the common ἀνάκρασις, presumably because its ending in -μα corresponded to χώρημα (receptacle), creating a balanced construction with homeoteleuton. In Greek grammar, a *krasis* is the combination of two vowels or syllables into one vowel or diphthong, which provides an intriguing analogy for the concurrence of divine and human natures in the Virgin.

the shavings found next to ground metals: See John Chrysostom, *Homilies on Uzziah* 2.2, ed. Jean Dumortier, *Homélies sur Ozias,* SC 277 (Paris, 1981) p. 92, lines 51–53: οἱ τὰ μέταλλα ἀνορύττοντες οὐδὲ τὰ μικρὰ ψήγματα παρατρέχουσιν, "For those who mine metals do not overlook even the dust."

seemingly small: The "seemingly small things" that Geometres proposes to discuss will occupy him at considerable length, introducing material that is not reproduced by Euthymios, and consequently doubling the length of his treatment of the Entry to the temple.

antithesis of Adam: See Romans 5:12–18.

10 *historical account*: In the following description of the Virgin, Geometres greatly expands upon a passage in Epiphanios, *Life of the Theotokos,* ed. Dressel, *Epiphanii,* 17. Whereas Epiphanios simply cites Proverbs 31:10 without comment, Geometres enlarges this into a detailed exegesis of nearly the entire chapter, Proverbs 31:1–26, sometimes quoting exactly but more often reworking the Greek of the original to fit the context; thus, the only quotations and paraphrases noted below are those that require elaboration or are from other sources. Note that the Septuagint text of Proverbs presents several problems in terms of the ordering of the verses, for which we have followed the standard chapter and verse division; see Johann Cook, "Textual Problems in the Septuagint of Proverbs," *Journal of Northwest Semitic Languages* 26 (2000): 163–73.

not only for her courage: Proverbs 31:10; see also Sirach 26:1. "Courage" (ἀνδρεία) was one of the four cardinal virtues and in Greek has verbal connotations of manliness and virility.

And he seeks her: An allusion to Proverbs 31:10: "Who shall find a virtuous (courageous) woman?"

love for virginity: The Greek word φιλοπαρθενία is a hapax.

into the masculine: See Proverbs 31:10, "Who will find a courageous wife?" where the adjective "courageous" (ἀνδρείαν) might also mean "manly." On this gender reversal, see Hans Boersma, *Embodiment and Virtue in Gregory of Nyssa: An Anagogical Approach* (Oxford, 2013), 113–14.

the law is a lamp: Psalms 118(119):105.

the arm is a symbol of the practical power: The same symbolism is identified by, among others, Evagrios, *Scholia on Ecclesiastes* 26, ed. Paul Géhin, *Scholies à l'Ecclésiaste,* SC 397 (Paris, 1993), 102: "The hands are a symbol of practical activity."

two sets of clothes: Genesis 45:22.

who is our high priest: See Hebrews 2:17, 3:1, 6:20, 8:1, and 9:11.

linen . . . the Virgin was spinning: Compare *Protevangelium* 10; see also Nicholas [Maximos] Constas, *Proclus of Constantinople and the Cult of the Virgin in Late Antiquity* (Leiden, 2003), 325–28.

is distinguished in the gates: Proverbs 31:23.

when he sits . . . in . . . the council: Geometres here works together Proverbs 31:23 and Luke 2:46–47, the latter a reference to the child Jesus in the temple with the Jewish teachers, on which, see below, 61.

God in his wisdom and power: See 1 Corinthians 1:24.

Phoenicians: Geometres's text of Proverbs 31:24 had τοῖς Φοίνιξι, a reading, according to Rahlfs's apparatus, preserved in *Codex Sinaiticus;* Alfred Rahlfs, ed., *Septuaginta, id est Vetus Testamentum graece iuxta LXX interpretes* (Stuttgart, 1935). Compare *Apostolic Constitutions* 1.8.3, ed. Marcel Metzger, *Les Constitutions apostoliques,* vol. 1, *Livres I–II,* SC 320 (Paris, 1985), 126.

coverings of shame: An allusion to the fig leaves or "garments of skin" given to Adam and Eve to cover their nakedness; see Genesis 3:21.

dyed purple in sin: A very similar phrase is found in Gregory of Nazianzus, *Oration* 39.20, ed. Moreschini and Gallay, *Discours 38–41,* p. 194, line 4. The Greek adjective φοινικέος, "dyed purple," introduces a wordplay on Phoenician (Φοίνιξ).

who put on honor and clothed himself in power: See Psalms 92(93):1.

11 *It will also be good to add . . . appropriate to the occasion*: A phrase borrowed from Gregory of Nazianzus, *Oration* 42.4, ed. Jean Bernardi, *Discours 42–43*, SC 384 (Paris, 1992), p. 60, lines 17–18.

Many daughters . . . exceeded them all: Geometres's final meditation here is on Proverbs 31:29.

She was most gracious to behold . . . proportioned in stature: Physical descriptions of the Virgin became common in the middle Byzantine period and may perhaps reflect developments in post-Iconoclastic theology and iconography, which was marked by heightened devotion to the Virgin, and which established distinctive physiognomies for each of the saints. For a similar description, see Epiphanios, *Life of the Theotokos,* ed. Dressel, *Epiphanii,* 18. In general, see Henry Maguire, *The Icons of Their Bodies: Saints and Their Images in Byzantium* (Princeton, 1996), 5–47.

12 *made himself poor . . . and become obedient*: See Matthew 11:29; Philippians 2:8.

so that the proportion between them was preserved: Compare the Greek here to a passage in Plato's *Theaetetus* 167d3: σῴζεται γὰρ ἐν τούτοις ὁ λόγος οὗτος, "upon these positions my doctrine stands firm." The context, however, renders the translation of related words quite different.

at once frightful to demons and desired by angels: A phrase borrowed from John Chrysostom, *Homily on Uzziah* 3.5, ed. Jean Dumortier, *Homélies sur Ozias,* p. 104, line 5.

13 *garden inaccessible*: See Song of Songs 4:12.

produced without digging: The phrase is borrowed from Romanos, *On the Nativity of Christ,* ed. José Grosdidier de Matons, *Hymnes,* 5 vols., SC 110, 114, 128, 283 (Paris, 1965–1981), vol. 2, p. 50, no. 10.1.5; compare John of Damascus, *Homily on the Dormition* 2.14.7, ed. Kotter, *Schriften,* vol. 5, p. 531.

sealed book: Isaiah 29:11.

king's couch . . . surrounding it: See Song of Songs 3:7, referring to Solomon's couch.

lampstand of gold: Zacharias 4:2.

the royal and priestly evergreen rod: The rod is a common biblical

symbol of authority: see, for example, Exodus 7:12 and Psalms 44:7(45:6). The idea of the "evergreen" or "everblooming" rod originates in the story of Aaron's rod in Numbers 17:8. Compare Hebrews 9:4, where the furniture of the Holy of Holies, including Aaron's rod, is described; other elements are also referred to below. For reference to the same story, see also below, 16.

the urn concealing the divine manna: Exodus 16:33; Hebrews 9:4.

the table bearing the bread: See Exodus 25:29; Leviticus 24:6.

the tablets of the law: Hebrews 9:4; see Exodus 32:15–16.

the ark covered on all sides with gold: Hebrews 9:4; see also Exodus 25:10 and Revelation 11:19.

proves the truth . . . and is in turn proven by them: Geometres seems to invoke the category of circular or reciprocal causality, discussed by Aristotle, *Prior Analytics* 59a32, and Diogenes Laertius, *Lives of Eminent Philosophers* 9.89, among others; on which, see William David Ross, *Aristotle's Prior and Posterior Analytics* (Oxford, 1949), 438–39.

14 *a light shone forth brilliantly . . . birth to my son*: Mary's vision of light and the voice announcing the divine birth, which may have been inspired by Samuel's vision in the temple (1 Kings 3:1–14), are not mentioned in the *Protevangelium,* and Geometres likely derived this episode from Epiphanios, *Life of the Theotokos,* ed. Dressel, *Epiphanii,* 18–19, though it also appears in the *Questions of Bartholomew.* On this last, see Cunningham, "The *Life of the Virgin Mary* by Epiphanios," 315–16.

mystery . . . unknown even to the angels: The phrasing here is close to that used in the tenth-century *Synaxarion of the Church of Constantinople,* ed. Hippolyte Delehaye, *Synaxarium ecclesiae Constantinopolitanae e codice Sirmondiano nunc Berolinensi: Propylaeum ad Acta sanctorum Novembris* (Brussels, 1902), 557–58.

15 *fourteen years old*: Following the *Protevangelium* 8.2, Euthymios, *Life of the Virgin* 15, states that she was "twelve years old," though "fourteen" is a common variant reading; see J. K. Elliott, *The Apocryphal New Testament: A Collection of Apocryphal Christian Literature in English Translation* (Oxford, 1993), 60n19.

the law itself expressly prohibited this: Here and in what follows,

Geometres is indebted to Gregory of Nyssa, *Homily on the Birth of Christ* (GNO vol. 10, part 2, p. 253, lines 4–15): "When she was grown up, the priests took counsel as to what they could do about her without sinning against God. To subject her to the law of nature and enslave her through marriage to one who would take her to wife was utterly unacceptable. Indeed it was regarded as sacrilege for a man to be master of something consecrated to God, but neither was it lawful for a woman to consort with priests in the temple."

might elude observation . . . incite his Opponent: The idea that the details of the incarnation had to be kept secret from the devil is a commonplace theme in patristic literature.

the prophetic words of Isaiah: See Isaiah 7:14: "Behold, the virgin shall conceive in her womb and give birth to a son, and they will call his name Emmanuel."

16 *judgment through the rods*: See Numbers 17:1–11, where, after Moses had collected the staffs of the leaders of the twelve tribes, Aaron's is said to have miraculously blossomed with buds and almonds, indicating that he and his descendants would occupy the priesthood.

filled the place of the traitor . . . casting lots: See Acts 1:15–26. The traitor is Judas Iscariot.

Zacharias, the father of . . . John the Baptist: See Luke 1:5–13.

his turn to serve: See Luke 1:8.

serve at the baptism of her son: Matthew 3:13–17.

And behold your kinswoman Elizabeth: Luke 1:36. That Mary and Elizabeth were the children of two sisters is suggested by Eusebius, *Supplement to the Questions to Stephen* (PG 22:973), who says they were ἐκ τῶν αὐτῶν προγόνων, "of the same forebears," and affirmed by Epiphanios, *Life of the Theotokos,* ed. Dressel, *Epiphanii,* 16; see Brock, "Genealogy of the Virgin," 68.

The rod of Joseph . . . as Aaron's had before it: See Numbers 17:8.

Thus was Joseph . . . guardian of the Virgin: See *Protevangelium* 8–9.

17 *the one who made himself poor . . . through his divinity*: See 2 Corinthians 8:9.

He was a carpenter by trade: See Matthew 13:55.

architecture of the Spirit: A phrase borrowed from Gregory of Nazianzus, *Oration* 19.8 (PG 35:1052C).

Joseph . . . a righteous man: Matthew 1:19.

18 *The beauty that Pharaoh saw . . . of Joseph*: See Genesis 41:38–39.

to teach them wisdom: Psalms 104(105):22.

to instruct them: Nehemiah 9:20.

feast of Tabernacles and the resting of the Ark: On these events, see Numbers 10:35, 3 Kings 8:2, and 2 Chronicles 7.

the birth of his son John was announced: See Luke 1:8–22.

the lamp should precede the light: See John 8:12.

the voice precede the Word: See Matthew 3:3; John 1:1.

friend arrive before the bridegroom: John 3:29.

Behold, Elizabeth . . . has conceived a son: Luke 1:36.

19 *the sixth month*: That is, after Elizabeth's conception.

fountain of life: See Psalms 35:10(36:9) and *Protevangelium* 11.1. In Byzantine literature, the "fountain" of the Annunciation is usually described as a "well" (φρέαρ), connecting it symbolically with a range of biblical wells.

primeval darkness . . . light was created: Genesis 1:1–3.

morning should hasten toward morning: A literal borrowing from Romanos, *On the Baptism of Christ,* ed. Grosdidier de Matons, *Hymnes,* vol. 2, p. 270, no. 17.1.6.

20 *Rejoice . . . O favored one*: Luke 1:28.

pain long associated with childbirth: The pain of childbirth to which Eve was condemned; see Genesis 3:16.

the Lord is with you: Luke 1:28.

through this word . . . as the Word, reasonably: There is a play on the Greek word *logos* (word) here that is difficult to reproduce in English; Geometres uses the same phrase in his *On the Annunciation* 11 (PG 106:820B).

fig juice stirred into milk: a reference to Aristotle's analogy of fig juice curdling milk to explain human conception: see Aristotle, *De generatione animalium* 1.20.729d.

moved the whole of human nature and shaped it around himself: Compare Gregory of Nyssa, *Against Eunomius* 3.2.54 (GNO vol. 1, part 2, p. 70, lines 5–10): "Long ago he took dust from the

ground and shaped man, and now he takes dust from the Virgin, and did not simply shape man but shaped him around himself (ἑαυτῷ περιέπλασε); long ago he created, but after that he was created."

the woman had recourse to the man: Genesis 3:16.

pain was bound to childbirth: An allusion to the dialectic of pain and pleasure in the theological anthropology of Maximos the Confessor; on which, see Christoph Schönborn, "Plaisir et douleur dans l'analyse de S. Maxime, d'après les *Quaestiones ad Thalassium*," in *Maximos Confessor: Actes du Symposium sur Maxime le Confesseur,* ed. Felix Heinzer and Christoph Schönborn (Fribourg, 1982), 273–84.

21 *Blessed are you among women*: Luke 1:28.

through one woman and one man: See Romans 5:12. Geometres extends Paul's Adam-Christ typology to include Eve and Mary.

accustomed to these sights: Her angelic nourishment during her time in the temple and her vision; see above, 9 and 14.

for . . . she was greatly troubled . . . greeting this might be: Luke 1:29.

Fear not, Mary . . . you have found favor with God: Luke 1:30; "favor" here translates χάρις, which may also mean "grace."

22 *And behold . . . you will conceive . . . and bear a son*: Luke 1:31.

According to the prophet . . . spirit of salvation: See Isaiah 7:14; 26:18.

you shall bear a son and call his name Jesus: Luke 1:31.

his earthly birth . . . heavenly birth: Here Geometres is indebted to Pseudo-Chrysostom, *On Melchisedek* 2 (PG 56:259A): καὶ ἀπάτωρ τὴν κάτω γέννησιν, ἀμήτωρ τὴν ἄνω, "his earthly birth is fatherless, his heavenly motherless." The language is taken from Hebrews 7:3, which describes Melchisedek, an Old Testament figure of Christ, as being both ἀπάτωρ, "fatherless," and ἀμήτωρ, "motherless." In the tenth-century *Book of Ceremonies* 1.2 (V2), the protocols for the imperial celebration of the feast of the Nativity called for the chanting of the hymn: "He who is without a mother (ἀμήτωρ) in heaven is born without a father (ἀπάτωρ) on earth"; see Ann Moffat and Maxeme Tall, trans., *Constantine Porphyrogennetos: The Book of Ceremonies* (Leiden, 2012), 37–38.

beloved son: See Matthew 3:17, 17:5.

he holds this name . . . promised land: The reference is to Joshua, whose name is an English variant of Jesus; both mean "savior."

he will be great . . . Son of the Most High: Luke 1:32.

utter extreme of the hypostatic union: A rendering of the Greek ἄκραν ἕνωσιν, a phrase used by Cyril of Alexandria and incorporated into the proceedings of the Council of Ephesus; ACO vol. 1.1, part 7, p. 43, line 16.

exchange of idioms: A rendering of the Greek phrase ὀνομάτων ἀντιπεριχώρησιν, also known as the "interchange of properties" between the human and the divine natures in the one hypostasis of the incarnate Word. The term *antiperichoresis* is rare in earlier patristic literature (the preferred term being *perichoresis*), though it is attested in Leontios, *Against the Aphthartodocetists* (PG 86:1320B, which mistakenly identifies the text as book 2 of *Against Nestorios and Eutyches*); see Brian E. Daley, ed., *Leontius of Byzantium*: *Complete Works* (Oxford, 2017), 342, who renders the word as "reciprocal relationship."

you will call him Jesus . . . the throne of his father David: Luke 1:32.

And of his kingdom there will be no end: See Luke 1:33.

when all things will be subjected . . . God the Father: A paraphrase of 1 Corinthians 15:27–28.

23 *How can this . . . be? . . . I have not known a man*: Luke 1:34.

no carnal impulse: Compare John 1:13, οὐδὲ ἐκ θελήματος σαρκός, "nor of the will of the flesh." Here and in the discussion that immediately follows, including citing the support of Dionysios the Areopagite, Geometres follows Epiphanios, *Life of the Theotokos,* ed. Dressel, *Epiphanii,* 22.

the great and divinely inspired Dionysios: The name of Dionysios the Areopagite, an Athenian nobleman who was converted to Christianity by Saint Paul and who became the first bishop of Athens, was adopted by the later (fifth- or sixth-century) author of a significant corpus of theological works. See *ODB* vol. 1, pp. 629–30.

God-bearing body: This phrase is from Dionysios the Areopagite, *On the Divine Names* 3.2, ed. Beata Regina Suchla, *Corpus Diony-*

siacum, vol. 1, *De divinis nominibus* (Berlin and New York, 1990), p. 141, line 6. Geometres later cites a lengthy excerpt (below, 106) from the same work.

For not a man . . . power of the Most High: A paraphrase of Luke 1:35.

already completely pure: Geometres echoes Gregory of Nazianzus, *Oration* 38.13, ed. Moreschini and Gallay, *Discours 38–41*, p. 132, lines 22–24: "He was conceived by a virgin who was purified beforehand (παρθένου προκαθαρθείσης) in both soul and flesh by the Spirit." For commentary, see Christian Kappes, "Gregory Nazianzen's Prepurified Virgin in Ecumenical and Patristic Tradition: A Reappraisal of Original Sin, Guilt, and Immaculate Conception," in *The Spirit and the Church*, ed. J. Isaac Goff and others (Eugene, 2018), 147–98, at 147–49.

Christ is the power and wisdom of God: 1 Corinthians 1:24.

overshadow you: Luke 1:35; Psalms 90(91):4.

Shadow of the Father: This unusual image is also employed by Geometres, *On the Annunciation* 16 (PG 106:825C). Its earliest use appears to be in Gregory of Nyssa, *On the Nativity of the Savior* (GNO vol. 10, part 3, pp. 255–56). It may have also been inspired by the iconophile theology of the preceding century; see, for example, Theodore of Stoudios, *Antirrheticus* 3.4.1 (PG 99:429A–B): "If every shadow inseparably follows its own body, and if it is possible to see in the body the shadow which follows it, then no one could say that Christ is imageless."

the Radiance . . . his paternal similitudes: At Hebrews 1:3, Christ is called the "radiance (ἀπαύγασμα) of the glory of God."

that which will be born . . . will be called, the Son of God: Luke 1:35.

24 *behold Elizabeth . . . called barren*: An almost exact quotation of Luke 1:36.

no word from God will be void of power: Luke 1:37; compare Genesis 18:14, where a similar statement is made concerning Sarah's miraculous pregnancy.

nothing is impossible with God: See Luke 1:37; the wording of the Greek here is closer to the usual translation of the verse in English, although the rendering of the verse provided above is more accurate.

Behold the handmaid of the Lord . . . departed from her: See Luke 1:38.

Joseph did not know her . . . firstborn son: Matthew 1:25. A traditional exegetical puzzle. Geometres seems to know the commentary on Matthew's use of the preposition "until" (ἕως) in a homily attributed to Basil of Caesarea, *On the Nativity of Christ* 5 (PG 31:1462BD), as well as in a work by Photios of Constantinople, *Amphilochia* 171 (*Epistle* 30), ed. B. Laourdas and L. G. Westerink, *Photii patriarchae Constantinopolitani Epistulae et Amphilochia* (Leipzig, 1983–1988), vol. 1, pp. 80–81.

He did not know the mysteries concerning her: An explanation of Geometres's rather elliptical phrasing is found in Epiphanios, *Life of the Theotokos,* ed. Dressel, *Epiphanii,* 21: "*He did not know her until she had born her son* [Matthew 1:25], that is, he did not know about the mysteries of God concerning her or the hidden depth of the things that had been fulfilled in her."

until the revelation: See Matthew 1:19. Geometres is referring to the appearance of an angel to Joseph in a dream, revealing to him that "the child that was born is of the Holy Spirit."

the Virgin came under examination: A reference to the threat of her examination by one of the midwives; see *Protevangelium* 20.1.

which remained hidden: See Luke 2:19.

ran to Elizabeth: See Luke 1:39.

the hill country: See Luke 1:39.

the former's Son . . . purified by him: A reference to Jesus's meeting with John the Baptist, who would baptize him in the Jordan River; for Geometres's treatment of this, see below, 64–66.

25 *the voice . . . before the Voice*: On the Baptist as the herald of Christ, see John 1:23 and Isaiah 40:3.

leaping: Literally, "his leaps." Geometres uses the same word ἅλμασιν as the *Akathistos Hymn* 5.5; compare Luke 1:41.

mother of the Lord: Luke 1:43.

she was perplexed: Elizabeth's perplexity is implicit in Luke 1:43.

the muteness . . . cannot be spoken: See Luke 1:20–23. For "words that cannot be spoken," see also 2 Corinthians 12:4.

Abraham and Sarah: See Genesis 17:16–19 and 21:1–2. Abraham

was promised by God that Sarah would bear a son, despite her very advanced age.

mother of the Lord . . . blessed beyond all other women: See Luke 1:42.

blessed is the fruit of your womb: Luke 1:42.

that "cursed" fruit, which had the opposite effect: The fruit of the tree of the knowledge of good and evil; see Genesis 2:17.

nor through sin but indeed is sinless: See Hebrews 4:15; 1 Peter 2:22.

takes away the sin of the world: See John 1:29.

26 *she was both a prophetess and the subject of prophecy*: See Basil of Caesarea, *Commentary on Isaiah* 8.208 (PG 30:477B): "No one would dispute that the prophetess, to whom Isaiah drew near in foreknowledge, is Mary, if he remembers the words she uttered prophetically, 'My soul magnifies the Lord,' for then you will not hesitate to call her a prophetess, because 'the Spirit of the Lord came upon her' and 'the power of the Most High overshadowed her.'" For commentary, see Aloys Grillmeier, "Maria Prophetin: Eine Studie zur patristischen Mariologie," *Revue des Études Augustiniennes* 2 (1956): 295–312.

handmaid . . . humility . . . regard: See Luke 1:47–48.

fulfillment of those things spoken to her by the Lord: Luke 1:45.

magnifies the Lord: See Luke 1:46.

she would be blessed everywhere by all generations: See Luke 1:48.

27 *name and his mercy . . . from their thrones*: This passage quotes heavily from Luke 1:49–52.

28 *And he exalted the humble*: Luke 1:52.

those who hunger . . . sent away empty: Luke 1:53.

29 *But he helped his servant Israel*: Luke 1:54.

he who is strong did mighty things: See Luke 1:49.

the child in her womb . . . from the very beginning: Geometres may be referring to a sermon, *On the Nativity of Christ*, dubiously attributed to Basil of Caesarea, which, on the basis of Matthew 1:20 ("that which has been born in her is of the Holy Spirit"), argues that "the Lord's body was not formed through the ordinary constitution of human flesh, for immediately at the moment of its conception it was perfect, and did not take shape through a process of gradual formation" (PG 31:1465A–B). In

what seems a parallel formulation, Epiphanios, *Life of the Theotokos,* ed. Dressel, *Epiphanii,* 25, states that Jesus did not come forth as a "newborn baby" but rather as a "child," citing Matthew as proof, which may be a reference to Matthew 2:11, which speaks of the infant as a παιδίον, or "child." (We are thankful to Mary Cunningham for this suggestion.) The same point is made in the following paragraph.

without the sin: Hebrews 4:15.

30 *he was a just man*: Matthew 1:19.

send her away in secret: See Matthew 1:19.

releasing him: There is wordplay involving the verb ἀπολύω in the Greek here. The same word is used for Joseph's plan to send Mary away as for his release by the angel from his concerns.

Joseph, son of David . . . is of the Holy Spirit: These phrases are direct quotations from Matthew 1:20.

taken the place of human seed: A Christological formula found a number of times in Maximos the Confessor; see, for example, *Ambigua* 2.2, ed. Nicholas [Maximos] Constas, *On Difficulties in the Church Fathers: The Ambigua,* Dumbarton Oaks Medieval Library 28 and 29 (Cambridge, MA, 2014), vol. 1, pp. 12–13; compare John of Damascus, *On the Two Wills of Christ* 9, ed. Kotter, *Schriften,* vol. 4, p. 192, lines 54–56.

the Spirit . . . is God: John 4:24.

31 *the Jewish rulers and leaders will cease*: A paraphrase of Genesis 49:10.

resides the expectation of the nations: Genesis 49:10.

a light unto the revelation . . . of Israel: Luke 2:30–31.

for not all who are descended from Israel belong to Israel: Romans 9:6.

kings and rulers will depart from Judah: Compare Genesis 49:10; the wording here is slightly different from the paraphrase of the same passage above.

My kingdom is not of this world: John 18:36.

a decree went forth . . . should be enrolled: An almost exact quotation of Luke 2:1.

raised up an iron rod . . . destroying them: See Revelation 2:27.

32 *he will be called a Nazarene*: Matthew 2:23.

the Christ comes from Bethlehem: John 7:42.

made himself poor for us: See 2 Corinthians 8:9.

no prophet had ever arisen from it: See John 7:52, "No prophet is to rise from Galilee."

you are not the least . . . of Judah: Matthew 2:6; see also Micah 5:2.

humbled himself: See Philippians 2:8.

33 *the law*: A reference to Caesar's decree.

that great and creative light: Presumably the light of the star of Bethlehem or the Nativity, but perhaps also a reference to Christ the "creator and light of the world," for which see John 1:3–5.

from the house and homeland of David: Luke 2:4.

did away with . . . distress of childbirth: An element of the penalty imposed for the disobedience of Adam and Eve; see Genesis 3:16.

no room at the inn . . . in a manger . . . swaddling clothes: See Luke 2:7.

34 *she was present at the Nativity, assisted in the delivery*: Geometres follows Epiphanios, *Life of the Theotokos,* ed. Dressel, *Epiphanii,* 24, "[At the Nativity] Elizabeth, along with some other relatives of theirs, brought them [that is, Mary and Joseph] whatever they needed when she learned of the place they stopped to rest."

dividing walls . . . brought to an end: See Ephesians 2:14.

great and first shepherd: Building on John 10:11.

peace and goodwill on earth: A paraphrase of Luke 2:14.

Fear not . . . Christ the Lord: Geometres intersperses quotations from Luke 2:10 with his own additions.

today and in the city of David: See Luke 2:11–12.

the light and their Savior: The Greek word φωστήρ, which has the basic meaning of "star," also brings with it the significant connotation of "light."

others, including . . . words of the shepherds: See Luke 2:15–18.

35 *pondered . . . treasuring them in her heart*: See Luke 2:19.

innovations of natures: A phrase derived from Gregory of Nazianzus, *Oration* 39.13, ed. Moreschini and Gallay, *Discours 38–41,*

176, describing the incarnation. Maximos the Confessor, *Ambigua* 41, ed. Constas, vol. 2, pp. 102–21, comments extensively on the phrase.

without corruption: That is, without compromising the physical integrity of his mother's body.

in a manner beyond perception . . . spiritual Fleece: The reference is to an episode, recorded in Judges 6:37, in which Gideon placed a fleece on a threshing floor to catch dew, when testing God's purpose for Israel in the struggle with the Midianites. There is a further reference at Psalms 71(72):6. The fleece, as here, came to be seen as a figure of the Virgin. Geometres's wording is close to that of Eusebius of Caesarea, *Commentary on the Psalms* (PG 23:800C): "If he 'descended like rain on the fleece,' it was in a manner beyond perception (ἀνεπαισθήτως) or sound, and thus the mystery of his conception and birth from the Virgin was neither heard nor understood, not even by those dwelling nearby."

he not only eluded the others but even his own mother: As noted above, 15, the notion that Christ's birth "eluded" (λαθεῖν) observation is quite common in patristic literature. Geometres's repeated use of λαθών here is, however, probably derived from the hymnology for the feast of the Nativity. Compare the first antiphon of the vespers: Λαθὼν ἐτέχθης ὑπὸ τὸ σπήλαιον, ἀλλ' οὐρανός σε πᾶσιν ἐκήρυξεν, "Being born in a cave you eluded observation, but heaven proclaimed you to all," etc., which is repeated seven times; and the first ode of the canon, written in the eighth century by Kosmas: Χριστὸς ὁ Θεὸς δυνάμεις λαθών, ὅσας ὑπερκοσμίους, ὅσας ἐν γῇ, "Christ our God eluded the powers, both those above the earth and those upon it."

36 *the movement of the star and the Magi converged*: See Matthew 2:2.

a divine power: See John Chrysostom, *Homily to the Goths* 8.5 (PG 63:507, lines 40–41; see also 63:508, lines 13 and 21–22), where the star is described as "a divine and invisible power (θεία τις καὶ ἀόρατος δύναμις) transformed into the appearance of a star."

sometimes it moved, and sometimes it stood still: On the peculiar movements of the star, see Gregory of Nyssa, *On the Nativity of the Savior* (GNO vol. 10, part 3, pp. 245–46).

diviners of horoscopes: See Gregory of Nazianzus, *Oration* 39.5, ed. Moreschini and Gallay, *Discours 38–41,* p. 158, lines 7–10; and Basil of Caesarea, *Hexaemeron* 6.5, ed. Stanislas Giet, *Homélies sur l'Hexaéméron,* 2nd ed., SC 26bis (Paris, 1968), 348–52.

37 *Where is he who has been born . . . troubled*: See Matthew 2:2–3.

Herod: Herod I, the Roman client-king of Judaea who ruled from approximately 37/6 BCE until about 4 BCE, although the latter date is disputed.

you will no longer . . . come forth from you: See Matthew 2:6; compare Micah 5:2.

laying down his own life for the sheep: An almost direct quotation of John 10:11.

come from Bethlehem: See Micah 5:2.

the rulers and leaders of Judah would cease: Similar phrasing to that employed by Geometres at 31, above, and drawing again upon Genesis 49:10.

the king of the Jews: Matthew 2:2.

we have come to worship him: Matthew 2:2.

watchers keeping watch at night: Luke 2:8.

if not that when we too are . . . holding vigil: This is one of the few places where Geometres makes a direct reference to the context, namely, a vigil held in church.

38 *Herod was deeply troubled . . . comes from Bethlehem*: See Matthew 2:4–6; Micah 5:2.

interpreting the words of the prophet . . . from the beginning of eternity: A reference to and quotation from Micah 5:2.

being so jealous . . . deaf to the truth as well: Compare here, for example, John Chrysostom, *Homilies on John* 37.3 (PG 59:210): "Just as those who are mad often stab themselves with a sword, so too do the envious have only one aim, namely, maltreatment of the one they envy, in the process losing sight of their own salvation." See also here Prokopios of Gaza, *Commentary on Isaiah*" (PG 87:2373): "Like blind people, standing in the light of

the sun, they endeavored to make themselves voluntarily deaf to the words of scripture."

39 *they rejoiced with great joy*: See Matthew 2:10.

gold . . . frankincense . . . myrrh: Matthew 2:11.

mortification . . . bodily members: See Colossians 3:5.

40 *gave himself . . . and a ransom*: See 1 Timothy 2:6; compare Matthew 20:28 and Mark 10:45.

41 *on the eighth day*: That is, the eighth after the birth; see Luke 2:21.

circumcision of the flesh and freedom from the passions: See Romans 2:25–29.

purification, forty days after the birth: The forty-day purification period was established by Leviticus 12:2–4. For the events of Jesus's purification, see Luke 2:22–38; the exact timing is not mentioned there.

the perfect number of the decad . . . the four virtues: The "decad" is the number ten, related to the tetrad or tetractys, a triangular figure consisting of ten points arranged in four rows (also representing point, line, plane, and tetrahedron); see Maximos the Confessor, *Responses to Thalassios* 40, trans. Maximos Constas, *On Difficulties in Sacred Scripture: The Responses to Thalassios* (Washington, D.C., 2018), 231n40. In the Byzantine tradition, the tetrad was associated with the four cardinal virtues, often understood as the "four elements" constituting the noetic realm of the virtues; compare Maximos the Confessor, *Ambigua* 21.4–10, ed. Constas, vol. 1, pp. 425–37.

slaughter of the infants: See Matthew 2:16–18.

the going up to Jerusalem and the purification: Here Geometres follows Eusebius, *Gospel Problems and Solutions* 16 (PG 22:933–36); compare Symeon Metaphrastes, *Life of the Virgin* 14, ed. Vasilii Vasil'evich Latyshev, *Menologii anonymi Byzantini saeculi X quae supersunt,* vol. 2, *Menses Iunium, Iulium, Augustum continens* (Saint Petersburg, 1912; repr., Leipzig, 1970), 356–57.

two years: A calculation taken from Eusebius, *Gospel Problems and Solutions* 16 (PG 22:933).

flight into Egypt: See Matthew 2:19–23.

that which has been neglected . . . by all: Taken verbatim from Aelius Aristides, *Panathenaic Oration* 3.

42 *most irascible . . . as the history affirms*: See Matthew 2:16 and *Protevangelium* 22.1, 23.2. By "history" here Geometres is probably referencing the principal historian of Herod's reign, Josephus, who gives a negative view of Herod's character following his account of the king's execution of his sons, *Antiquities of the Jews* 16.11.8. For that episode, mentioned by Geometres shortly below in the present paragraph, see the following note.

The solution . . . historical account: In the following passage Geometres presents a brief and partial narrative of two important events in Herod's reign. According to the account of Josephus, *Antiquities of the Jews* 15.7.4, Herod's second wife, Mariamne, was executed on charges of treason in 27 BCE after years of conflict between her, her mother Alexandra, and Herod's sister, Salome. Around 7 BCE, Herod had his two sons by Mariamne, Alexander and Aristobulus, executed for treason after bringing charges against them to the emperor Augustus, apparently based on false evidence; see Josephus, *Antiquities* 16.11.1 and 16.11.7.

43 *on children who had done no wrong*: The slaughter of the innocents; see Matthew 2:16–18.

turned the Morning Star into darkness . . . godless apostate: Geometres refers to the fall of the devil, who was understood, on the basis of a number of scriptural passages, to have originally been an archangel. For the particular connection with the "morning star," see Isaiah 14:12; the Greek word ἑωσφόρος was translated into Latin as Lucifer, whence the English name for Satan or the devil.

struck down by God . . . food for maggots: Josephus, *Antiquities* 17.6.5.

rich man in flames: See Luke 16:24, the parable of the rich man and Lazarus.

44 *A voice was heard in Ramah . . . they were no longer*: See Matthew 2:18, citing Jeremiah 38(31):15. Rachel's death in childbirth near Bethlehem and her tomb there are recorded at Genesis

35:16–20. On the symbolic relationship of Rachel's tomb to the *Kathisma* (an important site of Marian pilgrimage) and to the church of the Nativity in Bethlehem, see Rina Avner, "The Initial Tradition of the *Theotokos* at the *Kathisma:* Earliest Celebrations and the Calendar," in *The Cult of the Mother of God in Byzantium: Texts and Images,* ed. Leslie Brubaker and Mary B. Cunningham (Farnham, 2011), 9–29.

45 *great and the son of the Most High*: Luke 1:32.

swords passed through your soul: See Luke 2:35.

on what was also the first day: That is, Sunday.

he is given the name "Jesus," . . . foretold: Luke 1:31, and see above, 22.

46 *After the completion . . . holy to the Lord*: A paraphrase of and quotation from Luke 2:22–23, which cites Exodus 13:2. The expression "every male that opens the womb" refers to the firstborn male child.

makes things holy and is made holy: See John 17:19 and Hebrews 2:11.

a pair of turtledoves or two young pigeons: Luke 2:24, citing Leviticus 5:11, 12:8.

require interpretation: Literally, "contemplation" (θεωρία).

love of solitude: This phrase renders the Greek φιλέρημον. On the symbolism, see, for example, Origen, *Fragments on Luke* 63, ed. Max Rauer, *Die Homilien zu Lukas in der Übersetzung des Hieronymus und die griechischen Reste der Homilien und des Lukas-Kommentars,* GCS 49, Origenes Werke 9 (Berlin, 1959), p. 253, fragment 63, lines 8–9: "Turtledoves symbolize chastity and love of solitude (φιλέρημον)."

Cain, Reuben, and Esau: the firstborn sons respectively of Adam, Jacob, and Abraham, who in different ways proved to be weak and wicked men. Here, as elsewhere in this section, Geometres follows Amphilochios of Iconium, *On the Theotokos, and on Symeon and Anna,* ed. C. Datema, *Amphilochius Iconiensis Opera,* Corpus Christianorum Series Graeca 3 (Turnhout, 1978), 43.

conceived . . . brought forth in sins: See Psalms 50:7(51:5).

47 *power and wisdom of God*: See 1 Corinthians 1:24.

This gate will be closed . . . and the gate will be closed: An adaptation of Ezekiel 44:2. On this see Amphilochios of Iconium, *Homily*

on the Theotokos, and on Symeon and Anna, ed. Datema, *Amphilochius,* p. 45, lines 73–74; and Constas, *Proclus of Constantinople,* 132–33.

he will be called . . . every male: See Luke 2:23. Geometres uses a selection from the words of Luke to make a different point of his own; the Greek dative τῷ Κυρίῳ can mean both "to the Lord," as in the original passage, or "by the Lord," as here.

the one who is born . . . Son of God: A further reworking of the words of Luke 2:23.

48 *Symeon*: In this paragraph Geometres is commenting on the episode recorded in Luke 2:25–35.

a man like God for the God made man: The Greek wordplay, τῷ θεανθρώπῳ θεάνθρωπος, is impossible to render neatly in English. Literally, it means "a god-man for the God-man."

Ancient of Days: Daniel 7:9, 7:13.

49 *being moved by the Spirit . . . your people Israel*: Geometres is interpreting Luke 2:30–32, from which he quotes freely in this passage.

darkness of ignorance . . . he himself is light: See Luke 1:79; Isaiah 9:2.

from them . . . came Christ: Romans 9:5.

Israel . . . sees all things clearly: Geometres follows a traditional interpretation of "Israel" here; he is perhaps closest to Cyril of Alexandria, *Glaphyra on the Pentateuch* (PG 69:85): "The name 'Israel' means an intellect that sees God." See further Robert Haywood, *Interpretations of the Name Israel in Ancient Judaism and Some Early Christian Writings* (Oxford, 2005), 156–93.

50 *resolution of his doubts*: See Matthew 1:20.

Joseph . . . and his mother: Luke 2:33. The version of Luke that Geometres is using names Joseph here, but the standard text simply speaks of him as "the father."

blessed them both: Luke 2:34.

Behold this child . . . many in Israel: Luke 2:34.

51 *the preparation of salvation . . . all the peoples*: See Luke 2:31.

fall and rising of many . . . in Israel: See Luke 2:34.

preaching the Gospel . . . to all the Gentiles: See Mark 13:10.

buried with Christ . . . glorified with him: These phrases are in-

spired by Gregory of Nazianzus, *Oration* 1.4, ed. Jean Bernardi, *Discours 1–3,* SC 247 (Paris, 1978), 76.

52 *weak and strong*: See 2 Corinthians 12:10.

And a sign that is disputed: Luke 2:34. Geometres repeats and expounds on the possible meaning of this phrase throughout the paragraph.

it is an object of ridicule . . . of hatred: See 1 Corinthians 1:18.

Christ himself is the sign . . . creator of signs: In the Gospel of John, Jesus's miracles are called "signs."

weeds grown by the wicked farmer: The reference is to the parable of the weeds (ζιζάνια); see especially Matthew 13:25.

his body was illusory: A reference to Docetists or "Phantasiasts," who believed that the body of Christ was a mere appearance or "phantasm," a charge also leveled against the Iconoclasts at the Seventh Ecumenical Council. See ACO vol. 2.1, part 4, p. 534, line 5; p. 552, lines 28–54; p. 556, line 12; p. 590, lines 15–16; and p. 854, line 21.

without human reason or mind: A reference to the heresy associated with Apollinarios, who denied that Christ had a human intellect, which he claimed was displaced by the divine Logos.

as if through a tube: The notion that Christ passed through the body of the Virgin like "water through a tube" was first argued by Valentinus and other early Christian Gnostics, and regularly condemned by later Church fathers; see Constas, *Proclus of Constantinople,* 295–96.

the child in her womb was fully formed: See above, 29.

53 *not only of the more joyous . . . more sorrowful*: In what follows, Geometres closely follows Amphilochios of Iconium, *On the Theotokos, and on Symeon and Anna,* ed. Datema, *Amphilochius,* 63–69, who understands the "sword" of Symeon and the "sign that is spoken against" as the Virgin's troubled thoughts at the time of the crucifixion. The earliest source for this interpretation is Origen, *Homily on Luke* 17.6, ed. Henri Crouzel, François Fournier, and Pierre Périchon, *Homélies sur saint Luc,* SC 87 (Paris, 1978), 256–58.

you yourself: Luke 2:35.

you will all fall away: See Matthew 26:31; Mark 14:27.

a sword shall pierce your soul: Luke 2:35.

so that thoughts . . . may be revealed: Luke 2:35.

consequentially but not causally: See, for example, John of Damascus, *On the Orthodox Faith* 92 (4.19), ed. Kotter, *Schriften*, vol. 2, p. 93, lines 32–33: "It is customary for scripture to speak of some things as causes (αἰτιολογικῶς) which really are chance effects (ἐκβατικῶς)." Or see also Theophylaktos of Ohrid, *Commentary on John* 9 (PG 124:44B), where the contrast is also drawn, using the same terms: οὐκ αἰτιολογικῶς ἀλλ' ἀποβατικῶς.

but even the thief who was crucified with him: For the penitent thief, see Luke 23:40–43. Both Matthew 27:44 and Mark 15:32 indicate only that those crucified with Jesus "reviled" him.

54 *Joseph received the oracle . . . the flight into Egypt*: See Matthew 2:13. There Joseph is informed through a dream (κατ' ὄναρ), which Geometres here calls an "oracle" (χρησμός).

the great John the Baptist . . . before he could speak a word: See above, 25.

born shortly before Jesus: John the Baptist was six months older than Jesus.

preparatory offerings . . . even to Hades: An allusion to the apocryphal and hymnological tradition (see the *Gospel of Nikodemos* 18) that John the Baptist preached to the dead in Hades prior to Christ's death and descent into the underworld.

Elizabeth and her son . . . into the wilderness: As recounted in the *Protevangelion* 22.3; on which see Epiphanios, *Life of the Theotokos*, ed. Dressel, *Epiphanii*, 27.

Bridegroom . . . friend: See John 3:29, where John the Baptist describes himself as the "friend of the bridegroom."

unleashed . . . their rage on Zacharias . . . mingling blood with blood: That is, Zacharias's blood with the blood of the animal sacrifices. Geometres is here following and directly quoting Origen, *Homilies on Luke*, a work that survives in fragmentary form in the *catenae*. Origen suggests that Zachariah the son of Barachiah, mentioned in Matthew 23:35 ("Zachariah . . . whom you

murdered between the sanctuary and the altar"), was the father of John the Baptist. In the critical edition of these fragments, the citation in question is said to be from Origen's *Commentary on Matthew;* see Rauer, *Homilien zu Lukas,* p. 308, fragment 189; and Erich Klostermann, ed., *Origenes Matthäuserklärung,* vol. 2, *Die lateinische Übersetzung der Commentariorum series,* GCS 38, Origenes Werke 11 (Leipzig, 1933), 42–43. The *Protevangelium* 23–24 reports that Zachariah's refusal to tell Herod's soldiers where his son was hiding resulted in his murder. The account is clearly related to the story of the murder of Zachariah the son of Jehoiada, who was stoned to death in the court of the temple in 2 Chronicles 24:20–22.

55 *the flight of the demons of Egypt*: The apocryphal *Lives of the Prophets* 2.8–9 recounts that the Egyptian idols fell from their pedestals when Christ arrived; see James H. Charlesworth, *The Old Testament Pseudepigrapha,* vol. 2 (Garden City, NY, 1983), 387.

the Enemy: The devil.

serpents and scorpions: See Luke 10:19; compare Exodus 7:10–12.

came later to the Egyptians . . . figure of Israel: Here and below Geometres is alluding to the history of the captivity of Israel in Egypt, as recounted in Exodus.

inundating . . . drowning the legions: Geometres describes the defeat of the demonic legions of Egyptian religion through the presence of Christ by using language alluding to the destruction of the Egyptian army in the Red Sea; see Exodus 14:26–28.

a new mother of God: That is, in place of the goddess Isis, the mother of Horus by Osiris.

Behold the Lord . . . coming to Egypt: Isaiah 19:2.

Out of Egypt have I called my son: Matthew 2:15; compare Hosea 11:1.

the child would be called a Nazarene: See Matthew 2:23.

56 *he does not say this to contradict Matthew*: See Luke 2:39. Geometres closely follows John Chrysostom's version of the chronology here, *Homilies on Matthew* 9.4 (PG 57:180, lines 28–36). On the different chronologies of the infancy narratives in Matthew and Luke, see Raymond E. Brown, *Birth of the Messiah: A*

Commentary on the Infancy Narratives in the Gospels of Matthew and Luke (New York, 1993), 76–79, 84–86, 214–25, 412–70, 513–16, 587–96, and 616–17.

57 *golden freight*: A reference to Christ in Mary's womb.

58 *the royal image and the coin*: An allusion to the parable of the lost coin in Luke 15:8–10. Geometres is here drawing on Gregory of Nazianzus, *Oration* 38.14, ed. Moreschini and Gallay, *Discours 38–41*, 136: "he sought the coin, the royal image confounded with passions." See further, Gabrielle Thomas, *The Image of God in the Theology of Gregory of Nazianzus* (Cambridge, 2019), 112–13.

he saved the one who was now pursuing him: Herod was Jewish, and thus Geometres associates him with the Jews saved from Egypt in the time of Moses.

59 *his kingdom was . . . four provinces*: See Peter Richardson, *Herod: King of the Jews and Friend of the Romans* (Columbia, SC, 1996), 131–52.

remnants of his former evils: Geometres has borrowed this phrase from John Chrysostom, *Homilies on Matthew* 9.4 (PG 57:180, lines 12–13).

Archelaos . . . was ruling in place of his father Herod: Matthew 2:22. See John Chrysostom, *Homilies on Matthew* 9.4 (PG 57:180, lines 19–21). Archelaos, also known as Herod Archelaos, was the son of Herod the Great by his wife, Malthace. He acceded to the throne after the death of his father, but did not receive the title of king, ruling as ethnarch of Judea, Samaria, and Idumea (4 BCE–6 CE). His accession to the throne was the signal for Mary and Joseph to return with Jesus from Egypt to Nazareth. After a relatively short reign, he was deposed and replaced by a series of Roman governors, including Pontius Pilate (26–36 CE); see Josephus, *The Jewish War* 1.562, 2.93–98; and Maurice Sartre, *The Middle East Under Rome,* trans. Catherine Porter and Elizabeth Rawlings (Cambridge, MA, 2005), 96–97.

his brother Herod: Herod Antipas (or Antipater), who ruled as tetrarch of Galilee and Perea (4 BCE–39 CE). He ordered the

beheading of John the Baptist and was present at the trial of Jesus; see Sartre, *The Middle East Under Rome,* 97–98.

to the land of Israel: See Matthew 2:20–21.

he would be called a Nazarene: See Matthew 2:23.

how Archelaos was reigning . . . same time: Geometres follows (as earlier in this section) John Chrysostom, *Homilies on Matthew* 9.4 (PG 57:180, lines 14–19).

the historical account: Presumably Josephus, *The Jewish War* 1.117–84.

Aristoboulos: Aristoboulos II, high priest and king of Judea from 67 to 63 BCE; see James C. VanderKam, *From Joshua to Caiaphas: High Priests after the Exile* (Minneapolis, 2004), 340–45.

another Herod: Herod Antipas. See above note in this section, on "his brother Herod."

Pilate: Pontius Pilate, the governor of the Roman province of Judaea from 26/7 to 36/7 CE, presided over the trial of Jesus and ordered his crucifixion.

in accord with the prophecy: Genesis 49:10, on which, see above, 31 and 37.

his rebellious brother Hyrcanus: John Hyrcanus II, high priest (76–67, 63–40 BCE) and ethnarch of Judea (ca. 47–40 BCE); see Josephus, *The Jewish War* 1.109–273; and VanderKam, *From Joshua to Caiaphas,* 337–39.

taken prisoner by Pompey: The Roman general and statesman Pompey had been asked to intervene in the dispute over the throne between Hyrcanus II and Aristoboulos II. In his subsequent siege and conquest of Jerusalem (63 BCE), he brought about the end of Jewish independence and reduced Judea to a client state of the Roman Republic. Hyrcanus was reinstated as high priest but without his royal title, while Aristoboulos was taken to Rome for Pompey's triumphal procession (Josephus, *Jewish Wars* 1.128, 1.143, 1.145–53); see VanderKam, *From Joshua to Caiaphas,* 342–45; and Sartre, *The Middle East under Rome,* 40–42.

and it is clear . . . authority even over his own children: See above, 42.

60 *progress in stature and grace . . . wisdom*: See Luke 2:52.

the entire fullness of the divinity dwelt within him: An almost exact quotation of Colossians 2:9.

61 *at the time of the feast*: Passover. The account that follows bears comparison with Symeon Metaphrastes, *Life of the Virgin* 23–24, ed. Latyshev, *Menologii*, vol. 2, pp. 363–64.

Child . . . looking for you in great distress: Luke 2:48.

Why were you looking . . . Father's house: Luke 2:49.

Whoever has seen me . . . the Father: John 14:9.

"If you have known . . . know me too": See John 7:14.

62 *The Infancy of Jesus*: A reference to the second-century *Paidika,* often referred to as the *Infancy Gospel of Thomas,* which is not to be confused with the *Gospel of Thomas;* see Reidar Aasgard, *The Childhood of Jesus: Decoding the Apocryphal Infancy Gospel of Thomas* (Eugene, OR, 2009); and Frédéric Amsler, "Les *Paidika Iesou,* un nouveau témoin de la rencontre entre judaïsme et christianisme à Antoich au IVe siècle?," in Clivaz, Dettwiler, Devillers, and others, *Infancy Gospels,* 433–58.

more beautiful than the sons of men: Psalms 44:3(45:2). Compare Epiphanios, *Life of the Theotokos,* ed. Dressel, *Epiphanii,* 29, who in his account of the young Christ in the temple, states: "He was exceedingly handsome in his countenance, even as the prophet says, 'You are more beautiful than the sons of men.'" Geometres quotes the same verse from Psalms below, 89.

no razor ever came upon his head: See Numbers 6:5; compare Judges 16:17.

63 *he traveled with them down to Nazareth*: See Luke 2:51.

no one should seek his own good: 1 Corinthians 10:24.

The good shepherd laying down his life for his sheep: See John 10:11.

cherishing them in her heart: See Luke 2:51.

join his body . . . fitting manner: Ephesians 4:16.

No man has ever spoken like this: John 7:46.

No one has ever done . . . man has done: Compare John 9:32.

64 *He was thirty years old*: See Luke 3.23.

65 *peculiar diet*: See Matthew 3:4.

He himself was not the Christ . . . immediately after him: A paraphrase of John 1:19–20, 1:26–27.

reserved miracles for himself: See Romans 11:4.

Christ is coming after me . . . now stands among you: See John 1:30 and 1:26.

Behold the Lamb of God . . . sin of the world: John 1:29.

purified by us: "By us" in the sense of accepting baptism from John.

precluding destruction . . . by means of corruption: Note the distinction here between "destruction" (διαφθορά) and the four successive uses of "corruption" (φθορά). John of Damascus, *On the Orthodox Faith* 72 (3.28), ed. Kotter, *Schriften*, vol. 2, p. 171, lines 2–11, defines φθορά as the blameless bodily passions (including death), to which Christ was voluntarily subject, and διαφθορά as the body's "complete dissolution and reduction to the elements of which it was composed," to which Christ was not susceptible, citing Psalms 15:10.

he raises up . . . from its lower life: Geometres is closely following Gregory of Nazianzus, *Oration* 39.16, ed. Moreschini and Gallay, *Discours 38–41*, 184: "But now Jesus comes up out of the water, and he raises up, together with himself, the world from its lower life" (συναναφέρει γὰρ ἑαυτῷ τὸν κόσμον)."

66 *the entire fullness of the deity*: Colossians 2:9.

after our purification: A reference to the sacrament of baptism.

beloved Son: Matthew 3:17; Mark 1:11; Luke 3:22.

67 *he was ministered to by angels*: See Matthew 4:11.

he received John's disciples . . . John of virginity: See John 1:35–40. In Greek, the name "Andrew" is derived from the word for courage, while tradition holds that John remained a virgin throughout his life.

Andrew brought Peter: See John 1:40–42.

Galilee . . . Philip and Nathanael: See John 1:43–51.

68 *On the third day . . . the wedding at Cana*: See John 2:1.

His mother was also present: Epiphanios, *Life of the Theotokos*, ed. Dressel, *Epiphanii*, 31–32, oddly makes no mention of Mary's presence at the wedding.

transformation: The Greek term μεταβολή, appearing here and in cognates below, is that used in the Byzantine liturgy to signal

the transformation of the bread and wine into the body and blood of Christ.

sweet: Compare Exodus 15:23–25, where the bitter waters of Marah were made sweet.

ecstatic: Ἐκστατικόν. See the *scholion* to Maximos the Confessor's commentary on the Wedding at Cana, in his *Responses to Thalassios* 40, ed. C. Laga and C. Steel, *Quaestiones ad Thalassium I*, Corpus Christianorum Series Graeca 7 (Turnhout, 1980), p. 275, lines 12–13: "The 'good wine' is the Word, who makes human nature stand outside of itself (ἐκστατικὸν) in the process of divinization."

Wisdom herself desires to mix in a mixing bowl: See Proverbs 9:2.

the one who prompted her eagerness: The host or the wine steward.

Whatever he tells you to do, do it: See John 2:5.

the bridegroom abandoned . . . became a disciple: According to Byzantine tradition, the bridegroom was Simon the Zealot, also called the "Canaanite," who became one of the Twelve Apostles; see pseudo-Anastasios of Sinai, *Disputation with the Jews* (PG 89:1248B). Epiphanios, *Life of the Theotokos,* ed. Dressel, *Epiphanii,* 31–32, seems to be the earliest writer who states that the wedding at Cana ended with the bridegroom parting from his wife and following Christ (we are thankful to Mary Cunningham for this information). Geometres takes the idea further and adds that the bride became a disciple of the Virgin.

69 *Bethsaida*: A place believed to have been located on the northern shore of the Sea of Galilee. John 1:44 describes it as the home of the apostles Philip, Andrew, and Peter, and in Mark 8:22–26 and Luke 9:10–11 Jesus is said to have performed miracles nearby.

healed Peter's mother-in-law: Matthew 8:14–15; Mark 1:29–31; Luke 4:38–39. Matthew and Mark indicate that the miracle took place in Capernaum.

Zebedee: Geometres follows Epiphanios, *Life of the Theotokos,* ed. Dressel, *Epiphanii,* 32, in taking Zebedee as a place-name, as well as the name of the father of James and John (see below).

Gennesaret: Gennesaret may refer either, as here, to the Sea of

Galilee (otherwise called Lake Tiberias or Kinneret) or, more specifically, to the small plain bordering its western shore between Capernaum and Magdala that is mentioned in the New Testament at Matthew 14:34, Mark 6:53, and Luke 5:1. There is a long tradition of eulogy for the place going back to Josephus, *Jewish War* 3.10.7–8, to which are indebted Geometres's ekphrasis here, as well as Epiphanios, *Life of the Theotokos,* ed. Dressel, *Epiphanii,* 32–33. On Geometres's ekphraseis, see Panagiotis Agapitos and Martin Hinterberger, *Εἰκὼν καὶ Λόγος: Ἕξι βυζαντινὲς περιγραφὲς ἔργων τέχνης* (Athens, 2006), 129–61; and Christos Simelidis, "Two *Lives of the Virgin:* John Geometres, Euthymios the Athonite, and Maximos the Confessor," *Dumbarton Oaks Papers* 74 (2000): 125–59, at 131.

this is what Gennesaret means in Hebrew: Geometres may have misread Epiphanios, *Life of the Theotokos,* ed. Dressel, *Epiphanii,* 32, who says that "Gennesaret is also called 'Bowl' (φιάλη) because it is equal on all sides," but does not claim that this is the meaning of Gennesaret in Hebrew, which is possibly derived from the word for the trees or cane reeds that grow in the vicinity.

well over fifty stadia . . . into a circle: Taking the *stadion* as roughly equaling six hundred feet, Geometres's estimation of the lake's diameter is around six miles; it is in fact about thirteen by eight miles.

the house of their father Zebedee: See Luke 5:10.

the mother of the men . . . service to all: See Matthew 20:20–28.

sons of thunder: Mark 3:17.

70 *the healing of the paralytic*: See Mark 2:1–12, who identifies the location as Capernaum; compare the other synoptic versions at Matthew 9:2–7 and Luke 5:17–26.

members . . . one head, namely, Christ: See 1 Corinthians 12:12. The Greek term μέλη contains the meaning of both "members" (of a group) and "limbs" (of a body).

able to carry . . . homeland and house: See Matthew 9:6; Mark 2:9–12; Luke 5:23–25.

the world itself could not contain: See John 21:25.

he also both baptized and was baptized: See above, 64.

his sons sought . . . not permitted to do so: Geometres is apparently interpreting the otherwise anonymous episode of Luke 9:59–60 as referring to James or John.

the house in which . . . meager or insignificant: Geometres follows a traditional interpretation of the reference in Mark 1:20 to Zebedee having "hired servants" as an indication that the family was wealthy.

part of it . . . house in Zion: Geometres here follows Epiphanios, *Life of the Theotokos*, ed. Dressel, *Epiphanii*, 33–34, who describes the same episode.

disciple took her . . . to his own home: See John 19:26–27.

Joanna: Luke 8:3, where she is described as the wife of Chuza, Herod's steward.

unless one renounces all that one has: Luke 14:33. The full verse reads: "So therefore, whoever of you does not renounce all that he has cannot be my disciple."

took up her cross: See Matthew 16:24; Luke 14:27.

71 *feast of Tabernacles*: See John 7.

the Lord . . . drove away the moneychangers: See Matthew 21:12–13; Mark 11:15–17; Luke 19:45–46; John 2:13–17.

Magdala . . . Mary Magdalene: Magdala was a town on the western shore of the Sea of Galilee, north of Tiberias. Luke 8:2 first mentions Mary Magdalene among the group of women accompanying Jesus, but nowhere in the New Testament is she said specifically to come from Magdala.

plagued by all seven spirits of wickedness: See Luke 8:2 and Mark 16:9. Geometres's wording shows that he understands this as a reference to the concept of the seven deadly sins.

72 *will never be capable . . . worthy of the Virgin*: On the inability of language to express the mystery of the Virgin, see above, 1.

never in any way separated . . . each of the natures: Geometres expresses the classic teaching about Christ's two natures in one hypostasis (or person), promulgated by the Council of Chalcedon in 451 CE; see ACO vol. 2.1, part 2, pp. 128–30.

74 *was not the Passover prescribed by the law*: Geometres is referring

to the question of whether the Last Supper was a Passover meal. That seems to be the view of the Synoptic Gospels (see, for example, Mark 14:12), whereas John describes Jesus's trial and crucifixion taking place before the first day of Passover (see John 18:28, 19:24), when the sacrificial lambs were being slaughtered in the temple. The classic study of this question by Joachim Jeremias, *The Eucharistic Words of Jesus,* trans. Norman Perrin (London and New York, 1966), first published in German in 1935, argued for the Synoptic view, but the Johannine chronology is now recognized as more plausible; see Gerd Theissen and Annette Merz, *The Historical Jesus: A Comprehensive Guide* (Minneapolis, 1998), 423–26.

Pentecost: *Shavuot,* or the Feast of Weeks (see Tobit 2:1; 2 Maccabees 12:32), is a harvest festival celebrated seven weeks and one day after the first day of Passover (Deuteronomy 16:9), or seven weeks and one day after the Sabbath referred to in Leviticus 23:16. The Christian feast of Pentecost marks the descent of the Holy Spirit upon the Apostles while they were in Jerusalem celebrating the Feast of Weeks; see Acts 2:1–31. It is celebrated on the fiftieth day after Easter Sunday.

uttermost humble service and submission: A reference to Jesus washing his disciple's feet.

beautify their steps with speed: See Romans 10:15; and Isaiah 52:7: "How beautiful are the feet of those who preach good news!"

75 *handed over but did not go forth*: Psalms 87:9(88:8).

like a sheep . . . cry out: See Isaiah 53:7.

My friends and neighbors stood at a distance: See Psalms 37:12(38:11).

76 *Annas and Caiaphas*: Caiaphas was the Jewish high priest at the time while Annas, a former high priest and still evidently influential, was his father-in-law. They questioned Jesus at the time of his arrest and trial; see John 18:12–14, 18:19–24 and Matthew 26:57–66; compare Mark 15:53–65 and Luke 22:54.

had all turned away: Psalms 13(14):3, quoted at Romans 3:12.

had all lost their minds . . . is no God: Psalms 13(14):1.

Come let us kill: See Mark 12:7, where, in the parable of the vineyard, the tenants kill the son of the owner.

righteous man . . . inconvenient Messiah out of the way: See Wisdom 2:12. Geometres clearly has in mind here the entire passage, 2:12–20, where the ungodly are said to lie in wait for the righteous man, who is described as inconvenient to them, seeking to test and kill him to see if God really is his father. There is a wordplay in the Greek between Χριστὸν (Christ) and δύσχρηστον (inconvenient), which might be captured by the phrase "irredeemable Redeemer."

all of them thus raged and plotted in vain: Compare Psalms 2:2, quoted at Acts 4:25.

a nestling and a shepherd: Geometres here picks up the simile of the bird and the heifer and, as often in this work, inverts the relationship: Jesus, as son but also God, is both Mary's nestling and shepherd.

77 *A purple robe was wrapped in mockery*: Geometres's wording is closest to John 19:2 and Mark 15:17; compare Matthew 27:28 and Luke 23:11.

78 *clothes himself with light as with a garment*: Psalms 103(104):2.

divided by profane lots: See Matthew 27:35, Mark 15:24, Luke 23:34, and John 19:23–24, all following Psalms 21:19(22:18).

which shone like the sun: An allusion to the Transfiguration of Christ; see Matthew 17:2 and Luke 9:29. It is impossible to capture Geometres's wordplay in this passage between ἥλοις (nails) and ἡλιακὰς (like the sun).

a sword pierced through your own soul: Luke 2:35; see above, 53.

you surpassed your son in your sufferings: Euthymios, *Life of the Virgin* 78, renders the verb in the passive voice and thus does not require Geometres's qualification that this may be something perhaps "too bold to say."

79 *fierce and murderous glances*: The same expression occurs in a work, dated to 905, by John Kaminiates, *The Capture of Thessaloniki* 49.14, ed. David Frendo and Athanasios Fotiou (Perth, 2000), 81–82.

like dogs or wild beasts: See Psalms 21:17(22:16).

I am a worm and no man . . . shook their heads: Geometres comments upon an almost exact quotation of Psalms 21:8–9(22:7–8).

who wagged their heads: Matthew 27:39, citing Psalms 21:8(22:7).

their foolish or rather deranged words: Compare Romanos the Melodist, *On the Three Youths in the Furnace,* ed. Grosdidier de Matons, *Hymnes,* vol. 1, p. 376, no. 8.11.3–4 (τὰ ῥήματα τῶν λαλούντων, / ληρήματα φλυαρούντων, "the words of the speakers are the silly talk of babblers"), and Romanos the Melodist, *On the Resurrection,* ed. Grosdidier de Matons, *Hymnes,* vol. 4, p. 402, no. 40.13.4 (ληρήματά μου τὰ ῥήματα, "my words are silly talk").

The reproaches . . . fell upon me: Psalms 68:10(69:9).

I waited for one . . . but I found none: Psalms 68:21(69:20).

They gave me gall . . . vinegar to drink: Psalms 68:22(69:21).

each one that struck her was like a thousand swords: See Luke 2:35, and above, 45.

not able . . . men to their senses: Geometres borrows his phrasing from Theodoret of Cyrrhus, *Commentary on Isaiah* 1, ed. Jean-Noël Guinot, *Commentaire sur Isaïe,* 3 vols., SC 276, 295, 315 (Paris, 1980–1984), vol. 1, p. 150, lines 41–42.

through darkness: See Matthew 27:45; Mark 15:33; Luke 23:44.

Place of the Skull: A translation of the Aramaic "Golgotha," rendered in Latin as "Calvaria," and as "Calvary" in English. See Matthew 27:33; Mark 15:22; Luke 23:33; John 19:17.

when you go down . . . testify on my behalf: A combination of Exodus 19:10, 19:21 and Deuteronomy 31:28, taken again from Theodoret of Cyrrhus, *Commentary on Isaiah* 1, ed. Guinot, *Commentaire sur Isaïe,* vol. 1, p. 148, line 15, which Geometres follows closely through the quotation from Jeremiah, cited below.

Hear, heaven . . . earth hear my words: Deuteronomy 32:1.

Heaven was astonished . . . says the Lord: Jeremiah 2:12.

80 *many dogs now surrounded him*: See Psalms 21:17(22:16).

many young bulls . . . surrounding him: See Psalms 21:13(22:12).

the sinews of their necks were iron: See Isaiah 48:4.

81 *the one who takes away the sin of the world*: John 1:29.

inflicted great plagues on Egypt: For the ten plagues inflicted on Egypt, see Exodus 7–12.

purple robe of mockery: See above, 77.

luminous cloud: a reference to God appearing as a pillar of cloud by day to shelter the Israelites (Exodus 13:21–22). The same expression was used by Theodoret, *Questions on Leviticus,* 22, ed. John F. Petruccione, *The Questions on the Octateuch,* vol. 2, *On Genesis and Exodus* (Washington, DC, 2007), 50–51, and is heavily attested in Byzantine hymnography as an Old Testament figure of the Virgin and often linked with Isaiah 19:20: "See, the Lord rides on a swift cloud (νεφέλης κούφης) and is coming to Egypt." See, for example, the Canon of the Akathistos, composed in the ninth century by Joseph the Hymnographer (PG 105:1024): Χαῖρε, ἡ ἄφλεκτος βάτος, νεφέλη ὁλόφωτε, ἡ τοὺς πιστοὺς ἀπαύστως ἐπισκιάζουσα, "Hail, O unconsumed bush, and radiant cloud unceasingly overshadowing the faithful."

like an eagle . . . on your back: See Deuteronomy 32:11; Odes 2:11.

crowned them with glory and honor: Hebrews 2:7, citing Psalms 8:6(5).

a shield of favor: Psalms 5:13(12).

They have struck you . . . spat in your face: See Matthew 26:67, 27:30; Mark 15:19.

the sea covered their enemies: Exodus 14:16–29.

manifested the light of your face upon us: Psalms 4:7(6).

glorified the face of Moses: See Exodus 34:29–35.

with your spittle . . . blind man: See Mark 8:23; John 9:6.

gave strength . . . hands and feet: See Hebrews 12:12; compare Isaiah 35:3.

In return for: These anaphoric clauses beginning with ἀντὶ (in return for) are likely inspired by the hymnology of the Passion.

Barabbas: A criminal who was chosen by the crowd over Jesus to be released by Pilate. See Matthew 27:15–26; Mark 15:6–15; Luke 18:13–25; John 18:39–40.

82 *the loving and beloved disciple*: John the Evangelist.

the very Wisdom of God: Lampe translates the Greek word αὐτοσοφία as the "absolute wisdom (of God)"; see, for one example among many, Origen, *Against Celsus* 3.41, ed. Marcel Borret, *Contre Celse,* vol. 2, *Livres III et IV,* SC 136 (Paris, 1968), p. 96, line 7.

Woman, behold your son!: John 19:26.

Woman, what have you to do with me?: John 2:4, which may also be rendered as "What does this matter to me and you?"

Who is my mother? . . . brothers are these: See Matthew 12:48–50; Mark 3:33–34.

his own love and honor for him: That is, Jesus's love and honor for John.

Behold your mother! . . . took her into his home: John 19:27.

83 *I thirst*: John 19:28.

they rushed, alas, to give vinegar and gall: For gall, see Matthew 27:34, and for vinegar, Mathew 27:48, Mark 15:36, Luke 23:36, and John 19:29–30. There is a wordplay in the Greek here between ὄξος (vinegar) and ὀξέως (quickly) that seems impossible to capture in English.

none of the things prophesied: See Psalms 68:22(69:21).

turned the rain and the streams into blood for them: Exodus 7:14–24.

made the bitter waters of Marah sweet: See Exodus 15:23–25.

suckled them with honey: Deuteronomy 32:13.

from the spiritual rock that accompanied them: 1 Corinthians 10:4.

are the grapes of bitterness . . . wrath of dragons: Deuteronomy 32:32–33.

wormwood: See Revelation 8:11.

offered him wine . . . did not want it: Mark 15:23; compare Matthew 27:34.

84 *cried out . . . yielded up his spirit*: Geometres combines wording from Matthew 27:50, Mark 15:37, Luke 23:46, and John 19:30.

as the earth split . . . veil of the temple: See Matthew 27:51.

the victor ten thousand times over: The rare Greek word μυρίαθλος is used mostly to describe the sufferings of Job and was first applied to the Virgin by George of Nicomedia. Geometres uses the word in his iambic encomium on the *Life of Saint Panteleemon,* ed. Leo Sternbach, *Ioannis Geometrae Carmen de S. Panteleemone* (Krakow, 1892), p. 41, line 1038, where the words μυρίαθλα σκάμματα describe the countless trials of the saint.

85 *dregs . . . not yet been wholly poured out*: See Psalms 74:9(75:8).

Do not chafe . . . scourged: A direct borrowing from Basil of Caesarea, *I Will Pull Down my Barns* 3 (PG 31:268B).

no part of his body . . . the great lance: Here Geometres seems indebted to a hymn of Holy Thursday: Ἕκαστον μέλος τῆς ἁγίας σου σαρκὸς ἀτιμίαν δι' ἡμᾶς ὑπέμεινε· τὰς ἀκάνθας ἡ κεφαλή· ἡ ὄψις τὰ ἐμπτύσματα· αἱ σιαγόνες τὰ ῥαπίσματα· τὸ στόμα τὴν ἐν ὄξει κερασθεῖσαν χολῆς γεῦσιν· τὰ ὦτα τὰς δυσφημεῖς βλασφημίας· τῇ μὲν χλεύῃ χλαμύδα οἱ ὦμοι· ὁ νῶτος τὴν φραγγέλωσιν καὶ ἡ χεὶρ τὸν κάλαμον· αἱ τοῦ ὅλου σώματος ἐκτάσεις ἐν τῷ σταυρῷ· τὰ ἄρθρα τοὺς ἥλους· καὶ ἡ πλευρὰ τὴν λόγχην. "Each member of your holy flesh endured dishonor for our sake: your head the thorns; your face the spittings; your cheeks the blows; your mouth the taste of gall mixed with vinegar; your ears the impious blasphemies; your back the scourge and your hand the reed; your whole body the stretching on the cross; your joints the nails and your side the lance." The hymn is attributed to Theodore of Stoudios; see Kallistos Miliaras, "Ἱστορικὴ ἐπισκόπησις τοῦ Τριωδίου: Τὸ σχέδιον καὶ ὁ καταρτισμὸς αὐτοῦ," *Nea Sion* 29 (1934): 153–61, 177–84, 330–46, 452–67, 502–16, at 513.

so that it might once again give birth: That is, his wounded side.

fountain . . . of the Spirit: See John 19:34, for the blood and water flowing from Jesus's side; and 1 John 5:6–8, partially quoted here, for the interpretation. Following 1 John, Geometres refers the water and blood to the sacraments of baptism and Eucharist; compare Theodoret of Cyrrhus, *On the Incarnation* 27 (PG 75:1468): "The side of Christ is a fountain of life giving life to the world by means of two streams of which the first is the baptismal font that renews us and clothes us in an immortal garment; the second nourishes those who are born at the holy table, just as infants partake of milk."

My heart . . . pain was renewed: Psalms 38:3–4(39:2–3).

received back . . . she was owed: See, for example, the homily ascribed to John Chrysostom, *On the Nativity of the Savior* (PG 56:389–90): "Just as Adam brought forth a woman without a woman, so too the Virgin gave birth to a man without a man.

Women thus owed a debt (χρέος) to men, and today Eve's debt has been repaid by the Virgin." See also John of Damascus, *On the Orthodox Faith* 87 (4.14), ed. Kotter, *Schriften*, vol. 4, p. 201, lines 75–77: "To the Son of God she gave her flesh and blood... and thus she paid the debt for the first mother. For just as Eve was formed from Adam without physical coupling, so too did the Virgin bring forth the new Adam in accordance with the law of gestation (κύησις) by surpassing the nature of generation (γέννησις)."

86 *entire fullness of the divinity*: See Colossians 2:9.

hewed from the rock: Mark 15:46. Golgotha was a large rocky area towering thirteen meters above the ground and was the site of an abandoned quarry; see Theissen and Merz, *The Historical Jesus*, 180.

the new Adam: See Romans 5:12–21.

Stone . . . Cornerstone . . . Foundation: See Matthew 21:42, quoting Psalms 117(118):22; and Ephesians 2:20, referencing Isaiah 28:16.

garden on account of Eden: Genesis 2:8.

Place of the Skull . . . Adam who fell: A reference to the tradition that Adam was buried beneath the place where Christ was crucified (see above, 79). The tradition is well known in Byzantine art, which depicts the skull of Adam at the foot of the cross in the iconography of the Crucifixion; compare the corresponding "Chapel of Adam" directly below the site of the crucifixion in the Church of the Holy Sepulcher in Jerusalem.

87 *secretly out of fear*: John 19:38, in relation to Joseph of Arimathea.

while others stood at a distance: Psalms 37:12(38:11). The same verse is used in 75, above.

88 *asked, he received*: See Matthew 7:7.

more prudent . . . buried it for himself: An allusion to the parable of the merchant and the pearl in Matthew 13:45–46.

89 *when his friend died . . . with moderation*: A reference to Christ weeping at the tomb of his friend Lazarus (John 11:33–35). See also 1 Thessalonians 4:13: "We do not want you to be ignorant, brethren, concerning those who have died, lest you grieve as others who are without hope."

melts mountains by his glance: See Psalms 96(97):5.

He who looks on the earth and makes it tremble: Psalms 103(104):32.

he who looks into . . . their emotions: See Psalms 7:10(9). The Greek word νεφρούς, translated here as "emotions," literally means "kidneys."

whose eyes examine the sons of men: See Psalms 10:5(11:4).

Who instructs and enlightens the blind: See Psalms 145(146):8.

more beautiful than the sons of men: Psalms 44:3(45:2). The same verse was quoted above, 62.

90 *Joseph and Nikodemos*: See John 19:38–40.

91 *standing by the cross were not only his mother*: John 19:25.

the difficulty concerning this question: The number of women named "Mary" who were present at the crucifixion, along with the other myrrh-bearing women and their relationship to one another, is a traditional exegetical puzzle. Epiphanios, *Life of the Theotokos,* ed. Dressel, *Epiphanii,* 37, puts the total number of women (named in scripture) at seven, and the number of Marys at three, that is, Mary Magdalene, Mary the mother of James the Less, and Mary the wife of Clopas. It is highly unusual that he does not include the Virgin Mary among the women who waited outside or otherwise visited the tomb of Jesus (see below).

the women who had followed . . . from a distance: Geometres is closest in his wording here to Luke 23:49, but the same points are made in Matthew 27:55 and Mark 15:40.

Mary of Clopas and Mary Magdalene: See John 19:25. Mary of Clopas is mentioned only by John.

there were also many women . . . the sons of Zebedee: Matthew 27:55–56.

Mark also . . . without identifying them: See Mark 15:40; Luke 23:49.

I thirst: John 19:28.

sat opposite: Matthew 27:61.

as dawn . . . anoint Jesus: Geometres combines points taken from Matthew 28:1, John 20:2, and Mark 16:1.

Mary Magdalene . . . where he was laid: Geometres follows Mark 15:47 most closely in his wording but is actually discussing the

problem posed by Matthew 27:61, since Mark states specifically that the other Mary was Mary the mother of Joses, but Matthew says only that "Mary Magdalene and the other Mary" were "sitting opposite," that is, outside the tomb.

Take the child and his mother: Matthew 2:13. Symeon Metaphrastes, *Life of the Virgin* 35, ed. Latyshev, *Menologii,* vol. 2, p. 370, makes the same argument and cites this and the following three biblical passages, along with John 2:12 and Matthew 12:47.

the mother of Jesus was there: John 2:1.

his mother spoke to the servants: John 2:5.

standing by the cross . . . his mother: John 19:25.

unadorned term: That is, "mother."

were managing . . . according to the circumstances: An attempt to capture Geometres's play on the verb οἰκονομέω, which refers here both to the human activity of the women themselves and to the divine oversight that he sees as lying behind it.

inseparable from the tomb: Epiphanios, *Life of the Theotokos,* ed. Dressel, *Epiphanii,* 37, makes the unusual claim that, while the myrrh-bearing women went to Christ's tomb seven times that night, "the Theotokos was not present at the tomb because she was supine with unspeakable grief; and while the angel appeared to Mary Magdalene at the tomb, Christ appeared to his mother in the house of John the Theologian."

92 *the earthquake . . . to the city*: As he himself notes below, Geometres closely follows the wording of Matthew 28:2–4. Some of the language and phrases here are, however, also borrowed from George of Nicomedia, *Oration* 9 (PG 100:1496B).

The other evangelists . . . and his words: See Mark 16:5–7; Luke 24:4–7, 24:23; John 20:12–13.

Thus, it was around her . . . weaker in disposition: In this paragraph, Geometres follows and expands on George of Nicomedia, *Oration* 9 (PG 100:1497AC), keeping at times the latter's language and wording.

the Life and the Resurrection: John 11:25 with the order reversed.

and said, "Hail": Matthew 28:9.

the pain and the fear of Eve: See Genesis 3:16.

Wisdom itself: On the Greek word αὐτοσοφία, see above, 82.
seemed like an apparition . . . his disciples: See Luke 24:39–41; John 21:4–5; and compare Matthew 14:26.
Word . . . reason: Geometres plays on the Greek word λόγος, which contains the sense of both "word" and "reason."
not only as someone . . . noetic initiation: Geometres borrows phrasing from George of Nicomedia, *Oration* 9 (PG 100:1496D).
94 *Blessed . . . favored one*: Luke 1:28.
the disobedience: That is, the eating of the fruit and the fall from paradise, Genesis 3:1–7.
women were subject to pain and men were under a curse: See Genesis 3:16–17.
clothed in the whole power from on high: Luke 24:49.
Holy Spirit . . . overshadowed her: Luke 1:35.
95 *Opponent*: The devil.
with one accord . . . and his brothers: Acts 1:14.
called by the term "mother" . . . have supposed: See above, 91.
like fellow soldiers . . . of the all-Holy Spirit: see Ephesians 6:11–18.
96 *Father, forgive them*: Luke 23:34.
Those who have written extensively about her: Perhaps a reference to Epiphanios, *Life of the Theotokos,* ed. Dressel, *Epiphanii,* 38, who mentions the "indentations of her knees in the marble floor of her house," citing as his source Andrew of Crete, *Homily on the Dormition* 2.1 (PG 97:1073A).
97 *as their common trainer . . . securing their victories*: Geometres employs a vivid wrestling metaphor.
when Peter . . . imprisoned: See Acts 4:3.
the stones that struck Stephen: The martyrdom of Saint Stephen is described in Acts 7:58.
beheaded along with James: See Acts 12:2.
98 *the same son ordered her to turn back*: Christ.
Aelia: Aelia Capitolina was the Roman name for Jerusalem after the destruction of the Second Temple in the second century.
the opposition Paul experienced: See, for example, 2 Corinthians 11:23–28.
100 *trying to set her on fire together with the house*: Geometres's source

may have been the *Transitus* of pseudo-John the Evangelist, ed. Constantin Tischendorf, *Apocalypses Apocryphae* (Leipzig, 1866), 106, though additional, nonextant Greek sources could have also been available to Geometres and Euthymios. For a discussion of this passage in earlier debates regarding the provenance of the Georgian *Life,* see Phil Booth, "On the Life of the Virgin Attributed to Maximus Confessor," *The Journal of Theological Studies* 66 (2015): 149–203, at 166.

101 *Absolutely no one . . . unaware*: A phrase borrowed from Gregory of Nazianzus, *Oration* 43.6, ed. Bernardi, *Discours 42–43,* p. 128, line 20.

102 *the hollows made by her knees*: That is, from her frequent kneeling in prayer and making prostrations. See above, note to 96.

Father of mercies: 2 Corinthians 1:3; compare Luke 6:36.

one who makes the sun . . . the unjust: See Matthew 5:45.

was crucified for our sake . . . his enemies: See Romans 5:7–8.

made himself indigent . . . everyone rich: See 2 Corinthians 8:9.

103 *clothed in . . . diverse colors*: Psalms 44:10(45:9); and see above, 6–9.

behind the veil of the sanctuary: See Hebrews 10:20.

an archangel was again sent: See Luke 1:26.

104 *bent to the ground and venerated her*: The miracle of the trees, found in apocryphal accounts of the Dormition, is cited by John of Thessaloniki, *On the Dormition of the Theotokos* 3, ed. E. W. Brooks, *Lives of the Eastern Saints,* vol. 3, Patrologia Orientalis 19.2 (Paris, 1925), p. 379, lines 18–21, trans. Brian Daley, *On the Dormition of Mary: Early Patristic Homilies* (Crestwood, NY, 1998), 50.

she returned to Zion: Antoine Wenger, *L'Assomption de la T. S. Vierge dans la tradition byzantine du VIe au Xe siècle* (Paris, 1955), 366n2, suggests that Geometres is alluding to the tradition that the Virgin died on Mount Zion, in the house of John the Evangelist.

just as the Israelites . . . the mountain: The assembly of the Israelites at Mount Sinai or Horeb; see Exodus 19:2, Deuteronomy 10:4, for example.

conspicuous and overshadowed mountain: See Isaiah 2:2; Micah 4:1; Habakkuk 3:3; Zacharias 1:8.

unhewn mountain: see Daniel 2:34.

the unquarried cornerstone: See Isaiah 28:16, Ephesians 2:20, and 1 Peter 2:6 for the Greek term ἀκρογωνιαῖος (cornerstone). Compare Mark 12:10, citing Psalms 117(118):22; and Acts 4:11. The assertion that Christ is an "unquarried cornerstone" cut from an "unhewn mountain" is an allusion to the virgin birth found in many Byzantine homilies and hymns; see, for example, pseudo-Modestos, *Encomium on the Dormition* 6 (PG 86:3292BC); John of Damascus, *On the Nativity of the Virgin* 6, ed. Kotter, *Schriften,* vol. 5, p. 175, 21–24; and Peter of Argos, *On the Conception of Saint Anna* 11, ed. Kyriakopoulos, *Ἁγίου Πέτρου,* p. 30, lines 179–82.

bind together . . . separated: A reference to the concurrence of the divine and human natures in the hypostatic union; see John of Damascus, *On the Nativity of the Virgin* 6, ed. Kotter, *Schriften,* vol. 5, p. 175, lines 24–25: "Christ the cornerstone is the one hypostasis joining together things that were divided (τὰ διεστῶτα συνάπτουσα), both divinity and humanity."

the mountain upon which . . . to make his dwelling: Psalms 67:17(68:16). Geometres similarly associates the Virgin with biblical mountains in his homily on the Annunciation (PG 106:836C).

105 *after her son . . . adopted son*: See John 19:26–27; and above, 82.

were two small garments: This episode is derived from apocryphal accounts of the Dormition. It is also related by, for example, John of Thessaloniki, *On the Dormition* 6, ed. Brooks, *Lives of the Eastern Saints,* vol. 3, p. 385, lines 24–28, trans. Daley, *Dormition,* 54; and Symeon Metaphrastes, *Life of the Virgin* 38, ed. Latyshev, *Menologii,* 373.

enemies . . . drawing near: An allusion to apocryphal accounts of the Dormition, in which demons appear and attempt to seize the departing soul.

106 *the things that Dionysios . . . Here is the text*: The excerpted text that follows is from Dionysios, *On the Divine Names* 3.2, ed. Suchla,

Corpus Dionysiacum, vol. 1, p. 141, lines 1–17. From an early stage in the reception of *On the Divine Names,* this passage was understood as a reference to the funeral service of the Virgin; see John of Scythopolis, scholia to *On the Divine Names* 3.2 (PG 4:236C): "Perhaps by the body which was the 'source of life' (ζωαρχικόν) and which 'received God' (θεοδόχον) he means the body of the holy Theotokos, who at that time fell asleep." On Dionysios, see above, 23. The apostle Timothy is the addressee of the entire work and is thus the "you" addressed in the excerpt. Hierotheos is known only from *On the Divine Names,* where he is said to have been taught, baptized, and ordained by Paul, and to himself have instructed Dionysios.

This is observed by us with great care: At this point, Geometres omits about three lines from the text. Shortly below, after the words "that body which was the source of life" (ζωαρχικός), he also omits the word "God-receiving" (θεοδόχος), which he cites at the end of this chapter and, earlier, in 28.

should sing praises: See Andrew of Crete, *On the Dormition* 1.12–16 (PG 97:1065B–1072A), who devotes much of this homily to speculation on the content of these hymns.

supremely divine: The word θεαρχικός, translated here as "supremely divine," is a Dionysian term for the divinity that was associated with the Virgin by Andrew of Crete, *On the Dormition* 1 (PG 97:1068B); see Daley, *Dormition,* 128n8.

strength: Geometres here employs the word εὐσθενεία, a variant reading found in some manuscripts of *On the Divine Names;* the standard reading is ἀσθένεια (Suchla, *Corpus Dionysiacum* vol. 1, p. 141, line 10, apparatus). Andrew of Crete, *On the Dormition* 1 (PG 97:1061BC), and John of Damascus, *On the Dormition* 2, ed. Kotter, *Schriften,* vol. 5, p. 538, line 55, cite the same passage from Dionysios, and both have ἀσθένεια (see Daley, *Dormition,* 230n34).

worked harder than the others: See 1 Corinthians 15:10.

illumined . . . he was persecuting: See Acts 9:1–19.

After another fourteen years: See Galatians 2:1.

this rapture . . . the third heaven: See 2 Corinthians 12:2. Here,

Geometres follows Epiphanios, *Life of the Theotokos,* ed. Dressel, *Epiphanii,* 41, which he greatly expands and develops. On Paul's rapture in the Byzantine tradition, see Maximos Constas, "The Reception of Paul and of Pauline Theology in the Byzantine Period," in *The New Testament in Byzantium,* ed. Derek Krueger and Robert Nelson (Washington, DC, 2016), 147–76, at 170–73.

the birds of heaven: See Genesis 2:19; Psalms 8:9(8); Matthew 6:26.

planets: Isaiah 13:10; Matthew 24:29; Revelation 6:13. The planets (ἀστέρες) are the five celestial bodies (Jupiter, Saturn, Venus, Mars, and Mercury) that, along with the sun and the moon, move along their own paths in their spheres.

fixed stars: Exodus 32:13; Hebrews 11:12. The fixed stars (ἄστρα) are the stationary celestial bodies (including constellations) of the outer sphere of the heavens.

beyond the ocean . . . paradise itself: Wenger, *L'Assomption,* 374n1, sees here an echo of Byzantine speculation regarding the location of the terrestrial paradise: earth is surrounded by the waters of the ocean, beyond which is found paradise. Others contend paradise is close to the source of the Nile, thought to be one of its four rivers; see Jean Daniélou, "Terre et Paradis chez les Pères de l'Église," *Eranos Jahrbuch* 22 (1953): 433–72; and Antoine Wenger, "Ciel ou Paradis: Le séjour des âmes, d'après Philippe le Solitaire, Dioptra, Livre IV, Chapitre X," *Byzantinische Zeitschrift* 44 (1951): 560–69, at 569.

firmament: Genesis 1:7.

concealed by the firmament and thus hidden: Genesis 1:6–7 speaks of a lower and a higher heaven.

The third rank . . . would be the seraphim: Dionysios counts nine ranks or choirs of angels, organized into three orders each containing three ranks. The highest rank in the lowest order is occupied by the principalities, while the seraphim occupy the highest rank in the highest order. On Paul's ascent through the angelic orders, see Maximos the Confessor, *Ambigua* 20, ed. *Constas,* vol. 1, pp. 415–17.

107 *promised me will be fulfilled*: See Luke 1:45.

108 *seraphim, cherubim, and thrones*: The highest triad of angels.

self-emptying: See Philippians 2:7.

"Peace be with you" . . . fear of the Jews: See John 20:19.

109 *myriads of angels*: Compare Matthew 26:53, which mentions twelve legions of angels.

purple of mockery: See above, 77.

form and beauty: Isaiah 53:2.

the divinity which produces beauty: The Greek word καλλοποιός (literally, "beauty-producing") is used by Dionysios the Areopagite, *On the Divine Names* 4.7, ed. Suchla, *Corpus Dionysiacum,* vol. 1, p. 151, lines 1 and 5: "Beauty is that which has a share in the beauty-producing cause of all things," likely drawing on Plotinus, *Ennead* 6.7.32.

110 *She now magnified*: See Luke 1:46.

opening her all-holy mouth: In a tradition stretching back to Homer (*Iliad* 9.408–9), the soul was believed to leave the body through the mouth; see Ioli Kalavrezou, "Exchanging Embrace: The Body of Salvation," in *Images of the Mother of God: Perceptions of the Theotokos in Byzantium,* ed. Maria Vassilaki (London and New York, 2005), 103–15, at 108.

just as she had once . . . childbirth: Parallels between the Nativity and the Dormition became common in middle Byzantine art; see Henry Maguire, *Art and Eloquence in Byzantium* (Princeton, 1981), 59–68, who notes that whereas these parallels were common in earlier patristic literature, they entered Byzantine art during the tenth century, the earliest examples surviving in Cappadocia.

unapproachable light: See 1 Timothy 6:16.

heaven and paradise: Wenger, *L'Assomption,* 198–99, detects a trace here of earlier apocryphal traditions, according to which the Virgin's body attained only the earthly paradise and was not resurrected and united with her soul.

111 *the holy Hierotheos*: See above, 106.

her own bath: An allusion to the bath the Virgin is said by many apocryphal accounts to have taken before her burial; see, for example, John of Damascus, *On the Dormition* 11, ed. Kotter, *Schriften,* vol. 5, p. 528, lines 14–16.

the couch of the king . . . sixty: See Song of Songs 3:7, referring to Solomon.

golden lampstand: Zacharias 4:1.

she is the Holy of Holies: For Geometres, the Virgin is both the new Holy of Holies and, as he develops the allusion in the subsequent passage, the new ark.

mercy seat: The Greek phrase, ἱλαστήριον ἐπίθεμα, forms part of the description of the ark in Exodus 25:16; compare 25:20–21.

new workshop: The "workshop" was a common image for the womb, found in Philo, *On the Life of Moses* 2.85, and introduced into homilies on the Theotokos by Proclus of Constantinople; see further, Constas, *Proclus of Constantinople,* 149–50. See also Geometres, *On the Annunciation* 10 (PG 106:820A).

Uzzah: See 2 Kings 6:3–8. Uzzah was one of two men driving the cart transporting the ark; when the oxen stumbled, he put out his hand to steady it but was struck dead by God for touching it.

this man sought to disturb the bier: Here, and in the following three chapters, Geometres recounts the episode of Jephonias (in some sources said to be the Jewish high priest), who deliberately sought to overturn the Virgin's bier. The episode is found in the apocryphal accounts and in subsequent homilies; see, for example, John of Thessaloniki, *On the Dormition of the Theotokos* 13 (PO 19:280–81); Theoteknos of Livias, *Encomium on the Assumption* 19–20 (Wenger, *L'Assomption,* 281–82, trans. Daley, *Dormition,* 75–76); and Germanos of Constantinople, *Encomium on the Dormition* 3 (PG 98:368D–369C, trans. Daley, *Dormition,* 176–77).

112 *envious one . . . creator of envy*: The devil; see Wisdom 2:24; and John of Damascus, *On Holy Saturday* 8.2, ed. Kotter, *Schriften,* vol. 5, p. 125.

acclaimed by . . . children's hymn: That is, during Christ's triumphal entry into Jerusalem (on Palm Sunday); see Matthew 21:9, 21:15–16; Mark 11:9–10; Luke 19:37–38; John 12:13.

get his wings caught: For the proverbial phrase τοῖς ἰδίοις πτεροῖς ἁλισκόμενος, "caught by his own wings," which comes from Aeschylus frg. 139.4–5 *(Myrmidons),* see Christos Simeli-

dis, "Aeschylus in Byzantium," in *Companion to the Reception of Aeschylus,* ed. Rebecca Futo Kennedy (Leiden and Boston, 2017), 179–202, at 193–94.

114 *saying of the Lord*: See John 8:44.

his hands were reattached: Euthymios, *Life of the Virgin* 114, states that Peter is the one who joined the man's arms to his body.

115 *hymns of . . . royal triumph*: The Greek word βασιλευτήρια is coined by Geometres.

light swallowed by darkness . . . its presence: Compare John 1:5.

taking a piece of the burial linens: See Germanos of Constantinople, *On the Dormition* 3 (PG 98:369A–B).

117 *the house of life . . . treasure of mankind was not found inside*: That is, the body of the Virgin was not found. Compare here Epiphanios, *Life of the Theotokos,* ed. Dressel, *Epiphanii,* 43, who makes the unusual claim that the apostles witnessed the Virgin's body being taken into heaven.

a clear messenger: The Greek word used is ἄγγελος (angel), an allusion to the angel at the tomb at Christ's resurrection.

human nature: The Greek word φύραμα, meaning a kneaded lump of dough or clay, is a New Testament metaphor for human nature; see Romans 11:16; 1 Corinthians 5:6–7; Galatians 5:9.

118 *conveyed the news . . . to the present day*: Geometres here identifies the Dormition as part of the apostolic tradition handed down from the apostles to their successors.

our city: Constantinople.

has inherited . . . her belt and mantle: On the celebrated relics of the Virgin preserved at Constantinople, see, for example, Stephen J. Shoemaker, "The Cult of Fashion: The Earliest 'Life of the Virgin' and Constantinople's Marian Relics," *Dumbarton Oaks Papers* 62 (2008): 53–74.

119 *Leo the Great*: Emperor Leo I (r. 457–474 CE).

Galbius and Candidus: The story of Galbius and Candidus is extant in multiple redactions, which Wenger, *L'Assomption,* 113, reduced to two groups, placing the version by Symeon Metaphrastes in the second (see also Wenger, *L'Assomption,* 294–302 and 306–11). Because the story was well known in Constantinople, Geometres did not need to treat it in great detail; see

the following chapter. In contrast, Euthymios, *Life of the Virgin* 119–24, whose Georgian audience was probably unfamiliar with the story, provides a lengthy account, taken verbatim from Symeon Metaphrastes (see Simelidis, "Two *Lives of the Virgin*," 150, with note 183), perhaps to encourage pilgrimage to Constantinople among his fellow Georgians.

120 *treated in detail . . . writers before us*: Wenger, *L'Assomption*, 195, sees this as a reference to the extensive treatment of this episode by Symeon Metaphrastes, *Life of the Virgin* 44–53, ed. Latyshev, *Menologii*, 376–83, though he acknowledges there existed multiple accounts of the story, to which Geometres refers.

separated after their dissolution: Whereas the Virgin's soul was separated from her body, Christ's divinity, by virtue of his divine omnipresence and hypostatic union with his flesh, remained simultaneously present to his body in the tomb and to his soul in Hades; see John of Damascus, *Homily for Holy Saturday*, ed. Kotter, *Schriften*, vol. 5, p. 138, lines 32–39: "Even though his divine and sacred soul had been separated from his life-giving and immaculate body, yet since the hypostatic, inseparable union of the two natures in the womb of the holy Virgin and Theotokos Mary, which occurred at conception, the divinity of the Word abided without interruption in both of them: the soul as well as the body, so that there abided even in death itself a single hypostasis in Christ, the soul and body subsisting in the hypostasis of God the Word even after death and constituting the same hypostasis."

121 *confirming . . . exemption from dissolution*: "Separation" (διάλυσις) refers to the separation of soul and body at the moment of death, in contrast to the body's exemption from dissolution and corruption (ἀκαταλυσία). According to Geometres, the Virgin underwent the natural separation of soul and body but was not subject to the corruption and dissolution of the body; see Wenger, *L'Assomption*, 398n2.

Seize upon: The Greek imperative ἅρπασον plays on the term for the "rapture" (ἁρπαγή) of the disciples and the resurrection of the dead at the Second Coming of Christ.

will not precede those who were dead: See 1 Thessalonians 4:15.

the meeting there: Ἀπάντησιν; see 1 Thessalonians 4:17.

learn also the meaning of her translation: Geometres introduces a typological and symbolic interpretation of the Dormition. His aim throughout the work has been to draw his audience into the experience of the Virgin's life, and he now discloses the manner in which they may spiritually participate in it; see Wenger, *L'Assomption,* 400n3.

outward wanderings: A phrase borrowed from Gregory of Nazianzus, *Oration* 4.9, ed. Jean Bernardi, *Discours 4–5: Contre Julien,* SC 309 (Paris, 1984), p. 100, line 4.

122 *some sensory spectacles . . . to this day*: Commercial markets and fairs were held in conjunction with major religious feasts, and there is evidence that August 15, the Feast of the Dormition, formed part of a major market for produce and vending; see Speros Vryonis, "The Panegyris of the Byzantine Saint: A Study in the Nature of a Medieval Institution, Its Origins, and Fate," in *The Byzantine Saint,* ed. Sergei Hackel (Birmingham, 1981), 196–226, at 222.

splendors: The Greek word φαιδρύματα occurs elsewhere only in Clement of Alexandria, *Paedagogus* 3.11.64.1, ed. Otto Stählin, *Clemens Alexandrinus,* vol. 1, *Protrepticus und Paedagogus,* GCS 12 (Leipzig, 1963), p. 272, line 5, trans. C. Mondésert and C. Matray, *Le pédagogue: Livre III,* SC 158 (Paris, 1970), 130, where the spelling in some manuscripts is φαίδρυσμα; and in Geometres's third encomium of the apple, *Progymnasmata* 6.21, ed. Antony Littlewood, *The Progymnasmata of Ioannes Geometres* (Amsterdam, 1972), p. 25, line 21, and the note on p. 93.

this most beautiful and useful season of the year: For a similar description, see Geometres, *On the Annunciation* (PG 106:840C–844A). Praises of the seasons, especially spring, were common in Byzantine poetry and rhetoric; see Maguire, *Art and Eloquence,* 42–52.

summer and also autumn, of which today's feast marks: Note that the feast of the Dormition, which is celebrated on August 15 on the Byzantine (Julian) calendar, corresponds to August 28 on the modern (Gregorian) calendar, with meteorological autumn beginning on September 1.

123 *The sun departs . . . Virgo*: As Geometres correctly notes, the sun leaves Leo for Virgo on August 23. This astronomical event was known to early Greek astronomers and is commonly noted in Byzantine astronomical works.

corn-bearing: σταχυηφόρος. The brightest star in the constellation Virgo was called Στάχυς or Spica, meaning "an ear of corn." Its appearance in the sky coincided with harvest time; see Aratus, *Phaenomena* 96, ed. Douglas Kidd (Cambridge, 1997), 80, 97, with commentary at 215–16.

The first time . . . the second: Geometres's language here is highly condensed and allusive, and we have supplied additional words and phrases to bring out the sense. The two moments described here are, first, the elevation of Christ's human nature (and by extension all human nature) to heaven at his Ascension, and, second, the elevation of the Virgin's human nature to the "new and theanthropic nature" of her ascended son.

cherubim . . . seraphim . . . thrones: The seraphim are at the summit of the nine ranks of the Byzantine celestial hierarchy, followed by the cherubim and then the thrones. On cherubim and seraphim, see above, 108. On thrones, see Colossians 1:16.

124 *We thank you*: For discussion of Euthymios's translation of this section (*Life of the Virgin* 128–29), see Simelidis, "Two *Lives of the Virgin*," 146–48.

ransom: The Greek term is λύτρον, for which see Matthew 20:28 and Mark 10:45; compare 1 Timothy 2:6 and 1 Peter 1:18.

deliverance: Geometres introduces a wordplay here, since the Greek term λυτήριον (deliverance) is a cognate of λύτρον (ransom). Wenger, *L'Assomption,* 406n1, argues that this passage "forcefully affirms" the Roman Catholic doctrine of Marian co-redemption, associated with the redemption offered by Christ and extended in time by Mary. However, this misses the way in which Geometres differentiates and disassociates the two (λύτρον vs. λυτήριον), since the assistance offered by the Virgin is wholly dependent on salvation in Christ, while the latter in no way depends on the personal sacrifice of his mother; see Simelidis, "Two *Lives of the Virgin,*" 148.

125 *did not abandon us*: See above, 2.

not made us orphans a second time: See John 14:18: "I will not leave you as orphans." Antoine Wenger, "L'intercession de Marie en Orient du VIe au Xe siècle," *Études mariales* 23 (1966): 51–75, at 62–63, argues that the Virgin's power of intercession is a corollary of her translation to heaven. See, for example, Germanos of Constantinople, *On the Dormition* 3 (PG 98:365B): "In you we have received a promise of eternal life, and in you we have acquired a mediator (μεσῖτιν) with God."

you stand as the queen . . . virtues and graces: See Psalms 44:10(45:9); and above, 7–9.

But hear us . . . desire your beauty: See Psalms 44:11–13(45:10–12); and above, 8.

126 *another intercessor*: John 14:16. The Greek term παράκλητον is also sometimes translated as "comforter," "advocate" or rendered simply as "Paraclete." It is striking that Geometres applies an attribute of the Holy Spirit to the Virgin as intercessor. Euthymios, *Life of the Virgin* 130, seems to have been troubled by Geometres's bold comparison and is at pains to clarify the meaning of the phrase and to avoid any ambiguity; see Simelidis, "Two *Lives of the Virgin,*" 150–51. The term was, however, probably already used as a Marian attribute in the second century by Irenaeus; see, for example, *Demonstration of the Apostolic Preaching* 1.3.33, ed. Adelin Rousseau and Irénée de Lyon, *Démonstration de la prédication apostolique,* SC 406 (Paris, 1995), 130: "It was necessary for Adam to be recapitulated in Christ . . . and Eve in Mary, so that a Virgin might become an advocate for a virgin (ut Virgo virginis advocata)."

127 *removed the curse*: The curse on Eve; see Genesis 3:16.

brought the hostility to an end: Ephesians 2:16.

we have been mingled with God: The language of mingling and mixture became problematic in later Christological discourse but was freely used by Gregory of Nazianzus, not only to express the Incarnation but also to describe the intimacy of the believer with Christ; see Andrew Hofer, *Christ in the Life and Teaching of Gregory of Nazianzus,* (Oxford, 2013), 110–21.

you give graciously to whomever you wish: Compare the parallel formulation in Geometres, *On the Annunciation* 49 (PG 106:845C).

deification: The Greek term θεουργία literally means "divine work, activity, or miracle," but it also carries the connotation of deification.

128 *novel miracles . . . ancient marvels*: For a collection of such miracles compiled in the tenth century, see the *Anonymous Miracles of the Pege,* ed. Alice-Mary Talbot, in Talbot and Scott Fitzgerald Johnson, *Miracle Tales from Byzantium,* Dumbarton Oaks Medieval Library 12 (Cambridge, MA, 2012), 204–97.

129 *one body*: 1 Corinthians 12:12.

having one head, Christ: See Ephesians 4:13.

domestic and foreign wars . . . and plunders itself: See the Introduction for discussion of the situation to which Geometres may be referring here and the clues this passage may offer for dating the work.

May you do this here . . . and there: That is, in this life and in the next.

pasturing them . . . by waters of rest: See Psalms 22(23):2.

orders and contemplations: This would seem to be a reference to the orders and contemplations of angels; see Dionysios the Areopagite, *On the Celestial Hierarchy* 7.2, where the orders of angels are uplifted to their divine source through "contemplation," understood as a form of direct participation.

From home to home: The Greek phrase οἴκοθεν οἴκαδε is a proverbial expression first found in Pindar, *Olympia* 7.4.

Bibliography

Further Reading

Boss, Sarah Jane, ed. *Mary: The Complete Resource.* London and New York, 2007.

Brubaker, Leslie, and Mary B. Cunningham, eds. *The Cult of the Mother of God in Byzantium: Texts and Images.* Farnham, 2011.

Constas, Maximos. "The Story of an Edition: Antoine Wenger and John Geometres' *Life of the Virgin Mary.*" In *The Reception of the Virgin in Byzantium: Marian Narratives in Texts and Images,* edited by Thomas Arentzen and Mary B. Cunningham, 324–40. Cambridge, 2019.

Cunningham, Mary B. *The Virgin Mary in Byzantium c.400–1000: Hymns, Homilies and Hagiography.* Cambridge, 2021.

——. *Wider than Heaven: Eighth-Century Homilies on the Mother of God.* Crestwood, NY, 2008.

Daley, Brian. *On the Dormition of Mary: Early Patristic Homilies.* Crestwood, NY, 1998.

Kalavrezou, Ioli. "Images of the Mother: When the Virgin Mary Became *Meter Theou.*" *Dumbarton Oaks Papers* 44 (1990): 165–72.

Mimouni, Simon Claude. *Dormition et Assomption de Marie: Histoire des traditions anciennes.* Théologie historique 98. Paris, 1995.

Nissiotis, Nikos. "Mary in Orthodox Theology." In *Mary in the Churches,* edited by Hans Küng and Jürgen Moltmann, 25–39. Edinburgh and New York, 1983.

Simelidis, Christos. "Two *Lives of the Virgin:* John Geometres, Euthymios the Athonite, and Maximos the Confessor." *Dumbarton Oaks Papers* 74 (2000): 125–59.

Smid, Harm Reinder. *Protevangelium Jacobi: A Commentary.* Translated by G. E. van Baaren-Pape. Assen, 1965.

Vassilaki, Maria, ed. *Mother of God: Representations of the Virgin in Byzantine Art.* Milan, 2000.

Index

All references are to chapter numbers.